SOFTWARE RELIABILITY HANDBOOK

SOFTWARE RELIABILITY HANDBOOK

Edited by

PAUL ROOK

Centre for Software Reliability,
City University, London, UK

ELSEVIER APPLIED SCIENCE
LONDON and NEW YORK

ELSEVIER SCIENCE PUBLISHERS LTD
Crown House, Linton Road, Barking, Essex IG11 8JU, England

Sole distributor in the USA and Canada
ELSEVIER SCIENCE PUBLISHING CO., INC.
655 Avenue of the Americas, New York, NY 10010, USA

WITH 15 TABLES AND 75 ILLUSTRATIONS

© 1990 CROWN
First Edition 1990
Reprinted 1991

Some of the material in Chapters 2 and 12 is based on parts of Chapters 11 and
19 in *Software Engineering,* 3rd edition, by Ian Sommerville. © 1989 Addison-
Wesley Publishing Co. Reprinted with permission.

British Library Cataloguing in Publication Data

Software reliability handbook.
1. Computer systems. Software. Reliability
I. Rook, Paul
005′.3

ISBN 1-85166-400-9

Library of Congress Cataloging-in-Publication Data

Software reliability handbook/editor, Paul Rook.
  p.   cm.
Includes bibliographical references.
ISBN 1-85166-400-9
1. Computer software—Reliability. I. Rook, Paul.
QA76.76.R44S655 1990
005.1—dc20

Printed by The Universities Press (Belfast) Ltd.

Foreword

Sometime soon, software reliability is going to become a highly visible and important field. Unfortunately, given human nature, its thrust into prominence will only happen once we experience the software equivalent of the Chernobyl, Bhopal, or space shuttle Challenger disasters. Such a disaster is likely to happen in the next few years, for the following main reasons:

1. *Software is becoming central to many life-critical systems*. Many of these involve extremely large assemblages of highly complex software. Large next-generation aircraft will have over one million source lines of software on-board; next-generation air traffic control systems will contain between one and two million lines; the upcoming international Space Station will have over two million lines on-board and over ten million lines of ground support software; several major life-critical defense systems will have over five million source lines of software. Other software systems will not be as large, but will be equally life-critical: nuclear powerplant control systems, power distribution systems, and medical support systems.
2. *Software is created by error-prone humans*. Bailey, in *Human Error in Computer Systems* (1983), gives the following experienced human error rates in preparing information such as computer programs and data for computer processing:

   - System-level errors 10–25%
   - Data preparation errors 10%
   - Transcription errors . . . . 2·5%
   - Data entry errors . . . . 0·5%

   Thus, a one million line software program will have several hundred thousand individual errors which will be introduced during its creation.
3. *Software is executed in the real world by error-intolerant machines*. A piece of computing equipment never questions whether its orders might have typos, transcription errors, or 'obvious goofs' in them. It proceeds to

execute its orders at the same breakneck pace, whether the orders concern life-critical situations or entertainment video games.

4. *Software development and maintenance is driven more by budget and schedule concerns than by reliability concerns.* The (paraphrased) words of Gus Grissom, the Apollo astronaut, are relevant: 'It makes me think twice when I remember that all of these rockets and crew capsules are being built by the lowest bidder'.

Combining these four ingredients does look like a recipe for an almost certain software disaster. Are there any ways that we might keep it from happening?

Fortunately, there are a number of good techniques available. There are techniques for avoiding and detecting sources of error before they become part of the software. There are techniques for building software which will recognize and deal with many of the common sources of typos, transcription errors, and obvious goofs. There are management techniques for conducting software risk assessments, and for organizing the software development and maintenance process to design and build quality and reliability into the software.

To date, however, these techniques have been scattered about the software engineering literature, making it difficult for an organization to gain perspective on the key software reliability issues and to mount an effective initiative to address them.

That is what is so important and valuable about this *Software Reliability Handbook*. It brings together the best known techniques for achieving and assessing software reliability from both the technical and the management standpoints. It distinguishes between the mature, ready-to-use portions of the field and the less-understood but often oversold portions. And it provides or identifies implementation guidelines for putting the techniques into practice.

The key issues in achieving software reliability are:

(a) how do you determine and specify the degree of software reliability that you want?
(b) how do you create and maintain reliable software?
(c) how do you assess the reliability of the resulting software?

This handbook does a good job of addressing all three of these key issues.

(a) *How do you determine and specify the degree of software reliability that you want*? I believe that the key to answering this question is provided by the discipline of software risk assessment. Dale's Chapter 1 on 'Software Reliability Issues' provides a good presentation of the various types of software risks, and a careful discussion of the candidate reliability metrics appropriate for measuring and monitoring each type of reliability risk. Rook and Wingrove's Chapter 7 on 'Project Control and Management' provides an overview of software risk management concepts, and discusses how they help determine the most appropriate development and management process for a software project. Kitchenham and de Neumann's Chapter 11 and Appendix D on software cost modeling provide a framework for assessing software reliability cost-benefit relations, and a good perspective on the capabilities and limitations of current software cost estimation techniques. Frewin's Chapter 8 on 'Procuring and Maintaining Reliable Software' provides practical guidance on specifying reliability and related software requirements, and on organizing the software procurement process to minimize the risk of getting an unreliable software supplier, process, or product.

(b) *How do you create and maintain reliable software?* There are several keys to creating and maintaining reliable software. Each is addressed by chapters in the Handbook.

- *Design for software reliability.* Sommerville's Chapter 2 on 'Software Design for Reliability' provides an assessment of design guidelines, illustrated with specific examples. Moulding's Chapter 4 on 'Software Fault Tolerance' addresses design techniques for fault tolerance, including a particularly good section on the relative cost and effectiveness of alternative software fault tolerance techniques.
- *Careful software development.* Reade and Froome's Chapter 3 on 'Formal Methods for Reliability' discusses the state of the art and the state of the practice of formal methods, including a summary of their capabilities and limitations.
- *Early and continuing error elimination.* Hall's Chapter 5 on 'Defect Detection and Correction' provides a particular emphasis on defect detection techniques applicable in the early software life cycle phases, in which defects are far less expensive and troublesome to fix.
- *Managing for reliability.* Rook and Wingrove's Chapter 7 on 'Project Control and Management' defines a closed-loop control process for software project management, and provides a management perspective on the use of the software reliability techniques provided in the other chapters. Rook's Appendix B on 'Software Development Process Models' elaborates on the leading software process models and their ways of dealing with software reliability issues. Frewin's Chapter 9 on 'Software Quality Management' focuses on the importance and benefits of a formal software quality management function, and discusses the associated quality management organization's roles, responsibilities, and operational procedures.
- *Automated aids.* Sommerville's Chapter 12 on 'Software Development Environments' discusses the roles of various software reliability-enhancing tools, and the architectural considerations involved in integrating these tools into an integrated project support environment (IPSE).
- *Careful product control.* Frewin's Chapter 8 on 'Procuring and Maintaining Reliable Software' addresses the practices of change control and baseline configuration management, two of the primary keys to maintaining reliable software once it has been developed.

(c) *How do you assess the software's reliability?* Kitchenham's Chapter 10 on 'Measuring Software Development' and Appendix C on 'Software Development Metrics and Models' provide workable definitions of software size and defect metrics, practical guidelines for software data collection and analysis, and good evaluations of the strengths and difficulties of the leading software size, complexity, reliability, and quality metrics. Littlewood's Chapter 6 and Appendix A on software reliability growth models provide an essential perspective on the assumptions underlying most software reliability growth models, and a good comparative analysis of the capabilities and limitations of the leading models available. Frewin's Chapter 8 on 'Procuring and Maintaining Reliable Software' covers the use of the software acceptance test as a way of ensuring that a delivered software product is satisfactory with respect to reliability and other desired software features.

A good many compendia with objectives similar to those of this handbook fall short of their promise. The individual contributions end up uneven, either in the expertise of the authors or in the perfunctory nature of some of the contributions. The contributions are often incompatible, in terms of definitions, objectives, or technology assessments.

However, this *Software Reliability Handbook* fulfills its promise well. The authors are top experts; they put a lot of work into their contributions; and a consistent perspective on software reliability pervades the book.

The Alvey Directorate, the editor, and the authors are to be commended for a fine job. As people decide to take software reliability seriously, this book will provide them with a solid starting point.

BARRY W. BOEHM
Professor of Computer Science,
University of California Los Angeles,
Los Angeles, USA

Preface

The reliability of software is becoming increasingly important, and I am very grateful to Barry Boehm for his Foreword which introduces the subject so well. The reliability of a system depends on both the hardware and the software that together comprise the system. Although faults in design can continue to give problems, the issues and the techniques for meeting severe reliability requirements in hardware have been understood for some time. In the case of software both the techniques and a positive attitude of software developers to the achievement of reliability are much less well established. They are particularly crucial in the development of software-dependent safety-critical systems.

There are genuine differences between software and hardware:

—software has no physical existence;
—software includes data as well as logic;
—few software quality metrics exist;
—it is deceptively easy to introduce changes into software;
—effects of software changes propagate explosively;
—software developments have traditionally made very little use of pre-existing components;
—software may have much higher complexity than hardware (to the extent of attempting to implement functionality of a complexity that would be unacceptable for hardware).

However, in many important ways software development is like hardware development and can be managed and controlled using very similar techniques to those used in any other engineering discipline. The differences listed above are the very factors which make a genuine engineering approach essential for the successful development of reliable software.

Improvements in the technology of software development have reached the point where the major issues have been identified and considerable progress has been made in addressing them. Methods for technical software development are well defined and practical working tools to support improved software production are commonly available. Experience shows that application of the right methods can bring significant improvements in quality and productivity, and the purpose of this Handbook is to bring together the various aspects of software development into an integrated coverage of the subject of developing reliable software.

Chapter 1 introduces the concepts of reliability as the objectives to be achieved in the developed software, and Chapters 2–6 concentrate on the techniques for the creation of reliable software, and measurement and prediction of product reliability in test and operation.

However, control of software faults is only one part of control of reliability, and many software system failures are not attributable to software faults. Statements have been made that as little as 25% of software failure reports are attributable to faults in the code. The remainder are attributable to such causes as incorrect configuration control, side-effects of changes, incorrect documentation or user misunderstanding of the documentation or the software, failure to correctly capture the requirements in the software specification, and failures in inter-operation with the hardware. All of these problems may manifest themselves as 'software failures' and the high rate of occurrence compared with coding errors emphasises the importance of specification, design, verification and validation, documentation and communication, quality assurance, configuration management and project management in the development of the software.

Chapter 1 refers to this aspect of reliability in the discussion of explanatory models at the end of the chapter. Explanatory variables refer not only to characteristics of the product but also to factors in the development process which determine the reliability of the product produced, and in the second half of the Handbook, Chapters 7–12 concentrate on the reliability of the process of production of software, and control of the variety of factors which significantly affect reliability of the product. Chapter 8 emphasises that the major benefit is obtained by the *user* of the reliable software, who pays a much greater cost for unreliability of the software product than the producer.

The Handbook chapters are intended to provide straightforward reading. Therefore technical material which needs to be covered in order to support the subject of software reliability, but which would be a diversion from the direct theme of a chapter, has been put into appendices. The chapters bring together all the different aspects of software reliability as a reference point for everyone responsible for the development of software systems; technical staff, managers and customers. Our goal has been to ensure that the subject matter is based on real experience rather than hypothesis and that it is complete and comprehensive, but only to a certain depth so that it can be read by all those involved. The experts who require more depth in a particular aspect are referred to the further reading and the extensive set of references. All the contributors have cooperated in attempting to make the material in the different chapters consistent so that there is a common strategy in covering the different aspects of the subject. Where this is achieved, the credit is due to the expertise of the authors. Where success is less than complete, then blame the editor's attempt at the difficult task of encapsulating the state-of-the-art in a challenging and evolving field.

I am deeply indebted to the contributors for their help and support, and also for the assistance from the staff of CSR. I have much appreciated this opportunity to act as editor as a contribution to the field of software reliability, and offer this Handbook to the software development community in the hope and expectation that it will represent a valid contribution to the successful production of reliable software systems.

PAUL ROOK

List of Contributors

C. J. DALE

Centre for Software Reliability, City University, Northampton Square, London EC1V 0HB, UK and *National Centre of Systems Reliability, UK Atomic Energy Authority, Wigshaw Lane, Culcheth, Warrington, Cheshire WA3 4NE, UK.* Present address: *Cranfield Information Technology Institute, Fairways, Pitfield, Kiln Farm, Milton Keynes MK11 3LG, UK*

G. D. FREWIN

Centre for Software Reliability, City University, Northampton Square, London EC1V 0HB, UK and *Standard Telecommunication Laboratories, London Road, Harlow, Essex CM17 9NA, UK*

DR P. K. D. FROOME

Adelard, 28 Rhondda Grove, London E3 5AP, UK

PROF. P. A. V. HALL

Brunel University, Uxbridge, Middlesex UB8 3PH, UK

DR B. A. KITCHENHAM

Centre for Software Reliability, and *City University, Northampton Square, London EC1V 0HB, UK.* Present address: *National Computing Centre, Oxford Road, Manchester M1 7ED, UK*

PROF. B. LITTLEWOOD

Centre for Software Reliability, and *City University, Northampton Square, London EC1V 0HB, UK*

Prof. M. R. Moulding

Centre for Software Reliability, City University, Northampton Square, London EC1V 0HB, UK and Royal Military College of Science, Shrivenham, Swindon, Wilts SN6 8LA, UK

Prof. B. de Neumann

Centre for Software Reliability, and City University, Northampton Square, London EC1V 0HB, UK

Dr C. M. P. Reade

Brunel University, Uxbridge, Middlesex UB8 3PH, UK and Rutherford Appleton Laboratory, Chilton, Didcot, Oxon OX11 0QX, UK

P. E. Rook

Centre for Software Reliability, City University, Northampton Square, London EC1V 0HB, UK

Prof. I. Sommerville

University of Lancaster, Bailrigg, Lancaster LA1 4YR, UK

A. Wingrove

Centre for Software Reliability, City University, Northampton Square, London EC1V 0HB, UK

Support for the production of the *Software Reliability Handbook* was provided by:

The Alvey Directorate of the Department of Trade and Industry, Kingsgate House, 66–74 Victoria Street, London SW1E 6SW, UK

Contents

Foreword v

Preface ix

List of Contributors xiii

1. Software Reliability Issues **1**
   1.1 Introduction 1
   1.2 Definitions 1
   1.3 Statement of Reliability Requirements 5
   1.4 Achievability of Reliability Requirements 6
   1.5 Certification, Warranties and Legal Issues 9
   1.6 Reliability Assessment Based on the Development Process . . . 11
   1.7 Data Collection 14
   1.8 Research Directions 17

2. Software Design for Reliability **21**
   2.1 Introduction 21
   2.2 Formal System Specification 28
   2.3 Object-oriented Design 29
   2.4 An Object-oriented Design Example 36
   2.5 Object Implementation 44
   2.6 Summary 48
   2.7 Further Reading 48

3. Formal Methods for Reliability **51**
   3.1 Introduction 51
   3.2 Formal Methods 52
   3.3 The Nature of Specifications 53
   3.4 Formal Methods and Reliability 56
   3.5 The Main Approaches to Formal Methods 58
   3.6 Current Use of Formal Methods 69

3.7   Important Issues for Effective Use of Formal Methods   72
3.8   Prospects and Conclusions   80
3.9   Further Reading   82

4. Software Fault Tolerance **83**
4.1   Introduction   83
4.2   Overview of Software Fault Tolerance   84
4.3   Towards an Implementation Framework for Software Fault Tolerance   90
4.4   Robust Software Using Ada's Exception-Handling Facilities   92
4.5   *N*-Version Programming   96
4.6   Recovery Blocks   99
4.7   Comparison of *N*-Version Programming and Recovery Blocks   105
4.8   Practical Application of *N*-Version Programming and Recovery
      Blocks   107
4.9   Summary   109

5. Defect Detection and Correction **111**
5.1   Introduction   111
5.2   Life-Cycle View   112
5.3   General Principles   114
5.4   Defect Detection and Correction throughout the Life Cycle   120
5.5   Further Reading   135

6. Modelling Growth in Software Reliability **137**
6.1   Introduction   137
6.2   A Conceptual Model of the Software Failure Process   138
6.3   Prediction of Software Reliability   143
6.4   Software Reliability Growth Models   144
6.5   An Example of Use of the Models   146
6.6   Methods of Analysing Past Predicting Accuracy   147
6.7   Summary and Conclusion   152

7. Software Project Control and Management **155**
7.1   Introduction   155
7.2   Project Control and Project Management   157
7.3   Establishing the Software Development Process   167
7.4   Managing the Software Development Process   176
7.5   The Process Definition Diagram   183
7.6   Risk Management and Choice of Process   199
7.7   Productivity, Quality and Software Development Methodology . . .   205
7.8   Further Reading   209

8. Procuring and Maintaining Reliable Software **211**
8.1   Introduction   211
8.2   The Roles and Responsibilities of the Software Procurer   212
8.3   Contracting for the Development of a Software Product   213
8.4   Procurer's Involvement in Product Development and Testing   226
8.5   Product Handover, and Analysis of the Procurement   234

8.6   Maintenance of Software 234
8.7   Establishing the Baseline 237
8.8   Managing Changes Against the Baseline 239
8.9   Continuous Assessment of Product Status, and Support for Future
      Procurement. 243
8.10 Summary: The Roles of Procurement and Maintenance in Achieving
      Reliable Software 244

9. **Software Quality Management** **247**
9.1   Introduction 247
9.2   Definition of Software Quality Management 249
9.3   The Value of Software Quality Management 252
9.4   General Elements of Software Quality Management 259
9.5   Process Engineering 269
9.6   Three Angles on Software Quality Management 279
9.7   Summary 301
9.8   Further Reading 301

10. **Measuring Software Development** **303**
10.1 Introduction 303
10.2 Terminology 303
10.3 The Nature and Use of Software Metrics 304
10.4 Practical Problems 308
10.5 Analytical and Conceptual Software Models 314
10.6 Metric Evaluation and Model Validation 315
10.7 Metrics Through the Life Cycle 317
10.8 Guidelines for Interpreting Metric Values 328
10.9 Further Reading 331

11. **Cost Modelling and Estimation** **333**
11.1 Introduction 333
11.2 Cost Estimation 336
11.3 Cost Models 340
11.4 Sizing Models 344
11.5 Improving Cost-Model Estimates 360
11.6 Cost-Estimation Risk 368
11.7 Summary 376

12. **Software Engineering Environments** **377**
12.1 Introduction 377
12.2 Environment Facilities 378
12.3 Environment Architecture 381
12.4 Ada Support Environments 389
12.5 CASE Workbenches 391
12.6 Introducing an IPSE 394
12.7 Environments and Reliability Management 396
12.8 Summary 397
12.9 Further Reading 398

Appendix A. Software Reliability Growth Models **401**
   A.1   Jelinski–Moranda (JM) Model   401
   A.2   Bayesian Jelinski–Moranda (BJM) Model   403
   A.3   Littlewood (L) Model   404
   A.4   Littlewood–Verrall (LV) Model   405
   A.5   Duane (D) Model   406
   A.6   Goel–Okumoto (GO) Model   407
   A.7   Littlewood Nonhomogenous Poisson Process (LNHPP) Model . .   407
   A.8   Musa–Okumoto (MO) Model   407
   A.9   The *u*-Plot Method for Detecting Consistent Bias   408
   A.10 The Prequential Likelihood Ratio for Detecting Noise and Bias   . . .   409

Appendix B. Software Development Process Models **413**
   B.1   The Waterfall Model   413
   B.2   Classical Life-Cycle Phases   416
   B.3   Interaction between Teams   418
   B.4   Software Development Activities   420
   B.5   Matrix of Phases and Activities   422
   B.6   Software Development within System Development   426
   B.7   Software Project Organisational Structure   428
   B.8   The Contractual Model   429
   B.9   Object-oriented Processes of Software Development   430
   B.10 Prototyping   431
   B.11 Incremental Development   433
   B.12 The Spiral Model for defining Development Phases   435
   B.13 The Ada Process Model   437
   B.14 Conclusion   440

Appendix C. Software Development Metrics and Models **441**
   C.1   Introduction   441
   C.2   Selection Criteria   442
   C.3   Software Science   447
   C.4   Software Metrics   449
   C.5   Quantitative Software Models   476

Appendix D. Software Development Cost Models **487**
   D.1   Introduction   487
         D1.1 Model Validation and Verification Criteria   487
   D.2   Examples of Empirical Factor Models   489
         D2.1 COCOMO—the COnstructive COst MOdel   489
         D2.2 TRW Wolverton Model   498
         D2.3 The SDC Model   498
         D2.4 Walston–Felix   499
         D2.5 SOFTCOST   501
         D2.6 PRICE SP   503
         D2.7 ESTIMACS   504
         D2.8 Bailey–Basili Meta Model   505

D.3   Examples of Constraint Models 507
    D3.1   Putnam's Model 507
    D3.2   Parr 515
    D3.3   Jensen 515
    D3.4   COCOMO Schedule Equation 516
    D3.5   COPMO 516

References 519

Index 533

1

Software Reliability Issues

Chris Dale

1.1 Introduction   1
1.2 Definitions   1
1.3 Statement of Reliability Requirements   5
1.4 Achievability of Reliability Requirements   6
1.5 Certification, Warranties and Legal Issues   9
1.6 Reliability Assessment Based on the Development Process .   11
1.7 Data Collection   14
1.8 Research Directions   17

1.1 Introduction

This chapter identifies and explains a number of important reliability concepts as they apply to the specialized area of software reliability. It also includes a general discussion of various aspects of reliability assessment and related issues. Subsequent chapters deal with the detail of specific techniques for achieving, measuring and predicting reliability, and the function of a reliable development process to assure production and maintenance of software of the required reliability.

1.2 Definitions

Reliability is a term which in everday speech tends to be very subjective. Thus, a reliable item is one that is trusted, or can be depended upon with confidence, or is of sound and consistent character or quality. It is not difficult to understand what is meant by an unreliable motor car. The problem arises when one tries to make the concept into an objective one, and quantify the degree of reliability possessed by an item: should one consider the annual repair bill, or the frequency of failures to start, and does a failure of the windscreen wipers in dry weather count as unreliability?

Unfortunately, there has been an over-use of the subjective version of the definition in the software world, which is at least in part due to the difficulties associated with objective measures. Thus, imprecise phrases like 'the software must be adequately reliable' creep into specifications. In this book 'reliability' is used in two senses: the vague, 'English-language' usage of the term will be found in many places, but where precision is needed the term will be used in its strict, mathematically defined sense (see below). In general, the context will make clear which definition is being used—the technical or non-technical; where confusion is thought likely, the usage is explained.

There are a number of measures associated with reliability which are more-or-less intuitive, appropriate or useful in a variety of circumstances. Some of the more common terminology is defined below. It should be noted that none of these notions is unique to the field of *software* reliability; they are, however, explained here as they apply within that field.

Failure
An event that is viewed as determining the instant in time at which a system has ceased to function in a satisfactory manner. Thus, the term failure may refer to complete system disfunction, to degradation of functionality, or to the generation of incorrect outputs. Whether a particular event constitutes a failure is not always apparent: a failure to meet the user's expectation may not be a failure to meet the specification, for example. In any assessment of reliability it is vital to be clear what is regarded as constituting failure, in order to avoid ambiguity in interpretation of reliability quantities. The concept of failure must be defined carefully with a specific application in mind. For example, a spurious alarm generated as a result of a fault in the software of a safety system might not be considered to be a failure of the safety function, but would be regarded as a failure from the availability viewpoint.

Reliability
The probability that a given piece of software will execute without failure in a given environment for a given period of time. Alternatively, the probability that a given function will be performed successfully on demand.

Rocof (*Rate of occurrence of failures*)
The current rate at which failures are occurring—more formally, the first derivative of the function describing the number of failures observed up to and including the present.

MTTF (*Mean time to failure*)
The time which is expected to elapse between the current time and the next failure.

MTBF (*Mean time between failures*)
The time which is expected to elapse between one failure and the next failure. In a systems context, this includes any repair time following the original

failure. This is not always relevant to software, because in many cases it is possible to reload the software and continue operation with a very small delay. The other problem with this measure is that any software repair action will change the MTBF—this is not generally true with hardware systems, where repair often comprises replacement of a failed component by one of identical reliability characteristics.

Availability
The probability that the software will be functioning in a satisfactory manner at a given future time, conditional upon its satisfactory functioning at a defined start time. Under certain conditions this measure will tend towards the proportion of time available.

Time to target
The further time which is expected to elapse (for example, during testing and debugging) before a given target is achieved, such as the target reliability to be achieved before release to customer use.

Expected
This term implies the mean of the statistical distribution of the quantity to which it is applied.

Median
This term implies the point of the statistical distribution that a given quantity is equally likely to fall either side of—i.e. there is a 50% chance that the observed value will be greater (or less) than the median.

Reliability growth model
Probabilistic description of the sequence of random variables representing the successive inter-failure times of the software, assuming that the reliability is improving (at least in some average sense) as a result of fault removal.

Some important concepts have been deliberately left undefined; this is because they can only be defined with reference to a particular system. Time is one such quantity whose definition must be carefully considered; it should be defined to correspond, in some sense, to the stress placed upon the software during its execution. Thus, processing time would be appropriate for a piece of software operating in a time-sharing environment, clock-time for systems running continuously over a period of time, and number of executions or demands for many kinds of system that interact with either people or other systems. It is sometimes the case that the 'best' metric is not easy to collect; in such cases an appropriate substitute may be adequate (e.g. calendar time instead of execution time).

The particular metric that is used in any given application must also be chosen with care. Some examples for each of the metrics reliability, rocof,

Table 1.1. Software reliability metrics and their domains of application

Metric	Domain of application	Examples
Reliability	Failure particularly undesirable	Avionics, process control
Rocof	Frequency of failures important	Operating systems
MTTF	Utilization stable	Control systems, software packages
Availability	Down-time important	Telecommunications
Time to target	During development	Operating systems, large real-time systems

MTTF, availability and time to target are given below, and are summarized in Table 1.1.

Reliability

This is appropriate for systems whose failure is particularly undesirable (such as avionics software) and for many kinds of systems whose continuous operation over a period of time is important (e.g. process control). When the term is applied to successful performance on demand, it is applied to alarm or shut-down systems whose function is to monitor some process and take appropriate actions when unsafe conditions are detected. In such cases, the converse of reliability is often used as the metric, and termed 'probability of failure on demand'.

Rocof

This indicates the frequency with which undesired events can be expected to occur, and is the most universally useful and applicable of these metrics. It is of particular relevance to such things as computer operating systems, where it is of interest to know how often failures are likely to occur.

MTTF

This metric, often quoted in the field of system reliability, is of somewhat limited usefulness for the quantification of software reliability. It can be useful for systems that are relatively stable, both in terms of usage and fault content—in which case MTTF is often found to be a more intuitive measure than its reciprocal, the rocof. It must be remembered that the MTTF is the reciprocal of the rocof only when failure times follow an exponential distribution. This might apply in the case of control systems, or software packages, when the utilization of the software is relatively stable. However, MTTF can be very misleading in cases where rocof is not stable, such as during testing and debugging: the MTTF is no longer the reciprocal of the rocof, and in some cases can even be infinite despite the fact that the rocof is non-zero. This is clearly likely to mislead.

Availability

This metric is very useful for systems whose failure is less of a worry than the down-time that may follow. Telecommunications software is an example of this kind of system.

Time to target

This metric is of particular relevance during development, when there is great interest in the time (calendar or execution) which can be expected to elapse before a given target reliability is reached. Many kinds of large system are amenable to this treatment, including operating systems and real-time systems.

It can be seen from the above examples, and the associated discussion, that it is of great importance to choose the appropriate metric for a given application. This point is of especial pertinence to the statement of reliability requirements that must be made as part of the software requirements definition.

1.3 Statement of Reliability Requirements

The statement of software reliability requirements will be based upon, and in many cases will be similar to, the system reliability requirement. A reliability apportionment exercise may lead to an implied requirement on the software as a whole, or a number of requirements on individual software subsystems. In any case, it is important that the statement of reliability requirements be quantitative, and be made in terms that can be measured by observation of software execution. Thus, statements such as 'the software shall be fault-free' or 'the software shall have fewer than x faults per 1000 lines' must be avoided—the first cannot be measured, and the second can be measured only in ways that are not directly related to the user-perceived failure behaviour, i.e. the execution of the software in time.

It is important that the reliability requirement should reflect the various demands on individual functions of the software. Thus, a protection system of some sort may be required to have a reliability greater than p for its 'shut-down when required' function, and a rocof less than λ for its 'keep running if safe' function. This example illustrates that a mixture of metrics can sometimes be necessary in the requirements statement, and leads to the important point that the conditions under which the measurements are made must be specified carefully.

It is vital that any statement of requirements should be for an appropriate level of reliability. The required reliability must clearly be sufficiently high for the application in question, but must be kept reasonably low because of considerations of achievability and testability. Thus, demands for perfection must be avoided—perfection is (at least) difficult to achieve and impossible to demonstrate. Similarly, high levels of reliability are difficult (and costly) to achieve and can be demonstrated only by extensive (and expensive) verification, validation and testing activities.

For example, a requirement should be stated for a failure on demand probability of 10^{-4} only if it is possible to make the necessary investment to ensure that this level can be both achieved and assessed. The current state of the art provides little help in assessing software reliability at this level. The implications are that the overall top-level systems design should take into account the achievability and assessability of the reliability requirements placed upon software, and that overall design iteration should take place if the software requirements are either unachievable or unassessable, for economic or technical reasons.

The points made in this section can be summarized by stating that the reliability requirements for a given piece of software must be carefully expressed in a quantitative, measurable fashion, with the use of metrics, definitions and measurement units that are appropriate for the task in hand.

1.4 Achievability of Reliability Requirements

Following establishment of the requirements for reliability of the software in question, it is important to assess the achievability of the requirements. This can be regarded as the beginning of the process of assessing the reliability of the product, and should be done by reviewing the planned development process of the product in question with the aim of establishing whether or not it is likely to result in a product of the required reliability. There are currently no well-developed techniques to enable this assessment of achievability to be carried out in a scientific fashion. This does not mean the activity should not be carried out, but rather that the analyst should be aware of the qualitative and subjective nature of the activity, and should take care in interpretation of the analysis. The main value of the assessment of achievability of requirements lies in the possibility of discovering at an early stage deficiencies in the plan, enabling revisions as necessary.

Since assessing the achievability of reliability requirements is neither an easy task nor one for which formal procedures exist, this section attempts to give some guidance on the general principles involved and to suggest ways in which they may be applied, rather than to give specific advice on techniques to be used.

The task is essentially one of comparing a stated reliability requirement with a planned development process, and judging their mutual compatibility, taking due account of the nature of the software product to be developed. This judgement will in many cases have to be a subjective one based on the experience of the analyst. Demands for various kinds of control on the development process, such as the extent and precise nature of code inspections, code verification, and testing, will clearly be influenced by the requirements for reliability.

In an ideal world, the assessor would be able to draw upon documents detailing, in quantitative terms, the typical effect that various factors have on reliability. The hardware reliability engineer can turn to such information (especially in the electronics field), which, when used carefully, can be very valuable. The best that the software reliability engineer can hope for is to draw on the experience of (preferably) his own organization in developing similar products in the past. Where information is available from past projects concerning the nature of the product, the way in which it was developed, and its eventual achieved reliability, the assessor is in a much better position to be objective in his judgement about achievability of requirement. Due allowance will have to be made for divergences (in product or process) of the new piece of software from those for which the desired information is available. This introduces a topic which is discussed later in this chapter as it applies to reliability, and also in other chapters of this book—data collection: an important reason for investing (effort) in collection of data is the greater confidence and integrity that it will bring to the assessment process in the future.

Guidelines and checklists on 'good software development practice' can aid the assessor in his task, especially in cases where historical data is lacking. One particular document that has been produced with the assessment task in mind is a Health and Safety Executive report giving general technical guidelines on the use of programmable electronic systems in saftey-related applications (Health and Safety Executive, 1987). This describes in detail a method for assessing the safety integrity of programmable electronic systems, including the hardware and software. The philosophy behind the software-related parts of this document is to use a series of checklists, as aids to the assessment of safety integrity. As the title suggests, these guidelines have been produced with safety in mind. Safety is not the same as reliability, but in this case the two subjects are of sufficient similarity for these guidelines to be applicable. The application of these guidelines to process assessment is discussed in Section 1.6 of this chapter.

The result of an exercise to establish the achievability of reliability requirements may be recommended revisions to the development process (e.g. additional or more formalized verification activities at various development stages), or even to the reliability requirements. This latter requires a reapportionment of reliability to various (hardware or software) system components, or an appropriately agreed change to the overall system requirements.

For example, it may be recommended that formal specification and proving methods be used for certain safety-critical elements of a system, as the most effective means to achieve the reliability required for particular aspects of functionality. Such a recommendation must, of course, be cognizant of the current limitations of formal methods.

A question sometimes arises regarding the level of reliability that can be achieved in a piece of software. The theoretical answer is the absolute reliability which would be achieved by a perfect piece of software; this corresponds to the arbitrarily high reliability which can be achieved for a hardware system (in the absence of design faults) by replication of components and other forms of fault tolerance. These are the theoretical possibilities only. Although a piece of software can in theory be absolutely reliable, this is something that can never be demonstrated: an achievement is a rather empty one if it cannot be verified.

In attempting to quantify the best reliability that can reasonably be expected from a piece of software, it is instructive to consider what is regarded as achievable by systems in general, and why. Even in a highly redundant system, where components of the system are included for the sole purpose of being available in the event of failure of other components, failure probabilities lower than 10^{-4} or 10^{-5} per demand are rarely claimed or justified. This is largely due to the presence of design errors, and other so-called common-mode effects, where a single event leads to failure of several redundant components.

Returning to software, it is often felt that one should exercise greater caution in claiming reliability achievement for software-based systems, because they are in general more complex than their hardware counterparts, and because the technology is less well understood. This suggests that a limit of 10^{-3} or 10^{-4} should be established, beyond which claims of reliability can be accepted only in very special circumstances. There are a number of reasons for not allowing lower levels. These include the 'law of diminishing returns' applied to the various activities comprising the software development cycle. For example, successively larger amounts of effort have to be applied in testing to produce, in general, successively smaller improvements in reliability. Particular reasons for limiting what can be claimed in the case of diverse systems are common-mode or dependency effects. In any development there will be factors that tend to lead to commonality of faults in the respective diverse implementations. Perhaps the most obvious of these is the common specification often used to produce a number of pieces of software. More subtle effects include the fact that human beings as programmers are likely to make similar errors in performing similar tasks (Knight & Leveson, 1986a).

Related to the question of achievability is the question of cost. A particular requirement may be judged to be achievable but expensive. Cost–benefit considerations may have to be borne in mind when deciding whether an expensive requirement should be relaxed. It is important that the viewpoints of both customer and developer are taken into account here. The cost implications of lowering the reliability requirements are likely to be:

- decreased purchase cost
- reduced development cost
- increased maintenance cost
- increased cost to customer as a result of additional failures and their consequential costs

Some of these cost issues are discussed further in Chapter 11.

1.5 Certification, Warranties and Legal Issues

Most pieces of software are useful only because they are part of an overall system designed to do some particular job. There are a number of such systems which are subject to certification requirements: examples include civil aircraft requiring a certificate of airworthiness, and nuclear power plants which require a license to operate. Where certification covers aspects of these systems that include software, such as may be the case with avionics, the question of software certification arises in a natural way. There is in general, however, no clear agreement on even the meaning of software certification, not to mention the question of how it should be done. To illustrate this point, some examples will be discussed.

Certification of compilers for programming languages such as Pascal has been addressed in recent years by organizations including the British Standards Institution, to whom producers of compilers can submit their product for certification. The naive purchaser or user of a certificated compiler may imagine that there is some form of guarantee or assurance that the compiler in question is bug-free. This is not the case, however: compilers are certified by carrying out a series of fixed tests, and confidence in the integrity of the compiler in general is dependent upon the assumption that these tests represent a large proportion of the functionality of the compiler. There is clearly an (unstated) limit to the reliance that can be put on a product certified in this way.

Another interpretation of the term certification as it applies to software is the notion of correctness: this is not a simple issue, however. There is no such thing as a correct piece of software, in an absolute sense; software can be correct only with respect to something, such as a specification. Given that the specification in question is a formal one, it is in principle possible to prove that the software is correct with respect to its specification. The current state of the art does not permit this to be done in practice, other than in a very restricted sense; the technology is not yet sufficiently advanced to permit proof in most cases, though there is little doubt that the use of the technology of formal methods can produce benefits in terms of reliability. A further problem here is that the specification is itself an abstraction of a 'real-world' requirement, and that abstraction may be imperfect; proof of correctness with respect to the requirement would be very difficult to demonstrate. Also, the requirement in question is typically volatile, and user expectations may be different from the requirement. A more detailed discussion of formal methods is contained in Chapter 3.

The discussion of certification has, up to this point, made little mention of reliability; the rest of this section will concentrate on certification as it applies to reliability. There is an important distinction which must be drawn between the achievability of a particular level of reliability, and the demonstration that this level has been achieved in practice. There is no doubt that the proper application of software engineering techniques can sometimes produce very reliable software. The fact that the best techniques have been used does not however, of itself, enable one to make any statement of the level of reliability that can be associated with a particular product—though, potentially at least, it may be possible to talk about the level of reliability one would expect a typical product of a certain kind to have, given that a particular development strategy had been adopted. Demonstration of the reliability of a given product can only be attained by measurement of the reliability of that particular product.

Thus, certification that a given level of reliability has been achieved by a particular product is possible only on the basis of either actual product operation (possibly as part of some overall system) or by a regime of testing that can be related to actual use. The only known way of relating software testing environments to usage is to attempt to mimic usage (or various kinds of usage) in the testing environment. This is in itself a very challenging activity, which limits the extent to which certification is of value.

Given that a representation of usage (or of the relevant subset of usage) has been successfully produced during testing, then certification of reliability can be carried out by use of the quantitative methods described in Chapter 6. For certification purposes, it will sometimes be the case that only a subset of the normal operating environment is relevant. For example, the safety of a plant may be (partially) protected by a software-based system, so that certification of safety involves the software aspect. In such a system, the software function would typically involve monitoring certain parameters, and initiating plant shut-down when dangerous conditions arise. Thus, certification of the safety function must concentrate on the small subset of the operating environment that represents those conditions defined as dangerous.

It must be emphasized that certification of the proper application of a given development process does not constitute a certification of software reliability. Though it is reasonable to expect that a high-quality development will usually lead to a high-quality product, this cannot be guaranteed; assessment of product reliability based on observation of the development process will be discussed in Section 1.6.

When testing is carried out, the correctness or otherwise of the output resulting from each test case has to be assessed against something: normally this would be a specification, but it may in some cases be a less precise entity such as the requirement, or what the user wants or needs. When certification is based on testing, it is clear that this certification must be dependent on the view that is taken in determining the outcome of the individual test cases. It is worth clarifying the views that might be taken. These are:

- User needs. This is the system necessary to perform the particular function(s) in question; it is not always clear what is actually needed to do a particular job—many accidents could have been avoided with the benefit of hindsight.
- User wants. This is what the user genuinely believes he needs.

- Requirement. This is the user statement of his wants—which will almost certainly not coincide with what he really wants.
- Specification. This is typically an abstraction of the requirement, and encompasses the producer's understanding of the requirement.

In reality, it is only feasible to certify reliability against a specification—this is the only one of the four items listed above that can be sufficiently precise. It is unfortunate that certification will often, to the man in the street, be perceived as applicable to the needs of a particular system; this is, as discussed above, several stages removed from that which it is possible to certify.

There has recently been renewed interest in the question of certifying the correctness of software. The problem with correctness is that it is an absolute—software is correct (with respect to its specification) or it is not; usually it is not. As already mentioned, it is not in general possible to prove software to be correct, and any failed correctness proof leaves one without any measure of the degree of correctness. This is why, in most cases, certification of some appropriate level of reliability is a more practicable aim. It is also important to realize that incorrect software can be perfectly reliable in operation, since reliability is determined by the interaction between the software and its operating environment.

It will be clear from the above that there are a number of serious limitations to the ability to certify reliability. In summary, these are as follows.

(a) Certification must be based on reliability measurement during use, or during testing that is representative of use.
(b) Certification is only achievable against a specification, which may in itself be imperfect.
(c) Certification of correctness is not generally feasible—even if the software is correct with respect to its specification.

It is also clear that these limitations have potential legal problems associated with them. These will not be discussed in any detail, beyond making the comment that 'fitness for purpose' is something a consumer is legally entitled to expect, and this is in the domain of user needs, not specification.

1.6 Reliability Assessment Based on the Development Process

This section discusses both the value and the limitations of basing reliability assessment on the development process.

The best developed methods for assessment of software reliability are based upon observation of failures of the product, augmented by appropriate statistical analysis; these methods are discussed in Chapter 6. Such methods are the only way of measuring reliability of the product, since they are based upon direct observation of the product failure behaviour. As currently developed they have, however, two important shortcomings.

(a) They are concerned purely with product reliability measurement; other information concerning, for example, the methods that have been used to develop the product, is ignored. As will be seen in Chapter 6, these methods require considerable amounts of failure data to provide accurate estimates; the ability to use additional information to give greater confidence in estimates based upon small amounts of failure data would be valuable.

(b) They can be used only when the final product exists, because of their dependence on failure data. Thus, their earliest point of possible application is to data gathered during the testing phase of development. Fifteen years ago there was a lack of emphasis on validation and verification (V&V) in the early stages of software development, so that much reliance was placed on testing, and the testing phase could to some extent be relied upon to produce the required data. Today, however, there tends to be emphasis on V&V activities throughout development, thus decreasing both the dependence that developers place upon testing, and the data that the reliability assessor can expect to be able to utilize at this stage. The emergence of formal methods of software development is likely to reduce the importance and role of testing even further.

Thus, the best-developed aspects of software reliability assessment are not capable of utilizing information about the software development process, and can be applied only at a late stage of the development cycle.

In many instances, software reliability assessment is of interest only because the software in question is destined to be part of an (engineering) system of some sort, and there is a need to assess the reliability of that system as a whole. Those readers familiar with systems reliability assessment will know that reliability assessment can be carried out at the earliest stages of development; even at the feasibility stage it is often possible to express valid judgements about the reliability that is achievable by a given system. Certainly, by the time the design stage is reached, it is possible for many types of system (such as electronic) to produce quantitative statements of the reliability likely to be achieved by the eventual manufactured system.

These capabilities for system reliability assessment exist for three main reasons.

(a) Systems are made up of components, and identical components are used in many kinds of systems, so that the experience of using components leads to the availability of component-failure data. The reliabilities of the components are thus 'known' and can be used, together with the knowledge of the structure of the system, to produce estimates of the system reliability.

(b) The laws of nature can be used to support or even replace the use of failure data on components. This enables such things as differences of materials or operating environments to be taken into account

(c) Failures due to faults in the system design can often be ignored, because they are much less frequent than those due to physical failure of components and/or because the historical component failure data implicitly includes the 'normal' effect of system design faults on component failures.

It is clear from this that it is unreasonable to expect to have similar capabilities for quantitative software reliability assessment at the early stages of software development: software is not built of existing components of known reliability, and probably will not be for some considerable time; and there are no (known) laws of nature that can be applied to try to substitute for this lack of software component reliability data. This does not, however, dispense with the need to be able to assess reliability early in the life cycle. Rather, it limits the expectations and confidence that can be placed in any assessment that is carried out.

In addition to the need to assess software reliability because of the need to do so for systems in general that contain that software, there are a number of other motivations for the early assessment of software reliability. These include the need for the project manager to be able to monitor and control the process of developing software; early warning of problem areas leads to a more effective solution—this is as true of reliability as it is of other aspects of requirements. There is a continuing need to reassess the achievability of reliability requirements, based upon progress to date and plans for future development.

Assessment of the development process is also a necessary complement to any quantitative assessment of the product that is carried out later. For example, any confidence that is placed in the results of a reliability prediction produced during the testing phase must depend upon the confidence in the specification against which the software is tested, and the degree of confidence that the testing environment is indeed representative of the usage environment. Furthermore, particularly in the case of high-integrity systems, there may quite simply not be enough failure data to permit high confidence to be placed in the software reliability based on this alone. The assessor or licenser of such systems clearly needs to have confidence that the development of the software is in accordance with the proper professional standards, in addition to any failure data based prediction; even taken together, these two kinds of information will not always suffice.

The current state of the art in reliability assessment based upon observation of the development process is very limited. Approaches that can be adopted are closely related to quality-assurance activities, and have associated with them a good deal of subjectivity. There is currently no available quantitative approach for software comparable to those for many kinds of hardware-based systems; any assessment of software reliability based upon observation of the process of software development is, at present, necessarily qualitative in nature.

One well-documented approach appears in the HSE guidelines for programmable electronic systems in safety-related applications (Health and Safety Executive, 1987). These guidelines contain checklists applying to all stages of the development process, in recognition of the fact that reliable software is a result of actions carried out throughout development. As an illustration, Fig. 1.1 shows part of the software specification checklist. These particular guidelines are of greatest usefulness in the situation where, in addition to the customer and the developer of the software, there is a third party responsible for assessing or licensing the software. They are, however, readily adaptable to the situations where either the customer or the developer are themselves interested in the assessment; in the later case, the checklists may become an integral part of the quality-assurance activity—though care must be taken to ensure that assessment and quality assurance remain distinct from V&V and testing.

Whatever methods are used, reliability assessment (and where ·possible, measurement) and assurance against reliability requirements should be carried out on the intermediate products of each phase of the development process; however imperfect the methods, it is better to do this than to await the final product right at the end of the process. These intermediate assessments are facilitated by well-defined phase ends and reviews, leading to the definition, establishment and reinforcement of a process aimed at creating reliable software, rather than just building it and trying to put reliability in at the end by extensive testing and debugging.

In conclusion of this section, it is worth restating that there are limitations to any ability to assess reliability of software based only on observation of its process of development. Perhaps the most important limitation, which will apply almost irrespective of any future developments, is that a given process will produce products with a range of reliability characteristics; the process may be indicative of the achieved level of reliability, but measurement of reliability can be carried out only on the product.

1.7 Data Collection

As discussed in Section 1.6, the assessment of hardware reliability depends heavily upon the availability of data concerning component failures. There is also a role for data collection in the area of software reliability assessment; the assessment procedure outlined in Section 1.6 and the Health and Safety Executive document cited is in essence a particular kind of monitoring of the software development process and can be regarded as a form of data collection, applied in this instance to the development process of the product of interest.

Thus, the collection of data about the software development process can be seen to be a direct aid to the assessment of software reliability of the product about whose development process data is collected. There are also less immediate benefits to be gained from data collection. One of the reasons that

Checklist No 10A : Software specification

Item No	Item				Comments
10A.7	Are design reviews carried out in the development of the software specification involving users, system designers and programmers?	Y	N	NA	
10A.8	Is the final specification checked against the user requirements by persons other than those producing the specification before beginning the design phase?	Y	N	NA	
10A.9	Are automated tools used as an aid to the development of the software specification in	Y	N	NA	
	(i) documentation?				
	(ii) consistency checking?				
10A.10	Within the software specification, is there a clear and concise statement of:	Y	N	NA	
	(i) each safety related function to be implemented?				
	(ii) the information to be given to the operator at any time?				
	(iii) the required action on each operator command including illegal or unexpected commands?				
	(iv) the communications requirements between the PES and other equipment?				
	(v) the initial states for all internal variables and external interfaces?				
	(vi) the required action on power down and recovery? (eg saving of important data in non-volatile memory)				
	(vii) the different requirements for each phase of plant/machine operation? (eg start-up, normal operation, shutdown)				
	(viii) the anticipated ranges of input variables and the required action on out-of-range variables?				
	(ix) the required performance in terms of speed, accuracy and precision?				
	(x) the constraints put on the software by the hardware? (eg speed, memory size, word length)				
	(xi) internal self-checks to be carried out and the action on detection of a failure?				
10A.11	(i) Is there a software test specification?	Y	N	NA	

Fig. 1.1. Example of checklist. (Reproduced from Health & Safety Executive (1987).)

assessment during development is so difficult is that the level of understanding of cause and effect, as it applies to software reliability, is very low. There is little dispute with the statement that reliability of software is determined above all by events during its development, but there is little beyond anecdote and intuition to indicate which events during development have the greatest influence on reliability in use of the software produced. The collection, storage and analysis of data about the development of software products, and their subsequent reliabilities, can be an invaluable aid to discovering a much clearer relationship between the process and the reliability of the product, both within a given organization and more generally. Thus, data collection can ultimately lead to improvement, and possibly quantification, of the ability to assess reliability during development.

A particular instance of the usefulness of data collection is in comparing the efficacy of candidate software engineering techniques or methodologies (perhaps that currently used and a newly suggested one). The experimental use of both techniques on broadly similar projects, allied with collection of data about (for example) costs, timescales, and reliability can enable objective judgements about the relative merits of the competing methods.

Data collection as it applies to the whole development process will not be discussed further at this point, as this important topic is focused on in Chapter 10. This section concentrates on the particular aspects of data collection associated with the application of the quantitative software reliability assessment methods that are discussed in detail in Chapter 6.

Typically, software reliability models make use of failure data concerning the times at which failures have been observed to occur. This time metric has to be chosen appropriately for the software in question, and most models can be modified to cope with data about numbers of observed failures in given time intervals as an (inferior) substitute for the failure times themselves.

Where the models are to be used to assess the reliability of the software in its usage environment, based upon failures observed during testing (a common scenario), the models furthermore demand that the environment simulated by the testing is representative of use. It is therefore important that a record is kept of the sets of input data used during testing, so that it is possible to determine how well the test environment matches the usage environment. (This data will often be stored for other reasons, so is not necessarily a burden.)

The point has to be made that usage environments are not easy to characterize. Examples such as compilers, whose input data comprises (correct and incorrect) computer programs, and operating systems, serve to illustrate this point. Even in simpler cases, the usage environment can be an elusive concept. In a plant-protection system controlled by software, for example, the 'safe' system state(s) may be well understood and easy to describe; the potential accident scenarios, when the successful operation of the protection system becomes of especial importance, will typically be very difficult to anticipate—especially when it is remembered that characterization of the usage environment necessitates 'knowing' the frequency with which particular sets of input will be encountered.

This last example also illustrates the fact that multiple usage environments often exist. Reliability estimates may be required for each one, each necessitating its own dedicated set of tests.

There is an important problem with the replication of usage environments, besides the above-mentioned difficulty of doing so. This is the lack of understanding of the relationship between usage environment and failure: a relatively minor change to the usage environment may suddenly expose a new cluster of faults in an area of code previously rarely executed, and conversely a fundamental and sizeable change in the environment will often have no effect whatever on reliability. This is a little counter-intuitive, as in most engineering contexts a small change in environment will cause a small change in failure characteristics. A corollary of this property is that a small error in determining the usage environment can cause a massive error in estimating the reliability. This problem may be addressable by a form of sensitivity analysis, to judge the effect of perturbations in the assumed environment on the reliability estimates, but this is very much an untried hypothesis.

Although, as the discussion above shows, characterization of usage environment is difficult, it is often worthwhile. As well as enabling good estimates of operational reliability based upon testing data, it has the advantage of focussing attention on those areas of the software that are going to be heavily used. Also, the necessity of involving the customer in establishing what the user environment is likely to be will have a much wider beneficial effect in terms of validation of the software: involvement of the customer is likely to heighten awareness among the development team of what it is the customer actually wants.

1.8 Research Directions

In this section an attempt is made to indicate a number of areas in which current and future research may lead to significant advances over the next few years. The topics discussed here are utilization of knowledge of the structure of software, fault-tolerant software, and explanatory variables; these will be discussed in turn. Real progress in these areas, built on the foundations described in this book, will lead to great improvements in the achievement of reliable software.

The idea of estimating the reliability of a piece of software from a knowledge of the way the software is built up of individual modules of 'known' reliability is not new: methods have been suggested by Littlewood (1979a), Shooman (1976) and Cheung (1980)—indeed, these techniques are in some ways parallels of system reliability techniques that are much older. As developed at the moment, however, these models have a number of practical drawbacks. Typically, they assume that the software comprises a number of modules of known reliability, linked together in a known structure. The frequencies of execution of the individual paths through this structure are known, as are the probabilities of failure on transition between the individual modules. As can be seen, the application of these models is dependent on obtaining a good knowledge of many parameters, most of which are in themselves very difficult to estimate.

These drawbacks have led to very limited application of these models. This picture might change if a general trend were to be established towards reusable software and libraries of modules of known reliability. Some of these structural models may, however, be applicable in the slightly different context of fault-tolerant systems, which are described in detail in Chapter 4. In such systems, structure is 'added' with the aim of giving some protection against faults that may be resident in individual modules of a program. Typically, a number of diverse implementations of the same algorithm are executed and a vote or acceptance test of some sort determines which of the alternative algorithms is to be believed on any one occasion. There has been a good deal of debate about the extent to which diverse implementations may contain non-diverse faults, leading to what is known as the dependent failure problem.

Until recently there has been very little evidence either way to resolve this question, but it now appears that a significant proportion of faults are likely to exist in a number of diverse implementations of the same specification. This gives added stimulus to the search for models that can take due account of both the structural considerations implied by diversity, and the dependence that is now known to exist between the failure characteristics of diverse implementations.

Another interesting research area in the software fault tolerance field concerns back-to-back testing. Given that a number of implementations of a piece of software have been produced, it is possible to build a test harness that simultaneously submits common test data to each of the diverse implementations. Comparison of results can be done automatically, with agreement of output implying either that all versions have computed correctly, or that all have made the same mistake. Disagreement may be due to a fault in one or more versions, or due to minor numerical differences caused by the limitations of computational accuracy. There is great potential here for carrying out vast amounts of testing automatically. This can serve either or both of two purposes. It can be used as a means of testing (and debugging) the diverse system as a whole, or as a means of testing the individual copies. The system may then be implemented either as a diverse or a conventional system.

The economics of this latter suggestion—produce diverse software purely for testing purposes—have not been thoroughly investigated, but it may well turn out, for certain types of software, to be an efficient way of achieving high reliability. The other economic question that is sometimes discussed in this context is whether it may be cheaper to achieve high reliability through a number of 'ordinary' programs executing within some voting framework than it is to devote the resources necessary to obtain a single 'excellent' program.

These arguments need to take account of the 'dependent failure' problem arising from the commonality of specification (which may be wrong) as well as from the common inclusion of a fault in more than one program.

The third important area of research may bring about a unification of the methods and ideas in Section 1.6 of this chapter and those in the Chapter 6. The suggestions in Section 1.6 attempt to allow information about the way in which the software has been developed to be used in assessing reliability; the methods of Chapter 6 are incapable of doing this. Explanatory models may overcome this difficulty by allowing information about development and usage of software to be utilized side by side with failure data in a single model.

An explanatory model is, then, one that includes explanatory variables, which are included to 'explain' the effect of certain factors on the reliability. The development of such models is highly dependent on the collection of data that permits the link to be made between reliability measurements and the way in which the software in question has been developed or is being used. The point must be made, however, that explanatory variables indicate what effects are observed on average, or in general; only the failure data can be expected to contain the signature of the individual product.

The most immediate benefit here would be the availability of models that use all of the available information about the software to estimate its reliability. In particular, the models would allow (at least relative, qualitative) assessment of reliability during development, followed by assessment based on failure data as and when that became available; the failure data would have a progressively greater effect as it accumulated over time. Furthermore, such models would enhance the ability to predict reliability under differing usage scenarios.

The combination of these models with good data collection will lead to a much improved knowledge of which techniques work and which do not, for what application (etc.); furthermore, it will be possible to quantify the extent to which these techniques have been successful, thus permitting a scientific balance to be made in cost versus reliability trade-offs, for example.

The explanatory variables described above correspond to cost drivers in estimating models discussed in Chapter 11. The development and use of explanatory variable models for software reliability will enable many of the important themes of this chapter to become a natural part of the reliability assessment process:

- the need for clear definitions and statements of reliability requirements;
- the importance of a process designed to produce a product with the required reliability, and containing activities and events that permit the stepwise assessment of reliability;
- the value of the collection and analysis of data and metrics from the software development process.

At present, these are generally based on individual insight and manual methods. Successful development of techniques and support tools will facilitate reliable development of reliable software with wider confidence throughout industry.

2

Software Design for Reliability

Ian Sommerville

2.1 Introduction 21
2.2 Formal System Specification 28
2.3 Object-oriented Design 29
2.4 An Object-oriented Design Example 36
2.5 Object Implementation 44
2.6 Summary 48
2.7 Further Reading 48

2.1 Introduction

This book is concerned with the production of reliable software systems and it is obvious that one of the principal factors governing the reliability of a software system is the design of that software. Although Chapter 1 argues that the relationship between perceived reliability and the number of faults in a software system is a complex one, it is generally true that the fewer the faults in a software system, the better the reliability will be. Thus, general objectives of the design process are to produce software that contains as few faults as possible (fault avoidance), software that behaves predictably in the presence of faults (fault tolerance) and software that is readily repaired (fault discovery and removal).

This chapter is particularly concerned with describing an approach to software design where faults are less likely to be introduced into the software. In addition, the approach should also simplify the removal of those software faults that do occur. The following three chapters are concerned explicitly with fault-avoidance, fault tolerance and fault removal. The techniques discussed there complement the approach to design that is suggested here.

The chapter is primarily a tutorial on modern software design techniques and we are particularly concerned with discussing a technique known as object-oriented design. This technique was first used in the design of software for artificial intelligence applications but it has much wider applicability. It offers significant benefits in designing software for both embedded real-time

21

systems and some classes of data-processing systems. The chapter is aimed principally at software developers and project leaders, but software project managers should read the chapter introduction and the final summary for an overview of how object-oriented design can lead to software that contains fewer faults and is readily changed.

Of course, the problem in all software design tutorials is that the design techniques are stated as being useful for large system design yet can only be illustrated using small, manageable examples. There is no way that this can be avoided and we have to rely on the intuition of the readers to recognize similarities between the problems presented here and those in their own application domain.

Let us start by considering the design process itself. The conventional view of this is that design progresses through functional specification to high-level design, data design, detailed design and implementation. We propose a more general model (into which the conventional approach fits) but which has a variable number of stages. This model views the design process as a sequence of steps where each step consists of a specification phase followed by a realization phase that sets out the *structure* of a design that realises that specification. Realizations become less abstract as the system is specified in greater and greater detail. The final realization step is the implementation of the software system.

Figure 2.1 shows a possible sequence of specification and realization steps for a system that has both software and hardware components and whose software is made up of a number of interacting programs. The design model set out in Fig. 2.1(a) is different from the conventional view of the design process, where the output from one of the stages is taken to be the specification for the

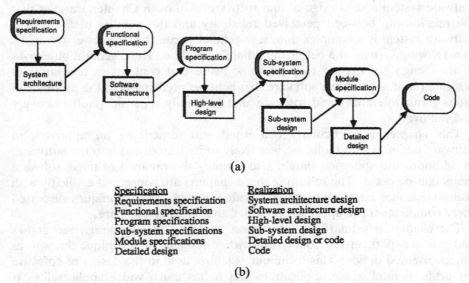

(a)

Specification	Realization
Requirements specification	System architecture design
Functional specification	Software architecture design
Program specifications	High-level design
Sub-system specifications	Sub-system design
Module specifications	Detailed design or code
Detailed design	Code

(b)

Fig. 2.1. (a) The design process. (b) Stages in the design process.

following stage. For example, normal practice is to take the high-level design and use this as a specification of the detailed design.

The problem with the conventional approach is that it can be difficult to separate specification and realization. The reasons for this are partly to do with human nature and partly to do with the fact that specification documents may have to serve both as a basis for a contract and as a basis for further design. In order to establish feasibility, some early design may be necessary and it is natural to include this in the contractural document. As a result, specification documents are, sometimes, a mixture of specification (what) and premature design (how). One serves to confuse the other and deliberately forcing a separation these notions makes for a more understandable design.

The structural description of the software at any particular level in the software process (except, perhaps, the most detailed design) should always be supplemented with a precise specification that provides a complete description of the realization at that level. This specification may be in natural language or in some formal notation designed to express software specifications. Thus, the realizations in the left-hand column in Fig. 2.1(b), have associated specifications which are those in the right-hand column of the following row. Structuring the design in this way factors out the design detail so that comprehensibility is maintained without losing completeness and precision.

It is not, generally, possible to translate a specification into a realization automatically. Human ingenuity is required to analyse the specification and determine how this is best realized. For example, a specification may describe a number of logical components and, given other system requirements, the designer may choose to realize them as parallel tasks. In other circumstances, a more appropriate realization might be as procedures in a sequential program. One of the benefits of an object-oriented design is that it allows the design to be considered as a set of components without forcing the designer to make such realization decisions.

Object-oriented design should not be confused with object-oriented programming. Object-oriented programming languages such as Smalltalk-80 (Goldberg & Robson, 1983) allow object-oriented designs to be implemented directly and incorporate notions such as inheritance and run-time operation binding. Object-oriented design can be practised irrespective of whether or not an object-oriented programming language is used. This is discussed later, in Section 2.5.

Reliability *per se* should be a design objective but it is not a design characteristic that can be assessed by static analysis of the design. Rather, we suggest that software reliability is dependent on the design exhibiting other characteristics that maximize its checkability and understandability, minimize its complexity and, hence, maximize the modifiability of that design. The characteristics we believe to be most important (as far as reliability is concerned) are the visibility of the design (which should be maximized) and the coupling of the design (which should be minimized). These are defined as follows.

- *Design visibility*. The visibility of a design is an assessment of how well the characteristics of a design specification are reflected in the realization of that design. This means it should be possible to take any part of the specification and identify where that part is realized. Realizations must be expressed in a form that is readily understandable and structured to reflect the specification structure.
- *Design coupling*. The coupling of a design is an assessment of the dependencies of the units of that design. Low coupling means that the design is made up of mutually independent modules with few shared data structures. Coupling metrics are discussed in Chapter 10.

These are the most important design characteristics as far as reliability is concerned for the following reasons.

- The achievement of reliable software depends on stringent validation during software development. This validation is simplified if each design entity may be considered in its own right without reference to other design units.
- Static design analysis has been demonstrated (Mills *et al.*, 1987) to be a very effective means of detecting design faults. If the transition between design levels is clearly visible, this analysis is simplified and the probability of finding errors in that transition is increased.
- The repair of faults in software subsystems is least likely to cause faults in other subsystems if the systems are mutually independent. Furthermore, the discovery of faults is simplified if the software design is visible. However, even with mutually independent subsystems some classes of fault such as timing faults may be introduced when one of these subsystems is modified.
- The use of shared data structures must be minimized if low coupling is to be achieved. This means that errors arising from misunderstandings about the use and organization of data structures between programmers or programming teams are less likely.

There does not appear to be any software metric that is related to design visibility. Some of the metrics that appear to be useful for assessing program understandability such as De Young/Kampen's readability measure (1979) may have some relevance, but design visibility is concerned with the equivalence of different system representations. It is obviously essential for a representation to be understood before such equivalence can be demonstrated, but an assessment of the visibility as defined above can probably only be made subjectively during design reviews.

The metrics that have been developed to estimate the coupling of modules such as those by Yin & Winchester (1978) and Henry & Kafura (1981) have been developed using Structured Design (Constantine & Yourdon, 1979) and it is not clear whether or not their notion of coupling is applicable to other design methods. It involves analysing a program structure chart that records procedural relationships and, although this would appear to be suitable for more general use, more research work must be done before a universal coupling metric can be derived.

Design visibility is best achieved by making use of a consistent approach to realizing a specification (consistency is the key here, no particular approach can be prescribed). Judicious use should be made of graphical design representations in combination with textual and tabular descriptions in formal and informal notations. Graphical notations are particularly important because the natural structuring that they impose simplifies the task of human understanding.

This is illustrated in Fig. 2.2, which shows the design for part of an electronic mail system. This collects mail from the user's terminal, performs some address translation, processes the mail in preparation for dispatch and hands it over to a network manager for transmission. Figure 2.2(a) is a simplified, incomplete description of the subsystems and, in practice, more detailed, complete subsystem descriptions would be produced. Notice that each description references a specification that provides more information about the entity being described. This specification might be formal, using techniques such as those described by Cohen *et al.* (1986) or informal, expressed in natural language or some formatted description language.

Notice also the numbering of table entries corresponds with the numbers on the design diagram. This numbering makes it easy for the designer to ensure that all diagram entities have actually been described in the table. The key to design visibility and comprehension is structured documentation of this form where the reader is given the opportunity to assimilate information before having to pursue the design in greater detail.

Increasingly, automated tools are being used in the documentation of designs. In the above example, a graphical editing system might be used to produce the diagram and this could be linked to a data dictionary system where information about the design entities is maintained. Apart from the obvious advantages of computer-produced documentation such as easy modifiability, the most effective design-support tools also provide design checking. They can ensure that all diagram entities have a data dictionary entry (for example) and can maintain simple consistency rules. The use of such systems is recommended whenever possible.

Low coupling in a design is achieved by delaying design decisions, so that the scope of any particular design decision is minimized, and by information-hiding so that system information is accessible only to those operations that must have access to that information. In particular, access to the representations of data structures should always be carefully controlled.

A system that exhibits low coupling is made up of a number of independent subsystems that communicate via precisely specified interfaces. Each subsystem should be an independent entity that does not depend on *any* features of other subsystems and it should be possible to replace or modify any subsystem without changing other parts of the overall system. Thus, if

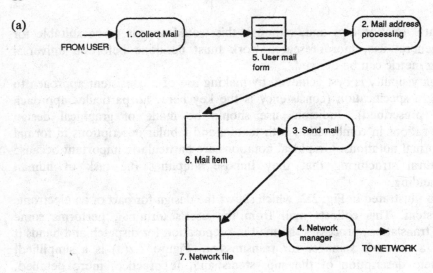

(a)

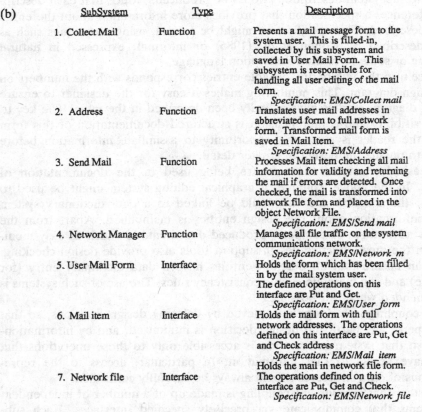

(b)

SubSystem	Type	Description
1. Collect Mail	Function	Presents a mail message form to the system user. This is filled-in, collected by this subsystem and saved in User Mail Form. This subsystem is responsible for handling all user editing of the mail form. *Specification: EMS/Collect mail*
2. Address	Function	Translates user mail addresses in abbreviated form to full network form. Transformed mail form is saved in Mail Item. *Specification: EMS/Address*
3. Send Mail	Function	Processes Mail item checking all mail information for validity and returning the mail if errors are detected. Once checked, the mail is transformed into network file form and placed in the object Network File. *Specification: EMS/Send mail*
4. Network Manager	Function	Manages all file traffic on the system communications network. *Specification: EMS/Network_m*
5. User Mail Form	Interface	Holds the form which has been filled in by the mail system user. The defined operations on this interface are Put and Get. *Specification: EMS/User_form*
6. Mail item	Interface	Holds the mail form with full network addresses. The operations defined on this interface are Put, Get and Check address *Specification: EMS/Mail_item*
7. Network file	Interface	Holds the mail in network file form. The operations defined on this interface are Put, Get and Check. *Specification: EMS/Network_file*

Fig. 2.2. (a) Part of an electronic mail system design. (b) Informal descriptions of mail system entities.

subsystem errors exist or are introduced, they are localized and do not affect other parts of the system.

Considering a system as logically independent subsystems allows decisions on concurrency to be delayed. Because each subsystem is a stand-alone entity it may either be initiated in a sequential program or may execute concurrently with other subsystems. Readers familiar with the MASCOT approach to software development (Simpson, 1986) will notice the similarities between MASCOT and this view; in MASCOT, the subsystems are concurrent functions (activities) and the interfaces are IDAs.

The subsystems making up a system may be implemented either as functions, processes or as abstract objects (discussed below). The interfaces between these subsystems should always be implemented as abstract objects.

Figure 2.2(a) shows a functional view of the electronic mail system and this approach to software design is easily understood, widely used and, we assume, familiar to most readers of this chapter. It is the basis of methods such as Structured Design (Constantine & Yourdon, 1979) that have been used successfully in very many projects. It is a valid approach to software design but we believe that an alternative, object-oriented approach offers some advantages over functional decomposition as a design technique. We concentrate in the remainder of this chapter on this technique of software design.

It is important to emphasize at this point that there is not a single design method that is applicable to all systems in all application domains and that object-oriented design is not necessarily a method that should be applied universally. For some classes of data-processing system, we would not recommend the use of object-oriented design but would recommend the use of JSP (Jackson, 1975) as this has proved to be eminently suitable where the data being processed conforms to a relatively simple structure. Similarly, for systems where minimal state information is maintained in components a functional approach or a data-flow approach to design is perhaps more appropriate.

However, an object-oriented approach is well-suited to the construction of embedded software systems with high reliability requirements and other approaches to software design are often inappropriate for such systems. The reason for this is that a natural view of many embedded systems is as a set of entities that maintain their own state and whose actions are dependent on that state. Object-oriented design is based on the notion of state localization and thus generates designs that have low coupling in this situation. It is possible to realize an object-oriented design as either a sequential program or as a set of cooperating processes.

The examples here are drawn from the real-time systems domain and we demonstrate that embedded systems can be structured as a set of interacting objects. Space does not permit a description of alternative design approaches but the reading list included with this chapter includes references to these techniques.

2.2 Formal System Specification

This is perhaps an appropriate place to set out how we view the place of formal methods of software design in the engineering of reliable software. A formal approach to design fits into the above model but requires that both the specifications and the realizations should be expressed in some notation whose syntax and semantics are formally specified. Formal system design involves developing a mathematical proof that the realization in fact meets the specification as defined.

A formal development method (illustrated in Fig. 2.3) involves transforming an initial formal specification through a series of stages until an executable program is produced. Each transformation is mathematically verified so that the correspondence between the initial specification and the ultimate realization is guaranteed. This is a laudable aim but for most classes of system it is not yet practically achievable. As discussed in Chapter 3, proving correctness of a design is very expensive, requires the use of specialized staff and, even when a proof has been developed, there are no absolute tests that will ensure that that proof is correct. Until automated verification tools are available, formal system development is unlikely to be practical for the majority of software developments.

One situation where formal program verification may be justified is in the validation of relatively small, critical system components. Failure in one of these components might jeopardize the entire system and the extra validation costs incurred in using formal verification may be justified.

However, whilst proving the correctness of a realization is not currently cost-effective, the same does not necessarily hold true for expressing the specifications of one or more levels using a formal notation. This is currently the subject of a great deal of research and, at the time of writing, some experiences of using formal specifications in production software projects have been reported (Earl *et al.*, 1986; Hayes, 1987). These are generally positive.

They emphasize that the advantage of formal specification is that the adoption of formal specification techniques forces a complete and rigorous analysis of the system requirements. Errors and omissions that, without formal specification, would not be discovered until detailed design and implementation are detected at an earlier stage in the software process. Faults that are due

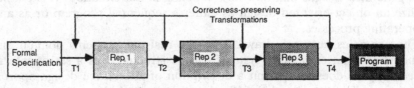

Fig. 2.3. Formal transformations.

to misunderstandings of or inconsistencies within the specification are likely to be avoided. An overview of formal specification is given in Chapter 3 and, for interested readers, a good introduction to this area is given by Cohen *et al.* (1986).

The cost-effectiveness of using formal specifications is difficult to measure and, to some extent, choosing to use formal specifications must largely be an act of faith. However, it is recommended that formal specification techniques are worthy of consideration and evaluation but that informal techniques that emphasize the structure of the design are an essential supplement to these techniques, particularly for abstract expressions of the software design.

2.3 Object-oriented Design

Object-oriented design is a design method that is based on information hiding. It differs from the more familiar functional approach to design in that it views a software system as a set of interacting objects, with their own private state, rather than as a set of functions.

An object is an entity that has a state and a set of operations to inspect and modify that state. Objects communicate by passing messages to each other and these messages initiate object operations. This view fits in with our previous statement that systems should be made up of independent subsystems communicating via abstract interfaces. In object-oriented design, both subsystems and interfaces are considered to be objects.

The advantages of object-oriented design may be summarized as follows.

- All shared data areas are eliminated as communication between objects is via message passing. This reduces overall system coupling as there is no possibility of unexpected modifications to shared information. It also enhances design visibility as the design complexity is reduced.
- Objects are independent entities that may readily be changed because all state and representation information is held within the object itself. No access and hence no deliberate or accidental use of this information by other objects is possible with the result that changes may be made without reference to other system objects.
- Objects may be distributed and may execute either sequentially or in parallel. Decisions on parallelism need not be taken at an early stage of the design process.
- An object appears to be an appropriate component for software reuse. The re-use of components should lead to higher-reliability systems because these components should have been validated in operational systems.

The basic premise which underlies information hiding as a design strategy is the notion that the binding of logical control and data structures to their realizations should be made as late as possible in the design process. The logical behaviour of an entity is independent of its representation, so the representation should be concealed from other parts of the program.

Communication between design entities is minimized (thus increasing the understandability of the design) and the design is relatively easy to change as modification only affects a minimal number of entities. The possibility of unforeseen effects of the software change is reduced because it is immediately obvious which entities are affected by the change.

In the discussion of object-oriented design, we use Ada as a design description language. Ada has been chosen because of its availability and because it is likely to become the predominant language for the development of real-time embedded computer systems. The most important Ada construct for discussing object-oriented design is the Ada package.

For readers unfamiliar with Ada, packages are summarized in the following section. This section may be skipped by those readers who have at least a reading knowledge of Ada.

2.3.1 Ada packages

The Ada package construct is an information-hiding construct that allows the software designer some control over the visibility of declarations made in his or her program. Unlike Pascal, say, where all visibility or scope control is lexical and depends on the nesting of procedures, the use of packages allows a set of declarations to be gathered together. Only those parts of the program that require access to the declarations in that set need make the package visible. Declarations may be made within packages that are confined entirely to that package and that are only used by the procedures and functions published in the package interface.

Ada packages have a specification part and a body part. The specification part declares the package interface and sets out those entities (normally only constants, types and subroutines if an object-oriented approach is adopted) that are accessible from outside the package. The body part provides the implementation of the entities declared in the specification part. Thus, for each procedure or function whose name and parameters are set out in the specification, the corresponding Ada code implementing that procedure or function must be provided in the package body.

Example 2.1 is an Ada package specification for an object class **Process_ queue** where entries are made at the end of the queue and removed from the front of the queue. This specification is annotated with comments (starting with- -) which explain the individual declarations in the package. Assume that the entries in this queue are of type **PROCESS_ID** which is declared elswhere in a **Process** object.

Example 2.1. An Ada package specification for a queue.

```
package Process_queue is
-- The following type declaration is 'exported'.
-- This means that objects of type Queue.T can be declared
-- in the user's program. Notice that the name of the type is
-- simply T but, when used, the type name is prefixed by the
-- package name thus giving the meaningful name Queue.T.
-- The type is declared as a private type which means that the
-- only predefined operations on that type are assignment and
-- equality. Its structure is not visible outside the package.
-- Apart from assignment and equality, the only functions
-- which operate on that type are those declared in the
-- Queue package

   type T is private ;
   -- The append procedure adds items to the queue.
   -- The in out designator means that Q is altered by the procedure.
   procedure Append (Q: in out T ; Item: PROCESS_ID) ;
   -- The remove procedure takes an item from the front of the
   -- queue. The out designator means that Item is initialized
   -- by this procedure. It is actually set to the value removed from
   -- the queue.
   procedure Remove (Q: in out T ; Item: out PROCESS_ID ) ;
   -- The Is_full function is used to determine if there is room to add
   -- a new item to the queue. Notice that this is used in preference
   -- to comparing the size of the queue with some maximum value.
   -- Thus, queue sizes may be changed without program changes.
   -- Information hiding again!
   function Is_full (Q: T) return BOOLEAN ;
   -- The size function returns the number of items on the queue.
   -- It returns a value of type NATURAL (0 or more)
   function Size (Q: T) return NATURAL ;
private
   -- The private part of an Ada package sets out the
   -- representation of those types which are declared to be private
   -- types. As far as the designer is concerned, this is irrelevant
   -- but it must be included in Ada programs so that the Ada
   -- compiler can allocate space for objects of these types. In this
   -- case, we simply declare the queue as a record type with
   -- components the current front and end and the queue values.
   -- There are a number of alternative implementations.
   Q_size: constant := 100 ;
   type Q_INDEX is range 1..Q_size ;
   type Q_ARRAY is array (Q_INDEX) of PROCESS_ID ;
   type T is record
      Front: Q_INDEX ;
      Rear: Q_INDEX ;
      Values: Q_ARRAY ;
   end record ;
end Process_queue ;
```

The package body implementing this queue would include the code defining the queue procedures as well as any other housekeeping information required. It is often the case when practising object-oriented design that the designer is only interested in the object specifications. This is possible because the objects are independent and details on how they are to be implemented may be postponed.

Packages are, in fact, more general than discussed here and it is possible to define so-called generic packages that can be instantiated according to the types of entity they manage. This level of detail, however, is unnecessary for the remainder of the discussion of object-oriented design.

Ada packages may be used to implement objects but the reader should not therefore assume that Ada is a true object-oriented language. Objects in Ada do not have full 'civil rights' and particular problems are caused by the fact that objects defined as packages may not be passed as parameters to other objects. Furthermore, exception handling is not properly integrated with the object-oriented approach, which can cause problems in real-time systems implementation.

It is also possible to use Ada tasks to implement objects in which case the objects are parallel rather than sequential entities. Ada tasking is fairly complex and we do not cover it in this chapter. However, the reader who is involved with real-time systems implementation should be aware that the requirement for parallelism does not exclude an object-oriented approach being taken during the system design.

2.3.2 Information hiding

The notion of information hiding was introduced earlier in this section. To illustrate how this approach to design can simplify system maintenance, consider the following simple example.

A temperature control system is required for individual rooms in a building. Each room has a heater unit, a temperature sensor and a thermostat that is used to set the required temperature. Users of the system set their desired temperature and the control system maintains that temperature by monitoring sensor values and switching the heater accordingly.

An obvious design for this system is to maintain an array of temperature values that is indexed by room number. Thus array element Temperature_required (15) holds the desired temperature for Room 15 and so on. As expressed in an Ada-like PDL, the system design might be expressed as shown in Example 2.2. The design description language used is close to Ada but, to avoid clutter, we relax the need to declare names before they are used when the name is self-explanatory.

Assume that the number of rooms in the building is held in a constant called Number_of_rooms. Assume also that an array also exists that records the current status of each heater and that, again, this is indexed by room number.

Example 2.2. A heating control system.

```
type Heater_settings is  (ON, OFF) ;
Temperature_required: array (1..Number_of_rooms) of INTEGER ;
Heater_status: array (1..Number_of_rooms) of Heater_settings ;

for i in 1..Number_of_rooms loop
    if Temperature_sensor (i) >= Temperature_required (i) then
        if Heater_status(i) = ON then
            Switch_heater (i, OFF) ;
            Heater_status (i) := OFF ;
        end if ;
    else
        if Heater_status (i)= OFF then
            Switch_heater (i, ON) ;
            Heater_status (i) := ON ;
        end if ;
    end if ;
end loop ;
```

This is a simple and straightforward design such as might be discovered in a number of control systems. Notice the use of the functions **Temperature_sensor** and **Switch_heater**. Given a room number as a parameter, these functions interrogate the temperature sensor in that room and switch the heater in that room. Of course, this loop would normally be embedded in another control loop which repeats the cycle indefinitely.

An alternative system design tries to hide as much information as possible (Example 2.3). In this approach, we view the system as being made up of **Room** objects each of which has a state that includes the actual temperature and the required temperature and a heater object that can respond to messages to switch on and off and to discover its state. Ada, in common with most other languages, does not support explicit message passing, so message passing is modelled here by calling functions or procedures that are part of the object. Thus, to send a message to switch on a heater, a function called **Switch** within object **Heater** is called.

The control loop that maintains temperatures is shown as Example 2.3.

Example 2.3. A heating control system using information hiding.

```
Rooms: array (1..Number_of_rooms) of Room.T ;

for i in 1..Number_of_rooms loop
    if Rooms (i).Temperature > Rooms (i).Required_temperature then
        if Rooms (i).Heater.Setting  = ON then
            Rooms (i).Heater.Switch (OFF) ;
        end if ;
    else
        if Rooms (i).Heater.Setting  = OFF then
            Rooms (i).Heater.Switch (ON) ;
        end if ;
    end if ;
end loop ;
```

Example 2.4 shows an Ada PDL package specification for the Room object class (or type). The package **Room** does *not* define an object but defines a class of objects. Individual objects are created by instantiating this class. This instantiation is simply carried out by declaring a variable to be of type **Room.T**.

Example 2.4. The specification of a Room object type.

```
package Room is
    type T is private ;   -- this means the type representation is not accessible
    function Temperature return INTEGER ;
    function Required_temperature return INTEGER ;
    procedure Set_temperature (Temp: INTEGER) ;
    package Heater is
        type STATUS is (ON, OFF) ;
        function Setting return STATUS ;
        procedure Switch (V:STATUS ) ;
    end Heater ;
private
    -- For implementation reasons, Ada requires the representation of the type
    -- Room.T to be declared here. When used as a design description language
    -- there is no need to make these declarations.
end Room ;
```

The designs shown in Examples 2.2 and 2.3 appear similar, but the advantages of the information-hiding approach become clear when we postulate the following (reasonable) changes to the system.

The heating control system is to be modified so that there is no longer a one-to-one relationship between rooms, sensors and heaters. That is, there may be more than one heater in a room and the system switches all heaters on or off depending on the sensor value. In addition, the system must also be able to handle shared heating situations where a number of rooms have a shared heater and temperature setting but individual sensors. The heating is switched on and off depending on the average value of all of the sensors associated with the area.

We leave it to the reader to try to modify Example 2.2 to accommodate this situation. It must, in fact, be completely rewritten because it is dependent on the assumption that the one-to-one relationship between rooms, heaters and sensors exists. This relationship has been used to optimize the design of the shared data structures used in the system with the result that when the relationship is changed, almost everything else in the system must be changed.

Example 2.3, on the other hand, need not be changed. All changes are localized within the package Room. In order to make the required changes, the function Switch in object Heater must be modified so that it can switch more than one heater and the function Temperature in object Room must be changed to accommodate the situation where the temperature is the mean of a number of individual sensor values.

A room is considered to be an individually controlled area as far as the heating system is concerned. It may actually encompass a number of different rooms in the building, so a better name for the object would have been something like Heated_space!

The key difference between these software designs is that the object-oriented view localizes the required changes. If an error is discovered in the heater control software (say) and it has to be changed, the maintenance programmer need not think about any parts of the program except the **Heater** object. Unexpected interactions with other parts of the program as a result of the system change are very unlikely indeed.

2.3.3 Inappropriate object-oriented design

The above example showing the advantages of information hiding suggests that an object-oriented rather than a functional view of systems is the most appropriate if the subsystems making up that system are to be as independent as possible with minimal subsystem coupling. However, this view of system design is not always the most natural and, at some levels of abstraction, a functional view is easier to derive from system requirements than an object-oriented view. Information hiding is still used (the function details are hidden) but, because very little state information must be maintained, an object-oriented approach is unnecessary.

For example, consider an automated teller machine in a bank where the customer selects a particular function by pressing the appropriate function key. A natural view of this system is a functional one rather than an object-oriented one and this interaction might be coded as shown below in a simplified way (Example 2.5).

Example 2.5. A cash-dispenser system.

```
loop
  loop
      Print_input_message ; --" Welcome - Please enter your card"
      exit when Card_input ;
  end loop ;
  Account_number := Read_card ;
  Get_account_details (PIN, Account_number, Account_balance, Cash_available) ;
  if Validate_card (PIN) then
      loop
          Print_operation_select_message ;
          case Get_button is
              when Cash_only  => Dispense_cash (Cash_available, Amount_dispensed) ;
              when Print_balance => Print_customer_balance (Account_balance) ;
              when Statement  => Order_statement(Account_number) ;
              when Cheque_book => Order_cheque_book (Account_number) ;
          end case ;
          Eject_card ;
          Print ("Please take your card or press CONTINUE") ;
          exit when  Card_removed ;
      end loop ;
      Update_account_information (Account_number, Amount_dispensed) ;
  else
      Retain_card ;
  end if ;
end loop ;
```

The important characteristic of this code is that again it is made up of independent subsystems (Dispense_cash, Print_customer_balance etc.) and that any one of these may be changed without reference to the others. Because the cash dispenser machine responds to customer function requests, a functional approach to system decomposition is appropriate. At this level in the design, information hiding using functions is being practised, as representation details are not visible.

None of the functional subsystems need retain state information (their action is independent of previous actions) and the overall system state is very simple. All that must be maintained are the customer's account number, personal identification number (PIN), account balance, cash available, cash dispensed and whether or not a statement or a cheque book has been ordered. Of this state, only the cash dispensed and the cheque book or statement order is not read-only with updates to the other variables made by the central computing system. Thus, an object-oriented approach would be of little benefit in this case.

The key objective is to achieve a system design where the subsystems are mutually independent and communicate via abstract interfaces. The distinction between a functional and an object-oriented approach is that data representation decisions have to be made earlier when a functional view is adopted and state information is shared. This tends to increase the coupling of the system and to make it more difficult to change. Whilst a functional view may be more natural at some levels in the design, as soon as representation decisions have to be made, we recommend that the designer's approach should become object-oriented.

2.4   An Object-oriented Design Example

The process of software design is a creative one that is reliant on the skill and experience of the designer. It is not possible to set out 'design rules' that, if followed, will automatically lead to a 'good' design. Rather, good design can only be illustrated by example. We rely on the intuition of human readers to learn from example and improve their own design skills. Object-oriented design is therefore illustrated in rather more depth by considering an example of a weather data-collection system.

Clearly, it is impractical to reproduce a full requirements document for such a system here and we simply present a high-level overview of the system functions. Because object-oriented design allows detailed decisions to be postponed, design can actually begin without a complete requirements specification and can easily be modified as requirements are added or changed.

This means that an object-oriented approach can be used to develop system prototypes that may actually evolve into the production system. Normally, evolutionary prototyping is not a recommended practice if reliability is of paramount importance, as the structure of prototypes tends to degrade very quickly as they are modified to meet changing requirements.

However, with an object-oriented approach, the system structure tends to be relatively robust and fairly major changes can be incorporated without degrading the structure. An object-oriented approach to prototyping is particularly effective when combined with the use of an object-oriented programming language like Smalltalk.

The example we show here is a data-collection system described as follows:

A weather data-collection system is made up of a large number of automatic weather stations that collect environmental data, perform some local data processing and periodically, send the collected, processed information to an area computer for further processing.

The data that is to be collected are the air temperature, the ground temperature, the wind speed and direction, the barometric pressure and the amount of rainfall.

Notice that this description says nothing about the frequency of collection or the data processing that is required. Nevertheless, it provides sufficient information to begin the object-oriented design process.

The first stage in object-oriented design is to identify the entities that are part of the system. In general, this initial identification of objects must be refined as the design progresses and we shall see this refinement process as this example is developed. In a system like this one, which includes a mix of hardware and software, it is perhaps useful to identify 'hardware' objects first. The reason for this is that the hardware usually constrains the design of embedded systems and there is little point in developing an elegant top-down design that cannot be mapped onto the available hardware.

The term 'hardware' object is not a precise one, but in this context we mean an object that interacts directly with some hardware unit such as a thermometer, clock or switch. The hardware unit may include embedded software to drive it. By contrast, a 'software' object is an object that only interacts with other system objects. The 'hardware' objects that can be identified from an analysis of the data collection system description are:

- weather_station
- air_thermometer
- ground_thermometer
- anemometer (measures wind speed)
- wind_vane (measures wind direction)
- barometer (measures pressure)
- rain gauge
- clock (required for timing collections and transmissions)
- modem (for communication with remote computer)

Each of these objects has associated operations although, in most cases the only defined operation is an operation to return the current reading. The operations and brief descriptions are set out in Fig. 2.5(b).

To achieve visibility in a design, it is often useful to document it as a diagram. Diagrammatic descriptions are valuable because of their immediacy

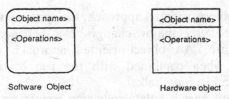

Fig. 2.4. Object description notation.

but, unfortunately, there has been relatively little work done in this area. Booch (1987) suggests a technique that involves irregular shapes, but this is unsatisfactory as it does not adapt well to automated graphical editing systems. An alternative is suggested here.

We need at least two different kinds of diagram to document an object-

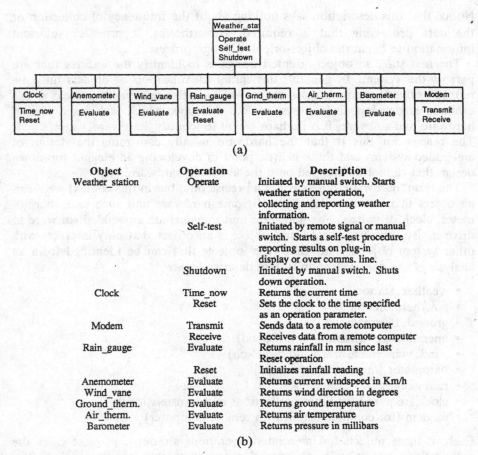

(a)

Object	Operation	Description
Weather_station	Operate	Initiated by manual switch. Starts weather station operation, collecting and reporting weather information.
	Self-test	Initiated by remote signal or manual switch. Starts a self-test procedure reporting results on plug-in display or over comms. line.
	Shutdown	Initiated by manual switch. Shuts down operation.
Clock	Time_now	Returns the current time
	Reset	Sets the clock to the time specified as an operation parameter.
Modem	Transmit	Sends data to a remote computer
	Receive	Receives data from a remote computer
Rain_gauge	Evaluate	Returns rainfall in mm since last Reset operation
	Reset	Initializes rainfall reading
Anemometer	Evaluate	Returns current windspeed in Km/h
Wind_vane	Evaluate	Returns wind direction in degrees
Ground_therm.	Evaluate	Returns ground temperature
Air_therm.	Evaluate	Returns air temperature
Barometer	Evaluate	Returns pressure in millibars

(b)

Fig. 2.5. (a) Weather-station hardware object hierarchy. (b) Hardware object descriptions.

oriented design:

(1) A network diagram showing which objects exchange messages. In many cases this will be approximately hierarchical, as much inter-object communication is between a parent object and its subobjects.

(2) A hierarchical structure chart showing how objects are decomposed into subobjects.

Figure 2.4 shows how objects may be represented on each of these diagram types. Each object is denoted by a rectangular box containing the name of the object. Operations on the object are defined in the lower part of the box. In situations where many operations are defined, these may be shown by ellipses (. . .). In this case, the reader must refer to a more detailed object description, perhaps presented in a tabular form, for operation information.

Figure 2.5(a) shows the hardware objects in the weather-station system. This is a hierarchy diagram showing that the Weather_station object consists of a number of subobjects. The Thermometer, Rain_gauge, Clock, etc. are used by the Weather_station object. As we shall see, the weather station object does not communicate with these objects directly but with intermediate level software objects. Hierarchy diagrams are distinguished from communication diagrams by the fact that, in communication diagrams, the lines joining objects are arrowed.

The weather station is essentially an information package with a switch on it with three positions, namely, On, Off, and Self-test. It is connected via a telephone line and modem to some remote computer and information is transmitted along this line. A possible package specification of Weather_station is given in Example 2.6.

Example 2.6. A Weather_station package.

```
package Weather_station is
    type T is private ;
    procedure Operate ;
    procedure Self_test ;
    procedure Shut_down ;
private
-- structure details are not relevant here
end Weather_station ;
```

We shall not define all of the operations on Weather_station but only consider the Operate operation (Example 2.7). To simplify the description of this design, we extend the Ada/PDL here to allow delay statements within a procedure. We show a procedure (Operate) using the delay statement within a loop. In fact, delay can only be used within tasks but this is really an implementation consideration. Of course, the implementation of this system would have to use parallel processes as the data collection operations must run continuously. This is indicated as a header comment in the procedure. We assume the existence of a clock object with an operation Time_now which returns the current time.

Example 2.7. Weather station operation.

```
procedure Operate is
```

-- This must be implemented as a task to allow it to be delayed
----
```
    Weather_info: Weather_data.REC ;
    --DURATION is a standard Ada type for representing time periods
    --CALENDAR is an Ada package which defines a type TIME
    Next_time: CALENDAR.TIME ;
    Transmission_gap : DURATION ;
begin
    loop
            -- assume the loop terminates when selecting Shutdown generates
            -- an interrupt. Not shown here.
            -- Transmission_gap is the time between scheduled transmissions
            Next_time := Clock.Time_now + Transmission_gap ;
            -- Create a package of weather data for transmission
            Weather_data.Create (Weather_info) ;
            -- Check the validity of the created data package and
            -- perform error corrections
            Weather_data.Check (Weather_info ) ;

            -- Send the data to the remote machine
            Weather_data.Transmit (Weather_info) ;
            delay Next_time - Clock.Time_now ;
        end loop ;
    end Operate ;
```

Notice in this example how the timing is carried out. Because data transmission tends to be error-prone and to require retries, the time required to carry out the creation, checking and transmitting of a weather record cannot be predicted. Therefore, rather than delaying for a fixed time before the next cycle, the time for the next transmission is computed before computations are carried out and the delay computed after these computations. This therefore takes into account the computation and transmission time.

The Operate procedure uses a 'software' object called Weather_data. To identify other software objects and their relationships with Weather_data, we need more system information.

All of the weather parameters except the rainfall are collected every minute. Every hour (once 60 data collections have been made), the temperatures, the wind speed and the pressure are processed to determine mean, maximum and minimum values. The amount of rainfall is collected hourly immediately before this processing. The mean wind direction is computed and all wind directions that vary from this by more than 25 degress are returned for transmission to the remote computer.

This outline description allows us to identify the software objects shown in Fig. 2.6. Again, this is a hierarchy diagram showing an object and subobjects. At this stage, it is not appropriate to look at the structure of the subobjects in more detail although they may themselves be implemented as further

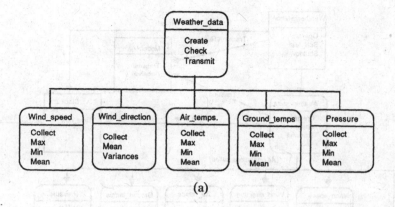

(a)

Object	Operation	Description
Weather_data	Create	Creates a weather data record consisting of all information to be transmitted to remote computer.
	Check	Checks each field of the weather data record for validity. If apparently invalid, the field is tagged with a 'doubtful' indicator
	Transmit	Sends the weather data record to the remote computer.
Rainfall	Evaluate	Returns the rainfall during the current time period.
	Reset	
Wind_speed	Max	Returns the maximum wind speed during the current time period.
	Min	Returns the minimum windspeed
	Mean	Returns the mean wind speed during the current time period.
Wind_direction	Mean	Returns the mean wind direction during the current time period
	Variances	Returns a list of wind directions which vary more than 15 degrees from mean in current time period.

(b)

Fig. 2.6. (a) Weather-station software object hierarchy. (b) Software object descriptions.

hierarchies of subobjects. Figure 2.6(b) is a description of some of these software objects. The table is not complete—the operation description for the other objects is similar to that shown and, for space reasons, has not been duplicated.

Now that both the major hardware and software objects have been identified, we can document the communication structure of the system as shown in Fig. 2.7. Notice the use of arrowed lines to indicate communication. A specification of the interface to the **Weather_data** object is shown in Example 2.8.

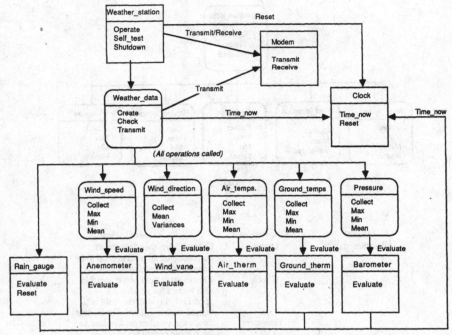

Fig. 2.7. Weather-station object communications.

Example 2.8. The Weather_data object.

```
package Weather_data is
    -- define a type to hold the packaged weather information. Its
    -- structure is hidden so it is declared as a private type.
    type REC is private ;
    procedure Create ( Data: out REC ) ;
    procedure Check (Data: in out REC) ;
    procedure Transmit (Data: REC) ;
private
    -- structure details are not relevant
end Weather_data ;
```

The **Weather_data.Create** procedure calls on the objects representing the collected temperatures, wind speeds, etc. to compute their means, maxima, minima, etc. and composes there into a transmission record. Notice that this procedure need have no knowledge of how the collected information is represented within the subobjects. A fragment of this procedure is shown as Example 2.9. Assume that the weather information is held as a record with named fields called REC. This procedure would be included in the body of the package **Weather_data**.

Example 2.9. Creating a weather record.

```
procedure Create (Data: REC) is
begin
      Rain_gauge.Evaluate (Data.Rainfall) ;
      Wind_speed.Mean (Data.Mean_wind_speed) ;
      Wind_speed.Max ( Data.Max_wind_speed) ;
      Wind_speed.Min (Data.Min_wind_speed) ;
      ...
      -- Start collecting the next lot of data
      Rain_gauge.Collect ;
      Wind_speed.Collect ;
      Wind_direction.Collect ;
      ...
   end Create ;
```

An example of the interface specification of the Wind_speed sub-object is shown in Example 2.10.

Example 2.10. The Wind_speed object interface.

```
package Wind_speed is
      type T is private ;
      procedure Mean ( Average_speed: out T ) ;
      procedure Max (Max_speed:  out T ) ;
      procedure Min (Min_speed: out T ) ;
      procedure Collect ;
   private
      -- structure details are not relevant
      end Wind_speed ;
```

The implementation of Wind_speed is concealed completely within the body of the package. It may be changed without changing any of the objects that call on the operations defined on Wind_speed. There is no need for any other objects to have access to the collected wind speed information. Of course, the data structure within Wind_speed could also be implemented as an object with its representation concealed. This should be declared as a subobject of Wind_speed (Example 2.11).

Example 2.11. The object Wind_speed_store.

```
package Wind_speed_store is
      procedure Put (Speed: T) ;
      procedure Get (Speed: out T) ;
      procedure Clear ;
      function All_done return BOOLEAN ;
      end Wind_speed_store ;
```

However, the designer may not feel that this level of decomposition is necessary and may actually represent the data structure directly in the Wind_speed object. This is the model we have assumed in Figs 2.6 and 2.7.

The object-oriented approach to design makes this system robust and tolerant to change. For example, say a new weather parameter, such as relative humidity, is to be collected. The only changes required to the system are to introduce a humidity object and to change the Weather_data object so that humidity is collected. Of course, we have not considered processing and the processing operation may also have to be changed when a new parameter is introduced.

Space does not permit us to continue this system decomposition, but the reader should now have a general picture of how this is a feasible and useful approach to software design. To reiterate, the key to designing a software system that exhibits low coupling and high visibility is to use information hiding to its fullest extent and to delay all decisions on representation until the most detailed design stages. If this approach is adopted, shared data areas may be completely eliminated and data representation details do not affect the software structure, thus allowing subsequent data changes without structural modifications.

2.5 Object Implementation

An object is an entity that has a state, a number of inspection functions to interrogate that state and a number of update functions to change that state. It may be composed of a number of subobjects. The access and update functions and some of the subobjects may be accessible from outside the object, but the state information cannot be accessed except via the functions published in the object interface.

An object-oriented approach to design is not dependent on any particular implementation language. However, programming languages such as Smalltalk (Goldberg & Robson, 1983) that support object-oriented design provide facilities for type or class hierarchies to be constructed where operations are defined for a particular type and these operations are inherited by other types that are derived from that type. This facility is extremely useful if there are a number of similar objects with some common operations that are specific to particular objects.

An Ada-based notation is used here to describe objects but Ada is not an object-oriented programming language in that it does not support a general model of inheritance nor does it allow run-time binding of operations to objects. These facilities involve significant run-time overhead and so cannot be supported in a language intended for the implementation of embedded systems. However, the information-hiding facilities in Ada do make it relatively straightforward to implement an object-oriented design using that language.

It is sometimes suggested that inheritance is fundamental to object-oriented design and there is no doubt that its availability simplifies the implementation of object-oriented systems. However, we disagree with this notion and suggest that representation hiding and state localization are the fundamental characteristics of an object-oriented design.

To illustrate the notion of inheritance in the weather station system, let us assume that temperatures are computed by collection of some raw value from a sensor then application of some correction to this figure because of prevailing local circumstances. This correction is different for air and ground temperatures. We could define a single object class temperature (Example 2.12):

Example 2.12. The object Temperature.

```
package Temperature is
    type T is range -50..50 ;
    function Get_value return T ;
    procedure Self_test ;
end Temperature ;
```

Given this basic type, we could go on to define **Ground_temperature** and **Air_temperature** objects that inherit the operations **Get_value** and **Self_test** but which provide their own correction facilities. In Ada, this inheritance uses the derived type mechanism.

Example 2.13. The object Ground_temperature.

```
with Temperature ;
package Ground_temperature is
    type T is new Temperature.T ;
    function Correct (Temp: T ) return T ;
end Ground_temperature ;
```

The **with** clause means that the object **Temperature** is made visible to the object **Ground_temperature**. A similar package could be constructed for **Air_temperature**. The advantage of this approach is that if some change is to be made that affects all of the objects in a class (say, the temperature sensors are to be replaced), only the single superclass need be changed and this change is then automatically inherited by all subclass members. The disadvantage, in Ada, is that private types may not be inherited and this negates much of the advantage of using packages in the first place. Ada-derived types should not therefore be used for object inheritance.

The approach used in Ada is but one model of inheritance and there are several other approaches that may be adopted. The whole topic of inheritance is a very complex one and we do not discuss it further here. It must be emphasized that we see inheritance as a programming rather than a design concept.

It may be appropriate to make use of inheritance of object operations in a software design if the system is to be realized in a language that supports this inheritance of operations. However, if some other implementation language is to be used, we do not recommend that inheritance is used, as the manual transformation of inheritance information that is then necessary is a potentially error prone process.

As discussed in Section 2.3.1, it is also possible to implement objects as Ada tasks. Objects thus implemented execute in parallel and this approach is particularly suitable for real-time systems implementation. We have deliberately avoided a discussion of tasking here because of its complexity. The advantage of taking an object-oriented approach to design is that decisions on parallelism become implementation rather than design decisions and the design can be expressed using packages with a translation phase where these packages are realized as tasks.

Ideally, an implementation language should provide facilities that allow this information hiding to be implemented directly, and programming languages such as Ada or Modula-2 have built-in facilities that simplify the translation of an object-oriented design to an executable program. However, it is sometimes impractical to use such a language for system implementation and a lack of information-hiding facilities means that a disciplined approach to design realization must be adopted by the system programmer. Given this disciplined approach and that the implementation language has facilities for programmers to define their own types, an object-oriented design may readily be realized. Indeed, it is possible to produce language pre-processors that accept object definitions and transform these to the appropriate declarations in Pascal, C, or whatever implementation language is used.

If the implementation language does not allow users to define their own types, an object-oriented view of the system design is still desirable, but systematic transformation of object declarations is difficult and effective implementation is reliant on the skill and discipline of the system implementor. Careful mappings must be made between the logical object types and the built-in types of the language and disciplined use must be made of language operations.

Whatever language is used for implementation, we recommend that a language that supports information hiding should be used as a PDL to describe the software design and that the information-hiding facilities should be systematically transformed into statements in the implementation language. As an example of how this can be done, consider Example 2.14, which sets out the interface to an object of type Menu, where a menu is a list of choices presented to the user, one of which is selected to initiate an action.

Example 2.14. A menu object.

```
with TEXT_IO ;
package Menu is
    type T is private ;
    Number_of_items: constant NATURAL := 15 ;
    type USER_CHOICE is range 1..Number_of_items ;
    procedure Display (The_menu: T) ;
    function Get_choice (The_menu: T) return USER_CHOICE ;
    procedure Initialize (The_menu: in out T ;
                          Menu_file: TEXT_IO.FILE_TYPE) ;
private
    type MENU_STRING is new STRING (1..20) ;
    type MENU_CHOICES is array (1..Number_of_items) of MENU_STRING ;
    type MENU_SIZE is new USER_CHOICE ;
    type T is record
        Size: MENU_SIZE ;
        Choices: MENU_CHOICES ;
    end record ;
end Menu ;
```

This **Menu** object is assumed to be made up of a variable number of choices (maximum 15) and the strings displayed are read in from a file by the **Initialize** procedure. The function **Get—choice** returns the number of the string chosen by the system user. Notice that representation information has been specified here. This allows a simple transition to a language where information hiding is not supported.

A systematic transformation of this object specification into a language like Pascal is straightforward. The problem with Pascal is that the rules of the language are such that constant, type, variable and procedure declarations are collected together so that all of the declarations associated with a single object cannot be grouped in the program. To circumvent this, a disciplined commenting and naming procedure must be adopted as shown in Example 2.15, which shows the Pascal declarations for this object.

Example 2.15. A Pascal implementation of the menu object.

```
{ Constant declarations for Menu object }

constant MenuNumberOfItems = 15 ;

{Other constant declarations }

{ Type declarations for menu object }

type   Menustring = array (1..20) of char ;
       MenuUserChoice = 1..MenuNumberOfItems ;
       MenuChoices = array(1..MenuNumberOfItems) of MenuString;
       MenuT = record
           Size:1..MenuNumberOfItems ;
           Choices: MenuChoices ;
       end ;

{ Other type declarations }

{ Procedure and function declarations for menu object }

procedure MenuInitialize (var M:MenuT ; MenuFile: file) ;
    { Body of Initialize procedure }

function MenuGetChoice ( M: MenuT ): MenuUserChoice ;
    { Body of GetChoice function }

procedure MenuDisplay ( M: MenuT ) ;
    { Body of Display procedure }

{ Other procedure and function declarations }
```

The transformation of the object specification to Pascal has involved prefixing all of the names with the object name (Menu) and including comments that identify the menu declarations. When using objects that are declared of *MenuT,* the Pascal programmer should *never* access the representation directly but should always use the functions and procedures defined on the object type.

A similar approach can be used for transformations into other programming languages although, in some cases, better object packaging is possible as, unlike Pascal the language may not have rules governing the order of declarations. For example, the C programmer can defined objects where all of the object declarations are in a single 'include' file.

2.6 Summary

The key points made in this chapter are as follows.

- Object-oriented design involves building a system from a collection of objects that maintain their own private state and operations to modify and inspect that state. There is no global shared data.
- Reliability in a design cannot be measured directly, but the most important contributory factors are design coupling (component interaction) and design visibility (the ease of relating different design representations)
- Formal system specification is useful because it reveals errors and inconsistencies early in the design process.
- A general design strategy that helps minimize design coupling is information hiding. Information hiding means that state information is only made available to those system components that have need of that information.
- Object-oriented design contributes to reliability because it reduces the interaction between design components. Hence, errors in the design should be simpler to detect and repair.
- Object-oriented design is not necessarily appropriate for all systems. Systems where little state is maintained can be implemented using a functional approach.
- Objects can be realized as either sequential entities such as Ada packages or as parallel entities such as Ada tasks.
- Object-oriented design can be practised when a programming language that does not support objects is used for implementation. Discipline and standards are necessary to support the objects in a language like Pascal.

This chapter has suggested that an object-oriented approach to software design leads to software systems where the subsystems are mutually independent and where changes to subsystems can readily be introduced without affecting other subsystems. Software reliability is thus enhanced by adopting an object-oriented strategy in the software design process.

2.7 Further Reading

The earliest reference to information hiding as a design technique was in 1972 in a paper by Parnas published in the Communications of the ACM. At the same time, work was going on in the development of abstract data types and Smalltalk, which was the first object-oriented programming language. The design of Ada (published in 1979) recognized the importance of this work and the Ada package facility allows an object-oriented approach to be adopted. This is best described by Booch in a book first published in 1983 and revised in 1987.

Parnas, D. (1972). On the criteria to be used in decomposing systems into modules. *Commun. ACM.*, **15**(2), 1053–8.

This easy to read paper overturned conventional ideas about software design when it was first published and is still recommended reading.

Goldberg, A. & Robson, D. (1983). *Smalltalk-80—the Language and its Implementation*. Addison Wesley, Reading, MA.

This is the definitive book on Smalltalk-80 which was the first programming language completely based on an object model. It is tough going at times but worth reading.

Booch, G. (1987). *Software Engineering with Ada* (2nd edition). Benjamin Cummings, Reading, MA.

This is an unusual Ada primer as it combines an introduction to Ada with a discussion of how to apply object-oriented design using Ada. It is recommended reading in conjunction with this chapter, particularly for those readers unfamiliar with Ada. One slight criticism is that the author perhaps oversells an object-oriented approach. As discussed in this chapter, it is not a universal solution to our system design problems.

Constantine, L. L. & Yourdon, E. (1979). *Structured Design*. Prentice-Hall, Englewood Cliffs, NJ.

An exposition of the Structured Design method. This has been widely and successfully used, particularly in the United States. The book covers all aspects of the method including data-flow diagrams, structure charts and data dictionaries. Unfortunately, all the examples are drawn from a single application domain (data processing) and it is this author's opinion that some of the examples would be better designed using Jackson's technique. However, it is clear that this method is appropriate for some types of embedded system design and it is a pity that this is not discussed in this book.

Jackson, M. A. (1975). *Principles of Program Design*. Academic Press, London.

This book describes Jackson's methodology of system design, which is based on deriving a program structure from the structure of the data to be processed. This method seems to be particularly suitable for data-processing systems based on an input/process/output model, where the data which is being processed has a known structure. It is probably less suitable in situations where the processed data has a complex structure that requires some parsing before processing can take place.

Cohen, B., Harwood, W. T. & Jackson, M. I. (1986). *The Specification of Complex Systems*. Addison Wesley, Wokingham.

This is a fine introduction to formal techniques of system specification. The authors do not overwhelm the reader with mathematical formalisms and use a linking example (an electronic mail system) in the discussion of algebraic and model-based specifications and in the specification of concurrent systems.

3

Formal Methods for Reliability

Chris Reade and Peter Froome

3.1 Introduction 51
3.2 Formal Methods 52
3.3 The Nature of Specifications 53
3.4 Formal Methods and Reliability 56
3.5 The Main Approaches to Formal Methods 58
3.6 Current Use of Formal Methods 69
3.7 Important Issues for Effective Use of Formal Methods . . . 72
3.8 Prospects and Conclusions 80
3.9 Further Reading 82

3.1 Introduction

Formal methods have been advocated for many years as an important technique for enhancing the reliability of software products. In trying to explain how the use of formal methods should improve the reliability of software, we note some subtle, indirect effects and other important factors that need to be taken into account.

As yet, formal methods have not played any significant role in large-scale software production, but their use in the computing industry is growing, and in recent years there has been more and more experience with intermediate-level use. Favourable reports of the benefits as well as reports on the difficulties encountered are helping to focus attention of researchers and practitioners on the problem areas.

The forthcoming UK Interim Defence Standard 00-55 will make the use of formal methods mandatory for the production of software that has the potential to cause loss of life (Ministry of Defence, 1988). This standard is aimed at the defence industry in the first place, but the techniques it advocates are also likely to be applied to civil safety-critical software.

We hope to show in this chapter that there are many aspects to formal methods and 'stepping stones' that allow formal methods to be put to practical use alongside current development methods to improve reliability. We begin by considering the nature of formal methods and the issues relating formal

51

methods and reliability. After that we look at some of the main techniques and issues surrounding the development of formal methods and at current experience with their use.

3.2 Formal Methods

Formal methods revolve around the use of formal specifications (i.e. specifications using mathematical notation) in the software development process. Such specifications may then be used in various ways to produce verified designs. One way to do this is to produce an implementation using established (non-formal) design methods, without making direct use of formal specifications, and then to use formal (mathematical) reasoning to establish that an implementation meets (is correct with respect to) a specification. Such *post hoc* verifications tend to be extremely difficult even for relatively small programs and are thus likely to be impractical for large-scale software production in general. Consequently, advocates of formal methods suggest that verification has to be considered during the design phases and closely linked with design methods. Designers should then be fully aware of the proof obligations generated by design decisions, and the need to verify may even influence design decisions.

Verification can be carried out at two levels of thoroughness: *formal* and *rigorous*. If complete detailed proofs (as might be found in a formal logic text book) are carried out, then the proof is said to be formal. Formal proofs proceed by the simple matching of syntactic structure; they are extremely time-consuming to carry out manually and cannot be trusted unless checked mechanically, because people make mistakes with proofs just as they do with programs. However, sufficient support for such proofs is rarely available. In an attempt to make verification more practical, some advocate the use of rigorous verification (Jones, 1980) as an alternative. In a rigorous verification, the outline of a proof is indicated but the fine detail is omitted (the level of proof one might find in a maths text book). The advantage of rigorous verifications is that they are easier for software engineers to produce (and follow), but their disadvantage is that they cannot be mechanically checked (or generated) and are thus more susceptible to error. The forthcoming UK Interim Defence Standard 00-55 on safety critical software insists on a rigorous level of verification.

A more radical solution to the problem of verifying implementations is to combine design and proof even more intimately. This envisages a technique for formal development of software using systematic 'transformations' (directed by a designer) to generate an implementation from a specification. When this is possible, implementations are guaranteed to be correct (with respect to the specification from which they were generated) provided that only verified transformations are used in the generation. This is usually called *transformational programming* and is the most advanced approach to formal software development. However, use of this technique is considered to be impractical for large-scale software production at present.

A less formidable aim than complete proofs of correctness of implementations is the use of formal specifications and reasoning to eliminate errors very early on in the development process. This can have a great impact on the development cost and may avoid difficult changes at late stages of development.

Clearly there is no single 'method' for the formal development of software, but rather a collection of techniques and tools relating to formal specifications that might be used to support software development. Most formal methods in use are really only notations for specification with occasional guidelines for their use in design and development. In this chapter, therefore, we will use the phrase 'formal method' to cover the use of formal specifications in software development generally rather than narrowing our attention to complete formal development methods such as transformational programming.

So how does this relate to reliability? We note that even when an implementation is formally verified (proved correct with respect to a formal specification), this is no guarantee of reliability. In particular, it is possible that the formal specification is not a description of what is really wanted, and the design may be functionally correct but bad for other reasons (such as being poorly structured and unmaintainable). Current experience seems to suggest that it is the *synergy* between the use of good design methods alongside formal methods that enhances reliability by allowing errors to be discovered much earlier and allowing designs to be validated much earlier. In the next two sections we discuss the nature of specification and the design process to see where formal methods should play a role in improving reliability.

3.3 The Nature of Specifications

Specifications are used to describe aspects of behaviour (and structure) abstractly by suppressing irrelevant information but without losing precision in describing that which is relevant. Specifications do not have to be expressed in a formal notation with a precise meaning, but it can be a serious handicap if they are not.

Firstly, getting precision in natural language can be much more difficult. Meyer (1985) illustrates several dangers inherent in using natural language alone to specify software, and advocates the use of formal specifications as a supplement to explanatory text (as do many other practitioners of formal methods). Not only does the presence of a formal specification resolve possible ambiguities and inadequacies in explanatory text, but the construction of the formal specification can also lead to a better understanding of the problem and therefore acts as a basis for writing a much clearer explanation in natural language.

Secondly, much more can be done with formal specifications than informal ones. For example, sophisticated tools can be developed to work with formal specifications analogous to the tools we already have for manipulating programs (compilers, structure editors, syntax checkers, type checkers, etc.).

Another important point we wish to make here is that we do not consider the act of specification (i.e. constructing specifications) to be restricted to the first stage in the process of software development. Instead, we regard specifications as important objects with which we work throughout design and implementation, and this includes the programs produced. A program is a specification even though it may be a rather low-level one emphasizing the details of how some function is to be computed rather than just what is computed.

This pervasive use of specifications is partly reflected in the description of the design process given in the previous chapter (Chapter 2, Fig. 2.1) where specifications appear at several levels of the design process. Even without the prospect of being able to perform formal proofs, specifications are essential conceptual tools for design. Making them more formal should not be regarded as just a necessary step towards formalizing proofs, but rather as a way of getting more return from the construction of specifications. Cohen (1982) proposes an alternative 'contractual' description of a design process that emphasizes contracts between customers and suppliers based on formal specifications. A diagram of Cohen's model is shown in Fig. 3.1, with the central boxes named to fit in with some terminology we introduce below.

The central boxes are viewed as the subject of a contract between a customer (on the left) and a supplier (on the right). The supplier, at one phase, becomes the customer at a lower phase, and each phase is completed when the customer acknowledges that a supplied item meets the terms of the contract. The contractual nature of specifications raises their importance so that much effort is likely to be spent in getting specifications right. Of course, it is possible to change contracts by mutual agreement, so this model does not preclude the possibility of iteration in the development. However, changes of mind by the customer and suggested changes of specification to improve performance would be taken very seriously as contractual changes. We will not pursue this model here (Appendix B discusses models of the software development process) but it usefully introduces an analytical structure for the use of formal methods in software engineering.

With this view of specifications in software development (repeated at progressive levels of decomposition), it is useful to classify different types of specifications according to their nature. This classification is given by Horning (1983) and has evolved from trying to apply formal methods to software design on a larger scale.

The large specifications that describe various aspects of the behaviour of a complete system (usually produced from requirements analysis) will not, in general, contain details of design. Such specifications are termed *system specifications* by Horning. (Note that the word *system* is intended to indicate the global behaviour and should not be read in the sense of the combination of

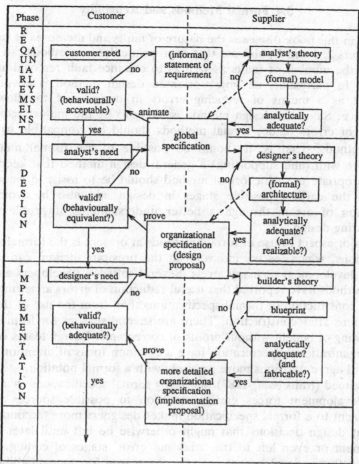

Fig. 3.1. Cohen's contractural model of software development. (Adapted from Cohen (1982), reproduced with permission of the Institution of Electrical Engineers.)

hardware and software in an engineered product.) In contrast, the (small-scale) specifications that are generally used to describe detailed properties of (small) components of an implementation (such as single procedures) are called *local specifications*. Between these two forms, we have *organizational specifications*, which describe a system's behaviour in terms of the behaviour of components along with the structure of the system design. Such specifications will usually be large and arise from the process of design. A proof that a realization meets a higher-level specification will often involve showing that properties required in a system specification follow from an organizational specification. We also use the term *structural specification* for the part of an organizational specification that details the structure. (This is the structure of the design being specified and it should not be confused with the structure of the specification itself. The structure of specifications is an important issue when large-scale specifications are being considered.)

3.4 Formal Methods and Reliability

Chapter 6 in this book discusses the nature of faults and measures of reliability and Chapters 2, 4 and 5 point out that appropriate design methods can be used to reduce the number of faults as well as to enhance fault removal and fault tolerance. In particular, an object-oriented design method is advocated in Chapter 2 as a means of reducing errors in design and to allow easier maintenence. Since the design method is likely to be the major factor in the reduction of errors made, formal methods should be compatible with good design methods. That is, it should be possible to use formal methods in conjunction with (and supporting) a general design method that keeps errors low. Appropriate use of a formal method should be to assist in weeding out errors at the earliest possible stages in design and also in avoiding the introduction of errors through a better understanding of problems being solved during design.

The major aspect of use of formal methods at present is the formalization of specifications, which, as we indicated in the previous section, can influence software development at many levels. Several software developers employing formal methods have reported that useful reduction of errors arises more often from the construction of formal specifications than from the use of the formal specifications after construction. There are several reasons for formal specifications being of benefit without proofs of correctness. Design teams constructing an organizational specification have a common focus of attention and can record and agree decisions more precisely with a formal notation.

It is claimed (Mills *et al.* 1987) that using formal specifications as a basis for design development forces earlier attention to possible sources of error. Commitment to a formal specification makes designers more 'accountable' for important design decisions that might otherwise be left until later stages of development or even left to the 'trial and error' stages of coding. In many practical software development projects, the reason for poor reliability can be attributed to dealing with fuzzy user requirements that change from moment to moment. Developing a design with formal specifications can help to bring the need for changes to the attention of both developers and customers at relatively early stages, which considerably increases the confidence in the development and can have a beneficial impact on development costs (see Boehm, 1981).

A particularly valuable technique that is applicable to formal specfications is that of animation. Animation allows specifications to be explored more carefully, which can mean the much earlier discovery of errors. Animation can also be used during design, to guide the design and assess the consequences of design decisions. This is particularly valuable for validating customer requirements.

Animation may be done by the direct examination and mathematical manipulation of the formal specification, carried out with the aid of mechanical proof editors or symbolic execution tools. This is the better method, since it allows the behaviour to be investigated for whole classes of inputs simultaneously. Alternatively, however, animation may be by the production of a prototype directly from the formal specification. This approach does enable the specification to be demonstrated to potential users, but may suffer from incomplete coverage. Animation by prototyping may be carried out by one of the following means: use of an executable subset of a specification language (e.g. Me Too (Henderson & Minkowitz, 1984; Henderson, 1986) for VDM); translation into a non-procedural programming language (e.g. Prolog, Miranda or Smalltalk); or translation into a procedural programming language with support for the abstract data types used in the specification. Protyping by means of a procedural language will generally involve more effort than the other options, and may give rise to problems due to the way the abstract data types are realized.

Animation should always be undertaken to examine aspects of the specification or design that have been identified in advance. The animation is likely to be a partial model; indeed, it may be undesirable for the animation to represent the entire system if it amounts to a full implementation that prejudges many design decisions.

During implementation, local specifications can be used as (contractual) interfaces when dividing up work between teams. Working with formal specifications also allows simplification of interfaces to be spotted more easily and allows designers to observe the structure of specifications. These aspects can be important for maintenance and hence reliability.

Horning (1983) also argues that specifications are always useful. Specifications provide a 'tangible record of the understandings that were acquired during their construction'. They can be used by clients, designers, implementors and users as well as during maintainence and as the basis for providing documentation and user manuals. They can even be a means of passing on knowledge of a general nature useful to designers of other systems. Availability of knowledge (especially formal knowledge) about particular application domains or standard interfaces (e.g. for workstation windowing systems or desk-top publishing systems) may also reduce the cost of using formal methods. (As pointed out by Good (1983a), a large amount of the theorem-proving effort goes into developing theories about the application domain. Such work can be reused for application domains where a lot of software is being developed.)

Through construction of specifications, software engineers can obtain a better understanding of the ways in which behavioural descriptions can be packaged better for human consumption.

Apart from this, formal specifications are clearly a prerequisite for the provision of some potentially useful software engineering tools. Transformation tools that generate executable code automatically from a formal specification are one class of such tools and we mention some of these later. There are other tools related to animation and rapid prototyping from specifications, although these are not yet well developed. Even so, they are likely to have a great impact on reliability, since they help with early validation against requirements and allow suppliers to check that a design is providing the system a customer really wants rather than what the supplier thought the customer said was wanted. Even if a prototype is not produced from a specification, other 'reasoning' tools might help to deduce consequences from a specification that could be used to check requirements. Consequences could be formally derived by the designer and translated back for the customer to consider, or questions posed about the design could be formalized to be checked against a specification. Formal tools to assist in this process could prove useful. (A small illustration of this is given at the end of Section 3.5.3).

This use of formal specifications is considered by some to be just as important as the prospect of formal verification of implementations. In fact, validation and testing in general can be greatly assisted by having formal specifications to work from. Mills *et al.* (1987) claimed that IBM's 'Cleanroom' method of software production (where correctness proofs are used in conjunction with testing) is much more effective in finding faults than using debugging and testing. This is because errors in software arising from errors in proofs tend to be more susceptible to discovery through testing than are the less-systematic errors usually encountered in implementations that have not been verified.

Full proofs of correctness can be and are being applied to critical systems of a few thousand lines of source code with beneficial effects on reliability. Such an approach may also reduce the cost of assessment and licensing, which currently often doubles the cost of safety-critical software.

However, it is important to remember that rigorous arguments may be very beneficial. When sufficient support is not available for formal proofs to be carried out effectively, rigorous arguments should help to bring out many potential design errors if done in a systematic way (as advocated by Jones (1980)).

In summary, formal methods can play a role in many aspects of software development: design, coding, testing and validation, maintenance, etc. Formal specifications are useful even without correctness proofs, and informal, rigorous arguments can be used to improve confidence in design when formal proofs are not practical. It is the early focus of attention on potential problems and precision in design, forced by the use of formal specifications, that has most impact on the reliability of the software produced.

3.5 The Main Approaches to Formal Methods

In this section we look at some of the main methods being used today for the specification of *sequential* processes. Methods for concurrency are addressed in Section 3.7.1. The methods have (perhaps not surprisingly) a great deal in common and many of the differences are superficial. They use well-founded mathematical formalisms to describe behaviour in an abstract way and they provide a notational framework (in the form of a specification language). A distinction is often made between formalisms using 'model-based' specifications and those using 'property-based' specifications (such as the algebraic methods) and we will explain this distinction below. However, there are strong connections between these two approaches and a mixture of both is possible in all the main methods in use.

3.5.1 Model-based approach

This approach is exemplified by Z and VDM. In both methods, standard, well understood, basic mathematical notions provide the building blocks and the notation is drawn from elementary set theory and logic. For example, sets, tuples, sequences, relations and mappings (functions) are used. 'Models' are built up from such objects using conventional means for expressing constraints with predicates and quantifiers. In the case of Z, there is little explicitly stated 'method' to go along with this except for the suggested use of 'schemas'. Schemas are a notational device for structuring specifications and are an addition to conventional mathematical notation. As an illustration of the notation, here is a simple schema expressing the properties of a stack operation *POP*:

$$
\begin{array}{l}
\hline
POP \\
\hline
st, st' \in seq\ X \\
r! \in X \\
\hline
st \neq [\ ] \\
st = [r!]\ ^\frown st' \\
\hline
\end{array}
$$

In a schema there is a declarative part (above the central line) that introduces some variables, and a constraints part (below the central line) that describes further properties of the variables. In this case, the behaviour of *POP* is described in terms of three values introduced in the declarative part of the schema. These are two stack values *st* and *st'* that are sequences of values of type *X* (elements of type *seq X*), and *r!*, which is a value of type *X*. (We assume that type *X* is a parameter of the definition.) By convention, when describing an operation, primed variables are used for the resulting values of state components when an operation is used: thus, *st'* represents the resulting state of the stack that is affected by the use of the *POP* operation. Conversely, *st* denotes the value of the stack before the use of *POP*. By another convention, a variable ending in '!' represents an output value, so *r!* represents the result produced by *POP*. Below the middle line of the schema, we express relationships between these values that describe when it is meaningful to use *POP* and the exact effect that the operation has. The first constraint says that the stack value before the use of *POP* must not be the empty sequence [ ], and the second constraint relates the resulting stack value to the original stack value. It says that the stack before the use of *POP* (i.e. *st*) is equal to the sequence of values beginning with *r!* and followed by the values in the sequence *st'* that remain in the stack after the *POP*. The symbol ˆ is used for concatenation of sequences. If $s = [x_1, x_2, \ldots, x_n]$ and $t = [y_1, y_2, \ldots, y_m]$ then $s \hat{\ } t = [x_1, x_2, \ldots, x_n, y_1, y_2, \ldots, y_m]$.

The example illustrates the way in which operations with side-effects are described in terms of their overall effect (and not just in terms of the function relating explicit arguments to results). Such operations with side-effects are commonly used in procedural programs, so it is important that they should be natural to specify. However, in early stages of design, it may be more appropriate to use more functional descriptions with explicit parameters instead of global state variables. (This is particularly true when the structure of a global state is unknown—i.e. to be decided.) Thus, we might specify a partial function *pop* that operates on all non-empty stacks of items of type *X*:

$$
\begin{array}{|l}
pop : seq\ X \nrightarrow seq\ X \\
\hline
dom\ pop = \{st \in seq\ X\ /\ st \neq [\ \ ]\} \\
\forall a \in X\ \forall st \in seq\ X\ pop([a] \hat{\ } st) = st
\end{array}
$$

Here, *pop* is introduced as a partial function (its type is given above the line and the symbol ↦ denotes partial functions). Below the line are constraints that specify the behaviour of the partial function. The domain of the partial function (i.e. the arguments for which the function is defined) consists of those sequences that are not empty. The last line states that for any *a* (of type *X*) and any *st* of type *seq X*, the result of applying *pop* to the concatenation of [*a*] and *st* is just *st*. Since all non-empty sequences can be expressed as such a concatenation, the constraint completely specifies the function.

It is important to note that specification languages like Z and VDM do not dictate the level of specification, and allow for descriptions of both functional and procedural objects (operations with side-effects).

When designing formal specifications, an appropriate abstraction is achieved by finding the 'right' level of specification for objects at each stage of the design, and this is an art that is best learned from practical experience. Much can also be learned from working through documented case studies such as those collected in *Specification Case Studies* (Hayes, 1987) and there are several training courses on Z currently being advertised.

A clear method is not yet as well developed for Z as it is for VDM, but more and more people are becoming experienced in using it. It requires only relatively low-level mathematical skills, and it is taught in many undergraduate computer science/software engineering courses. Recently, Nielson (1988) has suggested a 'hierarchical refinement' approach to the development of implementations from Z specifications that is similar to the techniques used with VDM.

With VDM, much the same ways of describing data are used along with Pre- and Post-conditions to describe the effect of functions and procedures. For example, *POP* might be described as:—

$$POP \; (\;) \; r : X$$
$$\textbf{ext wr } st : seq \; of \; X$$
$$\textbf{pre } st \neq [\;]$$
$$\textbf{post } [r] \; \hat{} \; st = \overleftarrow{st}$$

Here, *POP* is introduced on the first line as an operation with no explicit arguments ( ) and a result *r* of type *X*. On the next line it is stated that the operation also makes use of an external variable that it can write to and read from (*ext wr*). The variable is *st* and has type *seq of X* (cf. *seq X* in the Z example). The third line introduces a *pre*-condition that must be satisfied before *POP* is to be used (namely, that *st* is not the empty sequence). Finally, the fourth line provides a *post*-condition that must be satisfied after the use of *POP* (assuming the *pre*-condition held before). The notation $\overleftarrow{st}$ is used to refer to the value of the variable *st* before the operation, while *st* now refers to the resulting value in this description of the post-condition. As before, the old value of *st* is required to be equal to the new value prepended with the result *r*.

VDM is somewhat older than Z, and much of the early work was focused on the particularly difficult problem of specifying large programming languages such as PL/1 (and more recently Ada). Consequently, some of the more sophisticated ideas and structures from denotational semantics have been incorporated. VDM has a design and development aspect as well as a notation for specification, with the progressive commitment to a particular structure being defined in the implementation language from local specifications. The development steps generate 'proof obligations'—formulae that need to be proved in order to establish that the design step is correct. Similar proof obligations arise in Z specifications as well. (An illustration of such a transformation is given in Section 3.5.3.)

The notation used in both VDM and Z is now stabilizing. The definition of VDM is being considered by a BSI committee and the syntax should be published in 1990 (see Sen, 1987). A definitive notation for Z is contained in the Z reference manual (Spivey, 1988a). However, some evolution of the methods will continue, especially to handle concurrency (see Section 3.7.1).

A modularization scheme for VDM has recently been defined as part of the BSI standardization activities. Many of the deficiencies recognized by users of VDM are being addressed in the construction of RAISE (A Rigorous Approach to Industrial Software Engineering), which is to be a 'second-generation' VDM. This is supported by an ESPRIT project (due for completion in 1989) and aims (according to Prehn, 1987) to provide

- a wide spectrum language (a notation for describing both specifications and designs);
- a 'method' for rigorous development (including a language for expressing development steps);
- educational and training material for use in industry.

We have singled out two particular model-based approaches here because they have played a particularly prominent role in the attempt to introduce formal methods into industry. However, there are several other methods that could be included in this category of 'model-based' approaches (some are mentioned by Cohen *et al.*, 1986).

3.5.2 Algebraic approach

An alternative 'property-based' approach to specification emphasizes indirect specifications through formal descriptions of properties and relationships that hold between operations on data objects. This is instead of giving an explicit model of the data objects. Note that 'property-based' does not mean the absence of models, but rather that classes of possible models are implicitly associated with specifications (in some standard, pre-specified way). The majority of property-based approaches use algebras as the underlying models (hence 'algebraic' approach). Algebraic approaches provide elegant specifications in certain cases, but in general require great care to ensure completeness and consistency.

The properties and relations are expressed with 'axioms' in some formal logic. These are frequently equations but not always. The choice of a formal logic is particularly important, because highly expressive logics (such as full first-order predicate logic) make it easier to describe relationships, but they also make it easier to describe impossible restrictions (so that a specification is unimplementable) and they can make it much more difficult to do proofs. There can be considerable benefit in limiting oneself to weaker logics (such as the logic of equations or conditional equations) wherever possible, because they provide a tighter framework for writing specifications and can form a basis for more powerful support tools to assist in reasoning. When reasoning about specifications is particularly simple, a great deal can be learned about a design before it is implemented. (An example is given in Section 3.5.3.) Specifications may also have more pleasant mathematical properties (such as guaranteed existence of a model) with equational logic. Although they might seem restrictive at first, (conditional) equations are surprisingly expressive and with a suitable framework they are adequate for most specifications. From the simple examples usually encountered in introductions to the algebraic approach (such as 'stacks' and 'queues'), one might easily be misled into thinking that this method is only suitable for describing the simple data-objects manipulated in low-level programs (i.e. for local specifications). In fact, the same abstract means of specification can be used to describe complex modules and interfaces as well as larger systems and even the semantics of programming languages. This is because algebraic specifications can be made very modular and they focus attention on the way complex systems are built from components. Section 3.5.3 illustrates the differences in the approaches with simple examples.

There has been considerable research into the algebraic approach to specification which arose from early work by Guttag (1975) and the ADJ group at IBM Yorktown Heights (Goguen *et al.,* 1978; Thatcher *et al.* 1978) on abstract data types. The introduction of abstract data types into programming provided a mechanism for hiding implementation details and gave a powerful modularizing mechanism for both programs and specifications. The formal model used for abstract data types was the mathematical notion of an algebra and this was the source of many useful formal tools and techniques for working with such objects

Guttag, Horning and Wing (1985) have recently been working on LARCH, which is a practical system developed from earlier work and experience with Musser's (1979) AFFIRM proof system. LARCH distinguishes a general-purpose algebraic specification language that is to be 'shared' by all implementations of the system, and several extensions based on different programming languages (those that are to be used as the implementation vehicles for particular developments).

We should also mention another algebraic specification language, CLEAR (Burstall & Goguen, 1981). This language is mentioned not because it has been used extensively in developing real systems, but rather because it was designed specifically to tackle the problem of structuring large specifications. Many other specification languages have adopted or modelled their large-scale structuring facilities on those provided by CLEAR (discussed in Section 3.7.2).

Although there is a great deal of theoretical work surrounding the algebraic method, there is much less application in industry. However, many of the ideas developed for the algebraic approach, such as structuring specifications and indirect specification, have influenced and have even been directly incorporated into other methods (e.g. VDM). Perhaps the most significant feature of the algebraic approach is the relatively advanced state of development of formal support tools that can aid in reasoning about specifications and derive implementations. Examples of algebraic specification languages with such integrated tools are OBJ (Goguen & Meseguer, 1982) and the RAP system (Broy *et al.,* 1986; Geser & Hussman, 1986) which we return to in Section 3.7.3.

Further details of approaches to software specification may be found in Gehani & McGettrick (1986), Cohen *et al.* (1986) and Staunstrup (1982).

3.5.3 An example

We will illustrate some of the points discussed above with a small example. It is not practical to give an extended example or a complete introduction to a particular formal method here, and the reader is referred to the cited references for these. Instead, we adapt and simplify (part of) an example given by Guttag & Horning (1980) to illustrate the difference between the use of models and the algebraic approach and to show a simple transformation step.

The example concerns an interface for a computer terminal (screen) where window displays are to be used. The interface is already partially designed, and the design is described with a formal specification. (This emphasizes the point that formal specifications should be developed during design and not just seen as the starting point of the design.) The partially designed interface involves several sorts of objects that are still to be fully designed. Amongst these, we mention 'Pictures' and 'Views' and we will have a type for each of the sorts of objects we are specifying (or using). Informally, we can think of pictures as objects that can be displayed and have an 'Illumination' (e.g. black, white, other) associated with each 'Coordinate' within the picture. We can also determine whether or not a given coordinate is in a picture. Similarly, views can be thought of as collections of pictures positioned at different coordinates (pictures may overlap), and each picture in a view can be identified with a name (a 'PictureId'). Views can be displayed in a similar way to individual pictures and we can retrieve a list of (the names of) those pictures in a view that contain a given coordinate. Views are built up by adding named pictures at fixed coordinates to existing views. There is also an 'empty' view and a standard 'background' picture. From the description so far, we see that we also have objects with types **Coordinate**, **Illumination**, **PictureId** (and **PictureIdList**), the exact nature of which we will not need to know at this point.

Note that the classification of objects into types and the development of clearly specified interfaces for objects is typical of the object-oriented design methodology that was discussed in Chapter 2. It fits in particularly well with the algebraic approach to specification.

Now, to be more explicit about **Picture** and **View**, we provide a list of the basic operations that we intend to use on objects of each type. At this point, we only give the names of the operations and their type (functionality). For **Picture** we want

$$PicAppearance : Picture \times Coordinate \rightarrow Illumination$$
$$In \qquad : Picture \times Coordinate \rightarrow Bool$$
$$Background \quad : \qquad\qquad\qquad \rightarrow Picture$$

(amongst others). The first function (**PicAppearance**) expects as argument a pair consisting of a **Picture** and a **Coordinate** and returns an **Illumination** (the **Illumination** associated with the given **Coordinate** in the given **Picture**). The second function (**In**) expects similar arguments and returns a **Bool** (**True** or **False**) that determines whether or not a **Coordinate** is in a **Picture**. Finally, **Background** can be thought of as a constant of type **Picture** (or equivalently as a function with no arguments that generates a fixed value of type **Picture**).

For **View** we want

$$ViewAppearance : View \times Coordinate \rightarrow Illumination$$
$$AddPicture \qquad : View \times Coordinate \times PictureId \times Picture \rightarrow View$$
$$FindPictures \qquad : View \times Coordinate \rightarrow PictureIdList$$
$$Empty \qquad\qquad : \qquad \rightarrow View$$

(amongst others). The informal description of these follows, but a formal description is yet to be given. **ViewAppearance** tells us the illumination of coordinates in a view (probably calculated from the pictures in the view).

AddPicture expects as argument a (current) view along with a coordinate, name and picture and returns a new view (obtained by adding the named picture at the given coordinate). The argument coordinate indicates where the picture is to be placed relative to the view. (Details of calculations of 'relative' coordinates will be encapsulated within the description of type **Coordinate**, which we will assume has an operation **Minus** for calculating relative positions.) **FindPictures** returns a list of picture names (**PictureIds**) when applied to a **View** and a **Coordinate** (the names of those pictures containing the given coordinate in the given view). **Empty** is the empty view.

In the model-based approach we would specify the operations listed above by providing a mathematical model to represent the values of each type and describe the operations in terms of these. For example, we might specify that values of type **View** are given by (represented by) sequences of triples where each triple contains a value of type **Coordinate**, a value of type **PictureId** and a value of type **Picture**. This might be expressed by

$$\text{View} = \text{seq of (Coordinate} \times \text{PictureId} \times \text{Picture)}$$

The intention is that the most recently added picture with its name and coordinate is at the front of the sequence and the other pictures in a view are similarly recorded in the rest of the sequence, as in

$$\text{aview} = [(\text{coord3, id3, pic3}), (\text{coord2, id2, pic2}), (\text{coord1, id1, pic1})]$$

A description of each of the operations on views with this model is given below.

AddPicture(v, c, id, p) = [(c, id, p)] ˆ v	list concatenation is denoted by "ˆ"
ViewAppearance(v, c)	
= if v = [ ]	If v is the empty sequence
then PicAppearance(Background, c)	the illumination given by the background
else let (c', id, p) = head v	else consider the topmost/first/head picture
if In(p, Minus(c, c'))	If c is in the first picture (relative to its position in the view)
then PicAppearance(p, Minus(c, c'))	get the appearance from this picture
else ViewAppearance(rest v, c)	get the appearance from the rest of the view
FindPictures(v, c)	
= if v = [ ]	If v is the empty sequence
then Null	the empty list of identifiers
else let (c', id, p) = head v	else consider the topmost/first/head picture
if In(p, Minus(c, c'))	If c is in the first picture (relative to its position in the view)
then Insert (id,	add id to the list found
FindPictures (rest v, c)	from the rest of the view
else FindPictures (rest v, c)	else just those from the rest of the view
Empty = [ ]	the empty view is represented by the empty sequence of triples

We have given details of the functions using conditional recursive definitions, but we might have been more abstract, as in:

FindPictures(v, c) = [id | (c', id, p) is in v and In(p, Minus(c, c')) = True]

which simply says that FindPictures(v, c) in the sequence of those identifiers (id) such that (c', id, p) is in the view v (a list of such triples) and for which In(p, Minus(c, c')) is true. (This also assumes that PictureIdList = seq of PictureId.)

We use functions in the specification at this stage rather than operations with side-effects because it is not yet clear what a global state might look like and we might wish to consider relationships between many views without focusing attention on a particular global view.

For a complete specification, we should specify each of the other types of objects mentioned similarly (but we omit these specifications here).

An important point to note is that this specification has not committed the design to a particular implementation, as we will illustrate. Suppose, at a later design stage, we decided to include a form of bitmap (a mapping from coordinates to illuminations) for views as well as pictures to that the illumination does not have to be re-calculated from the original pictures in a view every time we use ViewAppearance. We can express this by providing a new representation for Views and describing a transformation from the older representation to this more detailed one. If we specify that

View1 ::   bitmap: Coordinate → Illumination
             viewpics: View

then a value of type View1 has two components, which are called, respectively, bitmap (a function of type Coordinate → Illumination) and viewpics (a View—i.e. a sequence of triples). The bitmap component can be applied to any coordinate and should return the illumination value of that coordinate (for that particular view). A value of type View1 can be written in the form mk–View1(f, v) and the component labels are also selectors, so

$$bitmap(mk–View1(f, v)) = f$$
$$viewpics(mk–View1(f, v)) = v$$

In fact, we will further constrain this type by specifying that a certain relationship holds between the bitmap and the viewpics components. This is expressed with an invariant predicate inv–View1 that is required to be true for any valid value of type View1. The modified definition of View1 is thus

View1 ::   bitmap: Coordinate → Illumination
             viewpics: View
        where
             inv–View1(mk–View1(f,v)) ≡ For all c in Coordinate
                                          f(c) = ViewAppearance(v, c)

The definition of inv–View1 says that for mk–View1(f, v) to be a valid element of View1, the bitmap f must produce the same illumination value as that calculated from the view v by the function ViewAppearance (for each coordinate c).

To show that the new representation is adequate, we should provide a 'retrieval' function from View1 to View showing which abstract value (in View) is associated with each new value (in View1). In this case it is trivial, since the old representation is a direct component of the new representation:

$$\text{retr--View(v1)} = \text{viewpics(v1)}$$

(or equivalently)

$$\text{retr--View(mk--View1(f, v))} = v$$

We just ignore (throw away) the bitmap component. Figure 3.2 illustrates the relationship between View1 and View. The next step is to describe the new implementation of the operations with the new representation and to check that they have been faithfully represented. We will define an implementation of ViewAppearance, which we will call View1Appearance. If it is to be a correct implementation, it should satisfy the following property (for each v1 in View1 and c in Coordinate):

$$\text{View1Appearance(v1, c)} = \text{ViewAppearance(retr--View(v1), c)} \qquad (*)$$

This could be taken as a definition, but the purpose of the implementation was to have the appearance already calculated and represented by the bitmap component of v1. Accordingly, we define

$$\text{View1Appearance(v1, c)} = \text{let } f = \text{bitmap(v1)}$$
$$f(c)$$

Now we can check that (*) holds. Firstly, for any View1 v1, we know that v1 must have of the form mk--View1(f, v) and must satisfy the constraint given

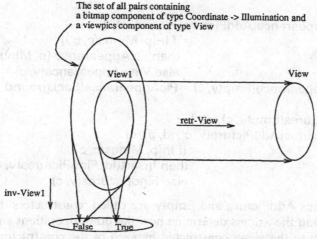

Fig. 3.2. Relationship between View and View1.

above by inv–View1. That is,

$$f(c) = \text{ViewAppearance}(v, c)$$

for any Coordinate c. So given such a View1 v1 = mk–View(f, v) and Coordinate c:

View1Appearance(v1, c) = View1Appearance(mk–View1(f, v), c)
$\qquad\qquad\qquad\qquad$ = f(c) (by the definition of View1Appearance)
$\qquad\qquad\qquad\qquad$ = ViewAppearance(v, c) (by the constraint above)

and

ViewAppearance(retr–View(v1), c) = ViewAppearance(viewpics(v1), c)
$\qquad\qquad\qquad\qquad\qquad\qquad\qquad$ = ViewAppearance(v, c)

so we have

View1Appearance(v1, c) = ViewAppearance(retr–View(v1), c)

as required.

A corresponding implementation of AddPicture would require the updating of the bitmap component to ensure that the resulting View1 satisfied the constraint inv–View1 = True.

This sort of transformation is called *data-reification*, and it is normally used to convert a more abstract design into a more concrete implementation-oriented design. (We will not present the full transformation here.) We have used a VDM-like notation, taking a few liberties to simplify the presentation.

As the next illustration, we present an alternative algebraic specification of the type View for comparison. This shows how we can express the same abstract behaviour of the listed operations without describing the details of any model. The type of the operations are laid out exactly as before. Their behaviour is specified by the following equations:

Axioms

ViewAppearance(AddPicture(v, c', id, p), c)
$\qquad\qquad\qquad\qquad$ = if In(p, Minus(c, c'))
$\qquad\qquad\qquad\qquad\qquad$ then PicAppearance (p, Minus(c, c'))
$\qquad\qquad\qquad\qquad\qquad$ else ViewAppearance(v, c)
ViewAppearance(Empty, c) = PicAppearance(Background, c)

FindPictures(Empty, c) = [ ]
FindPictures(AddPicture(v, c', id, p), c)
$\qquad\qquad\qquad\qquad$ = if In(p, Minus(c, c'))
$\qquad\qquad\qquad\qquad\qquad$ then Insert(id, FindPictures(v, c))
$\qquad\qquad\qquad\qquad\qquad$ else FindPictures(v, c)

The operations AddPicture and Empty are called 'constructors' because they build views and the axioms determine how the other operations should behave when applied to the views constructed by each of the constructors. Note that nothing is said about what values of type View should look like. Each of the models illustrated earlier (View and View1) will satisfy the axioms given here, and any other acceptable model will as well.

The final illustration shows how the specification can be used to investigate consequences of the design. In Guttag & Horning (1980) the following question is posed:

Is it the case that pictures are not transparent or even translucent? That is, if two pictures overlap does the bottom one have no effect on what one sees in the top one?

The question is reformulated as a more general question:

Suppose we took a picture (p) and placed the picture (at c' say) on top of any two views (v1 and v2). Now suppose that we took a coordinate (c) that lies in the picture p (placed at c'). Then, is the appearance at c the same in each case (i.e. for v1 and v2)?

This is then encoded as a logical statement:

For all c, c', p, id, v1, v2
In(p, Minus(c, c'))   IMPLIES
ViewAppearance(AddPicture(v1, c', id, p), c)
= ViewAppearance(AddPicture(v2, c', id, p), c)

The answer is YES and this result can be derived automatically. The statement follows directly from the axioms given in the specification in Guttag & Horning (1980) and the same is true for our simplified and adapted version.

Note that such reasoning with a formal design can sometimes answer very general questions about the design that could not be answered by a prototype. With a normal prototype, one can usually only test for particular instances of general questions and must therefore trust that there are no anomolous cases that remain uncovered by a finite number of tests.

3.6 Current Use of Formal Methods

As discussed in Section 3.7.2, formal methods are untried with very large-scale software developments and the reports on industrial applications concern intermediate-scale developments and small trials. The two formal methods currently most widely and increasingly used (relative to others) are VDM and Z. For each of these methods, recent books have been published with examples documenting experience with the methods in industrial use. Collections of case studies for software developments have been published for Z (Hayes, 1987) and VDM (Jones & Shaw, 1988).

There has been some notable work where the emphasis in the use of formal methods has been on specifying existing software or interfaces for large systems. A prime example is the work on formalizing part of IBM's CICS

(Johnson, 1988; Hayes, 1985) (a very large system in widespread use) using Z. The formal specification was used to describe existing software, with the object of establishing essential properties of components precisely so that they can be developed further and re-implemented more easily with new hardware. There are many other benefits recorded as well: documentation can be improved (omissions found and new documentation generated more easily); new programmers can be introduced to the existing software much faster through formal specifications; testing is enhanced and inspections are more productive. Johnson (1988) records that most users were 'enthusiastic' about the use of Z and found it helpful.

A large specification in Z has been produced for the ASPECT Public Tool Interface (Systems-Designers, 1986). The formal specification was regarded as an essential requirement in order that both tool designers and ASPECT implementors have a precisely defined interface to work from (independently of each other). The full text of the specification is large, although much of it is explanatory text with small chunks of mathematics (schemas) interspersed.

Similar work using VDM is the formalization of the interface for the PCTE. This is the VIP project, which has produced two final reports (VIP Project Team, 1988*a,b*). The formalization uses an extension of VDM involving temporal logic (see Section 3.7.1) to handle interference of processes and some modularization constructs. VDM has also been used in a safety-critical area in the formal specification of a nuclear reactor protection system (Bromell and Sadler, 1987).

Titterington (1986) reports on a comparative study of the use of three specification methods introduced into an industrial environment where programmers did not have experience with formal methods. The methods were VDM, OBJ (an algebraic specification language) and ML (a high-level functional language). The report gives some quantitative measures of the cost of using formal specifications, but not enough to determine whether there were any overall savings. The software produced was on a small scale, but the report concludes that there was little cost increase in the use of formal specifications in a simple way.

Looking beyond the simple use of formal specifications, there have not been any full proofs of correctness of significant systems (to our knowledge) but there is some experience with rigorous developments. There have also been some important achievements related to specific problems (e.g. compilers, protocols), parts of systems (critical components) and very regular systems (especially for hardware). In general, use of automatic theorem provers like that of GYPSY (see Good, 1983*b*) is limited but is increasing and they have been used on small but critical parts of systems. However, full automation of proofs is not feasible in general and the purpose of most proof systems is to provide intelligent assistance.

The IBM Cleanroom concept (Curritt *et al.*, 1986; Dyer, 1987; Mills *et al.*, 1987), which we mentioned in Section 3.4 is a successful instance of the rigorous use of formal methods. Programs are specified formally and developed rigorously using checklists of the proof steps involved. Testing is carried out by a body independent from the programmers. In a typical case consisting of 3200 lines of PL/1 program, four errors were found per thousand lines on initial test, and none was found on delivery. The Cleanroom experience suggests that benefits come from both the 'accountability' induced by requiring formal specifications and the combination of rigorous proof and testing.

One specialized area where formal methods have been used on relatively complex problems is the specification of large programming languages (PL/1, Ada, CHILL, Standard ML). Formal definitions of programming languages are significant for software reliability because they are a fundamental step in ensuring that implementations are correct and they have also led to the discovery of language design flaws. There has also been considerable work on the rigorous development of compilers from specifications (e.g. Clemmensen & Oest, 1983).

There has been other significant work on specific components of systems that are to be highly used and therefore worth the effort of a full proof of correctness.

Recently, a proof of a floating-point unit of the INMOS IMS T800 transputer was verified with respect to the IEEE standard (Shephard, 1988). This involved several separate steps. Firstly, the IEEE specification was formalized in Z and then an occam program implementing the specification was proved to be correct. A description of the hardware implementation of the floating-point unit was provided by a very low-level occam program that matched the structure and actions of the components on the chip. Finally, a transformation system for occam (written in Standard ML) was used to establish the equivalence of the two occam programs. The methods and tools used were quite advanced, but this involves important, re-usable work. The development was completed in under half the time estimated for an informal approach.

The specification and proof of a complex hardware component is illustrated by the 32-bit Viper processor, invented at the Royal Signals and Radar Establishment and now in commercial production. This was originally specified in LCF/LSM, and the development was formal down to the circuit network (Cullyer & Pyggott, 1987). Proofs were originally carried out by hand, and later machine-checked using Higher Order Logic (another derivative of Edinburgh LCF, which superseded LSM).

Another example where formal methods were used with a critical hardware component is SIFT (Mellier-Smith & Schwartz, 1982), a fault-tolerant flight control system. This case deserves special mention here, because there was an extreme reliability requirement (e.g. the system controls fuel usage, which is so economized that it could be impossible for a human to take over control in the event of failure). Observation and testing were not considered to be good enough to establish reliability because of the vast number of possible faults (with very low probabilities) that had to be considered. Fault-tolerant algorithms, duplication of tasks and voting methods were used to ensure reliability. Formal proofs were used to substantiate the reliability claims. This was achieved by separating the problem into two components. A predicate *system-safe* is defined to be true if and only if the replication of tasks is sufficient to ensure that voting will mask any faults. Under the assumption that system-safe is true, the system was proved to function correctly. Proofs were carried out using STP (SRI International) to establish correctness of the system down to the level of the Pascal executive programs. The second part of the proof used a Markov model to calculate an upper bound on the probability that system-safe could be false, and this guaranteed the reliability figures.

Although it is not economically feasible to do comparative studies (with a controlled development), reports of work such as that discussed in Mills *et al.* (1987) and Bromell & Sadler (1987) do suggest a reduction in work in later development and maintainence stages (with good improvements in reliability) when the extra effort is placed on formalizing specifications in earlier stages. It may be that this is a consequence of the fact that formalization forces more attention to possible problems early on rather than to the fact that it provides means for solving the problems. This aspect of formalization has been applied to the assessment of safety-critical systems (Bloomfield & Froome, 1986), where VDM was found to be very useful in specification analysis of a reactor protection system.

It seems that formal methods do not give much help with requirements analysis, nor with the actual production of a formal system specification from the informal requirements, although some work is being done in this area. The FOREST project (Cunningham *et al.,* 1985; Finkelstein & Potts, 1986; Maibaum, 1988) is researching techniques for the capture of requirements and requirements analysis in conjunction with formal methods so that initial formal specifications can be generated more directly with support tools. Also, at the early design stages, it is clear that formal development methods are not adequate in isolation. However, existing formal methods fit in well with the use of other commonly used design methods (in particular Object Oriented Design and JSD (Chedgey *et al.,* 1987; Crispin, 1987). This suggests that formal methods can be introduced gradually, supplementing existing, non-formal approaches without having to take big risks by abandoning the latter.

3.7 Important Issues for Effective Use of Formal Methods

It is likely that formal notations/methods will become more widely used for developing tools and environments for use with less formal methods. But their non-expert use is limited at present, and most potential users, put off by the mathematical concepts, are not ready to use them.

If formal methods are eventually to make a major impact on software productivity, quality, security and reliability in many applications, then it is necessary to overcome the present severe limitations of lack of tools, forbidding mathematical notations and lack of true methods. Software developers should ideally be able to work in the context of industrially established methods (descendants of SSADM, JSD, Yordon, etc.), using text notations and diagrams with graphical interfaces that they and the customers can understand yet underpinned by mathematical notations with defined semantics and manipulation rules. Similarly, the link to 4GLs and code generators should be underpinned by the formal notations, without demanding mathematical training of the users. This is the goal of industrialization of formal methods and the development of advanced support environments populated with appropriate tools to make them practicable for widespread use.

In this section we look briefly at the issues of concurrent systems, large-scale specifications, support tools, high-level languages and graphical interfaces, which are necessary for such industrialization of formal methods.

3.7.1 Dealing with concurrency

One very active area of research in formal methods concerns systems involving concurrency. Concurrent systems are notoriously more difficult to make reliable and to reason about than sequential systems and the majority of large systems fall into this category. They are likely to be increasingly important in the future because of hardware developments and needs in applications.

The problem comes from the fact that, when building any system, not only does one have to reason about and design components but one also has to reason about and design possible interactions between components in the integrated system, and the interactions can be far more complex for concurrent systems than for sequential ones. Furthermore, non-determinism is often a necessary descriptive tool for abstracting over the complex behaviour of systems and this can be particularly difficult to deal with. Non-determinism means that several different behaviours might be possible in the same (observable) situation. One impact of non-determinism is that results found in tests may be irreproducible, so testing is much less useful and the need for practical formal methods becomes even more important. Emphasis in research in this area has been on formal proof systems rather than transformational development. This is probably because, firstly, the latter is seen as less practical than in the sequential case and, secondly, the reliability of many concurrent systems (or components of them) is so critical that a great deal of effort spent on proofs is deemed worthwhile.

There are numerous approaches to the problem of concurrency. There are also some elegant, general mathematical models for describing concurrent systems with comforting algebraic properties to make reasoning about them and transformations on them more tractable. These might collectively be called *process algebras*. Most notably, they include CCS (also SCCS (Milner, 1980, 1988)) and CSP (Hoare, 1985), which is very similar, and LOTOS (ISO, 1988).

Typical of such algebras is a small collection of primitives for combining component processes to form larger systems. For example in CCS, if P_1 and P_2

are processes and a is an event (or communication), then

- $P_1 + P_2$ represents a process that non-deterministically chooses to behave either like P_1 or like P_2;
- $P_1 \mid P_2$ represents a process that behaves like P_1 and P_2 acting in parallel (possibly communicating);
- a . P represents a process that 'performs' event a and then behaves like P;
- τ . P represents a process that 'performs' some internal (but invisible) event and then behaves like P. The special symbol τ stands for any such internal event and is a major feature of the algebra in CCS.

From this very simple basis, we obtain useful algebraic laws that can be used in transformations and in establishing equivalences between implementation and specifications (both described with the same formalism). For example,

$$P \mid Q = Q \mid P$$
$$P + Q = Q + P$$
$$(P \mid Q) \mid R = P \mid (Q \mid R)$$
$$(P + Q) + R = P + (Q + R)$$
$$a . (P + \tau . Q) + a . Q = a . (P + \tau . Q)$$

but, in general,

$$a . (P + Q) \neq a . P + a . Q$$

Actually, the use of ' = ' in the equations needs to be qualified, because there is more than one interesting notion of equality depending on the model chosen. One possibility for = is *observational equality,* which holds between two processes if they cannot be distinguished in the context of any observing system.

In addition to algebraic laws, there are also some other proof methods such as the 'bisimulation' proof technique. The bisimulation technique has been used to show observational equivalence on examples such as the alternating bit protocol (Larsen & Milner, 1986) and a CSMA/CD protocol (Parrow, 1986).

Process algebras have already been supplemented with temporal logics in various ways to provide a variety of useful reasoning methods. Temporal logics provide simple ways of expressing many temporal constraints, such as: *if property P holds at some time* (*in some state*) *then Q holds at some subsequent time* (*state*). In particular, deadlock and livelock conditions can be expressed quite naturally. For a recent example, Barringer (1986) discusses the role of temporal logic in specification of concurrent systems.

The application of some of these methods has been quite productive in special areas such as protocol design, specification and analysis (see, for example, Bochmann *et al.*, 1982; Sarikaya & Bochmann, 1987). LOTOS (ISO, 1988) is an ISO standard protocol specification language based on CCS, with additional features from CSP and CIRCAL. It combines CCS with the abstract data type language ACT ONE in order to overcome the weakness of CCS in this area, although the standard allows for other formalisms to be used for the description of abstract data types if preferred.

Jones (1983) proposes extensions to VDM for reasoning with concurrent processes and an extended application with more details is given by Woodstock and Dickson (1988). The method described uses 'Rely' and 'Guarantee' conditions as well as Pre and Post conditions in order to separate out specifications of parallel components that may interfere with shared parts of the state concurrently.

Petri Nets are another well-researched tool for describing and analysing concurrent systems to specifying concurrent systems and have been used in industry for some time. Petri Nets can also be classified as a process algebra (see Boudel *et al.*, 1985), although, in practice, algebraic properties of Nets are rarely used. They tend to be used just for structural descriptions of concurrent systems along with some analysis tools that help to establish that Nets satisfy certain desirable properties (such as being 'deadlock free'). Comparin *et al.* (1985) give some guidelines for using nets with large scale specifications, and Reisig's recent text book (1985) has a detailed bibliography of work on Petri Nets and applications.

3.7.2 Large-scale specifications

It is often difficult to take in and fully comprehend the meaning of just a few lines of a terse mathematical specification and it is important to supplement formal specifications with careful explanation in natural language. A small specification can encapsulate a great deal of information. Nevertheless, moving to large-scale developments inevitably means having to deal with large specifications that will be impossible to understand in one reading.

Clearly, mechanisms are needed for structuring specifications so that the components of the specification are small enough and independent enough to consider easily in isolation. We also need to be able to comprehend how the components of a large specification fit together, so this needs to be easily explainable as well. Note that the structuring of specifications for the purposes of explanation to other people need not be simply related to the structure of the design being specified. A bad mismatch here may be a serious problem for keeping track of large designs as they evolve, but object-oriented design methods should help to keep the structure of the specification and the design closer together.

Some of the main formal methods in use today are acknowledged, by most people involved with them, to be lacking in this area and little is known about what sort of structuring should (or could) be used. There is some work related to this, however. We mentioned a module feature for VDM earlier and also CLEAR (Burstall & Goguen, 1981), which is aimed at providing structuring mechanisms. The mechanisms of CLEAR are analogous to some structuring mechanisms found in modular programming languages and allow larger 'theories' (specification components) to be composed from smaller theories. For example, parametrization of theories, instantiation of parametrized theories (application), and extending theories (sharing a common subtheory) are the main structuring mechanisms.

An important aspect of CLEAR is that the structuring mechanism is largely independent of the underlying logic used and can provide a structuring mechanism for use with different logics. The idea of an 'institution' is introduced by Goguen & Burstall (1984) to describe combinations of specification languages with their associated logic (proof system and class of models considered). The purpose behind this is to find ways of dealing with large specifications and complex systems where more than one institution might be used for expressing and reasoning about different aspects of the system. For example, one might want to use temporal logic to reason about the timing constraints in a real-time system and also equational reasoning to simplify properties of data-objects.

Once again, we know of no experience of industrial use of such work, but LARCH (Guttag *et al.*, 1985) involves an attempt to use structured algebraic methods in a practical environment and findings there may be very informative.

3.7.3 Formal development tools and systems

It seems worth mentioning an analogy made by Sintzoff (see Pepper, 1984) between use of formal methods now and the problem of parsing in the early 1950s. Then, the introduction of formal grammars to describe the parsing problem was a crucial step and led the way to the development of effective parsing tools. These tools were unlikely to have been thought of without the neat formal system used to describe the problem. Development of tools for use with formal specifications is just beginning.

The basic tools that may be used with formal methods divide into three categories: firstly, a word processor that handles any special characters—this is essential for all but the tiniest specifications; secondly, a syntax and type checker—this is essential for any serious work; and thirdly, a proof checker or editor—this is not necessary unless formal proofs are to be carried out. (A distinction is made here between a proof checker, which merely confirms that a proof discovered by some other means is indeed correct; a proof editor, which provides some help with discovery by carrying our simple rewriting automatically; and a theorem prover, which discovers complete proofs, usually by applying pre-programmed tactics.) In addition, configuration control tools are required to relate specifications to developments and keep track of the level of verification of each step.

Tools currently available or actively under development are:

- The Interactive Proof Editor and LEGO, developed by LFCS at Edinburgh
- The proof assistant MURAL being developed at Manchester University and Rutherford Appleton Laboratories as part of the IPSE 2.5 project (see Section 3.8)
- Symbolic execution tools for IPSE 2.5
- The concurrency workbench for CCS, which will solve some CCS equations and show equivalence

- Forsite Tools for Z
- VDM Toolset
- HOL proof-generating system
- ISABELLE developed by Larry Paulson at Cambridge
- Decision procedures for temporal logic being developed at Manchester University
- Tools for OBJ
- Spade Pascal Proof checker marketed by Program Validation Ltd
- REFINE development system developed by RSI Palo Alto
- Boyer–Moore Theorem Prover
- GYPSY
- LARCH

There are also more advanced tools related to transformational programming (transformation systems) and the animation of specifications. A very good survey of transformation systems can be found in Partsch & Steinbruggen (1983). There is also an excellent discussion and collection of position papers to be found in Pepper (1984), which is recommended reading. This is a report of a NATO workshop looking at transformation systems and programming environments and their possible application in industry in the future.

The general feeling of researchers seems to be that transformation systems are well enough developed to start doing extensive industrial trials. The purpose of such trials would be to discover where further work is needed to make the transformation systems practicable as well as to collect knowledge concerning the design and implementation of large systems. However, we should be patient: in the field of chemistry, a gap of 10 years between completion of experiments and full industrial use is the norm!

Meanwhile, further research is continuing to produce and refine other potentially useful tools. As well as the more obvious tools, there are some very powerful specialist tools (such as rewriting theorem provers). For example, there are various systems that give support for equational reasoning and which make use of the Knuth–Bendix algorithm (see, e.g. REVE (Lescanne, 1983) and ERIL (Dick, 1985)). Such tools bring the processes of specifying, designing and implementing closer together, and bring the paradigm of 'programming as reasoning' into the forefront. The automatic generation of functional programs from algebraic specifications is a feature of systems like RAP (Broy *et al.*, 1986; Geser & Hussman, 1986).

Tools such as these could play an important role in rapid prototyping and, as we mentioned earlier, it is important for designs to be checked against the user's needs as early as possible to avoid implementing the wrong system. The automatic implementations generated are useful not only for prototyping purposes but also for exploration of the design and deriving consequences of the constraints. Current experience suggests that the applicability of such tools is limited at present, but there is much active research in this area.

3.7.4 High-level languages

We have focused on the use of formal specifications and the use of proofs of design steps as a means of improving reliability in software products. We have also looked at some tools that help with reasoning and design. In this context, we want to consider the use of certain high-level programming languages and language features as another form of tool that supports formal development. Some of the more recent languages (in particular, declarative languages, which include the functional and logic languages) have been designed with proofs (of program correctness) very much in mind. That is, the constructs used for describing algorithms and data are very much easier to reason about and closer to the style of description found in specification languages. These languages usually exclude many of the error-prone constructs found in conventional languages, such as pointers and other explicit memory control operations. Full procedural languages are rarely designed this way, but subsets of Ada (Carre & Jennings, 1988) and Pascal (Carre & Debney, 1985) exist that are cleanly defined as an aid to verification. Declarative languages go a step further, and take the control of memory out of the programmer's hands and deal with it automatically, so that correct use of such constructs only needs to be established once and for all in the language implementation rather than for each program.

As an example, here is a recursive data type declaration in Standard ML (Harper *et al.*, 1986):

datatype View = Empty
         | AddPicture of (View × Coordinate × PictureId × Picture)

which says that a value of type View is either Empty or constructed by applying the operator AddPicture to a quadruple of a View, a Coordinate, a PictureId and a Picture. The constant

Empty

of type View and the constructor (= constructing operator)

AddPicture : View × Coordinate × PictureId × Picture→ View

are introduced by the type definition. This is very close to the sort of descriptions of data types and data objects in specification languages. In a conventional language such as Ada or Pascal, the type would (most naturally) be implemented using pointers, and this means that each data-object and operation on data-objects of the type is a potential source of very common programming errors. In addition this makes reasoning more difficult and makes programs less readable.

As another example, consider the following definition in Miranda style (Turner, 1985) of a function described in Section 3.5.3.

FindPictures(v, c) = [id | (p, id, c′) ← v; In(p,Minus(c, c′))]

This says that FindPictures(v, c) is the list of identifiers (id) such that (p, id, c) is in the view v and In(p, Minus(c, c')) is true. The description is a quite abstract specification, but it is also a runnable program.

The efficiency of such languages used to be the main reason for not using them in serious applications, but this is much less of a problem and their advantages in programmer productivity and improvements in reliability make them highly advantageous in some areas (e.g. for rapid prototyping). Where run-time efficiency is a problem (usually in the use of space rather than speed) transformation from declarative to conventional languages is also a possibility.

Common use of such languages in industry may well be a long way off, but such use is increasing and is likely to grow more rapidly with further architectural support. Even on conventional hardware, languages like Standard ML and PROLOG can perform sufficiently well to make them viable alternatives to conventional languages in several application areas. In particular, the sophisticated module structure of Standard ML designed for support of large-scale programs, combined with its recent publicity with an award from the BCS in 1987 should have an influence on its likely use in industry.

Another aspect of recent high-level languages such as Miranda and Standard ML is their polymorphic type systems. These are sophisticated type systems that allow programs to be statically checked for type correctness (i.e. at compile time) without excessive constraints that might inhibit the description of generic, multipurpose operations and modules. Furthermore, these type systems allow the types of objects to be inferred automatically with little information provided by the programmer. Such a type system could easily be classified as a built in, formal tool. Type checking is a kind of partial proof of correctness; inferring that function f has type int$\rightarrow$bool is a proof that f can only return results of type bool when supplied with arguments of type int, and checking that f is only applied to appropriately typed arguments is part of the proof of correctness of a program involving f. Industrial use of such advanced languages is very limited, but it is growing.

It should also be remembered that although PROLOG is classified as a programming language, it can be seen as a semi-automatic theorem prover that is sufficiently practical that it can be used in general-purpose problem solving. This points the way to future language developments that are being researched, in which programming and specifying are brought closer together, and could have a major impact on software engineering practice in the future. (See Reade (1989) for further details about functional programming.)

3.7.5 Graphical interfaces

We mentioned at the start of Section 3.7 that there is a great need for graphical tools to alleviate the problem of complex notation. Such tools are quite well developed in the support of (informal) object-oriented program development, where objects can be created and programmed by use of pointing devices and menus. There are also well-developed graphical tools used in hardware design. Some current research is aimed at adapting such tools to take care of much of the formal aspects of design (Fourman *et al.*, 1988*a,b*).

3.8 Prospects and Conclusions

As formal methods become more acceptable, they are likely to have more impact on software engineering practice generally. In particular, it may become less and less cost-effective to do programming without appropriate support tools. Smaller design teams with very specialized knowledge and sophisticated tools may prove to be more productive than 'armies' of developers that rarely produce reliable software on time and to budget. Such 'expert' design teams are more likely to be able to control large developments successfully if they have sufficient and sophisticated support tools, and their small size will allow easier communication and decison making. We may also see a split between developers of sophisticated products and more naive users of those products who are still 'programming' with them. Implicit formal support may be embedded in such products to protect naive users from errors. This would follow the trend in the development of high-level programming languages.

There are other larger (longer-term) projects such as IPSE 2.5 (Jones *et al.*, 1986; Lindsay *et al.*, 1986), which are aimed at an even fuller integration of formal methods into program development, blurring the distinction between reasoning and programming. In many ways, the development of environments to support software production with formal methods is feeling out new ground. It is not yet clear what is likely to be practical, cost-effective or useful. Despite this, it is becoming clearer that there are possibilities for a 'core' support for reasoning that is independent of particular formal methods, specification languages and logics. Such core support might take the form of general-purpose (customizable) formal reasoning tools with a theorem-proving engine along with tools for building graphical user interfaces for easier interactions. IPSE 2.5 is a step towards future integrated project support environments where formal methods are to play a significant role. A large part of this effort is concerned with the use of formal reasoning in the design process. The formal reasoning component of IPSE 2.5 is therefore seen as a significant part of the environment.

For the present, it is difficult to predict how quickly formal methods will be adopted because of the various factors discussed here. A senior industrialist recently commented on one of the design methods mentioned here, saying that 'it was a very good piece of work but not very useful to industry because it was too mathematical'. It may well be that the notation and style could well be improved (especially by the use of graphical interfaces) to make formal methods more palatable. However, there is a limit to such easements, because it is usually the behaviour being formally described that is the major complexity and one cannot always blame the formalism as the source of the complexity. Often, the system needed is more complex than had been expected and the use of formal methods facilitates early realization of the extent of the complexity required. Brooks (1987) discusses this point in trying to establish what is the major problem of software engineering.

Focus of attention on the real costs of unreliable products, and legal requirements on software quality may force an earlier adoption than might otherwise have been envisaged. The forthcoming UK Interim Defence Standard 00-55 shows that standardization and procurement agencies are prepared to live with the current shortcomings of the methods in order to improve the quality of software in critical areas.

Different aspects of formal methods are not equally cost-effective in increasing reliability. Emphasis on formal specification in design alone can give comparatively high benefits with lower cost. More advanced formal methods are unlikely to be cost-effective on a large scale until support tools have been developed further. However, they can be usefully deployed on small but critical components. Clearly, another major influence on the use of formal methods is the availability of the right sort of tools. The tools are needed not just at the theorem-proving end, but also at the requirements engineering end and to alleviate the problems of mathematical notation. The FOREST project (Finkelstein & Potts, 1986; Maibaum, 1988) is concerned with tools for deriving formal specifications from requirements and the development of high-level languages and graphical interfaces should help with notation problems. As formal methods become integrated into industrial practice, much is likely to be learned about deficiencies and cost-effectiveness of tools. This in turn will help to direct research.

It is possible to give some pragmatic advice based on current experience to managers wishing to get started with formal methods. It is desirable to start on a reasonably small project that will produce at most a few thousand lines of source code, and concurrency should be avoided. If the project is to start from an informal specification, it is important that this specification is adequate and at a high enough level of abstraction. A rigorous rather than formal approach (as defined in Section 3.2) should be adopted.

The choice of formal method to be used will depend upon the particular application, because there is no universally applicable method. However, the following criteria may be useful in making the decision: soundness of mathematical basis; public access to syntax and tools; successful industrial use in the application area; suitability for design as well as specification; availability of training; national or international standard definition; and existence of industrialized tools.

A commitment to adequate training is essential: project managers will require a one- or two-day awareness course, and development staff should attend an initial one- or two-week technical course in the chosen method with provision for subsequent on-site training. Assistance from someone with greater experience of formal methods will also be required: this may be obtained from consultants, although in the longer term larger companies should consider training a staff member to the required level, or employing someone of this standard.

Managers must revise their normal monitoring procedures to reflect the change in emphasis towards correct specification (at multiple levels) and away from early coding with lengthy testing to correct errors.

Finally, there is a clear need for an investment in tools to support formal methods, both to remove the error-prone drudgery and to derive more benefit from the use of a formal method (although some of these may be relatively inexpensive). A simple syntax and type checker for the method will be required in addition to the editing and configuration control tools. Organizations should be prepared to make these investments in order to reduce costs later in the life-cycle, especially during maintenance and licensing, bearing in mind that some customers may be prepared to pay a premium for software that is formally developed with the assurance of correctness and reliability.

3.9 Further Reading

A recommended, general introductory text book on specification is Turski & Maibaum (1987). Cohen *et al.* (1986) also give an introduction to formal methods with a survey of methods and examples. An introduction to the basic mathematical concepts is given by Denvir (1986). The use of formal methods with object-oriented software construction is discussed in Chapter 7 of Meyer's (1988) highly readable book.

Introductions to Z (Spivey, 1988*a*) and VDM (Jones, C. B., 1986) are available and we have mentioned collections of case studies for these respective methods (Hayes, 1987; Jones & Shaw, 1988) that are very useful. There are also introductory texts on the use of algebraic specifications, e.g. Bergstra (1989). A collection of papers on software specification techniques edited by Gehani and McGettrick (1986) includes an introduction to CLEAR (Burstall & Goguen, 1981) which is concerned with the construction of large-scale specifications.

The papers and discussions edited by Pepper (1984) are recommended for anyone wishing to look further at the issues related to program transformation.

4

Software Fault Tolerance

Michael Moulding

4.1 Introduction 83
4.2 Overview of Software Fault Tolerance 84
4.3 Towards an Implementation Framework for Software Fault
Tolerance 90
4.4 Robust Software Using Ada's Exception-Handling Facilities . 92
4.5 N-Version Programming 96
4.6 Recovery Blocks 99
4.7 Comparison of N-Version Programming and Recovery
Blocks 105
4.8 Practical Application of N-Version Programming and Recovery Blocks 107
4.9 Summary 109

4.1 Introduction

In Chapter 2 emphasis was placed on object-oriented design as an example of software design approaches which are aimed at avoiding the introduction of faults into the software, and which assist in the removal of faults during subsequent verification, validation and testing. Collectively, these approaches attempt to prevent faults from existing in the operational software, but for realistic systems they are unlikely to be totally successful and a number of residual faults will remain. Consequently, in the cost-effective engineering of reliable software, it can be appropriate to supplement fault prevention with design approaches which attempt to suppress the effects of residual faults. Such fault-tolerance approaches are the subject of this chapter and we will investigate the major schemes which have been devised to achieve this and discuss some associated design and implementation issues. However, we shall commence with an overview of software fault tolerance and in so doing uncover some important concepts and terms.

Before commencing with the technical material of the chapter, it is important to understand that, although the suppression of residual software faults has been introduced as a primary objective of software fault-tolerance schemes, it cannot be considered in isolation. Such schemes must be careful not to compromise the structural quality of the software, since this plays such an important role in fault-prevention approaches and, in keeping with the discussion in Chapter 2, we must emphasize the need for software fault-tolerance designs to exhibit high visibility and low coupling between software components. Indeed, much of the research in this topic has been directed towards the architectural issues of software fault-tolerance designs and this is reflected in our treatment of the subject here.

4.2   Overview of Software Fault Tolerance

In order to discuss the basic principles of software fault tolerance, we must first obtain a simple abstract model to describe software systems. Such a model is illustrated in Fig. 4.1 and portrays a software system as a number of components which co-operate under the influence of a design to service the demands of the system environment. The design can be considered as the algorithm which is responsible for defining the interactions between components, establishing connections between components and the system environment, and for providing any supplementary processing for the system to achieve its required behaviour. The components, which themselves may be viewed as systems in their own right, may be categorized as being either *synchronously* or *asynchronously* related to the design which employs them. Synchronous components are passive and, when invoked by their calling environment, will complete before the environment may resume, whereas asynchronous components are active and, once invoked, will operate asynchronously with their environment. The top-down decomposition of a sequential program into a hierarchy of procedures is a common form of design using synchronous components. The design of the system is embodied in the algorithm of the

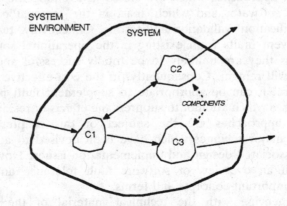

Fig. 4.1. Abstract model of a software system.

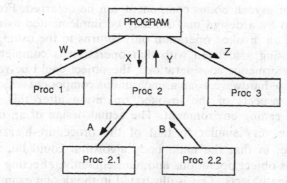

Fig. 4.2. Hierarchical structure chart for sequential program. (Annotated arrows specify data communicated.)

program main body which invokes the individual procedures and passes data between them. A structure chart, as illustrated in Fig. 4.2, is often used to describe the procedure hierarchy and identify the communication which takes place between a procedure and its calling environment. In contrast to this, program designs utilizing asynchronous components are often expressed in the form of a network of communicating parallel processes, as illustrated in Fig. 4.3. Here, the role of the program main body, which embodies the design of the system, is to construct the network and, in frozen systems (MASCOT Suppliers Association, 1980) where the network is static, the main body algorithm plays no further part in the operation of the system. Once activated, the processes will instigate their own communications and the design notation concentrates on explicitly defining their connectivity.

The choice of procedure-hierarchy and process-network representations to illustrate synchronous and asynchronous component designs reflects a traditional *functional* view of software design. However, the simple abstract design model is equally appropriate for the object-oriented approach described in Chapter 2. Under such circumstances the individual components will be objects which offer synchronous interfaces via their procedure operations. The internal design or realization of an object is hidden by these interface operations and, consequently, decisions regarding the selection of the object as

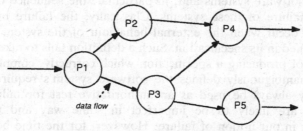

Fig. 4.3. Network of processes.

a synchronous or asynchronous component can be deferred. For example, an object employed by a design may initially be implemented as a synchronous object such that an invoked operation only returns to the calling environment when all processing associated with that operation is completed. However, after system performance considerations, the object could be re-implemented to run on separate hardware as an asynchronous component which continues to process certain aspects of the invoked operation after this operation has returned to the calling environment. The actual design of an object-oriented program can be very similar to that of the procedure-hierarchy program, described above, in that the main body algorithm could be responsible for invoking various object operations and, consequently, effecting the transfer of messages between objects. This is illustrated in the design example of Chapter 2, where a structure chart is used to define the object hierarchy.

From the simple abstract design model we can establish that a design has associated with it two separate specification stages. The first stage of specification defines the system requirements which the design must satisfy; the second stage defines the properties of the components which are identified by the design. Clearly, the model is recursive in that each component can itself be considered as a system in its own right and thus may have an internal design which can identify further subcomponents. The recursion will continue until, at the lowest level, a design is purely algorithmic, or employs re-usable software components of pre-defined specification. This separation of design from specification is an important issue in software fault tolerance and is consistent with both the discussion in Chapter 2 (Fig. 2.1), which advocated the use of separate specification and design realization phases in a software development cycle, and the description of Cohen's contractual model of software development presented in Chapter 3 (Fig. 3.1). It is regrettable that the specification of components is often carried forward implicitly in the designer's head and that the only description of a component is its design at the next level. In many respects the need for explicit component specifications outweighs arguments concerning whether such specifications should be mathematically formal or not. We do, however, encourage the adoption of any techniques which will draw attention to the role of specifications and improve their quality.

So far we have used the simple abstract model of software systems to describe their static architectural features. Before we can discuss software fault tolerance with respect to this model, we must extend it to describe the dynamic behaviour of software systems and, in particular, the sequence of events that leads to the failure of these systems. Classically, the failure of a system is considered to occur when the external behaviour of the system first deviates from that defined in its specification. Such a definition fails to take into account the difficulty of producing a specification which correctly, completely, consistently and unambiguously defines the software system's required properties and thus may always be used as an authoritative test for failure. Practical specifications are likely to be imperfect in some way and this must be accounted for in our notion of failure. However, for the time being, we shall ignore the imperfections of software specifications and return to this issue when we have investigated the dynamics of software failure.

The dynamic behaviour of a software system is characterized by the series of *internal states* which the system adopts during its processing. Certain elements of an internal state will coincide with the interface between the system and its environment, and these form the *external state* of the system via which its external behaviour is realized. Each internal state will comprise the set of data values within the scope of the design: output values produced by the components (i.e. their external states) and the values of any variables maintained directly by the design (e.g. variables used by the main body algorithm of a sequential program). Under normal processing conditions, the system will advance from one valid internal state to the next by means of a *valid transition*. However, if a *fault* is encountered in the software during its processing, an *erroneous transition* may occur which transforms the system to an invalid internal state containing one or more defective values or *errors*. Once the system state is damaged in this way, subsequent invalid states can be produced from valid transitions. Alternatively, if the natural processing repairs the damage, for example by overwriting an incorrect variable with a new correct value, then the system can revert to a series of valid internal states. If an error in an internal state maps on to the external state, for example when an incorrect value is output, then a failure of the system will result. Consequently, all system failures can be attributed to errors in the internal state of the system but not all errors need result in failure. All errors and, therefore, all failures are attributable to faults in the system.

Within the context of the simple abstract model of software systems, faults may be categorized, at any level of abstraction, as either design faults or component faults. To illustrate this point, consider that the system of Fig. 4.1 has failed during its operation. This may have resulted from the failure of the system design algorithm to perform its intended function (a design fault) or, alternatively, may derive from the failure of a system component to operate according to its specification (a component fault). Of course, all software components can be considered as systems in their own right and, owing to the abstract nature of software, will eventually decompose purely into a set of designs. Therefore, all software faults can be considered as design faults at some level of abstraction within the software system. Nevertheless, the concept of software component faults is valuable when discussing the deployment of software fault tolerance within a software system, and is likely to gain in significance with any trend towards re-usable software components.

The object of software fault tolerance is to prevent software faults from causing system failure. A general arrangement for achieving this for the abstract model of a software system is illustrated in Fig. 4.4. In order to allow the system to operate successfully in the presence of a system design fault, the software must be constructed from a number of diverse system designs which have a low probability of exhibiting common-mode failure (by producing similar erroneous output for the same processing conditions). A fault-tolerance

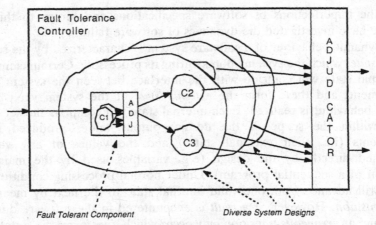

Fig. 4.4. Abstract model of a fault-tolerant software system.

controller can then be added which organizes the execution of the various designs and, with the aid of an adjudicator function within it, determines the overall system output. Redundancy applied at this level can also give protection against component faults if different components are used by the various diverse system designs. Alternatively, protection against the failure of individual components can be provided by having diverse component designs which can be organized by a fault-tolerance controller in the same way as at the system level. The precise way in which the controller operates is a function of the particular fault-tolerance scheme which is employed. Nevertheless, there are four major activities which will be performed by any such scheme:

(1) *Error detection*. When a diverse design executes, it is necessary to determine whether a fault has been encountered. Faults are not directly detectable but the effects of a fault, namely one or more errors in the internal state of a system (or component), can be used to identify the presence of a fault. In order to avoid system failure, it is important that such internal errors are detected before they can propagate to the external state of the system, and the most obvious way of achieving this is for the adjudicator to vet the output of an executing design.

(2) *Damage assessment*. When the internal state of the system (or component) contains one or more errors, the extent of this damage must, in general, be assessed. Often, this is achieved by having damage-confinement structures present within the system which limit the propagation of errors.

(3) *Error recovery*. Having assessed the extent of the damage to the internal state of a system (component), this damage must be repaired so that failure of the system (component) can be averted.

(4) *Fault treatment*. Allowing the fault to remain in the system following

recovery can lead to further errors. Removing the fault will require the offending software design to be configured out of the system for some processing period.

The foregoing discussion of software faults implicitly assumes that software specifications at both the system and component level are perfect and, consequently, can always be used to define system or component failure. In reality this will not be so and greater insight into software faults can be gained by considering the fallibility of specifications. At the system level, the specification may contain errors; it may not accurately reflect the requirements which the environment places on that system. Consequently, behaviour which is correct with respect to the specification may be viewed as a perceived failure in terms of the *expectation* of the environment. Furthermore, incompleteness, inconsistencies and ambiguities in the system specification are likely to cause the specification to be interpreted in a way which does not reflect the true requirement, thus resulting in additional perceived failures. By applying these arguments to both the system and component specifications of the simple abstract model of a software system the following origins of software faults can be derived:

System specification faults
Errors
Misinterpretations
System design faults
Component faults
Component specification faults:
Errors
Misinterpretations
Component design faults
Subcomponent faults

Consider first the application of software fault tolerance to the system level. This will not deal with system specification errors but may provide some protection against misinterpretations, since these may not be common to each of the diverse system designs. The use of diverse system designs will strive to protect against system design faults, and component faults (whether they be specification, design or subcomponent) should not cause common-mode failure between system designs which employ different components. Correspondingly, fault tolerance applied at the component level will not cope with erroneous component specifications but may cope with component specification inter-pretation problems. Similarly, the use of diverse component designs employing different components will strive to protect against component design faults and subcomponent faults. Thus, the higher the level at which fault tolerance is applied, the greater the range of faults that are addressed and, in particular, the greater the potential protection against specification faults, but the higher the cost in terms of software redundancy. However, no protection can be provided against an erroneous system specification: a deficiency which software fault tolerance shares with other specification-driven techniques such as formal verification.

4.3   Towards an Implementation Framework for Software Fault Tolerance

In the preceding overview discussion, the adjudicator function within the software fault-tolerance controller has been introduced as the main method of achieving error detection. In practice, adjudicator checks will not detect all errors and, consequently, should be supplemented with the following.

(1) Error detection *measures* within a software design which will check for anomalous data values. Assertion statements are a common form of error detection measure. These attempt to demonstrate that certain properties of the software design hold during its execution.

(2) Error detection *mechanisms* provided by the underlying virtual machine upon which the design executes. These will attempt to ensure that the software design does not attempt to use the virtual machine in an invalid way. The most powerful forms are those associated with the hardware; for example, memory-protection mechanisms which will detect an invalid memory access by the software.

Clearly such measures and mechanisms must be able to indicate the presence of errors to the fault-tolerance controller so that the remaining phases necessary for fault tolerance can be instigated. Exception handling provides a way of achieving this: the controller will provide an exception *handler* which will be automatically invoked when a measure or mechanism *raises* an exception to indicate the detection of one or more errors. A major benefit of this approach is that the abnormal processing of the fault-tolerance controller following error detection is clearly separated from the normal processing associated with a software design.

Within the simple abstract model of Fig. 4.4 there will exist two levels of exception handler: one at the component level and one at the system level. If a fault-tolerance controller at the component level cannot continue correct operation following the detection of an error within the component, then it itself may raise an exception to the system-level controller. Generally, exceptions propagated in this way may be categorized as:

• *Interface exceptions*. These indicate that a software design is being used incorrectly; for example, it may be asked to process data which it does not expect. At the component level, this would indicate that a design fault exists at the system level, or that the component specification is faulty (does not reflect the way the component is intended to be used). At the system level, an interface exception would be indicative of a system specification fault, or the misuse of the system by its environment (e.g. operator abuse).

- *Failure exceptions*. These indicate that the fault-tolerant system or component has failed owing to an internal fault which it cannot mask.

Evidently, the goal of software fault tolerance is to prevent the propagation of failure exceptions. Nevertheless, their identification is useful since they can be used to instigate fault-tolerant actions at a higher level, or at the system level they can be used to raise an alarm condition to the system environment. Interface exceptions raised from the component level are also of value, since they provide error detection to the design level which utilizes the component. They are very similar in nature to the exceptions raised by error detection mechanisms, since both indicate that the design at a certain level is misusing the facilities which are provided for it. Logically, the components of a design could be viewed as an extension to the virtual machine on which the design executes and, continuing this rationalization, suggests that the virtual machine should also be capable of raising failure exceptions. This is indeed the case and, in particular, is the way that tolerance to hardware faults may be organized. However, in the remainder of this chapter we shall not consider further the fallibility of the virtual machine but instead concentrate on the way that software fault tolerance may be applied to the applications software.

When an exception is handled by a fault tolerance controller, in general, damage assessment and error recovery will follow. An important dynamic structuring concept which assists in these activities is the atomic action which has been defined as follows (Anderson & Lee, 1981):

The activity of a group of components constitutes an atomic action if there are no interactions between that group and the rest of the system for the duration of the activity.

If the system is known to be in an error-free state upon entry to an atomic action, and an exception is raised during its execution, then only those components which have participated in the atomic action need be recovered by the fault-tolerance controller. However, it is important that such atomic actions are enforced by the underlying virtual machine, since the errant applications software cannot be trusted to adhere to this planned dynamic behaviour. The recovery itself can be categorized as follows.

- *Forward recovery*. The system is returned to an error-free state by applying corrections to the damaged state. Such an approach demands some understanding of the errors which exist.
- *Backward recovery*. The system is recovered to a previous error-free state. No knowledge of the errors in the system state is required.

Software faults, whether they be design faults or specification faults, are by their very nature unpredictable, as are the errors which they introduce. Consequently, backward error recovery provides the most generally applicable approach for software fault tolerance. However, for those limited cases where the characteristics of a fault are well understood, forward recovery can provide a more efficient solution. Moreover, the two techniques can be viewed as complementary and their combination will be discussed later in this chapter.

When error recovery is completed, the fault-treatment phase of software fault tolerance will normally be carried out, and this will usually involve the use of one or more diverse designs in order to obtain continued correct operation. However, some limited form of software fault tolerance can be possible without the use of diverse designs; for example, by detecting and recovering an error, and either ignoring the operation which generated it or by providing a pre-defined and heavily degraded response to that operation. In such cases the software cannot be considered as truly fault-tolerant since some perceived departure from specification is likely to occur. However, this approach can result in software which is robust in the sense that catastrophic failure can be averted. In the following section of this chapter, robust software will be discussed in the context of the exception-handling facilities provided by the programming language Ada. The remaining sections will then concentrate on the two main comprehensive software fault-tolerance schemes of N-version programming and recovery blocks, both of which include diverse software designs for fault treatment.

4.4   Robust Software Using Ada's Exception-Handling Facilities

It has long been recognized that a major source of unreliability in software is the inability of a software design, whether it be at the system or component level, to cope with invalid inputs. Over the years, this realization has led to a software design style known as *defensive programming*, in which the software is required to perform extensive checks on its input so that invalid values can be identified and remedial action taken, such as informing the calling environment that the required operation has been denied. The overall defensive programming strategy is to attempt to enumerate all the things which can go wrong and include features within the software design to deal with these. Importantly, a software design might also need to deal with errors detected by the underlying hardware; for example, overflow or underflow during arithmetic operations.

Inevitably, the programmed validity checks of the defensive programming approach will result in run-time overheads and, where performance demands are critical, many checks are often removed from the operational software; their use is restricted to the testing phase where they can identify the misuse of components by faulty designs. In the context of producing complex systems which can never be fully tested, this tendency to remove the protection afforded by programmed validity checks is most regrettable and is not recommended here.

Using the software fault-tolerance terminology introduced above, defensive programming requires the inclusion in a design of error-detection measures to check for invalid inputs, and forward recovery handlers to remove the predicted errors detected by either programmed measures or hardware mechanisms. Of course, such an approach will provide very limited protection against residual design faults, since errors introduced by these will be hard, if not impossible, to predict; backward recovery would be more suitable here. Moreover, the absence of any diverse designs means that an operation cannot be completed successfully in the presence of a software fault; either a failure exception must be raised or a heavily degraded response for that operation must be pre-programmed as part of the recovery handler. Nevertheless, the defensive programming approach will help to ensure that software behaves in a robust fashion when predictable errors occur.

One of the major difficulties of conventional defensive programming is that the fault-tolerance actions are inseparably bound in with the normal processing which the design is to provide. This can significantly increase design complexity and, consequently, can compromise the reliability and maintainability of the software. Modern programming languages with strong data typing like Pascal, Modula-2 and Ada do much to reduce the need for programmed validity checks. By carefully selecting data types to reflect the range of values which a variable may hold, and the permissible operations which are available to it, much of the run-time checking previously performed in untyped languages can now be conducted at compile time. Where run-time checks are still needed to enforce the data typing, these can be automatically included by the compiler, thus not compromising the complexity of the software design. The compiler essentially supports the abstraction of a strongly-typed virtual machine which raises some (interface) exceptions at compile time and the remainder at run-time—by virtue of embedded run-time checks. Of course, if the hardware supports data typing, then the compiler can map many of the run-time checks directly on to hardware instructions and significantly reduce their overheads. Consequently, when compared with conventional defensive programming, a strongly-typed language can not only reduce the complexity of the software but also improve its run-time performance.

The Ada language distinguishes itself from Pascal and Modula-2 in that it defines how run-time exceptions may be handled by the applications software. The other two languages make no such provision but instead allow the particular virtual-machine implementation to control this. In fact, Ada's exception-handling facilities closely model those introduced for the software fault-tolerance implementation framework, discussed above. In broad terms, each program block may declare one or more exception handlers to service particular exceptions raised during the execution of that block. If no exception handler exists in a block for a particular exception, then the exception is propagated out to the enclosing block (which caused the inner block to be executed) and a handler is sought for it there. This outward propagation continues until either a handler is found or the exception is propagated out of the program to the environment. If a suitable handler is found, it is executed and then control is transferred out of the block where the handler resides to the enclosing block; that is, an exception results in a premature exit from the block. A number of pre-defined exceptions are provided in Ada and result from the Ada virtual-machine run-time checks. In addition, applications software may declare other named exceptions which error detection measures within the software may explicitly raise. The simple program of Fig. 4.5 illustrates how these facilities may be used to provide a robust program which is resilient to certain predictable errors.

```
with FLOAT_IO, TEXT_IO;
procedure REAL_ROOTS is

    A,B,C, TEMP, R1,R2: FLOAT;
    IMAGINARY_SQ_ROOT, SQ_ROOT_FAILURE: exception ;

    function MULT (X, Y: FLOAT) return FLOAT is
    begin
        return X*Y;
    exception
        when NUMERIC_ERROR =>
            if (X<0.0 and Y<0.0) or (X>0.0 and Y>0.0) then
                if (X<1.0 or Y<1.0) then
                    return FLOAT'SMALL;
                else
                    return FLOAT'LARGE;
                end if ;
            else
                if (X<1.0 or Y<1.0) then
                    return -FLOAT'SMALL;
                else
                    return -FLOAT'LARGE;
                end if ;
            end if ;
    end MULT;

    function SQ_ROOT (X: FLOAT) return FLOAT is
        TEMP: FLOAT;
    begin
        if X < 0.0 then raise IMAGINARY_SQ_ROOT; end if ;
        -- body of function contains statements which will compute
        -- square root of X and assign this to local variable TEMP
        return TEMP;
    exception
        when IMAGINARY_SQ_ROOT => raise;
        when others => raise SQ_ROOT_FAILURE;
    end SQ_ROOT;

begin
    TEXT_IO.PUT ("Please input coefficients in order A, B, C: ");
    FLOAT_IO.GET(A); FLOAT_IO.GET(B); FLOAT_IO.GET(C); TEXT_IO.NEW_LINE;
    TEMP := SQ_ROOT( MULT(B,B) - MULT(4.0,MULT(A,C)) );
    R1 := (-B + TEMP) / MULT(2.0,A);
    R2 := (-B - TEMP) / MULT(2.0,A);
    TEXT_IO.PUT ("Roots are: ");
    FLOAT_IO.PUT(R1);   TEXT_IO.PUT (" ");   FLOAT_IO.PUT(R2);   TEXT_IO.NEW_LINE;
exception
    when IMAGINARY_SQ_ROOT => TEXT_IO.PUT_LINE ("ERROR - roots are IMAGINARY");
    when SQ_ROOT_FAILURE => TEXT_IO.PUT_LINE ("SORRY - square root routine has FAILED");
    when others => TEXT_IO.PUT_LINE ("SORRY - unpredicted failure has occurred");

end REAL_ROOTS;
```

Fig. 4.5. Exception handling in Ada.

The purpose of the program of Fig. 4.5 is to calculate the real roots of a quadratic equation which is specified by an operator in terms of its three coefficients. As is normal practice in Ada, the program is written as a parameterless main procedure. The *with* clause preceding the main procedure heading allows the program to import the library packages FLOAT_IO and TEXT_IO and use their procedures by qualifying the procedure name with the package name (those readers familiar with Ada will note that the *use* clause has been omitted in order to ensure that all references to library package procedures are clearly visible—an approach which is strongly recommended here in order to make the program easier to understand and, hence, contributing to fault avoidance). The two library packages can essentially be considered as input/output extensions to the Ada virtual machine.

The program itself employs two functional components which are declared in the declarative region of the main procedure, along with six floating-point variables and two *exceptions*. The first of these functions MULT provides robust multiplication for floating-point numbers. The body of the function simply attempts to return with the product of the two operands. If underflow or overflow occurs as a result of this, the pre-defined exception NUMERIC_ERROR will automatically be raised. Consequently, in the exception section of the procedure there is a handler declared for this. Its action is to return a result which corresponds to either the smallest (underflow) or largest (overflow) floating-point number of appropriate sign, thus effectively recovering the error with a pre-defined result of degraded accuracy. The second program function SQ_ROOT provides the square root of a floating-point number. For simplicity, the algorithm for this has been omitted but its effect is to compute the square root of the floating-point number operand into the local variable TEMP which can then be returned as the function result. Before computing this, however, a measure within the function first checks whether the operand is negative and raises the IMAGINARY_SQ_ROOT exception which was declared in the main procedure. The exception section of the SQ_ROOT function contains two handlers: one for the IMAGINARY_SQ_ROOT exception explicitly raised within the function, and one for any other exception raised during the execution of the function, such as a computational error in the square root algorithm. The action of the IMAGINARY_SQ_ROOT handler is simply to raise this same exception to the calling program; the other handler explicitly raises the exception SQ_ROOT_FAILURE which was also declared in the main procedure.

It can be noted that the exception-handling strategy of the SQ_ROOT function is somewhat different from that employed in the MULT function. No attempt is made to recover from errors within the function; instead, named exceptions are propagated out to the calling program so that it may deal with them in an appropriate way. One of these exceptions is an interface exception which identifies that the function was called with an invalid (negative) operand; the other is a failure exception which indicates that the function has failed owing to some residual fault.

The action of the body of the main procedure is simply to obtain the coefficients for the quadratic equation, compute its roots using the MULT and SQ_ROOT functional components, and output these results. Exceptions raised during the execution of this code are serviced by three handlers: one for each of the exceptions raised by the SQ_ROOT function, and one for any other exceptions which may occur. In each case, the handler provides forward recovery for the program by producing an appropriate response to the operator in lieu of the required computation.

The above example demonstrates how exception handling separates the normal processing aspects of a program from the abnormal actions required to achieve robust operation. However, it is difficult to generalize about the required actions of exception handlers because these will depend very much on the particular application. This is typical of the forward recovery approach. For example, the loss of accuracy when overflow or underflow occurs within the MULT function may be unacceptable in some programs and, instead, a failure exception may need to be raised so that the operator can be informed that a suitably accurate result cannot be obtained. Evidently, the forward recovery action of a software system or component under erroneous conditions is an important aspect of its specification, but often this is not adequately addressed. Ideally, a specification should identify various levels of degraded functionality for predictable errors. Sadly, this is seldom the case and it is left to the designer to interpret what might be regarded as acceptable forward recovery action under such circumstances. The absence of suitable attention to erroneous conditions in specifications is also reflected at the programming level in Ada, where a subprogram (procedure or function) heading, which specifies the subprogram interface to a calling environment, does not identify the exceptions which are explicitly raised and propagated out of that subprogram; exceptions form part of the hidden interface along with global variables accessed, and can only be determined by examining the code (design) of the subprogram.

4.5 *N*-Version Programming

In contrast to the robust software approach described above, where the presence of a fault will affect the operation of the system, the *N*-version programming scheme, illustrated in Fig. 4.6, attempts to mask software faults so that the system environment is unaware of their presence. This is achieved by utilizing three or more (*N*) versions of a program, each of which has been independently designed from the same specification and is activated by a *driver* module (D) which provides all versions with read-only access to the same input data. The driver then collects the individual outputs from the versions and, in the simplest case, performs a majority vote in order to determine the overall output from the *N*-version program. Consequently, a fault in any one version can be effectively masked.

Relating the *N*-version scheme to the general principles of software fault

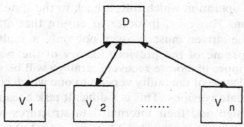

Fig. 4.6. *N*-version programming.

tolerance introduced in the overview section of this chapter shows the driver module to be a specific implementation of the software fault-tolerance controller, and that the voting check provides the adjudication function. In principle, there is no reason why the *N*-version scheme cannot be applied at both system and component levels, thus providing various nested levels of fault tolerance. However, as suggested by its attendant terminology, the application of *N*-version programming is normally limited to the outermost, system, level of the software.

In terms of the four major activities which must be performed by a fault-tolerant system, detection of errors in the state of the system is provided by the voting check which, by virtue of the disparity of an erroneous output, also locates the faulty version. Damage assessment is based on the premise that each version executes as an isolated atomic action and thus any damage must be confined within it. This atomicity can be achieved physically by running each version on dedicated hardware or, logically, by sharing one or more computers between versions and using appropriate protection mechanisms. It is important to recognize that atomicity is not simply concerned with preventing the versions from communicating with each other. It also means that the failure of a version must not affect the operation of the other versions, and the virtual machine which supports the operation of the various versions must provide this insulation. With atomic execution, error recovery is achieved by the driver ignoring the output values identified by the voting check as erroneous. Fault treatment can be considered as simply ignoring the results of the version identified as being faulty.

When an *N*-version program is invoked, all versions are normally executed. Consequently, each version can retain data between calls and, therefore, can be designed as an *object* which hides its internal structure. This has the advantage of increasing the design independence of the versions and reduces the data which must be passed to a version upon invocation. However, if the versions do retain data, then a driver will not be able to re-use a version which has produced an erroneous output, since its internal state might have become inconsistent with the other versions. If the fault-tolerance properties of the *N*-version system are not to be degraded under these circumstances, it will be necessary to provide some form of recovery of the internal state of a faulty version. One simple method of achieving this would be for each version to offer a *recover-last* operation which rolls it back to the state that it was in prior to its last operation. However, in order to ensure that all versions are in a consistent state, the driver must recover not only a faulty version, but all others, thus losing some of the previous history of the system. If this is not acceptable, then a more elaborate recovery strategy will be required which will recover the internal state of the faulty version to one which corresponds to those of the other up-to-date versions. This is a difficult task because the versions are of independent design and their internal data structures will, in general, be different. Essentially, a translation algorithm is required which will map from the internal state of one version to that of another.

The success of the *N*-version programming approach critically depends upon the voting check identifying the erroneous output of a faulty version. In order to increase the effectiveness of the voting check, it is normal practice to include in the specification for the versions intermediate cross-check values which will be delivered to the driver module together with the output results. By using these cross-check values, the voting check can now detect errors in the internal states of the versions as well as in their external states. The cross check values will, of course, limit the design independence of the various versions, since their internal processing must converge at these points, and an engineering trade-off must be made to determine the degree to which they are employed.

The voting check itself must be simple in order to minimize the possibility of design faults within it but, unfortunately, the design of voting checks may not be trivial. One complication occurs when the results involve non-discrete values such as real numbers, since different algorithms may produce slightly differing correct results. Consequently *inexact* voting is required which partitions the output from the various versions into equivalence classes prior to voting. Providing there are more than $N/2$ outputs in the largest equivalence class, then any of these could be used as the system output; alternatively, the median of the largest equivalence class could be adopted. The inherent difficulty with such an approach, however, is defining the class boundaries, since the normal variation in results from the versions will, in general, vary from one computation to the next.

Practical considerations can also serve to complicate the voting mechanism. For example, the driver module will, in general, have to time-out versions which do not produce their output within a specified time period and, in real-time systems, it may be necessary to compute the voting check on the fly, as results emerge from versions, so that a majority result can be output before all versions have completed. Of course, majority voting may not be suitable for all applications. For example, in safety-critical systems, a unanimous voting strategy may be needed; if all versions do not produce the same, or equivalent, results then a failure exception must be raised so that the system can be placed in a fail-safe state. In summary, the type of voting check employed in an *N*-version programming scheme will depend very much on the particular application and will, in general, require careful consideration.

When implementing *N*-version programming for real-time systems, it is attractive to use a multiprocessor configuration where each version runs on its own dedicated hardware. This reduces run-time overheads and provides physical separation for atomic execution. Moreover, if different processor types are used in each case, then this overall design diversity can provide protection against both hardware and software design faults. Such a mapping approach would, however, limit the degree to which N-version programming could be applied to various nested components within a system, since each fault tolerant component would then require its own set of (N) processors. Of course, this limitation does not concern those applications where N-version programming is used only at the outermost level of a program.

4.6 Recovery Blocks

The recovery-block approach, like N-version programming, attempts to prevent residual faults from impacting on the system environment but, unlike N-version programming, it is aimed at providing fault-tolerant functional components which may be nested within a sequential program. The basic features of a recovery block are illustrated in Fig. 4.7. A number of software modules of different design are produced from the same specification. There will exist a primary module which represents the preferred design and a number of other alternate modules which we shall assume, for the time being, all offer the same functionality. On entry to a recovery block, a recovery point is established which allows the program to restore to this state, if required. The primary module is executed and an acceptance test checks the state of the program for successful operation. If the acceptance test fails, then the program is restored to the recovery point taken on entry to the recovery block, the first alternate is executed and the acceptance test is applied again. This sequence continues until either an acceptance test is passed or all alternates have failed the acceptance test. If the acceptance test is passed, then the recovery point taken on entry is discarded and the recovery block is exited. If all alternates fail the acceptance test, a failure exception will be raised. Since recovery blocks can be nested, then the raising of such an exception from an inner recovery block would invoke recovery in the enclosing block. Generally, any exception raised during the execution of an alternate will indicate premature

```
ENSURE          acceptance test
BY              primary module
ELSE_BY         first alternate
ELSE_BY         second alternate


ELSE_BY         nth alternate
ELSE_ERROR
```

Fig. 4.7. Recovery block structure.

failure of that alternate and thus instigate the same recovery action as for acceptance test failure. Run-time assertion statements within a module and hardware error-detection mechanisms can be used to raise exceptions in this way.

In the context of the general principles of software fault tolerance previously discussed, the recovery-block structure itself defines the actions of the fault-tolerance controller and the acceptance test provides the adjudication function which is the primary method of error detection. Ostensibly, damage assessment is not required because backward error recovery will eliminate all damage to the program. However, in a multi-processing environment, backward recovery will only be applied to a single process (or at most a defined set of interacting processes, as discussed in a following section) and, thus, practical schemes will require protection mechanisms within the machine to confine the damage to that part of the system which will be backward-recovered. This constitutes implicit damage assessment. Fault treatment within a recovery block is achieved by the execution of a new alternate following recovery.

Although recovery blocks are based on the notion of backward error recovery, forward recovery techniques can also be used in a complementary way. If, for example, a real-time program communicated with its (unrecoverable) environment from within a recovery block then, if recovery were invoked, the environment would not be able to recover along with the program and the system would be left in an inconsistent state. However, if appropriate forward recovery action were applied at the environmental interface, for example by sending the environment a message informing it to disregard previous output from the program, then the system could be returned to a consistent state.

It should be noted that not all modules will be executed each time the recovery block is invoked. Consequently, they must not retain data locally between calls, since they could become inconsistent with each other; they must be designed as memoryless functional components and not objects.

4.6.1 Recovery-block acceptance tests

The overall success of the recovery-block scheme rests on the ability of the acceptance test to detect errors. There are a number of distinct approaches which can be adopted, including:

(1) *Reversal checks.* The acceptance test takes the results from a module and attempts to calculate what input values should have been applied. These are then compared with the true input values to determine whether the results are acceptable. For example, if a recovery block provides a square-root function, then the acceptance check could square the result and compare this with the input value.

(2) *Coding checks.* Consider a database system in which data records carry a checksum of the data contained within the record and this is maintained

by the software as the data is updated. Re-computing the checksum after a module had completed its processing could provide the acceptance test with a means of detecting corruptions to data in a record. This is an example of a coding check.

(3) *Reasonableness checks*. The purpose of this type of test is to determine whether the state of the system following the execution of a module is consistent with the designer's view of the system. The acceptance test for the aircraft tracking recovery block of the following section is an example of a reasonableness check. Often, such checks will require access to the values of variables prior to the execution of a module so that they can be compared with their corresponding values after execution. The virtual machine which supports the execution of recovery blocks should normally provide this facility.

(4) *Structural checks*. Consider the situation where a recovery block maintains a chained list of data which is linked in the forward direction only. If the list is enhanced to a doubly-linked list with backward, as well as forward, pointers, then an acceptance test can check whether there has been corruption to the list structure by reading the list in both directions. Thus structural redundancy (Taylor *et al.* 1980) within the list has allowed structural checks to be performed.

As with the voting check in *N*-version programming, an acceptance test must be simple otherwise there will be a significant chance that it will itself contain design faults. Moreover, the acceptance test will also introduce a run-time overhead which could be unacceptable if the test is complex. In summary, the development of simple, effective acceptance tests is a difficult task. Most tests (with the possible exception of reversal checks) will not provide a guarantee of correct execution, and so it is important that they are supplemented with assertion statements within the modules in order to provide additional error-detection capabilities. Equally important is the provision of a strongly typed virtual machine which is capable of detecting errors via run-time checks.

4.6.2 Recovery-block alternates

In a recovery block, all modules are available on entry to the block, regardless of previous faults, and they are always executed in the strict sequence defined by that block. The rationale for this is that a design fault will only be uncovered by a rate combination of processing conditions which are unlikely to recur when the recovery block is next executed. The sequential nature of the execution of primary and alternate modules gives rise to three basic strategies for providing design diversity within a recovery block.

(1) *Equally weighted, independent designs*. Each module is designed to provide exactly the same functionality, in the optimum way, and diversity is achieved by having independent developers (ideally using different development methods and tools) for each module. In this case,

the sequence in which the modules are executed is arbitrary and the design approach is the same as in the *N*-version approach.

(2) *Prioritized, fully-functional designs.* Each module provides the same functionality but there is a strict sequence in which their execution is preferred. For example, the alternates may be older, less-refined versions of the primary and, consequently, uncorrupted by faults which may have been introduced during such enhancements. Alternatively, the alternates may be deliberately designed using less efficient, but perhaps more robust, algorithms. The fact that these alternates should rarely be executed mitigates their inefficiencies.

(3) *Functionally degraded alternates.* The primary module will provide full functionality, but subsequent alternate modules will offer progressively degraded functionality. The alternates may be older versions of the primary which have not been corrupted by functional enhancements or they may be deliberately degraded to reduce software complexity and/or execution time. Note that the use of degraded alternates must weaken the acceptance test. However, the effect of improved acceptance testing for primary and high-functionality alternates can be provided by adding assertion statements to these modules.

Functionally degraded alternates are particularly useful in real-time systems, since there may be insufficient time available for fully-functional alternates to be executed when a fault is encountered. An example of a degraded-alternate recovery block is illustrated in Fig. 4.8, where the recovery block provides a simplified radar-tracking function for aircraft. Upon invocation, the recovery block will be passed a track record containing the track parameters of an aircraft (e.g. last smoothed position at time, smoothed velocity, etc.) and a plot record indicating the latest measured position of the aircraft from the radar at a certain time. In its primary module, the aircraft's new smoothed position and velocity will be calculated from its last smoothed position and velocity, and the radar measured position. The acceptance test which is then applied will check whether these smoothed position and velocity results are reasonable within the physical velocity and acceleration constraints of the aircraft. If this test fails, the first alternate provides degraded functionality in that it simply calculates the current predicted position of the aircraft from its last smoothed position and velocity, assigns this to the current smoothed

ENSURE	changes in aircraft smoothed position and velocity are within physical limits
BY	Smoothed Tracking Algorithm (track data, plot data)
ELSE_BY	Prediction Only Algorithm (track data, current time)
ELSE_BY	Null
ELSE_ERROR	

Fig. 4.8. Recovery block with functionally degraded alternates.

position, and leaves the smoothed velocity untouched. Further failure of the acceptance test results in the second alternate simply leaving the track record in its initial state.

The degenerate case of degraded alternates corresponds to a recovery block which contains a primary module and a null alternate. Under these conditions, the role of the recovery block is simply to detect and recover from errors, and to ignore the operation which uncovered the fault. Of course, this approach means that the occurrence of a fault will result in a loss of service to the environment, as in the case of robust software, discussed above. The important difference is that forward recovery employed by the robust software approach can only remove predictable errors from the system state, whereas backward recovery used in recovery blocks can cope with the unpredictable errors caused by residual design faults.

The decision where to use degraded alternates can be based on the identification of high- and low-integrity data paths in a system (Moulding & Barrett, 1987). For example, the passage of radar data through an aircraft tracking program can be considered as a low-integrity, high-volume data path; degraded alternates would be appropriate here because the loss of an individual radar plot is unlikely to have a long-term effect on the system. On the other hand, aircraft positional information input by a pilot would correspond to a high-integrity, low-volume data path; each item of data is important and thus every attempt to process it correctly must be made. Consequently, full-functionality alternates should be used. Where data integrity and volume are inversely related, as above, the alternate choices are sympathetic to run-time performance constraints; high-volume paths will have reduced alternate execution overheads because the alternates will be degraded, and the run-time overheads of full-functionality alternates are mitigated by the low data rates associated with this processing.

4.6.3 Recovery blocks in concurrent systems

When a regime of communicating processes employs recovery blocks, each process will be continually establishing and discarding recovery points, and may also need to restore to an established recovery point. If recovery and communication operations are performed in an unco-ordinated fashion, then it is possible that the *domino effect* (Randell, 1975) will occur. This is illustrated in Fig. 4.9(a), where the horizontal lines describe the progress in time of two processes P1 and P2, the vertical lines indicate communication between processes, and the open square brackets correspond to the establishment of recovery points. If, at the most advanced stage of its progress, P1 wishes to recover to its last recovery point, then this can be achieved without affecting P2. However, if process P2 wishes to recover to its last recovery point, then this will cause recovery beyond a communication with P1. In general, this communication must now be considered invalid (e.g. P2 may have passed P1 erroneous data) and so P1 must recover to its penultimate recovery

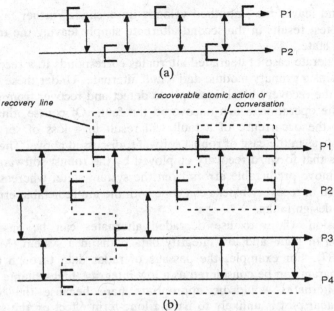

Fig. 4.9. Backward error recovery in concurrent systems. (a) Domino effect. (b) Recovery lines and conversations.

point. In so doing, this invalidates further communication and causes P2 to recover to its penultimate recovery point. This sequence will continue until either a consistent pair of (possibly ancient) recovery points are found, in which case the system may proceed, or the processes will be left in an inconsistent state when all recovery points of one or both processes have been used up.

One simple solution to the domino effect is to prevent processes from communicating with each other when they are in a recovery block. However, this can be unacceptably restrictive and a more general solution is to establish *recovery lines* in the system, as illustrated in Fig. 4.9(b). A recovery line connects a mutually consistent set of recovery points and can be achieved by the insertion of additional pseudo-recovery points (Shin & Lee, 1984) which do not correspond to the recovery blocks of the individual processes but are forced on a process by the run-time virtual machine in order to guarantee consistent recovery. Such an approach will, of course, add significant complexity to the virtual machine, and also result in a recovery structure which is dynamically generated and thus lacking in design visibility. An alternative strategy which can provide better design visibility of the intended recovery structure is for processes to co-operate to form recoverable atomic actions called *conversations* (Randell, 1975).

On entry to a conversation, a process establishes a recovery point and, thereafter, may only communicate with others that have also entered the conversation. If a process wishes to recover whilst in a conversation, then all other processes of that conversation are forced to recover also. When a process wishes to leave the conversation, it must wait until all other processes are ready to leave. This, of course, introduces a synchronization overhead, but that is the price paid for controlled recovery. Conversations, like recovery blocks, can be nested, as illustrated in Fig. 4.9. Here processes P1–P4 initially enter an outer conversation. Some time later, P1 and P2 form an inner conversation which, after two communications, completes and returns P1 and P2 to the outer conversation. At some future point in their processing, P1–P4 will synchronize to complete the outer conversation. Note that, for effective operation, the atomic nature of conversations should be enforced by the underlying hardware of the virtual machine.

4.7 Comparison of *N*-Version Programming and Recovery Blocks

In principle, both *N*-version programming and recovery blocks provide the basis for achieving software fault tolerance. In practice, a software designer must make an objective decision as to which technique is likely to be most effective for a particular application. In order to uncover the relative advantages and disadvantages of the two schemes, they are compared below in terms of their ability to detect errors, their propensity to encourage effective diverse designs, and the run-time overheads which their adoption is likely to impose.

4.7.1 Error detection

The practical effectiveness of any software fault-tolerance scheme rests critically on its ability to detect errors in the internal state of the system before they can impact on the system environment. The voting check in *N*-version programming provides a powerful error-detection approach where precise results can be specified, but the need for inexact voting in other cases will introduce complexity to the voting check and may, consequently, reduce the effectiveness of this approach. However, acceptance tests for recovery blocks are often much more difficult to devise and, in many cases, they will provide no guarantee that a module has executed correctly. To some extent, the fallibility of acceptance tests can be mitigated by the provision of run-time assertions and virtual-machine run-time checks, and the use of nested recovery blocks does mean that an error which is not detected at a low level might be identified by an acceptance test at a higher level. Nevertheless, a movement towards acceptance tests which are aimed at establishing the run-time correctness of the software is highly desirable, and the use of formal methods to identify such tests is likely to be of value here (Melliar-Smith 1983). Only when acceptance testing is based on such correctness notions can it be considered to rival an effective voting check.

4.7.2 Software diversity

In order to provide a continued service in the presence of residual software
design faults, both N-version programming and recovery blocks require diverse
software modules. Both schemes can achieve such diversity by attempting to
produce independent designs from the same specification, but recovery blocks
offer the additional approaches of prioritized fully functional designs where
diversity is deliberately planned at the expense of design efficiency, and
degraded designs where the diversity is achieved at the expense of functionality. In particular, the degenerate case of null alternates in recovery blocks can
provide an effective fault-tolerance strategy for real-time systems, and this has
no counterpart in the basic N-version approach. However, where independent
designs are to be produced, recovery blocks do suffer from the limitation that
the algorithms for each module must all operate on the same global data
structures, and this limits the degree to which such designs can be made
independent. The ability of modules of the N-version scheme to retain locally
their own data structures allows a greater level of design independence to be
achieved, but some loss of independence will result from the specification of
cross-check values for voting checks.

4.7.3 Run-time overheads

High software reliability is commonly a primary requirement of embedded
computer systems where the need to maintain real-time responsiveness is also
critical. In such applications the run-time overheads imposed by both
N-version programming and recovery blocks will be an important consideration for the software designer. Where the target hardware for a system
contains a single processor, N-version programming will introduce a high
run-time overhead since all individual versions must execute serially. However,
where separate hardware processors are available to run each version
concurrently, the performance of the N-version scheme will correspond to the
execution time of the slowest version which is to participate in the voting check
(a synchronization penalty), and the duration of the voting check itself. In
contrast, the execution time of a recovery block is normally that of the primary
module, acceptance test, and the operations required to establish and discard a
recovery point. However, when an error is detected, backward recovery, serial
alternate execution and repeated acceptance testing will result in an increased
run-time overhead. Thus, the overhead of recovery blocks is less predictable
than N-version programming and this must be accommodated in time-critical
applications by ensuring that there is sufficient slack time in the processing
cycle of the system to cope with a worst-case overhead. In fact, a special
variant of the recovery block, known as the *deadline mechanism* (Campbell *et
al.*, 1979), has been specifically proposed to address this issue. However, even
within the constraints of the general recovery block scheme, much can be done
to reduce both the magnitude and variability of the run-time overhead. For

example, hardware assistance for the recovery of main memory will reduce the overhead of recovery-related operations; a *recovery cache* (Lee *et al.*, 1980) has been successfully developed for this purpose and, more recently, a technique aimed at providing memory devices which are intrinsically recoverable has been devised (Hyland, 1985). Furthermore, functionally degraded alternates will reduce execution overheads, and the use of null alternates can be an effective option for real-time systems. However, a more subtle and fundamental run-time overhead of recovery blocks is the synchronization penalty of conversation-type structures used to co-ordinate recovery between concurrent processes. Here, the onus is on the software designer to select conversation structures which map on to the natural synchronization of the design, thereby minimizing the overhead (Halliwell, 1984).

From these comparisons it is evident that the choice of scheme must depend upon both the characteristics of the application and the hardware configuration on which it will run. Generally, the critical importance of error detection in software fault tolerance would suggest that where voting checks may be easily constructed, and replicated hardware is available to reduce run-time overheads, N-version programming is most appropriate. In contrast, the recovery-block scheme is a generally applicable approach which maps naturally onto nested component structures, and is most appropriate for those systems where hardware resources are limited and voting checks are inappropriate (Anderson & Lee, 1981).

In many respects, N-version programming and recovery blocks are complementary in terms of their relative merits. This has led to hybrid schemes which combine various features of each approach (Anderson, 1985). For example, one or more alternates of a recovery block could be run in parallel with the primary (providing their executions were atomic); the run-time overhead of alternate executions would be minimized, and their outputs could be used to support the acceptance test. Alternatively, acceptance tests could be used in N-version programming to assist the voting algorithm, and a version could employ run-time assertions to detect internal errors and signal the driver to disregard its output.

4.8 Practical Application of N-Version Programming and Recovery Blocks

Although these two basic techniques of software fault tolerance have been available for more than a decade, uncertainties regarding their overall cost-effectiveness have inhibited their widespread adoption in industrial and commercial systems. However, limited forms of N-version programming have been employed in safety-critical systems to provide additional confidence in the light of stringent reliability requirements. For example, dual-version programming ($N = 2$) is used to provide error detection in computerized point switching, signal control and traffic control in the Gothenburg area by the Swedish State Railways (Taylor, 1981), and the approach has now been adopted in several railway installations elsewhere (Haglin, 1988). In these applications, differing outputs from two versions result in the rail network being placed in a safe state (signal lights set at red). Dual-version programming has also found considerable application in the avionics industry (Voges, 1988), as exemplified by the slat-and-flap control system of the Airbus Industries A310 aircraft (Martin, 1982). In this case, two diverse programs are executed on separate diverse computers and their outputs compared to provide error detection which is used to instigate manual backup procedures to ensure safe flight and landing of the aircraft. This approach has been taken one step further for the pitch control of the *fly-by-wire* A320 aircraft (Traverse, 1988). Here, four-version software diversity and two-version hardware diversity are combined in a dynamically reconfigurable architecture to tolerate both software and hardware design faults. However, a limited form of mechanical backup is still provided.

In order to understand the key issues involved in the development of software fault-tolerance systems, a number of experimental evaluations have been conducted using the two basic schemes. *N*-Version programming has been under investigation at the University of California–Los Angeles (UCLA) since 1975. Initial work established the basic principles of the approach and this was followed by an experiment which investigated the impact of specification on residual faults (Avizienis & Kelly, 1984). Recent work has been concerned with the development of a test bed for *N*-version experiments (Avizienis, 1985; Avizienis *et al.*, 1988), and its use to investigate issues such as inexact voting strategies and recovery of failed versions.

Further evaluation of *N*-version programming has been performed in a project on diverse software (PODS) which has been jointly conducted by the Safety and Reliability Directorate (SRD) and the Central Electricity Research Laboratory (CERL) in England, the Technical Research Centre of Finland (VTT) and the Halden Reactor Project (HRP) in Norway (Bishop *et. al.*, 1986). Three versions of software for a reactor overpower protection system were developed independently by CERL, VTT and HRP, and then combined in an *N*-version configuration to determine the effect on software reliability. Of the nine residual faults detected, six resulted from difficulties with the *customer* specification and two were attributable to modifications made during testing. Two faults were common between versions and, consequently, would have caused the three-version unit to fail, when encountered. All other fault combinations were effectively masked by the majority voting.

The presence of common design faults raises questions regarding the independence of versions and an investigation of this issue (Knight & Leveson, 1986*a*) has demonstrated that in a large-scale experiment, involving a 27-version program submitted to one million test patterns, common-mode failures of two or more versions were encountered on 1255 occasions. This was viewed statistically as demonstrating that the failures of versions were NOT independent, but care is needed when interpreting this result. It does not mean that the 27-version program ever failed to produce the correct output, since no more than eight versions ever failed at the same time. Nor does it mean that reliability improvements could not be achieved if the versions were grouped into smaller voting units. In fact, in a later experiment (Knight & Leveson, 1986b) when three-version programs were randomly constructed from the 27, the average probability of failure for a three-version unit was found to be 19 times less than the average for individual versions. The significance of these results is that reliability prediction calculations for N-version programs based on the assumption that independently designed versions would fail independently is invalid, and that this will result in reliability predictions which are optimistic. However, significant reliability improvements can still be achieved.

Recovery blocks have been the subject of a long-term research programme at the University of Newcastle upon Tyne since the early 1970s, and in 1981 a project was set up to evaluate the cost-effectiveness of applying recovery blocks to a naval command and control demonstrator. The software was based on MASCOT (MASCOT Suppliers Association, 1980) and a scheme was devised to establish conversation-type recovery structures for a regime of communicating MASCOT activities (Moulding, 1986). The practical development work of the project included the design and implementation of a MASCOT virtual machine which supported recovery blocks, together with extensions to the CORAL programming language to allow the software fault-tolerance applications to be written in this high-level language. The results of experimentation on the completed demonstrator revealed that 74% of potential failures were averted by the software fault tolerance. The price of this improvement was approximately 60% increased development costs, 33% extra code memory, 35% extra data memory and 40% additional run-time (Anderson et al., 1985b). Research at the Royal Military College of Science has recently extended this work to the design of a demonstrator modelled on functions provided at the London Air Traffic Control Centre, and the results have reinforced confidence in the general applicability of this software fault-tolerance approach (Moulding & Barrett, 1987). Continuation of the work is aimed at investigating the use of formal specification techniques to improve the independence of module designs, and for identifying effective acceptance tests and run-time assertions. Future planned work is to integrate software fault-tolerance into the methods and tools employed across a typical software engineering life cycle. This will include extensions to the Ada programming language for both N-version programming and recovery blocks, and the integration of software fault-tolerance considerations into conventional software analysis and design methods employed for real-time systems.

4.9 Summary

This chapter has been concerned with explaining the ways in which software may be designed so that it can tolerate its own residual design faults, and so provide high-reliability operation. The general principles and terminology of software fault tolerance have been explained within the context of a simple abstract model of a software system and an implementation framework for software fault tolerance, based on exception handling and including the notions of atomic actions and backward and forward recovery, has been identified. The utility of exception handling in separating the abnormal fault-tolerance actions of software from its normal processing has been demonstrated with a simple Ada program which uses forward-recovery techniques to provide robust operation when predictable errors occur. Such robust software solutions attempt to ensure that the software does not fail catastrophically, but they cannot mask the presence of a fault from their environment. In order to provide continued correct operation in the presence of faults, diverse software designs must be employed and the main emphasis of the chapter has been concerned with describing the principles and practice of *N*-version programming and recovery block schemes which provide the framework for introducing such design diversity.

Over the past decade, a number of experimental evaluations have been made into the utility of software fault tolerance and these have generally shown that such schemes have proved effective in improving the reliability of software. An attendant technology has emerged which is available for practical exploitation and only when this occurs will uncertainties regarding cost-effectiveness be resolved. No doubt the provision of re-usable virtual machines (Avizienis *et al.*, 1988; Moulding & Barrett, 1987) to support software fault-tolerance schemes would do much to encourage the uptake of this technology and it is hoped that future developments will contribute to this. Of course, as the applications software becomes increasingly reliable through the use of software fault tolerance, this may expose reliability deficiencies in the design of the virtual machines. Thus, the construction of virtual machines to support software fault tolerance may well need to incorporate this technology to achieve the desired levels of reliability (Avizienis, 1986).

The *Achilles' heel* of software fault tolerance, which it shares with other specification-driven approaches, is an erroneous system specification, since any diverse designs derived from it will be perceived to exhibit common-mode failure by the system environment. Formal specification techniques will do much to reduce the possibility that system specifications are misinterpreted but, since they are merely an abstraction of the real-world problem, they can never be shown to be error free. However, by introducing diversity into the specification process, increased confidence in their correctness can be gained and it is interesting to note that the back-to-back testing of formal executable specifications, which have been independently produced, has been proposed as a way of improving the correctness of specifications (Avizienis, 1986). This is one of a number of ways in which formal methods and fault-tolerance techniques may be combined to improve the reliability of software, and it is hoped that, in time, the engineering of cost-effective reliable systems will be achieved through a *measured* blend of conventional validation and testing (discussed in Chapter 5), formal specification and verification techniques (presented in Chapter 3) and software fault tolerance. Such would be the hallmark of a mature engineering discipline.

5

Defect Detection and Correction

Patrick Hall

5.1 Introduction 111
5.2 Life-Cycle View 112
5.3 General Principles 114
5.4 Defect Detection and Correction throughout the Life Cycle . 120
5.5 Further Reading 135

5.1 Introduction

If we are to produce high-quality reliable software, then it is important at all stages of development to look actively for defects or potential defects, and take corrective action for any detected. Defect detection is usually called 'testing', a term that is also frequently used to denote defect correction or 'debugging'. Here we are careful to separate these two activities.

This chapter is concerned with the strategic issues concerned with the detection of defects and their removal and the principles underlying them, and not with tactics and the specific techniques for constructing tests and executing them successfully using tools. For specific techniques, the books by Myers (1979) and Hetzel (1984) are recommended. For the current position on tools, the STARTS Guide (National Computing Centre, 1987) is recommended.

Section 5.2 takes a broad look at defect detection and correction throughout the life cycle, taking several different views of the life cycle. In the following section a generic phase in a life cycle is described, and the role of defect detection and correction in relation to this is determined.

The generic life-cycle phase is rather abstract, and in Section 5.4 the issues are made concrete through the discussion of the defect detection and correction methods appropriate to particular phases of the life cycle.

The whole strategy of testing, particularly defect detection, is central to the process of producing quality software. The life-cycle view and the places within this where defect detection will take place will be laid out in the Quality Plan for the particular project being undertaken. While each development project will have special needs that particularize their approach to testing, the general principles discussed in this chapter will always apply.

5.2   Life-Cycle View

The development of software takes place through a number of phases. While there is broad agreement about the nature of these phases, each company may follow its own variation of the life-cycle, using its own terms. Appendix B of this book presents the principles of life-cycle models, contrasting phases as periods in the project at the end of which milestones will be achieved to mark progress on the project, and activities such as design and test that occur during all phases of the project.

At the end of each phase, it is important to pass on as few problems as possible to later phases. If a problem such as a design flaw or a misunderstood requirement is passed on, then it will become manifest later. To correct it may require major rework, tracing the problem back to source and repeating the development from there. It is much more expensive to repair the defect later—perhaps by a decimal order of magnitude for each phase through which the defect passes undetected. This means that defect detection (and its subsequent correction) must be practised at all phases of the life cycle, to catch defects as early in the life cycle as possible.

However, we must recognize that the input to each phase may contain undetected defects that could cause it to produce the 'wrong' output to the following phase. Thus, when testing the result of a phase, as well as ascertaining that you have produced what was asked for, of detecting defects with reference to the direct inputs, it may be appropriate to refer back to earlier phases, or even right back to the customers and users where the original need arose. The outcome of a test may not only be to apply corrections to the products of the immediately preceding phase, but also to apply corrections to the products of earlier phases.

In testing, there are two terms that are conventionally used. The terms are *verification* and *validation,* to distinguish between the extremes of defect detection with respect to immediate inputs and defect detection with respect to the human originators of the requirement. The distinction has been neatly captured by Barry Boehm as:

> *Verification*: testing that you have built the system right.
> *Validation*: testing that you have built the right system.

Some aspects of software may only be able to be tested late in the development cycle, or perhaps only at the end. Examples of these are performance and reliability. In principle this should not have to be the case. We should be able to make appropriate evaluations of intermediate products and from those predict the value for the final product. But currently we do not know enough to do that. The taking of such measurements or *metrics* is described in Chapter 10 on Metrics.

So far the discussion has focused on defects in the products. But the processes that produce these products may themselves be faulty, and be causing the defects observed. An important component of testing is the accumulation of statistics, to provide evidence of defects in the processes, and the information necessary to be able to take corrective action.

5.2.1 The vee-model life cycle

When discussing testing, it is usual to expand the implementation phase into a sequence of smaller phases within the 'vee-model', as in Fig. 5.1. This model has been based upon a simpler form given in the STARTS Guide (National

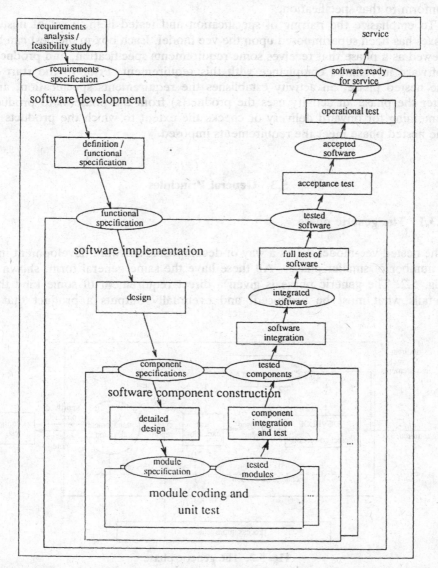

Fig. 5.1. The vee-model of the software development life cycle, with nested phases.

Computing Centre, 1987)—this is also discussed in Chapter 7 and Appendix B.

Note that the service phase can itself be treated as a sequence of development cycles all conforming to the vee-model.

In the vee-model, the horizontal axis denotes the passage of time from left to right. The downwards vertical axis on the left shows the elaboration and decomposition of the proposed software during design, and the upwards vertical axis on the right shows composition of the actual software during integration. The vee-model emphasizes that for each specification document on the left there is a corresponding tested software item on the right that claims to conform to that specification.

To emphasize the pairing of specification and tested item, a set of nested boxes has been superimposed upon the vee model. Each box in the nest can be viewed as a phase that receives some requirements specification, and produces software in claimed compliance with this requirement. Prior to the start of the nested phase, an activity establishes the requirements specification, and after the phase an activity uses the product(s) from the phase(s) to produce something for onward delivery or checks the extent to which the products of the nested phase meet the requirements imposed.

5.3   General Principles

5.3.1   The generic phase

The nested vee-model shows a way of decomposing software development into a number of smaller phases. All these have the same general form, shown in Fig. 5.2. The generic phase is given a direct requirement of some kind that details what must be produced, and eventually outputs a product that is

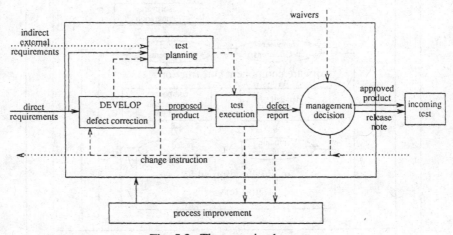

Fig. 5.2. The generic phase.

claimed to meet that requirement. Internally the generic phase may decompose into some development activity followed by some test activity to seek out any defects and report these. The test is planned both on the basis of the direct requirements, and possibly on the basis of the requirements for earlier (outer) phases, and possibly also from knowledge of the structure of the proposed product. Test execution produces a report that leads to a *management* decision: if defects are found the product may be rejected, and the development process repeated; this continues until a management decision has been made to deliver the product.

Further discussion of defect detection and testing will be in terms of this generic model.

5.3.2 Requirements and testability

The products of a phase is tested with respect to the imposed requirements. For this test to be possible it is important that the requirements are *testable*. This means that any requirement should include a means of verifying conformance with that requirement. This could be implied, as when the requirements are expressed quantitatively and precisely.

For example, the phrase 'fast response' could be replaced by the phrase '90% of all enquiries should complete within 1 second, and all enquiries within 2 seconds, regardless of the complexity of the enquiry'.

5.3.3 Development and testability

The development of the product must recognize the defect detection and correction stages that follow, and development must be undertaken to facilitate these. This requires attention to a number of issues.

Requirements must be *traceable* through to the part or facet of the product that meets that requirement, and equally every part and facet of the product must be *traceable* back to the requirement that justifies its presence. Some form of *compliance* table or matrix may be produced to assist this, showing for each paragraph of the requirements document the paragraph in the later product document where this requirement is met. Alternatively, the information may be recorded in the configuration management system providing that the system can handle the fine grain of information required for traceability. Traceability assists in the verification of the product against its requirements.

Traceability is assisted by *modularization*. The product should decompose into sensible parts for which there is an internal cohesion within the parts and low coupling or interdependence between the parts. This has been discussed in Chapter 2 on design for development products that are software, but the principle holds equally well for other products such as documents.

Modularization also is important for defect correction, since the modules make natural units that can be isolated from each other in the process of fault location, and natural units that can then be repaired or replaced. We will assume the hierarchical decomposition of software, terming the higher-level parts 'components', and the lower level parts 'modules'. Modules are separately compilable elements, independently developed by individual software engineers.

Redundancy helps, since it enables internal inconsistencies to be identified. Frequently one is advised that redundancy is bad practice just because it can lead to inconsistency and consequential doubt about which of the alternatives is to be adhered to. A form of redundancy has been described in Chapter 4 on failure-tolerant design methods. Another example of good practice in redundancy is that followed in formal specifications in Z, where the specification is given twice, once in mathematics and once in English, following the same modularization pattern. In software, an example is input checking in defensive coding, which affords powerful defect detection but costs in performance.

We may take the approach that redundancy is encouraged during development, but once everything is consistent, the redundancy is removed for the delivered product. However, in the highly reliable systems that are of concern in this book, this argument is not acceptable, and clearly the extra checks of defensive coding and similar practices need to be retained within the operational system. This would enable the 'graceful degradation' of the operational system to be arranged when inconsistencies are encountered—by their detection, we can avoid catastrophic failure.

5.3.4 Test planning and preparation

The testing to follow the development activity needs to be carefully planned, and not improvised when the time arrives to carry out the tests. It is important that all direct requirements are tested for. If appropriate, indirect requirements may also be tested, possibly involving the intended users of the software in a review or a validation test. In constructing the tests it may be helpful to take into account the internal structure of the product.

In addition to conformance to particular requirements, there may also be general requirements to which conformance is necessary. These are requirements like standards and industrial good-practice, and the defects in these areas that should be sought out during testing should be stated during the test planning and preparation. Internal consistency should also be considered.

It is fairly common practice to split the preparation activity into two steps. Initially *test requirements* or *test specifications* are established, to determine what should be tested for as in the previous paragraph, and to what level of thoroughness. Then on the basis of these test requirements, *test plans* or *test procedures* are produced. These plan in detail how the tests will be carried out. Test cases may be produced together with a means of determining whether the correct output has been produced.

The IEEE standard on testing (IEEE, 1983) divides these stages into more steps, but following essentially the same principles.

Note that the test requirements and test plans require testing themselves!

This would typically be done by a formal review of the documents, but they may be tested further during test execution, for example using a test-coverage measure.

Test planning and preparation should ideally be carried out by people independent of the developers of the product to be tested. The developer is naturally predisposed to find that his product is correct: the tester should be disposed to find it full of defects.

5.3.5 Test execution

Armed with the test plans, tests are then carried out on the proposed product when this is available. Establishing the tests may be quite elaborate: tools may have to be created, computer scripts prepared, perhaps even real users arranged for validation tests.

The form of the test could be very simple, a *review* or *inspection*. This consists of a group of people systematicaly considering the product. Nevertheless, this still needs planning and preparation, and produces a report on the basis of which management may or may not release the product. Alternatively, the test could be very complex, requiring perhaps the parallel running of a new system and an old system over several months, with the results being compared as the test proceeds.

During test execution it may be required to assess the adequacy of the tests themselves, for example in the form of test coverage measures. Some tests may be free-running, and it may be necessary to determine when to finish the tests: for example in performance measurement more tests may be necessary when there is great variation among the results of the tests.

The output from a test is always some form of report concerning what defects were found. Note that it is not the function of the test execution activity to pass or fail the product, but simply to characterize it for follow-up action.

Frequently tests need to be repeated after some change has been made: these tests should be more general than simply consideration of that part of the item that has been changed, so as to ensure that no unfortunate secondary defects have been introduced making the item *regress* rather than progress. Such repeated tests are referred to as *regression tests,* and are particularly relevant in the testing of code using suitable tools.

As with test planning, test execution should ideally be carried out by someone other than the developer of the item under test.

5.3.6 Management decision

The execution of the test produces a report that characterizes the product to the extent required by the test plans. On the basis of this report, a decision must be made whether to rework the product or to release the product for use in later phases. The decision is essentially a management decision, though it may frequently be taken at the end of the test execution as if part of the same activity.

To highlight this point, it may be appropriate to release a product with known defects, on the basis that these defects will not seriously affect the subsequent use of the product. A document may be released with a chapter missing on the grounds that the rest of the document provides valuable information that will enable other work to proceed. An election forecasting system was released even though it was making bad forecasts, on the grounds that bad forecasts before the election were better than no forecasts or good forecasts after the election.

If the managerial decision is to release the product with known defects, then the recipients must agree through the issue of a *waiver* or equivalent, or at least must be informed through the issue of a *release note* describing the problem. Where the product is one delivered to a paying customer, this usually makes sound commercial sense, though of course there are occasions where the commercial sense is not to reveal the defects.

If the managerial decision is to reject the product and send it back for rework, then some form of *change instruction* will need to be raised. This would indicate what changes are required, and would usually be supported by the report from the test execution. The changes required will mostly be to the product, but we may require changes to earlier products such as the requirements imposed, or to the test plans, or even to the development process itself through changes to items like standards and tools.

Decisions here should be properly founded on some form of *risk analysis* (e.g. Chapter 19 in Boehm, 1981; Boehm, 1988a; Chapter 6 in Gilb, 1988) balancing the expected or possible losses that could be incurred from the premature release against the costs of fixing immediately plus the costs of delaying the release.

5.3.7 Defect correction

Once it has been decided to correct a defect, and possibly a change instruction has been raised, then it is necessary to correctly identify the *fault,* and make what changes are necessary to rectify this fault. It is important to note the distinction between defect detection, which shows the presence of the defect, and fault location which actually identifies the underlying cause of the defect.

When defects are found, it may not be obvious what to correct: the original creative process that produced the product may have to be repeated, and some alternative produced. The defect-correction activity is very much a problem-solving activity, but it can be tackled systematically. There exists a literature on fault diagnosis aimed at the mechanization of this; contained within this is much useful advice for those involved in fault location (see for example, Keravnou & Johnson, 1986).

Getting someone involved other than the original producer is helpful, for they will bring to bear a different point of view. Particularly useful will be any ancillary records kept during the original work of the alternatives considered and why they were rejected. These could be working papers, or personal log books, and could even have been included in the deliverable documents as appendices or annexes.

Fault location may require further investigation of a nature similar to defect detection. However, the objectives are now very different. The item may be changed experimentally to help in the process. When making changes it is important to do this systematically, making changes one at a time so as to identify the root cause.

It is important that items are built with ease of repair in mind. For example, documents should be prepared using automatic formatting tools that include automatic section, chapter, and figure renumbering, as well as page renumbering. The normal word-processors produced for office use are usually not good enough, and neither are most electronic publishing systems: what is needed are *document preparation* systems that include these features to facilitate change.

For code, *automatic rebuild* tools are important: these tools use a description of the components or modules that are necessary to construct the system, and the way they should be interconnected, and then compile, link and undertake other processes appropriate to building the system. If the system has been built before, then only those parts that have been changed will be recompiled or otherwise rebuilt.

In making repairs, it is vitally important to maintain the quality of the item being repaired, retaining or modifying structure as appropriate to avoid its progressive degradation into an item that is impossible to maintain and repair any further.

Records should be kept of the defects found, and the underlying faults. These records enable us to learn from our mistakes. The process of development which introduced these faults should be investigated to determine the cause, and the process corrected. Tests, inspections, and audits, should be modified to ensure that they discover any reoccurrence of the fault.

5.3.8 Incoming tests

Once a product is released, it could in principle undergo a further *incoming* or goods-inwards test. The purpose of this would be to satisfy the recipient that the item delivered is what was expected and required.

However, if the development process is visible to the recipient, and in particular the test plans and test reports are visible, then incoming testing may not be necessary, or may be very rudimentary. In the planning of a complete project, this will have been recognized, omitting incoming tests for internal deliverables, but including them as some form of acceptance test for externally produced items, such as those procured on subcontract.

5.3.9 Process improvement

During the execution of the phase, information should be gathered from all sources available. This information would include statistics about the defects found and the cause diagnosed during defect correction, but could include other information. This information is analysed from time to time, and improvements in the processes used during the phase would be undertaken. The ultimate objective would be to produce zero defects, a clean-room environment for the production of software, as has been aspired to by Harlan D. Mills (Mills *et al.*, 1987).

5.4 Defect Detection and Correction throughout the Life Cycle

All phases shown in the vee-model are described below. For each of these, the eight issues raised in discussion of the generic phase are picked up and discussed specifically for their application to this phase. The sequence in which the phases are discussed is to describe the larger 'nested' phases before proceeding to discuss the more conventional phases contained within. Thus, for example, the Software Implementation phase that starts with the specification and ends with the acceptance tests is described before the discussions of design and coding.

5.4.1 Requirements/feasibility phase

5.4.1.1 *Requirements and testability*
The inputs to this phase are formal or informal documents that indicate that a need for the software product does exist, and authorizing the conduct of at least this phase, the requirements or feasibility study. In addition, local or industry standards may be cited for conformance.

While it is hoped that the statements made in the various input documents are precise and quantified, these will usually be of a rather general nature such as 'a system is needed to control the stock during the building of the next oil-rig'. Nevertheless, they should be precise enough to ensure the testability of the Feasibility Report or Requirements Specification produced by this phase.

5.4.1.2 *Development and testability*
The study will involve interviewing a (possibly large) number of potential users and beneficiaries of the proposed software system, resolving conflicts, etc., possibly using a method like CORE (National Computing Centre, 1987).

The output from the phase is a report that will indicate whether or not the need can be met by a computer system and, if so, at what cost. If feasible, the requirements may be spelled out in some detail, derived from the material collected at interviews with client's staff.

In preparing the Requirements, it is important that these requirements should be made testable. If they can be quantified, so much the better. For example, the following frequently encountered terms could be made more precise and testable as indicated below:

- *High-performance*: give response times and through-put volumes.
- *Portable*: give range of targets to which the software is to be ported.
- *Reliable*: give an actual reliability goal in terms of mean time to failure or availability or similar, as described in detail in Chapter 1 on Software Reliability Issues.
- *User-friendly*: this is difficult to quantify, though learning time or error-rate could be used. Alternatively particular properties of desirable interfaces could be defined, or particular interfacing methods could be cited, like pop-up menus and multi-windows.

5.4.1.3 *Test planning and preparation, and test execution*
The Feasibility Study report or Requirements Specification document is reviewed. The preparation required is that for normal reviews and inspections. This is essentially a validation exercise, the most important participants in the review being the customers of the proposed software, though of course the authors of the document and the prospective implementers would also be important.

5.4.1.4 *Management decision*
The report from the review will lead to a management decision either to rework the Requirements Specification, or to forward it to the customers or clients.

5.4.1.5 *Defect correction*
Rework of the Requirements Specification could be trivial, such as a change of format to conform to Standards required, but it could be substantial should major issues concerned with the software have to be reconsidered or even be considered for the first time.

5.4.1.6 *Incoming tests*
Once received by the customer, the Requirements Specification is unlikely to undergo further incoming reviewing, since the customer should have been heavily involved in the review held by the developer.

5.4.1.7 *Process improvement*
Any substantial defect correction must indicate the need for improving the Requirements Analysis and Feasibility Study methods. Perhaps a formal method will need to be adopted, or appropriate tools procured for use on future projects.

5.4.2 Software Development nested phase

5.4.2.1 *Requirements and testability*
The input to the Software Development nested phase is the requirements
document produced by the Requirements Analysis or Feasibility Study phase.
The start of this phase may well be initiated by a contract that could impose
various standards upon the work. In particular it could impose particular
methods, formats for deliverables, and even the use of particular tools for use
at various stages in the Software Development project.

The output from this phase is the software ready for service following the
acceptance test conducted with respect to the Requirements and Functional
Specification, and following the initial trial operational use. The software ready
for service includes the documentation to support it, such as user manuals,
training materials, and maintenance documentation. It has already been
emphasized that the Requirements Specification should include testable
statements, so that final tests of the software can be made objective.

5.4.2.2 *Development and testability*
The development here consists of the production of the Functional Specification by the Definition or Functional Specification phase, followed by the
Software Implementation nested phase that is contracted to produce software
in conformance with that Specification. This conformance would be assessed
both within the Software Implementation nested phase in its Integration and
Test, and in the Acceptance Test, which forms an incoming test for the
products of the Software Implementation nested phase.

Testability is a major issue within all this development, and in particular the
Functional Specification must be testable, to be able to ensure that the tested
software delivered by the Software Implementation nested phase does
conform.

5.4.2.3 *Test planning and preparation*
Testing is a very important aspect of the Software Development nested phase,
and this needs careful planning. The test to be carried out is the Acceptance
and Operational test, based upon the Requirements Specification (and possibly
also including some incoming tests derived from the Functional Specification).

Test plans are created, either as part of the Definition/Function Specification activity, or more usually as a separate activity by an independent team.
The plans will usually include typical scenarios of usage, and may even include
trial use by the user as a beta-site test or parallel running. Extended trials with
loosely defined completion criteria may also be planned.

The acceptance test plan will very likely be prepared by user staff, or in close
cooperation with them. This plan could systematically work through the
requirements and give execution tests that can be applied to the system on its
delivery to the customer. Alternatively it could plan for parallel running of the
system, or trial use internally or externally (alpha- and beta-site testing). Note

that there may be contractual dimensions to the acceptance test, since development or implementation contracts that commence with the requirements specification or the functional specification may well only be agreed to be completed with successful passing of the acceptance tests. Thus, it is important that these are produced and agreed early in the project: too frequently these are left to the end, and become the focus of a dispute between the customer and the development team about who had agreed to produce them.

The user documentation should be planned to be thoroughly studied and the software product used following its instruction.

5.4.2.4 *Test execution*
The test plans are followed. If appropriate, the set of tests there are run using a test harness or a test-data generator.

5.4.2.5 *Management decision*
Following the acceptance test, management may decide to release the software into service. This will be based not only upon the technical issues raised in the acceptance test, but may also be based upon commercial considerations, such as the need to make the product available to selected customers in spite of known defects. Known defects may be cleared with the intended customers, either through the use of release notes documenting the defects, or through waivers in bespoke development.

5.4.2.6 *Defect correction*
If the decision is to correct a number of defects found during acceptance testing and trial use, the fault may lie in the Functional Specification or in the Software Implementation or the acceptance tests themselves. Usually the location between these three is fairly obvious.

5.4.2.7 *Incoming tests*
After delivery a further user incoming test would only exceptionally be undertaken. Usually the results of the main acceptance and operational tests will be very visible to the user, since they will typically take part in these tests.

5.4.2.8 *Process improvement*
The recording of defects and their causes may well lead to action to improve the methods of Functional Specification, of Test Planning, or may suggest the imposition of further controls over the Software Implementation phase nested within this phase.

5.4.3 Definition/specification phase

5.4.3.1 *Requirements and testability*
The input to the Definition or Functional Specification phase is the requirements document produced by the Requirements Analysis or Feasibility Study

phase. As already indicated, this should be as quantitative and detailed as is possible.

5.4.3.2 *Development and testability*
During this phase the requirements will be filled out to produce the functional specification, possibly involving extensive interviews with potential users of the software. In addition, a scenario may be produced, or the specification animated, or some other form of prototype produced.

The output of the phase will be a functional specification, describing in detail what the software should do and the various performance, reliability, quality, and other attributes that it should have. Tools may be used extensively, and the specification may be contained in some database, such as a Data Dictionary.

Other documents may also be produced by this phase. These could include user manuals, operators' manuals, and acceptance test and integration test plans. These may only be produced in draft form in this phase, with the intention of taking them through into final form in later phases.

5.4.3.3 *Test planning and preparation*
All these deliverables would be reviewed prior to delivery. User participation is important, to provide the element of validation, so that the specification and other documents are checked not only with respect to the documented requirements, but also with respect to the underlying user needs.

To aid in the review with respect to requirements, a compliance matrix may be produced. This shows for each clause or paragraph of the requirements document where in the specification this is met, and also for each clause of the specification where this is required. Traceability in both directions is important.

All the intended checks and cross-checks to be made in review need to be planned for, particularly the intended use of any prototype, or the use of formal proof.

5.4.3.4 *Test execution*
To aid in the review against needs, the prototype may be exhibited at the review, and indeed may be one of the deliverables that are formally approved. Where both the specification and the prototype are deliverable, it is important that their mutual consistency is demonstrated. The customer may have made his decision to proceed on the basis of the prototype, but both customer and implementer may be contractually bound to the specification. Clearly, where the prototype has been produced by animating the specification, there should be no problem.

In the event that the requirements themselves were recorded in a formal notation, it may be appropriate to seek formal proof of consistency between the specification and the requirements. Formal notations for requirements (as opposed to specifications—see Chapter 3 on formal methods) are still a research topic, and are unlikely to be encountered in practice for many years.

5.4.3.5 *Management decision*
The management decision required is whether to proceed to Software Implementation (Design). This may or may not involve the customer of the system. It is possible that even with a Functional Specification with substantial defects, it may be decided to proceed while fixing the defects in parallel.

At this stage it may also have been revealed that some requirements are mutually incompatible or lead to an unnecessarily complex system. Management may seek waivers for these, or may raise change requests against the Requirements.

5.4.3.6 *Defect correction*
Should defects be found at review, the repair of these would follow the same general principles described earlier under the Generic phase, and for the Feasibility study.

5.4.3.7 *Incoming tests*
Where Software Implementation is undertaken by some separate contractor, there may be some further evaluation of the Functional Specification as a basis for this further contract.

5.4.3.8 *Process improvement*
Again, feedback from the records kept of defects and their causes could lead to changes in the software definition and functional specification process to improve it.

5.4.4 Software implementation nested phase

5.4.4.1 *Requirements and testability*
The functional specification is input to this software implementation phase, leading to the production of software tested with respect to this specification. An important property of the Functional Specification is its testability to enable this verification to take place.

5.4.4.2 *Development and testability*
In response to the Functional Specification, a high-level design is produced. This identifies a number of components, and is input to the software components construction phases that elaborate this design, to produce the components that are then integrated. The components are not tested again, but evidence of testing of the component prior to delivery may well be sought.

5.4.4.3 *Test planning and preparation*
The integration of components is planned based upon the architectural design. The full software tests are planned to co-ordinate with this, based upon the Functional Specification. These tests need to be as comprehensive as possible, subject to the limitations of time and acknowledging the fact that they cannot

hope to be exhaustive. Some knowledge of the methods used in software design and construction is also necessary, since different methods may lead to different kinds of failures. Representative cases for all functions should be included, as well as all varieties of error-handling.

Other properties of the software, like its reliability and its performance, may also be assessed. These would very likely involve test-data generators and automatic monitors of the software, and could involve test runs of many days, or even weeks. They would usually follow the functional tests associated with the integration of the components.

5.4.4.4 *Test execution*

The full software test and integration plans are followed, and the comprehensive set of tests there run using a test harness or a test-data generator. As a measure of the adequacy of the tests, some form of coverage measure could be used. This would not be as detailed as for module tests, but at least every function (and possibly every statement) should be exercised, or the failure to exercise them explained. As with module testing, a suitable tool should be used. This would instrument the code so that each function or statement sequence increments a counter when executed.

Part of the Integration Test could involve the complete rebuilding from sources of all the code, to ensure that all object and executable code does conform to the sources. The build process should be mechanized: for this, the build tools used during development may be inadequate, since here we want to put together specific versions of sources. A full configuration management system will be required. However, we may in addition want a limited incremental build using latest revisions of specific modules, to cope with cycles of rework following System Test failure.

5.4.4.5 *Management decision*

In many software development projects, the software may fail its system test many times, and be returned for repair. Perhaps half the total development effort would be spent on the cycle of test–repair–integrate–test.

In the newer diagrammatic and mathematical approaches, more care is taken during specification and design, and this leads to less time spent in the test–repair cycle, and in principle failure during component integration and system test should become the exception.

Either way, the execution of the system test leads to a report for management consideration. Even if the system has residual defects, it may still be released for sound commercial reasons.

5.4.4.6 *Defect correction*

There are systematic ways of proceeding to locate a fault in the software and to correct it. The main techniques are as follows.

- Isolate the software components from each other. Frequently, when defects occur, items of software interact in ways that are difficult to envisage, through storage corruptions. The software components need to have fire walls put between them and this could mean rebuilding the code using multiple processes or removing parts of the code and replacing them by simple dummies.
- Gather extra information by selective tracing. The ability to trace key data values should have been built into the software during its development. The tracing should be able to be re-activated easily, and one can distinguish several levels of tracing. The simplest level is likely to have been left in the code, and will either continually produce its information in some 'buffer' or file or will be capable of being switched on when required. The more detailed levels may need to be incorporated by recompiling and rebuilding the code.
- Add extra redundant checks. Some of these may be compiler generatable, such as array-bound checking, others will be a form of defensive coding.
- Use debug tools that enable you to single step, change data values, and so on. These tools should operate at the level of the source language being investigated.

The problem with all these techniques is that they change the code, either its storage location or its timing, and the defect could then disappear.

It is possible for some machines to obtain hardware that will trace the execution of a program by monitoring the processor's bus, and correlating addresses back to the level of the source using symbol tables and storage allocation maps. These do not change the code, but may not be available and could overwhelm one with detail.

An important ancillary tool here is one that makes it easy to rebuild a system. The frequent cycle of test–repair–rebuild makes this imperative. Note that some tools may not be adequate, since the tool must log the actual revision numbers used in a particular system build, and thus enable the rebuild of earlier versions of the complete system with precisely the versions of the constituent parts used originally.

5.4.4.7 *Incoming tests*
On receipt of the tested software by the outer Software development phase, the software then undergoes the acceptance tests. While this is more than an incoming goods inspection, the presence of this acceptance test makes any other incoming test unnecessary. Moreover, the system test may have been visible to the recipients of the tested software, helping them to gain confidence in the system prior to their own acceptance tests.

5.4.4.8 *Process improvement*
Problems in system test can be very revealing about defects in the software development process. Frequently the problems will be traceable back to

Table 5.1

Symptom	Diagnosis	Remedial action
System failed due to storage corruptions	Inconsistent versions of components sharing storage built	1. Tighten up on change control and version management, introducing tools to aid in this 2. Reduce use of shared storage to minimum by redesign of the critical components of the system
As above	Failure to check for null pointer	Procure tool to trap attempts to follow null pointer
Large volume of trivial errors discovered that should have been handled during unit test	1. Slippages in development left little time for programmers to thoroughly test their code 2. Some programmers had attitude of why test it, if it was to be tested later	1. Improve estimating methods through setting up of database of previous implementation experience 2. Tighten up progress monitoring through introduction of weekly progress milestones and reports 3. Introduce test harnesses to make testing and retesting easier 4. Make evidence of testing an obligatory part of the delivery of units into integration, with programmers responsible for failures in their code

inadequate management controls, failures in budget and schedule control allowing quality procedures to lapse, or not controlling configuration properly.

All defects discovered should be reviewed, and a wide-ranging enquiry instituted into how the defect could have been avoided, and how software development could be done better. Table 5.1 shows the kind of improvements that can be made.

5.4.5 Design phase

5.4.5.1 *Requirements and testability*
The principal input to this phase is the functional specification for the system to be produced. This document must be detailed in its treatment of function, and quantitative where it can be, thus rendering testable the functions that must be realized in the design. Other input might be the user manual and test plans for further elaboration.

5.4.5.2 *Development and testability*
Design is now largely a technical activity, and will proceed according to some method determined either by the contract or by the quality plan. The design phase will deliver an intermediate document recording the outline or architectural design. This must be reasonably precise, to enable its own review against specification, and to enable later the review of the detailed design and the establishment of integration plans.

In addition, the user manual and test plans may have been progressed (as required by the quality plan). Note that on large projects, these would typically be produced during parallel activities by independent teams.

5.4.5.3 *Test planning and preparation, and test execution*

All outputs from this phase are reviewed. Some user participation in the review is appropriate, but may not be a major element. The architectural design is reviewed with respect to the specification, and also with respect to various technical objectives, whether the system is feasible, the size and performance of the system, potential for deadlocks, and so on. It is vitally important that the architectural design is adequate, since mistakes here could be very expensive to repair later.

5.4.5.4 *Management decision*

Management will need to be very sensitive to problems here, and may permit parts of the follow-on detailed design to proceed while holding up other parts for remedial action. The review or inspection of the architectural design will be very important, particularly the comments from independent experts.

5.4.5.5 *Defect correction*

If the architectural design is found to be inadequate, it may require complete reworking, perhaps with a complete change of approach.

5.4.5.6 *Incoming tests*

Once the architectural design has been approved, it will form the basis for detailed design. In the process of reading and understanding the design further problems may be discovered and the design reworked correspondingly.

5.4.5.7 *Process improvement*

As indicated above, problems with the architectural design could signify major problems with the architectural design process, and the need for reconsideration of the methods of design.

5.4.6 Software component construction nested phase(s)

Note that for a small system, there may be no component phase, with the system being decomposed immediately into code modules.

5.4.6.1 *Requirements and testability*

Input here is the High-Level or Architectural Design of the software that contains the specifications of the components of system, or there may be separate Component Specifications for each component to be produced. As emphasized above, this must have been carried through to sufficient detail and precision to enable detailed design and integration planning and the testing of the outcome of these.

Output from Software Component Construction phase will be the integrated and fully tested components of the software ready for further integration to form the full software.

5.4.6.2 *Development and testability*

For each component, a detailed design is produced, identifying a number of modules that will be specified, and then coded (and tested) independently. As these individual modules are delivered, they will be integrated, built together and in the process tested to see that interfaces have been conformed to and that there have not been any misunderstandings.

5.4.6.3 *Test planning and preparation*

The test plans here are the integration test plans for each of the software components. This determines the sequence in which the modules will be tested and integrated with other modules, what extra software in the form of test stubs and drivers need to be written, and what test cases to use.

A comprehensive set of test cases will be required, to match all stages of the integration plan. The test cases may possibly be derived from the component test cases.

The integration plan needs to be very carefully prepared. It is unwise to accept all the modules and build them together, and then run the component tests, for when something goes wrong, it may be very difficult to locate the fault. From a pure defect-detection point of view this may seem appropriate, but it is usual to integrate the component progressively, adding one new module at a time. The integration plan would determine this sequence.

Integration may progress by a number of strategies:

- Top down: starting with the main or master module, which contains the program's entry-point, using stubs for all the modules called, and then progressively replacing these with the real modules, progressing downwards until all the lowest level modules have been added.
- Bottom-up: starting with the modules that call no others, then adding to these those that call them, and so on. No stubs are necessary, but a sequence of harnesses and test cases are.
- Thread: either a top-down or bottom-up thread of processing is integrated to give a complete function that is demonstrable.

Integration may have been assisted by a design that builds in extra checks, such as defensive coding at the interfaces, so that no module assumes that it will be used correctly. Such defensive code, and other code included to aid defect detection and correction, should be able to be removed either through conditional compilation or through dynamically settable switches.

Associated with the integration plan may be a number of build scripts. The plan and the scripts may themselves be tested before use in integration, using a review or inspection.

5.4.6.4 Test execution

As with the integration of components to form the full software product, part of the integration test here may involve the rebuilding from sources of the object code. Configuration control will be important, with tools to rebuild automatically from new sources as these are recycled for correction.

5.4.6.5 Management decision

Once the software components have been successfully built and tested, they will be ready for further integration to build the software system. The decision to release the components for further higher-level integration involves an internal technical judgement with no management involved.

5.4.6.6 Defect correction

See notes under Software Implementation in Section 5.4.4.

5.4.6.7 Incoming tests

The components are delivered for integration and then full software test. It is so important for successful integration that the components have been thoroughly tested that the person or team doing the integration may separately require the evidence of testing. Indeed, in some organizations this team may have the delegated authority to reject components that have been inadequately tested, effectively performing the managerial function discussed above.

5.4.6.8 Process improvement

Problems found during integration usually indicate problems with interfaces or unexpected side-effects—either the interfaces have either been inadequately specified, or changes have been inadequately controlled. Either way, remedial action is necessary.

Occasionally, problems may reveal more fundamental defects in the development process. For example, various kinds of resource contention could be met: these could be very difficult to correct at this late stage, and extra procedures for eliminating these early in design would be introduced.

5.4.7 Detailed design phase

5.4.7.1 Requirements and testability

The architectural design, which identifies the major components of the system and their interactions, will be input into this phase. Clearly this document should be sufficiently detailed for further design work to progress, and be validated for consistency with the architectural design. The use of some formal design notation could be beneficial.

5.4.7.2 Development and testability

The output of this detailed design phase will be the full specification of the modules to be produced and later integrated. These specifications should be very precise, so that these can be tested fully once produced, before they are integrated. Even if formal notations have not been used elsewhere, they should at least be used here for the specifications: a notation such as a previously defined pseudo-code, or rigorously defined subset of Ada, or a mathematically based notation such as Z (e.g. Hayes, 1987), could be appropriate.

5.4.7.3 *Test planning and preparation, and execution*
The detailed design and module specifications will be reviewed or inspected, and the usual planning for this would be undertaken.

5.4.7.4 *Management decision*
It is important that the various documents output from this phase do pass their review. It will be tempting to code prematurely. Either the same staff will be involved and be eager to start coding, or other more junior staff will have been assigned to do the coding, and there will be a desire to utilize the programming staff, but this should be avoided: rather any 'idle' staff should be deployed on other activities such as feasibility trials in areas of implementation uncertainty, tool making, or system-test planning. Only when sound module specifications have been produced should coding commence.

5.4.7.5 *Defect correction*
Where defects have been found, design activity will have to be repeated, as was discussed previously for earlier phases of the life cycle.

5.4.7.6 *Incoming tests*
While, in principle, the module specifications should not need further inspection by the programmer who will implement them, nevertheless the act of familiarization with the specification will raise issues that need resolution. This will be particularly true for less-formal specifications.

5.4.7.7 *Process improvement*
As always, defects need to be analysed, and this analysis may indicate some entrenched facet of the design process that needs improvement.

5.4.8 Module code and test

5.4.8.1 *Requirements and testability*
The input here is the module specification produced by the detailed design phase.

5.4.8.2 *Development and testability*
From the module specification, the module is designed, coded, compiled, and unit tested. The outputs from these activities are the tested modules, ready for integration.

5.4.8.3 *Test planning and preparation*

The code may be 'tested' statically in a number of ways. Very important will be formal reasoning about the code: that it does correctly implement the functions required. This could involve formal proof, or symbolic execution of the code. Various other tests of the code may be done, either manually or using tools, to measure its complexity, to extract control or information flow. The code may also be inspected or read by some other person as a further test of its correctness and its maintainability.

Finally, the code will be compiled and run, and tested dynamically. To do this required that test cases are constructed beforehand—that is, the tests are planned. For module testing, there are many well-established techniques for constructing tests systematically from the specification. In outline, these examine the required behaviour of the software and divide the inputs into partitions within which the behaviour is essentially the same and over which one may deduce that if the software works correctly for one case, it will very likely work correctly for all cases in the partition. The boundaries of the partitions represent discontinuities of behaviour, and the correct positioning of the boundary should be tested by selecting test cases on and/or close to the boundary. To these tests can be added further tests inspired by knowledge of typical mistakes that are made. However, these tests will not in themselves be enough. It is the nature of computing mechanisms that they introduce further discontinuities of behaviour, and with knowledge of the internal mechanics, the partitions generated from the specification would have to be refined. Put another way, if only the test cases derived from the specification are used, not all the code or code-sequences may be exercised or 'covered'. Test cases derived from the specification are conventionally called *black-box* tests, while those derived from the internal structure are called *white-box* tests.

5.4.8.4 *Test execution*

The running of tests is made much easier through the use of tools. A test harness enables batteries of tests to be run many times, thus avoiding limited tests on bug fixes, with the risk of failing to find side-effects introduced by the bug fix (this is a form of regression testing). Stubs enable modules to be tested in isolation, without the other modules used being present. Test-data generators enable large volumes of data to be used in a test, possibly for a performance or endurance test more usual in later stages of testing.

It is usual to measure the thoroughness of dynamic testing by instrumenting the code and monitoring the execution to measure the proportion of the code (statements, branches, paths, or similar) that are actually executed. This gives a coverage measure, which, while very useful, does not take into account the intended function, the specification.

5.4.8.5 *Management decision*

It is important that the modules that are delivered to integration test have been thoroughly tested and thereby demonstrated to conform to their specifications.

Otherwise, at integration, effort will be expended in building the software and exercising large volumes of code unnecessarily, and, when faults do arise, there will be difficulties in locating the fault and identifying which module needs to be repaired.

Management must enforce thorough testing, requiring evidence to be presented to substantiate claims of thorough testing. Test reports or test logs, and even perhaps reports from independent test runs, should be required.

Management may of course release a unit for integration with known defects when to delay it would hold up integration work that could progress in spite of the known defects.

5.4.8.6 *Defect correction*

The main techniques for locating faults in modules are similar to those for components discussed earlier. They are repeated here with small changes.

- Isolate the pieces from each other. Frequently, when defects occur, items of software interact in ways that are difficult to envisage, through storage corruptions. The separable pieces of software need to have fire walls put between them, but this would usually not be possible, and a strategy such as removing parts of the code and replacing them by simple dummies may have to be adopted.
- Gather extra information by selective tracing. The ability to trace key data values may be supplied with the compiler, but may have to be built into the software during its development. The tracing should be able to be re-activated easily, and one can distinguish several levels of tracing. The simplest levels is likely to have been left in the code, and will either continually produce its information in some 'buffer' or file or will be capable of being switched on when required. The more detailed levels may need to be incorporated by recompiling and rebuilding the code.
- Add extra redundant checks. Some of these may be compiler-generatable, such as array-bound checking.
- Use debug tools that enable you to single step, change data values, and so on. These tools should be operated at the level of the source language being investigated.

The problem with all these techniques is that they change the code, its physical location and timing, and the defect could then disappear.

It is possible for some machines to obtain hardware that will trace the execution of a program by monitoring the processor's bus, and correlating addresses back to the level of the source using symbol tables and storage allocation maps. These do not change the code, but may not be available, and could overwhelm one with detail.

5.4.8.7 *Incoming tests*

The modules are delivered for integration and then component test. It is so important for successful integration that the modules have been thoroughly tested that the person or team doing the integration may separately require the evidence of testing. Indeed in some organizations this team may have the delegated authority to reject modules that have been inadequately tested, effectively performing the managerial function discussed above.

5.4.8.8 *Process improvement*

Failure in the test stages of module production almost certainly indicates faulty module design and code practice. Of course some level of human fallibility will occur, and some norm would be determined by experience. Beyond that, the methods used (or person responsible) for faulty modules should be investigated, and if necessary more rigorous coding methods should be introduced.

5.4.9 Service

Once in service, some defects may remain and manifest themselves. The software will need to be changed to correct these defects, but the software may also be undergoing change in response to changing user requirements or to add facilities delayed for later delivery. For each set of changes, the system tests have to be repeated. The tests may not be as comprehensive as the original system tests, but should exercise the whole system to make sure that there are no unintended side-effects from the bug fix. Such tests are known as *regression tests*.

This whole activity or modification during service is termed 'maintenance'. Typically, over half of the expenditure on a software product occurs during this period of maintenance. Each cycle of maintenance involves all the processes and activities of initial development, and all the considerations discussed above apply. Of particular importance is configuration management, to control the versions of software released. Further information is given in Chapter 8 on maintenance.

5.5 Further Reading

This chapter has concentrated on the principles underlying the detection and correction of errors, and left many specific techniques unexplained. For guidance in the systematic construction of test cases and in the management of the test process, the reader is refered to the following books.

Hetzel, William, (1984). *The Complete Guide to Software Testing*. Collins, London.

Myers, Glenford D. (1979) *The Art of Software Testing*, Wiley-Interscience. Tools to assist in testing are well understood, but not readily available. The STARTS Guide is very helpful here.

National Computing Centre. (1987). *The STARTS Guide* (2nd edition). National Computing Centre, Manchester.

Central to a lot of testing is the control of versions of software, documents, etc. Two good books on this are:

Babich, Wayne A. (1986) *Software Configuration Management.* Addison-Wesley, Reading, MA.

Bersoff, Edward H., Henderson, Vilas D. & Siegel, Stanley G. (1980). _*Software Configuration Management and Investment in Product Integrity.* Prentice-Hall, Englewood Cliffs, NJ.

For further ideas on software maintenance, the following collection of papers may be useful.

Parikh, G. & Zvegintzov, Z. (1983). *Tutorial on Software Maintenance.* IEEE Computer Society.

6

Modelling Growth in Software Reliability

Bev Littlewood

6.1 Introduction 137
6.2 A Conceptual Model of the Software Failure Process. 138
6.3 Prediction of Software Reliability 143
6.4 Software Reliability Growth Models 144
6.5 An Example of Use of the Models 146
6.6 Methods of Analysing Past Predicting Accuracy 147
6.7 Summary and Conclusion 152

6.1 Introduction

The first reliability growth models aimed specifically at software, rather than hardware, appeared about 15 years ago. Whilst it would be desirable to be able to recommend a single definitive model to potential users, the present state of the art does not justify such a recommendation. Research studies show that the accuracy of the various models is very variable, and no single model can be trusted to perform well in all contexts.

One can speculate about the reason for this state of affairs. There is clearly great variability in the difficulty of the problems represented by different software projects. Indeed, there is great variation in the underlying problem domains themselves. The development of each particular software product is a complex intellectual and social process that will inevitably exhibit features unique to that product. Given the inadequacy of mathematical models in other similar walks of life (economics, sociology), it is not surprising that we are currently not able to devise complete mathematical descriptions of either the software development process or the behaviour of the software product.

However, the picture is not entirely bleak. It will be shown later in this chapter that it is generally possible to obtain reasonably accurate reliability measures for software. More importantly, we shall show techniques whereby the *actual accuracy* attained in a particular context can be assessed. This means that users of software reliability models can generally be confident of the reliability figures obtained for their product.

6.2   A Conceptual Model of the Software Failure Process

The problem that currently has the most-developed solution concerns the reliability growth that takes place when faults are removed from a program.

Consider Fig. 6.1. Using the data $t_1, t_2, \ldots, t_n$ collected in the past, we wish to predict future failure behaviour. Thus, the *current reliability* of the program is a statement about the random variables T_{n+1}. Here we use upper case for random variables and lower case for their realizations, the observed t_i. Notice that even a statement about how reliable the program currently is involves *prediction* via the as-yet-unobserved T_{n+1}. All other predictions involve the random variables T_{n+k} ($k \geq 1$).

Table 6.1 gives an example of some real software failure data. This was collected by John Musa at Bell Labs. in the mid-1970s, and relates to a real-time command and control system (Musa, 1980). The table reads left to right in rows, and the recorded times are execution times, in seconds, between successive failures. Notice that there is clear overall growth in reliability: later times tend to be much larger than earlier ones. However, within this trend there is great variability and this seems typical of such data. There are several zeros in the table, which are apparently accounted for by rounding the raw times.

This data was collected with great care, and the project was entirely under Musa's control. He reports that fixes were introduced whenever a failure occurred, and execution did not begin again until the identified failure source had been removed. Thus, there are no repeat occurrences of individual faults. Whether this is in general a reasonable assumption is open to question: there seems to be at least anecdotal evidence that 'fixes' often do not remove the target fault. Equally, it is possible that an attempt to fix one fault may introduce other new ones. These are issues to which we shall return later.

In this example, and for the remainder of this chapter, 'time' will be taken to mean *continuous* execution time (between execution starting after a failure and stopping at the next failure). It is relatively easy to obtain *discrete* time versions of most of the popular software reliability growth models so as to handle data of the kind 'n_i failures occurred in the $(i-1)$th period of observation of length x_i'. Clearly, there are advantages in having the complete failure record in which the time of each failure is logged, but this is often

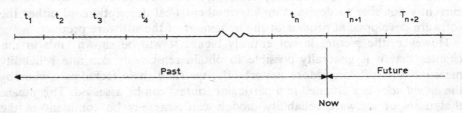

Fig. 6.1. The problem is to make predictions now about the future using only data collected in the past.

Table 6.1. Execution times in seconds between successive failures (Table reads left to right in rows)

		Inter-failure times		
3	30	113	81	115
9	2	91	112	15
138	50	77	24	108
88	670	120	26	114
325	55	242	68	422
180	10	1 146	600	15
36	4	0	8	227
65	176	58	457	300
97	263	452	255	197
193	6	79	816	1 351
148	21	233	134	357
193	236	31	369	748
0	232	330	365	1 222
543	10	16	529	379
44	129	810	290	300
529	281	160	828	1 011
445	296	1 755	1 064	1 783
860	983	707	33	868
724	2 323	2 930	1 461	843
12	261	1 800	865	1 435
30	143	108	0	3 110
1 247	943	700	875	245
729	1 897	447	386	446
122	990	948	1 082	22
75	482	5 509	100	10
1 071	371	790	6 150	3 321
1 045	648	5 485	1 160	1 864
4 116				

impractical. In many computer systems it is possible to obtain quite easily a very good approximation to continuous execution time. For example, in transaction-processing systems the number of transactions will usually approximate well.

It will be assumed in all cases that debugging is taking place so that we are in the presence of reliability growth. However, the detailed assumptions about the nature of this growth vary from one model to another. Not all models, for example, require the stringent assumption of Musa that each fix is perfect (see, for example, Littlewood & Verrall, 1973).

Perhaps the most stringent restriction that is present in all models is the assumption that the conditions of use in the future are the same as those in the past. Obviously this is needed, since the models use the evidence of past behaviour to predict future behaviour, and any discontinuity of use in the future would not be estimable from the past. This requirement places severe demands on the data-collection process. It essentially requires that, in order to predict operational reliability, the input data for the models must come from operational use. Most software testing regimes do not emulate operational use in this way; indeed it is often assumed to be a very inefficient process (Myers,

1979). However, new research is tending to suggest that this efficiency problem may not be serious (Duran & Ntafos, 1980). What does need to be said, however, is that constructing an accurate emulator of operational use can sometimes be very difficult.

There does seem to be conflict between the view of testing as *achievement* and the view of testing as *measurement*. If, as will become more usual, it is necessary to measure the actual achieved reliability of a piece of software, it may be worthwhile to adopt a testing procedure that facilitates this, even at the expense of finding faults a little less efficiently. It should be said, though, that support for the claims of efficiency of conventional testing are largely anecdotal. There seem to be no empirical studies to support such assertions.

The way we express our reliability predictions in a particular case will depend on the use to which they are to be put. We might be interested solely in the current reliability of the product, perhaps so as to make a judgement about termination of testing, and this could be expressed in various ways: mean time to failure, $E(T_{n+1})$; ROCOF; probability of failure-free execution for some specified mission time, t; etc. Equally, we might be interested in longer-term prediction, for example of the time needed to achieve a specified target reliability. The point is that in all these cases the predictions are probabilistic in nature. Before looking at the specific models in detail, it is worthwhile to examine in general terms the nature of the uncertainty that forces us to adopt this probabilistic approach.

Figure 6.2 shows the basic simple conceptual model that underlies the different software reliability models. Here execution is seen as the selection of a sequence of input cases from a space, I. The way these are selected will be characteristic of the operational profile. It would, for example, vary from one user to another and possibly result in differing perceptions of the reliability of the program.

This observation is clearer from an examination of Fig. 6.3. Here we denote by the subset I_F, all those input cases which the program cannot currently correctly process. Thus when an input case is selected from I_F, the program will produce unacceptable output and we shall say it has failed.

We can think of the operational profile of a particular user as represented by a probability distribution over the points of I. Different users might have different probability distributions over the inputs. In particular, the probability associated with I_F, which can be thought of as the probability that a particular input choice results in a failure, will be different for different users. That is, they have different reliabilities.

Execution of the program in a particular environment, i.e. according to a particular operational profile, involves the successive selection of test cases according to the appropriate probability distribution. A simple assumption would be that these selections are, at least approximately, independent. Then a period of execution might be a succession of successful test cases terminating in a failure. The number of input cases until failure would be geometrically distributed under the independence assumption. The time to failure would be

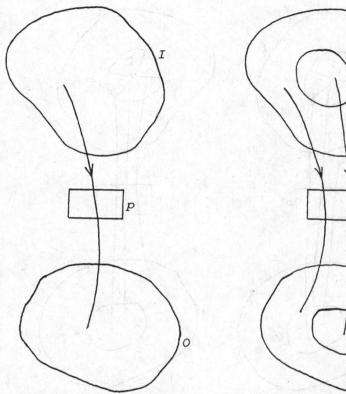

Fig. 6.2. A program p as a mapping from the input space, I, into the output space, O, that is $p: I \rightarrow O$.

Fig. 6.3. Program execution viewed as a mapping. (Note the successful and the failed executions here.)

approximately exponentially distributed under the extra, reasonable assumption that I_F is very small compared with I.

We now need to model how the failure behaviour changes as a result of fixes (or, at least, *attempts* at fixes).

Figure 6.4 extends the above ideas to include the notion of faults as a partition of the input space I_F. Thus (1), (2), (3), ... in Fig. 6.4(a) can be thought of as individual faults: an input case from any of these will result in failure. Assume now that input cases are selected until the first failure occurs, and this is caused by selecting a case from (1). If we could be assured of fixing this fault, and not introducing new faults as a result of the fix, the fault set I_F will become I_F', as shown in Fig. 6.4(b). Execution can continue as before, but the program is now more reliable because there is less chance of selecting an input from I_F' than from the previous I_F. This is because the probability distribution over I remains unchanged and I_F' is contained in I_F. Inputs from the old (1) can now be processed without failure, as shown in Fig. 6.4(b).

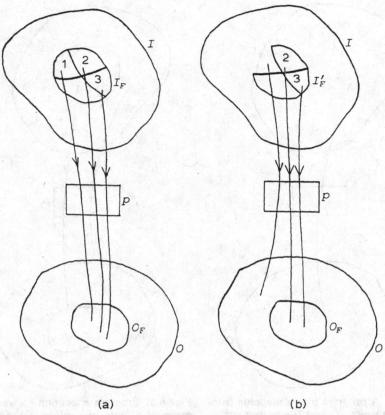

Fig. 6.4. The execution model showing 'bugs' as subsets of a failure region of input space. The effect of a successful bug fix is to remove such a subset, making the failure region, and hence the rate of occurrence of failures, smaller.

Under the same assumptions, the process repeats itself. The program executes until it fails, whereupon a fix is introduced which makes I'_F even smaller, the program is now more reliable, and so on.

The chance that a particular fault will cause a failure on a single input choice depends on the size of the region of I_F corresponding to the fault, and on the probability distribution over I. Clearly, these probabilities vary from fault to fault. Some faults are 'large' in the sense of having a high probability of manifesting themselves, others are 'small' (notice that this idea of large and small has nothing to do with the seriousness of the consequences of such manifestation).

There will be a tendency for the large faults to show themselves earlier than the small ones, but this will be a random process. If there are very many small faults in the program, some of these may show themselves quite early in debugging. The important point is that, even if we know the magnitudes of the faults in a program, the process of detecting them is such that they will occur in an unpredictable order.

This model is quite simplistic as it stands. One important drawback is the assumption that a clean fix is inserted with certainty whenever a failure takes place. In practice, we shall not be sure that our fix has been successful in many cases, nor shall we be sure that new faults have not been introduced.

To summarize the situation so far, there are two sources of uncertainty about the program failure process that prevent us knowing deterministically when failure will occur. The first is the nature of the input selection mechanism. We do not know which inputs will be selected next, and we do not know which inputs are in I_F and thus will precipitate failure. The second source of uncertainty is the nature of fault removal. When a failure occurs, we attempt to identify and fix the fault that caused the failure. However, we are never sure of the efficacy of the fix, nor do we know how much of an improvement in reliability will take place even if the fix is perfect. These points must be borne in mind in the following discussion of models of the software failure process.

6.3 Prediction of Software Reliability

The data of Table 6.1 can be thought as realizations of the random variables $T_1, T_2, T_3, \ldots$ (Fig. 6.1). We now need to use the ideas of the previous section to describe the probabilistic behaviour of this sequence.

In many of the models, it is assumed that the first source of uncertainty introduces a purely random process. That is, the nature of the input selection mechanism is such that at each stage the time to next failure is exponentially distributed. The second source of uncertainty then concerns the way the exponential distribution parameters change as a result of the bug-fixing attempts. If we accept that there is uncertainty here also, then we must represent this sequence of exponential distribution parameters itself as a stochastic process. This will result in a complete probabilistic description of the sequence $\{T_i\}$, and it is this mathematical description that we shall call the *reliability growth model*.

Such a reliability growth model will contain parameters that will distinguish its application to different data sources. In a particular case it will be necessary to estimate these unknown quantities. This *statistical inference* procedure will generally need to be repeated at each stage i, using the available data $t_1, t_2, \ldots, t_{i-1}$.

Since our ultimate objective is one of predicting future failure behaviour, the final step is to combine the model and the statistical estimation in a *prediction procedure*.

Although we talk loosely about different 'models', we really require complete *prediction systems* comprising the three steps: (i) mathematical (stochastic) model, (ii) statistical inference and (iii) prediction procedure. The accuracy of the predictions will depend on these and we could introduce inaccuracy at any of the three steps. Of course, the underlying mathematical model itself is an important part of the triad and it seems unlikely that good predictions will be ultimately attainable unless the model captures reality closely. However, a good model is not itself sufficient. Indeed, recent work (Littlewood & Keiller, 1984) suggests that certain deficiencies in the models can be overcome by the use of statistical tools, described in Section 6.6, which have been developed to analyse the accuracy of complete prediction systems.

A conventional statistical approach to this problem might suggest that the three steps of the prediction system be examined separately in each application. Thus, if all steps were trustworthy, it might be reasonable to place trust in the predictions themselves. Unfortunately, this approach has several drawbacks. Conventional goodness-of-fit testing for the underlying model is impossibly hard for most of the software reliability models. Properties of the maximum-likelihood estimators of unknown parameters, which are the usual approach to the second step, are usually not obtainable. Finally, and perhaps most importantly, it is not easy to determine the relative contributions of the different steps to 'good prediction'.

Accordingly, we advocate that users analyse the predictions themselves by comparing them with eventually observed actual behaviour. We show how this can be done in Section 6.6. First we shall compare some reliability growth models and, in Section 6.5, show how they work when analysing the data of Table 6.1.

6.4 Software Reliability Growth Models

In Appendix A we describe in some detail eight models, the basic elements of which are given below. Perhaps the best known model is due to Jelinski and Moranda. The JM model assumes a finite number of faults to be present in a program, and each fault to contribute equally to the unreliability. Reliability growth occurs when fixes (assumed perfect) are carried out whenever faults are uncovered by their causing failures. The statistical analysis of the failure data, required for the second part of the prediction system, is by the method of maximum likelihood. The Bayesian version of this model (BJM) uses a Bayesian analysis of the data, otherwise it is essentially identical to JM.

The Littlewood–Verrall (LV) model treats the fixing process itself as a stochastic process. The rate of occurrence of failures of the program is assumed to change at fix attempts in an unpredictable way: i.e. there is a likelihood, but not a guarantee, that a fix will improve the reliability.

The model due to Littlewood (L) is an attempt to combine the finite fault count property of JM with uncertainty about the effect of a fix. Here, different faults contribute differently to the unreliability (some are revealed at higher rates than others). Thus, even if a fix is successful, there will be uncertainty

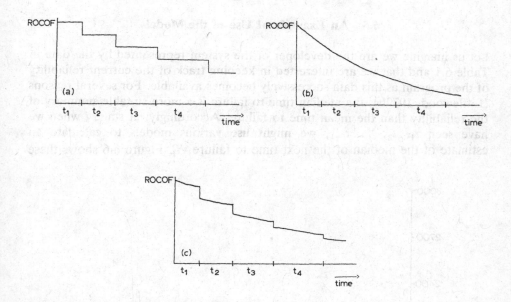

Fig. 6.5. ROCOF plots for various models: (a) JM model; (b) NHPP models; (c) LV and L models.

about the 'size' (rate) of the fault removed, and so uncertainty about the magnitude of the improvement in the reliability of the program.

The other four models (Duane, Musa-Okumoto, Goel-Okumoto, Littlewood NHPP) are nonhomogeneous Poisson process (NHPP) models. The rate of occurrence of failures in these NHPPs is a *continuously* changing function: the different models then arise from different choices of this function. There is a sense in which such models are 'wrong': we know that changes in the rate should be finite jumps (for better or worse) at the fix attempts. However, they may be good approximations to the jump process if the jumps are small. Indeed it can be shown that, on the basis of a single realization, t_1, $t_2, \ldots, t_n$, it is impossible to distinguish between certain jump processes and related NHPPs.

The ROCOFs of the models thus fall into three main types shown in Fig. 6.5. The JM model ROCOF is a step function: improvements in reliability only take place at failures (fixes), and these are *equal*. The Poisson process models show continuous change in elapsed time, and fixes have no direct effect. The L and LV models incorporate both continuous change in elapsed time and discrete changes at fixes. One way to interpret these continuous changes is to adopt the Bayesian subjectivist view of probability (and thus of reliability). Here a probability represents the measure of a subject's strength of belief. In our case it is then intuitively appealing to be reassured by periods of failure-free working, and so increase our confidence in future behaviour: i.e. reliability improvement.

6.5   An Example of Use of the Models

Let us imagine we are the developer of the system represented by the data in
Table 6.1 and that we are interested in keeping track of the current reliability
of the program as this data successively becomes available. For several reasons
(Littlewood, 1979*b*), the median time to failure is a more suitable summary of
the reliability than the mean time to failure. Accordingly, at stage *i* when we
have seen t_1, t_2, . . . , t_{i-1}, we might use various models to calculate an
estimate of the median of the next time to failure, T_i. Figure 6.6 shows these

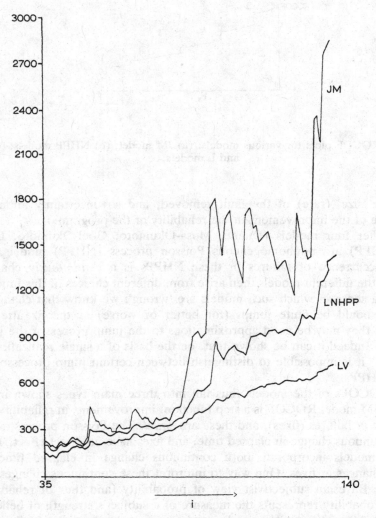

Fig. 6.6. Median plots for JM, LNHPP, LV, data from Table 6.1. Plotted here are
predicted median of T_i (based on t_1, t_2, . . . , t_{i-1}) against *i*.

median predictions plotted against i; here the models used are JM, LV and LNHPP.

Figure 6.6 shows great disagreement between the medians calculated from the different models. We might reasonably ask which, if any, we can trust. Results such as this are typical: if we applied other models to this data we would get further disagreement. We have no reason, *a priori,* to prefer one model over the others. Indeed, even if on earlier projects we somehow knew that a particular model had performed well and given accurate reliability predictions, we could not be certain that the same model would work well here.

A closer inspection of Fig. 6.6 shows that, in the early stages, there is reasonably close agreement between the median predictions. Then there is a quite sudden increase in the LNHPP and JM predictions that is not revealed so dramatically in LV. Is this jump really present in the true reliability? Not only are LNHPP and JM more optimistic than LV in the later stages, but they are also 'noisier', particularly JM. We might also ask whether this noisiness is really present in the true reliability (perhaps occasional decreases in reliability caused by bad fixes?), or whether it is an artefact of the procedures used to estimate the model parameters.

If our sole objective is to give a reliability estimate for the program at the end of testing, i.e. at stage 136 in Fig. 6.6, plots such as this are a great disappointment. A cynic might suggest that the vendor would use the JM estimate, the client the LV estimate.

The disagreement revealed here is typical, and appears to be a major impasse. An analysis of several data sets by 10 models (Abdel-Ghaly *et al.,* 1986) shows that, although some models can be rejected because they give very poor answers, no single model always performs well. In addition, there seems to be no way that models can be matched with data sources so that in each case the most suitable model is selected for the data in hand. In fact, we currently do not understand fully why model accuracy varies so much from one context to another.

6.6 Methods of Analysing Past Predicting Accuracy

There seems no alternative to treating each data source separately and attempting to select the best model for future predictions by analysing the accuracy of past prediction *on that data source.* In order to do this, we first need to understand the ways in which prediction systems can be inadequate. For simplicity we shall consider here only the problem of predicting *current* reliability, but the techniques we shall describe are also applicable to certain types of longer-term prediction.

Given that we have observed data $t_1, t_2, \ldots, t_{i-1}$, a total description of current reliability would be knowledge of $F_i(t) = P(T_i < t)$ the distribution of the next, unobserved, random variable T_i. A prediction system will give an estimator of this, $\bar{F}_i(t)$, based on the data. The operation of calculating $\bar{F}_i(t)$ can be repeated for each value of i. In principle, a comparison should be possible between the predictions $\bar{F}_i(t)$ and the later observed t_i. A rather crude procedure, for example, might calculate the median of each $\bar{F}_i(t)$ and then later note whether the observed t_i were greater than this median; roughly one-half of the time this should be the case if the prediction system is in close accord with reality. We need other, more sensitive methods of detecting departures between $\{\bar{F}_i(t)\}$ and the unknown true $\{F_i(t)\}$.

Clearly the problem is hard. There is a sense in which it is impossibly hard: since the sequence of random variables $\{T_i\}$ is non-stationary, the number of ways $\{\bar{F}_i(t)\}$ can depart from $\{F_i(t)\}$ will increase with i. However, we shall show how certain particularly important departures between prediction and reality can be detected.

In the previous section we saw how, for median predictions, three prediction systems can give very different results. It is clear, for example, that for later predictions either JM is too optimistic or LV is too pessimistic (or perhaps both). Which is the case? Is the compromise candidate, LNHPP, better than the others? There is also the question of the noisiness of JM medians: does this reflect a noisiness of reality (decreases in reliability occurring because of poor fixes) that is not being detected by LV, or is it a spurious artefact of the prediction system?

The first of these questions is similar to the issue of *bias* in conventional statistics. It is the question of whether a prediction system is erring *consistently* in some way. For example, here this could be consistent optimism or consistent pessimism. Of course, any prediction must be a function of previous observations of the interfailure times, and so predictions must exhibit 'sampling fluctuations'. The first important question is whether the predictions are in some sense 'on average' close to the truth, or whether they consistently deviate. In particular, we would like to know whether the $\bar{F}_i(t)$ are on average close to the true $F_i(t)$. We could call a prediction system with this desirable property 'unbiased' and be confident that it would not exhibit consistent departure from reality. Specifically, simple summary predictions such as the median time to failure would not deviate consistently from the truth.

Although it is important that a prediction system give approximately unbiased results, this is clearly not sufficient. A user wishes to be confident that each prediction is close to the truth, not merely that the prediction errors (perhaps large) in some sense cancel themselves out on average. It is possible, for example, that a series of predictions fluctuates wildly above and below the truth, yet still retains the property of unbiasedness. No single prediction in such a case could be trusted to be close to the truth.

A second aspect of predictive accuracy, therefore, is 'noisiness'. By this we loosely mean random fluctuations about the truth from one prediction to the next. It may be, for example, that the behaviour of JM in later stages of Fig. 6.6 exhibits such noisiness. However the picture is not a simple one: we never know that the reliability is changing (increasing) relatively smoothly so that non-smoothly changing predictions can be rejected. It may be that as debugging continues the reliability sometimes increases and sometimes decreases owing to bad fixes. Thus, in Fig. 6.6 it may be the case that JM is accurately tracking some genuine reversals of fortune and LV is incorrectly smoothing these out.

Notice that these questions are quite separate from the notion of unbiasedness, discussed earlier, which concentrates on average performance. For the data analyses shown in Fig. 6.6, we are concerned with two separate questions: firstly, what is the average, long-term evolution of the reliability represented by the medians? Secondly, what is the true local behaviour from prediction to prediction?

In Appendix A we give details of two simple procedures that give partial answers to these questions: the u-plot and the prequential likelihood. More information about these, including detailed analyses of several data sets using many models, is available elsewhere (Abdel-Ghaly *et al.*, 1986). Here we shall show how they allow us to choose between the different models for the data of Table 6.1.

The u-plot gives information solely about biasedness. Figure 6.7 shows u-plots for JM, LV and LNHPP based on 100 successive predictions of next time to failure for the data of Table 6.1. As explained in the appendix, a good prediction system would give a plot near to the line of unit slope that is drawn here as a continuous line. Deviations from this line are an indication of predictive inaccuracy: the larger the deviation, the stronger the evidence for this. There are various ways these deviations can be examined to see whether they are significantly large: the simplest is the Kolmogorov distance, which is the maximum vertical deviation between plot and line. In this case the values of 0·187 (JM) and 0·144 (LV) are significant at the 1% and 5% levels, respectively. This means that neither prediction system is performing very well, but the 1% significance level suggests that JM is notably worse.

In fact, the plots tell us much more than this. The JM plot is everywhere above the line, LV is almost everywhere below. It is shown in Appendix A that this means that JM is too optimistic and LV too pessimistic. We might therefore conclude that, in Fig. 6.6, the truth lies somewhere between the optimistic JM and pessimistic LV medians: perhaps LNHPP is closer to actual failure behaviour than either of the other sets of predictions. This is confirmed by the u-plot: LNHPP has a Kolmogorov distance of only 0·081, which is not large enough to be statistically significant. The tentative conclusion, then, is that there is not evidence here to suggest that LNHPP is 'biased' and so, at least for this criterion, is superior to LV and JM *for this data source*. Its performance on other data sources should not, however, be presumed to be superior to that of other models; rather, in each case an analysis of this kind should be conducted.

The problem of 'noisiness' of predictions, as mentioned earlier, is a difficult one because we must be careful not to reject a model that is producing noisy predictions justifiably (because the true reliability is fluctuating genuinely

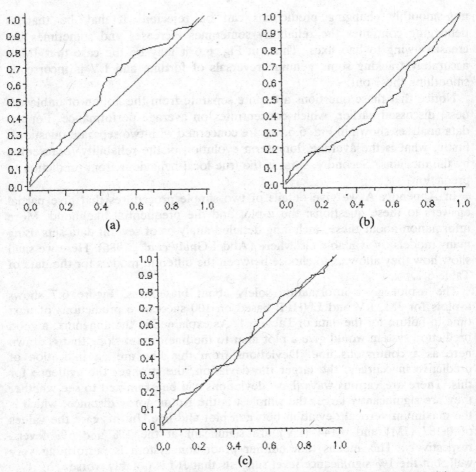

Fig. 6.7. *u*-Plots for the data of Table 6.1: (a) JM, maximum deviation 0·1874; (b) LV, maximum deviation 0·1437; (c) LNHPP, maximum deviation 0·0805.

about a long-term growth pattern). If we knew that there was a relatively smooth improvement in reliability taking place, with only minor reverses, we could simply obtain comparative measures of the (presumed incorrect) noisiness of the prediction systems and select the least noisy. In the absence of such knowledge we need a means of distinguishing between predictions that are justifiably fluctuating and those that simply exhibit random noise (and so cannot be trusted for individual predictions).

Unfortunately, techniques that can discriminate as finely as this do not exist. We are therefore forced to look for other tools. Prequential likelihood (see Appendix A) is a method of comparing prediction systems generally; it is sensitive to *both* of the departures from accurate representation of the truth discussed above. It will respond to unwarranted noisiness (when the true reliability is changing smoothly) and to unwarranted smoothness (when the true reliability is changing noisily as a consequence of occasionally bad fixes). However, this response is confounded with any other deviations between prediction and reality, such as bias, that the prediction system may exhibit. Prequential likelihood should thus be seen as a completely general method of discriminating between different prediction systems on the grounds of their predictive accuracy.

Table 6.2(a) shows a prequential likelihood comparison of JM and LV on the data of Table 6.1. Here are shown values of the *prequential likelihood ratio* (PLR) at 10 step intervals for JM versus LV prediction. If PLR is increasing, this is evidence that JM is performing better; if PLR is decreasing, that LV is performing better (explained in Appendix A). A PLR that fluctuates around unity suggests there is little to choose between the two prediction systems. In this case there is little to choose between LV and JM until about the 60th prediction; after that LV shows a definite superiority. Of course, we do not know whether this superiority is due to JM being more seriously biased than LV, or whether it is due to JM being unwarrantably noisy, as Fig. 6.6 suggests might be the case. The PLR analysis does tell us, though, that there is evidence for taking LV to have been more generally accurate than JM in past predictions for this data.

Table 6.2(b) shows a comparison between LNHPP and LV. Once again there is little to choose between the prediction systems for the first half of the predictions. As before, this is not surprising, since the median plot shows these predictions to be in fair accord until this stage. After that there is some evidence from the table that LNHPP is superior to LV, but there are reversals of fortune. These may be due to a trade-off taking place between 'bias' and 'noisiness': there is slight evidence from the median plot that the LNHPP medians fluctuate more than those from LV, even though they are less pessimistic. If indeed this is the case, a user could in different circumstances prefer either model. If consistency were preferred, one could use LV and

Table 6.2. Prequential Likelihood Ratio Comparison of JM, LV and LNHPP Models Operating on the Data of Table 6.1

(a) JM and LV models		(b) LNHPP and LV models		(c) LNHPP and JM models	
n	PLR_n	n	PLR_n	n	PLR_n
10	1·19	10	1·16	10	0·975
20	0·318	20	0·593	20	1·86
30	0·252	30	0·759	30	3·01
40	0·096	40	0·502	40	5·23
50	0·745	50	1·83	50	2·46
60	6·50	60	7·56	60	1·16
70	0·088	70	5·75	70	65·34
80	0·001 77	80	1·24	80	700·56
90	0·000 081 3	90	0·66	90	8 118·08
100	0·001 19	100	30·85	100	25 924·37

perhaps compensate informally for its known pessimism. If unbiasedness were preferred, LNHPP could be used, accepting the risk that individual predictions may fluctuate above and below the truth more than is the case for LV.

Table 6.2(c), finally, shows the comparison between LNHPP and JM. As we would expect, this shows LNHPP exhibiting very superior performance to JM for the later predictions. Of these three models, then, there is strong evidence that JM is worst. There is slight evidence that LNHPP is better than LV, and a user might reasonably conclude that LNHPP should therefore be used for the next prediction. An analysis of this kind could be performed whenever a new prediction was to be made, and the best model selected at that stage in the light of predictive accuracy so far. It seems to be the case that comparative performance of models changes fairly slowly, if at all, so it will usually be unnecessary to conduct these analyses of predictive accuracy at every step. For very large data sets it will be best only to take into account the most recent predictive performance in deciding which model to use for the next prediction: the past becomes less relevant as a guide to future accuracy as it recedes further.

In summary, then, a user of software reliability models does not need to know *a priori* which model is most appropriate for the program under examination. It is best to use many available prediction systems and use for the current prediction that system which has given the best result at earlier stages of the data set.

Of course, there can never be a guarantee that such a policy will work: it assumes a kind of continuity between past and future of which we can never be certain. In particular, in our context, we must be careful that no obvious discontinuity has been introduced, such as a change from an artificial test environment to an operational use environment. This reinforces the importance of ensuring that testing for reliability *measurement* must take place in a context that accurately reflects the conditions under which the software will actually operate.

6.7 Summary and Conclusion

The main point is that it is usually possible to obtain accurate reliability predictions for software, and to have confidence in their accuracy in a particular case. It should be stressed that not *all* data sources yield accurate reliability predictions, but the techniques we have described will provide a user with a warning in such cases.

Readers wishing to measure or predict the reliability of software would do well to treat sceptically any claims that a particular model will be sufficient for their needs. All the recent evidence points to the individual models performing with variable accuracy over different data sets, and there is obviously no 'universally best' model. Having said this, some models are generally worse than others in most contexts. However, even this observation is not sufficiently strong to be able permanently to reject any models. The safest solution is to try many (as many as possible) on the data set that is of interest, and select the one (or more) that is giving the best answers.

Of course, this is a computationally intensive approach. Most models require the maximum-likelihood estimates of parameters to be successively re-estimated via search algorithms. Fortunately, there now exist efficient ways of doing this. For example, the software (Reliability and Statistical Consultants Ltd, 1985) used for the examples in this chapter runs on an IBM PC-AT, or compatible, with maths coprocessor. This software allows nine models to be fitted to each data set, and carries out the analysis of predictive accuracy so that a user can intelligently select the predictions to use. For the data of Table 6.1, which involved 100-parameter re-estimates for each of the nine models, together with calculation of reliability predictions and analysis of these, the run time on the PC was about 40 minutes.

Using this approach, our experience (Abdel Ghaly *et al.*, 1986) has been that it is generally possible to obtain reliability predictions that are accurate and, perhaps more importantly, to have some confirmation of their accuracy. The main obstacle to the use of these models remains the difficulty of collecting the right kind of data. This is essentially the problem of ensuring that the environment in which the software operates during this collection of failure data is similar to that in which it will operate during operational use. The construction of such an environment artificially is not easy, but it is possible sometimes to do this in an industrial context (Curritt *et al.*, 1986), effort well spent if there is a strong need to know how reliable a program will be for a user.

It should perhaps be emphasized that the techniques described here are generally only suitable for situations in which fairly modest reliability levels are required. There seems to be a law of diminishing returns operating for debugging. The return in reliability improvement from investment of effort in testing becomes smaller and smaller as the 'larger' faults are found, and the program ends up containing perhaps very many faults with infinitesimally small rates. Thus, in safety-critical applications, where a failure rate of 10^{-9} per hour is a typical requirement, reliability growth techniques cannot be expected to give the necessary confirmation of achievement in realistic time scales. Equally, a law of diminishing returns of this kind might suggest that we eventually reach a stage where it is not cost-effective to continue fixing faults: the benefit of a slight improvement in reliability is out-weighed by the cost of the fix. This effect is accentuated by the oft-reported phenomenon of old code being intrinsically more expensive to maintain than new.

This is still an active research area, and it is likely that we shall see some improvements to model capability in the next few years. Recent work, (Littlewood, 1989) for example, has shown that the techniques of Section 6.6 can be used for improving the accuracy of predictions by learning from the analysis of past errors. However, the most important message of this chapter is that software reliability prediction techniques are available now and, for appropriate data, they work well. We hope that readers will be encouraged by their ease of use to set up appropriate data collection mechanisms.

7

Software Project Control and Management

Paul Rook and Alan Wingrove

7.1 Introduction 155
7.2 Project Control and Project Management 157
7.3 Establishing the Software Development Process 167
7.4 Managing the Software Development Process 176
7.5 The Process Definition Diagram 183
7.6 Risk Management and Choice of Process 199
7.7 Productivity, Quality and Software Development
   Methodology 205
7.8 Further Reading 209

7.1 Introduction

Nearly every software development project is faced with numerous difficulties and when a project is successful it is not because there were no problems but because the problems were overcome. The problems usually arise from technical difficulties or inadequacies in the technical development but become critical managerial problems if the project control structure is ineffective.

Project Management is the specific activity of achieving project control. Software project control is not inherent, and an assumption that control of the software development will come from within the project is demonstrably a lack of good management. As a necessary prerequisite for a successful project, the project manager is responsible for determining the development process, establishing it and ensuring that it is really being used, supported and updated as necessary. Software development depends on documentation and communication and is only manageable if a structure is imposed and controlled. It is necessary to set out precise definitions of tasks and task-products in the software development process, the achievement of which then provides unambiguous milestones for measurement of progress, thus bridging the gap between technology and management of events, resources and budgets. If this is not done, then the project manager cannot manage because the means of management are not there. As well as meeting all the other constraints on product and project, the manager is responsible for the *reliable production* of the (reliable) software.

Software project control is dealt with in this chapter on the basis of a common understanding between software technical staff, the project manager and senior management. If the principles to be applied in determining the process for a software development project can be agreed and understood at levels from an understanding of the Process Definition Diagram (see Section 7.5) then the project is much more likely to be successful for everybody concerned. Some emphases in the chapter are oriented to large real-time software projects, where indeed the problems are such as to require a high degree of explicit definition and formalization of methods of working and responsibilities. However, the principles are still valid for small or less-demanding projects, or styles of development used in other applications, and the reader should be prepared to glean the principles and tailor their application appropriately. Where the software is being developed as part of a system, an integrated system approach is essential, with the differences between hardware and software recognized and accommodated in a total system development process.

The primary structure for project control is described in Section 7.2, identifying the three constituents of management; Project Management, Quality Management and Configuration Management and briefly discussing the activities involved and the relationship to Technical Development.

The next four sections deal with the software development process, which has to be grasped by the project manager in order to achieve project control. Section 7.3 deals with establishment of the process, Section 7.4 discusses the use of the process to achieve project control and Section 7.5 illustrates the principles of a well-defined process with an example and a process definition diagram. Reference is made to life-cycle models of the software development process in order to use phases for process definition and baselined phase-products for milestones in project planning. In order to keep to the main subject of project control, the discussion of the principles of software life-cycle models and their internal operation is covered separately in Appendix B. The choice of a particular process for a project is based on a determination of risk in the development. Section 7.6 deals with risk analysis and the choice of process phases and reviews on the basis of risk management so that the project remains under control.

If the project is to be successful, it is necessary that productivity be sufficiently high to meet the timescale required with the resources available. Of course, productivity should not be the antitheses of quality, and indeed, addressed properly, improved productivity enables improved quality. Section 7.7 deals with productivity and quality in the context of the wider management issues that encompass the activity of project management on the local project.

Project success is an amalgamation of meeting the target of developing the product on time and within budget, meeting the customer's requirements for functionality, performance, reliability and quality, and also satisfying the wider objectives of the organization. This chapter deals with the means available to overcome the very real problems presented by the task of successfully managing the development of software products. However, there is not room within the scope of the *Handbook* to cover all aspects of project management and we concentrate on those aspects that deal with ensuring the reliability and effectiveness of the development process for *software* projects. Our goal is to put in place the bridge to the technical methods of software development, covered in the previous chapters, so that software projects are as controllable as projects for any other engineering discipline. Those aspects of project management that are fundamentally necessary but equally applicable to any project, such as leadership, planning, time management, decision making, effective communication, people management and training, etc., are only briefly referred to. For more depth in these topics, reference should be made to the books listed under Further Reading.

7.2 Project Control and Project Management

A control system for a project is based on the common principle of establishing suitable feedback loops to ensure that the controlled system can be guided toward its objective. Figure 7.1 illustrates, in a simplified form, such a project control system. Technical Development is what is being controlled, with Project Management as the controller. Feedback loops operate not only directly from the Technical Development but also through the functions of Quality Management and Configuration Management.

The diagram illustrates a continuous process, as indicated by the inner loop feeding back intermediate development products as the basis for continuing technical development activities. The Quality and Configuration Management functions operate continuously during the development process, not simply on the products finally delivered to the customer. Quality Management is responsible for both measurement of conformance to the procedures defined for the process and measurement of the quality achieved for the products according to the standards. Together they can be used to ensure that declared achievement of a milestone can be relied on. Configuration Management is responsible for the custody of baselined products.

Whilst the inner loop represents the work on the product, the outer feedback loops represent the basis for control. The upper feedback loops will always be present, and represent the paths for changes. The project manager must ensure that they are sufficiently controlled through appropriate procedures; for example, change requests being handled through a change control procedure. The lower feedback loops represent the progress monitoring functions which will not be present unless established by the Project Manager. Project control is based on obtaining information to make decisions, replanning as necessary to meet timescale and budget, reassignment of work and feedback to the Project Manager that the decisions have been implemented and whether the consequences of the decisions have had the desired effect.

Standards and Procedures are necessary for the meaningful definition of tasks in software development. Only with such definitions can the project

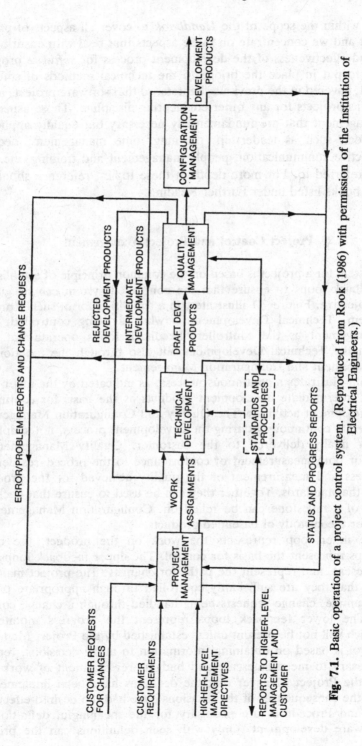

Fig. 7.1. Basic operation of a project control system. (Reproduced from Rook (1986) with permission of the Institution of Electrical Engineers.)

manager be confident that the assigned task is adequately defined and that its completion is unambiguous.

The project control system depends on the existence of clearly defined managerial responsibilities within an organization, related to the four main functions: Project Management, Quality Management, Configuration Management and Technical Development. Figure 7.1 organizes the concepts of project control into an operational structure; the rest of this section deals briefly with the parts of the structure, and the remaining sections of the chapter deal with the various aspects of making the structure work in practice for software development projects.

7.2.1 Project Management

Project management technique can be regarded as the set of procedures, rules, practices, technologies and know-how that the manager applies to plan, organize, staff, direct and control an engineering project aimed at producing a particular product within constraints of resources, budget and time scale. The principles and practice can be universally applied to the management of any organization or activity. The *IEEE Tutorial on Software Engineering Project Management*, (Thayer, 1988), is an excellent starting point for reference on all the various aspects of software project management. Thayer's introductory paper on pages 15–53 of the Tutorial gives a comprehensive top-down view of the activities involved. As stated in the introduction, this chapter does not have space to cover all aspects of project management, and we concentrate on those aspects that ensure that the software development process is understood, defined and brought to the state where it becomes manageable using standard project management technique.

Figure 7.2 shows Project Management, expanded from the single box in Fig. 7.1, as a set of interacting tasks. These illustrate the principle that the ability to control a project depends on the quality of information that the tasks generate and the use made of it.

7.2.1.1 *Decision making*

The most important aspect of project management consists of making decisions (or ensuring that decisions are made) which includes making sure that timely technical decisions are made regarding the product as well as making the more obvious project decisions. Whilst authority and decision making can, and must, but appropriately delegated, ultimate responsibility for decisions still rests with the project manager. The responsibility includes customer relationship, specification, correctness of design and implementation, quality, use of allocated resources and staff, meeting timescale and budget, standards and procedures, anticipation and resolution of problems and ultimate delivery and acceptance of the product.

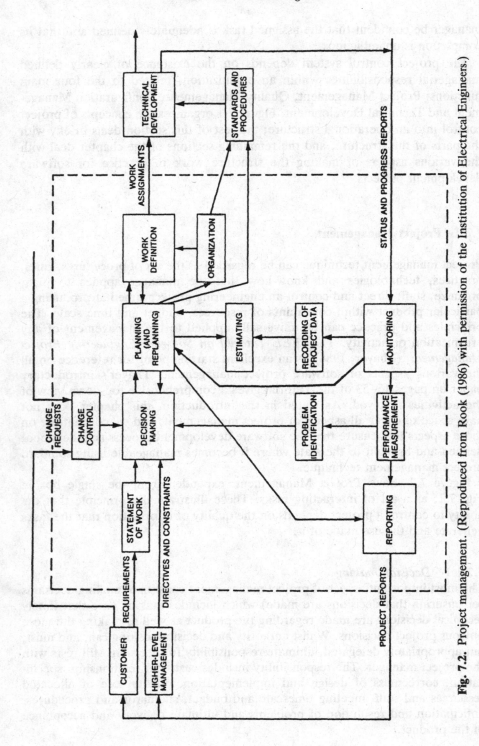

Fig. 7.2. Project management. (Reproduced from Rook (1986) with permission of the Institution of Electrical Engineers.)

7.2.1.2 *Estimating*

Planning and managing the project depends on a method of estimating the development resources required in terms of cost, effort and timescale. The estimating method must be able to take into account the sensitivity of the development cost to various product, project and environmental factors. Cost estimation must also be able to take past experience into account, particularly the relevant experience of the department or business in the development of similar software.

Estimating for software development is rightly regarded as a difficult problem, and for any chance of success must depend on:

- a trial design;
- a standard way of organizing a software development project process (right down to task level, and the discipline to stick to this method of working so that assumptions are not invalidated);
- a trusted estimating method using data from previous projects.

Even with this foundation, there are still problems, as discussed in Chapter 11 of this *Handbook,* and accuracy of estimation is inseparable from risk management, discussed in Section 7.6, and the need for frequent re-estimation to deal with changing realization of the scope of the work.

For a discussion of software estimating methods and procedure, reference should also be made to *Software Enginering Economics* (Boehm, 1981). As a basis for project control, reliable estimates are best obtained (and for important projects second-best should be unacceptable) from a combination of the techniques of expert judgement, summation of effort for individual tasks and metrics based cost models using data from previous projects. All three techniques depend on an understanding of the software development process used for the project as well as on the definition of the software to be implemented.

Estimates obtained in the form of activities and phases of the software development process lead the project manager to analyse and control the project in a way that builds on the strengths of the phase-based process. The correspondence between the detail of the estimates, the plan, the assignment of work, the team responsibilities in the organization and the measurement of progress strengthens the emphasis on defining the method of working on the project and ensures that it corresponds to actual practice rather than just good intentions. It also allows projects to be tracked easily, and facilitates frequent re-estimation, thus giving early warning of the need to re-examine budgets and plans.

7.2.1.3 *Planning*

Planning includes the activities of defining milestones, assigning resources, scheduling and budgeting. It depends on the estimates and on the Work Breakdown Structure used for work definition. The project manager produces a project plan (to be publicly viewed and reviewed) which shows estimates, product and subproduct schedules and relationships, and the allocation of resources to the tasks. It is accompanied by a definition of the Project Organization and the standards and procedures to be used in Technical Development. Refer to the paper by Fairley (1987) in the *IEEE Tutorial on Software Engineering Project Management* for more detail on the project management plan.

It is important to recognize that the project plan must explicitly address risks and contingency and must be dynamic: reference Risk Management Plans discussed in Section 7.6. Through the normal processes of iterative analysis, design and implementation changes, resource problems, customer or environment changes, and re-estimates, the project plan will require regular updating and revision. Copies of each version of the project plan should be properly stored in the project history file together with the reasons for revision.

7.2.1.4 *Work definition*
Definition of the Work Breakdown Structure (WBS) is an interactive part of planning and the choice of WBS depends fundamentally on the chosen techniques for the technical development and the overall method selected for the software development process. The detailed work packages (the lowest level of the WBS) define a structure of subproducts for project work and management visibility. The WBS not only requires management and customer agreement on the specification of the subproducts and the final product but also requires agreement on the methods of working to be used for the whole project.

7.2.1.5 *Progress monitoring*
Monitoring involves measuring actual development progress and handling minor revisions to schedule and resource-requirements within the responsibilities of the teams. Project progress is also related to quality assurance through technical reviews and walkthroughs. Based on written reports and meetings, monitoring involves the evaluation of expected progress of subproducts against actual progress and also the recording of project history in the project data file.

7.2.1.6 *Management reporting*
The project manager reviews the status, progress and identified problems as a foundation for decisions. Comparison of monitored actual progress with expected performance yields relevant information for the project teams, management and the customer.

The information for management should be a filtered subset of the information needed by the project manager when tracking progress within the project. The information needed by management is to answer questions such as 'Is the project on schedule?' and, if not, 'Can the team handle the schedule slippage within its own area of responsibility, or does management need to do something to help the project return to a controlled state?' The information on measured achievement must be presented effectively to both higher management and the customer so that project progress can be approved at critical points and the correct decisions made.

7.2.2 Quality Management

'Quality' is generally taken to mean not only conformance of the product to its stated requirements, but also meeting defined standards and with the connotation of good professional practice in software development. Quality is built into the product by the activities of the technical development staff as a continuous process and is everybody's responsibility—it cannot be added by any testing or control on products. Verification, Validation, Testing and In-process Quality Control on intermediate products as development progresses do, however, provide early warning of problems; changes can be made at much lower cost than in the later stages of development provided, as always, that proper change control procedures are followed.

Since check-out of final products, rejecting those that do not meet quality criteria, does nothing to ensure success of a software development project, the emphasis of Quality Management in software development is not only on in-process quality control of intermediate products, but also on the development process itself, which is seen as fundamental to the ability of the project to produce products of acceptable quality.

Thus, assurance of quality—'Quality Assurance'—includes checking whether the development staff are following the intended process (in all their work, not just the VV&T activities) to *assure* the quality of the components produced. Verification, Validation and Testing (VV&T), described further in Section 7.4.3, are carried out by technical development staff, but Quality Assurance is carried out by staff either from a separate QA department or staff specifically assigned to quality assurance work in the project.

Quality Management covers the responsibility of obtaining, training (technical skills in quality assurance) and managing the quality assurance staff, and planning and managing the work of:

- provision of independent advice on all quality issues, especially on the choice of standards and procedures at the beginning of each project;
- preparation of the quality plan;
- monitoring the process as actually employed on the project;
- auditing the quality (conformance to standards and requirements) of products (including the intermediate development products, especially the early ones) as the project progresses to find out whether the procedures are being effective.

The quality plan is described in Chapter 8 (Sections 8.3.7 and 8.4.1), which deals with it from the Procurement point of view. The last two areas of work listed above are specified by the quality plan: the process is monitored against its definition in the plan, the quality of the products is monitored against the targets set in it. The plan also defines the procedures and reports appropriate to this work. Later in this chapter, Section 7.3.5 discusses the key role of the quality plan as the basis of the triangular relationship between the customer, PM and QM.

In a large software development, the quality assurance staff are crucially valuable to the project manager. No-one else will be able to verify that the process is operating as intended and therefore whether it is ensuring the quality intended in the final product. The project manager is not able to do it directly, because of the immediate work on all the tasks described in Section 7.2.1. In the absence of assurance of quality, project control is open loop as far as the quality of the items that are being produced, with the consequence that the quality of the final product will be a surprise (and unlikely to be a pleasant one). Successful quality assurance gives the project manager the means to be sure of both measuring progress through events corresponding to production of items *and* measuring the quality of the items produced based on the intended process being followed. Refer to Chapter 9 for a full discussion of Quality Management.

It is also natural for the quality assurance staff to take responsibility for the collection of data. This data provides the basis for modelling and predicting the quality of the product (e.g. reliability modelling as discussed in Chapter 6) from error (incident) logging, error correction logging, defect analysis (based on rates of error detection and removal) and recording of all project data (events, sizes, effort expended against planned and unplanned items), documentation and change control for subsequent audit and analysis. This data is also the source of all information for metrics and cost modelling (discussed in Chapters 10 and 11).

7.2.3 Configuration Management

The successful development and maintenance of a large software product requires strict control over the documentation and the code constituting the product. This is the responsibility of Configuration Management, which covers the following activities:

- clear identification of software items and documents, and their successive versions and variants;
- definition of the configuration of software products, and their related configuration items;
- physical control over the master files of software code and documentation;
- control of introduction of changes to these files by a change control board and change procedures;
- maintenance of a system of configuration records, reflecting the definition of products in the field.

On a large project, the sheer quantity of work necessary for adequate configuration management, and the need for efficiency to be able to react to the demands made on it by development staff, requires not only a separate organizational responsibility, but also automated tool support. A complete CM tool (or set of tools) has to include facilities for:

- support for technical staff in controlling the local versions during development;
- baseline establishment and maintenance (possession of baselined components—separation from development versions);
- change control;
- build management (building standard versions and variants of products from baselined components);
- data collection.

Chapter 12 (Sections 12.2 and 12.3.3) emphasises the importance of configuration management support in the software development environment.

During software development, the specification is subject to continuous pressure for change, to correct errors, introduce improvements, and respond to the evolving requirements of the customer. Configuration management supports the disciplines of baselining that are necessary to prevent the chaos of uncontrolled change. The output of each development phase is verified and validated against the relevant preceding baselines. The configuration management procedures ensure that this output is, in turn, baselined and that subsequently only up-to-date definitions and baselines are used. Once a baseline has been formally established, its contents may only be changed by the operation of the formal change control procedure. This has the following advantages:

- No changes are made thereafter without the agreement of all interested parties.
- The higher procedural threshold for change puts a barrier against unconsidered changes.
- There is always available a definitive version of the product, or of any of the controlled intermediate products (baselines).

Baselining is discussed further in Section 7.4.2, and Chapter 8 goes into more detail on baselining and configuration management (in Sections 8.7 and 8.8). Although the discussion in Chapter 8 is from the point of view of maintenance, much of it also applies to the Configuration Management responsibility, tasks and procedures during development—which should, indeed, be seen as the initial steps of establishing possession of the product for the organization and for the purpose of supporting it in operation for the users.

7.2.4 Technical Development and Technical Control

The project manager is responsible for the selection, or confirmation, of the technical methods to be used in the project. Software development techniques such as formal specification, object-oriented and fault-tolerant design, correctness proofs and test methods, as covered in Chapters 2–5, are examples of suitable techniques when the emphasis is on the required reliability of the software product. The choice of such techniques, together with documentation standards and configuration management and quality assurance procedures, must be matched to the characteristics of the development, the imposed schedules, and other operational considerations. Once selected, the methods must be implemented, supported with tools and training for staff, and integrated into the operational process. Careful selection of software development techniques is fundamental, since the project cannot succeed without suitable technical skills applied by the staff. However, no matter how sophisticated the design and programming techniques, they are not sufficient to ensure a successful software product unless the technical development is *fully integrated* with a systematic approach to software project management.

There is a potential dichotomy between Project Management and Technical Development. In most cases the project manager does not have the time, and sometimes also lacks the technical understanding, to be sufficiently involved in the technical work to realize the consequences of technical problems until too late. The danger is that the project manager is only linked through reported progress and even the link between project progress and quality assurance, discussed in Section 7.2.2, is insufficient: problems may not become apparent until the effects are seen in the phase-products. The technical integrity of a complex development can only be ensured by strategically looking ahead. The activities are performed by members of a number of teams and it is vital to co-ordinate the technical drive to define, design and produce the software.

This focus on the central integrity of the Technical Development is referred to as 'Technical Control'. The role of technical controller on a large project may be referred to as 'system architect', 'project architect', 'chief engineer' or 'chief programmer' (as used by IBM), or the position may correspond to the leader of the design team.

Primary examples of the responsibilities of Technical Control are the maintenance of the integrity of the design in the presence of detailed changes after the completion of the structural design phase, and test planning. Test planning is a strategic activity from the very start of the project which defines and co-ordinates all the test methods, modelling, tools and techniques to be used throughout the life cycle. It also identifies critical components that need the most testing, what test data is required, and when it is to be prepared. The technical controller must determine the verification and validation strategy and monitor the effectiveness of reviews so that errors are detected and corrected early, and the technical risk is controlled. When subcontractors are involved in the project, Technical Control becomes even more important in co-ordinating the technical aspects of all work between the subcontractors and the integrity of the subcontract products. In the context of Fig. 7.1, Technical Control is regarded as part of the Technical Development, and is defined as the continuing activity of making certain that what is being produced is technically correct, coherent and consistent. It can be clearly distinguished from such concerns as schedule, budget, organization, staffing, etc., which are solely the responsibility of Project Management.

Whilst it is reasonable on very small projects for the project manager to undertake both project management and technical control, on large projects such a combination of roles is not workable. It is rare to find people who combine both the strong management talent and strong technical skills necessary for large projects. More importantly, on a project of even reasonable size, each activity is necessarily a full-time job, or more. It is hard for the project manager to delegate the project management tasks to allow time for technical work. It is impossible for the technical controller to delegate technical control work without compromising the conceptual integrity of the product. The bottom line is that for a software project of any significant technical difficulty there *must* be one person fundamentally responsible for Technical Control, and on a project of sufficient size (it depends on the application, but the boundary is no higher than 5–10 staff) it *cannot* successfully be the same person as is responsible for project management.

Clearly, the relationship between the project manager, the technical controller and the project staff can present a problem. There is opportunity for pathological connections (reference Fig. 7.3) and questions to be answered for staff to know who to report to in which context. It is sometimes possible to run a project with the technical control exercised by the senior manager in charge of the project and almost all project management tasks delegated to a second-in-command. It is much more usual for the project manager to be in command, with the technical controller having the technical authority. In this case, it is important that the technical controller does have enough authority for decisions without being in the direct management line above all the project teams. Whilst there is no universal solution, the theoretical problems usually have a clear answer in practice in any specific project. Whatever the solution in terms of responsibilities, hierarchy and organization, it must be worked out and made clear to all staff. What we are dealing with is the crucial bridge between software development technique (which sometimes is in danger of being no more than merely technically clever) and software project management (which is being effective). Brooks deals with the subject with both humour and insight in Chapter 7 of *The Mythical Man-Month* (Brooks, 1975), comparing the roles of project manager and technical controller to those of producer and director.

7.3 Establishing the Software Development Process

In some cases a standard method of working will already be in use, together with the appropriate support facilities. In other cases the project manager will have to select and establish a process specifically for the project. In either event, project management has the final responsibility of ensuring (or confirming) the suitability of the process for the project and defining precisely the details of its operation.

Establishment of the process for the software development project depends on the following five principles:

- Define the project process for all the work involved, covering technical development, project management, quality assurance and configuration management.
- Establish the organization to match the process of work on the product.
- Carry out a project initiation phase to ensure that the process is in place and understood.
- Use tools to make the work more efficient by automating the tasks and supporting the process.
- Set the project goals on a contractural basis, with metrics and targets to be achieved, so that effective use can be made of real feedback to control the process.

7.3.1 Definition of the process

It is management's job to steer the individuals and teams on a project in a common direction so that their creativity is productive, the products interface with each other, are finished within the project cost and schedule constraints, and together accomplish the project goals. A project can only operate effectively when each member knows the answers to basic questions regarding the job such as:

- Who do I work for?
- What is expected of me?
- Why is it expected of me?
- What tools and facilities are available to me?
- How do I do what is expected?
- What training is available to me?
- What must I produce?
- When must it be produced?
- Who do I give it to?
- How will my product be evaluated?

Establishment of the relationship between the functions of project management and the technical activities depends on the engineering professionalism of the technical staff. Codes of practice, accepted standards, training in these and professional integrity in working to industry procedures are the mark of a mature engineering discipline. Where these properly exist there is no misconception when a task is assigned and no ambiguity as to whether the product of the task has been completed to the standard required. The codes of practice are a significant contribution to providing answers to the above questions posed by individuals in the project. The rest of the answers are provided by the process of working and organizational responsibilities which have to be established by the project manager.

Definition of the overall process for the whole project starts by determining the phases and reviews, and then the software development activities. The next step is a Process Definition Diagram showing the relationship of the tasks and the task-products to the major stages in the process. An example of such a diagram, for a particular version of a software development process is shown in Fig. 7.7. A diagram in this form is an invaluable basis for discussions with senior staff to progressively search out all the tasks that need to be added to the initial diagram. They thus bring their expertise and share in the decisions that finalize the process.

Promulgation of the agreed Process Definition Diagram is the project manager's most effective communication tool in ensuring that everyone on the project understands the process to which they are working and the relationship to the actual tasks in hand.

7.3.2 Establishment of the organization

On the basis of estimates for the sizes of the tasks in the various phases and the defined activities, the work breakdown structure leads to task assignments to teams and a mapping onto an organizational structure, using the principles referred to in Section B.7 in Appendix B, with responsibilities clearly shown on the Process Definition Diagram.

Since it is observable that the structures of products displays only too well the structures of the organizations that produced them, it is generally preferable to set up the organization to correspond to the process for the product that it is wished to produce. Figure 7.3 illustrates the commonality of principles in good software design and good organizational 'design'. Design of the software development process and of the project organization for a significant software development is a worthwhile intellectual challenge. The same skills and techniques that are used for the design of a significant software system should be applied to the design of the project process and organization and will bring commensurate gains in effectiveness for the software development project.

7.3.3 Project initiation

Everything that is done right in software development project management is done early. If the necessary foundation for the process is not adequately established at the beginning, then, on a large project working to meet a deadline, there is never sufficient time subsequently to back-track and set up better means of project control.

Figure 7.4(a) shows the potential incidence of trouble as the software development progresses. Establishing a management structure at the earliest possible stage of a project provides the necessary basis to identify and control problems before they become critical. It is impossible to provide a model management structure which would be universally (or even generally) applicable to a wide range of software development projects. The application for which

Software	Organization
Each software unit should be small so that it can be easily understood.	Each software team should be small so that it can be effectively controlled.
Each software unit should be only loosely coupled to other software units.	Each software team should be assigned units of work which minimise unnecessary communication among software teams.
Each software unit should be highly cohesive (perform one function).	Each software team should be assigned work units that are highly cohesive.
The scope of effect of a software unit should be a subset of the scope of control.	Teams should be grouped together (reporting to one manager) in such a way that the decisions made within the managerial group have minimal effect on the work of other managerial groups.
As software is decomposed into a hierarchy of units, higher level units perform decision-making and lower level units do the actual work.	In an organizational structure the managerial hierarchy takes the decisions (longer range and more abstract decisions at higher levels of management) and the lower organizational levels perform the actual production work.
'Pathological' connections (communication links not following the hierarchical software structure) should be avoided, or at least fully documented.	Organizations should not have to rely on pathological connections (such as dependance on arbitrary communictions between programming teams to find out the consequences of design decisions).

Fig. 7.3. Common rules for structuring software and organizations.

the software is being developed, the degree of complexity and difficulty, the skills and experience of the development personnel and the existing structure and 'culture' of the development organization are all major factors in deciding what level and detail of management are both necessary and possible.

Moreover, as is discussed in Chapter 8, these decisions involve the customer (procurer, user or both) and need to be taken as part of accepting contractural (or even implicit) obligations of budget and timescale. The fate of many large software projects has been determined, even before technical development began, because management levels have been set at what was possible rather than what was necessary, or because what was necessary had been grossly underestimated. Cost and time overruns are frequently a reflection of the lack of the necessary management resources to avert technical disasters caused by lack of early detection and control of difficulties. Of course, the consequences of the tar-pit described by Brooks in *The Mythical Man-Month* is that the technical staff bear the burden of trying very hard to do the impossible, and the opprobrium of failure.

On the other hand, too much management control with many levels of bureaucracy will create unnecessary costs and swamp what might have been a comparatively simple project with overhead that cannot make timely decisions.

The ability to determine the optimum level of management and technical control for a project is always facilitated by experience of similar previous projects. Unfortunately, the nature of software is such that, even with similar

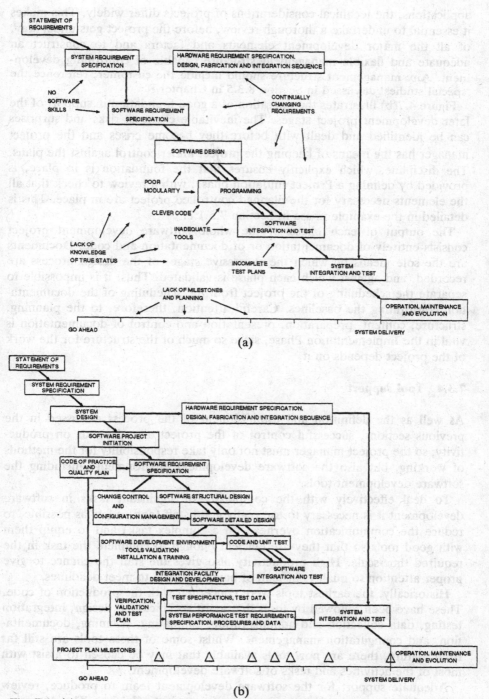

Fig. 7.4. (a) Sources of trouble in software development. (b) Building a foundation in the software project initiation phase.

applications, the technical considerations of projects differ widely. This makes it essential to undertake a thorough review, before the project gets under way, of all the major development elements and factors and to construct an adequate and flexible management structure capable of controlling development. Any management structure should include the customer; reference the 'special studies' discussed in Section 8.3.5 in Chapter 8.

Figure 4.7(b) illustrates the operation of a good foundation in support of the later development project stages. The inevitable changes, risks and surprises can be identified and dealt with before they become crises and the project manager has the means of keeping the project under control against the plans. The discipline, which explicitly ensures that the foundation is in place, is provided by defining a Project Initiation phase, with a review to check that all the elements necessary for the planned controlled project are in place. This is detailed in the example phase in Section 7.5.1.2.

The output of each phase of the whole software development project consists entirely of documentation or of documentation and code. Documents are the sole means by which the successive stages of the design process are recorded, and against which each phase is validated. Thus, it is impossible to separate the scheduling of the project from the scheduling of the documentation constituting the baselines. Careful attention, therefore, to the planning, structure, content, preparation, presentation and control of documentation is vital in the Implementation Phase, since so much of the structure for the work of the project depends on it.

7.3.4 Tool support

As well as the definition and establishment of the process discussed in the previous sections, successful control of the project also depends on productivity, so the project manager must not only take responsibility for the methods of working, but also the software development environment—including the software development tools.

To deal effectively with the complexity of significant tasks in software development it is necessary to use really good staff (and as few as possible, to reduce the communication overhead on a complex task) and to equip them with good tools so that they are efficient enough to complete the task in the required time-scale. High productivity also gives the staff the chance to give proper attention to quality, instead of having to rush to meet deadlines.

Historically, the earliest tools were concerned with the production of code. These have been followed by tools that assist specification, design, integration testing, data collection and administration, estimating, planning, documentation, and configuration management. Whilst some of these tools are still far from mature, there are now tools available that may be chosen to assist with most of the activities and tasks of software development.

Adequate support for the software development team to produce, review and update documents is very important for project efficiency. The documentation development tools should cover word-processing, editing, formatting and printing (including diagrams), which not only work together but are integrated with the configuration management tool(s) (for instance to identify automatically any changed sections in reissued documents). Since so much of software development is, in fact, the production of documents, it is very easy to underestimate how much CPU power and disk file space is required compared with that to support coding and testing of the software itself.

However, the first step is not to select tools, but to determine the appropriate techniques and methods to be used in the process and then to select the appropriate tools to support the methods (though one criterion for choosing a method might be availability of tool support). The methods must be matched to the existing culture, the characteristics of the development, the imposed schedules, and other operational considerations. Once selected, the methods must be properly introduced, supported with training and monitored to ensure that they are really used and that the intended benefits are obtained.

If the software development tools and development environment are not already in use, they will have to be selected and established specifically for the project. Although the technical controller, quality manager and configuration manager will certainly be involved in the decisions, the project manager must ensure (or confirm) the suitability of the development facilities.

When the methods have been chosen, then the right tools not only increase efficiency but also have the further significant advantage of automatically defining part of the method of working, thus simplifying the definition of the process and ensuring conformance. Tools can encapsulate procedures and include tests against standards.

Even with a complete and appropriate set of tools, more is required for an effective software development environment. The tools need to be integrated so that they work together and perform further operations on transferred and shared data, based on an object management system (OMS). They also need a common human communication interface so that staff are comfortable that they are working in a coherent environment. This integration into a unified toolset is a primary function of an Integrated Project Support Environment, referred to as an IPSE.

A fully effective IPSE also supports the project process, and is itself a tool to support the method of working for the whole project. Although IPSE support for the process is thus a tool of project management, there will also be other project management tools specifically for the tasks of estimating, planning, work assignment, progress monitoring, analysis and reporting. These functions are supported by the explicit integration of project management tools into the IPSE, often referred to as the project manager's workbench (akin to the configuration manager's workbench, programmer's workbench, etc.).

Some IPSEs define a particular process, which makes them suitable candidates for use on a project for which their in-built process is applicable and sufficient. But note the expressed danger of choosing the IPSE first and then having to force the process and methods of working to conform.

More comprehensive IPSEs provide facilities for tailoring to any required process. This also includes the ability to extend and modify the defined project process as the development progresses and the incorporation of existing or separately supplied third-party tools, so that different integrated toolsets can be provided, as required, for different projects supported in the same IPSE.

An IPSE should assist the project manager with the following:

- determination of the process suitable for the project;
- determination of the organization, methods and tools required;
- instantiation of the process, efficiently and completely, by defining it in the IPSE;
- integration of all the chosen tools into a unified toolset;
- support for inter-staff communication with IPSE facilities;
- support for the process in operation, by the combination of the tools and IPSE itself;
- automated data collection, which provides the feedback for project control.

Whilst the above functions are only partly achieved in currently available IPSEs, their fuller realization is the aim of continuing IPSE development. Chapter 12 deals with software development environments and IPSEs.

7.3.5　Contractural basis for the project

There is a three-way relationship between the project manager, the customer and the quality manager:

- The customer's perspective is dealt with in Chapter 8, which covers statement of requirements, contracting for a project, role during the project and how to get value from the product after the project is completed. This results in three contractual documents:
  —statement of requirements;
  —quality plan for the process to assure the product of the required quality;
  —project contract for deliverables with costs and dates.
- The Quality Plan (discussed in Section 8.3.7, Chapter 8) also defines the activities which determine the correctness of operation of the intended process, measurement of the achieved quality against quality targets, and quality reporting mechanisms, all of which are responsibilities of the quality manager.
- It is the responsibility of the project manager to produce the product with the required quality as well as on time and to budget. To support this responsibility (and to make sure that quality reporting is as strongly established as progress reporting) the project manager and quality manager jointly use the Quality Plan as agreed with the customer. Hence the three-way relationship, which is illustrated in Fig. 7.5.

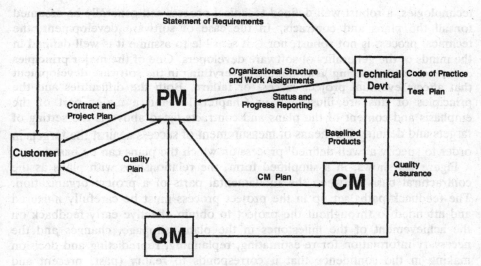

Fig. 7.5. Contractual foundation for a project.

For large bespoke software systems, this is a critical issue. For smaller projects, the issue may be less critical but is still an important aspect of concentrating the direction of the project by prior emphasis on the definition of the success criteria for the project.

An adequately founded project requires all the following plans and contracts:

- A STATEMENT OF REQUIREMENTS defining the required product. This leads to the User Manual and the REQUIREMENT SPECIFICATION.
- A CODE OF PRACTICE demonstrating ability to produce the product with technical development techniques, tools and trained skilled staff.
- A QUALITY PLAN defining the means of determining the success of the process in operation.
- A TEST PLAN defining verification, validation and testing throughout the project to determine the correctness of what is being produced.
- A CONFIGURATION MANAGEMENT PLAN defining product possession.
- A PROJECT PLAN defining the use of resources against task-estimates for the project.
- An ORGANIZATIONAL STRUCTURE defining authorities and responsibilities for applying staff resources to the development.
- A PROJECT CONTRACT (with the customer, marketing or internally with the business) defining the business success criteria.

In principle, the above contractual basis is no different than that for a project involving any other technology. The difference is that for most engineering technologies, a robust well-defined technical process can generally be assumed for all the plans and contracts. In the case of software development, the technical process is not robust, nor is it sensible to assume it is well-defined in the minds of the generality of software developers. One of the major principles of 'software engineering' is to quantify everything in the software development that affects eventual project success or failure. Both the difficulties and the principles of this are illustrated in Chapter 10, and a major part of the emphasis and content of the plans and contracts listed above is the setting of targets and defining the means of measurement of success against the targets in order to specify a 'well-defined' process on which the plans can be based.

Figure 7.5 shows, in a simplified form, the relationships with plans as the contractural basis between the fundamental parts of a project organization. The feedback paths set up in the project process must be carefully nurtured and attended to throughout the project to obtain effective early feedback on the achievement of the milestones in the plans, slippage, changes and the necessary information for re-estimating, replanning, repredicting and decision making in the confidence that it corresponds to reality (past, present and future). Feedback provides knowledge; knowledge is power—or at least the basis for making rational and effective decisions to continually re-orient the project to its end goals.

7.4 Managing the Software Development Process

Imposing a structure onto the process of a large development project reduces the complexity of the whole task by refining it to a number of tasks of reduced complexity. If this is carefully and properly done, following the principles discussed in Appendix B, then the ability of the project manager to control the project to successful completion can be enhanced without loss of the essential nature of the development.

The difference between a good structure and a poor structure for a given project is that the good structure will be able to work effectively at lower levels of delegation without everybody having to attend communication meetings to review each other's work in order to make progress. An attempt to run a badly structured project process at too low a level of detail results in slower progress because of trying to manage all the communications (meetings and paper-work), or overstaffing (which makes the problem worse) or reliance on pathological connections between groups.

For a well-structured process, the parts are chosen so that the communication paths between the parts are minimized and are therefore amenable to the organizational authorities and responsibilities. This is quite feasible at the higher levels of the structure but becomes increasingly difficult as the structure is defined at lower and lower levels. However, well thought-out the structure and the organization may be, there are levels below which the communication required by explicit structuring starts making the work more complex.

Thus, despite the advantages of carefully structuring the process and establishing a corresponding organization, there is a limit to how far the overall complexity can be reduced. There will still be tasks that are relatively large and complex within the structure. If an attempt is made to ignore this and reduce all the work to straightforward small tasks then the technical staff will feel that the business is trying to reduce them to mere automata without the opportunity to creatively apply their skills to the undoubted technical problems of design and implementation.

7.4.1 Life-cycle phases

In order to structure the software development project it is necessary to define the development process by adopting some model as an expansion of the Technical Development function shown in Fig. 7.1. A model which defines phases in the development of a software product is referred to in software engineering as a 'Life-Cycle Model'. The basic principles of Life-Cycle Models can be interpreted in many ways to define different sets of phases, and Appendix B discusses the basic principles and goes into more detail on the relationship between various models of the software development process.

Descriptions of management methods for software projects are best related to these phases. The process chosen by the project manager will determine the actual number and type of phases for any particular project, depending on the size and complexity of the project and the appropriate methodology.

For the purposes of management, the crucial characteristic of a phase is that it has a clearly defined beginning and end as points in time. Based on this principle, we will refer to an example of a process with the following, so-called 'classical', life-cycle phases:

- Feasibility Study
- Project Initiation
- Requirement Specification
- Structural Design
- Detailed Design
- Coding
- Unit Test
- Integration
- Integration Test
- Acceptance Test
- Operational Test
- Project Completion
- Operation (In-Service and Maintenance)
- Product Phaseout (Replacement or Disposal)

where the phases follow in sequence, except Project Completion which occurs during Operation.

Not all projects will have all of these phases. Small and simple projects may merge phases. Large and complex projects may need to have some of the phases divided. Where the software development is part of a system development, the software phases will generally be interleaved with the system phases for hardware design and combined integration.

For many larger innovative projects, Feasibility is a project in its own right, producing requirements, reports of options and even prototype products which will be precursors for the main development project. Often, and particularly when the designers of the software have experience of similar products, Feasibility will be a very minor activity and will merge into Project Initiation.

A development process with a completely pre-determined set of phases is only appropriate for some projects. Where the project is dealing with unknown technology, an uncertain statement of requirements or an unprecedented situation in any significant way, then it is much more suitable to use a process where either the phases are iterated around a cycle based on prototyping, or evaluation of evolving research. An alternative approach which is more suitable for some products is to separate the required functionality into a series of increments, with the well-understood functionality implemented in the first increment and an (initially) unknown series of further increments to tackle further extensions of functionality which are initially less well defined. These various process models are covered in Appendix B, and Section 7.6 deals with the question of choice of process for any particular project.

For all of these cases, the following principles still apply. Each development phase is defined in terms of its outputs, or products. The products of the phases represent the points along the development path where there is a clear change in emphasis, where one definition of the emerging product is established, reviewed and used as the basis for the next derived definition. As such, they are the natural milestones of the development progression and offer objective visibility of that progression.

7.4.2 Baselines

To use this visibility for effective management control, a software development process based on the Life-Cycle Model uses the concept of baselines. A 'baseline' established at any stage in the development process is a set of information which defines the product at that stage.

The completion of each phase is determined by the satisfactory review of the defined products of that phase and the products placed under Configuration Management. These products then form the baseline for the work in the next phase. The products of the next phase are measured and verified against previous baselines before themselves forming a new baseline. In this way confidence in project progress is progressively built on successive baselines.

It should be noted that the phase boundaries represent discontinuities in the product development. Representations differ between phases. For example a specification is very different from a design in terms of the viewpoint (what the system does versus how it does it) and hence the semantics and notation of the documentation. Often, in a large project, the staff involved in different phases are different. Discontinuities are weak points in any process, so although phases provide the basis for managerial control points, extra care must be taken to avoid misunderstandings and undetected ambiguities. This is one area where technical control (as discussed in Section 7.2.4) is essential. It is also the reason for specific data collection discussed in Chapter 8 (Section 8.7).

A common representation of the phases of software development is the V-diagram—an example of which is shown in Fig. 7.6. In this diagram the rectangular boxes represent the phases and the oval boxes represent the baselined phase products. The form of the diagram has the advantage of showing the symmetry between the successive decomposition of the design and the building of the product by successive stages of integration and test. Figure

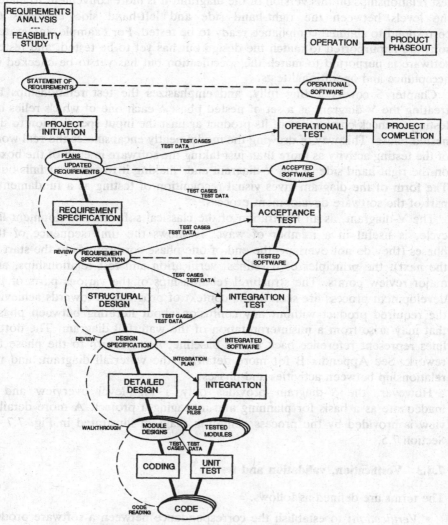

Fig. 7.6. The software development life cycle.

7.6 also shows the verification relationships, as dotted lines. The product of each specification and design phase is verified against the previous baseline. The product of each integration phase is tested with test cases and test data derived from the corresponding design or specification baseline on the left-hand side of the diagram.

The diagram is similar to that shown in *The STARTS Guide* (National Computing Centre, 1987), and illustrates the same principles, though with more detail. The simplified diagram in *The STARTS Guide* matches the levels between the right-hand side and left-hand side elements to correspond to tested compliance (so, for example, integrated tested software has been tested as fully meeting the intentions of the design). With the extra detail showing the test relationships on this version of the diagram, it is more convenient to match the levels between the right-hand side and left-hand side elements to correspond to claimed compliance ready to be tested. For example, integrated software is purported to match the design but has yet to be tested, and tested software is purported to match the specification but has yet to be checked in acceptance and operational tests.

Chapter 5 covers testing fully, and emphasizes the test relationships by treating the V-diagram as a set of nested phases, each one of which relies on testing to check compliance of its product against the input specification to the nested phase. This way of drawing the model neatly encapsulates the real work of the testing activity as more than just taking the software in each of the boxes on the right-hand side of the V-diagram and 'shaking it to see what falls out'. The form of the diagram gives visual recognition of testing as a fundamental part of the software development process.

The V-diagram, as an illustration of the classical software development life cycle, is useful in a number of ways. It shows the time sequence of the phases (they do not overlap—the end of one phase corresponds to the start of the next), the principles of baselines, verification and test relationships, and major review points. The structural relationships of the various parts of the development process are seen in the context of progression towards achieving the required product without any confusion about iterating between phases that may arise from a misinterpretation of the waterfall diagram. The dotted lines represent reference back to the baseline, *not a* return to the phase for rework. See Appendix B for more detail on the waterfall diagram, and the relationship between activities and phases.

However, the V-diagram provides only a high-level overview and is inadequate as a basis for planning and managing a project. A more detailed view is provided by the process definition diagram illustrated in Fig. 7.7, in Section 7.5.

7.4.3 Verification, validation and test

The terms are defined as follows.

- *Verification*: to establish the correspondence between a software product (documentation or code) and its specification—'Are we building the

product right?' The goals of verification are:
—confirming the transformation from the previous phase;
—assuring the consistency of the current representation;
—ensuring that the current representation is a suitable basis for future phases.
- *Validation*: to establish the fitness of a software product for its operational mission—'Are we building the right product?'
- *Testing*: running the code to produce test results. Test planning starts from the specifications and designs (on the left-hand side of the V-diagram) to produce test cases and test data ready for the tests on the right-hand side of the V-diagram.

VV&T activities cover the tasks of checking the correctness of the products of each phase (baselines) and are performed by the software development staff. As will already be apparent from the V-diagram, most of the work goes into verification and testing. It requires a specific determination to actually do validation, usually at the time of the phase reviews as part of the risk analysis (see Section 7.6).

VV&T should be carried out by staff within the project organization but, as far as possible, not by the originators of the work. Verification may be the responsibility of a series of different teams as the project proceeds through the life-cycle phases. For testing, it is common practice to establish a separate test team with professional emphasis on the technical skills of testing and familiarity with the test tools.

7.4.4 Reviews

Formal reviews at baseline stages of development are the most powerful determinant of the successful control of progress of a project. The review team should include not only development personnel but also experts from other projects and disciplines and, whenever possible, customer and user personnel.

The involvement of the user cannot be over-emphasized. One of the most frequent causes of unreliability or failure to achieve the required performance of a product is associated with the requirements and the user's expectations of their implementation in the final product. Getting the requirements right, (reference Chapter 8, Section 8.3.2), is arguably both the most essential and most difficult activity in a software project. Close involvement of the customer/user throughout the development process, as discussed in Section 8.4 of Chapter 8, is essential, but nowhere is it more effective than at project reviews.

It can be seen from Fig. 7.6 that verification takes the form of reviews when what is being reviewed refers to the project as a whole. This applies to the earlier phases on the left-hand side of the V-diagram, when prototypes, draft user manuals and test cases are very valuable in implementing otherwise theoretical specifications.

Reviews are also used at the end of the phases on the right-hand side of the

V-diagram, but here they are not so much the vehicle for discovering problems as reviews of the status of problems shown up in the testing, which is the primary basis for checking the correctness of the products of the phases.

In the lower part of the V-diagram, where the verification is on parts of the product (modules or groups of modules) then walkthroughs, code readings and unit test inspections are much more appropriate, involving only the few staff immediately involved in a small, efficient meeting.

The various forms of reviews, including walkthroughs and code readings, have been clearly demonstrated to be very effective; see Fagan (1976), Weinberg and Freedman (1984) and Britcher (1988). Walkthroughs are not just small reviews, they have a quite different format, and staff should be explicitly trained in how to run them and their appropriateness in finding different sorts of errors.

7.4.5 Practical application of the Life-Cycle Model

The concept of distinct phases of software development, representing the achievement of pre-defined states during the development of the product, can be regarded as a device, used by project management, to deal with complexity and to improve visibility.

The chosen phase definitions are the basis for real control of software development, but that control has to be explicitly planned and based on the methods of working used and applied by development staff. It does not happen naturally; project management has to *make* its own version of the Life-Cycle Model realistic.

It might be assumed, simplistically, that all the work on an activity is completed in the phase of the same name (specification in the specification phase, design in the design phase, etc.) and that the phase cannot be considered complete, and the next phase started, before all the work and documentation of that phase has been completed to specified standards and approved at a review. Although the intended rigour of such an approach might be commendable, it is quite unrealistic to interpret the life-cycle model in such a simplistic way.

In a real software project:

- Exploratory work on the primary activity associated with a subsequent phase is usually required before the current phase can be completed (for example, design investigation is almost invariably required before it can be stated that a user requirement can be met).
- Problems encountered in a later phase may involve reworking the products of earlier phases—failure to recognize this leads to earlier documentation becoming inaccurate and misleading.
- The user's perceived requirement may not remain constant during a protracted software development process, and it may be necessary to consider changed requirements and consequent design changes during later phases.

In practice, particularly on large-scale projects, the precise breakpoints between phases are not easy to define and depend, to some extent, on management decision. Milestones are rarely achieved completely. Because completely rigid phase control is impractical, status and risk analysis at milestones is particularly important. This can only be obtained from conscientious emphasis on thorough technical and management reviews.

The above difficulties do not lead to the conclusion that the life-cycle phases are impractical. Having escaped the simplistic interpretation, the Life-Cycle Model does represent a basic recognition of what is actually involved in the technical work of software development. The definitions and concepts in the model represent the best current understanding of software development practice, gained from experience in applying software engineering to a wide range of development projects. Moreover, the software Life-Cycle Model is reasonably matched to projects where integration of software and hardware is necessary within a system—in other words, it brings software to the same level of defined and manageable process as can be relied on in other engineering disciplines.

7.5 The Process Definition Diagram

The software development process, defined according to the principles given in the previous sections, is the basis for a number of diagrams and documents for the project, including the organizational structure diagram, work breakdown structure diagram, time-based PERT and Gantt charts in the project plan, Code of Practice (Standards and Procedures) and task definitions. However, none of these give an easily understood, integrated overview of the actual project process on which they rely. A diagram for the specific purpose of displaying the defined process should be drawn as follows:

- The activities of software development are resolved into tasks—the conclusion of the task is defined by a task-product which passes the criterion of a previously defined standard.
- The organizational responsibilities are shown for each task-product.
- The interaction of the tasks, each task depending on products from preceding tasks, is defined by procedures.
- The whole project process (either predetermined to completion of the project using a set of phases such as those in the classical life-cycle, or steadily evolving as phases chosen to manage risk as discussed in Appendix B and Section 7.6) is defined by grouping the task-products and small processes to correspond to the phases by drawing a diagram showing transition from state to state through the duration of the project, where each state corresponds to the achievement of the end of a phase.

Thus the Process Definition Diagram takes the form of a state-transition diagram linking the different aspects of the process by explicitly showing the top level relationship between:

- *all* activities involved in the software development process;
- top level of the work breakdown structure;
- task-products (to be baselined);
- standards and procedures;
- organizational responsibilities;
- phases of the process for the project.

Such a diagram, by integrating the definition of the process for a specific project, facilitates the following:

- Initial description, argument, resolution and confirmation of completeness of the planned process, between the project manager, senior management, quality assurance, senior technical staff on the project and the customer.
- Promulgation of the project process, graphically, for all concerned in and with the project, in a way that can be pinned on office walls and readily updated to keep visible the interaction of responsibilities within the process. Its early creation underlines the need to define the process and ensures that everybody understands it.
- The choice of metrics (out of all possible metrics discussed in Chapter 10) which are definable as values of attributes of the task-products on the diagram. The values can be set as targets, estimated as the tasks progress and measured as achievements. This gives the data to be collected and analysed which is part of defining the project process. It must, for a successful product, address the measurement of quality and reliability as well as productivity (project progress against milestones).
- Derivation of the quality plan for the project—which includes definition and plans for monitoring the quality and reliability of the process as part of assuring the quality and reliability of the product.

The diagram will, inevitably, be different for every project (although in a good organization it will be derivable from existing practice and previous projects) and will need to be updated as the understanding and application of the process evolves. Figure 7.7 shows a suitable form of the Process Definition Diagram for the worked example described in Section 7.5.1. The diagram is intended to illustrate the sort of visible, straightforward definition of the process that should be the basis for every project. It must not be confused with the PERT diagram, which may be used as a planning tool. That is concerned with progress on planned interrelated activities, and whilst it may cover all task interrelationships (all too often to a level of detail where such interrelations are fictional), it will hardly be involved with invocations of standards and procedures, and is not drawn with the primary aim of illustrating the process and organizational inter-responsibilities.

The form of the diagram emphasizes an object-oriented approach—each rectangle is an object to be reviewed, with all the overtones implied in

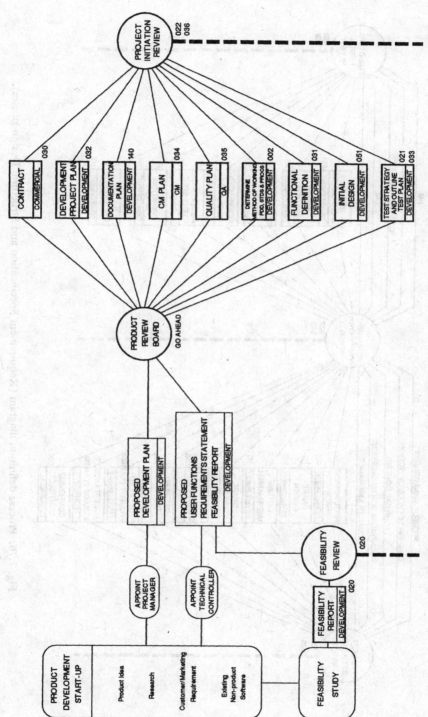

Fig. 7.7a. Process definition diagram (Feasibility Study and Project Initiation phases).

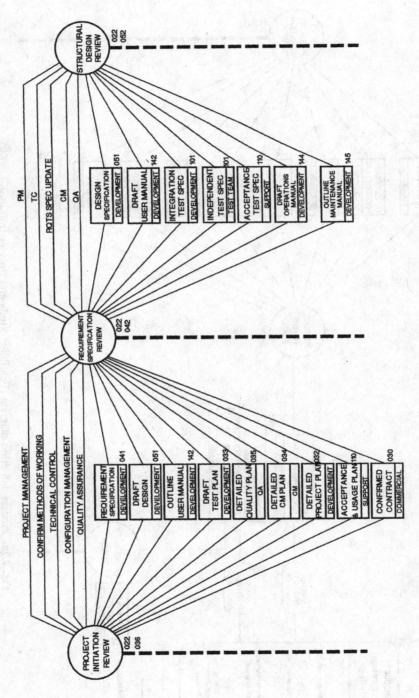

Fig. 7.7b. Process definition diagram (Requirement Specification and Structural Design phases).

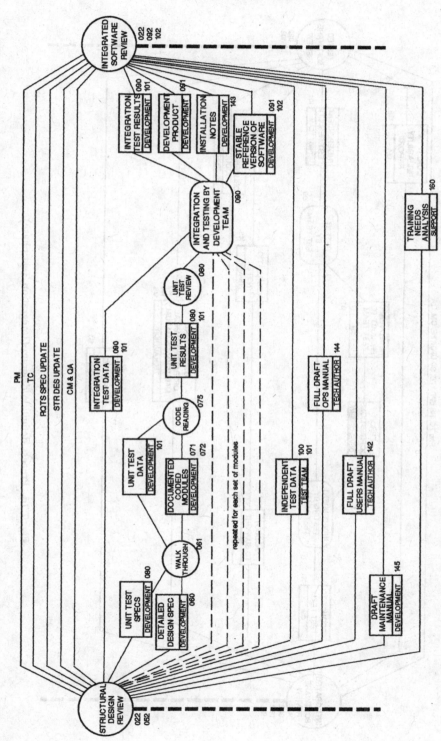

Fig. 7.7c. Process definition diagram (Programming and Integration phases).

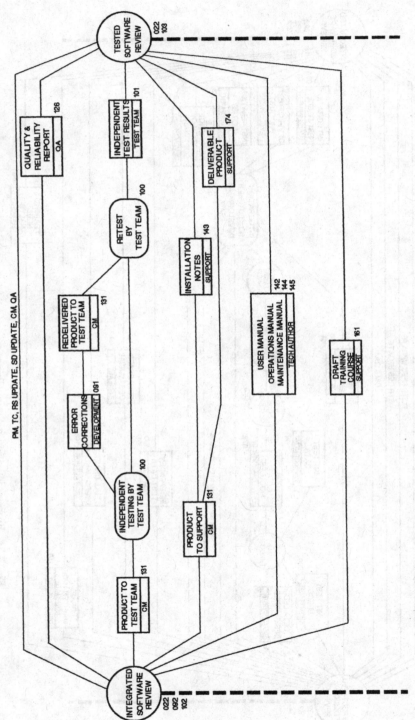

Fig. 7.7d. Process definition diagram (Integration Test phase).

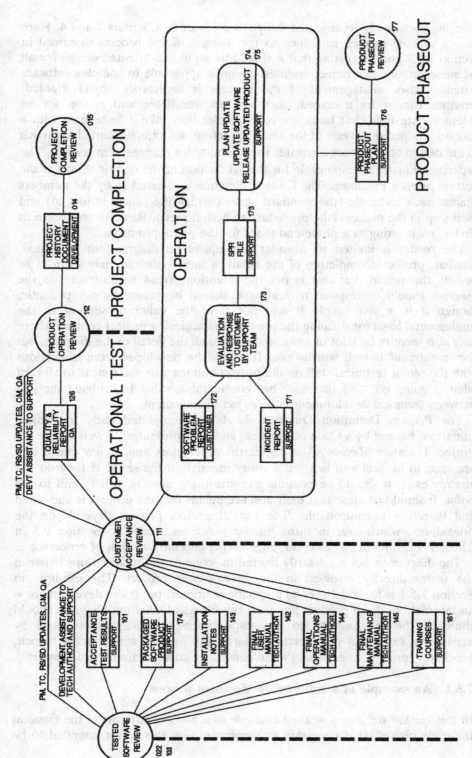

Fig. 7.7e. Process definition diagram (Product Acceptance and Operational phases).

referring back to object-oriented design of software in Chapters 2 and 4. Here we are making explicit reference to the 'design' of the process discussed in Section 7.3.2 and suggesting that it should be an object-oriented design for all the same reasons that object-oriented design is applicable to complex software systems. Also, management of the process is *necessarily* object-oriented: activities cannot be managed, they are uncontrollable and go on for an indeterminate time, but tasks are controllable; they take a finite time with a defined product at the end of the task. Therefore, an object-oriented approach to the design of the process ensures its suitability for management control. The department or team responsible for the production of the item is shown at the bottom of each rectangle. The Code of Practice is referred to by the numbers against each rectangle (the standard against which the object is judged) and each step in the process (the procedure to be followed). Reviews are shown as circles, each acting as a phase-end focus for the phase-products.

The reader is invited to consider the equivalent diagram for an actual, familiar, project. Completion of the detail of such a diagram may seem to be heavily theoretical, but that is not the intention. What is illustrated on the diagram should correspond to reality; it should be pragmatic not pedantic, though if it is too simple it will not have the value of serving as the fundamental basis for defining the process and achieving project control. There may also seem to be a lot of work to complete all the detail of the diagram, but the investment is well worthwhile. It should be developed from discussions with the senior technical staff on the project and used to make clear to all staff what is going on, and therefore has considerable value in bridging the gap between technical development and project management.

The Process Definition Diagram should be completed early in Project Initiation, backed by a Code of Practice, and fully promulgated well before the Project Initiation Review. The standards, procedures and review check lists are seen to be real and not just a dusty manual on the shelf. If they do not already exist, it should be possible to write them quickly, briefly and to the point. It should be clear that their absence means that the process is undefined and therefore uncontrollable. The overall project process depends on the procedures, which are, in turn, smaller processes. Refer to Section 9.5 in Chapter 9 for detail on selection, engineering and introduction of processes.

The diagram is not necessarily limited in scope to the relationships between the teams directly involved in the development project. The example in Section 7.5.1 is for a delivery to a specific customer, but if the development is an internal one for a product line then the Process Definition Diagram should show all the relationships to the responsibilities and items produced by marketing, sales and commercial departments dealing with market launch, brochures, pricing, sales strategy and general customer training and support.

7.5.1 An example of a software development process

In this section we give a worked example of a process in terms of the classical life-cycle phases. It is necessary to emphasize that this is not intended to be seen as the 'correct' set of phases—there is no such thing. As already stated, there are many alternative ways of constructing the alternative processes suitable for particular projects (further discussed in Appendix B and Section 7.6). It is not possible in the scope of this chapter to work out all the principles for even a selection of the alternative processes, and we have chosen the classical life-cycle phases as providing the most general reference point from which the reader can translate into the chosen process for a specific project. Each project must ensure that it has its own suitable process—it is not possible to pick a standard process off the shelf and use it without at least some tailoring to local circumstances.

The example takes the form of a list of the phases, each consisting of:

- a brief discussion of key aspects of the activities in the phase; for more information on the activities and the tasks refer to Appendix B (Section B.4 and Fig. B.9).
- the phase products;
- the named review to complete the phase;

together with the Process Definition Diagram in Fig. 7.7 and the corresponding list of standards and procedures in a suitable Code of Practice in Fig. 7.8.

7.5.1.1 *Feasibility study*

The first step in tackling a problematical software development is usually to carry out a feasibility study. The cost and duration of such a study will depend upon the size and complexity of the proposed development. The depth to which it goes in carrying out experimental work depends on what is needed to identify technical problems and to validate design assumptions, so that there is a basis for technical control in the development project. It may even be necessary to depend on a research contract. It is usually necessary to involve the customer/user to get the requirements right. This includes understanding the needs and exploring the limits of what it is feasible to implement within the constraints of budget and design. The outcome of the feasibility study is not only whether the proposed development is feasible, but also an assessment of capability to do the job and a much better idea of the size of the job for predictions and initial estimates on which plans for the project can be based.

FEASIBILITY STUDY PRODUCT

- Feasibility report

The Feasibility Review terminates the feasibility study, which should be treated as a project in its own right, terminated by the production and review of the report. It may be the necessary precursor to a subsequent development project, but it is not the first phase of, or an adequate foundation for, the development project—which must set up its own foundation in the project initiation phase.

001	Index	
002	Software Development Process	
003	Glossary of Terms and Abbreviations	
Project Management		
010	Project Planning and Work Definition	
011	Estimating and Metrics	
012	Progress Monitoring/Reporting Procedure	
013	Change Control Procedure	
014	Project History Document	
015	Project Completion Review	
Technical Control		
020	Feasibility Report and Review	
021	Verification and Validation Strategy	
022	Procedure for Development Reviews	
Project Initiation		
030	Contract Standard	
031	Functional Definition Standard	
032	Project Plan Standard	
033	Test Plan Standard	
034	CM Plan Standard	
035	Quality Plan Standard	
036	Project Initiation Review	
Requirement Specification		
040	Capture of Requirements	
041	Requirement Specification Standard	
042	Requirement Specification Review	
Structural Design		
050	Design Techniques	
051	Design Specification Standard	
052	Structural Design Review	
Detailed Design		
060	Detailed Design Specification Standard	
061	Design Walkthroughs	
Coding		
070	Structured Programming	
071	Module Documentation Standard	
072	General Coding Standard	
073	C Coding and Layout Standard	
074	Ada Coding and Layout Standard	
075	Code Reading and Source Code Reviews	
Unit Test		
080	Unit Testing and Unit Test Review	
Integration		
090	Top-down Integration and Testing	
091	Development Product Standard	
092	Integrated Software Review	

Product Test
- 100 Independant Testing
- 101 Standard for Test Specs, Data and Results
- 102 Acceptance of Product from Development
- 103 Tested Software Review

Customer Acceptance
- 110 Customer Acceptance Plan Standard
- 111 Customer Acceptance Review
- 112 Product Operation Review

Quality Assurance
- 120 QA in Software Development
- 121 Creating Standards and Procedures
- 122 Project Specific Standards and Procedures
- 123 Concessions Procedure
- 124 Error Data Recording and Analysis
- 125 Quality Audit Procedure
- 126 Quality and Reliability Reports

Configuration Management
- 130 CM during Software Development
- 131 Product Control(Product Library Operation)
- 132 Documentation Control

Documentation
- 140 Documentation System
- 141 Documentation Standard
- 142 Standard for User Manuals
- 143 Standard for Installation Notes
- 144 Standard for Operations Manuals
- 145 Standard for Maintenance Manuals
- 146 Documentation Production
- 147 Documentation Review Procedure

Development Environment
- 150 Environment Facilities and Support
- 151 Software Tool Update Procedure
- 152 Extraction of Files from Archive

Training
- 160 Training Course Development Procedure
- 161 Training Course Standards

Product Support
- 170 Product Support Services
- 171 Customer Incident Handling
- 172 Software Problem Reporting Procedure
- 173 SPR Handling Procedure
- 174 Deliverable Product Standard
- 175 External Product Release Procedure
- 176 Product Phaseout Plan Standard
- 177 Product Phaseout Review

Fig. 7.8. An example of the standards and procedures covered in a software development code of practice.

7.5.1.2 *Projection initiation*

There are many ways of embarking on a project, and entry into the Initiation Phase is often very ill defined—what is important is that the appointed project manager ensures that the *end* of this phase is well defined, with a thorough review of the foundation for control of the project in subsequent phases. As well as setting in place the basis of project methods of working (process definition diagram, standards and procedures, technical methods and tools) and the establishment of project control operation (work assignment, progress monitoring, metrics collection and analysis (quality monitoring), reporting and budget accountancy), the project manager must ensure that external aspects are agreed; contractural issues and customer/user involvement during development, confirmation of requirements, technical control, the freedom to tackle technical risks by prototyping and incremental development, change control and commitments in the plans to deliveries and acceptance tests.

PROJECT INITIATION PHASE PRODUCTS

- Functional definition (statement of software requirements, including definition of the user manual, backed by an initial design study)
- Contract (formal or informal)
- Quality plan (approved strategy and resources for achieving the required quality)
- Documentation plan
- Configuration management plan
- Initial design (derived from the approved, validated system architecture, with basic hardware–software allocations and concept of operation including boundaries between the users and the system, with definition of the technical strategy for implementation)
- Test strategy and outline test plan
- Method of working on the project (approved process definition diagram showing how the project organization will develop the defined product together with specification of all the standards and procedures to be used, with particular emphasis on project control mechanisms)
- Project plan (approved top-level plan based on adequate estimates, milestones related to the process definition diagram and assignment of resources; showing organizational responsibilities and schedules for major elements of the work breakdown structure)

The Project Initiation Review covers the above items (to project standards and following the project procedure) and also verifies that the method of working on the project is fully in operation. A satisfactory answer to the question 'Do we have the project under control?' determines the completion of the phase and transition to the following development phases.

7.5.1.3 *Requirement specification*

This phase not only deals with fully capturing the requirements to produce a 'complete' specification, but also involves a major emphasis on establishing the technical control, test strategy, test plans and tool support/development environment for subsequent phases. Increased precision in the detail of the specification and design enables estimates and plans to be refined, risks to be assessed (and the appropriate techniques of prototyping, customer involvement, simulation and incremental development invoked to deal with them). The change control procedures must be established and put into operation during this phase in order to control the cost of changes in subsequent phases.

REQUIREMENT SPECIFICATION PHASE PRODUCTS

- Requirement specification (approved, validated functional, performance, quality and interface specifications; verified for completeness, consistency, testability and feasibility and to a level of detail to deal with risk)
- Outline user manual
- Draft design specification (including the basic software architecture)
- Draft test plan (overall plans for verification and validation, excluding detailed test plans)
- Detailed quality plan (including metrics to be used, data collection and analysis)
- Detailed configuration management plan
- Detailed project plan (detailed development milestones, criteria, resource budgets, organization, responsibilities, work breakdown structure tasks, techniques, schedules, deliverables and plans for risk management)
- Detailed plan for acceptance and usage (acceptance criteria, training, conversion, installation, operations and support related to development deliverables and schedules as set out in the project plan)
- Confirmed contract

The Requirement Specification Review covers the above items and also verifies that product control (as defined in the quality, configuration management and test plans) is fully in operation. A satisfactory answer to the question 'Do we have the technical development under control?' determines completion of the phase. The updated plans require contractural confirmation with the customer.

7.5.1.4 *Structural design*

The design team concentrates on development of a good design to meet the requirements of functionality and performance. Transformation of the design to lower levels of detail and partitioning of the design into component specifications is the basis for definition of interfaces between components and subsequent assignment to a number of teams for implementation.

STRUCTURAL DESIGN PHASE PRODUCTS

- Design specification (verified for completeness, consistency, feasibility and traceability to requirements and with all high-risk technical issues identified and resolved; covering program component hierarchy, control

structures and data interfaces through to unit level, physical and logical data structure through to field level, and data-processing resource budgets (timing, storage and accuracy))
- Preliminary test specifications for integration testing, independent testing and acceptance testing
- Draft user manual
- Draft operations manual
- Outline maintenance manual

The Structural Design Review on the above items poses the question 'Is it now simply a matter of implementation?'. Of all the software design reviews, this review is the most crucial to the ultimate success of the project. Because the structural design phase is the last opportunity to make changes and correct errors without a significant cost impact, the complete design should be carefully verified and validated before the project moves into the implementation phases (detailed design, coding and unit test).

7.5.1.5 *Detailed design*

This phase is characterized by multiple teams working on the parts of the designed software at the detailed level (down to algorithmic level). Technical control includes a central design authority to preserve design integrity. Project control is crucially dependent upon the previously established methods of working, reporting and product control. Thoroughgoing quality assurance in the preceding phases is necessary if the required quality of the product is to be assured as part of the process. The methods of working and their confirmation and strengthening by quality assurance are by now part of the project culture and very difficult to change under the increasing pressure and the technical drive of the team to get on with implementing the design. From this stage onwards quality assurance is increasingly ineffective in changing anything—it is only a matter of observation and discovery. Anything that is found with wider ramifications than a single module becomes a matter of debugging implemented software, which is notoriously costly and uncontrollable.

DETAILED DESIGN PHASE PRODUCTS

- Detailed design specification for each unit (verified for completeness, consistency, and traceability to requirements and system design specifications and size and speed budgets
  —for each module (module size limitations as defined in the coding standard) specified name, purpose, assumptions, sizing, calling sequence, error exits, inputs, outputs, algorithms, and processing flow
  —database description through parameter/character/bit level
- Unit test specifications (standalone test cases)
- Completed and approved relevant parts of the integration and independent test plans and test data
- Completed relevant part of the draft maintenance manual

A Detailed Design Review satisfactorily completed (e.g. with a walkthrough), determines the completion of the phase for each module or group of modules. Note that previous phase ends were for the project as a whole, but for the detailed design, code and unit test the teams follow independent time paths for progress of their work on the modules.

7.5.1.6 *Coding*

CODING PHASE PRODUCTS

- Code module(s) (verified as complying with programming standards)
- Completion of module documentation
- Test data for unit testing (validated as covering all unit computations, using not only nominal values, but also singular and extreme values and exercising all input and output options, including error messages, all executable statements and all branch options)

The Source Code Review usually takes the form of code reading (by another member of the team) or, in the case of critical modules, a walkthrough with a number of attendees.

7.5.1.7 *Unit test*

UNIT TEST PHASE PRODUCT

- Unit test results

The Unit Test Review verifies that the unit test results show the unit performing correctly in all its operations, according to the unit test plan using test data derived from the detailed design.

7.5.1.8 *Integration*
The prerequisite for this step is the integration test data and the first set of unit-tested modules. Subsequent sets of modules will be available at intervals—planned to fit in with the integration strategy (such as top-down, critical processes first, etc.).

INTEGRATED SOFTWARE ITEMS

- Integration test data and results
- Development product (for central configuration management, from which new clean versions are installed for the independent test team and customer support team)
- Installation notes
- Test data for independent testing
- Full draft user manual
- Full draft operations manual

- Draft maintenance manual
- Training needs analysis
- Stable reference version of the product (for production of manuals and training courses)

The Integrated Software Review verifies that the integration test results show that the product is functionally integrated according to the integration test plan, using test data derived from the structural design.

7.5.1.9 *Integration test*

This is the real test of the integrated software. For thoroughness it is carried out by a test team independent of the development team(s). During the software implementation phases, this test team is responsible for the preparation of the test data from the structural design and the requirement specification. They take the integrated software and the full draft user manual and thoroughly test the product according to the plan for independent testing. Any faults found are passed back to the development team for correction and redelivery and re-installation of a new version of the product. This testing is internal and must be satisfactorily completed before delivery to the customer for acceptance testing.

TESTED SOFTWARE ITEMS

- Independent test results (satisfaction of planned test programme for the complete software product)
- Quality and reliability report
- Deliverable product (initial release)
- Installation notes (initial release)
- User manual (initial release)
- Operations manual (initial release)
- Maintenance manual (initial release)

The Tested Software Review poses the question 'Do we have a properly functioning and supported software product?'. This relies on verifying that the independent test results show the correct performance of the product in all its operations, according to the independent test plan; that the above constituents of the tested software product and the analysis of the quality metrics in the quality and reliability report meet the criteria in the quality plan for release of the product for customer acceptance, and that the support team is ready for the customer acceptance phase.

7.5.1.10 *Acceptance test*

This involves evaluation and acceptance by the customer against the acceptance criteria, with acceptance tests using data derived from the requirements specification. Faults found by the customer are corrected by the development team (in the case of the software) and by the technical author (in the case of the manuals) with updated releases delivered to the customer by the support team.

ACCEPTED SOFTWARE ITEMS

- Acceptance test results (verification of satisfaction of software require-ments, demonstration of acceptable off-nominal performance as specified)
- Deliverable packaged software product
- Installation notes and trained installers
- Final accepted manuals for users, operations and maintenance
- Training courses and trained lecturers

The Customer Acceptance Review answers the question 'Is the software product accepted and handed over to the customer?' by seeking confirmation of the customer's agreement that the product has met the original acceptance criteria and contractural acceptance of all deliverable software products including reports, manuals, as-built specifications and databases and that the product is satisfactorily supported.

7.5.1.11 *Operational test*
This phase deals with experience of initial operation of the product at the customer's site with continuing support from the development team to deal with problems. Analysis of the data from measurements of quality and reliability is used to determine the success of the product before the development project can be closed.

OPERATIONAL TEST PHASE PRODUCT

- Quality and reliability report

The Product Operation Review determines the completion of all specified conversion, installation and training activities and verifies the operational readiness of the software, hardware, facilities and personnel, and ensures that the product operation at the customer site is satisfactory and ready to be fully handed over to the support team for continuing in-service support and maintenance. If this phase is part of the contractural arrangements then there will usually be final formal confirmation of acceptance of all deliverable system products: hardware, software, documentation, training and facilities.

7.5.1.12 *Project Completion*
The objectives of the project completion phase are to ensure that all technical information is properly available and to provide the planning and organization necessary to ensure a smooth handover to subsequent projects related to the project now completing. Depending on contracts and technology, these may be maintenance support, further product line development, or subsequent con-tractural stages in a large-scale system development. The project completion phase also gathers and analyses quantitative data from the project, to improve

the numerical basis of future project planning, estimating and control, and to capture for wider business use the commercial, technical and management experience gained on the project so that lessons are learnt and methods updated where appropriate.

PROJECT COMPLETION ITEM

- A completed project history document comparing estimates and plans with actual development schedule and costs

The Project Completion Review is an internal project management review that confirms that all project actions are truly complete and that the project can indeed be closed, and also establishes that appropriate follow-on actions are identified through project and product analyses, that the information for these actions is available, and that responsibilities are assigned for their execution.

7.5.1.13 *Operation (in-service and maintenance)*

Corrections for implementation and specification errors, based on Software Problem Reports (SPRs), and evolution of required functions are controlled by a series of releases of updated software. The goal of maintenance is a fully functioning version of the software at each release. Each release is based on a sequence of steps following the same phases as development, tailored to the magnitude and risks of the changes involved, with even greater emphasis on change control and configuration management.

7.5.1.14 *Product phaseout (replacement or disposal)*

When the product is to be superseded, the purpose of this phase is to explicitly address the need for a clean transition of the functions performed by the product to its successors (if any).

PHASEOUT PRODUCT

- Product phaseout plan and report on completion

The Product Phaseout Review verifies completion of all items in the phaseout plan: conversion, documentation, archiving and transition to new system(s).

7.6 Risk Management and Choice of Process

The software development process is inherently subject to risks whose consequences are manifested as financial failures (timescale overrun, budget overrun) and technical failures (failure to meet required functionality, quality or reliability). The objectives of risk management are to identify, analyse and prioritize risk items before they become either threats to successful operation or major sources of expensive software rework, to establish a balanced and integrated strategy for eliminating or reducing the various sources of risk, and to monitor and control the execution of this strategy.

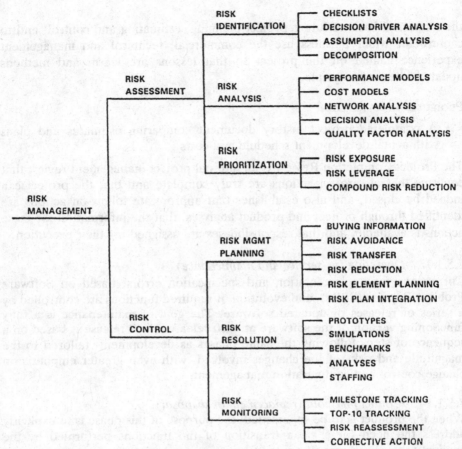

Fig. 7.9. Software risk management steps. (Reproduced from Boehm (1989) with permission of the IEEE.)

The *IEEE Tutorial on Software Risk Management*, (Boehm, 1989), gives a full introduction to the subject, from which Fig. 7.9 is taken. As shown, the practice of software risk management involves two primary steps, risk assessment and risk control, each with three subsidiary steps.

Figure 7.10, also from the *IEEE Tutorial*, gives a checklist of the primary sources of risk for software projects, based on a survey of a number of experienced project managers. The *IEEE Tutorial* also refers to further detailed checklists. These checklists can be used by managers and technical staff on a new project to help identify, and suggest resolution techniques for, the most likely serious risk items on the project, but they should be backed up as soon as possible by checklists derived from specific local experience.

After using all the various risk identification checklists, plus the other risk identification and risk analysis techniques shown in Figure 7.9, one very real risk is that the project will identify so many project risk items that the manager could get bogged down just investigating them. This is where risk prioritization

Risk Item	Risk Management Techniques
1. Personnel shortfalls	— Staffing with top talent, job matching; teambuilding; morale building, cross-training; pre-scheduling key people.
2. Unrealistic schedules and budgets	— Detailed, multi-source cost and schedule estimation; design to cost; incremental development; software reuse; requirements scrubbing.
3. Developing the wrong software functions	— Organization analysis; mission analysis; ops-concept formulation; user surveys; prototyping; early users' manuals.
4. Developing the wrong user interface	— Task analysis; prototyping; scenarios.
5. Gold plating	— Requirements scrubbing; prototyping; cost-benefit analysis; design to cost.
6. Continuing stream of requirement changes	— High change threshold, information hiding; incremental development (defer changes to later increments).
7. Shortfalls in externally-furnished components	— Benchmarking; inspections; reference checking; compatibility analysis.
8. Shortfalls in externally-performed tasks	— Reference checking; pre-award audits; award-fee contracts; competitive design or prototyping; teambuilding.
9. Real-time performance shortfalls	— Simulation; benchmarking; modeling; prototyping; instrumentation; tuning.
10. Straining computer science capabilities	— Technical analysis; cost-benefit analysis; prototyping; reference checking.

Fig. 7.10. A top ten list of software risk items. (Reproduced from Boehm (1989) with permission of the IEEE.)

becomes essential. As well as the obvious application of common sense, effective analytical techniques for risk prioritization involve the quantification of Risk Exposure (probability of unsatisfactory outcome multiplied by loss level) and Risk Reduction Leverage (reduction of risk exposure divided by cost of risk reduction investment). These techniques are generally necessary to ensure concentration on the key factors. Often there is a great deal of uncertainty in estimating the probability or loss associated with an unsatisfactory outcome. This uncertainty is itself a major source of risk, which needs to be reduced as early as possible. One of the best ways of reducing this uncertainty is to buy information about the actual situation, such as investing in a prototype.

When risk assessment has determined the major risk items for a project and their relative priorities, the next step is to establish risk control. One aid for this is the second column of Fig. 7.10 which identifies risk management techniques for the most common risk items.

There are two categories of risks to be distinguished: project specific risks and generic risks.

Project specific risks are those which only apply to a particular project, such as:

—personnel shortfalls
—unrealistic schedules and budgets
—inappropriate requirements
—shortfalls in externally supplied components and services
—technology shortfalls, unknowns and reliance on advances in the state of the art
—user–interface uncertainties
—ambitious performance requirements

Risks in this category are addressed by the steps in the lower half of Fig. 7.9 with a set of risk management plans to lay out the activities necessary to bring the risk items under control. The individual risk management plans have to be integrated with each other and with the overall project process and project plan. Once a good set of risk management plans is established, the risk resolution process consists of implementing whatever prototypes, simulations, benchmarks, surveys, or other risk reduction techniques are called for in the plans. Risk monitoring ensures that this is a closed loop process by tracking risk reduction progress and applying whatever corrective action is necessary to continue elimination of identified risks.

Generic risks are those which are common to the generality of software development projects, such as:

• costly, late fixes—addressed by early requirements and design verification and validation
• error-prone products—addressed by testing, verification and validation through the life-cycle
• uncontrollable process—addressed by planning and control
• uncontrollable product—addressed by configuration management and quality assurance
• poor communication—addressed by documentation and reviews

The degree to which these are expected to be significant for the particular software development determines the choice of the method of working for the project.

Even for the generic risks, risk management concepts are useful in planning the project, particularly in providing a context and a rationale for software verification and validation (V&V) activities, and addressing the key question of 'How much V&V is enough?'. The risk exposure view of software V&V suggests that the level of investment in software V&V should be a function of the relative loss caused by a software error in a system, and that software V&V should be part of an integrated risk reduction strategy which also includes other error elimination techniques (such as formal and rigorous methods for specification and design, fault tolerance techniques, walkthroughs and clean-room techniques, and operational loss limiting techniques).

Risk Reduction Leverage calculations can be used to assess the relative cost-effectiveness of V&V with respect to other techniques in reducing software risk exposure. These generally confirm that V&V investments in the early phases of the software life cycle have high payoff ratios, and that V&V is a function which needs to begin early to be most cost effective. Similar calculations can help a software project determine the most cost-effective mix of defect removal techniques to apply across the software life-cycle. Example approaches can be found in Chapter 3 of Jones, T. C. (1986) and Chapter 24 of Boehm (1981).

Risk monitoring may be tackled by simply following progress with respect to the various milestones in an overall Risk Management Plan. Another technique which has been highly successful is to use risk management to drive the nature of weekly or monthly management reviews of the project, by focussing on assessment of the top ten or so risk items on the project. This concentrates management attention on the high-risk, high-leverage management issues rather than swamping monthly reviews with large amounts of low-priority detail. The techniques of risk assessment and risk control stimulate a 'no surprises' approach to software management which demands improved project visibility and control, and significantly reduces the cost of software development by discovering and dealing with problems early rather than having to undertake rework at later stages.

As well as using risk assessment to determine the methods of working in the project, risk management is also the basis for the appropriate choice of the overall process for the project. There are three strategies that can be followed in choosing from the alternative software development process models, discussed in Appendix B, for a specific project:

—Treat the classical life-cycle phases as an all-purpose model and tailor its use to fit every situation. This may be valid for a site where the projects do not get into unprecedented new developments. The strategy may be adopted, more unrealistically, in circumstances where the customer (or rather the procurer) appears to demand it as the prescribed process. Using an unsuitable process, or the alternative of pretending to use it as an overlay on an actually different process, are not recommended strategies.

—Regard the various models in Appendix B as discrete alternatives, the most appropriate being selected for the specific project. Figure 7.11, from Boehm (1989) lays out such a set of alternative process models with the reasons for deciding on the most appropriate for given circumstances. This is a reasonable strategy when a specific alternative correctly fits the circumstances of a particular project, as will often be the case.

—Create an ad-hoc phase-by-phase process based on risk management for a specific process to fit the situation on a project. This strategy fits the circumstances where risks dominate the planning (rather than questions of accuracy of estimating for well understood software development). The necessary sequence would be to determine the objectives and constraints

GROWTH ENVELOPE	UNDERSTANDING OF REQUIREMENTS	ROBUSTNESS	AVAILABLE TECHNOLOGY	ARCHITECTURE UNDERSTANDING	PROCESS MODEL	EXAMPLE
LIMITED			COMMERCIAL PACKAGES		BUY COMMERCIAL PACKAGE	SIMPLE INVENTORY CONTROL
LIMITED			4GL, TRANSFORM		TRANSFORM OR EVOLUTIONARY DEVELOPMENT	SMALL BUSINESS - DP APPLICATION
LIMITED	LOW	LOW		LOW	EVOLUTIONARY PROTOTYPE	ADVANCED PATTERN RECOGNITION
LIMITED TO LARGE	HIGH	HIGH		HIGH	PRE-DETERMINED CLASSICAL PHASES	REBUILD OF OLD SYSTEM
	LOW	HIGH			RISK REDUCTION FOLLOWED BY CLASSICAL PHASES	COMPLEX SITUATION ASSESSMENT
		HIGH		LOW		HIGH-PERFORMANCE AVIONICS
LIMITED TO MEDIUM	LOW	LOW TO MEDIUM		HIGH	EVOLUTIONARY DEVELOPMENT	NEW DECISION-SUPPORT SYSTEM
LIMITED TO LARGE			LARGE REUSABLE COMPONENTS	MEDIUM TO HIGH	FIT CAPABILITIES TO REQUIREMENTS	ELECTRONIC PUBLISHING
VERY LARGE					RISK REDUCTION PLUS CLASSICAL PHASES	AIR TRAFFIC CONTROL
MEDIUM TO LARGE	LOW	MEDIUM	SOME COMMERCIAL PACKAGES	LOW TO MEDIUM	SPIRAL	SOFTWARE SUPPORT ENVIRONMENT
FIXED BUDGET OR SCHEDULE AVAILABLE					DESIGN TO COST OR DESIGN TO SCHEDULE	
EARLY CAPABILITY NEEDED LIMITED STAFF OR BUDGET AVAILABLE DOWNSTREAM REQUIREMENTS POORLY UNDERSTOOD HIGH-RISK SYSTEM NUCLEUS LARGE TO VERY LARGE APPLICATION REQUIRED PHASING WITH SYSTEM INCREMENTS		(ANY ONE CONDITION IS SUFFICIENT)			INCREMENTAL DEVELOPMENT	

Fig. 7.11. Software process model decision table. (Reproduced from Boehm (1989) with permission of the IEEE.)

for the project, decide which are the critical process drivers and analyse the construction of process phases using the spiral model (described in Section B.12 of Appendix B) to develop a process which minimizes the risk of not satisfying the critical process drivers.

The spiral model defines a risk driven approach to determining the software development process. It may be used to create an ad-hoc phase-by-phase process as in the third alternative above, or risk analysis may result in steps that fit into the classical phases, or determine the need for increased risk-protection from an evolutionary or prototype process, an incremental development process (Sections B.11 and B.13 of Appendix B) or any combination of these. Risk Management in the software life-cycle and the use of the spiral model as a process model generator are discussed in the *IEEE Tutorial* (Boehm, 1989) which also deals with how the various reviews and phase-products in a contract-oriented software development process correspond with the steps of risk management, use of risk management plans, and cycles in the spiral model.

7.7 Productivity, Quality and Software Development Methodology

The productivity of software development projects presents a major problem for most organizations. The efficiency of computer hardware continues its spectacular increase, but so often the rate of production and quality of custom-built code continues to be low and notoriously unpredictable. Clearly, part of the solution is to increase the use of standard software as far as possible rather than develop bespoke software. However, even if development of new software is unavoidable, a great deal is known about how to improve productivity, and even a doubling of productivity would make a significant difference for most organizations. Instead of being always behind schedule, and then prone to try to meet the impossible, which makes the situation even worse, the software developers would have the time to do the work right, and thereby be able to meet predictions of quality and delivery on time. A major motivation for improving software productivity is that software costs are large and growing larger. Software costs are increasing not because people are becoming less productive, but because of the continuing increase in demand for software and the growing significance of software in the production of complex systems. Any percentage saving from increased productivity will be correspondingly significant.

Software productivity can easily be stated as the quantity of output of software from the development process divided by the cost taken to produce the software. However this straightforward concept is not so easy to turn into real measurement. The most difficult metric is the size of the product: the traditional measurement in lines of code (LOC) is subject to much criticism but it does have the advantage of being relatively easy to define, its meaning is clear, and it is easy to measure once the software is developed. However if

LOC is to be successfully used in an organization there must be objective, well-understood counting rules, a definition of what is delivered in terms of compliance with a set of software quality standards, and definition and tracking of the language level and extent of re-use of source code. Examples of such definitions can be found in Boehm (1981) and Jones, T. C. (1986). Newer metrics such as function points have been successful in some areas, and many organizations are experimenting with their use, refinement and extension. Refer to Chapters 10 and 11 for coverage of alternative metrics.

In a sense, how we measure the size of the product does not matter since it can be seen that the project will produce what is required, and if it successfully meets the requirements for functionality and quality then the 'size' is not a variable that can be changed. In fact, it can be seen that if the same functionality and quality is met by a smaller amount of code, then that would probably be 'better' since it could be cheaper to maintain. Notions of size of software product cannot be separated from quality. However, it is necessary to use some metric if projects are going to collect data and determine improvements in productivity from introducing better software development practices.

There are two primary interactions between software costs and quality. The first is that a project can reduce software development costs at the expense of quality, but only in ways that increase the operational and maintenance costs. The second is that a project can simultaneously reduce software development costs and improve software quality by intelligent and cost-effective use of modern software techniques. The equation for productivity is improved by tackling the 'cost' of producing what is required, through the use of tools, modern programming practices and better people. The emphasis is on building quality in from the beginning and early error detection. Getting the right mix of the various components of quality (reliability, efficiency, ease of use, ease of change, etc.) can be a very complex job. Approaches which have had some success in managing multiple quality objectives are design by objectives in Gilb (1985) and the goals approach in Boehm (1981).

Cost models for software development give clear insights into productivity ranges and show the leverage of those factors that are under management control to reduce the costs of a project to produce a required product. The most significant influence on software costs is the number of source instructions. This leads to cost-reduction strategies involving the use of fourth-generation languages, re-usable components to reduce the number of source instructions developed, the use of prototyping and other requirements analysis techniques to ensure that unnecessary functions are not developed, and the use of already developed products. The next most significant influence by far is that of the selection, motivation and management of the people involved in the software process. In particular, employing the best people is usually a bargain, because the productivity range for people is usually much wider than the range of people's salaries. The other cost driver factors which are controllable by management are requirements volatility, hardware capacity, use of software tools and modern programming practices. Since large software development projects are highly labour-intensive, there are significant opportunities for the provision of automated aids to make the activities more efficient as well as the implication that human resource and management activities aimed at getting the best from people have high leverage on productivity.

Figure 7.12 is taken from Boehm (1987*a*) (extended in Boehm and Papaccio (1988)) and shows a comprehensive structure of the major sources of software development cost savings. Boehm's paper gives a thorough discussion of each of these opportunities for improving productivity and a particularly useful list of references for further reading.

In dealing with productivity it is important to carefully define objective metrics and relate them to quality and also realize that improving software productivity is not an end in itself. It is a means of better expanding the capability of the staff on the project to work effectively in creating a product of the required quality and must be placed in the context of the wider interests of the organization. Software engineering deals with the structuring of a relationship between technical and management aspects, and this has been the major theme of this chapter in defining the basis for achieving project control. The term 'software development methodology' is used to refer to a systematic set of procedures that integrates the technical development techniques with the management procedures controlling the development process and the deployment of tool support for software development. The managerial and technical

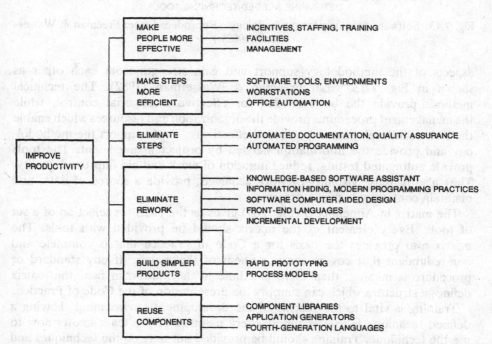

Fig. 7.12. Productivity improvement opportunities. (Reproduced from Boehm (1987*a*) with permission of the IEEE.)

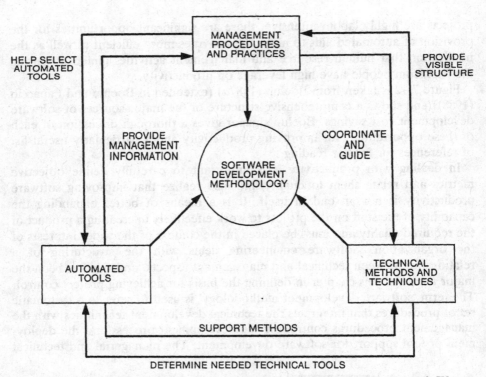

Fig. 7.13. Software development methodology. (Reproduced from Freeman & Wasserman (1982).)

aspects of the methodology support and gain strength from each other as shown in Fig. 7.13, from Freeman & Wasserman (1982). The technical methods provide the basis needed for effective managerial control, while the management procedures provide the organization and resources which enable the technical development to proceed effectively. Tools support the methodology and provide the information needed by project management. The tools provide automated testing, reduce iteration of work and aid improved quality. They also increase visibility of work achieved, provide a source of data, and maintain continuity between projects.

The matrix in Appendix B (Fig. B.9) gives us the basis for selection of a set of tools. Every element of the matrix should be provided with tools. The matrix also provides the basis for a Code of Practice that is complete and non-redundant if it covers every element of the matrix. If any standard or procedure is missing, then there is a hole in the matrix; in fact, the matrix defines a structure which can simplify the presentation of the Code of Practice.

Training is vital to the success of the development environment. Having a defined technique is useless unless every member of the team knows how to use the technique. Training should be provided not only on the techniques and tools but also in the Code of Practice.

Procedures and practices need to be backed by a corporate policy, promulgated in a Quality Manual, which declares the principles of achievement of real quality, backed by management commitment. It sets the quality norm for the organization, the climate and leadership style with an insistence that the standards and procedures are really to be used and that staff are required to be aware of them, responsible for their continued improvement, and for their application in software production (see Section 9.6.3 in Chapter 9).

The effectiveness of software development projects in efficiently producing a quality product depends on the maturity of the technical methods, the coverage of the techniques, tool use and environment support. But of even greater importance than these is the maturity of the process; the extent to which it has been proved over a number of projects, is well understood and supported by the standards and procedures and is part of the culture for the technical staff, project managers and senior management alike. In turn, software projects depend upon the effectiveness of the organization as evidenced by quality management maturity and software professionalism supported by sufficient development facilities and a good physical environment.

Given that making software engineering methodology really works is always difficult, it follows that success depends on more than just the wish to improve the control and productivity of software development. Management commitment and active support is necessary in order to achieve successful control of software development projects.

7.8 Further Reading

The Mythical Man-Month is a series of essays on software engineering. With the insight of real experience and persuasive humour, Fred Brooks makes the essential points on management of software projects. The book is very easy to read, especially for the non-technical manager, and should not be missed by anyone concerned with software project management.

Software Engineering Economics by Barry Boehm is still the most comprehensive textbook on understanding and modelling software development.

Controlling Software Projects by Tom DeMarco is for the practising project manager. It places a strong emphasis on metrics for software development as the necessary basis for project control.

Peopleware: Productive Projects and Teams, by Tom DeMarco and Timothy Lister deals with the management of people to counterbalance the structural approach on which this chapter has concentrated.

The *IEEE Tutorial on Software Engineering Project Management* edited by Richard Thayer is an excellent collection of papers, some of them written especially for the tutorial. The papers provide entries, with a wealth of further references, to all aspects of project management.

The *IEEE Tutorial on Software Risk Management* by Barry Boehm gives a state-of-the-art discussion of the subject, with a lot of new material as well as extensive reprints from existing reference papers.

8

Procuring and Maintaining Reliable Software

Gillian Frewin

8.1	Introduction	211
8.2	The Roles and Responsibilities of the Software Procurer . .	212
8.3	Contracting for the Development of a Software Product . .	213
8.4	Procurer's Involvement in Product Development and Testing	226
8.5	Product Handover, and Analysis of the Procurement	234
8.6	Maintenance of Software	234
8.7	Establishing the Baseline	237
8.8	Managing Changes Against the Baseline	239
8.9	Continuous Assessment of Product Status and Support for Future Procurement	243
8.10	Summary: The Roles of Procurement and Maintenance in Achieving Reliable Software.	244

8.1 Introduction

Users of software products are interested in 'reliability' in terms of their requirements for products that give a continuous supply of the functionality, performance and other qualities that they need. It is because requirements are so frequently inadequately investigated, badly expressed, and poorly realized (often resulting in a product with a complex mass of 'near-misses' to the requirements and design, which then give rise to systems that sometimes work and sometimes fail), taken with the many ways in which an item may be compromised once it is in service, that the processes by which items are procured and maintained become so important to the success of systems containing software.

'Procurement' is the software user's view of the processes by which wanted software products and services are obtained: 'maintenance' is the group of processes by which a product, once procured and satisfactorily installed, retains its value and performance. The two are closely linked by the 'Statement of Requirements' document, which acts as the 'shopping list' during procurement, and the standard of performance during the period of use and maintenance.

Other links exist because of the cyclic nature of user's needs. New functions or better performance are wanted: an answer is found by the procurement process: the new service is used until it, too, fails to meet demands and a new procurement is started: and so on. There should be a continuous thread of measurement, recording and analysis throughout, by means of which Statements of Requirements are refined and augmented, and the procurement process made more precise and better grounded in fact.

8.2 The Roles and Responsibilities of the Software Procurer

Any buyer must realize that the quality of the items obtained is directly related to the qualities of the procurement process. If the procurer is not able to handle the responsibilities (of specification, development, testing, approval and application of the products and systems obtained) in a professional manner, then there cannot reasonably be high expectations of the functionality or fitness of what is received. It is not our intention here to suggest that all the problems of reliability achievement lie with the procurer, but to show that there are many essential activities in defining, developing and using a product or system that can best be coordinated and undertaken by this focal position.

The Procurer is the person responsible for obtaining a product. This may be done against a requirement wholly or partially prepared by the Procurer, in the role of the intended user of the item procured. Alternatively, the Procurer may be acting as an agent for others: for example, those who will actually employ the item (its user), or those who will provide its services to users. In these cases, the Procurer is charged with fulfilling a requirement that has been supplied. Thus, a Procurer may be acting purely as an agent for others, or may be personally involved with the what and the why of the item being obtained. This distinction becomes significant when it is necessary for the Procurer to take a prominent role in representing the requirement to the items' producers or suppliers: if a procurement is undertaken with the Procurer acting as an agent, then to have a reasonable chance of ending the exercise satisfactorily there must be available throughout a substantial contribution of time, involvement and specialist advice from the users concerned.

The first and most important step in good procurement is the formation and agreement of a requirement that accurately represents what is wanted. The initial list of 'wants' must then be carefully screened and adjusted to result in a statement of requirements that is internally consistent, technically feasible and economically affordable (with 'affordability' relating to the *costs* of obtaining the item, maintaining it and using it, and measured against the *value, or benefit*, obtained from having, and applying, the product). The 'cost/benefit' analysis is necessarily imprecise in the early stages of procurement, as actual costs will not be available: however, benefits can be explored and assigned values, and thus a maximum acceptable cost identified. The cost/benefit statement should be the main item in justifying starting the procurement, and, as it is gradually amended by the addition of 'actual' costs and benefits, makes an important contribution to continuous management of both procurement and maintenance.

Once the first acceptable draft statement of requirements has been formed, a way of filling it must be found. Possible routes include:

- A bought-in item that can be applied without much adjustment or customization. This is the easiest case to handle because the item is already complete and proven in practice, although it may not be the cheapest or give the best performance because of the functions and facilities built in to meet the wider market.
- A bought-in item that needs significant work before it can be used in the desired way. Customizing work may be done locally or by the supplier.
- A bespoke development from an external or internal source. In this case the supplier designs and builds a product to fit the requirements. It is this case, especially as it relates to an external supplier, that is expanded upon below.

It is the responsibility of the Procurer to locate, examine and evaluate the various possibilities, and then to choose and carry through the most effective and timely route to the required product or services. Whichever is chosen, its detail should not be allowed to obscure the real message: that professional procurement (followed by effective product management) is essential if software products, and systems containing software, are to prove reliable in practice.

8.3 Contracting for the Development of a Software Product

The first step is to obtain a full, agreed, and achievable, Statement of Product Requirements. (For background, methods, tools and techniques, see Heninger, 1980; Yeh, 1980; Checkland, 1981; Tapscott, 1982; Gilb, 1985, 1986; Cutts, 1987; Redmill, 1987; Downs *et al.*, 1988.)

The statement should include both specific functions and all the more general qualities that make the difference between a product that is or is not acceptable to its owners, its users and those who must maintain a service to those users. 'Acceptability' has many dimensions, some of which are clearly technical and 'hard', and others that are more qualitative and 'soft'.

Because of the possible variety of users, uses and viewpoints, the requirements for a product can cover many different things, including:

- specific functions to be provided (these are 'hard' requirements), and the ease with which they can be customized, called up and controlled (the customizability and controllability of functions are 'soft' qualitative requirements):
- 'friendliness' of the software towards its users. An impression that the machine is well-disposed towards its users is created by such things as the

use of familiar language and concepts in the human–computer interface, a system which is tolerant towards user mistakes, and general supportiveness shown by providing 'help' facilities and meaningful messages. The requirement for 'friendliness' may be difficult to define, but is important in obtaining a product which will be used readily and correctly;
- costs of procurement and of ownership;
- length of the period between perceiving the need and actually obtaining the product solution, and the actual timeliness of that solution;
- ease with which the product can be interfaced to existing hardware and software, and adjusted to interface with future environments;
- reliability, usability, extensibility, and maintainability of the product solution obtained.

The range of legitimate interests means that the Procurer has to ensure that requirements are collected from them all, and that any conflicts are resolved.

Given the time needed for procurement, and the length of life of many useful products, it is also extremely important that the Procurer obtains a statement of requirements that will match not only present perceptions of what is needed, but also the ways in which that need is likely to alter. These alterations may result from causes external to the user population (say, changes in the pattern of work within the company, or in its computing provisions) or from users' gradual growth in familiarity with the product and its potential applications. While changes within the company and its computing environment can only be foreseen locally, the experience of any external supplier involved should be helpful in anticipating the way in which the manner of use will develop.

There is another problem area: requirements may not be technically feasible, either individually or when taken as a group. Thus, a supplier must be found who can be relied upon to analyse the requirements laid upon him, filtering out any that are impractical and pointing out necessary and useful additions, and then go on to deliver and help install the agreed product at the expected time.

Although it is seldom practical to make a full product specification or even a substantially stable requirements statement until the development of the product is well under way, it is essential that each of these documents is at all times as honest, complete, clear and consistent as is possible given the current state of knowledge and consideration. In particular, both *Requirements* (which are the external, user's, or buyer's views of the item being procured) and *Specifications* (which are the technicians', designers', creators' and maintainers' views) should be most carefully constructed and presented so as to make clear what is necessary and what is desirable, why these aspects are as they are, and how their existence or absence in the product could be tested.

Many requirements are not as obvious as a need for specific functionality: rather, they are inherent in the users themselves, the social, technical and administrative systems in which they function, and the changes in those users and systems that will be facilitated or forced by the new software item. These requirements (which are especially relevant to the reliability and utility of the procured item) may have to be 'discovered' by the Procurer rather than their being openly presented by the users, since they (the requirements) are often one or more of:

- subconscious, as in the assumptions and informal practices that develop to smooth the day-to-day operations of any company;
- unacknowledged, as in the shifts and stratagems by which many 'official' procedures are by-passed in order to save time and effort;
- embarrassing to acknowledge, as in the case of actual processes and controls that fall short of the ideal, and of practical but officially frowned-upon methods of covering up failures;
- difficult to find or to predict, as in activities undertaken to meet crises and other infrequently occurring circumstances, and then forgotten in relief when the pressure is over.

Nevertheless, the effective Procurer must make every effort to find the underground influences in existence at any time, monitor new factors as they arise, and both predict and attempt to influence those still to come.

The obtaining of 'honest, complete and clear' requirements needs tact on the part of those collecting and collating the statements, rigorous technical reviewing, and, perhaps, courage and self-knowledge among those making the assertions of their requirements. Software developers are accustomed to receiving statements of requirements that:

- are expressed in pseudo-technical or inaccurate terms, and thus tend to create confusion as to what is really meant;
- are based on grandiose and/or imprecise concepts, which cast doubt on the accuracy of the rest of the requirements;
- contain a mixture of *requirements* (which are what the product must do) with *design* (which is how the product will meet its requirements) and *method* (which is how the design and development will be undertaken);
- put very precise figures on qualities which are in fact unachievable, unnecessary, over-expensive, and impossible to demonstrate;
- use the statement of requirements as a political document, which is meant to underline the importance and urgency of the activities to be served by the new software;
- are otherwise misleading and unhelpful.

While much of this can be put down to unfamiliarity rather than to deliberate mis-direction, such a flawed requirements statement is dangerous if it is treated as if it were complete and accurate, and used as the guiding material for contract-making and product development. Rather, it should be used creatively as the starting point for discussions, explorations, and education, all leading to informed users and an improved statement.

8.3.1 Forming a contract

The activities undertaken by the Procurer to obtain a useful statement of requirements, to locate one or more possible suppliers and then to settle on one and to make a firm contract, are as follows:

(a) Prepare draft requirements.
(b) Plan and carry out the initial evaluation and selection of suppliers.
(c) Refine the draft requirements with the chosen (or short-listed) supplier or suppliers.
(d) If necessary, re-visit the selection of suppliers and the refinement of the requirements statement.
(e) Draft, evaluate, agree and formalize a contract and the contract-support arrangements—including all the responsibilities, information exchanges and other interactions between supplier, user-community, and Procurer.

These stages are confirmed and secured further by

(f) The Procurer continuing to support suppliers and future users through the periods in which the requirement is refined and re-stated as a product specification, the contract and the development project are set up, the product is made and tested, delivered, and maintained in use.

Although it is important that the first stages of preparing a requirements statement are undertaken without any input from a prospective supplier (since otherwise there is a significant risk that the user requirement will be distorted by what the supplier wishes to sell) it is sensible to seek informed technical support in refining that first statement; and the obvious sources of expertise lie in one or more of those potential suppliers. This follows not only from their demonstrated competence, but also from their technical and commercial interest in the project, which should ensure their commitment to getting the requirements right.

Looking at the last sentence more closely, as well as the benefits there are obvious risks associated with reliance on the suppliers 'demonstrated competence' and their 'technical and commercial interests'. What precisely should be demonstrated, how should it be evaluated, who is competent to make the assessment, and, is it certain that the interests of a supplier (particularly before a contract has been made) are necessarily those of the Procurer and the users being represented? These questions can only be touched on here, but should be considered.

8.3.2 Collecting and documenting the initial draft statement of requirements

While the final statement of requirements must be a formal, structured and supported document, it can be unwise to get into too great detail or into a pre-defined format in the very early stages. Doing so tends to depersonalize what is presented and to restrict the scope of the investigation, since an imposed structure suggests that most of the answers and evaluations are already established. Where there is a suitable format available, this can be used as a check on the completeness and interrelations of the requirements that are proposed—but remembering that such checks should always be secondary to the collection of as much unbiased and general opinion as possible.

The collector should consciously avoid imposing personal constraints, vocabulary, or attitudes on the potential users of the item. If the contributors are not familiar with the production of requirement statements, this initial period is a good time for them to practise the formation and the reviewing of such statements before too much is involved.

Each requirement statement should be expressed as clearly and concisely as possible, and should be accompanied by one or more examples of what is meant and, if possible, a suggested demonstration that would provide satisfactory evidence that the requirement had been met. Reviewers should look for any difficulties with the wording, such as ambiguities or serious omissions, and check that their understanding is accurate and complete by working through the examples and perhaps putting forward examples of their own. As soon as a body of statements is available, reviewers can also look at the interactions between requirements from different sources.

It is not appropriate to go into greater detail here on the concepts and mechanisms of 'requirements capture', but for further information see the references given at the head of Section 8.3 and the IEEE *Guide to Software Requirements Specifications* (IEEE, 1984).

The following points should be observed whatever the 'capture' method:

- The main shape and dimensions of the requirement should be agreed and documented before any outside help is involved.
- The formation of the requirement should be handled so as to encourage free expression of needs and concerns, and thus to promote the identification of those who 'own' them with all the activities needed to meet them. 'Ownership' of parts of a requirement can be a powerful incentive for future users to concentrate on getting their own clauses right, and for establishing the balance and priorities between conflicting needs. Many requirements statements include features that have been added because they might be of use in unspecified circumstances and at some unknown time. By allowing (or assigning) 'ownership', the Procurer avoids cluttering up the product and its development with items that no one really needs, and benefits from the personal interest taken in defining and demonstrating the ones that are known to be essential.
- The Procurer's prime responsibility is usually to the broad spirit of the exercise and the general good of the organization, rather than to the fine technical detail of specific elements within the requirement. This is related to the previous point, on 'ownership': the Procurer does not usually own the statement of requirements or the product that results from it. The

Procurer *does* own a professional responsibility for the whole task. If the principals insist on 'requiring' a software item that the Procurer believes to be wrong for them, reasoned argument can be applied but usually not a veto. While this is the general case for a Procurer, it is not invariably true: in very large organizations such as the MOD or British Telecom, and in major manufacturing, the Procurement function is so central and influential as to be able to form its own policies and detailed requirements, and to override individual users' requests if they do not fit in with the wider view.

8.3.3 Supplier evaluation and selection

Where there is a choice of possible suppliers, the Procurer should be careful to ensure that their capabilities and expectations are a good match with what is required. This evaluation may sometimes appear to be pointless because of strong influences from:

- 'political factors', which might, for example, make it difficult to use any supplier other than one that is in-house;
- prejudices associated with the nature of potential suppliers, such as a general feeling against small companies, or against international companies;
- the specific requirements (which might limit the choice to a very small number of declared specialists, where this was not necessarily the best course);
- any past or present relationship between the Procurer and the Supplier;

but there is still an established common procedure for supplier evaluation and subsequent selection that should be followed. This may turn out to be particularly important where the result is apparently completely constrained, as it can avoid blindly setting out on a course that cannot possibly be successful. By following the procedure, and by fully documenting its outcomes and indications, the Procurer is at least able to present and justify a rational case for the recommendations, and for the possible consequences of having any other course imposed.

Supplier evaluation procedures follow these steps:

(a) Find, prioritize, weight, and document significant supplier factors. It is important that the factors are chosen *before* their measurability, or the availability of relevant data, is considered. Otherwise, significant aspects of a suppliers ability to provide the required performance may be lost simply because no easy way can be seen to give it a rational and obtainable rating. The chosen factors usually include:

- competence—that is, the general technical and managerial capability of the supplier;
- stability—that is, the confident expectation that the supplier will remain in business during the procurement and the support period;

- capacity—that is, the ability of the supplier to provide sufficient and appropriate resources;
- directly relevant experience—that is, recent and successful projects of a similar kind to the procurement in question.

(b) Find suitable metrics, and values of those metrics, for as many as possible of the significant factors. For the four factors mentioned in (a) above, metrics could include:

- the number of items (each equivalent in some way to the one being procured) that have been delivered and have been judged satisfactory by their owners;
- the length of time the potential supplier has been in business;
- whether there is any doubt as to the supplier remaining able and willing to provide lifetime support for the item. This might be indicated by the length of time in business, the number of products being supported, and the number of years of support given to each to date;
- financial measures of the risk represented by this item to the supplier (for example, would its non-acceptance after completion be ruinous? Would staged payments be needed to ensure that the development could be completed? and so on);
- the technical, managerial and quality standards and procedures used by the supplier, and evidence that they are followed;
- whether there is evidence that the supplier has staff with the required training and experience, and whether the training is regularly up-dated;
- any evidence that can be found as to the quantities and qualities of staff, the commitment of named staff to the project, the way in which the more experienced staff are used throughout product development, the extent to which senior staff are used on more than one project at a time, and whether the same staff remain responsible for their products after delivery or whether other (and perhaps less-qualified staff) are used for support purposes.

(c) Search for quantitative and qualitative consequences associated with the factors and with specified criterion values of the metrics, in order that comparisons and cost–benefit analyses can be readily made. As examples of criteria, unless the required item is extremely unusual, it might be expected that

a potential supplier (or the senior project staff of that supplier, when working previously with other organizations) should have successfully developed at least three similar items in the last two to three years. Fewer items than three would seem unlikely to provide a sufficiently wide understanding, and a longer period would raise the possibility that the suppliers' experience would be out of date.

in either case, communication between supplier and Procurer would risk being incomplete or inaccurate, and the product could easily be based on misconceptions about the functionality and qualities required. Similarly,

a potential supplier who could not demonstrate several years of financial stability (or steady growth) would be judged a poorer risk (in respect of project integrity, and ability to provide lifetime maintenance and support) than one which had maintained a viable position for such a time.

(d) Establish profiles (say, for the classes 'acceptable', 'debatable', and definitely 'unacceptable') against which the potential suppliers can be measured. Build up lists of possible suppliers, and of sources of useful information and advice, including, for example, any 'reference customers' given by the suppliers, technical and commercial associations, the trade press, and so on,

(e) Undertake the necessary researches and then apply the selection scheme; augmenting, adjusting and adapting it (and always in a fully documented and appropriately confirmed way) as is desirable and necessary. For an example, certain outcomes may indicate that a given supplier, though not entirely ideal, may still be employed with reasonable security as long as extra-ordinary care (such as default clauses in the contract, regular Quality Audits by the procuring organization, or the application and control of prescribed methods) is taken.

Figure 8.1 gives an example of a Supplier Selection Checklist. The example is taken from an actual checklist used, but it is not intended to be definitive; rather it is intended as an example of the principles for argument. The checklist chosen to evaluate suppliers should have been tailored to the circumstances and be further developed as indicated by experience.

Although following the complete supplier evaluation procedure is recommended, it will not always be practical. One reason for this is its cost to the procurement, and another is the cost to each of the group of possible suppliers. For both, the expenses of the selection process must be balanced against the potential value of obtaining the product, or of gaining the contract. Suppliers will normally build into their rates an element to account for the general costs of selling their services, but may also need to charge for any extended or specific consultancy work called for when the selection process has reached its later stages.

8.3.4 Suppliers' roles in forming requirements

While a procurement will be managed by people with their own areas of expertise, and able to call on local advice and support, their joint knowledge and experience cannot be expected to match that of all the potential suppliers. Unless there are proscriptive factors (such as commercial or national security), suppliers' contributions should be sought during the period in which the contract is drafted, and the initial requirements statement refined into a fit

Factor	Points
(i) *Technical Competence*	

Is the supplier accredited by an authorized agency?
YES = 10 pts
NO = 0 pts

Has evidence been given of staff competence, and is it adequate for this procurement?
YES = 5 pts
NO DATA = 0 pts
MAYBE = 2 pts
NOT ADEQUATE = −20 pts

Has the supplier a well-defined development method, with good tool support and in-built checking and reporting?
YES = 20 pts
MEDIUM = 12 pts
POOR = 0 pts
NONE = −15 pts

What proportion of the time of technical staff is spent in training and/or research?
UNDER 5% = 0 pts
5–10% = 10 pts
OVER 10% = 5 pts

RANGE FOR THIS FACTOR +45 to −35

(ii) *Managerial Competence*

Are there clear and acceptable procedures for contract estimation, project planning, and control?
YES = 10 pts
PARTLY = 5 pts
NO = −10 pts

Is there evidence to suggest that contracts are met to time and budget?
YES = 15 pts
NO DATA = 0 pts
EVIDENCE NEGATIVE = −25 pts

RANGE FOR THIS FACTOR +25 to −35

(iii) *Stability and Reputation*

How long has the supplier been in business?
10 years + = 8 pts
5–10 = 5 pts
under 5 = 3 pts

How is the supplier generally regarded?
HIGHLY = 10 pts
AVERAGE = 5 pts
POORLY/BADLY = −20 pts

RANGE FOR THIS FACTOR +18 to −17

(iv) *Capacity*

How many technical staff are employed?
OVER 50 = 20 pts
30–50 = 10 pts
15–30 = 5 pts
UNDER 15 = −10 pts

What proportion of the suppliers staff would be employed on this contract?
UNDER 5% = 10 pts
5–15% = 8 pts
15–30% = 0 pts
OVER 30% = −15 pts

What proportion of the suppliers staff are actively working on contracts at any time?
OVER 90% = −10 pts

RANGE FOR THIS FACTOR +30 to −35

Fig. 8.1. Example of entries in a supplier selection check-list. Note that the points score is to be added under each heading.

(v) *Relevant Experience*

How many similar systems are known to have been developed and delivered by this supplier in the current 3-year period?	5 = 25 pts 3–4 = 20 pts 1 OR 2 = 10 pts OVER 5 = 30 pts NONE = −10 pts
If NONE, can it be shown that lead staff have had significant, recent and relevant experience while with other suppliers?	YES = 18 pts

RANGE FOR THIS FACTOR +25 to −10

(AND SO ON)

Fig. 8.1.—*contd.*

state to become both a contractual document and the starting point for technical work on the project.

The main contributions that can be made by the supplier (or group of potential suppliers) in this period are:

- technical reviewing of requirements;
- contributions to requirement refinement, in terms of mock-ups and demonstrations based on general-purpose tools and systems;
- informed predictions on in-service reliability; rates of change in requirements; support requirements, provisions and costs; expected and possible changes (in HW/SW/languages/relevant legislation, and so on) during the presumed lifetime of the procured item.

8.3.5 Special studies

'Special studies' are those made throughout the development of a software item, to ensure the continued correctness of the requirement and of the processes by which the software item is being designed and made. Some of these studies can be pre-planned, for example, those to be made in parallel with the development (including detailed cost-benefit and quality reviews at each major milestone), while others must be *ad hoc*. The need for (unplanned) studies might arise, for example, from supplier requests to vary the contract, or the Procurer's examination of development project reports, or from the design and trial of manual processes, user- and operator-training, and other supporting activities associated with the introduction of a computer system, by which the user-community readies itself for the eventual delivery of the new item.

The need for continuing reviews is supported by reports that have been made of the fates of software development projects, and of software products. Although the results vary, depending on the precise details of the classes of project and product, whether the results are expressed in terms of cost or value or numbers of items, when and where the study took place, and so on, they generally report that at least half (and sometimes up to 80% or more) were abandoned before project completion, or before a completed product was used, or as soon as an attempt was made to use the product. In addition, a recent report on the *Benefits of Software Engineering Methods and Tools* (Department of Trade and Industry, 1985), has estimated that during development, 66% of software projects overran on time-scale, 55% overran on budget, and 58% were affected by at least one major unexpected problem.

This evidence supports the need to make thorough and regular studies throughout the procurement period, so that difficulties and deviations can be recognized as early as possible and suitable actions taken, in order to avoid serious gaps opening between what is developed (and its costs and timing) and what is needed.

Risk, decision-making, and cost/benefit studies should be made before, during and immediately after making a procurement contract: and at regular intervals in the development period and in the active lifetime of the procured item. They should set out the dimensions and implications of significant factors in the product (and in the various contexts in which it will be used) and provide the basis for current and later technical and managerial decisions. Typical questions to be asked include the following.

- What are the most likely costs and schedules for the development contract? What are the main risks, and how severe are they? Could the risks be minimized by undertaking the elements of the project in a special sequence? Might some risks be avoided by the buying-in, adaptation and/or grafting together of existing and established products?
- Can critical points in the project be identified in advance, and are there reasonable alternative courses of action if reviews at these points indicate excessive risks?
- Should the development even be started? Having started, and in view of what has been learnt so far and/or current and expected factors in the environment, should it be continued? If the project is not presently acceptable, can the work to date be salvaged in some way, perhaps by re-starting the project at a more favourable time (for example, when improved supporting technology becomes available)?
- Given the state of the product/project at specified points in the development, should the project/product/contract be revised? Should stage payments scheduled for the review date be made?
- Are the proposed development method and quality controls appropriate (in terms of cost, risk, transparency, etc.) for the type of product and project? Are the methods and controls being followed? Are they proving to be effective? Should help and/or extra supervision be provided?
- What are the risks and benefits of various kinds of contractual arrangement, and how should a choice be made between them? Given a particular kind of contract (see Section 8.3.6 below), and supposing it fails, what retrieval measures and what alternative arrangements might be made to minimize loss and disruption?

8.3.6   Contract management

Typical contractual terms, and their main risks, include the following:

- fixed price (risks include development tailored to the price and not to the requirement, or the buyer's resources being wasted where the price is greater than the cost);
- actual costs plus a fixed profit percentage (this risks a supplier regarding the contract as the source of a steady income, and thus not being highly motivated to reach contract completion);
- staged deliveries and staged payments (where income depends on the making of a delivery, great care is needed by the Procurer to ensure the quality of what has been produced and put forward for delivery);
- fixed cost or fixed term with penalties for variations (while this is a reasonable form for contracts concerned only with precisely specified items and well-understood technology, bespoke software products are rarely in this class and thus have both quality and cost risks. Functionality, and process standards, may be trimmed by the supplier to keep within the agreed limits, resulting in a product that is unsatisfactory or unreliable in use);
- contract management by the procuring organization (which can be highly time-consuming, and possibly insufficiently informed owing to the difficulties of entering fully into the organization, attitudes and politics of a foreign site) or full devolution of project management to the supplier (with obvious risks to the inactive party);
- single supplier (whose failure or idiosyncracy could be disastrous for the buyer);
- main supplier plus subcontractors (risks and dependencies are multiplied in one way, but may also be reduced as appropriate specialisms are made available);
- feasibility study at cost followed by fixed price or fixed term (a short-sighted view is that if the study reports that the project is not feasible, then costs have been incurred without getting nearer the desired result).

To help ensure reliability, and to re-assure both the Procurer and the developer that the processes and products and procedures are proceeding as expected, it is essential that the contractual terms include the reporting of progress and of quality achievements in ways that are meaningful and useful. (The most 'useful' reports are ones that not only clearly show deviations from what is wanted, but also indicate the causes of the deviations and possible actions to remove, or capitalize on, the differences.) A Procurer would not normally want (or be allowed to see) project reporting at the same frequency and depth of detail as the project manager, although, if deviations occur that are serious enough to indicate that the project is in real danger, then all available expertise and information, of the Procurer and end-user as well as the developer, may need to be pooled in the effort to save it.

8.3.7 Quality plans

The Procurer must ensure that the contract is backed up by the organization and methods that will make it a practical reality. The main vehicle for defining the Project Quality System, and the production system to which it is applied, is the Quality Plan. This is a document embodying quality of objectives, methods and controls, and which should be in an advanced state of drafting at the point where the last pre-project costing and feasibility studies are made.

All developments, whether under contract or not, need to have Quality Plans. (Planning and achieving software quality are discussed more fully in Chapter 9.) Although the *costs* of constructing and following a strong Quality Plan are significant, the *value* of defining and ensuring the qualities of the process and the product, and in giving constant assurance that they are as required, would make it extremely unwise to omit from the contractual terms that there shall be a Quality Plan, and that its plans and procedures shall be fully implemented and demonstrated to be continually effective.

Items to be covered or referenced in the Quality Plan are:

- statement of the Quality Objectives;
- identification of 'applicable documents', such as the contract, the Statement of Requirements, the Project Plan, and any standards called up by the Plan or used in its construction;
- the project's organization, with described and assigned responsibilities. For a procurement, it is particularly important for future communications that the roles and responsibilities concerned with liaison between customer and supplier are fully thought out, agreed, and recorded;
- identification of the Project Deliverables, and the schedule for their release/acceptance, in relation to the Project Plan;
- an abbreviated version of the initial statement (it can be expected to change in detail later in the project) of the Project Plan, with its phases, milestones, major reviews, deliveries, etc.: to show its relationship with the planning and estimation of quality activities, and to help in the future management of changes as they should be reflected in all the relevant plans;
- the working methods to be applied throughout the project, and the supporting hardware, software, tools, special equipment and services that will support them;
- the measurement, recording, analysis and decision-making processes to be used in the Quality Management of the process, product and project;
- the methods by which the required process and product qualities are to be assured, expressed as plans and Codes of Practice for:
  — Configuration Management (as detailed in a crossreferenced Configuration Management Plan; see Buckle (1982));
  — Change Management;
  — Documentation Plan;

— Testing, and Test Management (as detailed in a crossreferenced Test Strategy Statement, and Test Plans; see Evans (1984) and Ould & Unwin (1986));
— Product Release (by the developer);
— Product Acceptance (by the Procurer and users).

Although direct product development is the most usual place to find Quality Plans, they can equally well be applied to any other activity, for example, the procurement itself. Every Procurer is advised to draw up their own Quality Plan, concerned with the procurement activity and paralleling the suppliers Quality Plan by the assurance, communication and management actions needed to round out and link the actions and responsibilities of the three parties to the contract: the supplier, product users, and the Procurer.

8.3.8 Cost/benefit analysis

An initial analysis of the costs, and benefits, of obtaining and using the software item will have been made early on in the procurement, in order to support the decision whether it should or should not be pursued. At that time, there could be little precision on most of the cost items, but these will have become clearer during the period in which the supplier is chosen and a contract formulated. That early analysis, and the decision, should be re-visited before the contract is finalized.

A number of risk analysis and cost/benefit items have already been listed in the latter part of Section 8.3.5. In determining the investment of procurement effort into the development process, the cost to the procurer (and the developer) has to be balanced with the benefits to be obtained. The following, at least, require consideration:

Factor	Benefit
(a) Strong involvement in formation of Requirements	Long-term savings Early familiarity with product
(b) Strong involvement in forming Quality Plan	Security of assurance of final product quality Effectiveness of system to allow something to be done early if quality is at risk
(c) Regular reviews	Long-term savings Early risk/problem identification

8.4 Procurer's Involvement in Product Development and Testing

Obtaining a workable statement of requirements, and an acceptable contract, are only the beginning of the activities necessary to result in a product that will meet (reliably) all the needs of its managers and users. It is the duty of each party to a development contract to do all that can be devised to ensure that everyone concerned is kept fully informed of every fact or intention that might affect the nature or acceptability of the end result.

One of these communication routes is between prospective users and the development, passing (in both directions) through the Procurer. Most of the Procurers' regular responsibilities to the development group should be clearly documented in the development project's Quality Plan, and the Procurement Quality Plan, and can be expected to include the items listed below:

- The definition and management of communication paths between the supplier, the Procurer, and the user community.
- The identification, formation, editing and submission of technical inputs from the user environment and user community to the developers; made by way of the Procurer and the communication channels defined in the Project and Quality Plans.
- User specification, testing and scoping activities, carried out to assist the supplier with:
  — the specification of the product;
  — product test planning, testing, and result evaluation;
  — product release, acceptance and installation.
- Project progress reporting and control, especially as they affect the planning and carrying out of pre-installation activities by the buyer/user.
- Project, process and product quality reporting and control, especially as it gives early indications of the probable end quality, functionality, form, and completion dates, of the projects' products. These indications or predictions are necessary for planning and carrying out procurement and user activities (such as the product acceptance procedures, defining and testing user applications, preparatory training, etc.) that need to be integrated with the arrival of the products.

8.4.1 Interfaces between the supplier, the users, and the Procurer

For convenience in using the Quality Plan, its contents will often be stated very compactly. For example, the user–supplier interfaces will have been given in only enough detail to allow anyone needing to make contact for a particular purpose to locate the correct person and method of approach. Within the supplying and procuring organizations, the brief summaries within the Quality Plan must be expanded into detailed statements of precise responsibilities and their supporting procedures and given resources.

For example, there will have to be considerable interaction between the user community, the product developer's staff, and the group providing the computing environment in which the product will operate. Some of these interactions may be made most suitably by informal conversations, while others must be handled more formally, with the provision and acceptance of specified documents or by minuted meetings of formally constituted groups.

In order to maximize the usefulness of these contacts, and to minimize the disruption they could cause, it is necessary (amongst other details) to:

- name the primary contacts on each 'side';
- define procedures for inspection and authorization of the information passed;
- define procedures and assign responsibility and resources for the review and maintenance of documentation;
- assign responsibility and resources for the collection or creation of sets of data for use as examples or as test materials, and to review test plans and test results: especially where these relate to the user's interfaces with the product.

One of the functions just mentioned as needing control by a responsible person (or, better, by *two* responsible persons, one with the supplier and one with the Procurer) is the acceptance, authorization and maintainance of project documentation. High rates of change in the documentation, and/or poorly managed changes to documentation, are prominent on any list of the causes of project and product failure. Properly handled, measurements of the number and extent of changes to project documents are good metrics of the quality of the work done in forming those documents, as well as reliable indicators of the potential quality and difficulty of future activities based on the documents.

Obviously, these need handling with care. For example, a low rate of change could equally well be due to excellent preparatory work or to poor performance in the detailed analysis and expansion of the documents during later stages of work; just as high rates of change could either result from necessary changes to poor-quality early document or from the uncontrolled addition of all kinds of afterthoughts, from either the Procurer's organization or the developer.

8.4.2 Inputs from the potential user, to the development team

The Procurer should be prepared to supply the following.

- Data and specimens relating to the area of operation of the required item, such that the developers have a clear understanding of what is current there and thus what must either be replaced or interfaced with by the new product.
- Scenarios and mock-ups of the working conditions, facilities, etc., expected from the new item, such that the expected man–machine system and its interfaces with the new product may be reviewed, simulated and refined.
- Access to those who must work with, support, and control the new item, (including training, work study, organization specialists, etc.). This is especially needed in order that they may contribute to the external aspects of design aimed at meeting their own needs, and critically review any

design or user documentation relating to their own and closely related areas of activity.

- Predictions, plans (and leading indicators and/or models, as appropriate) of the nature and quantities of use to be made of the system, the value of its contents and facilities, and of any known up-coming new constraints, crises or major changes.
- Current versions of the user-organization's cost/benefit studies (or requirements) for the procurement, installation, and operation of the system, including assessments of risk and of the costs of recovering from failures, in both the 'hard' (machine-controlled) and the 'soft' (human-supplied) parts of the system. These studies will help ensure that the objectives and success/failure criteria applied by both the supplier and the Procurer are mutually understood and are kept in line with each other.

8.4.3 Specification, testing and scoping

It has already been indicated that requirements and constraints are best given in such a way that every statement is accompanied by one or more examples of what it is intended to mean in practice, and how success or failure in meeting the need will be measured or assessed. The Procurer should require this approach to be continued by the developers throughout the gradual detailing of various levels of design, resulting in a very full and complete collection of 'tests' to be applied to every intermediate and final product of the development.

The tasks of *specification* (that is, of fixing a set of elements that will together and, within the constraints, meet the requirements), *testing* (that is, demonstrating that the requirements have been met, and the constraints not violated) and *scoping* (that is, by specification and by testing, to set the limits within which the requirements will be met) are a joint responsibility between the developer/supplier and the Procurer.

While the developer is best equipped to suggest the nature and interpretation of the tests relating to the internal operation of the product (e.g. white-box testing), the Procurer must take a major role in shaping and interpreting matters that relate to the actual use of the product (e.g. black-box testing and human-factors). This responsibility (and opportunity) cannot be ignored if the Procurer takes seriously the securing of qualities such as the reliability, applicability and usability of the eventual product. However careful and professional the supplier, the knowledge that the supplier can obtain of the user's organization and operations and staff cannot be expected to equal that of its members: not in accuracy, or completeness or in up-to-dateness.

The procuring organization may be involved in the following activities.

(a) *Acceptance/installation/release testing*
For security and peace of mind, procurement 'Acceptance' procedures should be applied to all the project's more significant working documents, designs,

prototypes, plans, tests and investigations, etc., as well as to the items listed in the contract as being deliverable at defined project milestones. It is not sufficient to delay attention to 'acceptability' until the major milestone at the end of the development stage of the contract, or to that reached when the item has been delivered and the supplier proposes to withdraw.

The Procurer therefore needs to know what items should be examined, when they are expected to become available (and when they actually do), and what their significance is for the project and the product. From these details, a practical programme can be set up and managed by which a reasonable coverage of items can be achieved. Depending on the results obtained from the earlier reviews or tests, the later programme can be intensified or lightened. However, it is preferable that the first plans are for quite rigorous coverage, since it is easier for many reasons (including the administrative, social and technical) to reduce the level during a project than to increase it. Suitable check-lists must be devised and maintained for each item or class of items, reviewers must be found and made available at the appropriate times, and a simple system set up for recording what has been done and its results.

A particularly important class of items for review are those that relate directly to 'testing', whether this is the routine testing of separate units as they are produced, or the larger-scale testing of subsystems built up from those items, or of the final completed product. Any kind of testing has four main steps, each needing review. They are test planning, the creation or collection of test materials, the test outcomes, and the evaluation of those outcomes. Product release and acceptance are frequently made only on the results of the last stages of testing subsystems and the end product: these results *will not be* sufficient indication of in-service reliability (or any other quality) *unless* they have been very carefully planned and carried out, and unless the design of the product, and lifetime control of inputs and other aspects of the product environment, are carefully integrated with all the 'testing' done and its results.

(b) *Performance testing*
This is testing directed specifically at the quantification of the functions provided by the product. The Procurer should have collected quantified requirements (such as minimum response times for various functions and/or numbers of simultaneous users, speed of processing for given quantities of input and output using certain equipment, speed of processing given that limiting capacities are reached or closely approached, and so on) together with materials and procedures for their demonstration—and these materials etc. should be offered to the developers as a supplement to their own performance investigations.

(c) *Stress testing*
This is testing directed to the conditions of loading and usage where it is suspected that the product may not be able to cope. While the product should

have been designed within the known limits of capacity and speed of its physical elements, it is a much more difficult and subtle matter to predict and prevent the kinds of stress that can be built up by sequences of errors and/or unusual demands; or by the product being run on equipment, and by support software, that are simultaneously being extended by several competing systems.

(d) *Bench marking*

The term 'bench marking' is applied to measuring the performance of one or more systems when each is given the same task. It may be used to compare competing products, or to investigate the operating capacities of a single product when it is put into different supporting environments. Bench marks for competing products might be used to define the performance required of the item being procured ('process faster than X', 'support at least as many users at once as Y'), and could be used as contractual terms.

Investigatory benchmarking supports the management of a collection of software, equipment, and other resources, in the service of multiple activities each with characteristics that may vary from time to time. For example, the Support System Manager may need to be able to run tasks on different configurations because of equipment failure, or because several high-priority tasks need to be serviced at one time. The information obtained from benchmarking will allow the tasks and equipment to be juggled so as to satisfy the maximum number of demands within the time available, or to provide the most beneficial mixture of satisfied demands, and so on.

(e) *Regression testing*

Because of the interactiveness, and complexity, of most software, there is always the possibility that any change to a product, however useful and well-tested in itself, can produce either complete failures or a reduction in service in other areas of the item. Thus, any alteration must not only be tested in its own terms, but must also be followed by the fullest possible (or fullest that can be afforded) check that no other functions have been accidentally corrupted.

An effective maintenance and support organization can be expected to keep a suitable set of tests for this purpose, and to up-date it with great care whenever changes are incorporated. The correct running of this set of tests is an assurance that the product has not 'regressed' (that is, become worse in some way), and the testing itself is known as 'regression testing'. Even if maintenance is in the hands of another organization (perhaps the supplier of the product, or the software system engineers of the user company) it is a sensible precaution for any user group to have its own set of regression tests, and to run them after any change, and (as a precaution) before any particularly significant work with the product.

The regression sets held and maintained by product developers, maintainers, and users are likely to be different in nature, since they are directed to slightly different purposes and will alter in response to different local pressures. If all the sets are available, their variation is in itself a useful extra precaution, and is to be encouraged.

(f) *Destructive testing*

Where a product is required to be highly reliable or secure in operation, it is useful to spend time in deliberate attempts to make it fail, in order that the knowledge gained can be applied in improved internal or external defences. By using both the developers of the product and the more inventively inclined members of the user community in these tests, a broad range of failure types should be covered. Although it is often difficult to capture the exact operations leading to the failures, it is important that every reasonable step is taken to make sure that the causes and conditions of each failure, as well as the actual manifestations of the failure itself, are clearly recorded and are (if at all possible) demonstrated to be repeatable.

As ·well as stressing the inherent reliability and security of the product, destructive testing helps in exploring the functionality and usefulness of any 'self-testing' aspects it may have. These are facilities and design features such as collection of information on the routes being taken through the software, secure storage of register contents for display when needed to help diagnosis, and special facilities for 'snap-shotting' the internal control mechanisms at critical points. Although these facilities should also be tested under less-exciting conditions, to check that they are capable of all their specified functions, it is in the crisis and disaster situation that their help is most needed, and thus demonstration of their ability to function under stress is very reassuring.

8.4.4 Progress reporting and control

However carefully the supplier of a 'bespoke' item has been selected, and however little risk there seems to be of the product delivery being late, incomplete, or not to requirements, there is still a need for the Procurer to keep in close touch with progress, and with quality achievement. This is not only in order to have early warning of any changes in cost and schedule, but also so that the user's programme of preparing for acceptance, receipt and use of the item(s) can be kept at the right level. The nature and timing of progress reporting must be agreed between the Procurer and the supplier's Project Manager: for the Project Management view of this relationship, see Chapter 7.

The design of the procedure by which progress is reported from developer to Procurer is worth all the time it takes to develop. An effective reporting system can be expected to provide the following:

- Clear and verified evidence of development achievements against the contractual terms. The formation of a sufficiently detailed but not over-elaborate set of schedules for final and intermediate deliverable and reportable items is a procurement necessity.

If the contract is in very broad terms, without breakdowns into schedules of deliverable items and the stages by which those deliverables are to be reached, then there will be little to report against. It is also possible that over-detailed schedules result in voluminous but meaningless reporting, and that insistence on meeting large numbers of not-very-significant targets could hamper and distort the project's work. The balance is not easy to make, but it must be attempted for the sake of both the supplier and the buyer, who are equally concerned that the product be completed with the required attributes and in the required time and cost scales.

- Data on which well-supported predictions of the project's future achievements can be based. Again, both buyer and seller should be very concerned that any significant deviations in the current project be identified as soon as possible, and that information useful when planning other projects is collected and presented in a usable form.
- Timely and relevant reporting. The contents and timing of reports needs to be related to what they can be expected to show, and what they can sensibly be used for. It is the Procurer's responsibility to co-ordinate local preparations (including application development, maintenance provisions, and user-training) with product delivery, and to ensure that any failures or slippages by the supplier do not have excessively discouraging and costly consequences for the expectant users.

8.4.5 Quality reporting and control

Quality Management, as carried out by the supplier to assure the effectiveness of the software development process, is covered in Chapter 9. It is not directly the concern of the Procurer, although it is appropriate for the Procurer to require that there be an adequate Quality Assurance System. However, the Quality Plan will have included specific reporting on the quality being achieved by its processes, and in its products. The Procurer should take these reports very seriously, since they are the first indications of whether the project is meeting its quality objectives. For example, it would be cause for concern if it were reported that parts of the process were exceptionally long or short, or that parts of the product had unusually high or low fault rates, change rates, and time spent in reviews and other tests.

Although the Procurer cannot be directly involved in analysing the causes and implications of such warning signs, since they are properly the concern of the development project's management, it is more than reasonable that the basic reports be received, and a part taken in planning any remedial actions and in monitoring their resolution.

Chapter 10 (Section 10.8) gives a brief discussion on analysis and alternative resolutions when abnormal values, with quality implications, are reported for the data collected against the metrics used on a project.

8.5   Product Handover and Analysis of the Procurement

Depending on the kind of procurement, and the nature of the contract, responsibility for the product may remain with its producers until satisfaction is demonstrated or may be handed over with the product as soon as some mutually agreed demonstrations of completion have been made. Whatever the nature and timing of this transfer, the procurement exercise should not be regarded as complete until the product has been installed, has gone through the defined acceptance procedure, and is then either brought into full and satisfactory use or formally rejected.

The handover period, and the analysis of all aspects of the procurement, are the phase in which the Procurer progressively passes responsibility for the product to its new owner or to the Maintenance Manager. The release/acceptance activities will have been specified in the Quality Plan, including allocation of responsibilities for the product, and for managing any repairs or adjustments to be made to it, during the early period of usage. While the Procurer may continue to act as the interface with the supplier until full acceptance and development contract-completion are reached, responsibility for the technical nature and care of the product should pass in a controlled manner to the person or group with Maintenance responsibility.

An important part of the handover is the transfer of all the documentation that will be included in the Maintenance baseline, the quality records collected during the development, and an analytical report based on the Quality records and the experiences of the release/acceptance period and high-lighting any known weaknesses and peculiarities in the product. This analytical report will be used as a resource in future procurements, and as a major input to planning and predicting the maintenance required by the product.

8.6   Maintenance of Software

'Reliability' can be defined as the ability of a product or system to perform consistently, as expected, and in an acceptable manner—provided that it is used for the specified purposes, in the prescribed manner, and in the defined environment. These provisions (specified purpose, prescribed manner, defined environment) might seem only fair and reasonable. Also, if we could assume for simplicity's sake that:

- all Procurement is perfect, and thus that all software products and systems have their full sets of required qualities and functions when brought into use;
- the hardware elements of the system will be sufficient, supported, and economic, throughout the usage period;
- the original group of users, and of related systems, will remain constant;

then we could also visualize a very simple and clear-cut Maintenance task that ensures consistent service by preventing any attempts at change.

However, in practice this is neither practical nor efficient. A rigid system will soon find itself abandoned as it becomes further and further removed from the evolving needs of its users, and fails to gain the improved efficiency that could have come from enhancing its supporting technology. Thus, a useful and surviving system has to live and change with continuing updates from an effective maintenance operation that is working to preserve the value of the system.

Causes of alteration include the following.

- *Actual and overt changes made to the product.* In order to repair 'faults', extend functionality, enhance performance, make use of devices not considered in the original, and enable interfacing and interaction with products and systems that were not foreseen when the original requirements (and their associated verification and validation) were made. These changes may be suggested or required by the system's developers, or by its operators and users.
- *Deliberate changes made to the environment and operating conditions of the product*; for example, use beyond the original group of users; porting to new equipment; extension of applications into areas that were expected but not operational at the time of taking on the product; extension of application into new and unexpected areas; re-balancing of performance to meet changes in the profile of types and volumes of demand.
- *Gradual and/or unplanned changes to the way the product is used.* The reasons for this include the effects of familiarity and perhaps sometimes of pressure, on operators and users, as well as slow and unrecognized changes in the nature, patterns and volumes of the demands made on the product or system.

As well as changing during use, the product as-introduced is seldom identical with the product as-required at the start of the procurement period. Even if the requirements were 'correct' at the time when they were collected and documented, there are many events and influences during product design and development and in the on-going activities of the users-to-be that can lead to differences between the first wish and the eventual fulfillment.

In order to supply 'reliability', and allowing for the facts that changes cannot be excluded, and a perfect starting position is rarely achieved, the Maintenance responsibility will have to provide the means of assuring several aspects of the product and its environment, including assurance of the following.

- The nature and environment of product application(s) are kept as close as possible to those defined in the Requirements, Specification, and Acceptance testing.
- The Reliability dimension is properly considered whenever any change in organization, methods or support provisions, are proposed.
- Significant changes in the patterns and manner of use of the product are predicted and/or identified, tracked, and suitably managed.

- All proposed product changes are managed, that is, they are identified, notified and recorded, analysed for their costs and benefits, examined for their necessity and feasibility, subjected to a specified yes/no decision making process, and then progressed or retired in an effective manner.
- Those product changes that are accepted and made meet the same processing and quality standards as those for the original product and are prevented from causing any unwanted consequential effects when included into the new totality.
- Products are constantly monitored for their performance and qualities, and suitably managed against the results of the monitoring. This should include especially prediction and identification of the point at which a product and/or its usage has become so different from its original state that re-design or replacement is necessary.

Where the 'Acceptance' of the item had to be qualified in any way, or where it was known at the time of acceptance that the conditions of use were neither stable nor predictable, the problems of Maintenance are correspondingly greater. 'Qualifications' mean that the product is only expected to be reliable in certain, given, circumstances, and an 'unstable environment' (whether of use or of product support) means that whatever these given circumstances were in which the product could be assumed to be reliable, they cannot be relied on to be present at any point or to remain so for any length of time. A prudent product or service manager in such a situation should avoid taking on a commitment that would imply taking responsibility for circumstances and events over which there can be no control, although the professional duty would still exist to define and avoid the dangerous area.

Whatever the commitment or responsibility, a Maintenance Manager will find that the practicalities of the task are much the same. They consist of establishing a firm and agreed 'baseline' position; of managing all aspects of change against this baseline; and of ensuring constant readiness to supply the information needed to support decisions on the status of the products presently in use, and on the detailed requirements for future replacement procurement. (For general background reading on software maintenance, see Glass and Noiseux (1981).)

It will be seen that the work of a Maintenance Manager is difficult and demanding, and needs a high degree of technical ability as well as tact if it is to be carried out effectively. In addition to managing the areas under direct control, there must be very strong lines of communication and interaction with procurement, product acceptance, provision of services, and management of all the product applications. To be effective, Maintenance activities, and Maintenance management, require a considerable investment in tools and training, and are heavy absorbers of staff time. Because of its importance to product users, and the range of items that might be under care at any time, Maintenance must always be adequately resourced and managed if it is to be successful. Specific actions include:

- establishing a full Baseline for each product;
- establishing and enforcing the disciplines that ensure that changes to the Baseline are made rationally, professionally, and visibly;
- reviewing the contents of each Baseline and its associated records regularly and intensively; ensuring that all its contents are worth keeping, and planning for timely revisions and replacements;
- maintaining a programme of data collection, and reviews (with contributions by product users, service suppliers, product developers, procurers and policy makers) in order to be able to:

(1) ensure that all the products used are cost-effective;
(2) secure maintained products against disturbing alterations in their application or support;
(3) ensure as far as possible that future procurements and alterations are soundly based on accurate information, such as:

    (a) the relative qualities and costs of supporting items designed and developed by different methods;
    (b) transaction volumes, including error cases;
    (c) past patterns of activity;
    (d) the most frequent local failure modes;
    (e) supplier assessments based on observed qualities-in-action;
    (f) user preferences for such things as style of MMI, provision of figures to enable manual controls and traces, etc.;
    (g) support means and support capacity.

In practice there are many different possible situations, depending on particular products, priorities and uses, so not all the details of the aspects discussed here can be expected to be universally applicable. Even so, they should be useful as a basic checklist of factors for consideration in any circumstances. For convenience, the discussion below is presented under three headings (Section 8.7 Establishing the Baseline, Section 8.8 Managing Changes against the Baseline, and Section 8.9 Continuous Assessment of Product Status, and Support for Future Procurement), which correspond roughly to the order in which a Maintenance Manager would approach the specific tasks.

8.7 Establishing the Baseline

Changes are only clearly and usefully seen in relation to a defined starting position. 'Baseline' documentation provides this definition, together with descriptions of the procedures and means by which changes will be initiated, recorded, managed, and related to the initial statements.

Although the exact forms and sources of the baseline documentation will vary, there should always be a set of documents held by the Maintenance function which cover in detail the following.

(1) *The original requirements,* including functionality, performance, usage patterns, predicted loadings, predicted movements in loading (and of the required performance with those loads), expected extensions to functionality, and expected changes in the Hardware and Software environments of use. These requirements are the major documents against whose contents a system of regular product records and reviews should be built.

(2) *Any changes to the requirements made during product design, development and installation.* Apart from their functions of modifying the Requirement and illuminating the way in which understanding and intentions developed, early change records are useful in signalling and identifying any significant problems in the smooth flow of product design and development. Each one indicates a potential point of weakness in the product, and of confusion in its documentation.

(3) *The defined release and acceptance tests,* plus test results and analyses, and any agreements that were reached on deviations from the tests as specified. This group of documents is essential as providing hard evidence of what was actually intended, and how it relates to what was actually received.

(4) *Any relevant reports from the development and/or installation activities*: for example, any that might highlight weaknesses in the design, the development process, or the quality of the product (particularly its extensibility and maintainability). Use of the word 'relevant' here is deliberately vague, since the range of possibilities is so large, including such things as changes in key personnel at sensitive points in the development, disputes over the processes and tools to be used, struggles to meet particular requirements or constraints, and the location of fault-prone software elements. Although this vagueness may make it hard to be sure that none of the relevant items have been missed, it is certain that the effort needed to find and apply the information will not be wasted.

(5) *A set of 'regression tests' and the mechanisms designed for their regular in-service review and any necessary integration and up-dating.* These tests (with their supporting methods and tools) are the means by which the continued functionality and performance of the product can be re-confirmed whenever needed.

(6) *A set of plans for suitable staffing, controls, tools and procedures* by which all adjustments and changes will be made to the product in a standard, managed, visible, secure and traceable manner.

(7) *An accessible specification of the design and construction of the product,* suitable for use in supporting the design of change-implementations, assessing the size and effects of any proposed changes, and the keeping of cumulative records of the quantity of changes per identified area of the product. This is the 'map' that will be used as the basis of decisions on whether given requests for change should be accepted or rejected, and on when all or part of the software should be replaced, re-designed, and/or redeveloped.

(8) *A database plus suitable metrics and procedures* for the collection, analysis and presentation of results, by which trends and changes in usage and

performance can be regularly and meaningfully examined and assessed. Wherever possible, elements of this collection should be collected and displayed automatically as a by-product of the normal operation of the product or system.

(9) *The contractual conditions and procedures concerned with 'support' from the product's suppliers.* This 'support' covers such things as:

- the automatic supply of any 'improvements' generated by the supplier after the item has been accepted;
- repairs and corrections made by the supplier in order to redress points at which the original requirement was not met;
- extensions and alterations made by the supplier at the request of the product's owners and users.

The organization and nature of support will be different for bespoke one-owner items, and for those that have been sold for general use or to a group of related users. Where there are multiple users or owners, each one must be clear as to the position to be taken on the acceptance of 'alien' changes: that is, of changes made to meet the needs of others and perhaps of little or no local relevance.

While *not* accepting these alien changes is a protection for a user against any unwanted consequences there might be on functions and performance that are satisfactory, the supplier's policy may be to prevent the difficulties and extra work of supporting a number of product variants by accepting responsibility only for those into which all the issued alterations have been incorporated. Thus, the risks and costs of being supported or unsupported by the supplier must be carefully considered jointly by users and the Maintenance Manager.

(10) *Plans for the conditions and procedures under which local requests, authorization and undertaking of changes, will be made and managed.* The organization and interfaces should be established before they are needed, or there is a serious risk that uncontrolled changes will get out of hand in a very short time. 'Ownership' of the product and its services may have to be vested in a strong neutral body, probably a Quality Control function with responsibilities to the whole organization, and for the entire body of software in use, if a flood of minor and conflicting amendments, and attempts to 'beat the system' by over-stating the urgency of requests, are to be avoided.

8.8 Managing Changes Against the Baseline

As it is not possible to exclude all changes, it is necessary to ensure that those that do occur are firmly managed and controlled. This is of sufficient importance to warrant being an identified activity in its own right: the function is known as Configuration Management, and covers the control of minor changes, of larger deviations that create separately identified 'versions and variants' of the initial software for defined purposes, and of the 'builds' (or instances that link known combinations of hardware and software units). The potential needs of Configuration Management are the reason why several of the 'baseline' items listed previously were concerned with the timely setting up of the framework for active reporting and control during maintenance activities. In order to implement these intentions at the right time, and with the appropriate priority and funding, there must have been prediction and costing of the potential scope and consequences of the 'change' area, followed by the assignment of responsibilities, setting up of procedures, and provision of appropriate authority, means and resources (Buckle, 1982).

The main areas of activity are listed and briefly described below.

8.8.1 Change control

All the items in the Baseline should be placed under Change Control. This means that requests for alterations must be submitted (in a locally decided format) to the appointed Change Control function and will only be implemented if that function decides that they will provide a nett benefit. The Change Control function may be supported by representatives of the user community, and the support services, in making its decisions but should not be directly controlled by either.

All requests for change should be fully documented and recorded, and their progress monitored and reported upon. Where a request is accepted, and the product and relevant documentation are altered in consequence, the change process should also include designing specific tests for the validity of the change and amending the relevant parts of the Regression Test set as required, and changes should not be accepted into the working product until both specific and regression tests have run satisfactorily. The 'specific tests' should include reviewing as much of the documentation as is necessary to ensure that all consequential changes have been thoroughly thought through, and all the required documentary amendments and records properly made.

8.8.2 Developing and integrating product changes

Once it has been agreed that a particular change should be made, direct responsibility for its development goes to software technical staff against a *plan* for its timing and staffing. Whenever possible, the same tools and methods (including the validation and verification processes and tools) should be used as those of the original development: this avoids differences that might have been introduced by variations in the tools and the way they are handled. It is also helpful, when the product was developed or substantially customized by in-house staff, to use those staff in maintenance also, as this reduces both the chance of mistakes caused by misunderstanding the structure and usage of the product, and the time needed to learn enough about the product and its support system to enable the design and creation of the change.

While the physical changes may have been to only one or two elements of the product, it will seldom be sufficient to test these only. Rather, closely related elements should also be examined for any consequential effects, and at least part of the whole-product regression tests should be shown to have no unexpected outcomes before the change is accepted and the revised product passed for service. This necessary testing overhead, as well as the better-quality work achieved when a set of changes are designed and implemented together, justifies a policy of grouping the making of changes into significant work packages. The alternative policy (of making all changes as and when they are raised, and thus apparently giving a good service in the short term) can turn out to be dangerous and expensive in the long run.

8.8.3 Baseline maintenance

Baseline items should not usually be physically changed in response to a single request, but each should have an appended record of all the approved changes since the last Baseline issue. Each item and its records should then be regularly reviewed, and a new version covering a number of changes formally issued when it is appropriate to do so. ('Appropriateness' includes such things as the number, size, and importance of the changes made; and the security and convenience of up-issuing a complete set at one time whether or not every one of the individual members would justify it for themselves.) The up-issue becomes the reference copy for the next round of changes. Earlier issues are kept secure, and the file of change requests and change histories are also retained, though possibly in a summarized form after the first year or so in the product's active life.

The situation just described is for unplanned (but controlled) up-issuing of versions: where a software item is known beforehand to need a number of significant extensions or enhancements, the contents and timing of each release can be planned, giving developers and users the opportunity to comment on, and to prepare for, the series of versions.

8.8.4 'Build' management

It is sometimes possible to regard a working software product as a monolithic item, and to 'apply' changes to it with little regard for its original design or its internal structure. This approach may be adequate for minor changes to simple products, but is inadequate to maintain integrity and reliability in the face of more significant changes, changes occurring in large numbers, and changes made to complex products. For these more demanding cases, the product must have been designed and made as a set of interlocking but separable components (see Chapters 2, 3 and 4).

When the required changes have either individually or as a group resulted in the need to declare new 'Baseline' versions of components or of the overall design, there should also be a new 'build' of the product from all the current versions. The new build should be thoroughly tested, both to guard against regression and to ensure that the changes have been effected, and then used to replace the current working version.

A complete system for build management would cover the following.

- Procedures and tools for the maintenance of a secure library of elements (or parts) that might be used in the complete product, and for the specifications (or designs, or 'build-lists') which govern the selection and combining of those elements into various versions of the product.
- Procedures and tools for controlling and achieving the selection, creation, integration and validation of a working product from a specified build-list.
- Test sets applicable to specific elements and versions of elements, and to the results of combining them into larger elements, and into complete products.
- Procedures and tools for controlling and achieving all the testing and demonstrations needed to assure that a specific build meets its specification and its requirements.
- Procedures and tools for controlling and assuring that all the necessary parallel actions are taken. For example, parallel actions could include up-dating user and product documentation, automatically building defined variants of the product to meet known local requirements and preferences, and ensuring that all concerned parties are aware of the new build and any special factors in its functions or performance that might affect them.

The selection, control, testing and issuing of a new, complete, baseline, product 'build' whenever it is justified by the total effect of all alterations made to the product since the last build, ensures that:

- the product can be re-built at any time, to a known and proven specification;
- any activities involving the product (assessment, performance testing, learning about its design and implementation, training in its use, porting, interfacing, etc.) can be assured of having the current version and of only needing to consider changes since the last Baseline was issued;
- the evaluation and design stages of change control and change implementation are always made against a version that is as complete, clean, and coherent as possible;
- where a number of changes are to be included, or where alternative versions of the changes are to be compared, the existence of the baselining and building systems make it easier to achieve and control the necessary range of versions;
- it is always possible to go back to an earlier baseline build, or to create one which includes only completely trusted versions (or variants) of its constituent elements, if required.

8.8.5 Data collection, analysis and use

Operational statistics have already been mentioned in Section 8.7.8. These complement the files of change requests and change histories to give a fuller picture of why certain problems have arisen, and help indicate such things as where it might be best to approach a problem report or change request through alterations to the use made of the product, or the organization of the way the service of the product is supplied, or working methods, or even different training for users and operators, rather than through attempting to change the product.

In general, manual collection of data should only be made where at least one regular and significant usage is planned: otherwise data collection will probably soon become incomplete and inaccurate. Automatic collection, where possible, should be consistent and readily analysed, although unexpected entries and trends may not be recognized or understood as quickly as in a people-based system.

Much of the recording of change management is suitable for a degree of automation, for example by:

- recording fault reports and change requests in standard computer-based forms; with accurate completion prompted, and the results posted (that is, routed and recorded to all the required people and files), by the system;
- manual assignment of reports, requests, and eventual changes, to specific areas in the baseline and database, and then automatic posting and analysis of progress reports and comments as required;
- automatic provision of maintenance performance reports and control sheets; to ensure that items are not 'lost in the system', that priorities are observed, and that resources appropriate to the current loadings are authorized.

8.9 Continuous Assessment of Product Status and Support for Future Procurement

All products and systems should be regularly reviewed to ensure that they are, and will remain, effective and efficient suppliers of the required services. In order to do this, Maintenance and Product Managers should be able to give at any time well founded assessments of the state of all the items under their care.

These assessments will be based on records like those noted in Sections 8.7.8 and 8.8.5 above, and will be partly qualitative and partly quantitative, covering such aspects as the following.

- Which products are currently active?
- How often, and for what transaction volumes, is each product used? How often and for what volumes is future usage expected to be? Who uses it?

For what purposes? With what value? Might there be a better (that is, easier, cheaper, more powerful, more adaptable, easier to maintain, etc.) alternative?

- What quantity of maintenance effort has been applied to each product (numbers of faults and changes, plus quantities of effort used)?
- What future maintenance requirements are expected? Will it be cost-effective to continue to support current products? Will the methods (that is, the group of standards, processes, tools and controls) used on current products continue to be used in the development of future products? What are the probable cost and quality consequences of supporting more than one method?
- (where appropriate) How satisfactory has the quality and cost of the supplier's support been? Are there any questions of its continued availability and cost? How satisfactory has the product itself been, in terms of faultiness, extensibility, reliability, usability?
- Is there reason to suspect that certain parts of the product (or areas of functionality or performance) are near their safe limits?
- Are there reasons to question the future use of the product? For example, is the local support environment (hardware, software, staffing, tools, funding, etc.) likely to change in ways that will affect it? Is the local pattern of computer usage going to alter (perhaps by integrating systems and/or functions into more powerful and effective units, or by inter-working between related companies and services)?

Answers to questions like these are appropriate to both effective Maintenance Management and to the formation of Requirements, and Acceptance criteria, for future Procurements. In particular, one of the greatest problems of procurement is to get sufficient and reliable information on what users actually do, and what qualities they expect from their supporting products: regular collection and review of maintenance and operating records are thus a very valuable resource.

8.10   Summary: The Roles of Procurement and Maintenance in Achieving Reliable Software

Reliability is the principal purpose of both the Procurer and the Maintainer of software products. The Procurer establishes what it is that the product should perform, and the supplier is able to provide, and ensures that the requirement, the supply process, and the user's expectations are kept in step. The Procurer's goal is to ensure that the product should be reliable in every known aspect at the point of coming into service: including a reliable capacity for being maintained so as to continue to provide effective value to its users.

Once in use, the Maintainer tracks and manages any changes in requirements, adjusting the product to meet them, or refusing to make any alterations that could harm its reliability. Eventually, if there are so many or so extreme changes in the environment and requirements, the Maintainer decides when the product cannot be stretched or adjusted any further without causing it to become unreliable in some or all of its functions.

At this point, all the knowledge gained by the Procurer and the Maintainer is brought together, to make the next requirement more precise, the next contract more secure, the next application more effective. That is, in total, to improve the overall reliability and cost-effectiveness of software usage.

9

Software Quality Management

Gillian Frewin

9.1 Introduction 247
9.2 Definition of Software Quality Management 249
9.3 The Value of Software Quality Management 252
9.4 General Elements of Software Quality Management 259
9.5 Process Engineering 269
9.6 Three Angles on Software Quality Management 279
9.7 Summary 301
9.8 Further Reading 301

9.1 Introduction

This chapter deliberately avoids being prescriptive about the organization and content of software quality management. The approach taken is low-key and small scale, which is felt to be appropriate since the qualities of a software product begin in the intentions, beliefs and actions of individuals. Although 'quality' activities and management must be coordinated, represented and funded at a high level in each project and in the projects' host organizations, they cannot be entirely successful unless they are founded and maintained in the ways that development staff work and think.

Although this book is about achieving a single quality, that is the specific quality of 'Reliability' as it applies to software products, it is not sensible to try to manage software development with such a narrow focus. Even though some of the attributes of a software item that contribute to 'low' reliability can be identified, this does not mean that they then necessarily become either preventable or manageable, or that the means and methods by which they are prevented, if concentrated on to the exclusion of other concerns, will not have malign consequences for other essential qualities.

All aspects of project and product design, the methods used during development, and the way in which the product is handled after that development, interact to give the eventual mix of qualities. When a particular type or amount of any one quality is sought at the expense of others, the results may not be as expected or wished. For example, high reliability, if

247

obtained at the expense of performance or size, might well lead to the product being unacceptable. Similarly, high performance obtained at the expense of flexibility and maintainability might be over-expensive in the long run. A highly 'productive' development process (where 'productive' is equated with speed of progress through the project plan) might be applauded for its low costs until the full impact of quality consequences (such as poor documentation or low flexibility) become evident. These examples illustrate the necessity for broad and consistent attention to all the qualities of a product.

Quality management is concerned with the fitness and function of products throughout their lives from requirement to retirement and with the appropriateness and manageability of all the processing methods that are applied in the definition, development, application and support of those products. However, despite all the importance of all its roles, software quality management does not generally have a high profile or a good reputation as a promoter of product reliability.

Some of the reasons for this are understandable: ranging from:

- the negative effects of trying to impose 'standards' that demand rigid attention to the 'what' and 'how' of quality activities at the expense of their 'why';
- an association with what are seen as being 'old-fashioned' ways of working, and suitability limited to controlling only large-scale manufacturing activities;
- attempts to carry over into software development industrial quality practices that do not meet the needs of software products and their producers; and
- unhappy experiences of insensitive application of quality-related standards and measures;

through to possibly more appropriate, and better-implemented practices, which are nevertheless: inadequately proved, characterized, and engineered.

Past failures and a poor press should never be used to justify present neglect: what has been done badly before is wide open to improvement, and it would be unwise to give quality management a low priority just because it often has an unfashionably low-tech image, and needs a modicum of care in its application.

The text of this chapter falls into five major sections. Section 9.2 gives a workable definition of Software Quality Management, with some notes on why the quality management of software developments is particularly troublesome. Difficult though it is, the creation and assurance of software quality must still be controlled: Section 9.3 has summaries of reasons *for* applying quality management methods to software, and then reasons why they are *not* always used. These pro and con points are presented to assist users, partial users and non-users of software quality management techniques to establish why they are doing whatever they are doing, and perhaps to help form the cost–benefit basis of arguments for adjusting current attitudes and practices where this is needed.

Section 9.4 is a compact list and description of the general functions or activities found to be necessary in most software quality management circumstances. This demonstrates the range and depth of the software quality management task, and might find a secondary use as a checklist when reviewing local provisions. Two key quality management objectives are emphasized: they are to maintain full and appropriate communications, and to ensure that the technical processes used in product design and development are capable of consistently good results and are themselves applied consistently, until updated with necessary improvements.

After coverage of Process Engineering in Section 9.5, Section 9.6 revisits the list of general quality management functions introduced in Section 9.4, in terms of the needs and scope of software quality management in three different positions within an organization. It is hoped that the chosen form of presentation will encourage the reader to browse through the factors, gaining immediacy (and perhaps encouragement and support) through being able to identify with the situations covered.

9.2 Definition of Software Quality Management

So far, 'quality management' has been written in lower case: this was to avoid confusion with any set of responsibilities and activities which have received the title 'Quality Management' within an organization or in the Standards literature. It has been possible to avoid a definition in the Introduction, but it is now necessary that one be given: although not a common one, it does summarize the objectives, and, by extension, ways of meeting those objectives that are relevant to the role-model that underlies this chapter. From now on, the role receives its upper case Q and M, and will be qualified by adding the word 'Software' whenever this role is to be distinguished from the Quality Management of other products.

Software Quality Management is *the specialist role that exists to assist software developers to make confident statements about the general merit or characteristics of their processes and products*. While this definition has the merit of brevity, it immediately raises the questions of why anyone would want to make such statements and, if they do, how they can ensure that the statements are truthful and supportable?

'Why' and 'How' can be explained quite briefly by looking at significant technical and managerial issues found in any kind of development project. Quality Management is about identifying methods and tools that are capable of giving the required results, and of qualifying that selection with the constraints and controls that are necessary to make those results most likely of achievement. It is concerned that achievements are made in ways that are manageable and economical, and advises on how and to what extent, cost reductions can be made without compromising the qualities of processes and products.

Once the decision has been made to match a given product requirement with a specified set of methods and tools, Software Quality Management will go on to assist the Project Manager to set up realistic project plans and the appropriate supporting environment. During the project, the Quality Manager will monitor processes and their results, and advise on any necessary adjustments. Finally, the Quality Manager will provide an independent assessment of the qualities of the product in terms that are appropriate to its release, sale and maintenance.

Project Managers actually carry product responsibility and *should* be able to do everything a Quality Manager does, and it may therefore be thought that there is no need to have both. However, the two roles have different experiences, viewpoints and priorities, and are complementary in their effects: with the Quality Manager providing both a wider view and a more detailed view on products and processes than a Project Manager can be expected to have. By applying the 'wider view', the Quality Manager tempers any tendencies to abandon good project practices out of sloth or for short-term reasons: the 'detailed view' seeks out qualitative variations and their causes and consequences, and thus supports the making of controlled changes to the project's processes when they are needed.

While a Project Manager is rightly concerned with completing the task in hand and thus to concentrate effort and attention to that which serves this end, a Quality Manager always has an eye to explaining what happened in past projects, and to finding ways of improving future ones. Thus, the one (the Project Manager) may find records and measurements tedious and wasteful while the other (the Quality Manager) regards them as an essential part of the engineer's technical armoury. The second view clearly promises the greatest good for the greatest number in the longer term, but without continued championship by Quality Management it is unlikely to prevail against immediate project pressures.

Redefining 'Quality Management' in terms of its activities, Quality Managers advise on, set up for a general department (or assist in setting up for a particular project), and monitor and assess all the procedures and supporting means (techniques, methods, codes of practice, standards, procedures, tools, training) that enable products to be confidently planned, produced and maintained with known and acceptable characteristics.

Typically, these characteristics include not only those specifically required for a given product but also more general qualities. These include process reliability and product reliability, and the product's 'fitness for purpose' (which includes such factors as its ease of use, ease of maintenance, extensibility, security, resilience, acceptable cost of creation and bearable costs to maintain).

One question that often arises is 'Are there special difficulties for *Software* Quality Management?' The task of Quality Management is much easier in some circumstances than in others. Consider those industries (usually those that are long-established, and have products that are widely used) where there are well-established expectations and procedures. Customers, consumers or users have clear ideas of the general characteristics, or 'qualities', of the industry's products and of the ways in which these characteristics can be described, recognized and measured. Additionally, they either have or can easily obtain enough experience of similar products to be able to recognize the costs and consequences to themselves of a product that is 'better' or 'worse' than average. Thus, they are equipped to make reasonably accurate statements of their requirements, and comparative judgements, when specifying and procuring products.

Similarly, well-organized makers and providers of established products (whether software or anything else) can have clear and reliable knowledge of previous production processes, and of their cost and quality implications. When a new product or process is introduced as an extension to an established range, there is the possibility of assessing it against a secure body of information and of continuing to work within guidelines and standards that have already been adopted to protect both producers and customers from dangerous products or misleading claims. In such favourable circumstances, Quality Management is a simple matter of choosing the development or production process that gives the 'best' balances between costs, risks and the satisfaction that will be felt by customers and users, and then checking at convenient intervals to ensure that nothing unexpected and undesirable has occurred.

Unfortunately, there are also areas of design and production where few if any of the ideal condtions exist. Software procurement, design, development and assessment are particularly far from being well established and widely understood. As major software items are expensive to obtain, and often potentially very harmful if something goes wrong, but are also increasingly essential for the management and control of many highly valued and necessary aspects of commercial, public and private life, effective Software Quality Management must be achieved.

Software systems are used to control nuclear power installations and military equipment, life-support systems, air-traffic movements and many other vital and complex areas. Applications like these are frequently made in environments where the necessary operational qualities are not fully understood, or are not definable and/or not measurable. Unfamiliarity and imprecision may be compounded by the use of unpredictable design and development processes, and the lack of any adequate methods or tools to monitor the qualities and characteristics of both processes and their products.

Local guidelines, and quality measures, are usually parochial and hopeful rather than proven, demonstrable and widely applicable; those provided for general use are very likely to be based in the technology and failures of five to ten years before. This time lag arises from many causes, including secrecy over failures, delay in appreciating what is needed and what technology and theory is available: and the inevitably long time scales of agreeing, publishing and promoting a national or industry standard. Also, in general, the more important (and/or the more potentially disastrous) products are one-offs and thus do not allow procurers, developers and users to develop that 'feel' for the interactions of complexity, familiarity or unfamiliarity, feasibility, risks, costs and qualities that is a major protection for all those working in more mature fields of engineering endeavour. In addition, as the need for experienced staff exceeds the supply, the two factors of relatively high staff turnover and lack of time to digest the lessons of one project before starting the next also contribute to a slow and laborious build-up of knowledge and good practice.

Thus, Management of the Quality of Software throughout specification, development, and control (which includes attention to the quality of 're-liability' as being of particular interest) is an especially difficult and especially important, branch of the profession of 'Quality Management'.

9.3   The Value of Software Quality Management

Software Quality Management is not as widely or as effectively employed as it should be. Software design and development began on a small scale; with individuals reaching very personal solutions to problems, within the narrow and quirky constraints of early computing machinery. Programs were neces-sarily compact and often very complex for their size but they were produced in man-weeks rather than hundreds of man-years. Reaching the stage of having a viable program that met a fair proportion of the initial intentions had to be enough: meeting all of an extensive and elaborate group of firm requirements, with all the desired qualities and within cost and time constraints was not to be expected. At that stage there was not enough commonality between computer applications or the hardware that supported them for the lack of common standards and processes to be significant. Reliability and other qualities were appreciated and sought but their achievement could only be left in the hands of the craftsmen software makers.

The case is now very different. The removal of many of the early constraints together with the 'market pull' of greater expectations and competition, and the 'technology push' of better tools and methods, have resulted in the necessity and the possibility of obtaining better software and that by way of manageable processes. Quality Management of processes and products is needed and there are the means by which it can be undertaken. However, there are still many software producers who are either unaware of the value of gaining this control and predictability, or have not chosen to take full advantage of it.

The case for or against whole-hearted Software Quality Management is sometimes founded on habits and assumptions rather than logical and quantitative analysis. This is not wrong in itself but does present a major difficulty for anyone seeking to examine whether the present standing and activities of Software Quality Management in a business are such as to maximize its contribution. To suggest lines of investigation and argument for those making their own local cases for funding a higher profile or a more flexible approach to Software Quality Management, summaries are given below of reasons for the intensive application of Software Quality Management and then (as a counter to excessive enthusiasm) of reasons that are frequently used against it.

9.3.1 Why should Quality Management be part of every software development?

Assuming that there can be no real argument against the propositions that software products in general are necessary, are expensive and may be dangerous if unreliable, then any technique that might assist in improving reliability must be taken seriously. It is in the nature of the wide, complex and changing world in which software products are developed and applied that the list of positive assertions below cannot be proved true for all situations. Any technique or organization can be poorly implemented, misapplied, or be inadequately resourced and supported. However, given that sufficient care is taken, there can be very little doubt that the propositions will be found sufficiently true, sufficently often, to be well worth investigating.

Why, then, should a strong Quality Management presence be made a part of all software developments and support activities?

- *Because Quality Management is cost-effective.* Prevention of error is not only better than cure, it is also cheaper. A quality review that results in discovering and clearing up a misunderstanding before it is built into the product can save a project from (as a minimum) re-work and (at worst) complete rejection of the end product and waste of all the resources used in its creation. Similarly, reviews of proposed changes to an existing product may prevent destruction of its performance and reliability.

- *Because there are few alternatives, and those that are available are usually only partially applicable or successful.* While some technologies and tools exist that improve parts of the development process or meet particular situations, they are rarely able to provide a sufficiently wide coverage to be adopted as the main or only 'quality' provider and assurer in a software or system development. For example, however high the potential of a formal design method or a high-level language system in the areas to which it applies, it must still be matched with an appropriate area of application and be built into a full and coherent process to cover all project activities and eventualities. The best source of a wide and flexible range of preventive, control and management facilities is still an informed and effective Quality Manager, working closely with both project staff and the project customer.

- *Because Quality Management is flexible and reactive.* Formal technologies, or pre-determined standards, can only be expected to recognize and cope with the situations that were foreseen when it was developed, and that present themselves in an easily recognized way. An experienced, inquisitive and creative Quality Manager uses and complements the available technology, and extends or replaces it when necessary.

- *Because one of the Quality Management specialisms is in providing unbiased and well-founded assessments, predictions, and alarms.* Assessments may be of processes or products, and predictions and alarms (or early warnings) may be related to elements within a project or in the later lifetime of its products. 'Well-foundedness' is achieved by regular and meaningful measurements, inspections and reports, supported by timely analyses and reviews of the information being collected. This service is invaluable for Project Management, Support Management, Senior Management, Product Marketing, and (perhaps of the greatest significance) to those who procure and use the end products.
- *Because Quality Management seeks out and plugs the holes other technologies cannot reach.* Even the best possible 'today' system eventually meets a situation that was not envisaged and that it is not programmed to handle. Before this failure is recognized, considerable damage may be done, and high costs incurred. Lateral thinking and an almost infinite variability of approach makes man the perfect last-resort safety and security back-up system, and the broad focus and experience of Quality Managers makes them the most likely members of a project to spot new conditions as they arise.
- *Because it works.* Software quality achievement is highly interactive and people-dependent. By concentrating on maintaining a high level of technical and conceptual communication Quality Management gives the broadest possible protection against losing either the coherence of the whole project and product, or the narrower-focus integration of the technical actions by which it is intended to achieve it. By engineering working procedures and processes to be as reliable and controllable as possible, Quality Management provides the means of making better products, and better-characterized products.

9.3.2 Why is Quality Management *not* always used, or not used well?

The points below summarize and answer some of the main attitudes and arguments working against introducing, extending or altering the Quality Management of software activities. Attitudes and assumptions about quality work can be particularly hard to identify and alter: some are based on real experience while others are irrational, but they are all influential on the success or otherwise of a Quality Management scheme.

- *Because Quality Management is thought to be old-fashioned, inappropriate, and/or over-restrictive: especially if applied to methods and products that are very abstract, formal, high-tech, etc.* Quality Management should not have any of the unpleasant attributes given above. Indeed, if it is being applied in such a way that any or all of them are present then the quality system needs re-thinking.

Although it is always to be hoped that newer methods have been designed and chosen because they give better results then previous ones, it is unlikely that any method (especially while still 'new') can be the complete answer to every possible problem and need and thus produce perfect results every time. Software and system development is a particularly trying field for 'general-purpose' methods because of the wide differences between one instance of a development and others: in the nature of the requirements, the degree of interaction between them, the volatility of those requirements, the ability of project staff, and so on.

Choosing technology, tools and methods for a project is thus always difficult. It should always be remembered when contemplating a new and high-technology item that manageability and user-acceptance are needed as well as technical brilliance. One of the practical considerations in selecting technology is the extent to which it can reliably support the Project Manager and the Quality Manager as well as the project's technical staff, readily and acceptably providing the services, information and first-line controls which are needed.

• *Because Quality Management is seen as being an optional add-on to a product development and maintenance, rather than as their strong central thread.* This unfortunate impression is sometimes encouraged by the more authoritarian literature on Quality Management, which can easily give the impression that the forms of Quality Management are more important than its objectives and content, and that these forms exist independently of a particular project situation. This apparent inflexibility leads to a belief that quality does not need thinking about and that it can be imposed without reference to the realities of the project, possibly much later than the other areas of technical project management.

The 'add-on' impression leads to dangerous behaviour such as:

—Omitting to include quality considerations and contributions as a full and important part of requirement specifications, feasibility studies, process selection and design, predictions of project progress and achievements, etc.
—Omitting to plan and cost quality activities at the right (that is, the earliest possible) time, and confining them to too short and narrow a portion of the product's life.
—Budgeting for Quality Management as some small proportion of a separately determined project cost, and not as the actual amounts needed to provide the facilities and functions necessary for project and product to meet their technical objectives.
—Allowing a significant amount of the project's early work to be done before a Quality Management appointment is made, or allowed to become effective. This may result in anything from minor re-work to a project that is entirely flawed by inadequacies in the processes used and in the interfaces between their products. Late entry into a project

makes it difficult or impossible for the Quality Manager to establish his or her position, and to introduce the procedures and checks the Quality System (and the project) needs. Communication and control have to be built into the total project process at the earliest possible point, and as a high priority for all project staff, or they cannot be fully effective in preventing and discovering faults in the project's concepts and products.

- *Because Quality Management is thought to be difficult, and not cost-effective.* Quality Management is not simple and should always be in the hands of the best available staff. Its funding, like that of all the other resources and activities needed for satisfactory project completion, should be at the levels shown to be required from a detailed analysis of the work to be done. If the need for technically and managerially experienced quality staffing and the level of the predicted quality costs are thought to be surprising and excessive then probably the actual and potential costs of trying to achieve the same results by any other method have not been sufficiently identified and evaluated.

Looking first at the requirement for staff: it has to be recognized that much of Quality Management is concerned with early identification of situations and complex interactions within a project and its processes which have present or future consequences for the qualities of end-products. Once identified, the potential for good or for ill has to be modelled and decisions made on whether and when to take action, on what that action should be, and how it can best be implemented. In order to do all this the people concerned need technical and organizational skills and a great deal of experience. They must also have the respect and confidence of project staff and a very close working relationship with them. While there may be some repetitive aspects to Quality Management that could be handled by less able persons, they must all be closely monitored by competent quality staff to ensure that no significant points are missed.

As to being expensive, cost may be regarded differently at the start and end of a project. An initial estimate that demands spending of (say) 10% or more of project resources on quality-related activities may seem very high when first presented: if this results in avoiding the many multiples of 10% frequently achieved in overspends and overruns, then it cannot reasonably be judged to be excessive overall. Similarly, quality activities during a development may seem unproductive in that they do not directly add functionality or performance to the product. However, the result of making a reliable and supportable product can be to save more on support and maintenance effort over its lifetime than was expended on the entire initial development, as well as providing better service than an item whose development was thought more obviously economical in the short term but that proved temperamental and rigid in use.

Although it is often asked for, presenting the quality budget as a bare percentage of a total project cost or as a net sum to cover all the primary activities is not the most effective way of putting across how the 'quality' resource will be used or of the consequences of making cuts in it. Indeed, putting forward a simple request for a specified total sum positively invites others to trim it down. Instead, a presentation that shows how the minimum quality resource requirement is built up from consideration of the structure of the product, and the plans and designs and other documentation required for all the elements and at all the levels (combined with the development and quality processes that have been planned to be applied to them all) makes it apparent that a cut in the quality resources can only be made by removing some of these inspections, reviews, demonstrations and other tests. It is then up to more senior management to decide whether their natural desire to reduce project costs will result in reducing the reliability and other qualities of the process and thus the products of the process.

- *Because Quality Management is thought to be only appropriate for industrialized processes, while software development is still largely ad hoc, 'creative' and unpredictable.* To be reliable, and capable of resulting in reliable products, it is necessary that as much as possible of the software development process is engineered or industrialized. This should not inhibit all the interesting and creative aspects of the human elements in the process, but should rather free them from as much tedium as possible. For example, the formal translations and consistency checks that must be made between creative stages are in many processes tedious, uninteresting, error-prone and often skimped if done by hand: if they can be performed by machine they will be done consistently and correctly. In addition, once a process has been automated it has a greater capacity for producing its outputs in a range of alternative presentations that it might have been too onerous to attempt by hand, but which can add a great deal to understanding, communication, and the efficiency of verification and validation.

- *Because Quality Management has assumed or been placed in a position that is excessively detached from the actions and concerns of projects and their staff.* While enough independence is needed to enable Quality Management to make cool assessments and unbiased decisions, too much will result in serious weakening of communication channels and thus potentially cause the loss, inaccurate transmission or late arrival of important information. The further the quality management functions are from the project in both conceptual and organizational terms, the more its work will be seen as irrelevant, intrusive and threatening: the treatment of Quality Management as an 'optional add-on', discussed above, is another aspect of this distancing.

- *Because current design and development methods are thought to have made formal Quality Management obsolete.* This appealing proposition does not seem to have been proved (or if proved, to have been reported) for any method now in use: Method developers do not appear to give priority to demonstrations of cost and quality performance that would support such a proof. Neither highly automated nor mathematically founded methods can dispense with Quality Management: rather, because any faults may be subtle and far-reaching, these methods need very close attention.

- *Because technical staff are thought not to like having their work monitored in any way.* Direct staff assessment is not a part of Quality Management, and most Quality Managers ensure that their reports and records are as secure as possible from any such usage by others. If it does become obvious that there are wide variations in performance, the quality interest is in finding out if there is any identifiable and removable cause: for instance, insufficient training, inadequate support, ambiguous specifications, poor tools and equipment. Properly handled, it is clear to all staff that the quality presence is there to help them and not either to spy on them or to try to reduce them all to automata!

- *Because of satisfaction with present processes, products and productivity.* This is the most acceptable reason for not applying, or not up-grading, Software Quality Management, but should only be put forward if satisfaction is well-founded and reflected in the views and actions of staff and customers. Even when the satisfaction seems well-founded at a given time, can any organization risk falling behind the rest of the industry on the next project or with future technologies? Can any organization be sure that its present standards of achievement will be maintained without a degree of precautionary independent auditing and checking, and will good practices persist without encouragement and supportive action? Even justified satisfaction should not be allowed to interrupt the continuity of research and development directed at further improvement in the achievements of software development processes.

9.3.3 Recommendation

Whatever the present style and degree of Quality Management and quality achievements, every software producer should regularly and critically review what is being done and whether it could be more technically and financially effective. Negative assumptions and attitudes should be identified, investigated and (if need be) countered; and more positive ones should be fostered. If local Software Quality Management activities seem to be under-achieving, under-funded, or under-estimated, then there should be effort put into looking at present and possible costs and benefits, and in giving the results (which can be fairly confidently assumed to be supportive of continued and probably of enhanced quality management) a high profile.

Experience suggests that even very small outlays on such investigations can be highly beneficial. For example, if the cost of releasing products with faults and inefficiencies has been established (however roughly, and over however small a number of products), it is usually clear that only a small proportion needs to be prevented to bring the nett costs and benefits onto the positive side. A few days spent in examining processes for the ways in which they permit (or encourage) errors, rarely fails to find preventive methods for that small proportion, at least.

While staff directly concerned with quality matters will be regularly involved in costing poor quality and in seeking its improvement, for best results they should be joined by project technical staff who have the most direct and recent experience of using the methods and processes and by those who have had to manage the post-production lives of products. 'Post-production' includes the selling, installation, use, maintenance and support of products, and will have encountered the practical consequences of any failure to meet the product specifications or to have the qualities that may have been unspecified but that are still essential for easy and effective handling of the product. A wide range of involvement in quality costing and assessment not only gives a broader insight into problems and possible solutions than could be supplied by Quality Management alone, but also contributes to the acceptability and integration of quality reports and recommendations across the organization.

9.4 General Elements of Software Quality Management

There are perhaps two main elements to be found in all successful Software Quality Management: one is ensuring that excellent communications are facilitated and maintained, and the other is to be able to engineer, select, enable and monitor for particular circumstances those design and development processes that have the highest chances of producing the required qualities in the end-products. 'Checking-out' (that is, the testing and demonstration of end-products to honestly convince their makers and their buyers and users that the specific functionality and general qualities are there) is also needed, but as it cannot create quality it is of lesser and later interest than the ways in which functionality and quality are put into the product as it is developed.

The main objectives and consequently the strategies used are recognizably constant for all kinds of Quality Management. However, the manner in which those strategies are transformed into working tactics is usually governed by the nature of the products and processes being managed, the host organization and the position and scope that Quality Management has been given. For example the detailed approaches that are appropriate and necessary for large-scale manufacture of electrical goods would not be the same as those that would best fit the design of individually bespoke and hand-made items of furniture. Making software is often still nearer to the second of these cases than the first, even if it is done within an organization where there are many projects and many software staff and thus an apparent potential for standardizing on one software development process.

Although there is a growing interest in the industrialization of software development it is not always practical, nor is it realized where it is possible. Some of the reasons for this can and should be countered, while others have no obvious solution at present. No Software Quality Manager should allow the absence of a complete answer to hold up what can be done to remove or tidy up those parts of the process that can be made more effective and efficient.

Looking at a business organization and the position of Quality Management, within it, the lot of an isolated and part-time 'software quality officer' within a single project is naturally different in many respects (though not in kind) from that of a Software Quality Manager who is responsible for a range of products and projects, and different again from that of the Software Quality Director of a company. While the more powerful positions are influential in setting up a climate and general environment in which 'quality' can be achieved, it is at a local and detailed level that day-to-day actions and interactions within a development actually do achieve it. A range of levels of influence and of quality management activity, from policy making for a company through to making inspections of piece-parts, is needed to ensure that the required results are possible, are economic and are obtained.

To cover as much of this ground as possible the common quality elements will be presented in two ways. The first is in this Section (9.4) as a summary of the common tactical quality management functions; a second view is given later (in Section 9.6) by looking through this list of functions as they relate particularly to three of the organizational positions from which 'quality' services and controls might be provided.

The basic Software Quality Management functions are as follows.

(A) Definition and support of an effective quality organization

The organization should derive from clearly stated and well-supported business-level quality policies and objectives, and from a defined and proven set of methods (or processes). This formality is as necessary (and useful) for a small sub-project as it is for a major undertaking.

The design and implementation of an organization includes.

- the specification of roles and responsibilities;
- the identification and design of interfaces between roles, and chains of authority and reporting;
- the assessment of resource needs, and agreement of budgets;
- the selection, appointment, and, if necessary, training of persons to meet the defined roles and responsibilities;
- formalizing the place of the 'quality' organization in relation to its surroundings; for example, by ensuring that the methods and codes of practice for general management include appropriate and timely reference to Quality Management services.

(B) Feasibility studies

These include all the professional and technical studies made before a full project is authorized. Quality Managers assist and support Project Management by providing detailed plans and estimates for quality activities and by reviewing the implications that all the project's plans have for each other. A particular responsibility is for the formation and agreement of an effective Project Quality Plan (see also Chapter 8 on procurement and maintenance) that ties together objectives, processes, organization and controls.

Functions (B) and (C) (feasibility studies, and process selection and engineering) are closely related and interact with each other. Examinations of technical feasibility cannot sensibly be done without having made at least preliminary judgements on the processes to be used (or possibly the short list of processes from which the selection will be taken). Similarly, the project plan and the predictions on which it is based would be seriously incomplete without details of the validation and verification activities inherent in the development process, and the recording and reporting functions that support project and process management, as discussed in Section 7.2.1 of Chapter 7.

The feasibility-study period is particularly important for Quality Management, since it is here that the interactions between technical and quality and managerial processes are designed, reviewed, costed and established as the framework of the project. If Quality Management is not a full member of the project management and technical team at the outset of these investigations and decisions, it may be impossible to retrieve the position once the project becomes active.

It should be remembered also that every feasibility study is itself a subproject, and thus needs its own objectives, plan, and reviews of its process and results, as well as retrospective reviews once the project studied is underway, to ensure that earlier decisions and expectations continue to be valid.

(C) *Process selection, engineering, and introduction*

The nature of the development process is influential on the results, costs and controllability that can possibly be achieved. The choice of process, or selection and integration of subprocesses, should therefore be made thoroughly and rationally. Although the Project Manager has the ultimate responsibility for the selection made and its consequences, for balance and commitment the selection procedure should also involve the Quality Manager (who will be charged with responsibility for ensuring that processes are followed and are effective) and other leading Technical Managers, as well as representatives of the project staff who will apply the process.

The Quality Manager's roles with regard to process selection include the following;

- providing historical data on which processes may be judged;
- ensuring that the chosen process selection procedure is appropriate, and is followed;
- ensuring that candidate processes are examined for their quality potential, as well as technical desirability, and productivity;
- ensuring that trials are carried out consistently and accurately;

- identifying control points, and control targets, that can be used to indicate that the process is behaving as required;
- taking responsibility for ensuring the effective, continued and consistent use of chosen processes once in action.

Candidate processes for the selection may come forward for the following reasons.

- They have been required by a customer (in which case the investigation and assessment may be regarded as a feasibility study, rather than as a part of a selection procedure).
- They are already in local use.
- They have been put together specifically for the current project/product purposes.
- They have been suggested by the project's technical staff.
- They are contained in a published Code of Practice.
- They have been put forward by specialist bodies.
- They have been derived from technical communications (books, journals, seminars, conferences, exhibitions, demonstrations and so on).

This list of several sources, and use of the work 'selection', may have been taken to imply that Quality Managers can expect to find a number of suitable processes to choose from. Unfortunately, there are very few software-related processes in existence (apart from some language compilations) that are really well engineered and that are suitable and available for general use. The term 'well-engineered process' is used here to mean one with stated applicability, defined theory (where appropriate), a useful and flexible range of functionality, fully defined and easy-to-use procedures, readily accessible operational requirements, measured performance characteristics, support tooling and suitable packaging (training, manuals plus available examples and advice, etc.).

While there are a few complete and well-engineered processes available, there are none that can be unhesitatingly recommended as being the 'best' in all circumstances. 'Best' would mean always having the highest scores on all measurable and desirable properties, including such things as:

- development and maintenance costs;
- prevention of errors;
- disclosure of errors;
- reliability in action;
- predictable and manageable achievement of all possible required product qualities, in required quantities;
- convenience of application;
- acceptability to users.

As local views on which factors constitute 'desirability', and on the relative importance of those factors, will differ, every process-procurement has to establish its own list of requirements and ways of measuring the degree to which a given process meets them.

Process selection, and process engineering, cannot be separated in practice. Many candidate processes must be engineered extensively before they can even be considered for entry into a selection process, since without it they are so ill-defined and unqualified as to not be comparable on most of the aspects of interest. Further, even when well-constructed processes are available and are selected, it is rare to be able to apply them effectively on a specific project without some local engineering effort. A brief treatment of process engineering is given in Section 9.5, and it should be emphasized that Process Engineering is the essential activity and skill for successful project control and product completion.

A well-engineered process provides support for Project Management as well as ensuring that generally desirable product qualities as well as those that have been specifically required, are achieved consistently and economically. Support for project and other management comes from including in each process sources of control data and technical data, and the provision of a network of data channels through which this information will reach appropriate decision-making people and processes in good time for action to be taken.

If reliable products are to be produced, then the entire production process (consisting of a number of linked subprocesses) must itself be reliable: this can only be assured if process engineering is applied consistently and professionally and all processes are introduced and maintained in an appropriate way. Introduction of a new process must be managed at different levels, including the production of operational manuals, provision of training and exemplars, and inclusion in all the relevant codes of practice. Maintenance will be directed to keeping the process workable and consistent, and identifying and acting on any need to make changes.

(D) *Quality control and quality assurance*

While there is agreement that two different functions exist, one relating to continuous quality activities during a process and the other to the closing of a process by assessing its end products, there is not complete unanimity in the literature as to which should be called 'assurance' and which 'control'. No attempt will be made here to give an authoritative resolution of the issue: instead, alternative terms ('In-process control' and 'Check-out') are used below, while the two familiar terms are left in the heading to assist browsers.

In-process control. This is the group of responsibilities and activities by which the specified qualities of processes and products are monitored and kept within control during active development or within other large-scale activities such as maintenance. It includes the setting of standards for the procedures and products, formation of a suitable monitoring system of procedural audits and product measurements, and managing that monitoring system and its outcomes.

For example, the combination of audits, measures and assessments known to be needed within a project should be embodied in a written plan (preferably within a formal Quality Plan) and that plan must be resourced and carried out in a way that is suitably integrated with the development process. Results should be reported and followed up in such a manner that 'negative' or 'destructive' deviations of the product and/or process are discovered and redressed, and such that information useful for forecasting and planning purposes is collected.

Check-out. This takes place when development of the process-products is complete and just before product-release. It is the group of demonstrations, tests and assessments made at the end of a project to (it is hoped) show that the combination of the chosen process and its in-process control has resulted in an acceptable outcome.

If this function shows up significant deviations from product specification, or from more general quality expectations, then the end of the development is a very expensive point at which to discover the need to alter or repair the product! Thus, the final check-out should never be allowed the status of a serious element in achieving or controlling the quality of a product: its proper position as a 'quality' exercise is as a showcase and delivery point.

(E) *Quality reporting*

Like all reporting, this is most effective when matched to particular objectives and audiences. For example, an accountant or administrator may be best served by reports that show the accumulation of costs against quality headings, the unspent portions of each budget, and estimates of when the budgets will be exhausted and whether these points of exhaustion will coincide with the end of calls on those budgets. Reports like this will show when adjustment or re-negotiation is needed and its probable extent, and whether quality costs (such as carrying out debugging, rework and reviews) are 'under control'. Too much technical detail (for example of small steps within processes, the items to which they are being applied, and the results being found) may not only be uninteresting but may actually serve to obscure the messages that are important for accounting needs.

However, reports to Technical Management should be at least as concerned with quality 'achievements' (whether positive or negative), as with quality costs. For example:

- What quantities, of what qualities, of useful output have been made up to each reporting point?
- What is the status of the most critical work items? What needs to be done about them?
- Are the chosen processes behaving as required?
- Are the less critical items being progressed in accordance with relevant plans and schedules?

- Where there are deviations from expectations: what caused them, what will their likely effects be and who should be taking what actions to contain or to exploit them?

Only two extreme forms of report have been touched upon above: in practice there are likely to be many different reporting requirements made on a Quality Manager, and a few simple rules should always be applied to help to keep them within bounds.

- The contents and forms of the main reports should be settled as far as possible before the project becomes fully active. In particular, the funding for, and main purposes of, reporting, need to be established before there is any possibility of the Quality Manager being regarded as a 'free' source of information.

  The collection, collation and analysis of information must be a prime interest of a Quality Manager, since it is based on the material that is needed to meet long-term quality objectives such as the abilities to model and predict. The ability to respond accurately and quickly to requests for information is a significant selling point for quality activities and the Quality Manager, although care is often needed to prevent too much time being spent in making responses to *ad hoc* demands.
- Whenever possible, data should be collected for multiple purposes, and reports should be such that their main points can be verified or supported against independent controls of some kind.
- One-off reports made for special purposes should be made with the cooperation of those to whose work they apply, and should be based as far as possible on the data usually collected, and on the reports usually made.

(F) *Configuration, and documentation, control*

These are well-known to be essential (and effort-consuming) services, and are often assigned to a separate Configuration Management function and re-sourced separately from Quality Management; see also Chapter 8, and Buckle (1982).

However the responsibilities are divided, configuration and documentation control acts as a specialist technical 'customer' to the project, as an enforcer of standards, and as a librarian. These functions are responsible for identifying deliverable products (whether plans, designs, documents, code, tests and test materials, build-lists or build-control instructions, etc.) and ensuring that it is possible at any time to produce the current version of each, and the path by which that version was reached. The work includes defining relevant status levels, setting baseline configurations from which changes are to be tracked, receiving and managing deliverable items, assigning them status levels as they are created and developed, and controlling the number of copies of each and their nature and usage, as the project progresses.

Elements in the control include:

- maintenance of secure libraries;
- quality checking of items offered for acceptance into the libraries;
- maintenance of the necessary parts, plans, tools, versions, etc., needed to ensure that items can be re-created;
- library management, including:
  —selection and maintenance of the media and tools used;
  —agreement and implementation of policies on access to items of given status;
  —policy and procedures for the number of copies of any item at any time;
  —removal and/or back-up of dis-approved or retired materials;
  —selection and possibly packaging of items suitable for re-use;
  —reporting against the planned intake of items;
  —notification of any present or foreseen problems.

(G) *Data collection for project, product and process records*

Some of these measurements and records will be suggested by (and perhaps 'owned' or required by) the technical and administrative management of the project or of the environment in which it is being carried out. Whoever owns the data, the Quality Manager is often the natural agent for their collection and the first stages of collation and analysis. Whether or not charged with the collection of particular data, the Quality Manager will always be well advised to collect and review operational information in order to have:

- the fullest possible picture of the current project, in order to help identify points of pressure, 'good' and 'bad' trends in performance, deviations for previous experience, etc.;
- useful materials to carry into other projects, especially to support feasibility studies, choice of process, process control, and so on;
- useful materials to carry into activities such as the planning and provision of common procedures, processes and support facilities.

In order to be acceptable to project staff, data collection should avoid obstructing or duplicating other activities and should be purposeful. That is, recording should be built into the development process and automated or facilitated as far as possible, and there should be a real and known benefit from having the data.

(H) *Audits and reviews*

An 'audit' is a check that a defined procedure is being followed: a 'quality review' (which will be distinguished from other Technical Reviews in the Development Process by its wider scope) is a check or an assessment on how well a given set of objectives is being (or is likely to be) fufilled.

A third level of regular examination can be supplied by organizing Quality Circles (see Mohr & Mohr (1983) for a description), in which staff within a given area meet regularly to discuss any quality-affecting factors that have come to their notice, and that they feel can be improved. Quality Circles are particularly appropriate places for discussing and making practical recommendations on physical factors (such as accommodation, access to people and equipment, noise, and irritants such as inappropriate heating and lighting) and poorly designed interfaces to tools and services. These are all known to affect the quality and quantity of work, but are often overlooked.

In practice, audits and reviews are often considered as interrelated faces of a single check-point, with a specific audit being followed by consideration of whether the procedure has met or will meet the objectives for which it was designed, and a wide-ranging review of possibilities and interfaces that might not have been covered adequately in the original procedure-design or the narrow-focus assessments based on that design.

A planned and agreed programme of audits and reviews should be part of normal quality control. However, the possibility of 'extra-ordinary' audits and reviews must also be within the scope of the Quality Manager's interests and responsibilities. 'Extra-ordinary' audits and reviews need special handling and reporting, and each one needs to be separately, publicly, and carefully justified if they are not to cause negative reactions among both project and quality staff.

Probably the most common calls for additional audits and/or reviews come from senior management with a need to balance the risks and returns of a number of projects (or products), or having been called upon to answer criticisms or doubts raised about the project. One of the tasks of the Quality Manager is to balance any irritation and delays caused by the use of project staff in these 'extra-ordinary' activities, with the needs for their technical inputs to, and personal acceptance of, the investigations themselves.

In addition to the programme of formal audits and reviews organized and 'owned' by the Quality Manager it is helpful and informative if there can be an appropriate 'quality' presence at the project's own internal technical reviews. Inclusion in a representative sample of these reviews is very helpful in allowing the Quality Manager to carry out the responsibility of ensuring project processes. This does not mean that every code-reading or design walk-through must be attended (which would be an inefficient use of time) but that enough coverage should be sought to give reasonable assurance that any process problems will be recognized as quickly as possible after they arise.

Quality attendance at the project's lower-level technical reviews should not be claimed as a right since this could be seen as interference or covert assessment and thus inhibit the openness and value of the reviews attended. Rather, a situation should be encouraged in which 'quality' attendance is invited, because its technical and administrative contributions are welcomed.

(I) *Communication and justification*
No process will be successful if its internal communications are inefficient: and no project can expect to interface effectively with its surroundings and services if its external communications are inadequate or flawed.

The quality of communication is essential for several good reasons, some of which are inherent in the nature of software products, their specification, and the available development means and methods. The 'softness' of software, the uncertainties of its development, and the habit of undertaking development of software in parallel with the development, creation or elaboration of the environment in which it will be applied, all lead to greater or lesser degrees of fluidity and correctness in the initial specification. Similarly, over the development and supported lifetime of a product, the concepts, methods and tools of software design and construction are all liable to evolve or to become obsolete, encouraging much changing of horses in mid-stream.

On examination, many software faults are found to result from differences in understanding of what is required and intended. Various groups of persons involved in a single development may have their own interpretations and assumptions: while work done inside one such group may be perfectly coherent and consistent, when the pieces from several groups are brought together there may be serious, subtle and far-reaching failures to fit together smoothly and completely. Any 'interpretation' or 'assumption' is dangerous, resulting in such problems as ambiguous documentation, incomplete documentation, and substitution of local or individual concepts for those that were (or should have been) defined for the whole undertaking.

The size and complexity of many software products, the lack of a single (accepted and adequate) vocabulary to describe them and their behaviour, and the number of equally valid ways of designing and instantiating any one of them means that they are difficult to think or talk about. The high costs and high profiles of some software projects and products (together with the difficulties of making reliable forecasts) can discourage complete candour in reporting and predicting possibly unpalatable outcomes. Thus, a single product will be viewed and discussed in different ways by the various individuals, teams and interests involved in its development and its later life.

Ensuring the maintenance of full, honest, consistent and communicable views, in forms that facilitate both easy comprehension and the location and evaluation of matches and mis-matches between them across the project staff and their products, is a function that Quality Management is uniquely able to carry out.

Quality reports and recommendations will only be efficiently communicated (in respect of the manner in which they are received and valued) if the Quality Management role has been established with the required standing and authority: one way in which this is done is by regular and effective justifications of what is being done and its costs and value. 'Justification' must be mastered by a Quality Manager; it is concerned with finding arguments and supporting evidence that will convince concerned audiences that correct decisions have been made and are being carried through. Justification within a project may be carried out to convince technical staff that chosen processes are working well, while external justifications are often made to demonstrate the cost-effectiveness of applying Quality Management at all. The insistence on constantly evaluating and justifying quality activities may be a hang-over from regarding them as a luxury or as an encumbrance: however, making the effort to find tangible and acceptable evidence is beneficial in itself as it keeps Quality Management realistic and in touch.

9.5 Process Engineering

Control and management of many of the factors that are known to influence, create or destroy product reliability can be designed into development processes and regularly verified to be there in practice. Other factors, for which the positive connection is less easy to prove and quantify but for which it is strongly indicated, are encouraged and supported by the existence of well-designed processes. The factors include:

- timely, full, and appropriate communication;
- timely, full, and appropriate recording and analysis of progress and quality;
- process consistency, controllability, convenience and reliability;
- control of the style and extent of product testing (both Validation and Verification);
- effective detection and handling of various kinds of fault;
- avoidance of the pressures and stresses caused by late identification of problems.

9.5.1 Selecting and improving available processes

The stages of the procedure are the same, whether dealing with an entire project-process or a subprocess.

(1) *Define the process requirements,* together with a plan for the measurements and tests to be used in the decision making procedure.

(2) *Define any process constraints* (such as cost to own, cost to introduce, time to introduce, hardware and software available for support).

(3) *Procure* (or get access to) *candidate processes.* This may present a difficulty when a process is embedded in an expensive tool-kit, or a tool-kit that is specific to hardware and support software that you do not have, requires lengthy training or makes heavy demands on the capabilities and experience of its users. Such limitations bring the complementary risks of either rejecting a good process without assessment because it would be awkward or expensive to try out, or, for much the same reasons, accepting one without adequate first hand experience.

(4) *Make preliminary selection,* rejecting or shelving those with least potential *or* greatest need for engineering work.

(5) *Perform any basic process engineering* (see Section 9.5.2) *needed* to bring the processes into an assessable state. This avoids frustration and time-

wasting when the product as-received has obvious and fairly easily removed problems, such as a lack of written procedures.

(6) *Make practical trials*: by testing, measuring and reporting each candidate process in accordance with the plan defined in (1).

(7) *Revise and repeat the tests and measures as needed,* until a supported decision can be made on the acceptability of each process. If none of the first processes examined meet enough of the stated requirements, it may be necessary to relax or revise the criteria; re-visit processes previously rejected; extend the basic engineering already done, until the better of the candidates come nearer the requirements; re-plan the project and/or re-design the product, to make the best possible compromise.

(8) *Undertake specific enabling engineering work*: for example, further customization and integration of technical and managerial aspects of the process, and preparing training and manuals, specifically for the project and product in hand, then re-measuring and re-reviewing intensively before making any project commitment,

(9) (If possible) *Repeat and review the tests and measurements*, and gather users' impressions, after a limited period of real-life use and from then onwards at intervals throughout the life of the process.

The most promising current development in support of process and project management is the gradual appearance of IPSEs (Integrated Project/ Process/Programming Support Environments, see Chapter 12). In using them, it is necessary first to select or to design the project's process so that it can be entered into the IPSE process-definition system, which will then give automated assistance to following the process consistently and under control.

Finally, in this 'process selection' section, a warning: however rational a decision making procedure is followed when selecting a method or process, there are pressures and temptations that need to be recognized. One is a mix of over-assessing the problems and poor results of the processes that have been used to date, and overrating the excellence and promise of unfamiliar ones. Another risk comes from wishing to become allied with the technical avant-garde by adopting the latest methods and technologies whether or not these have been shown to be most appropriate for the intended usage. Realistically, an even more pressing reason for accepting a particular process is that it has been imposed by forces (such as product customers, senior management, agreement by a trade association, etc.) outside the immediate project group.

Wherever the process suggestion may have come from, and whatever its 'pedigree' of previous success, no process should ever be put into use without going through the selection procedure:

- to ensure that the requirements are identified, and have been given criterion values;
- to validate that the process can meet the identified requirements and is therefore acceptable;

- to provide practical experience in its use, to ensure that avoidable risks are removed and that performance can be predicted;
- to ensure that local process engineering work is undertaken where it is needed and before its absence might have expensive outcomes.

9.5.2 Engineering a Process

This is the way in which a process is built up, and proved, against a Process Requirement Specification. The treatment here is necessarily very brief, and is restricted to a 'bottom-up' design and implementation—for a higher level view see Chapter 7 and Appendix B, which deal with the overall software development process.

Every process-procurement, and process-engineering, activity has to establish its own list of requirements, and ways of measuring the degree to which a given process design meets them. This follows from the range of different local needs and views on the environment in which the process will be applied; the various factors that might together constitute desirability in the process; the ways in which those factors should be measured; and their relative importance.

However, despite all the sources of difference, all well-engineered processes (if only because each has within itself the means of matching with particular needs, and of customization for given circumstances) will always be found to score reasonably well on selection criteria such as:

- a favourable balance between development, and maintenance, costs;
- good prevention errors, disclosure of errors, and easy error repairs, when compared with other processes;
- reliability in action;
- convenience of application;
- acceptability to users.

Well-packaged and well-engineered processes will also be recognized because they have:

- stated areas of and limits to applicability;
- defined concepts and theory (where appropriate);
- a useful and flexible range of functionality;
- fully defined and easy-to-use procedures;
- identified and easily manipulated functions which can be tuned or customized to meet local needs;
- readily accessible operational requirements;
- measured and repeatable performance characteristics;
- suitable packaging (training, manuals, support, etc.).

The procedure for the engineering of processes is as follows.

(1) *Identify the required process*
Identify its value, its area of applicability, its frequency, its implications for project and product, its expected users and its interfaces with other processes.

The term 'process' can be applied to systematic activities of a wide range of sizes: from the complete project down to the separate steps within, say, a document review procedure. Dividing the process in question into an appropriate set of subprocesses is crucial to its eventual utility: each one should be of a 'size' (in effort, time, or consequences) to merit the costs of control, and have inputs and outputs that are measurable and are worth measuring. For example, in the document review just mentioned, it would seem to be worthwhile measuring the number of faults found, the size of the document and the time taken to review and re-work it, since these are important for both quality management and project scheduling. The value of the document-review process would be worked out against such factors as whether the documents are deliverable products, whether their contents have technical influences on the rest of the product and project, the number of documents to be produced, and the probable time to be spent on each one. The costs of the process, and its precise value, cannot be established until a later stage in process development, but will certainly be influenced by the effectiveness with which it can be carried out and controlled.

(2) *Form process requirements*
A process is a product like any other, and needs a clear, accurate and complete statement of requirements before it can be produced. Where possible, these statements should be quantified in such a way that they can be used as managerial or technical controls when the process is being used.

For example, the probable 'cost of ownership' and 'running costs' should be predicted as accurately as possible, and then the actual costs collected and used as controls once the process is in regular use. 'Used as a control' does not necessarily mean that the process should be discarded if the expected cost is exceeded, but rather that observed costs that are significantly different from the expected will signal the need for reviewing the process and the project and product to which it is being applied.

(3) *Create process design*
In its most basic form (Fig. 9.1 could represent either a very small process *or* a high-level summarized view of a larger one), any process consists of performing an activity on one or more inputs, to give one or more outputs. Output from one process may become the input for another.

Inputs and outputs can be of various kinds, including statements of requirements, design documentation, procedure definitions, standards, the resources made available for the process (including staff, tools, instruments, access rights, etc.), and products (that is, things that did not exist before the activity). Some inputs (such as effort and other resources) are consumed during an activity, while others are used for guidance and control (standards, plans, designs) or as the means of what is done (tools, tool chains, forms, equipment).

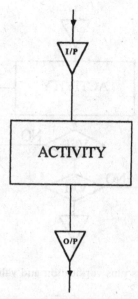

Fig. 9.1. The basic process.

A well-engineered process is not content with merely progressing from inputs to outputs: it tries to ensure that:

- the inputs are appropriate and timely;
- the outputs are acceptable and/or correct;
- the activity was carried out efficiently;
- there is the recording and reporting needed to support the needs of progressively more comprehensive processes, up to that which constitutes the entire project.

For these reasons, more elaborate forms of the basic process are created, and begin to link processes on more than one level. In Fig. 9.2, two kinds of checking have been added: they are Verification (was the activity performed correctly?) and Validation (did the activity fit into the wider needs of the project or product?).

Verification comes first, since there is little point in going on if the offered output is known to be faulty. A verification failure would normally require a return to an 'activity' within the process, after any obvious causes of failure have been removed. A simple example of this pairing of an activity followed by the immediate verification of the output is seen in the process in Fig. 9.3, where a manual coding activity is followed first by a manual code-check, and then that code (corrected as necessary) is input to a computer-compilation activity and the results are again verified.

Validation is a check that the whole process activity has been performed against the appropriate requirement, or design, or objectives *and* that these

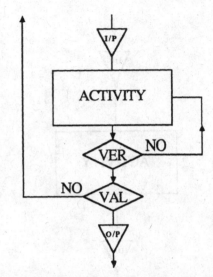

Fig. 9.2. A basic process plus verification and validation of the output.

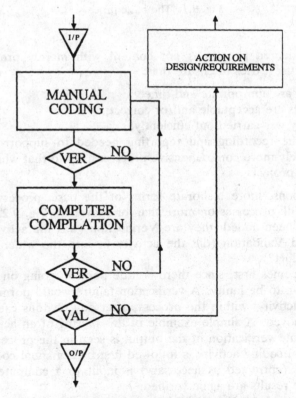

Fig. 9.3. A two-stage process with final validation.

have been met. If Fig. 9.3 is the coding and compilation of an elemental code item, then Validation would consist of testing the result first against the element design, and then to confirm that the element design is consistent with its specification and with other closely related designs and specifications.

(4) *Instrument the process*

'Instrumentation' is used here to mean two things: one is the provision of manual and automated aids, and the other is building-in of the means of process control. The first of these can be seen in the context of Fig. 9.3, where checklists could be used in aiding the verification of manual coding and a computer-based compilation provides both the translation of manual code into its machine executable equivalent and checking for those grammatical and logical errors and omissions that are in its compass to recognize.

The second aspect of instrumentation, that is the creation and application of process control, is harder to show adequately in simple examples. Controls may be loosely grouped as being: immediate, long-term and predictable, or long-term and requiring judgement. Let us expand on these a little.

- *Immediate controls.* These are triggered by comparing a measurement with a standard control value, and are such that there is a clear course of action to be taken as a result of the comparison. An example of this is the control point shown in Fig. 9.4. If the total number of faults found in the manual checking plus those reported by the compilations exceeded a given value then the code element would automatically be reported as a possible deviant and returned for a special technical design review. The actual control point would be supported by the measurement activities in which the errors were counted and recorded after the two Verifications.
- *Long-term and predictable controls.* These are similar to immediate controls, but operate over a longer period. Extending the previous example, if the process of Fig. 9.4 classified and counted the errors found in a code element during and after compilation, and if these were subsequently augmented by any errors that were found later in the development and could be confidently ascribed to the same element, then an automatic control process might be inserted towards the end of the project by which the 10 or 20% most-faulty elements overall were reviewed and re-worked as a group.
- *Long-term controls requiring judgement.* These will be concerned with matters important to Quality Management and Project Management, but on which decision making must involve many factors, not all of which are measurable or controllable by the project itself. They include such things as the relationships between project progress and its costs, or quality and costs, and will include factors that should be measured and recorded and reported on a regular basis by the project's processes. Measurement, recording and reporting will usually mix items that are determined by people and those that can be automated.

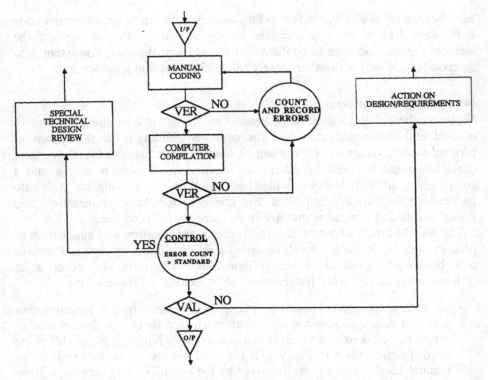

Fig. 9.4. A two-stage process with an additional control function.

All three kinds of control are aided and simplified by the use of appropriate tooling, and may not be practical without such automatic support as is provided by an IPSE. However, although such tools greatly assist the regularity and consistency of project processes and their reporting and control, there may be penalties in losing flexibility, and in the time and effort needed to set up all the required dimensions of the project and its intended product structures, and in devising and obtaining suitable metrics and rule systems on which control can safely be automated.

(5) *Verify, validate and characterize the process*
This needs to be done before a process is installed into a working situation, and at regular intervals thereafter. A general checklist should be devised before a process is designed, relating to such things as:

- the existence of suitable verification/validation after each activity;
- performance in terms of resources used and efficiency in preventing/encouraging certain things, in specified conditions;
- the effective matching of activities with control actions and control points;
- the items and concepts to be measured;

- identification of the circumstances where the whole process, or parts of the process, are particularly recommended or are advised against;
- the ease and accuracy of use of the process, its tools and documentation, by the expected user population;
- the kinds of technical and managerial reporting to be made.

Once the process has itself been verified and validated, the original checklist of requirements can be amended as seems suitable and actual performance figures (and their supporting evidence) attached where necessary to provide targets and planning constants. This checklist should then be augmented with any factors specific to a proposed use, and the pros, cons and performance figures confirmed before use as a standard process in a particular project.

9.5.3 Introducing new processes

It is not enough just to select or to engineer a process that meets its requirements. Processes must also be positively introduced into use if they are not to risk being ignored or misused. Some pointers to successful introduction are the following.

(1) *The existence of evidence that strongly suggests that a process is technically and economically efficient*
It may be thought that this first 'pointer' should outweigh the rest, but unless the process is adequately engineered and the evidence has been collected locally, recently, and professionally, it can be dangerous to accept any 'evidence' uncritically. A process that has been 'proved' right for one environment will not necessarily show the same performance elsewhere and the criteria, metrics and measurements used in one evaluation rarely map exactly into the needs and values of another.

(2) *Availability of local enthusiasm, experience, information and technical support*
It is always best to involve process-users in the selection procedure. Even if some of the processes are suggested on the untested grounds of hearsay, or association with people of high reputations, or of effective advertising, the resulting high initial expectations can help give positive benefits by leading people into strongly assuming that the process will work and thus into perseverance and good will if any difficulties arise. Without these benefits, any new approach may be scrutinized warily for its weak points and may be abandoned unjustly at the first sign that it might not be entirely perfect.

Whatever the theoretical value of a process may be, it cannot be expected to reach its full potential if users start out with suspicion or dislike; and if their initial attempts are hampered by a lack of information and training, and by the process having been poorly engineered and supported. Therefore, anyone evaluating, or introducing, a new process must pay attention to the way in which the users will be brought to accept it and apply it.

Two positive points in encouraging local support are:
- finding a respected local technician who is eager to take the lead in using the process, and in acting as an example, adviser and supporter for later users;
- finding that the supplied training and documentation are well received by trial users and can be objectively shown to be of sufficient quality to meet long-term needs (that is, that they are well presented, accessible, accurate, with examples of local relevance, organized at different levels to meet the needs of a variety of users, etc.).

(3) *Availability of automated support tools*
This would include, for example, program checkers, editors, animators, configuration controllers, and procedures for their manual verification. If the process is being engineered locally, a high priority will be placed on providing this support. Questions should be asked in any process evaluation about the amounts of manual and machine work it requires, and about the inherent capacity of the manual stages for creating complex errors that would be difficult and time-consuming to discover and redress without automated support.

(4) *Suitability of the project/process pairing for being managed*
The combination of the basic process with the project's management and control structures, and the design and development plan for the project's products should work together to meet technical and managerial needs. These needs include the following:
- Ways of judging progress towards completion that are easy to apply, can be applied at appropriate intervals and to suitably sized sub-items, and that will act to maintain confidence and control.
- Methods for avoiding and/or limiting mistakes, of sufficient power and scope to detect at least some of those that might have been introduced by happenings outside the declared scope of the process. An example of an 'outside' but influential event is the occurrence of a late declaration of an alteration to be made in the requirements.
- The ability to extrapolate in-service behaviour from aspects that are detectable or measurable early in the development process.
- Formal documentation of significant concepts and design decisions.
- Control of consistency and completeness between elements and stages of the process and its products.

(5) *Availability of exemplars of the application of the process in areas similar to that of the product in hand, and/or in the intended first application*
Technical judgements, training, and initial check-lists for inspections and reviews need to be based on examples of the process in action. Naturally, the Quality Manager will collect local data and instances as soon as is practical, but the exemplars are valuable both for basic information and as performance standards.

(6) *Cost, quality and schedule models*

Such models should be sought to support both managerial and technical choices between candidate processes, and enable sufficiently reliable schedules and plans to be proposed. Without these, the process cannot be sensibly chosen or brought into project use. If a process arrives without the support of such models, and is chosen for use on other grounds, then a high priority should be placed on gathering and analysing modelling information as quickly as possible.

The whole-project processes discussed in Chapter 7 (Section 7.5 and Fig. 7.7) are examples of ones that have been designed to meet the needs of Software Project Management. In practical use each one has to be fully defined, characterized, and thoroughly introduced to project staff so that they see the nature, relevance and importance of their own parts in its operation. Even the best processes can only perform within the extent to which their operators understand and accept them, making process introduction of equal importance to process selection and process engineering in ensuring the success of a project.

9.6 Three Angles on Software Quality Management

Quality management is achieved through the basic Quality Management functions, discussed in Section 9.4, which were derived from the definition of Software Quality Management as 'the specialist role that exists to assist software developers to make confident statements about the general merit or characteristics of their processes and products'. The manner in which the functions are carried out is influenced by the need to encourage and maintain complete and accurate communications—between buyers and suppliers, between elements in the project organization, between individuals in the project, and from one time to another in the lifetimes of the project and its products—and by the understanding that reliable products can only be made by using reliable processes.

The basic functions are looked at below from three of the organizational positions from which 'quality' services and controls might be provided. After a statement of the scope of the three positions, and a reminder of the identities of the functions, the section is grouped into three parts (Sections 9.6.1–9.6.3), each consisting of a short discussion of the position (or view) being taken followed by notes on the functions seen in that light. Each entry is identified by a letter (A–I) showing which function is being discussed, and by a code word ('project', 'group' or 'company') to indicate the viewing position. It is expected that this section will be used for reference, rather than read as a continuous text and the identifiers and codes are provided to aid location of topics of interest.

The three Quality Management positions are:

- *Project-based* (project): this implies Quality Management being taken as an individual responsibility, within and for just one software project.
- *Group-based* (group): Quality Management with responsibility for a group of software projects (for instance in a department) and for coordination between those projects, probably with agents or representatives working directly within each project.
- *Company-based* (company): this is a Quality Management responsibility for all aspects of software development and software services within a company or organization.

The functions have been described in general terms, in Section 9.4, under the heading General Elements of Software Quality Management and are as follows.

- A. Definition and support of an effective quality organization
- B. Feasibility studies
- C. Process selection, engineering and introduction
- D. Quality control and quality assurance
- E. Quality reporting
- F. Configuration, and documentation, control
- G. Data collection for project, product and process records
- H. Audits and reviews
- I. Communication and justification

9.6.1 Software Quality Management for, or within, a single project

The independence and scope of a Project Quality Manager will be heavily influenced by the extent to which the role is embedded in the project's technical activities and reporting structure. Although the quality role must be seen as a professional service to the Project Manager, it can be vital for the effectiveness of the quality work that the responsibility can be divorced from the project's short-term and technical interests when needed.

In different projects, Project Quality Management responsibilities may be taken:

- wholly by the Project Manager, or by his assignees within the project's technical staff;
- jointly by the Project Manager and a project Technical Quality Lead (perhaps placed within an organizational entity named the Project or Product Design Office);
- jointly by the Project Manager and a dedicated Quality Management function that is logically and organizationally independent of the project it serves.

Each of these can work for or against the interests of the quality function. For example, because of the high requirement for communication and continuity that is inherent in all software developments, the placing of responsibility with a Quality Management function outside the project's own management and technical structure is often not to be recommended, since it makes information capture and operating relationships difficult to maintain at a sufficiently high level.

Equally, without some separation (and, if problems arise, the potential for appeal to higher and non-project-oriented authority) it can be hard for the person with quality responsibility to retain sufficient independence and balance to be able to recognize, and where necessary publicize, undue attention to short-term concerns. If the person with quality responsibility for a single project has to identify strongly with any one interest, it is probably most healthy that it be with either the project's customer or with the long-term needs of the company, although the second must still be done from a position at least partly embedded in the project's structure for the reasons of communication and essential authority already given.

In this subsection, the particular case of the quality manager who is newly appointed, in-project, and 'stand-alone' (that is, unsupported by an existing and independent quality function) is used as the basis of discussion. This was chosen as an extreme (although not unusual) situation, and thus one which helps highlight common problems of Project Quality Management.

We look in turn at the list of general functions and relate them to the case of a newly appointed in-project Quality Manager.

9.6.1.A (project) *Definition and support of an effective quality organization*
If the particular project exists within an environment in which 'quality' activities and responsibilities are already accepted, then the task should be quite straightforward, consisting mainly of picking up (and adjusting as needed) the patterns and standards that are being used and found effective elsewhere. Project Management and project staff will be familiar with the quality policy and the way in which it is worked out and supported in practice, and are only likely to demur if this project is markedly different from the rest in its quality requirements and provisions.

However, if overt attention to quality, as signalled by the appointment of a Quality Manager, is not a common thing in local (software) experience, then every activity and interface will have to be negotiated separately and may even have to be developed and introduced gradually as the need for them is brought home by specific circumstances, incidents and accidents. Regular project quality reviews in which staff are encouraged to bring forward any worries about the development of undesirable trends or the effectiveness of current procedures, are a useful means of exploiting circumstances to get support for improvements in processes and controls.

Although the new Project Quality Manager may have to work on establishing and extending the role and its influence by a policy of opportunism, it is as well that the ideal organization aimed for is documented and publicized as soon as possible. This puts quality activities into context, and supports the

Quality Manager in setting out to gather the goodwill and information that will allow wider powers and roles to be taken up as and when they are seen to be justified.

9.6.1.B (project) *Feasibility studies*

A one-project Quality Manager may not be appointed until early studies, or even a period of actual activity on the project, indicates that the role is needed. If the appointed Quality Manager was not involved in those studies or experiences, then subsequent involvement with their results may come too late for the role to ever have the influence and support it needs from the Project Manager and other technical staff.

Whether present at the project initiation or not, a newly appointed Project Quality Manager should always as a first priority review and report on *all* the project's current controlling documents: feasibility studies, contracts, plans, specifications, received standards, process definitions, available tools and services, constraints, and so on. This may be the last or only chance to register professional quality views on risks to the project and the ways in which they may best be limited and monitored, before becoming involved in details and in any crises that arise.

At the Feasibility Study stage, Quality Managers and other managerial and technical staff may find themselves without the detailed information and comparative experience they need. If this is the case, the lack of knowledge should be identified and the scope of its consequences sketched in as far as possible; project plans and processes should then follow that have built in the controls and check-points needed to find when (and whether) the initial assumptions fail, and when enough new information has been collected to allow re-planning with more confidence.

9.6.1.C (project) *Process selection, engineering and introduction*

Process selection. Few Project Quality Managers have as much freedom as they would like to choose and install complete processes for their projects. It is more likely that they will be limited (by time, resources, and their sphere of influence) to taking part in a project's selection process and then helping refine the way the chosen process is engineered into a complete working method, designed to satisfy technical, managerial and quality objectives. Even when the Quality Manager has more freedom and power, it cannot be applied sensibly if there is little or no real experience and information outside the present project or previous local development style . However, the Quality Manager should be able to ensure that the selection and engineering procedures are themselves adequate, and that all the important interests (including those of Quality Management in the project and of collecting data to support future decisions) put forward properly considered statements of their requirements on the process and of ways in which satisfaction of these requirements can be demonstrated.

Process engineering. The Project Quality Manager will work with the Project Manager and senior technical staff in selecting processes (or in closely examining any that are imposed) and in ensuring that their engineering is as good as possible before the process characteristics are built into project plans and controls, and the processes themselves are introduced into project work.

Process introduction. Senior technical staff within the project can take responsibility for specific aspects or functions within the whole project process, producing and reviewing suitable documentation, giving training, and being available to give advice and support throughout the project. Voluntary involvement of this kind is an excellent thing, both directly for the quality of the processes, and for the creation of a project identity.

In the capacity of independent protector and spokesman for the project on quality-related matters, the Project Quality Manager has a particular concern for the following aspects of process.

- Does each process and each combination of processes have an effective combination of those actions that create outputs and those that test and report on what has been created? That is, is it reasonable to expect that the majority of errors will be found within a few hours, or days, of their introduction? Will they be found and corrected before their host-items (designs, code, documentation, etc.) have been passed on to other stages in the process or to other members of the project team? If there are known classes of error that cannot be detected within the process in which they were created, can their effects be limited and compensated for elsewhere in the overall process? Is such deferred action cost-effective, quality-effective and sufficiently reliable?
- Is there enough understanding of the error profiles to be expected from each subprocess and the process as a whole? Have these and their consequences (for example, the need for planned and controlled re-design and other re-work as required within the development project, and the implications for product reliability and other qualities once products are in service) been explored and built into the project plan and the product design criteria?
- Is there an acceptable balance between the manual and the automated stages? Are the methods and tools easy to use and do they have 'help' facilities and appropriate ways to detect and notify possible mistakes as they are made? Is there easy and complete traceability between manual and machine-created representations? Are errors detected in one product representation (for example, the requirements statement) easily mapped into others (for example, graphical designs and compilable code)? Are changes and corrections easy to make, and can they be easily controlled and reported as an integral part of the development process?

- Are adequate training and support available? Have provisions been made in project plans to cover the early stages of the learning and familiarization period?
- Has the process been provided with sets of reporting points and reporting terms (metrics, check-lists, performance standards, 'actuals' against quality and progress plans, etc.) that meet the operational needs of this project and the need to collect data to support later projects?

9.6.1.D (project) *Quality control and quality assurance*

In-process control. This is only effective where the relationships between the properties of processes, sub-products and intermediate products can be reliably measured and modelled and then extended into predictions about project and process performance and the properties of end-products. If this capability does exist, it can be used to set up firm predictions and controls. However, failing such precision and predictability the Quality Manager should ensure that the needs of the project in hand and future projects are balanced by setting up process management so as to do the following.

- Maintain the integrity of the chosen processes and designs as far as possible in the face of what might be only temporary deviations in performance and the environment, recording those deviations and their apparent causes and effects for future use.
- Make sure that any process adjustments are made in a considered and well documented way.
- Take throughout such measurements and qualitative observations that the project in hand forms a useful source of information for any later evaluations, predictions and characterizations that might be made to serve the needs of later projects.
- Test out proposed models and process controls within a real situation.

Check-out, just before product-release. If the development processes and in-process control activities are working well, then this final check-out should be little more than a formality. However, the single-project stand-alone Quality Manager may be without supporting experience and norms from other projects and products and thus particularly prone to making miscalculations when approving production processes and their complementary checks and controls, and when certifying that an end product is such as to meet all its agreed and assumed requirements. There is also the possibility that mismatches exist between the written requirement and the reality of product use, and a novice Quality Manager may not have the confidence or status to allow him to pursue investigations far enough to ensure that there are no surprises for supplier or user when the product is brought into operation. For the Procurer's view of this, see Chapter 8.

9.6.1.E (project) *Quality reporting*

If the Quality Manager reports only within the project whose quality is being managed, there may be a problem in finding suitable audiences; especially where the reports indicate the need for corrective action. The Project Manager may be (and usually is) more inclined to maintain progress, and to keep technical staff happy and busy, than to halt work while quality problems are investigated and new procedures installed. Reluctance to act is especially likely if the corrective actions and new procedures involve re-working items already marked off on the project plan as completed. One solution for such problems is for the Quality Manager also to report to a suitably motivated and sufficiently powerful person outside the project hierarchy: however, although this may be effective in getting changes made, it can tend to isolate the Quality Manager and make subsequent interactions with the project's technical staff more difficult.

The existence of powerful support can be a useful weapon, used to encourage the project team to behave as the Quality Manager wishes. Such a weapon can only be used once, and must be saved for extremity, but knowledge that it exists will often be enough to gain the desired end. For most situations where leverage is needed, a better tactic than the 'big brother' threat is to be able to use the project quality records in presenting convincing arguments. This ability to detect and help avoid potential troubles should be welcomed by the project team and encourage them to be open with the Quality Manager; especially when the weapon can be used on the project's behalf to influence external factors that are causing it distress. This is in contrast to the secretive and antagonistic behaviour that might result from a more authoritarian approach.

In routine reporting, whoever the recipients may be, the Quality Manager should aim always to include the positive side of what is recorded. For example, records and reports should show both the numbers of items reviewed and of those accepted, the numbers of faults found and of those found and cleared, the processing problems investigated and those that have been satisfactorily fixed. Also, if project staff trust that the quality-reporting system is sufficiently flexible to assist them by providing impartial and timely support to any quality-affecting report they might wish to make, openness and cooperation will be encouraged.

Without this simple and neutral reporting route through the Quality Manager, it is only too easy for busy project technicians to fail to report such matters as persistent stress caused by small but significant factors in the environment. Typically, small and simple irritations cause large and subtle errors through loss of concentration and resulting incomplete and inconsistent work. Irritations are often easily removable if someone can be found to do the leg-work. Typical examples of this cause of error are poorly thought-out interfaces with tools, unreviewed and untidy working documents being passed from one activity to another, erratic or inadequate services, inconvenient paperwork, unsuitable keyboard layouts, poorly presented print-outs of computer store contents, noisy and uncomfortable working conditions, insufficient terminals or computing power, etc., etc.

9.6.1.F (project) *Configuration, and documentation, control*

The need for these functions is principally affected by a project's size, difficulty, complexity, rate of change, number of staff and groups of staff, numbers of versions and variants, the length of the support and maintenance period and the range of uses and users of the product. A novice Quality Manager would be very unlucky to be faced by a project or product with very high configuration and documentation control needs, since these need firm and far-sighted procedural support from the outset. Help should be sought immediately if there is any possibility of becoming swamped by the quantity and variety of data that must be preserved and organized.

Retro-active control is extremely difficult to achieve and it seems to be in the nature of software and mixed software/hardware systems that configuration items are always more numerous and varied than expected. Thus, a pessimistic view (that is, one that tends to the high end of foreseen numbers of items, versions, adaptations and combinations) should always be taken when making feasibility studies and when setting up control procedures and supporting facilities within a project.

Although a Quality Manager is rarely directly responsible for configuration control or documentation control, the size and long-term importance of these functions means that they must be high on the list of activities requiring regular auditing. To make this possible, there must be built into the supporting tools and procedures adequate facilities for tracking and for display.

9.6.1.G (project) *Data collection for project, product and process records*

These records are the basis for evaluating, characterizing, controlling and improving the technical work of product development. Thus, the planning and carrying out of data collection and analysis are key to the achievement of reliable processes and reliable products, within a managed and manageable context.

The data arises within a project and may be regarded as the property of that project alone, with the Project Manager deciding what is to be collected and how it is to be used. However, those within a project, and subject to its pressures and constraints, may not be best placed to appreciate potential future benefits from regular data collection and may be tempted to give it a low priority at just those difficult times when it has the highest potential value. The balance between the value of records and the costs of making and keeping them is a difficult one to get right, and the project Quality Manager should expect to have to keep it under constant review.

Although much of the value of records comes from their support for the planning and control of later projects, the effort of collection must be associated with one or more immediate benefits if the persons being asked to make the primary records are to do so consistently and without complaint.

Fortunately, the benefits need not be financial: explanations of the eventual use of data, and displays of any models or interactions suggested by the data collected so far coupled with the opportunity for staff to join in reviews of the information, should be sufficient to maintain interest and accurate recording. Identification and involvement is particularly important if making the entries involves a significant break from more obviously progressive and technical activity, or if the recorders are required to do significant work in making discriminations between the different classifications into which the data might fall.

Where special formats and careful choices between alternatives are essential to the recording scheme, the Quality Manager will need to ensure that there is effective initial training (and perhaps re-training if the data quality changes after a period of use). Another small but potentially ruinous item to check is that there are always sufficient forms (or access to the recording system) available at the places where the data originates: forms filled in after the event are often inaccurate. Once data is collected, validation and preliminary analysis must be done and fed back promptly, in order to catch any problems as quickly as possible as well as demonstrating that the activity is being taken seriously.

A common example of the results of forgotten training and/or lack of interest in the data and/or recording after the event (plus over-complicated classification schemes), is a tendency for the recorders to save their energy by gradually moving towards using only a small sub-set of the range of classifications available to them and to formalize into a few standard phrases what are intended to be free-form descriptions of unclassifiable events. Anyone involved in analysing quantities of fault reports is likely to have met these effects and to be aware of how rapidly data can become apparently repetitive and empty of meaning. Regular data validation, for individual entries and for sets of records, is needed to distinguish between genuine clusters of similar events and the outcomes of an uncared-for recording scheme.

9.6.1.H (project) *Audits and reviews*
These are the main instruments by which the Quality Manager regularly investigates and advises on whatever may be needed to keep processes and products with their required quality characteristics. These investigations should cover issues of both verification (Is the process being performed in the defined manner? Are the products within their specifications?) and validation (Will these products and processes meet the overall requirements?). Although the Quality Manager's assignment to the project encourages rapid reaction to any problem, it is better for the quality of problem assessments and solutions if the formalisms of the audit and review are used to help in the description of the difficulty and the structuring and introduction of resulting actions.

Aspects of audits and reviews with which an in-project Quality Manager must take special care include the following.

- Documenting, explaining and gaining acceptance for the procedures well before there is a need for them to be applied. This is true for all quality procedures, but applies especially to any that are likely to be used in circumstances where there may already be an atmosphere of criticism and failure.
- Scrupulous adherence to the standards and procedures for calling and conducting project audits and reviews. As the principal person involved in setting standards, it is too easy for the Quality Manager not to feel bound by them: however, if they are to provide useful information, and the opportunity for project staff to clarify and communicate their own ideas, the meetings and reports must be made in a consistent way.
- Ensuring that any personal but unsupported views held by the Quality Manager are not allowed to guide or constrain discussions and their reporting. The privileged position of the in-project Quality Manager will give special insights into what is being done and how, and may have encouraged the Quality Manager to identify more strongly with some project staff than with others. Impressions and pre-judgements (however valid) must not be allowed to influence and colour the parts of the audit or review report which are concerned with current observations or with the expressed concerns and interpretations of the project staff present at the meeting. Where the Quality Manager has real and additional information, it must be thoroughly checked and then presented impartially.
- The ability to accept criticism of the procedures and rules which the Quality Manager has introduced. This covers recording criticism honestly and fully, preventing bias in its investigation, and fully supporting any changes which are needed.
- The ability to accept that the project's guiding procedures and rules, including any received from a higher authority in the company or as part of the contractual conditions, may prove to be unhelpful in the particular project however well proven elsewhere. A tendency to show undue respect for all kinds of authority, whether technical or hierarchical, is a recognized weakness of Quality Managers.

9.6.1.1 (project) *Communication and justification*

A Project Quality Manager must be aware at all times of a responsibility to ensure that all planned communication processes within the project and between the project and other interested parties (such as senior management, the project customer, and suppliers of services) are kept effective, open, accurate and up-to-date.

Justification is particularly pressing for a lone Project Quality Manager (that is, one without the support of a wider Quality organization), who must not allow the value of the quality role to be forgotten either inside or outside the project in case this results in situations from which it will be difficult to recover. Thus, there is a high priority for the Project Quality Manager to provide truthful and convincing evidence throughout the project lifetime that the exercise of quality management has indeed been cost-beneficial. Finding baselines from which improvements can be measured is always a problem, especially because expectations at the start of any project are frequently unreasonably high, with any previous failures or low achievements being regarded as due to unusual factors in the projects concerned or as being purely accidental, unavoidable, and unlikely to happen again. Each Project Quality Manager should expect to add to the direct in-project tasks a considerable expenditure of effort on retrieving and analysing results from other projects and on encouraging senior staff to consider and define rational quality and cost criteria against which can be set up telling demonstrations of the ability of Quality Management actions to promote desirable results and to limit the possibility of bad ones.

9.6.2 Software Quality Management across a group of projects

While the Quality Manager or quality leader appointed to care for a single project often arrives in that position without specific training or experience, it is unusual for a general manager or a senior technician to be appointed to Group Quality Management without either training or an apprenticeship of some kind. Such an appointment is also rarely made unless the group has some kind of commitment to quality achievement and perhaps a history of quality-related activities. Where these conditions exist, the Group Quality Manager is in a much stronger position than the in-project, unsupported and newly appointed individual of the previous section; having more support, authority and experience as well as more information on which to work. Although it is possible for a Group Quality Manager to be appointed without any of these advantages, it is the more favoured position that has been taken as the viewpoint below.

The most important differences between working for a group of projects and within (or for) only one project lie in:

- the opportunity to define a quality policy, quality objectives and generic standards and plans, to give consistency and stability to all other quality work;
- the Group Quality Manager's increased scope for collecting, interpreting and applying, project and process data;
- greater possibilities for the progressive refinement of tools and procedures, as they are used consecutively in a number of projects,
- increased difficulty of recognizing and meeting the special needs of any one of the projects in sufficient time and detail.

Whatever the longer-term plans, a newly-appointed Group Quality Manager must (in order to survive, as well as to give a recognizable 'house style' within which everyone can receive basic training and begin to work within a uniform quality 'style') rapidly devise, publicize and introduce essential codes of practice. A new Group Quality Manager will be judged by the speed and firmness with which the responsibilities are taken up. Failing to deliver clear and workable instructions from the outset will cause grave loss of confidence amongst the project group. As effective quality management works principally by example and moral pressure, such a loss has to be avoided.

Although it is possible that software methods and standards will have longer useful lives in the future, current experience suggests that any set will have to be regularly updated, with a major re-release every two to three years. Whether Group Quality Management is a new post or not, introduction of a new code of practice, and then negotiations of its precise application to each project provide a natural occasion for forming or renewing trust and close communication links between the projects and the Group Quality Manager.

Turning to look in turn at each of the general functions, and their particular meaning for the Group Quality Manager, we have the following.

9.6.2.A (group) *Definition and support of an effective quality organization*
The first essential for a coherent and effective organization is that there be a clear guiding policy. This will cover a longer term and wider area than the policy for any single project and those project-specific policies should be derived from it. The central policy should include an improvement programme with the collection and analysis of information across several projects, and the provision of general quality services and support activities such as auditing, training and the organization of Quality Circles.

The Quality Manager for a group of projects will neither wish nor be able to do everything needful alone and will have to have a recognized network of quality contact-and-communication persons working within the specific projects. The nature of the recognition could vary from formal full-time appointments to inclusion as one of the responsibilities of a senior member of a project's technical staff, but it must always be clearly stated and agreed that the role exists and has certain quality responsibilities within, and beyond, the project itself. It will be beneficial to the standing and growth of the appointees (and thus to Quality Management throughout the Group) to define and share out well-defined special responsibilities amongst them.

The 'special responsibilities' could include, for example:

- organization of quality audits;
- process engineering support;
- monitoring of the quality and performance of all support facilities;
- collecting and collating data;
- tool evaluations;
- tool and process introductions, including the preparation of manuals and organization of training and support.

The mechanisms of document and configuration management can also be the subject of special assignments, if it is convenient and effective to handle them centrally.

The making of special assignments should result in:

- appointees increasing their job satisfaction;
- opportunities for training and specialization;
- enhancing the experience and capability of the whole quality community as they move between assignments;
- providing competent and recognized points of contact on quality matters for both project staff and quality staff;
- efficient use of quality effort.

Together, the appointees and the Group Quality Manager will form a kind of super-Quality Circle, in which both 'good' and 'bad' experiences can be explored and characterized ready for inclusion among the group's common experience base and for introduction and use at suitable points in present and future activities.

9.6.2.B (group) *Feasibility studies*

Having the responsibility for a range of projects will widen the knowledge and experience which Group Quality Management can bring to bear on feasibility studies, making it easier to identify and apply special technical abilities whatever their sources: staff from other projects say, or senior members of the organization, or bought-in experts. Where the feasibility studies recommend special tools, training, methods or other facilities, their cost and benefit justifications will be made more easily if spread across a wider area and time than could be claimed for a single project.

However, special care must be taken to not abuse this greater freedom by taking the risk of imposing superficially attractive but insufficiently proven items or approaches on the whole group. In this matter, a degree of autonomy in the projects can be a valuable safeguard to limit the possibility of confusion, waste, resentment and poor results that might otherwise be caused by too enthusiastic adoption of new ideas.

9.6.2.C (group) *Process selection, engineering and introduction*

Process selection. As for feasibility studies, this becomes a balancing act between the influences of the past and the possibilities of the future. Each of these could act for or against innovation, and thus a selection process can become muddied by strong but sometimes irrational forces. Fear, inertia, restlessness and fashion all need to be recognized and taken into account when views are expressed.

With the chance to experiment and analyse across a number of projects and with long enough time frames, the Group Quality Manager should be able to set up a rational and controlled programme of exploration and evaluation. This will limit the scope for making disastrous mistakes in choosing not to consider process changes or in the selection of new ones, as well as providing objective criteria and controls for the processes in use.

Process engineering, and process introduction. An open-minded and broadly based Group Quality Management function should expect to receive a constant stream of suggestions for process improvements, and may be justified in setting up a small specialist process engineering section to:

- instrument tools and processes, with manual and machine-based data capture, inter-linking, reporting, error detection, etc.;
- customize received processes and tools as needed;
- keep in touch with the needs of projects;
- maintain knowledge of the literature and market-place, especially in terms of processes, tools, evaluations, and reports on experiences in process and tool applications;
- receive and evaluate suggestions;
- plan and justify procurements, including training and giving information to potential users;
- support projects when required;
- specify and carry out small changes and extensions to the local repertoire of processes and tools;
- plan and manage the installation of major new processes and tools.

If all this is organized centrally by the Quality organization, it can have several benefits (such as of ensuring that tooling is appropriate, widely and properly applied, and of a high standard)—but it may also risk boundary disputes. These could be with senior technical staff in the projects (who want to make their own choices, and implement them as and when they wish), and with software engineering specialists within any general 'computer services' group that may be present. Because of the importance of having reliable and well-controlled processes, it seems advisable that the Quality organization should have the major role: avoiding interface problems as far as possible by including project and service specialists as respected members of all the tactical and technical activities.

9.6.2.D (group) *Quality control and quality assurance*

In-process control. The activity will have been a major concern when engineering the process, with any external needs and requirements (for example, those of Group Quality Management and senior Project Management) being integrated as closely as possible to individual project's own organization and activities and with first-line actions being carried out by project quality staff.

If a Group Quality Manager attempts to take on the whole burden of quality control there will be difficulties in the following aspects.

- Managing to provide the time, effort and attention needed by all the projects. It is one of the fundamental laws of quality-life that errors, crises and failures occur in unpredictable and inconvenient clusters rather than in any known and allowable-for pattern: thus, it is not possible to make confident plans for when and how they will be dealt with.

- Building in some kind of chain of authority and judgement, to provide fair and fast responses to any queries or disputes. Project-level quality staff need to have their own defined spheres of responsibility, and the existence of higher powers to whom to appeal when necessary. If the Group Quality Manager attempts to operate at all levels, the authority of project quality staff will be diminished and there will be no recourse in extreme circumstances.

- Maintaining sufficiently close technical, and reporting, connections to enable the Group's technical and administrative 'control processes' to follow quickly enough, and with enough detailed knowledge, upon each 'creation' or 'translation' process. Obviously, the focus cannot be (and does not need to be) as close for Group purposes as it is for the project itself, although it must be detailed enough to alert the Group Quality Manager whenever a problem is large enough or lasts long enough to require attention outside the project itself. The general rule still holds, that Control that is either too late to contain all the consequences of an incorrect process or too shallow to identify the causes and effects of such a process is not only ineffective in preventing or reducing errors but by devaluing the control function and by introducing chains of consequential errors it becomes a positive force for quality deterioration.

Check-out, just before product-release. For credible assurance of product final qualities and functionality, communication between development activities and the Group Quality function should not be too high. In fact (except in providing high-level process assurance and in particular the prevention, detection, analysis and repair of faults) the separation of Group Quality Management from any one project/product should be kept clean and visible during the activities that lead to a completed product being pronounced by its makers as fit for service. The position changes once this point is reached: Group Quality will be held responsible for the quality of a product that has been released to a customer, and thus must be fully involved in its final assessment.

It is an effective additional assurance if both the final product check-out, and special checks on the most important subassemblies or other significant intermediate results, are carried out first by the developers and then by an independent authority such as a certifying body, or a commercial Validation and Verification service, or an in-house team headed by the Group Quality Manager (or an appointee), and staffed by persons not involved in the product development. Where product customers are available, their involvement in this exercise or in a parallel one is also highly desirable.

Unless there is an intention to perform random testing (perhaps in order to use the results in particular kinds of reliability modelling) the different testing teams should each be required to plan, manage and report their work in such a way that it can be demonstrated that in total the quality assurance process has covered both the internal and external specifications of the product in an identified, measured and acceptable manner.

9.6.2.E (group) *Quality reporting*

Once the Group Quality Manager has planned and introduced a general quality reporting scheme, there will be a reliance on the suitability of the items selected for reporting and the frequency and granularity of those reports to keep in touch with individual projects and with the whole body of projects.

It is not easy to design a scheme that is sufficiently detailed (but not unacceptably report-intensive) and can be relied upon to highlight anomalies in good time without resulting in a permanent state of panic. However good a scheme has been in the past, it will need to be reviewed frequently and to be supplemented by personal and qualitative pictures of current progress and quality from Project Managers and project quality staff. There is always tension between making revisions to reporting and recording schemes to meet new or short-term needs and the higher-level requirement to maintain consistency of reporting and thus its understandability and comparability.

9.6.2.F (group) *Configuration, and documentation, control*

With several projects, there must be a consistent approach to configuration and documentation control. This is an important part of the projects' total process, and greatly benefits from an integrated approach that ties together the creation, testing, and management, of items.

At the Group level, configuration and document control includes:

- the identification of 'responsible persons', and of a suitable allotment of finance and other resources;
- the specification of responsibilities and control procedures for use during product specification and development;
- a policy and associated procedures and controls, for use with existing products;
- (where possible) the provision of management tools and supporting services for the libraries of parts and other documents (such as designs, plans, tests, test results, build lists and partial builds, etc.);
- a common standard for the identification of parts and for awarding and maintaining appropriate status for each controlled item.

If there are software developers who doubt the need for such provisions (except for the very smallest and definitely one-time-use products), then a little archaeology among project, product, fault, complaint, query and change records should soon show the numbers of items and versions and variants that inhabit their software space and that it would have been beneficial to have had them under closer control.

In addition to providing the control and manageability needed to reduce the stress and resources associated with the unchecked production of parts, pieces, and patches, once in place the system assists real parts management. This is achieved, for example, by enabling selection of parts for re-use and guiding the nature and timing of regular 'preventive maintenance' for high-usage and/or frequently repaired parts. It may also eventually support an effective CAD-cum-factory-production style of software development and delivery.

9.6.2.G (group) *Data collection for project, product and process records*

Sets of data collected across different projects, products and processes, but in a common and controlled way for them all, are a valuable resource for quality and software engineering.

Data definition and collection is treated in more detail elsewhere in the handbook (Chapter 10), so there is no need to repeat the basic rules and suggested data profiles here. However, it should be repeated that no Quality Manager can hope (or pretend) to be able to achieve the objectives of reliable processes resulting in reliable and cost-effective products unless there is regular and well-defined collection and analysis of appropriate data items.

A short list of things that might be measured and recorded includes:

- numbers of faults found: possibly classified by their type, points of inclusion (that is, the process stages in which they were introduced), points of discovery (that is, the process stages in which they were identified), length of time from inclusion to disclosure and probable causes;
- costs of finding faults (that is, of checks, tests and reviews);
- consequences of faults: possibly classified by the resources used in their identification and removal and by the numbers and consequences of the secondary faults that can be seen to have been caused by earlier ones;
- performance (in terms of productivity and of achieved quality) of tools and processes;
- numbers of, and resources used up by, faults and failures in the projects' processes and use of tools; plus assessments of the costs and consequences of these faults and failures.

9.6.2.H (group) *Audits and reviews*

Across a group of projects, these will probably be undertaken at three levels of detail. The first is a regular programme (but semi-formal in that meetings are called by project staff, as and when there is either a product to be checked or a problem to be addressed) of product and process audits and reviews, performed mainly by project staff and forming the first-line of quality control in the project. Group Quality Management should receive reports from these, but should not normally attend them except if specially invited to support the project quality representative or perhaps as part of random checking.

Behind this, there will be a more formal sequence of pre-planned audits and reviews timed to coincide with 'milestones' such as, for example, the endings of defined project 'phases', examination of significant in-project results and external deliverables, the arrival of pre-determined reporting dates or levels of expenditure, and so on. This second line concentrates less on the details of actual products and more on the quality and progress being achieved overall, that is, on the aggregate import of the reports from the first-line checks and on the interrelations between processes, products and procedures. Group Quality Management should have an interest in these activities but should not need or wish to attend them all.

The third level is undertaken by the Group Quality Manager, either as part of providing regular overall project, process and product assurance or in response to serious concerns expressed by senior Management or the product customer.

9.6.2.1 (group) *Communication and justification*

Quality-related communication processes must be kept open and effective within projects, between projects and Group Quality Management, and between Group Quality Management and senior management. As well as regular reporting on progress, there is the special class of communication concerned with the affectiveness and survival of the Quality function. A Group Quality Manager has an urgent need (just like that of an individual with quality responsibility for just one project) to justify the existence and imposition of all the quality-related processes and to provide rational and convincing evidence that they should be continued and even extended. In this, the Group Quality Manager is in a much better position than the Quality Manager for an individual project, since there is a wider field and more time within which evidence can be gathered and procedures and processes refined.

While the Project Quality Manager must show that activities in the single project have been cost-effective, the Group Quality Manager has the easier task of showing that numbers of successive projects are gradually moving into an area of generally greater reliability and predictability. The occasional notably strange or unfortunate project provides a useful example and source of information and can be used productively at Group level, while for the individual Project Quality Manager it can be a disaster: even (and sadly sometimes even especially) if it was predicted that unacceptable results were coming unless avoiding actions were taken, but the advice was ignored.

9.6.3 Software Quality Management for a company or entire organization

The main differences between managing the quality of an identified group of projects and managing the quality of all the present and future projects of an organization lie in the greater authority needed and responsibility taken by the Company Quality Manager, and the correspondingly lesser possibility of being personally aware of the particular needs and characteristics of any given process or project or product.

The Company (or Corporate) Quality Manager must quickly set up fixed systems and standards in order to survive the multiplicity of demands for attention and to have any chance of keeping every project within reasonably acceptable bounds: in doing so detailed insight may be lost, and risks of missing new ways of going wrong or of going right may be raised. Because of this, the Company Quality Manager needs supporting technical staff outside the project structure plus strong links with quality staff within projects. For example, though it might be difficult for a Company Quality Manager to disentangle local anomalies or trends from the entire stream of data from all projects, centrally placed data analysts working with project quality staff should be able to identify them quite readily.

Equally, while the Company Quality Manager is responsible for setting up the guidelines and procedures within which quality aspects of development processes are chosen and implemented, the continuous programme by which promising processes are identified and engineered should be made the responsibility of a body of quality and software engineering specialists. Whether under the direct authority of the Company Quality Manager or another senior Technical appointment, such an engineering group would be the most suitable function to identify and be able to take up in the required time scales genuinely 'better' ways of working for individual projects with special needs or for the whole family of projects and products within the company. If such a function exists then the Company Quality Manager must ensure that quality needs are fully represented: if it does not, then the quality responsibility is to ensure that the need for this work is recognized and the gap filled.

In summary, a particular concern for the Company Software Manager must be to ensure that a reasonable balance is maintained between the general and the particular. Obligatory standards must be established to assure overall reliability of processes and products, but there must also be quality research and development activities and channels through which new or unusual needs can be identified and handled, so as to obtain the best possible balance between stability and growth.

Only the first three of the listed general quality functions are discussed in detail for the particular case of a Company Software Quality Manager (or perhaps its Director: Software Quality Management often justifies such a position since a Company's software activities affect both the smooth running of the Company and the acceptability and profitability of its products). All the remaining functions will be covered by these three and by the work of Software Quality Managers within the Company's Groups and Projects.

9.6.3.A (company) *Definition and support of an effective quality organization*

This is a position with great potential, and requires exceptional care when formulating policies and the organization to support them. All statements of policy have to be:

- beneficial (and, if possible, inspirational) in order to gain acceptance and support, and limit the scope for requests for exemptions;

- clear and compact, so that they can and will be widely used;
- conceptual rather than prescriptive, so that they are adaptable and long-lived;
- widely applicable, so that there is a minimal requirement for updating and extensions;
- truthful, so that staff can rely on being backed up in their applications of the policy;
- practical, so that the policy is a useful tool rather than an inconvenient constraint;
- self-limiting, so that excessive zeal is unlikely to lead to excessive costs or complications;
- easily translated into action.

Despite the difficulties of reaching a satisfactory policy, it is far better to spend time on formulating one and its expression in a supporting organization than to allow gradual and piecemeal development in the group consciousness of a 'feeling' for what is and is not acceptable. Such unstated assumptions always result in a reduction of respect and expectations, and can be worse for quality and performance than a policy that is stated but is not as good as it might be. At the very least, public promulgation allows the policy to be questioned and improved, while an unstated policy cannot even be discussed.

If newly appointed, a Company Software Quality Manager may well have authority and responsibility in advance of either the resources or the contacts to make them feasible. Obtaining and keeping all four of these necessary facilitators (authority, responsibility, resources, and working contacts) in good order must always be a primary objective. Good intentions that cannot be achieved are of little value.

Resources that are provided on a per-project basis may come too late, or too irregularly, to enable an adequate and consistent approach to:

- appointment of regular quality support staff, both within the technical staff of projects and in quality services (such as auditing, research, data management, etc.) outside the projects;
- undertaking of individual and organization-wide training;
- evaluation, specification, procurement and supported installation of inter-related sets of tools, methods, and procedures;
- provision of professional support to project and product design, planning and management, including feasibility studies, design and development reviews, advice and support on animations and demonstrations, special occasion audits, etc;
- provision of suitably independent and professional technical services such as customer liaison, product verification and validation, evaluation of (internal and external) products, support to marketing, support to sales, procurement, goods-inward inspections, system management, and so on.

9.6.3.B (company)   *Feasibility studies*

For the Company Quality Manager, the timing and focus of these studies moves farther back in project-time and to a more strategic level in the Company. Where a Group Quality Manager, or an individual Project Quality Manager, might protest strongly at being assigned a project that is clearly high-risk or low on direct returns, at a higher level in the company such projects might be judged worthwhile for their broadening of the company's experience into new technical or market areas or for maintaining a competitive presence despite the costs, or for using fixed assets that would otherwise be idle. In such circumstances, the Company Quality Manager has the difficult task of remaining as fair and honest as possible in the face of all pressures.

It is a Quality responsibility to ensure that projects with high risks, low returns and over-ambitious targets are recognized and registered as such with the senior management of the company. Even though in some circumstances these daunting conditions may be deliberately concealed at first from the project staff, to try to avoid their feeling defeated at the outset, facts must be admitted if the false ones are challenged. Quality Management at any level must be based on truth, and cannot operate effectively once it has been found capable of accepting and spreading false impressions. If a high-risk activity must still be undertaken, it deserves open acknowledgement, specially close monitoring, and the maximum possible support and involvement from the quality organization. Appropriate measures are unlikely to be taken if the situation is being misrepresented.

Project plans and predictions should be audited and analyses and reports made at project completions. The Company Quality Manager should soon have a good collection of local data and both the time and specialist support needed to analyse it suitably for the support of project planning and control. This support can be provided in more than one form, for example, by particular analyses of existing information to meet specific project purposes and by the formulation of models and rules.

While the Company Quality Manager is unlikely to be directly involved in forming models, rules and predictions, there will be a responsibility to ensure that they are produced and tested in a suitable manner for the expected usage. Among the dangers to recognize are of being either too selective or not selective enough in the application of the data and the 'general rules' deduced from it. Large projects are not necessarily more representative than small ones or the 'average' project a better guide than one which has been carefully selected to match the one in hand. Also, the most easily obtained data may swamp or ignore the less easily regularized but very significant details that are necessary to point to how and by how much the quality and productivity of processes and projects might be raised.

9.6.3.C (company)   *Process selection, engineering and introduction*

Process selection. A Company Quality Manager can obtain a breathing space on appointment by decreeing that there be a single and unobjectionable code of practice for project management, product design and development, documentation and configuration control, and for measuring and evaluating product qualities and staff productiveness. With this code of practice made stable for a significant period, and once the necessary tooling and training is in place, savings and improvements can be expected as all aspects are used, examined and refined. Senior management may also be very happy with the reduction or removal of the costs of research and development into processes and grateful for the more accurate predictions provided by a closed system.

However, the Company Quality Manager must make sure that it is not forgotten that the software and system business and its customers and staff do not stand still and that too long a retirement from the real world can be very costly if customer expectations and general levels of quality achievement move on. Thus, there must soon be added the channels and functions whereby additions and variations to the initial code of practice can be made.

Process engineering and introduction. If a process-engineering section is set up at Company level (similarly to that which might be found for a group of projects, see Section 9.6.2.C above), it may be in danger of losing contact with the needs and capabilities of those it serves and of attempting to force inappropriate technology onto projects in the interests of consistency and technological advance. Thus, it is important that this function be closely allied to the wishes, capacities, and current pressures of project managers and that introductions and other changes are always made jointly and at an acceptable rate.

The research and development programme will have to meet the interests and objectives of the company, projects, project staff and process engineers. The rate at which new processes are evaluated, engineered and introduced, with all their attendant facilitating activities (training, equipment, tools, languages and other representations, etc.) must be carefully balanced with the potentially adverse short-term effects of making changes while work is in progress. Also, in order to succeed, such a programme must be planned and supported at a high level in the organization, since it will almost certainly lead to all or most projects having some part of their work carried out in a spirit of experimentation and thus risking the programme being seen as a danger.

The Group Quality Manager can be instrumental in planning this activity, in obtaining the support and resources needed, in ensuring the quality of the engineering work done and in assuring worried managers that risk has been minimized and that the interest and involvement raised will certainly benefit the host-projects. Even when the main responsibility is with another functional line in the company (Software Engineering, say) the quality involvement must be high for recommendations and implementations to be of assured value.

All the topics, from A through to I, will be handled by the Company Quality Manager through a co-ordinated programme. This programme will include:

- the creation and dissemination of codes of practice;
- central control and support for these codes of practice (including the provision of supporting tools, services, databases, and persons with assigned responsibility and authority, as required): the 'supporting services' may include a central QA department, and a software-engineering specialist group
- consultation between, and training of, 'quality' and other technical staff;
- an accessible and rational system through which concessions and variations and their accompanying prediction, recording and control systems can be handled quickly and efficiently;
- an interlinked system of Quality Circles, Review Groups and Special Interest Groups through which local knowledge, interest and capability are constantly applied and refreshed;
- the representation and justification of quality activities at all levels in the company, resourcing, quality planning and control;
- setting up a complete quality system throughout the company and covering all its activities, founded in senior management responsibility. Such a system is described in the standard ISO 9004 (International Organization for Standardization, 1986);
- defining company quality policy and strategy, which might include going for assessment and certification against standards such as BS 5750 (British Standards Institution, 1987) or ISO 900, (International Organization for Standardization, 1987);
- explicit and on-going investment in quality costing and justification, in order to demonstrate and assure that cost benefits result from the application of quality thinking and quality actions;
- overt introduction and encouragement of quality attitudes and practices into all levels of the company.

9.7 Summary

Reliable products result from reliable processes: reliable processes result from effective process engineering, supported by good communication and timely and appropriate controls. No software development organization can expect regularly to achieve reliability or any other quality in its products without first making sure that reliability is a characteristic of its processes: and the only way to achieve and demonstrate the reliability of a process is by the application of Quality Management.

9.8 Further Reading

Literature appropriate to software quality management is not extensive. However, three books for background reading on general aspects of Quality

Management are recommended. They are *Quality is Free* by Philip Crosby (1979), *Quality Assurance for Computer Software* by Robert Dunn and Richard Ullman (1982), and *Managing Software Reliability: the Paradigmatic Approach* by M. G. Walker (1981).

It is difficult to make recommendations in the area of standards, since there are many standards-producing bodies and no clearly outstanding examples of Standards that are widely used, applicable to a number of different kinds of product and development style, and readily incorporated in existing (but not standardized) organizations. Only two are suggested here in addition to those already mentioned in the text, both because they are of the 'how to do it' kind rather than bare instructions as to 'what to do'. They are *Guide to the Achievement of Quality in Software* (Ministry of Defence, 1984) and *Software Considerations in Airborne Systems and Equipment Certification* (RTCA, 1985).

10

Measuring Software Development

Barbara Kitchenham

10.1 Introduction 303
10.2 Terminology 303
10.3 The Nature and Use of Software Metrics 304
10.4 Practical Problems 308
10.5 Analytical and Conceptual Software Models 314
10.6 Metric Evaluation and Model Validation 315
10.7 Metrics Through the Life Cycle 317
10.8 Guidelines for Interpreting Metric Values 328
10.9 Further Reading 331

10.1 Introduction

This chapter of the handbook describes how software metrics and models may be used to assist with the production of cost-effective, reliable software products. There is no attempt to provide a comprehensive or complete list of all possible metrics and models. The aim of this chapter and the accompanying appendix is to assess some of the more widely known metrics and models, and to identify those that have proved useful in practice.

This chapter discusses some general issues relating to software metrics and models, including a discussion of how they might be assessed or evaluated in a particular situation. Appendix C defines a standardized format by which metrics and models can be described, and then uses that format to describe a number of standard software metrics and models.

10.2 Terminology

The term 'software metrics' is used in this chapter to mean measures (in terms of amounts or counts) related to software products and the process of software production and support. The term 'synthetic' is used to indicate a metric value obtained from a formula or model.

In this context, the 'software products' from which software metrics may be derived should be taken to include all the intermediate products, such as design documents, specifications, code listings, test reports, etc., that are produced during software development and maintenance, not just the final software product. This fairly loose definition reflects the fact that the term software metrics is used as a general tag to cover all aspects of quantification related to software production and support. It may be considered an adequate definition, if it is agreed to allow the term 'measures' to include values obtained in at least three different ways:

- *By edict,* this occurs when project targets are set to indicate the constraints within which a product is to be developed, or the specific requirements that a product must satisfy. These targets may be set on the basis of commercial decisions such as getting a product into the market before other companies, or obtaining a particular contract.
- *By estimation,* this occurs when the value of a metric is needed at a stage in the development process when it is not available for direct measurement. Predictions or estimates may be based on estimation models or subjective guesses.
- *By measurement,* this occurs when the value of a metric can be obtained directly (occasionally 'back-estimation' is used to 'estimate' the value of some metric nobody collected at the time—on the whole it is preferable to measure directly rather than guess).

Targets, predictions and actual values are all needed within the context of project control. Targets provide the constraints within which a project manager must work (i.e. targets are what we want). Predictions provide an indication whether a project is likely to achieve its targets (i.e. predictions are what we think we will get). Actual values measure attributes of the project directly (i.e. actuals are what we got). They also feed forward into both the identification of targets for future projects and the improvement of estimation methods.

10.3 The Nature and Use of Software Metrics

In general there are two important classes of software metrics:

- metrics that assist in the *control* or *management* of the development process;
- metrics that are *predictors* (or *indicators*) of either product qualities or control metrics.

In practice, the same metrics may be used for both purposes, but the justification, and hence the criteria by which the metrics should be evaluated, will be different.

10.3.1 Control metrics

Control metrics are not specific to software—any industrial production or manufacturing activity would be managed and controlled by similar 'metrics'.

The metrics that are used most widely for project control are resource-related metrics such as effort, elapsed calendar time, machine usage for particular tasks/activities. These metrics support project control because they may be incorporated into a management planning and monitoring activity, where *estimates* of the effort, time-scale and machine usage are made as part of the project plans and *actual* values are used to monitor progress against those plans. Cost metrics and cost-estimation models are discussed in detail in Chapter 11.

Other metrics that are used for control are those that are used to estimate task completion, such as percentage of modules coded, or percentage of statements tested. They compare an estimate of the 'size' of the task, in terms of its expected output, with the 'amount' of the task output that has been completed at a particular point in time.

The last category of metrics that is often used in project control is defect-related metrics. From a Quality Engineering viewpoint, the discovery, and elimination of defects is the major cost of non-conformance. To control non-conformance costs, it is necessary to record information about the nature and origin of defects and the costs associated with their discovery and removal. From a Project Management viewpoint, the activity of testing and debugging various intermediate and final products cannot be planned without some estimate of the expected defect rate and effort required to diagnose and fix defects. It is therefore necessary to estimate defect rates based on past projects against both products and testing activities, and monitor current defect rates to ensure that the current product is behaving as expected.

10.3.2 Predictor metrics

Predictor metrics are used to estimate final product characteristics (often called product qualities) or to provide estimates of control metrics. Examples of such metrics discussed in Appendix C are fan-in/fan-out metrics, which are based on the relationships between system components (usually calls between modules), structural metrics, which are based on equivalent control-flow graphs of programs or data-flow diagrams, or readability indexes for software documents, which may be based on sentence length and syllable-per-word counts.

The use of metrics as predictors of product qualities rests on three assumptions:

- The metric measures some inherent property of the software.
- The inherent property itself influences the behavioural characteristics of the final product.
- The relationship between the metric and the final quality is understood (at least approximately) and represented in terms of a formula or model.

In practice, it is usually only the first two assumptions that are considered. Thus, for example, structural metrics are often assumed to be related to 'complexity' (McCabe, 1976). The larger the value of the metric the more complex a program is assumed to be. It is then assumed that complexity is related to various product qualities. For example, complexity is believed to be negatively related to reliability because more complex programs have more chance of containing residual errors. Similarly it is also believed to be negatively related to extendability, since more complex components will be more difficult to understand, and therefore more difficult to amend successfully.

As yet, there has been little attempt to formalize such beliefs into general formulas or models, because in practice it is difficult to determine appropriate measurements of final product attributes. However, quality predictors can be used as part of the project control process, if some decision rules are incorporated into the planning process. For example, it may be decided to provide either intensive testing or extended design of any modules with unusually large values of certain 'complexity' metrics.

The use of metrics as predictors of control metrics rests on the assumption that the metric being measured is related to the control metric, and the relationship can be expressed in terms of a formula or model. An example of this is Albrecht's Function Point metric, which uses a weighted sum of the number of inputs, outputs, master files and commands in a system as a predictor of development size (Albrecht, 1979).

From the above discussion, it is clear that metrics that can be used effectively for both project control and quality assessment are of particular value to project managers, since, having two roles, they are cost-effective to collect. The metrics that are used extensively for both project control, and predictions are: simple size measures, such as lines of code, and fault and error counts based on various fault classification schemes.

Because of their potential importance, these two types of metrics are discussed in more detail in the next two sections.

10.3.3   Dual-purpose metrics

10.3.3.1   *Size metrics*
Size metrics such as lines of code, number of machine-code instructions, etc., are used to assist project control by providing a mechanism by which project progress can be assessed (in terms of percentage completion).

Size is also frequently used as both a control metric predictor and a quality predictor. Size is used to predict project effort and time scales, but is also sometimes considered as a quality predictor. Large components are assumed, on average, to have a larger number of residual errors and be more difficult to understand than small components, and so are assumed to impact on reliability and extendability.

10.3.3.2 *Fault classification and counting*

Fault counts and fault analysis are used to permit the traditional quality assurance aspects of project control. Quality assurance is primarily concerned with cost-effective defect control, where defect control comprises defect prevention/avoidance, defect detection, defect removal, and defect analysis.

In a conventional manufacturing industry, production processes are established that minimize the opportunity for introducing defects into a product and maximize the efficiency of detecting and removing any defects that are introduced, with the aim of minimizing manufacturing costs. Defect analysis involves counts of the number of defects within classification schemes that indicate the nature of the defect, how it was introduced into the product, how it was detected, together with information about the cost of the defect and the defect-removal process. It is used to monitor the production process with respect to the cost of defect control, and indicate any potential problem areas.

In the software industry, the concept of cost-effective defect control incorporated into process control is equally important, but is made more difficult because:

(1) The effect of various development processes on the characteristics of a final software product are not well-defined in quantitative terms, e.g. the lifetime cost savings of using one technique rather than another has not usually been identified.
(2) Each software product is unique, so standardization and control of a development process (unlike standardization and control of a manufacturing process) will not guarantee the quality of a particular product.

These difficulties imply that active quality assurance is even more important for software production than for conventional manufacturing industries. However, for software, it is vital that quality assurance not only supports the control of the production process but also permits an assessment of the quality of the particular software product being constructed (relative to other products), and the ability to assess the effectiveness of different production processes.

It is generally assumed that defect avoidance, detection and removal lead to improved reliability. However, as Littlewood (1978) points out, it is unreasonable to assume either that each fault has an equal contribution to the overall failure rate, or that conventional defect-detection techniques reveal the same type of faults as life use. None-the-less, the removal of faults is likely to improve reliability, so the identification of appropriate strategies for efficient, cost-effective fault avoidance, fault detection, and fault tolerance should be the aim of software producers who wish to achieve consistent and predictable levels of product reliability. Defect analysis provides a useful technique to help achieve this aim. In addition, if project control procedures are established to cater for particularly difficult system components (e.g. by subjecting them to more stringent testing than other components), then defect analysis may be used as a support for detailed project monitoring and control processes.

10.4   Practical Problems

10.4.1   Interpretation of metric values

One of the major problems with the use of software metrics is that they do not, in general, have an interpretation scale, i.e. there is no means of interpreting a value of 100 lines of code in the same way that a value of 100°C can be interpreted. Metrics must usually be interpreted relatively, and there are three ways in which this may be done.

- *Comparison with plans and expectations.* Formal project constraints, either targets or predictions, may have been specified in a formal project plan. For example, the testing and debugging phase of a project may be planned on the assumption that unit testing will result in the discovery of 2 faults per 100 lines of code, and that they will be found and cleared at a rate of 4 per day. An actual value of 4 faults per 100 lines, found and cleared at a rate of 1 per day, can then be interpreted in terms of the implications of schedule slippages and additional staff requirements. In addition to formal plans, project managers usually have informal expectations about the way a project should progress, for example, it might be expected that the completion of unit testing and the move to integration testing should be accompanied by a reduction in the unit testing fault-detection rates. A manager would interpret an increasing or non-decreasing detection rate as an indication that unit testing needed to be extended, and integration testing deferred.
- *Comparison with other similar projects.* A metric value may be judged as normal or abnormal by comparison with the values observed for that metric on other similar projects. For example, an expansion metric that measured the ratio of design size to code size that was much higher than that observed in other projects might indicate an incomplete or inade-quate design. Other projects thus allow 'baselines' to be established by which deviations from the expected 'norm' can be detected. It is necessary to have some means of identifying 'similar projects'. DeMarco (1982) suggests projects produced by the same company, in the same language, which have the same processing bias (i.e. database-oriented, or function-oriented). It is often the case that norms derived from past experience are the basis for planned targets, although issues such as the availability of new tools or commercial pressures may result in differences.
- *Comparison with other similar components within a project.* This is very similar to comparisons with other projects, but in this case other components, for example modules, are used to set up the baselines. An example of this form of comparison would be to identify modules with unusually large or small error rates, by comparison with the average and range of error rates observed for all the modules in a product.

The methods of metric 'interpretation' suggested above are only suitable for identifying deviations from some agreed standard or norm, be it based on targets, or baselines. It does not provide an interpretation in the real world in the way 100°C is interpreted as boiling point (at sea level). A feature of software projects is that deviations from standards or norms may be a result of many different underlying causes, some of which may be good, some of which may be bad. For example, a high design-to-code ratio (i.e. a small number of design statements being expanded to an unusually large number of code statements) may be the result of an incomplete design, but it might also be due to inefficient coding, or alternatively, component reuse. It is beyond the scope of the metrics to determine all the possible causes of a particular abnormal value, or to distinguish which cause is operating in any particular circumstances.

An example of monitoring project progress with respect to baselines is provided by Doerflinger & Basili (1983). They identified a set of measurements that could be evaluated at various distinct stages in the development process. The measurements were compared with a baseline to detect whether the project was progressing normally. The baseline was obtained by calculating the average of each of the measurements from a group of similar projects, plus or minus one standard deviation. Measurement values for the project being monitored that were outside the baseline were identified as abnormal. Doerflinger & Basili offered a number of different explanations for each possible anomaly. For example, they suggest that a larger than expected number of lines of code per software change, at the 40% code completion stage of the project, might be caused by any one of the following conditions:

- good code
- easily developed code
- an influx of transported code
- closeness to build or milestone date
- computer hardware problems
- a poor testing approach

Doerflinger & Basili make it clear that the project manager must institute some additional procedures in order to determine which interpretation, if any, is likely to be correct, and thus determine what actions, if any, should be taken.

10.4.2 Data-collection procedures

One of the reasons why metrics are not used more widely in the software industry is that it is difficult in practice to obtain accurate measures. Ideally, metric values need to be repeatable, comparable and verified. By repeatable, we mean that two independent data collectors would obtain the same value if they were to measure the same item. By comparable, we mean that metric values obtained from different items have been obtained using the same procedures. By verified, we mean that values have been checked for clerical errors and inconsistencies. In order to achieve these requirements, it is

necessary to establish data-collection procedures and ensure that they are
adhered to.

These requirements should not rule out metrics based on subjective
assessment, which are often useful. However, they do suggest that the criteria
by which subjective assessments are made should be well defined.

Data-collection procedures must include the following:

- *Metric definitions*: it is not usually sufficient to define a metric by its name
  alone. A full definition should identify the units that apply to the metric,
  the type of software entity to which the metric applies, together with a
  description of the way in which the metric is to be collected. The need for
  extended definitions can be appreciated by considering the often-quoted
  'lines of code' metric. Without specific counting rules for blank lines,
  comment lines, declarations, multiple statements per line, and executable
  statements spanning more than one line, there is no way to ensure that
  values of the metric are repeatable. In addition, without identifying which
  language the code is written in, it is not possible to know whether values
  obtained for different programs are comparable. The Alvey Software Data
  Library project has devoted a good deal of effort to the problem of
  metrics definitions, and has recommended a standard format (Ross, 1986).
- *Organizational details*, which should identify the person(s) responsible for
  collecting data, the person(s) responsible for verifying data, the way in
  which data is to be recorded, and the way in which data is to be verified
  and analysed.

In practice, the ways in which data is recorded, verified and analysed are
related, and are likely to influence the success or otherwise of any data
collection activities. Data collection is unlikely to be successful unless:

- data collection is integrated into the development process (e.g. as part of
  the Quality Management System);
- it is automated whenever possible;
- data that cannot be collected automatically is collected at the time (i.e. is
  not based on recollection of past events) and is verified immediately;
- the time-scales between data collection and data analysis are minimized;
- data is treated as a company resource and facilities are available to keep
  historical records of projects, not only to monitor current projects;
- the problem of motivating software engineers to keep accurate records is
  not underestimated. Proper training in data-collection procedures and the
  use of software metrics, together with quick analysis facilities are
  essential, but not sufficient requirements.

Examples of existing data-collection schemes are given by Basili & Weiss
(1982a) and Kitchenham (1984).

10.4.3   The analysis of software metrics

The analysis of software metrics data is usually assumed to be a simple matter
of utilizing conventional statistical techniques to provide analyses of the

following type:

- summary statistics indicating the average value and variability of a set of data points,
- scatter plots, correlation and regression analysis for investigating the relationship between two metrics,
- contingency table analysis to investigate counts and percentages within classification schemes.

However, in practice software metrics datasets have a number of very undesirable properties. Data values are usually discrete, heavily skewed, non-negative and often contain a substantial number of outliers. These properties imply that the use of conventional statistical techniques, based on the assumption that the data is Gaussian (i.e. symmetrical, continuous, and possessing a 'bell-shaped' frequency distribution) is a little unrealistic.

There are four main methods for dealing with non-Gaussian data:

- using the true underlying distribution;
- using robust statistical techniques that are resilient to departures from the Gaussian distribution;
- using non-parametric techniques that are independent of the underlying distribution;
- applying transformations to the raw data that force the data values close enough to the Gaussian for use of conventional analysis techniques.

The method used in a particular situation will depend on the circumstances. In the rest of this section we describe some practical techniques for analysing software metrics data.

Using the true underlying distribution is ideal for analyses involving only one or two different metrics, but may not be suitable for multivariate analysis where many different metrics need to be analysed in a single model. It may also be difficult in practice to determine the 'true' distribution.

Robust methods seem useful for software metrics analysis, particularly univariate summary techniques such as Tukey's 'box plots' (Hoaglin *et al.*, 1983), which indicate the central location of a data set, together with the range and skewness of the data set, in a simple graphical form. An example of a box

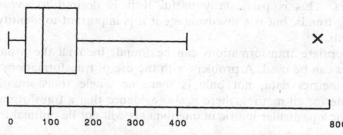

Fig. 10.1. Box plot produced from the lines of code values of 27 modules.

plot of lines of code obtained from a set of 27 modules is shown in Fig. 10.1. The vertical line within the rectangular part of the plot shows the position of the median, which for this data set was approximately 80 lines of code (LOC). The median is the value that divides the data set so that 50% of the values are less than it and 50% are greater than it. The position of the vertical lines that make up either end of the rectangular part of the plot are called the lower fourth, or F_L, (referring to the left-hand side of the rectangle) and the upper fourth, or F_U (referring to the right-hand side of the rectangle). In Fig. 10.1, F_L is approximately 40 LOC and F_U is approximately 160 LOC. F_L is obtained from the value that divides the values less than median, such that 50% are less than it and 50% are greater than it, and F_U is obtained from the value that splits the data values greater than the median. The median splits the data values in half, and the fourths split the data values into quarters. Thus, for a completely symmetrical data set the fourths would be equivalent to quartiles; for all data sets the rectangular part of the box plot covers a range of values that includes 50% of the data points. It is clear from Fig. 10.1 that the data set represented in the box plot is not symmetrical because the line representing the median is much closer to the left-hand side of the box than the right-hand side. The lines outside the rectangle in Fig. 10.1 are called the tails of the box plot and are calculated as follows:

$$\text{Cut-off point of the lower tail} = F_L - \tfrac{3}{2} \times d_F$$

$$\text{Cut-off point of the upper tail} = F_U + \tfrac{3}{2} \times d_F$$

where $d_F = F_U - F_L$.

The lower cut-off point in Fig. 10.1 is at zero LOC and the upper cut-off point is at approximately 420 LOC. Values in the data set that lie outside the tails of the box plots are regarded as 'outliers' or 'anomalous' values, and their values are shown explicitly on the plot. In Fig. 10.1, there is one outlier value at approximately 770 LOC.

For multivariate studies however, the use of robust methods is restricted to multivariate regression, because robust equivalents of other analysis techniques have not been defined.

Non-parametric techniques are particularly useful for analysing data that is in the form of counts or percentages within some classification scheme. A characteristic of many non-parametric techniques is that they reduce the effect of outliers. This is particularly useful if it is desired to investigate any underlying trends, but is a disadvantage if it is important to identify abnormal components.

If appropriate transformations can be found, then all the usual statistical techniques can be used. A problem with the use of transformations is that, for software metrics data, not only is there no single transformation that is appropriate for all metrics, there is also evidence that a transformation that is optimal for a particular metric in one data set will not be optimal for the same metric in a different data set (Kitchenham and Wood, 1986). A possible strategy for transformations is the following.

- Use the natural logarithm transformation for effort, duration, and cost data, in line with current software cost modelling (Boehm, 1981) and econometirc practice.
- Use the square root, or the cube of the square root transformations for failure, fault, and error counts; such transformations are optimal for data generated by a Poisson distribution.
- Use the natural logarithm, or the square root transformations for other software data; the square root transformation is particularly useful for metrics that can take the value zero.

An example of the effect of the logarithmic transformation can be seen by comparing Fig. 10.2(a) with Fig. 10.2(b). Figure 10.2(a) is a scatter plot of the size in lines of code plotted against McCabe's complexity metric (McCabe,

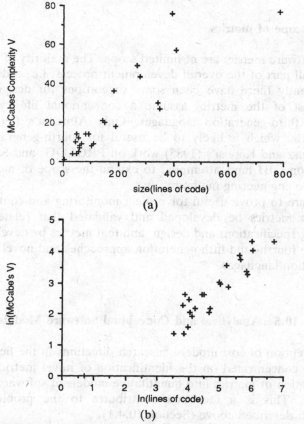

Fig. 10.2. (a) McCabe's V versus size (original). (b) McCabe's V versus size (transformed).

1976); each point corresponds to the pair of values obtained for one module. There appears to be an underlying relationship between the two metrics such that large modules also exhibit large values of McCabe's metric. However, it might be misleading to assess relationship using a conventional least-squares regression analysis on the raw data because it is highly skewed (i.e. there are more points exhibiting small values of both metrics than exhibiting large values), and the data appears to indicate a relationship between mean and variance (i.e. the data appears to be wedge-shaped, with the data points being more spread out for the large-valued data points, than for the small-valued points). The scatter plot of the transformed data is shown in Fig. 10.2(b). It can be seen that the transformation has reduced both the skewness and the non-stable variance. A regression performed on the transformed data is, therefore, more likely to result in valid statistical assessment of the existence and extent of any relationship between the two metrics. It is interesting, however, that a side-effect of the transformation has been to alter what is identified as an 'outlier' from a data point that has a particularly large value to one that has a particularly small value.

10.4.4   The scope of metrics

Currently, software metrics are of limited scope. The majority of metrics apply to only a small part of the overall development process, i.e. code and testing, although recently there have been some suggestions for design metrics. In addition, most of the metrics assume a conventional life cycle, and the conventional third-generation languages. Only Albrecht's (1979) work on function points, which is likely to be useful for fourth-generation developments, Markusz and Kaposi's (1985) work on PROLOG, and Samson *et al.*'s (1989) work on OBJ have attempted to extend the scope of metrics to more novel software engineering methods.

If metrics are to prove useful for project monitoring and control, then it is essential that metrics be developed and validated that relate to software requirements, specifications and design, and that metrics be developed that are useful for the fourth- and fifth-generation approaches and novel programming and specification languages.

10.5   Analytical and Conceptual Software Models

With the exception of cost models, research directions in the field of software metrics have concentrated on the identification of novel metrics, rather than the incorporation of metrics into quantitative models of software development and support. This is a fact that contributes to the problem of metric interpretation described above (Section 10.4.1).

Quantitative models incorporating software metrics may be classified into two kinds:

- *conceptual models,* which incorporate various management or engineering heuristics, such as the belief that unusual components or project metric values should be investigated, or the expectation that completion of one type of testing should be preceded by a reduction in the rate of detection of certain types of fault;
- *analytical models,* which are characterized by having defined inputs and outputs and an objective procedure for transforming the inputs into the outputs, usually as a result of some mathematical formula.

Both types of model are important. Analytical models are almost always developed by formalizing some conceptual model, and provide a framework within which the validity of a conceptual model can be tested scientifically. Conceptual models provide the means by which knowledge that cannot be stated algorithmically may none-the-less be articulated and utilized, for example in advice systems and/or expert systems.

Conceptual models, using software metrics, are basically concerned with the view that norms can be established for various facets of the development process, and that deviations from those norms should be investigated.

Analytical models, apart from cost models, tend to be one of three types:

- fault/error detection models, which consider the generation and detection of faults in terms of evaluating both a particular product with respect to residual faults and/or a defect detection strategy with respect to its theoretical efficiency;
- quality models, which attempt to predict the characteristics of the final software product from measures of software development metrics;
- process models, which attempt to model the quantitative characteristics of a particular development process, such as debugging, or coding.

Examples of each of these types of model are discussed in Appendix C.

10.6 Metric Evaluation and Model Validation

In our view, metrics that are part of the project-control process do not require formal evaluation. As long as they are direct measures either of costs, or of the completeness of the product being made or the processes being performed, and are used to support the usual project-management procedures, evaluation seems unnecessary.

Metrics that are used to predict either final product characteristics, or control metrics, do need to be evaluated. It is necessary to confirm that a relationship does exist between the predictor metric and the metric being predicted. Predictor metrics should only be incorporated into the control of the development process if such relationships have been confirmed.

This view of metric evaluation equates metric evaluation to model validation. A metric can only be used as a predictor if its relationship with the metric or attribute being predicted is formalized in a model. When models are formalized using statistical techniques like regression or discriminant analysis, then model evaluation can be based on cross-validation (Hoaglin *et al.*, 1983). Cross-validation is a technique whereby a model is formulated on one set of data, and then evaluated on a second data set. It can be done in two ways:

* *single cross-validation*, which, in its simplest form occurs when a single data set is split into two parts, a model is formulated using one part, and evaluated using the other part;
* *double cross-validation*, where one data set is used to formulate the model and a second independently collected data set is used to evaluate the model.

Model formulation is a three-step process:

(1) identifying the parameters/variables which are to be included in the model;
(2) identifying the functional form of the model;
(3) identifying the coefficients of the parameters/variables in the model (this step is sometimes called calibration).

Statistical techniques are of most use in the first and last steps of the process, and in particular the last step. It is unfortunate, perhaps, that it is the first two steps that are most critical for the evaluation of software development metrics. The example of cost-estimation models illustrates this point. It is generally accepted that the relationship between production effort and program size can be modelled as an exponential function:

$$\text{Effort} = a \times (\text{size})^b$$

where a and b are the model coefficients and effort and size are the model parameters/variables.

This general type of relationship has been observed in many environments (Boehm, 1981; Basili & Freburger, 1981). However, the value of b is close to 1, and in no case has there been any means of distinguishing the above model from the simple linear model:

$$\text{Effort} = a \times \text{size} + c$$

It has also been observed that the values of a and b vary a good deal from data set to data set. This has not, however, led to the belief that the model is invalid. It has led to the practice of calibrating any such model to the environment in which it is to be used.

In some cases regression-based evaluation is less straightforward. This occurs when the attribute that the predictor metric is believed to estimate is difficult to measure, either because it is not a static attribute (e.g. software reliability that is time-dependent), or because it is subjective in nature (e.g.

clarity of documentation). In the case of time-dependent attributes, techniques such as proportional hazards modelling (Wightman and Bendell, 1985), which allow additional 'explanatory' variables to act as weights on a basic reliability function, are needed to determine whether or not a metric influences final reliability. In the case of subjectively determined attributes, it may be necessary to evaluate predictor metrics experimentally by using software engineers to assess a selection of software items with respect to the attribute of interest.

The discussion above has concentrated on direct metric evaluation, but it is also possible to evaluate metrics indirectly. Indirect evaluation occurs when a metric is evaluated in terms of its relationship to a second metric and the second metric is known (or assumed) to be related to a quality or control metric of interest. For example, function points may be evaluated as suitable for use in cost-estimation models by identifying a relationship with program size (i.e. indirectly) rather than development effort (i.e. directly). This type of evaluation is particularly useful when alternative predictors are required that have beneficial properties such as availability at an earlier stage in the development process.

10.7 Metrics Through the Life Cycle

A number of metrics and models are discussed in detail in Appendix C. In the appendix, each metric is discussed independently. In this section, we consider metrics from the viewpoint of a project manager attempting to use metrics constructively throughout the software development life-cycle. The detailed recommendations about metrics and models given in the appendix, are presented here in terms of a number of related project-management procedures.

For the purpose of this section, we shall assume a conventional third-generation approach to software development, based on a life-cycle comprising requirements analysis, structural design, detailed design, coding, unit testing, integration testing, acceptance testing. Each of the stages (except acceptance testing) is discussed below in terms of which metrics should be collected and how the metric values should be used. Acceptance testing is excluded from discussion in this chapter because it is the point at which reliability can be assessed directly, and is, therefore, the main factor that distinguishes acceptance testing from unit and integration testing and is covered by Chapter 6 on reliability modelling.

It is assumed that during structural design, integration test plans are prepared; that during detailed design, black box module test plans are prepared; and that during coding, white box module test plans are prepared. Test plans are assumed to specify the test cases that must be executed during the corresponding testing stage.

It is also assumed that checking activities takes place during the system specification and design stages, and the terms inspection, review, and/or walkthrough are used to describe those activities (see Chapters 5 and 7). It is recognized that most software engineers differentiate between these activities, and that a more finely-grained monitoring system might be expected to detect different fault patterns from the different activities. However, for the purpose of this section, the terms are used interchangeably, and it is assumed that any fault data is based on aggregated data from all relevant checking activities for a particular life-cycle stage.

The general approach to using software metrics, which is applicable to each stage of the life cycle, involves the following.

- Setting quantifiable targets for all the activities and outputs associated with a stage. Quantifiable targets permit the amount of work required in each stage to be estimated for budgetary and scheduling reasons, and the percentage of work completed to be assessed at any point during a stage, and establish criteria for determining the completion of a stage.
- Measuring the actual values.
- Comparing the actual values with the target values.
- Formulating a plan to correct any observed deviations from the targets.

This is the usual process control approach that is found in many industrial situations. It is somewhat more difficult for software because for the following reasons.

- There will often be many possible causes for deviations from targets and for each cause there may be several different types of corrective action (see Kitchenham and Walker, 1986b). This implies that the project manager will need to institute some additional procedures to determine which, if any, of the possible causes is the actual cause, before any corrective actions can be taken.
- The targets themselves may be inappropriate, since there are no very accurate models available to estimate targets. This again causes complications when attempting to understand the reasons for deviations from targets. Sometimes, the actual values observed during a stage of the life-cycle can be used to re-estimate the 'targets', for example an estimate of size used to predict the time required for the-coding stage may be replaced with the actual size of code produced before deciding whether the actual time required was inappropriate. For a discussion of the political dimensions of target setting and estimating, and the effects that targets can sometimes have on actuals (e.g. an emphasis on productivity targets resulting in poor quality), see Tom DeMarco's excellent book *Controlling Software Projects* (DeMarco, 1982).

In addition to monitoring with respect to pre-set targets, we take the view that metrics may be used to identify anomalous components that are unusual with respect to other component values rather than with respect to targets.

This permits detailed project monitoring to be based on internally generated project norms rather than estimates based on other projects. This form of monitoring can be undertaken from the structural design stage (assuming that structural design includes the production of system-structure diagrams showing the links between components).

In this section, we will make specific suggestions about which metrics are of interest, how targets may be set, and what type of corrective action is appropriate for each stage in the life cycle. We will not repeat in this section discussions on the use of cost metrics, which are found in Chapter 11, and for simplicity, we will ignore the problem of enhancing an existing system. The suggestions given below are illustrative and, therefore, by no means complete. The ESPRIT-backed REQUEST project is attempting to develop a more complete model of the information required to support quality management, which includes checklists identifying the possible different interpretations of particular deviations from targets, and indicates various other kinds of information a project, or quality, manager might require to distinguish between the various possible interpretations (Hamer *et al.*, 1986).

10.7.1 Requirements specification

SETTING TARGETS
- Use values from other, 'similar' projects.
- Use expert opinion (guesses).
- Use company or group standards.
- Estimate point-value plus range; use box plots if values are available from other projects or from a number of different experts; and base the point estimate on the median, and the permitted range on the fourths (see Section 10.4.3).

RELEVANT METRICS
This implies those that should be estimated to obtain target values and that should be collected to monitor project progress.

- Size of product in lines of code (LOC) (for effort and timescale estimation, and estimating total number of faults).
- Number of faults that will be detected during product development per 1000 LOC, and breakdown of fault detection rate and fault origin rates per life-cycle stage (for documentation quality assessment, and estimation of rework effort).
- Size of specification in pages or words (for documentation completeness assessment).
- The fog index of natural-language specification (Gunning, 1962) (for document clarity assessment).
- Percentage of faults classified as missing or wrong (to assess document completeness and correctness).
- Number of unresolved faults at end of stage (to assess defect-removal efficiency).

10.7.2 Structural design

SETTING TARGETS
- As for requirements specification, except that the actual values of the metrics collected during the requirements stage can be used both to improve the selection of 'similar' projects for the comparison, and to provide inputs to other predictive models. Some models that may be used to generate targets are discussed below and in subsequent sections. In all cases, it must be emphasized that these are suggestions, which should be validated before being used in any particular circumstance.

SETTING PROJECT NORMS
- Module-based metric values are summarized in box plots, and values within the upper and lower tails of the box plots are assumed to be 'normal', while values outside upper and lower tails are assumed to be 'anomalous'.

RELEVANT METRICS
- Size of product in LOC, an estimate based on median size of similar projects may be checked against an estimate based on the median expansion ratio from specification size in pages to code size in LOC (to refine effort, time-scale, and total fault estimates).
- Number of modules (to provide a measure of product size against which the completeness of subsequent module based activities can be assessed). An estimate based on median number of modules from other similar projects may be compared with an estimate based on the formula:

$$NM = \frac{S}{M}$$

where NM is the estimated number of modules;
S is the estimate of the system size in LOC;
M is the median module size found in other similar projects.

N.B. If the above formula is used to estimate NM, then a suitable range for the target may also be determined using the upper and lower fourths from a box plot of observed module sizes.
- Number of faults per 1000 LOC, and breakdown of fault detection rate and fault origin rates for each life-cycle stage. Fault rate estimates should be refined as a result of the actual number of requirements faults detected during reviews and inspections. There are a number of different models that might be developed. The original estimate could be adjusted by the number of faults detected, using a formula of the form:

$$FR_N = FR_O \times \frac{FR_{A1}}{FR_{E1}} \quad \text{assuming } FR_{A1} > 0 \text{ and } FR_{E1} > 0$$

where FR_N is the new estimate of the fault rate per 1000 LOC;
FR_O is the original estimate of the fault rate;
FR_{A1} is the actual number of faults per 1000 lines found during requirements specification;
FR_{E1} is the original estimate of the number of faults per 1000 lines to be found during requirements specification.

Alternatively, a new estimate of the total number of faults that will be detected during product development could be generated from a model of the form:

$$F = b_0 + b_1 \times RS^{z_1} + b_2 \times RF^{z_2}$$

where F is an estimate of the faults that will be found during product development;
b_i, $i = 0$, 1, 2, are constants determined from other similar projects;
RS is the size of the specification in pages or words;
RF is the number of requirements faults detected;
z_i, $i = 1$, 2, are constants determined from other similar projects.

N.B. There is no guarantee that such a relationship exists, but should it be validated in a particular environment, it could be used to generate both a point estimate of the expected fault rate, and a suitable range of values.

- Size of natural language design document in pages or words (to assess document completeness).
- Fog index of natural language document (to assess document clarity).
- Ratio of design document size to specification document size, i.e. design size/specification size (to assess the translation process from specification to design).
- Number of integration test cases planned (to assist estimation of integration testing activities, and to assess the test plans). This could be based initially on a formula linking the median fan-in to a module, and the number of modules that are linked to a module as a result of shared data areas, and the expected number of modules to give:

$INT_{MIN} = FI \times NM$
$INT_{MAX} = (FI \times OLM) \times NM$
$INT_{EST} = (INT_{MIN} \times INT_{MAX})^{1/2}$

where INT_{MIN} is the minimum expected number of integration tests;
INT_{MAX} is the maximum expected number of integration tests;
INT_{EST} is the point estimate of the expected number of integration tests and is the geometric mean of the minimum and the maximum;
FI is the median fan-in per module based on values from other projects;

OLM is the median number of links to other modules via shared data structures based on values from other projects;

NM is the expected number of modules.

N.B. The values *FI* and *OLM* may be checked for validity during the structural design stage as soon as a reasonable number of design levels in the structure diagram have been completed. The target for integration tests may then be re-estimated. Similarly, at the end of the stage when *NM*, *FI* and *OLM* are known, the target may again be re-estimated.

- Number of requirements faults detected during the structural design stage (to assess the effectiveness of the early testing activities, and re-assess the quality of the requirements specification).
- Number of requests to change the requirements specification (to assess the stability of the product being developed).
- Number of unresolved faults at planned end of stage (to assess the efficiency and effectiveness of fault-resolution activities, and to check that sufficient effort is available for fault resolution).
- Number of faults that, although fully diagnosed, have not been corrected in the relevant documents, and number of outstanding change requests (to assess the efficiency of the fault removal activities, and to check that sufficient effort is available for fault removal).

METRICS THAT SHOULD BE COLLECTED TO PROVIDE MODULE-BASED ANALYSIS

- Structural fan-in and fan-out, and number of read, and write accesses to common data items (to identify whether the system decomposition is adequate—i.e. no overworked modules, no missing levels in the hierarchical decomposition, and all critical modules identified early).
- Number of integration test cases planned that involve each module (to check that each module will be adequately tested).
- Number of faults associated with each module (to identify any potentially fault-prone module as early as possible). It is assumed that during structural design only some faults can be attributed to a particular module.

10.7.3 Detailed design

SETTING TARGETS AND PROJECT NORMS

- As for structural design.

RELEVANT METRICS

- Size of product in LOC; this may now be estimated from the following formula:

$$S = MS \times NM$$

where S is the product size in LOC;

MS is the median module size based on values from other similar projects;

NM is the actual number of modules identified during structural design.

N.B. MS may be checked for appropriateness during detailed design using a formula linking module design size (DS) to code size via the median design to code expansion ratio observed in other projects:

$$MS = DS \times ER_{dc}$$

where DS is the median module design size in PDL, or other design notation components (e.g. boxes in a JSP structure diagram; Jackson, 1975);

ER_{dc} is the relevant design-to-code expansion ratio.

This formula may be used as soon as the detailed design for a representative subset of modules has been completed.

- Number of faults per 1000 LOC, and breakdown of fault detection rate and fault origin rates for each life-cycle stage. Fault-rate estimates should be refined as a result of the actual number of requirements and design faults found in the previous stages of development, using formulae analogous to those described in Section 10.7.2:

$$FR_N = FR_O \times \frac{FR_{A2}}{FR_{E2}} \qquad \text{assuming } FR_{A2} > 0 \text{ and } FR_{E2} > 0$$

where FR_N is the new estimate of the fault rate per 1000 LOC,

FR_O is the original estimate of the fault rate;

FR_{A2} is the actual number of faults per 1000 lines found during requirements specification and structural design;

FR_{E2} is the original estimate of the number of faults per 1000 lines to be found during requirements specification and structural design.

Alternatively,

$$F = b_0 + b_1 \times RS^{z_1} + b_2 \times RF_T^{z_2} + b_3 \times DS^{z_3} + b_4 \times HDF^{z_4}$$

where F is an estimate of the faults that will be found during product development;

b_i, $i = 0, \ldots, 4$, are constants determined from other similar projects;

RS is the size of the specification in pages or words;

RF_T is the total number of requirements faults detected;

DS is the design size based on natural language document size or number of modules (i.e. NM);

HDF is the number of structural design faults detected;

z_i, $i = 1, \ldots, 4$, are constants determined from other similar projects.

- Fog index for natural language-based detailed design descriptions.
- Number of 'black box' test cases per module (Myers, 1979). This may be based on a formula linking the median number of parameters on the interface and the median number of states (or data partitions for variables that do not have a small number of finite states) taken by parameters, as follows:

$$BB_{MIN} = NP \times NS$$

$$BB_{MAX} = NP^{NS}$$

$$BB_{EST} = (BB_{MIN} \times BB_{MAX})^{1/2}$$

where BB_{MIN} is the expected minimum number of black box tests
per module;
BB_{MAX} is the expected maximum number of black box tests
per module;
BB_{EST} is the expected number of black box tests per
module, and is the geometric mean of BB_{MIN} and BB_{MAX};
NP is the median number of parameters on a module
interface based on values from other projects;
NS is the median number of state or data partitions per
parameter based on values from other projects.

N.B. The target may be re-estimated once actual values for NP and NS become available from a representative subset of modules.

- Number of requirements faults and structural design faults detected during detailed design.
- Number of requests to change requirements specification and/or structural design.
- Number of unresolved faults at planned end of stage.
- Number of faults that, although fully diagnosed, have not been corrected in the relevant documents.

METRICS THAT SHOULD BE COLLECTED TO PROVIDE MODULE-BASED ANALYSIS

- Module size in design statements (e.g. pseudo-code statements or flow chart boxes, or JSP boxes).
- Number of parameters per module (to identify potentially complex, or over-worked modules early in the development process).
- Number of states or data partitions per parameter (to identify potentially complex, or difficult to test modules early in the development process).
- Number of black box test cases planned per module.
- Number of branches in each module (to indicate complex modules, and hard to test modules early in the development process).
- Number of faults found in each module.

OTHER METRICS OF INTEREST

- Number of modules recognized as necessary during detailed design but not identified during structural design (to assess the effectiveness of the structural design).

• Number of modules identified as necessary during structural design but discarded during detailed design (to access the effectiveness of the structural design).

10.7.4 Code

SETTING TARGETS AND PROJECT NORMS

• As for structural design.

RELEVANT METRICS

• Size per module in LOC, based on the formula linking code size to design size and expansion ratio discussed in the previous section.
• Expected number of faults per module, broken down into those expected to be found during code reviews and walkthrough, and those likely to be found during white box, black box, and integration testing. The initial overall estimate may be based on a formula of the type:

$$mf = b_0 + b_1 \times ds^{z_1} + b_2 \times kmf^{z_2} + b_3 \times f_o^{z_3}$$

where mf is an estimate of the module faults that will be detected during module code reviews, white box, and black box testing, and integration testing;
b_i, $i = 0, 1, 2$, are constants derived from other similar projects;
ds is the module size in design statements;
kmf is the number of module-based faults detected during structural and detailed design;
f_o is the module fan-out;
z_i, $i = 1, 2, 3$, are constants derived from other similar projects.

N.B. There is no guarantee that such a relationship exists, but should it be validated in a particular environment, it could be used to generate both a point estimate and a suitable range. The equation above could use estimated module size in LOC (assuming the expected design to code ratio is known), rather than design size, in which case the targets can be re-estimated when a representative number of modules have been coded and a better estimate of the expansion ratio from design to code is available.
• Number of white box tests planned per module. This may be based on a formula using the number of branches per module and an estimate of the data flow complexity (Oviedo, 1980):

$$wb_{\text{MIN}} = nb, \qquad wb_{\text{MAX}} = nb + df$$

where wb_{MIN} is the minimum expected number of white box tests
per module;

wb_{MAX} is the maximum expected number of white box tests
per module;

nb is the number of branches per module identified in
the detailed design of the module;

df is the median data flow complexity (which is related
to the number of variable references, excluding

definitions), based on results from other projects.

N.B. Targets can be refined once actual values of data flow complexity are
available.

- Number of requirements faults and design faults detected during code reviews and walkthroughs.
- Number of requests to change requirements specification and/or structural design during coding.
- Number of unresolved faults at planned end of stage.
- Number of faults that, although fully diagnosed, have not been corrected in the relevant documents.
- Number of outstanding change requests.

METRICS THAT SHOULD BE COLLECTED TO PROVIDE ADDITIONAL MODULE-BASED
ANALYSIS

- Number of data items.
- Number of branches.
- Expansion ratio between design statements and LOC.

OTHER METRICS OF INTEREST

- Number of modules recognized as necessary during coding, but not identified during detailed design.
- Number of modules identified as necessary during detailed design but discarded during coding.

10.7.5 Unit testing

SETTING TARGETS AND PROJECT NORMS

- As for structural design, but may be assisted by models of the testing and debugging process as suggested by Huff *et al.* (1986). Such models monitor testing metrics against targets set on a weekly or daily basis during the planned testing period.

RELEVANT METRICS

- Faults per module attributed to white box test cases and black box test cases. These values can be estimated using models analogous to those discussed in Section 10.7.3.

- Number of requirements and design faults found during unit testing.
- Number of requests to change requirements specification and/or structural design during unit testing.
- Overall percentage of planned white box test cases run successfully (i.e. producing the specified output, which could of course be an error message).
- Overall percentage of planned black box tests run successfully.
- Overall percentage coverage achieved in terms of lines of code, branches, and LCSAJs (Woodward *et al.*, 1980).
- Number of unresolved faults at planned end of stage.
- Number of faults that, although fully diagnosed, have not been corrected in the relevant documents.
- Number of outstanding change requests.

METRICS THAT SHOULD BE COLLECTED TO PROVIDE ADDITIONAL MODULE-BASED ANALYSIS

- Structural coverage in terms of lines of code, branches, LCSAJs.
- Percentage of planned black box tests run successfully.
- Number of black box test cases not identified during test planning but identified as necessary during unit test (to assess the effectiveness of test planning).
- Percentage of planned white box tests run successfully.
- Number of white box test cases not identified during test planning but identified as necessary during unit test (to assess the effectiveness of test planning).

OTHER METRICS OF INTEREST

- Number of modules recognized as necessary during unit testing but not identified during system design and coding.

10.7.6 Integration testing

SETTING TARGETS AND PROJECT NORMS

- As for unit testing.

RELEVANT METRICS

- Number of faults, based on project size, and faults found during previous stages. During integration testing it is expected that the majority of faults detected will be structural design faults, only some of which may be attributable to particular modules.
- Number of requirements faults and coding faults found during integration testing.
- Overall percentage of planned integration tests run successfully.

- Overall number of unplanned test cases required during test stage.
- Number of requests to change requirements specification and/or structural design during integration testing.
- Number of unresolved faults at planned end of stage.
- Number of faults that, although fully diagnosed, have not been corrected in the relevant documents.

METRICS THAT SHOULD BE COLLECTED TO PROVIDE ADDITIONAL MODULE-BASED ANALYSES

- Faults detected per module.
- Percentage of planned test cases affecting a module run successfully.
- Number of unplanned test cases involving a module required during the testing stage.

OTHER METRICS OF INTEREST

- Number of modules recognized as necessary during integration testing, but not previously identified as missing.

10.8 Guidelines for Integrating Metric Values

10.8.1 Generic classes of exceptions and their interpretations

Once a metric value is identified as abnormal with respect to its target value(s), it is necessary to determine the possible reasons for the particular abnormality. There are favourable and unfavourable interpretations for most abnormalities, and some general trends can be observed:

- Low fault rates associated with a product or intermediate product imply:
  (a) a good quality item;
  (b) an unexpectedly simple item;
  (c) an incomplete item;
  (d) a poor testing approach;
  (e) a large amount of code reuse or automatic code generation.
- High fault rates imply:
  (a) a poor quality item;
  (b) an unexpectedly difficult item;
  (c) a particularly stringent testing approach;
  (d) an unstable product.
- A high value of a static attribute of an item implies:
  (a) a poorly constructed item;
  (b) an unusually difficult item;
  (c) a critical item;
  (d) inclusion of unplanned functionality;
  (e) scope of the problem underestimated.

- A low value of a static attribute of an item implies:
  - (a) a well constructed item;
  - (b) an unusually simple item;
  - (c) an incomplete item;
  - (d) the scope of the problem over-estimated.

10.8.2 Distinguishing between different causes

In order to determine which interpretation is appropriate in a particular circumstance, the project or quality manager will have to institute some additional investigations, such as an extra project review or an independent audit of the project. In addition, managers may use their knowledge about other features of the project to assist their interpretations. Features that make favourable interpretations more plausible are:

- highly-experienced staff (either as a result of general software engineering experience or as a result of application experience);
- highly-motivated staff;
- a particularly well-understood product;
- provision of automated tools and procedures to support construction, testing and administration;
- good quality assurance procedures, both in terms of standards and standards enforcement.

Conversely, the features that make unfavourable interpretations more likely are:

- inexperienced staff;
- poorly motivated staff;
- staff with responsibilities to many different projects;
- a novel product (note that a novel product may have a favourable effect, if it causes staff motivation);
- using unfamiliar development methods;
- poor provision of tools;
- poor quality assurance;
- externally imposed budgetary and schedule targets that do not correspond to the requirements of the product.

10.8.3 Project problems and corrective actions

Some of the problems that may beset projects, and the corrective actions available in response to those problems, are outlined below. It should be noted that different responses to a problem need not be mutually exclusive.

Problem 1
The technical activities needed in a particular stage of development appear to have been inadequately performed, this can apply to checking and testing activities as well as system specification and design activities.

SHORT-TERM RESPONSES

- Re-do the current activities (or some of the activities) with more experienced staff.
- If the inadequately performed activity was a specification or design activity, extend the related activities, perhaps with more-experienced staff.
- Extend the time scales for subsequent specification and design activities.
- Use more-experienced staff for subsequent specification and design activities.
- Extend the time scales for subsequent testing and debugging activities.
- Intensify the testing criteria for subsequent testing activities.
- Use more-experienced staff for subsequent testing activities.

LONG-TERM RESPONSES

- Review and improve quality assurance procedures.
- Review and improve staff training procedures.

Problem 2

The overall scope of the project, a development stage, or a particular activity has been miscalculated (it is often the case that effort and time scales for rework and fault clearance activities are underestimated).

SHORT-TERM RESPONSES

- Re-plan project and re-estimate targets.
- If the scope of the project has been under-estimated, obtain more-experienced staff.
- If the scope has been over-estimated, release experienced staff to other projects.

LONG-TERM RESPONSES

- Review and improve estimating procedures.
- Review and improve project working procedures.

Problem 3

A stage has been started prematurely (usually as a result of pressures to meet schedule targets).

SHORT-TERM RESPONSES

- Stop current work and revert to activities of preceding stage.
- Extend activities of previous stage into current stage, replanning effort and work assignment.
- Extend time scales for testing and debugging current stage because of anticipated additional latent faults from previous stage.

LONG-TERM RESPONSE

- Review and improve criteria for entry to, and exit from stages and activities.

Problem 4

A particular component (i.e. a module) appears to be either fault-prone (it may be complex, badly written, or just large!) or critical (i.e. has many interconnections with other parts of the system).

SHORT-TERM RESPONSES

- Redesign the module into smaller components.
- Extend the time scales for testing the module.
- Intensify the testing criteria for the module (for example, increase the code, branch and LCSAJ coverage requirements for the module; Woodward *et al.*, 1980).
- Use more-experienced staff to continue the construction and testing of the module.

LONG-TERM RESPONSE

- Review and improve module reuse practice.

10.9 Further reading

A practical introduction to establishing a data collection and analysis programme is given in Grady and Caswell's (1987) book *Software Metrics: Establishing a Company-wide Program,* Prentice-Hall, Englewood Cliffs, NJ. The authors describe their experience of setting up a software metrics programme in Hewlett–Packard. They provide metrics definitions, and examples of the results of their program. Of great practical use is the description of the sales pitch they used to get metrics accepted in Hewlett–Packard, and the discussion of the response of the engineering staff to the metrics program.

11

Cost Modelling and Estimation

Barbara Kitchenham and Bernard de Neumann

11.1	Introduction	333
11.2	Cost Estimation	336
11.3	Cost Models	340
11.4	Sizing Models	344
11.5	Improving Cost-Model Estimates	360
11.6	Cost-Estimation Risk	368
11.7	Summary	376

11.1   Introduction

The purpose of this chapter is to give the reader an idea of what cost modelling aims to do, and what may reasonably be expected of it, as a software engineering tool. This introduction begins by reviewing cost modelling as a whole, but concentrates, where appropriate, upon the special problems associated with software.

Cost estimating as a systematic technique goes back to biblical times (Luke 14.28: For which of you, intending to build a tower, sitteth not down first, and counteth the cost, whether he have sufficient to finish it.) and, no doubt, beyond. In Hebrew, the phrase for 'how much will it cost?' is

כַּמָּ ת זֶ ה עוֹלֶ ה?

and means literally 'how high is it?'.

Cost estimating is, or should be, a fundamental engineering management tool, which if used and evaluated properly is crucial to good project management. Unfortunately, it is often the case that those entrusted with 'project management' have no appreciation of the limitations of these techniques and therefore tend to place an over-reliance upon the results of such analyses, often to the detriment of their particular project and ultimately to the detriment of the subject. They often, too, equate usefulness with simplicity—this is a dangerous paradigm, and should obviously only apply where simplification has been shown to be possible: simplicity *per se* can be dangerously ignorant.

Armed with these words of warning and advice, it is now appropriate to progress to a general explanation of cost estimating.

Cost analysis is the process that attempts to identify, examine, and evaluate all resources needed to acquire, operate, and support a system. It attempts to consider the overall cost of ownership, which consists of acquisition, operation and support, disposal, and in these days of 'green conscientiousness', sometimes, pollution costs. Taken together, the cost of these resources represents the life-cycle costs of a given system.

Acquisition costs consist of research and development costs and initial investment. Costs for R&D include all purchaser and contractor costs to design an item of equipment or, for software, to design and produce an operational set of computer code. Initial investment refers to those system costs required beyond the R&D activities to introduce a system into operational use and has two major components—production and support. Production costs include the non-recurring production costs incurred during the manufacturing process and the recurring production costs associated with each unit manufactured. The recurring costs tend to be subject to a learning-curve effect in which the cost per unit decreases as the quantity produced increases. The basis for this decrease is a combination of one or more of the following factors: technology, productivity, managerial efficiency, material utilization efficiency, etc. The rate at which items are produced can also be a significant factor in production cost. Support costs include all costs for specialized test and maintenance equipment, installation, test and check-out, training equipment, initial spares and other provisioning, and the construction of necessary facilities. These initial support costs are significant and their identification, estimation, and evaluation represent a major aspect of cost analysis.

The largest part of the total life-cycle cost is for operation and support. These costs are incurred during the in-service phase and consist of all the annual recurring costs of operating, maintaining, and supporting the acquired system. Included are the costs for personnel, fuel, maintenance, spares, training, supplies, and other needed support. These costs reflect the system's deployment, maintenance, and logistics-support concepts. Generally, operations and support-cost estimates utilize data derived from experience with similar systems or existing, deployed units.

Decisions made in the concept and acquisition phases determine the system's life-cycle cost: even before procurement starts, 70–90% of the life-cycle cost has been committed. Whilst the percentage varies, the conclusion is well supported. Decisions prior to procurement will significantly and unalterably shape the system's evolution and actual life-cycle cost. It is thus important that such decisions, at the outset, take into account the life-cycle cost ramifications.

During the concept phase, the factors influencing operations and support costs require both an engineering analysis and a cost quantification. The uncertainties in both factors are reduced as the process is repeated throughout the concept and acquisition stages.

Costs for disposal are treated differently by analysts depending upon the type of system, the organizational funding definitions, and the purpose of the estimate. In some analyses, it is assumed that disposal cost equals salvage value and hence can be ignored. For systems where, for example, nuclear waste material has to be disposed of, or concrete and steel structures have to be dismantled, disposal costs could be significant.

The analysis is, or should be, a continuing activity occurring throughout the total life of a system.

The recognition of reliability as a subject worthy of study and analysis brings with it the tacit recognition that costs of failures are important. In a sense, reliability modelling is the simplest form of cost modelling—however, current software cost modelling is in this sense over-simplistic. It is here that software cost modelling, at the present time, at least, loses contact with any science that one day may be relevant. The whole area has become highly empirical, with little, if any, recourse to any identifiable theory. This is not to say that such an approach will not produce relevant and useful models but rather to emphasize the dangers inherent in making unjustified assumptions.

The crux of the problem is that the models are 'over-sold'. Project managers, who often appear to be busy people, want a simple model with simple results, to analyse what must be one of the most complex procedures known to mankind, viz. engineering software of known quality to schedule and within budget. This is a contradiction in terms: Can we seriously expect to model such a complex procedure simplistically? The answer must be No! The project managers therefore have unreasonable expectations with regard to cost modelling/analysis, and this is due to a combination of factors that include overselling by enthusiastic purveyors of cost models, and an (un)characteristic naivety on the part of the managers who appear to be willing to believe anything in the quest for simplicity. The Hans Christian Anderson story of the Emperor's New Clothes is of direct relevance here, particularly as we appear to be in danger of suffering a similar outcome.

We therefore intend to review the more fashionable amongst the currently existing cost models and will attempt to indicate their strengths and weaknesses. ('Fashion' is indeed the correct term here, since it appears to be the sole selection criterion in practice for choosing any particular model rather than any scientifically based evaluation.) Furthermore, we will indicate how the subject should develop if it is to mature into a useful scientifically based methodology. The way ahead will not be straightforward, there are too many vested interests in 'commercial' models. However, we must move forward and incorporate the best features of any models into new models. As has been stated elsewhere (de Neumann, 1983), the only realistic way ahead is to create a climate for rational discussion of the models, whereby features may be publicly justified to all potential users.

It is worth reminding the reader at this point that we as cost estimators should always take the widest possible view, within the restrictions of a project, and consider all relevant costs. That is, we should always be looking towards considering system life-cycle costs, and take software costs as being cost elements of an overall life-cycle cost exercise. Thus, whilst we shall be considering cost-estimating models that apply to software, we shall on occasions revert to the wider view if it is appropriate.

There are a number of proprietary models and public domain models in existence, and in Section 11.3 we examine two of the best-known examples. Models, in general, concentrate upon the task of attempting to estimate the development costs of a piece of software. This estimating has to take place early in the lifecycle and naturally has to be evaluated in terms of variables that correlate to the final development costs. Of course, cost estimation should not take place in a vacuum, with its results either ignored, or used as political tennis balls. It is intended to be a purposeful activity, whose results influence the progression of a system from concept to the field by delivering sound guidance to the project management as to the outcome of viable alternatives so that informed decisions may be reached and justified. To this end, Section 11.2, by taking the viewpoint of project control, examines measurement and estimation of costs, and also considers some of the problems that some software practioners have with cost estimation.

Section 11.3 discusses the aims and types of cost models, and identifies a number of problems with conventional models. Section 11.4 deals with sizing models, including alternative approaches based upon sizing metrics other than lines of code. Section 11.5 considers ways in which the performance of cost models may be improved and ways of reducing the effects of the problems identified in Section 11.3. Finally, Section 11.6 considers the problem of risk assessment for various models. Detailed descriptions of a number of the cost models are given in Appendix D.

11.2   Cost Estimation

In this section, we consider the problems of software cost measurement and estimation from the viewpoint of project control. We look not only at the need for estimates, measurements, and a cost-estimation process, but also at some of the particular problems that software managers and developers have experienced when attempting to estimate project costs and time scales.

11.2.1   Project control

Project control is inextricably linked to measurement and estimation. We agree with DeMarco (1982) that you cannot control what you cannot measure, and would add that you cannot plan what you cannot estimate. Controlling a software development project means ensuring that a software product is produced on time, within budget, and to an agreed standard (i.e. quality). In order to do this it is necessary to:

- specify budget, schedule and quality targets;
- track performance against those targets;
- observe and react to deviations from targets.

This is yet another formulation of the basic project-control procedures discussed in the chapters on project management and metrics.

Looking at the components of project control, it is clear that we need estimates to allow us to specify the targets, and actual measurements to allow us to compare performance with estimates. However, the context within which the estimates and measurements are used depends on project plans which enable:

- estimates to be related to particular stages in the development process, and the outputs of particular stages;
- measurements to be obtained at the appropriate times;
- contingency procedures to be specified to cope with deviations from targets.

In this chapter, we will concentrate on the issues of estimation and measurement.

Chapters 7 and 10 have both made the point that the basic project control procedure of setting targets and monitoring progress against them is normal industrial practice. It is also the case that cost estimation as a basic support to project control is normal industrial practice. However, software cost estimation is generally considered to be more difficult, and in consequence less reliable, than cost estimation in other industries.

There are a number of good reasons for this. Clearly, software is pure design with no physical manifestation, and there are a number of estimating problems which result from this.

- We are attempting to cost the activity of constructing a solution to a problem rather than the activity of building a previously defined artefact, and all industries have difficulties estimating the development time and costs of prototypes (an obvious example is the aerospace industry).
- The type of problems we are attempting to solve are usually related to the requirements of human society, rather than the physical attributes of the natural world. Thus, there are seldom independent 'theories' to describe the attributes of a 'correct' software solution in the same way that the stress characteristics of materials might be used to check the properties of a design for a bridge or a building.
- The constituent components of a software solution are difficult to identify and do not have a deterministic relationship with the cost and characteristics of the complete solution. This may be contrasted with the estimation technique of a quantity surveyor, who can estimate the cost of building a wall because there is a direct relationship between the required dimen-

sions of a wall and the number of bricks needed, and there are accepted formulae for the number of bricks that can be laid per hour and hourly labour rates.

In addition, the software industry is a new industry and we simply do not have the wealth of experience with software production that we have in other industries. As a result, our estimating techniques are immature, tending towards either simple parametric models, or unsystematic analogies with past experience.

However, no matter how justified are complaints that software cost estimation is difficult, there is no excuse for not attempting to estimate, and not attempting to improve methods of estimating. A refusal to estimate is a refusal to manage, and should not be acceptable in any industry.

None-the-less, many software experts argue that we are worse at estimating than we need be. To understand the reasons for this, we discuss some of the characteristics of poor estimating procedures in the next section.

11.2.2 The reasons for poor estimates

The difficulties that many software managers experience when attempting to estimate project costs usually involve political as well as technical issues. The sort of problems which are often encountered are a widespread bias towards underestimating costs, and an associated inability to estimate worst-case scenarios, and an inability to improve estimates. Technical issues that contribute to these problems are the failure to establish an estimating procedure and the lack of experienced estimators.

Underestimation is often due to inexperience resulting in a misunderstanding of the nature of an 'estimate'. It is *not* the shortest time scale (and/or effort) with non-zero chance of success. An estimate of project cost should be the value that has 0·5 probability of being exceeded, other values will, therefore, have a greater or less than 0·5 probability of being exceeded. 'A cost estimate' should not be a point estimate, it should in fact be a range of values (determined by a lower and upper value) that has a given probability (e.g. 0·95) of including the actual cost. The identification of an upper and lower range provides the type of information needed to produce PERT charts of the links and dependencies among project activities, while in addition the upper range is essential for exploring 'worst case' scenarios (refer to Section 11.6 for the use of a probability distribution for risk analysis).

Inability to improve estimates is due in part to inexperience and in part to lack of an estimating process. Estimates are poor because estimators have little chance to practise. A software manager or developer is unlikely to work on more than two projects a year, and so makes only very infrequent attempts to form estimates and seldom actively re-estimates. (Managers are often only required to record slips against the original estimates, or to alter the estimates to accommodate the slips.)

Lack of an estimating process reinforces bad habits such as failure to re-estimate as a project progresses, and means that past experience is not used constructively. For example, there are no good, quantitative inputs to the estimation process and data are not collected, so there is no means of comparing actual costs with estimates. Thus, there is no feedback mechanism to improve the performance of the estimators or their estimation algorithms. The cost-estimation process is described in some detail by Boehm (1981) and DeMarco (1982).

Political issues that contribute to the problems of biased estimates and inability to improve the estimates include the following.

- Using externally imposed targets rather than estimates. This usually involves using underestimates in order to 'motivate the troops', or to obtain a competitive contract, or to impress or mollify a superior (temporarily). These may or may not be appropriate ways to manage a project, but unless they are accompanied by plans to reduce functionality, they are certainly poor ways to obtain accurate cost estimates.
- Using estimators who are too involved with the project being costed to be unbiased. DeMarco (1982) observes that most people are able to judge the amount of time someone else will need to do something without bias, but will underestimate the time they themselves will take to do something.
- Not being prepared to bear the cost of obtaining good estimates (which might be 5–10% of project development costs and might take some of a manager's best production staff out of development). Good estimates take time and effort to produce and maintain, and that time and effort is an overhead on a project throughout its development life cycle.

We agree with DeMarco that many of the technical and political issues can be alleviated by the establishment of an independent estimating group and the quantification of development methods. Thus:

- The cost of an estimating group may be spread across a number of different projects, and estimators will have the opportunity to gain experience at estimating over many projects.
- Unbiased and consistent estimates are more likely, since the estimators are not personally involved in any project. However, ultimate responsibility for the use of the estimates remains with the project manager.
- The responsibility for data collection can be centralized, and the independence of the collectors may enable the accurate collection of sensitive data to take place (e.g. actual hours per person per activity per phase).
- A group with a target based on the quality of estimates rather than a target to produce a product will be encouraged to improve their estimates by periodic re-estimation, and to use actual project data to improve their estimation procedures.
- The ability to link quantifiable attributes of the development methods to cost information provides a basic method for improving estimating methods.

The QA department are a possible choice for an independent estimating group since: the extra time spent in understanding the product can be justified, and they have a vested interest in ensuring that plans are not so tight that quality suffers. However, a rational prescription for improving cost estimates may still not be possible in an organization where political problems predominate. If managers do not wish to know what is happening, there is no way to make them listen.

The next three sections look in more detail at the technical issues of cost estimation; in particular we consider the contribution that models and metrics make towards the cost-estimation process and the way in which past experience can be used constructively to improve such models.

11.3 Cost Models

Cost model equations do not usually estimate cost in monetary terms, although many cost estimation tools provide estimates of actual cost. Model equations usually estimate a related feature such as:

- effort;
- time scale (sometimes called schedule, or duration);
- staffing levels.

There is also a tendency for models to concentrate on:

- development effort, excluding at the one end of the life cycle feasibility and requirements analysis effort and, at the other end, maintenance effort;
- the production of new products, using conventional development methods.

Many models have additional features to permit estimation of the cost of maintenance (without usually distinguishing between maintenance for fault correction, or product enhancement), and to allow for code reuse. However, such features are usually *ad hoc* additions rather than built-in features, and are usually less well founded theoretically and less well validated than the main parts of the model.

11.3.1 Cost-model classification

Researchers have made a number of attempts to classify software cost models (e.g. Conte *et al.*, 1986; DeMarco, 1982). This is useful, because it permits the general principles of model types to be investigated without the necessity of studying every model variant. This is particularly important for the study of cost models because, in some cases, the models form part of a commercial product and detailed description of the model algorithms are not available.

Unfortunately, classification schemes are by their nature subjective and there is no universal agreement as to the best one. We adopt a simple classification of cost models based on distinguishing between models that specify the *relationship* among various cost parameters (i.e. effort/cost, schedule, staff levels), and models that provide *an estimate* of the value of a cost parameter.

Models of the first type may be regarded as constraint models:

- Given the values of all but one of the cost parameters used in the model, they determine the value of the remaining parameter.
- Given two unknown cost values, they will indicate how the values of one will change in response to hypothetical values of the other.

Models of the second type are, in general, empirical factor models, since they are usually based on empirical studies in which factors describing the product or development process are related to various cost factors. They provide a direct prediction of a cost-parameter value given the value of one or more input parameters. (An alternative way of viewing this is that empirical factor models do not use a cost parameter as an input parameter.)

This classification scheme places the following models in the constraint model category:

- PUTNAM (Putnam, 1978)
- JENSEN (Jensen, 1984)
- PARR (Parr, 1980)
- COCOMO SCHEDULE formulas (Boehm, 1981)
- COPMO (Thebaut, 1983)

The following models are placed in the empirical factor model category:

- COCOMO EFFORT (Boehm, 1981)
- TRW WOLVERTON (Wolverton, 1974)
- SDC (Nelson, 1966)
- SOFTCOST (Tausworthe, 1981)
- ESTIMACS (described in Kemerer, 1987)
- PRICE S (described in Cuelenaere *et al.*, 1987)
- WALSTON–FELIX (Walston and Felix, 1977)
- BAILEY–BASILI Metamodel (Bailey and Basili, 1981)

Further classification of models is possible if the functional form of the models is known. Constraint models are either derived from the Rayleigh curve (or a variant of it), or an exponential model derived from expert opinion or statistical analysis. Empirical factor models are often what DeMarco calls 'corrected single-factor cost models'.

The cost models listed above are described in detail in Appendix D and in addition brief descriptions of Putnam's model and COCOMO are given in the next sections.

11.3.2 Putnam's model

Using the assumption that the relationship between staffing level and elapsed time could be modelled by a Rayleigh curve, and the results of a number of empirical studies, Putnam (1978) derived a number of equations relating system size (S_s), total life-cycle effort (K), and elapsed time to develop software (t_d). His basic equation is:

$$S_s = CK^{1/3}(t_d)^{4/3}$$

where S_s is the number of non-comment source statements (NCSS);
K is the total project costs in years excluding requirements analysis and specification but including maintenance;
t_d is the development time in years;
C is the *technology factor*, which is a parameter used to describe the effect on productivity of factors such as hardware constraints, program complexity, programming environment and staff experience. C is permitted to take one of 20 different values ranging from 610 to 57 314.
Putnam also uses the following equation;

$$D_0 = K/(t_d)^3$$

where D_0 is a constant for a particular class of project. It is 8 for new software with many interfaces, 15 for new stand-alone software, 27 for software being re-implemented.

Using both equations, further equations can be derived that include only a single cost parameter, giving two simple estimating models, one including K and the other including t_d.

In order to use Putnam's approach, S_s must be estimated, D_0 must be known and C must be derived. C may be derived from the relationships observed in other similar projects or by an assessment of the project environment.

Putnam's approach is incorporated into a commercially available cost-estimation system called SLIM.

11.3.3 COCOMO

Boehm's COCOMO model (1981) is based on the assumption that development effort is related to system size in the following way:

$$MM_{nom} = \alpha(KDSI)^\beta$$

where MM_{nom} is the effort in man-months for product development (excluding feasibility and requirements analyses and maintenance);
$KDSI$ is the number of thousand delivered source instructions excluding blanks and comments.
To obtain an estimate of effort, the size of the product must be estimated and the 'mode' of the development must be specified. The mode describes the

overall project environment in one of three different ways: organic (in-house development of well-understood programs); embedded (development of software with many external non-negotiable requirements and constraints); semidetached (intermediate between organic and embedded). COCOMO provides numerical values for α and β for each mode.

A more precise estimate may be obtained by adjusting the basic equation using 15 multiplicative factors (called cost drivers) that are used to describe the ways in which a particular project may differ from the 'average' project. Cost drivers include factors such as product complexity, staff experience, and the stringency of performance and reliability requirements. The use of cost drivers is part of the 'Intermediate' and 'Detailed' versions of COCOMO.

11.3.4 Problems with cost models

In practice, cost models have two major problems:

- Independent validation studies have indicated that models can give very poor predictions when used on independent datasets.
- The models require input variables that may be inaccurate, since they may be estimates or subjective ratings, leading to very inaccurate model outputs. Thus, the models can appear to give very different results when applied to the same problem (see Rubin, 1985; Mohanty, 1981).

There appear to be three main reasons for the first problem that are primarily technical in nature:

- difficulties in applying consistent counting rules for lines of code and effort, which is a problem for model users as well as model evaluators;
- the environment in which a model is derived and tuned may not be representative of the environment in which the model is to be used—this may mean that the coefficients in a model equation may be invalid, or the correction factors (cost drivers) inappropriate in a different environment;
- inconsistent use of subjective correction factors, which is a problem for model evaluators as well as for inexperienced model users.

The reasons for the second problem are more philosophical, they include:

- the basic estimating dilemma that the information needed to make good predictions about future events may itself occur in the future;
- the nature of software as a human problem-solving activity, making the identification of useful measurements and the production of accurate estimates difficult, as discussed in Section 11.2.1.

The reasons underlying the second problem suggest that we may need to accept a substantial degree of imprecision in the best cost estimates. Nonetheless, the underlying reasons for the first problem indicate that there should be practical approaches to minimizing the degree of inaccuracy.

The descriptions of models in Appendix D gives an indication of some of the approaches that can be taken. Cuelenaere *et al.* (1987) suggest the use of expert-system rules to impose consistency on the process of determining the values of cost drivers. The ESTIMACS model uses an alternative estimate 'size' that is based on counts that are available from requirements documents. Bailey and Basili (1981) suggest the construction of local models. Or, like the PRICE SP model, models may be tuned to the local environment before use.

In addition, experienced estimators try to obtain estimates from several different sources (such as expert opinion, or analogy) as well as estimates from a cost model, in order to check the plausibility of model-based predictions.

All these methods are useful. For example, Kemerer (1987) noted that the poor estimates obtained by direct use of the COCOMO and Putnam models could be improved by tuning the models to his dataset. In addition, after tuning COCOMO to their own dataset, Miyazaki and Mori (1985) improved their estimates from a mean magnitude of relative error (MMRE) of 1·66 and a proportion of estimates within 20% of actuals (PRED(·20)) of 0·06 to an MMRE of 0·20 and a PRED(·20) of 0·48.

In the next two sections we will look at various approaches to improving the predictive accuracy of models in more detail. In Section 11.4, we discuss approaches that can be used to improve the accuracy of cost-estimation models by improved methods of product sizing. In Section 11.5, we describe methods of improving the process of cost estimation, which include tuning models to a particular environment and developing special-purpose local models.

11.4 Sizing Models

In this section we consider two approaches to sizing:

- improving product LOC estimation;
- using alternative size metrics.

A criticism of all cost models that rely on lines of code (LOC) is that LOC is very difficult to estimate. There has, therefore, been a great deal of research by model developers and model users into improved methods of LOC estimation. This has resulted in the developments of LOC estimation tools that can be used to generate the inputs to cost models, some of which act as direct front-ends to proprietary cost-estimation tools. Methods of estimating LOC are discussed in Section 11.4.1.

An alternative approach to gauging the 'size' of a product is to use non-LOC-based product size metrics, which can be directly measured (as opposed to estimated) at an early stage in product development. Non-LOC size metrics are discussed in Section 11.4.2.

11.4.1   Improved LOC estimation methods

LOC estimation methods are of four basic types:

- estimation-refinement methods (size-in–size-out), which are methods of refining an initial LOC estimate;
- estimating by structural decomposition, which is based on decomposing a system into basic units of approximately equal size and generating the system size from an estimate of the basic unit size multiplied by the number of components;
- estimating-by-analogy methods, which generate a size estimate from comparison with the sizes of other similar software. These methods divide into two subclasses, comparison of application functions, and comparison of project attributes (which takes the approach of comparing cost driver-like attributes);
- estimating by predictive model, which uses a functional relationship between LOC and some other measurable characteristic(s) to predict LOC.

Each of these methods is discussed below with examples of particular models. In addition, this section includes a description of the PRICE SZ model, which cannot be properly classified because its internal workings are not in the public domain.

11.4.1.1   *Size-in–size-out*
Size-in–size-out techniques are used to refine an initial approximate size estimate. Techniques for estimate refinement include:

- combining several independent estimates from individual experts;
- relative size ranking, which involves ranking products or modules into a size order relative to some reference products or modules of known size;
- estimating LOC in terms of size ranges (usually a most likely estimate, and an upper and lower bound).

We discuss three examples of these techniques in more detail below.

Although these techniques are presented as methods of refining LOC estimates, there is no reason why they should not be used to refine direct estimates of effort.

(A)   WIDEBAND DELPHI TECHNIQUE
The Delphi technique is a means of eliciting and reconciling the opinions of a group of experts. The original technique originated at the RAND Corporation, the Wideband version is described by Boehm (1981).

The use of the Wideband Delphi technique for product sizing is a multistep procedure as follows.

(1) The coordinator presents each expert with a specification and an estimation form.
(2) The coordinator calls a group meeting in which estimation issues are discussed.
(3) The experts fill out the estimation forms independently and return them to the coordinator.
(4) The coordinator returns a form to each expert showing the median values of all the estimates and the expert's own estimate.
(5) A further meeting is called in which the experts discuss differences among the estimates.
(6) The expert's prepare another estimate independently, and steps (4)–(6) are repeated until a consensus is reached.

It is important to note that the experts do not communicate to one another what their particular estimates are, only the coordinator knows which expert made which estimate. This anonymity is intended to prevent members of the group being influenced by more assertive members.

The original Delphi approach did not include group discussion. The advantage of group discussion is to ensure that nothing of relevance to the estimating problem is overlooked. The effect of group discussion is usually to filter out extreme opinions.

(B) SOFTWARE SIZING MODEL (SSM)

SSM is a computerized software sizing system developed and marketed by Dr George Bozoki (Bozoki, 1987). SSM is based on three assumptions.

(1) During the early phases of development, qualitative information is more accurate than corresponding quantitative data.
(2) Estimators are more accurate at gauging the relative sizes of components than absolute sizes.
(3) There is a strong correlation between estimates of the relative sizes of components and the actual relative sizes of software components.

The model can be used as soon as the product can be partitioned into components (i.e. subsystems, functional components, or modules) whose operational and functional characteristics are defined.

SSM uses the following approach.

(1) The user initially inputs components names and/or descriptions. There must be at least two components whose size is known (called the reference components).
(2) The user provides relative ranking information of two kinds. Firstly, the components are considered in pairs and the user must indicate which is the larger. Secondly, the components must be ranked from largest to smallest.
(3) The user must identify each component with a size interval and provide a size range for each component identifying the lowest possible, most likely, and highest possible size values.

(4) SSM rationalizes the input data, to provide a size ordering of the components and relates the relative sizes to the reference components. SSM outputs the estimated size and standard deviation of the estimate for each component and the product as a whole.

(C) PROGRAM ESTIMATING AND REPORTING TOOL (PERT)

Putnam (1978) developed the PERT technique as a means of obtaining an overall system size estimate. It should not be confused with the activity planning technique of the same name. The technique has been incorporated into a number of models including SLIM and SSM.

PERT uses expert opinion of component size to provide a refined estimate as follows:

(1) The expert (or experts) provide an estimate of the lowest (L), highest (H) and most likely (M) size of the components.
(2) The expected size of the ith component E_i is found from the weighted formula:

$$E_i = (L_i + 4M_i + H_i)/6$$

(3) The expected system size is then

$$E_{tot} = \sum_{i=1}^{n} E_i$$

(4) The standard deviation per component is obtained from the range as

$$\sigma_i = (H_i - L_i)/6$$

(5) The standard deviation of the product as a whole is calculated from the square root of the sum of squares as follows:

$$\sigma_{tot} = \left[\sum_{i=1}^{n} \sigma_i^2 \right]^{1/2}$$

(6) If more than one expert opinion is used, the average or median values of the L, H and M values are calculated and used in the above equations.

The rationale behind the equations is that they are the formulae used to estimate the mean and standard deviation of a beta distribution.

11.4.1.2 *Structural decomposition*

This method of LOC estimation involves decomposing a system into its basic elements, which are assumed to be of a similar size. An estimate of system size is obtained by multiplying the number of elements by an estimate of the element size.

This method must be combined with another method in order to estimate the size of the basic element. The example of this method described below uses a predictive model based on Halstead's Software Science metrics (reference Section 11.4.1.4(B) and Section C.3 in Appendix C).

(A) State machine model

The state machine model is based on the assumption that software systems may be decomposed into six levels (Britcher and Gaffney, 1985):

(1) initial program specification, level 0;
(2) baseline software product level, level 1;
(3) integration level, level 2;
(4) module level, level 3;
(5) procedure level, level 4;
(6) source code, level 5.

Each level is composed of a number of discrete components (except level 0), where each component or 'function box' will expand to a roughly equivalent number of lines of source code. The state machine model uses the number of boxes at any level (from level 1 down) to estimate product size.

The size of any one function box is estimated by specifying the amount of data (variable count) it is to use and generate. At the procedural level the size of a function box is estimated using the following formula (Gaffney, 1984):

$$S = (4 \cdot 8078/N)V \log_e V$$

where $N = 1$ if $V < 100$, 2 if $100 \leqslant V < 1000$, 3 if $1000 \leqslant V \leqslant 10\,000$;
  S is the average number of lines of source code;
  V is the variable count for the box (which is equivalent to Halstead's operand count, n_2).

Once the size is calculated for one box, the value is multiplied by the number of boxes at the procedural level in order to estimate product size.

The state machine model has not been automated.

11.4.1.3 *Sizing by analogy*

The sizing by analogy approach involves comparing a new product to previously developed modules and systems with similar functions and requirements. It depends upon the construction of a size database consisting of descriptions of previously developed software functions and the numbers of source lines required to develop them.

When such a database is available, a new product can be sized by determining the similarities and differences between the database entries and the new product, selecting similar items, and using them to generate a size estimate. Different implementations of the same function provide an indication of the possible size range.

There are two approaches to sizing by analogy:

- comparison of application functions, where the approach is based on identifying software of a similar application type and function;
- comparison of project attributes, where the approach is based on comparing cost driver-like attributes.

Both types of sizing by analogy are described below by reference to commercial products that support the approaches.

Like estimate-refinement methods, it is possible to base direct effort estimation as well as LOC estimation on analogy, as suggested by Cowderoy and Jenkins (1989).

(A) COMPARISON OF APPLICATION FUNCTIONS

Estimates based on comparison of application functions are based on identifying products of a similar application type to the product being sized. The accuracy of such methods depends on the extent to which the data exhibits similarities to the new product. This in turn depends on the validity of the categorization scheme, and the amount of data in each category.

The actual lines of code needed to produce a product will depend on the personnel, language, and development methods used, so the more the database is tuned to a particular environment, the more likely it is to provide sound estimates.

QSM Size Planner. The QSM Size Planner supports the SLIM product with a sizing model that uses two levels of this approach to sizing by analogy and also a LOC predictive model based on function points (reference 11.4.1.4(A)), (Putnam, 1987).

The high-level version is based on fuzzy logic. It permits the selection of similar products from a database based on application category, overall size category, and size range within a category. The tool uses 11 application categories such as microcode/firmware, real time, avionics, business. The six overall size categories range from very small to very large, and within each category there are four size ranges (low, medium-low, medium-high, high). Once a user of the tool has defined the required software in terms of the three categories, the average size and the size distribution of software products in the QSM database with the same characteristics are obtained. The size estimate obtained from the database may be combined, if required, with a user estimate. The system uses Bayes formula to generate the combined estimate.

The low-level version of comparison of application functions in QSM Size Planner (referred to as standard component sizing) is used when the system has been deomposed into elements. As the development progresses through design and implementation, increasing use can be made of estimates or measures of 12 component inputs (subsystems, modules, screens, reports, interactive programs, batch programs, source lines of code, files, bytes, bits, words and object instructions) to identify the functions and software implementations in the application. The tool provides three point estimates (low, most likely, high), with confidence ratings, for all components applicable at that time. Each component is turned into an LOC estimate and Bayesian statistical weights are used to combine component estimates. Size Planner collects data so that historical data can be used to establish relationships between components and LOC and for tuning the database to site history.

The three techniques (fuzzy logic, function point analysis and standard component sizing) can be used as appropriate through the phases of the development life cycle and the different size estimates combined using Bayes formula to produce a composite estimate that should be of increasing accuracy as the development progresses.

(B) COMPARISON OF PROJECT ATTRIBUTES
Like comparison of application functions, this type of sizing approach uses a database of historical data. However, comparison of project attributes does not concentrate solely on functional similarities. The types of attributes compared can include required reliability, and complexity, as well as counts of the number of screens and reports produced. This approach is used by CEIS, which is described below.

Computer Economic Inc. Sizer (CEIS). The basic concepts of this approach were developed by Saaty (1980), and applied to software sizing by Joseph Lambert (1986). The basic procedure is to compare the attributes of a new task with the attributes of three reference tasks of known size. The system user determines the *relative* importance of the following six task attributes for the new project on a pairwise basis:

- complexity
- peak staffing level
- technology rating
- requirements volatility
- specification level
- required reliability

The CEIS tool checks the results of the comparison activity for consistency and, if they are consistent, the tool identifies attribute weights. Weights are obtained for the three reference tasks and the new task. The three reference tasks are compared with each other and the new task, and the tool is then able to generate a size estimate for the new task.

The accuracy of this sizing-by-comparison tool will depend on the comparability of the reference tasks, which in turn will depend either on having a very large historical database, or on using the tool in an environment where very similar products are produced.

11.4.1.4 *LOC estimating by predictive model*
LOC predictive models are derived from empirical observations of a relationship between LOC and some alternative size metric(s) that can be directly measured at an early stage of product development.

LOC predictive models are split into those based only on conventional function points, and those which use other metrics. Both types are discussed below.

(A) LOC ESTIMATION BASED ON CONVENTIONAL FUNCTION POINTS

These predictive models use function points (Albrecht, 1979) as their input metric. Function points are counts of external product features; they are described in more detail in Section 11.4.2.1.

LOC estimates are obtained by multiplying the function-point count by a source-language expansion factor. The expansion factor is obtained from empirical observations of the relationship between various source languages and function-point counts.

A recent report on sizing models (DACS, 1987) describes a number of function point-based tools, and notes that language expansion factors vary. The report attributes the variation to three factors.

- The expansion factors were derived from different data bases.
- Variations in programming skills and language experience have a major effect on size.
- Function-point analysis involves subjective assessments, so different analysts will obtain different function-point counts for the same system.

Tools that estimate LOC from function points should therefore include a means of calibrating the expansion factor to the local environment.

Conventional function points are used as one of the sizing techniques in the QSM Size Planner and in BYL, which is described below.

BYL (before you leap). BYL was developed by Donald Gordon and is described in the DACS (1987) report. It contains two major subsystems: one implements COCOMO, the other provides an LOC estimate using function-point counts.

The function-point count is obtained from weighted counts of the number of external inputs, queries, outputs, interfaces, and internal logical files as described in Section 11.4.2.1.

The LOC estimate is obtained by multiplying the function-point count by a source-language expansion factor. BYL has default expansion factors for 21 different source languages including Assembler, C, COBOL, Fortran, Pascal, and FOCUS. However, a user of BYL can calibrate the expansion factor to his or her own environment by providing BYL with the function-point analysis details and the number of delivered source instructions of a previously completed project.

(B) LOC ESTIMATION USING OTHER METRICS

LOC predictive models that use metrics other than just function point counts include the State Machine Model equation (Section 11.4.1.2(A)) which uses Halstead's software science metrics, and ASSET-R (Reifer, 1986), which uses both function points and Halstead's metrics.

ASSET-R (Analytical Software Size Estimation Tool—Real Time). ASSET-R is a mixed model incorporating function-point analysis, and using Halstead's software equations for the mathematical volume of the code to be produced. It was developed by Donald Reifer of RCI Inc. to extend the function-point approach to real-time systems.

The model is based on the following equation:

$$SIZE(SLOC) = (ARCH)(EXPF)[(LANG)(FPA) + MVOL_N]^{RF}$$

where *ARCH* is a constant describing the system architecture;

    EXPF is a technology expansion factor;

    LANG is a language expansion factor;

    FPA is an adjusted function-point count;

    $MVOL_N$ is a normalized operator and operand count;

    RF is a re-use factor;

    SLOC is source lines of code.

A number of inputs are required to derive the factors in the equation (except the system architecture constant and the language expansion factors, which are selected directly by the user).

To determine the value of the *ARCH* constant, the user is asked to identify which of seven possible system architectures are to be employed (i.e. centralized; tightly-coupled multiprocessor; loosely coupled multiprocessor; federated; distributed with centralized database; distributed with distributed database; other). The system determines the value of the *ARCH* parameter from a table. Similarly, to determine the language expansion factor the user is asked to indicate which of 14 possible languages are to be used, and the system provides a size-to-function-point conversion factor.

The technology expansion factor (*EXPF*) reflects the experience base of the product developer's organization. It is assessed from nine contributing factors:

- requirements volatility
- database size
- use of software tools
- applications experience
- programming language experience
- degree of real-time code
- environment experience
- analyst capability
- use of modern programming techniques

An important feature of ASSET-R is its extension of the function-point concept from the data-processing to the scientific and real-time domains. Determination of the function-point count for data-processing applications is based on the number of external inputs, outputs, internal files, external inquiries and external interfaces. For scientific applications, a count of the number of operating modes is added to the basic function-point count. For real-time applications, a count of the number of operating modes, stimulus/response relationships and rendezvous is added to the basic function-point counts. The counts are divided into those that relate to very simple,

simple, average, complex, and very complex items and are weighted appropriately before being combined into a single count, as described in Section 11.4.2.1. Function point counts are used to estimate the size of non-mathematical components of a software product.

MVOL is the mathematical volume based on Halstead's software science metrics. The operator and operand counts of mathematical components of the software product may be obtained by analysing the engineering equations in the product specification. Alternatively, the model will accept a count of the number of mathematical algorithms to be used rather than the operator and operand counts. The importance of this factor depends on the type of software product being produced.

The reuse factor is usually set to 1, but its calculation is internal to the system.

This sizing model is very similar to a cost model in terms of the number and nature of the inputs. It would, therefore, suffer from all the problems associated of over-fitting, instability, and incomplete validation that are found with cost models. It would also seem very unwise to use the estimate of size obtained from this system in a cost model other than the related SOFTCOST R model, which has a built-in adjustment, because another cost model might include the adjustment factors a second time.

11.4.1.5 *PRICE SZ*

The PRICE SZ model (Rapp, 1985) has to be treated separately from a discussion of the other LOC estimation methods, because information about the internal working of the model is not available in the public domain. We include a description of the model because it provides a front-end to the widely used PRICE S cost-estimation model.

PRICE SZ uses the following quantitative inputs to estimate size:

- number of pages of output
- number of alphanumeric displays
- number of graphic displays
- number of output streams
- number of input message fields
- number of operator actions
- number of input analogs
- number of input streams
- number of computed or created tables
- number of system states

The following qualitative environmental factors are used to adjust the factors:

- program application (military or commercial)
- system design skill of development staff
- program design skill
- coding skill

- integration with other system
- design review
- code walk-through
- top-down approach
- structure and modularization approach
- program requirements growth (anticipated growth of project due to the addition of new requirements)

In addition, four 'calibration factors' must be applied:

- functional bulkiness (experience of software team with language and tools);
- size calibration factor (describes the user's development practices);
- language expansion ratio (describes the combination of languages and compiler to be used);
- target size of the system.

Like ASSET-R, PRICE SZ seems like a cost model in terms of the number of parameters required. It is likely to suffer from exactly the same problems as a cost model with a large number of input parameters some of which are subjective and many of which are correlated, which is an over-fitted, unstable, difficult to validate model. In addition, it would be dangerous to use the size value output from such a model in a cost-estimation model (other than the related PRICE S model), because project factors might be accounted for twice.

11.4.1.6   *The accuracy of LOC estimating techniques*

LOC estimating techniques are intended to provide improved size estimates, but there have been few independent validation studies of the accuracy of such models.

The US Data and Analysis Center for Software (DACS) have produced a survey of LOC size estimation models and methods (DACS, 1987). The DACS report describes a comparative study that compared the results of applying nine different LOC sizing models to a single project. ASSET-R and SSM both got within 30% of the actual value; the next best result was from PRICE-SZ, which was over 130% distant from the actual; while the other sizing models tested were considerably less accurate. SSM gave an assessment of the probability of the actual value being in a given range that excluded the actual value at the 95% level; ASSET-R did not offer an assessment of the variability of its estimate.

Sizing models usually require a relatively large number of inputs, some of which are themselves estimates and/or subjective ratings, so many more evaluation studies of these techniques are required before any particular model or approach can be recommended.

11.4.2 Non-LOC size metrics

An alternative to attempting to improve the accuracy of cost models by improving estimates of lines of code is to develop models based on alternative measures of size. In this section we look at some of these alternative size metrics. We will discuss two types of specification metric: Function-point count (Albrecht, 1979; Albrecht and Gaffney, 1983) and the Bang metric (DeMarco, 1982), and a high-level design metric: Design Weight (DeMarco, 1982).

11.4.2.1 *Function-point analysis*

Function-point counts are based on system features seen by an end user. They were developed by Allan Albrecht (1979). This account is based on a refined version (Albrecht and Gaffney, 1983). Initial function counts are based on:

- number of simple, average and complex external inputs;
- number of simple, average and complex external outputs;
- number of simple, average and complex external inquiries;
- number of simple, average and complex external interfaces to other systems;
- number of simple, average and complex logical files in the system.

The unadjusted function count (UFC) is the weighted sum of the counts, where the complexity of each item is assessed according to factors such as the number of data elements it manipulates. The values of the weights given to the different data types are shown in Table 11.1a. Thus:

$$UFC = \sum (\text{number of elements of given data type}) \times (\text{data type weight})$$

The UFC is adjusted by considering the characteristics of the particular project. Adjustments are based on 14 factors shown in Table 11.1(b). The effects of the factors are rated at six levels of 'degree of influence' *(DI)* varying from 0 (meaning not present or no influence) to 5 (meaning strong influence), as indicated in Table 11.1(c). Using this assessment a technical complexity factor *(TCF)* is calculated:

$$TCF = 0.65 + 0.1 \sum DI_i$$

Then the adjusted function point *(FP)* count is calculated:

$$FP = UFC \times TCF.$$

The TCF can vary from 0·65 (if all factors have a *DI* value of 0) to 1·35 (if all factors have a *DI* value of 5). Therefore, the adjustment to the original function point count *(UFC)* is in the range ± 35%.

In order to provide an estimate of effort, function-point counts must either be used as direct inputs to a cost-estimation equation or be used to estimate LOC, which is then used as an input to conventional cost-estimation equation.

Table 11.1. (a) Unadjusted function point weights

System data types	Data type complexity weights		
	Simple	Average	Complex
External input	3	4	6
External output	4	5	7
Logical internal file	7	10	15
External interface file	5	7	10
External inquiry	3	4	6

(b) Items contributing to technical complexity factor

C1	Data communications	C8	On-line update
C2	Distributed functions	C9	Complex processing
C3	Performance	C10	Re-usability
C4	Heavily used configuration	C11	Installation ease
C5	Transaction rate	C12	Operational ease
C6	On-line data entry	C13	Multiple sites
C7	End user efficiency	C14	Facilitate change

(c) Factor weights
0 = Not present or No influence
1 = Insignificant influence
2 = Moderate influence
3 = Average influence
4 = Significant influence
5 = Strong influence

Several commercial cost-estimation tools use function points rather than LOC as a direct input, of which ESTIMACS (Rubin, 1983) is the best known. However, it is limited, in that it is tuned to commercial applications by using conventional function points as initially described by Albrecht.

Reifer's extension of the function-point approach to scientific and real-time applications is not limited to producing an estimate of LOC. When the ASSET-R model is used in conjunction with SOFTCOST-R or SOFTCOST-Ada, the non-LOC size values are direct inputs to the combined model for estimating cost and time scale.

There are few published accounts of attempts to validate Function points. Kemerer (1987) used Albrecht's effort-estimating equation (Albrecht and Gaffney, 1983) on a data set of 15 projects and found the MMRE (mean magnitude of the relative error) to be 1·03 and the proportion of projects for which the relative error was less than 25% (i.e. PRED(·25)) was 0·33. This result was better than the results obtained for COCOMO, SLIM or ESTIMACS. In addition, Kemerer found a strong correlation between function points and lines of COBOL.

A feature of Kemerer's study was that he found no evidence that the adjusted function-point count (FP) was a better predictor than the unweighted-function count (UFC).

11.4.2.2 *Bang metrics*

DeMarco's metrics (DeMarco, 1982) are based on counts derived from data flow diagrams, E–R models, and state diagrams. These notations are used to record the specification of a system when DeMarco's Structured Analysis and Design method is being used (DeMarco, 1978).

The Bang metrics are derived from the following primitives:

- number Functional Primitives (FP), which are the number of circles in a data flow diagram;
- TC_i, the number of data tokens associated with each FP;
- DEO the number of output elements crossing the person–machine boundary;
- OB, number of objects in the retained data model (i.e. the automated part of the data model);
- RE the number of inter-object relationships in the retained data model;
- RE_i the number of relationships associated with each object in the retained data model.

A 'function-strong' project has $RE/FP < 0.7$; a 'data-strong' project has $RE/FP > 1.5$, 'hybrid projects' have RE/FP in the range 0.7–1.5.

A Bang metric for a function-strong system is derived from data flow metrics. A Bang metric for a data-strong is derived from E–R model metrics. A hybrid system will need both types of Bang metric.

For function strong products, the Bang metric is based on the token count for each functional primitive, TC_i, and an adjustment for complexity based on the type of function (see Table 11.2(a)). The token count is corrected prior to the complexity adjustment using a variant of Halstead's Volume formula (Halstead, 1977):

$$\text{Corrected } TC_i = TC_i \times \log_2 (TC_i)$$

The corrected token count CTC_i is multiplied by its relevant complexity weighting w_i and the Bang metric is the sum of the weighted, corrected token counts:

$$\text{Bang} = \sum_{i=1}^{n} w_i \times CTC_i$$

For data-strong products, the Bang metric is based on the RE_i count. The correction factor is shown in Table 11.2(b). DeMarco does not state the basis of the figure explicitly, but it appears to be generated by using $RE_i + 1$, in the Halstead Volume formula.

We are not aware of any published studies of attempts to validate Bang metrics.

For hybrid systems both Bang metrics should be calculated and cost estimates should treat the database construction activities and the procedure development activities separately.

Table 11.2. (a) Complexity weighting factors for various classes of functions

Class	Weight	Class	Weight
Separation	0·6	Synchronization	1·5
Amalgamation	0·6	Output generation	1·0
Data direction	0·3	Display	1·8
Simple update	0·5	Tabular analysis	1·0
Storage management	1·0	Arithmetic	0·7
Edit	0·8	Computation	2·0
Verification	1·0	Initiation	1·0
Text manipulation	1·0	Device management	2·5

Source: DeMarco (1982). Reprinted by permission of Prentice-Hall, Inc., Englewood Cliffs, New Jersey.

Table 11.2. (b) Weightings for data-strong systems

RE_i	Corrected OB
1	1·0
2	2·3
3	4·0
4	5·8
5	7·8
6	9·8

Source: DeMarco (1982). Reprinted by permission of Prentice-Hall, Inc., Englewood Cliffs, New Jersey.

11.4.2.3 *Design weight*

DeMarco's design-weight metric (DeMarco, 1982) is derived from the module-structure information obtained when structured design techniques are used (Myers, 1978; Constantine & Yourdon, 1979). It is calculated from attributes of the links among modules and is in consequence related to module coupling and cohesion characteristics.

Design weight is a weighted count of the number of data tokens explicitly shared along normal module connections for each module (i.e. connections based on simple call statements), where the weight is related to the structure of the module inputs; see Table 11.3. Input structure counts are obtained for each module by:

- counting 1 for each iteration in the input data;
- counting 1 for each optional input data item;
- counting the number of alternatives—1, for each data item that can take on one of a number of values (i.e. an item that can take one of three alternative adds 2 to the count).

Table 11.3. Module design weight

Data tokens	Input structure							
	0	*1*	*2*	*3*	*4*	*5*	*6*	*7*
1	1·0	1·1	1·2	1·4	—	—	—	—
2	2·4	2·6	2·9	3·3	3·7	—	—	—
3	4·0	4·4	4·9	5·4	6·2	7·2	—	—
4	5·8	6·3	7·1	7·9	9·0	10·5	12·5	—
5	7·8	8·5	9·5	10·7	12·2	14·1	16·8	21·5
6	9·8	10·7	12·0	13·4	15·3	17·8	21·2	27·0
7	12·0	13·0	14·6	16·4	18·7	21·8	26·0	33·1
8	14·3	15·6	17·4	19·6	22·3	26·0	31·0	39·6
9	16·6	18·1	20·3	22·7	25·9	30·2	36·0	46·0
10	19·0	20·7	23·2	26·0	29·6	34·6	41·2	52·6
11	21·5	23·4	26·2	29·5	33·5	39·1	46·7	59·6
12	24·1	26·3	29·4	33·0	37·6	43·9	52·3	66·8
13	26·7	29·1	32·6	36·6	41·7	48·6	58·0	74·0
14	29·3	31·9	35·7	40·1	45·7	53·3	63·6	81·2
15	32·0	34·9	39·0	43·8	49·9	58·2	69·4	88·6

Source: DeMarco (1982). Reprinted by permission of Prentice-Hall, Inc., Englewood Cliffs, New Jersey.

The justification for weighting the data token count by the structure of the input data is that the structure of the input data should determine the structure of the procedure that manipulates the inputs. The relationship between the structure of data and program structure is the basis of the Warnier (1976) and Jackson (1975) program design methods.

The design-weight metric does not consider the effect of links between modules and common data structures or data bases, and so is likely to underestimate the amount of data processing performed by modules that read or update data structures.

We are not aware of any published validation studies of the design-weight metric.

11.4.2.4 *Problems with non-LOC size metrics*
Albrecht's function points have been criticized by Symons (1988) on a number of grounds.

- It is difficult to define the basic counts objectively (e.g. what is a 'logical internal file'?).
- The 'complex', 'average', 'simple' classification is over-simplified.
- The choice of weights for the initial classification and calculation of the technical complexity factor was determined subjectively and based on IBM experience.
- Internal complexity is treated twice, during the initial classification and during the calculation of the technical complexity factor.

- The effect on function-point counts of comparing a group of independent systems linked by interfaces and a single fully integrated system is counter-intuitive.

Symons has developed an improved set of counts and counting procedures, which he refers to as Mark II Function Points.

Like function points, DeMarco's metrics are not simple counts, they are based on complex tables of weights. The complexity weights for the function-strong Bang are subjective and environment dependent, and the basic Bang counts make use of the dubious Software Science concepts.

Some of the metrics are of limited applicability. The original formulation of function points was only suited to data-processing applications, although Reifer has extended their application to scientific and real-time application in his ASSET-R sizing model. Bang and design-weight metrics presuppose the use of a specific design methodology. They do not provide a direct estimate of effort, or schedule. They must, therefore, be incorporated as direct inputs into a cost model like ESTIMACS or incorporated into sizing models to produce an estimate of LOC that can be used in LOC-based cost models. Section 11.5.3 indicates how such metrics may be used in locally constructed cost models.

11.4.2.5 *Advantages of non-LOC size metrics*
The main advantage of these metrics is that they are available for measurement, rather than estimation, at an earlier stage in the development process than lines of code. However, it is also likely that the metrics are intrinsically better predictors of certain cost components because they are more closely related to the component activity than lines of code. For example, function points, which reflect the user view of a system, should by their nature be better predictors of user-documentation costs, user-training costs, installation costs, and acceptance tests than lines of code. Similarly, Bang metrics should be better predictors of system and integration testing costs.

A particular advantage of these metrics is that they are also appropriate for quality assurance and control. The issue of the relationship between quality and productivity is discussed in Section 11.5.4.

11.5 Improving Cost-Model Estimates

In this section, we consider further ways in which cost estimates can be improved, in addition to improving product sizing, which has been covered in the previous section. We consider three main approaches:

- improving the cost-estimation process;
- model tuning;
- developing local, process-linked cost models.

We end the section by considering the relationship between quality and productivity.

11.5.1 Improving the cost-estimation process

11.5.1.1 *Periodic re-estimation*

As a project progresses, more information about the software product and its development become available.

- A more detailed understanding of the software product is obtained in terms of the structure of the product and the functions performed by each product component.
- Actual measurements are available for some phases and activities in terms of effort, schedule, and staffing levels.
- Actual measurements of product attributes are available from requirements and design documents.

The availability of actual measurements of various product attributes has led to the development of alternative size metrics that are discussed in Section 11.4.2. In addition, however, estimates should be refined in the light of information about the observed progress and quality of the project. For example, the quality of the design may have been compromized in an effort to achieve time-scale targets.

Kitchenham and Taylor (1985) noted that the effort used in early phases of the development process correlated with effort expended in later phases, but there are no models that explicitly incorporate such relationships to assist re-estimation.

It is the availability of additional knowledge about the product that is usually exploited by cost models such as COCOMO, which encourage re-estimation. The Intermediate and Detailed versions of COCOMO are based on component and module size estimates, respectively. It is assumed that estimates of product component and module size will be of greater accuracy because of the better understanding of the detailed functionality of the product that accompanies structural design activities.

DeMarco (1982) points out that estimators (and by inference estimating models) should not be judged on the basis of a single estimate made early in the project life cycle, but on the convergence of a series of estimates produced at various points in the life cycle. He suggested a measure of the quality of estimates (the Estimating Quality Factor, *EQF*) that assesses a *series* of estimates by plotting the value of the estimate against the time it is used, as shown in Fig. 11.1. The *EQF* is obtained by dividing the area of the graph under the actual result line by the shaded area on the graph. The higher the *EQF* the better the estimate. DeMarco (1981) found that an *EQF* of 4 was above average. He recommends that estimators aim at an *EQF* of 10.

11.5.1.2 *Checklist for the use of cost-estimation models*

In order to use cost models effectively, whether they are locally derived models or proprietary models, it is necessary to ensure that the estimation process is properly defined and incorporated into the project working practices. The

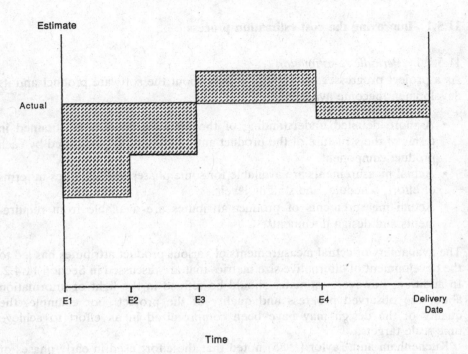

Fig. 11.1. Evaluating the quality of a series of estimates.

following checklist identifies the major processes and procedures which need to
be organized.

- Establish an adequately staffed and funded estimating group.
- Define a data-collection process that identifies *who* collects *what* items of
  data, *when, using which* data definitions, forms, data extraction tools, and
  procedures.
- Obtain a database for long-term storage of project data, with procedures
  for data entry and data validation.
- Define procedures for data analysis.
- Define an estimation process that uses the results of the data analysis to
  provide predictions at predefined points in the development process.
- Define a procedure for assessing the plausibility of estimates (this usually
  involves obtaining a number of different estimates and investigating any
  significant differences among them).
- Set targets for the estimating group based on monitoring the convergence
  of estimates.
- Define project-management procedures for monitoring project progress
  with respect to estimates, and for handling the effects of re-estimates (e.g.
  replanning).

11.5.2 Model tuning

The initial selection of a model involves choosing a model that is appropriate for the environment in which it will be used; however, any model will also need to be 'tuned'. This involves:

- *model installation,* which involves ensuring that the input parameters are used correctly and the outputs are in locally acceptable terms and correctly interpreted;
- *model calibration,* which involves changing the constants of the basic model algorithms on the basis of local project data.

We will discuss each issue briefly in the following sections.

11.5.2.1 *Model installation*
Model installation is needed to ensure that the basic inputs to the model conform to the model requirements, and that the model outputs are properly understood by model users. It also involves setting up the procedures for incorporating estimation into project control, and procedures for improving model accuracy.

(A) MODEL FAMILIARIZATION AND CONSOLIDATION
The first stage in model installation is ensuring that the assumptions concerning the basic inputs and outputs are understood.

For models using lines of code as an input parameter, it is important to ensure that the counting assumptions used in the model correspond to those expected by the model users. This includes considerations of whether or not the following items are included:

- blank lines and comments;
- code produced for testing purposes;
- data declarations;
- job control instructions.

For models that generate an estimate of effort, it is necessary to confirm:

- which activities are included in the estimate;
- which staff categories are included;
- the relationship between the model measurement scale and the environment scales (i.e. hours per person month used in the model and used by the model user).

For models that generate schedule, it is necessary to confirm whether or not the estimate is in terms of working days or calendar time (i.e. does it ignore weekends or not).

The above familiarization issues are relatively straightforward. It is more difficult to ensure that subjective parameters are interpreted and rated in a manner consistent with that of the model. In addition, it may be the case that the cost drivers included in the model are not relevant to a particular environment, or that the model does not cater for important features of a particular environment (e.g. the use of fourth-generation languages).

Cuelenaere *et al.* (1987) describe the problems experienced by the users of the PRICE SP model when attempting to interpret the meaning of the model inputs. All models that include subjective assessments cause problems of this sort for an inexperienced user. There is no obvious solution to such problems. A way around the problem is to use the expertise of people with experience of the model. Many proprietary models are sold or leased with consultancy, while Cuelenaere *et al.* (1987) suggest a means by which a large organization can make use of its own experience, by building an expert system to help estimators determine inputs consistently.

(B) ESTIMATION PROCEDURES AND PROJECT CONTROL
The use of model estimates must be incorporated into the process of project control, or there is no point in estimating at all. It is important to establish procedures for incorporating estimates into project plans, for monitoring actuals against estimates and for developing contingency plans to cater for significant deviations from plans.

In addition, the estimation process must be included in project procedures and plans to ensure that:

- the responsibility for obtaining the estimates is assigned;
- the schedule for the production of estimates and re-estimates is determined;
- the collection of model input data takes place;
- the collection of actual effort and schedule data takes place.

(C) PROCEDURES FOR IMPROVING MODEL ACCURACY
The final consideration of model installation is to prepare for the next stage of model tuning, which is model calibration. This involves ensuring that the data collected to support project control is not lost. It should feed into a database of local project data that can be used to tune the model even more finely to the local environment, as described in the next section.

11.5.2.2 *Model calibration*

Model calibration involves formulating a version of a cost model in which the model algorithms are selected or amended in the light of locally collected data. In Appendix D, we describe a number of models with built-in calibration facilities. PRICE SP cannot be used unless it is calibrated to local data, and SLIM may be used in calibration mode to generate the appropriate value of its technology factor from past data.

Boehm (1981) describes a method by which the COCOMO model can be calibrated to a new environment that should be appropriate to any empirical factor model that uses an exponential function. Boehm suggests that the simplest and most stable way of calibrating the COCOMO model is to establish the mode and use least squares to recalculate the value of the coefficient (α) in the equation

$$MM = \alpha(KDSI)^\beta \Pi(EM)$$

where β is fixed by the mode of the installation;

$\Pi(EM)$ is the overall effect of the effort multipliers of the cost drivers.

When data is available from a number of different projects, α is re-estimated as follows:

$$\bar{\alpha} = \sum_{i=1}^{n} MM_i \Pi(EM)_i \Big/ \sum_{i=1}^{n} [\Pi(EM)_i]^2$$

If α and β are both to be recalculated, the formulae are as follows:

$$\log_{10} \bar{\alpha} = (a_2 d_0 - a_1 d_1)/(a_0 a_2 - a_1^2)$$

$$\bar{\beta} = (a_0 d_1 - a_1 d_0)/(a_0 a_2 - a_1^2)$$

where

$$a_0 = n$$

$$a_1 = \sum_{i=1}^{n} \log(KDSI)_i$$

$$a_2 = \sum_{i=1}^{n} [\log(KDSI)_i]^2$$

$$d_0 = \sum_{i=1}^{n} \log[(MM)_i / \Pi(EM)_i]$$

$$d_1 = \sum_{i=1}^{n} \log[(MM)_i / \Pi(EM)_i] \log(KDSI)_i$$

11.5.3 The construction of local cost models

DeMarco recommends developing a series of different regression models using the measures available at the different stages of the development process (function points, Bang, design weight, code metrics). He suggests the following procedure.

- Decompose the projects into cost components, i.e. specification cost, design cost, coding cost, testing costs, project management costs, QA costs, documentation, etc.
- Determine the likely predictors (metrics) of each cost component.
- Collect data about the metrics and actual costs (preferably from new projects).
- Use regression techniques to confirm or refute the supposed relationship and to indicate the strength of the relationship (e.g. the MMRE, and/or PRED($\cdot$20) values).

This leads to a number of models that could be invoked at various stages in the development process. Thus, function points might be used in a number of different models to predict:

- overall cost
- specification costs
- acceptance test planning
- acceptance testing
- installation costs
- user training costs
- user documentation costs

Bang metrics might be expected to predict:

- overall cost
- design costs
- system test planning
- system testing

Design weight metrics might be expected to predict:

- overall cost
- code and unit testing cost (overall and per module)
- integration test planning
- integration test costs
- rework costs
- support costs

Code metrics might be expected to predict:

- overall cost
- unit test costs
- machine time for testing
- support costs

It would be necessary to confirm that predictions made at different stages in the life cycle converged on the final cost.

DeMarco suggests using simple linear regression to construct 'basic' cost models and then incorporating knowledge about the specific project in terms of subjective corrections to the basic predictions. He does not offer any advice as to which factors should prompt correction, although he suggests keeping the number of correction factors down to four or five.

The discussion of the Bailey and Basili Meta-model in Appendix D describes a more sophisticated method of constructing models that are calibrated directly to a particular environment. Bailey & Basili (1981) constructed their local model using lines of code as a size input, but there is no reason why function points, Bang metrics, and design weight should not be used as an input parameter instead of LOC, and models constructed in the manner they recommend.

It would seem appropriate in practice to use DeMarco's simple approach when records of only a few projects are available, and to use Bailey and Basili's approach when a larger set of data has been accumulated. With seven or fewer projects, statistical analysis would be inappropriate; the data should be used to assist more heuristic methods of costing, such as costing by analogy. With 8–20 projects, simple linear regression with subjectively determined corrections would be used, and with 21 or more projects non-linear regression and statistical determination of cost driver influence would be used.

Projects included in the analysis should be basically 'similar'. DeMarco suggests that initial identification of project as similar should be based on a two-dimensional classification, where one dimension identifies whether the project is function-strong, data-strong or hybrid, and the other dimension identifies whether the project is scientific or commercial.

Tools such as EML-I (Cowderoy & Jenkins, 1989) should make it more attractive for project managers to develop their own locally calibrated cost models by providing flexible interfaces for model construction. EML-I is particularly useful for large projects where many different calculations are required, for example when dealing with a detailed work-breakdown chart. For small projects, spreadsheets can be used.

11.5.4 Quality and productivity

The effects of poor quality are spoilage and re-work. These can account for 50–60% of life-cycle costs as a result of debugging during software production, correcting faults after release, and poor productivity of post-release enhancements.

Although this chapter has been concerned with cost estimation, it must be noted that there is a strong relationship between quality and productivity. There are no examples of stringent productivity requirements resulting in increased quality; there are however, a number of studies indicating that quality improvements increase productivity (primarily due to the decreasing re-work costs).

An additional advantage of looking for better measures of product size for cost-modelling purposes is that the same metrics can be used to assist quality control and assurance. Thus, specification and design metrics should be checked to monitor conformance to requirements, and the adequacy of test plans, and unusual values of metrics can be used to identify potential weak points in the specification and the design.

Final project quality needs to be measured and recorded in the same way as project cost data needs to be recorded. DeMarco suggests the following metrics:

- cost of defect detection and correction pre- and post-delivery (using six-month post-delivery costs as a baseline);
- defect density pre- and post-delivery;

- user change requests frequency (number per month post-delivery);
- persistence of defects (elapsed time between detection and removal of faults).

If objective measures of quality are identified and recorded, then we can use the same methods to develop quantitative quality models as we can use to develop quantitative cost models.

This basic approach is being taken by the ESPRIT project REQUEST, which is attempting to develop a constructive quality model called COQUAMO (in a direct analogy to COCOMO). COQUAMO is a three-part model involving prediction, monitoring and assessment (Petersen & Kitchenham, 1988). Initial quality predictions are based on the quality levels achieved in previous products of the main quality factors, which are then adjusted using a number of 'quality' drivers, producing a model very similar to intermediate COCOMO.

In this context, quality levels are quantified measures of product characteristics, e.g. maintainability measured in terms of elapsed time to respond to a problem report, reliability measured in terms of median time to next failure, etc. The quality drivers to be included in the model are still the subject of research (Petersen *et al.*, 1989). They will be derived from:

- product attributes such as quality requirements, success criticality, product difficulty;
- process attributes such as process maturity, tool use, method maturity;
- personnel attributes such as software experience and motivational level;
- project attributes such as the quality norm and leadership style;
- organizational attributes such as quality management maturity, and physical environment.

The relationship between technical development (specification and design metrics), quality (defect metrics and quality model drivers), productivity (cost model drivers) and project planning (cost model outputs) is the same co-ordinating principle as is discussed in Chapter 7 as the bridge between Technical Development, Quality Management and Project Management (Sections 7.2.4, 7.2.5 and 7.6). Section 7.6 discusses this as Software Development Methodology, which can be seen as making the combined principles work with present-day capabilities. Research in modelling is beginning to move, very slowly, away from mere cost modelling, and even quality modelling, towards Software Project Modelling, which encompasses all the above aspects on a basis of modelling the software-development process.

11.6 Cost-Estimation Risk

Most software cost models do not tell you anything about the risk. The purpose of this section is to determine and, where possible, quantify the risks involved in accepting the estimates derived from cost models.

A fundamental assumption of this analysis is that the data upon which the parameters are based is unbiased. Unfortunately, this is often not the case, and it is hard to verify that any given data satisfies this requirement. Often such data is biased for political or commercial reasons. This leads to an unquantifiable component to risk.

It seems that many people neglect the fact that cost estimation takes place against an uncertain outcome. That is, the actual costs of a system are sums of random costs induced by the stochastic nature of the development process. Thus, it is important, and extremely useful if possible, to estimate the variance of cost estimates so that the cost-estimation risk may be quantified.

In what follows we shall consider System (i.e. Equipment, Software, etc.) Costs. We also introduce the nomenclature of 'Prime Mission Equipment' Costs, and other support costs, such as logistics costs, or software maintenance, etc. Figure 11.2, which is not definitive, illustrates this concept.

By definition the Prime Mission Equipment Costs are all the costs (including software and hardware costs) involved in producing a system that is capable of fulfilling its Prime Mission (i.e. its first use for its main purpose).

The cost-estimation risk calculations attempt to quantify the uncertainties in the parameters used by particular models in terms of their effect upon overall life-cycle cost. For example, in the case of Logistic Support, we would be interested in uncertainties in the failure rates and unit prices, whereas, in the case of Prime Mission Software, we might well be interested in uncertainties in the model parameters of, say COCOMO, as well as in uncertainties in the quantity of delivered lines of code.

11.6.1 Risk analysis

Because of the great variety of cost relationships supposed by the various cost models currently in vogue, it is impractical to analyse the risks for each. We therefore aim to provide an analysis for the main types of relationships; these analyses can be extended in an obvious way to cover all existing models, and, no doubt, will also extend to future models. The different techniques for cost estimation are considered separately, and then it is shown how these can be combined to give the risk for a complete cost element.

Note that a sensitivity analysis of a model's direct results merely estimates the model's sensitivity to changes in its parameters. Since the models, at best, restrict themselves to estimating means, this is not sufficient to estimate the risks.

As regards the results given in this section, we are attempting to gauge the risk involved in accepting the cost projections calculated by the models. That is, we are attempting to assess the probabilities that the models' predicted costs will be exceeded. In order to do this we must assume that there is some semblance of truth encapsulated within the models; however, as has been stated earlier in this chapter, this may be difficult to justify. Where possible, we shall show how these risks may be evaluated using the Normal distribution.

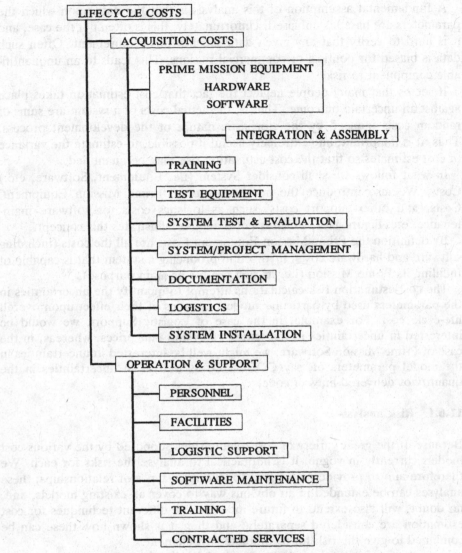

Fig. 11.2. The relationship between cost elements.

In other cases we shall utilize the Chebyshev inequality, as follows, to make a qualitative evaluation:

$$\text{Chebyshev inequality: } P\{|x - \mu| \geq \varepsilon\} \leq \frac{\sigma^2}{\varepsilon^2}$$

where X is a random variable with mean μ, and variance σ^2, which has values

x, and ε is a positive real number. This inequality is seldom tight, and thus generally the r.h.s. is optimistically high, thus making the estimate useless for quantitative purposes. If we restrict ourselves to considerations like 'knowing the actual cost is likely to be within some percentage of the predicted estimate' then the above inequality can be written as

$$P\left\{\alpha \geqslant \frac{\delta\sigma}{\mu}\right\} \leqslant \frac{\sigma^2}{\mu^2}\frac{1}{\delta^2} \qquad \text{(putting } x = \mu \pm \alpha\mu\text{)}$$

where $1 - \alpha$ is the acceptable percentage accuracy, and δ is a positive real number. This gives the justification for taking the ratio σ/μ as a qualitative guide to the risk.

The following subsections review the risks involved in accepting the results of some of the more commonly occurring equations used in cost modelling.

11.6.1.1 *Percentage calculations*

Many models estimate some of their costs as direct percentages of other estimated costs. For example, documentation costs are often estimated as being a fixed percentage of say Prime Mission Equipment Costs (*PME*).

Let C_α = total of percentage costs for one equipment type, i.e.

$$C_\alpha = \left(\sum_{i=1}^{N} \lambda_i\right) PME$$

where λ_i = percentage of *PME* for cost element i;
$\quad N$ = number of percentage cost elements;
$\quad PME$ = Prime Mission Equipment Cost.

Then

$$\text{Var}\{C_\alpha\} = \left(\sum_{i=1}^{N} \bar{\lambda}_i\right)^2 \frac{\Delta^2}{3} + \frac{\overline{PME}^2}{3}\sum_{i=1}^{N} \varepsilon_i^2 + \frac{\Delta^2}{9}\sum_{i=1}^{N} \varepsilon_i^2$$

where

$$\bar{\lambda}_i - \varepsilon_i \leqslant \lambda_i \leqslant \bar{\lambda}_i + \varepsilon_i$$

and

$$\overline{PME} - \Delta \leqslant PME \leqslant \overline{PME} + \Delta$$

Note that:

(1) If N is not too small, the distribution of C_α will be Normal ($N \geqslant 8$).
(2) A knowledge of *PME*, Δ, $\bar{\lambda}_i$ ($i = 1, 2, \ldots, N$) and ε_i is required to make this calculation.
(3) The calculation is only valid for all of one equipment type, and not the individual equipments of a type, i.e. $PME = M \times PME_j$, where PME_j = Prime Mission Equipment cost for each of the jth equipment type.
(4) If $N \leqslant 7$, then a ratio of the standard deviation ($\sqrt{\text{Var}}$) with the mean will give some indication of the risk, e.g. $0 \cdot 1$ = good, 10 = bad.

11.6.1.2 *Software maintenance*

Taking as an example the COCOMO model of software maintenance, then we find that, if we take the instance of embedded software, then

$$C_{SWM} = \sum_{i=1}^{I} ACT_i 3 \cdot 6 NL_i^{1 \cdot 2} C_{MM}$$

where ACT_i = Annual Change Traffic Ratio for software i;

NL_i = Number of lines of code for software i;

C_{MM} = Cost per Man-Month for software maintenance.

Then

$$\text{Var}\{C_{SWM}\} = (3 \cdot 6)^2 \frac{2}{3} \sum_{i=1}^{I} \frac{\alpha_i^2}{3} \text{Var}\{NL_i^{1 \cdot 2}\} \text{Var}\{C_{MM}\}$$

where

$$\text{Var}\{NL_i^{1 \cdot 2}\} = \frac{\overline{NL_i^{3 \cdot 4}}}{6 \cdot 8\lambda}[(1+\Lambda)^{3 \cdot 4} - (1-\Lambda)^{3 \cdot 4}] - \frac{\overline{NL_i^{4 \cdot 4}}}{(4 \cdot 4\lambda)^2}[(1+\Lambda)^{2 \cdot 2} - (1-\Lambda)^{2 \cdot 2}]^2$$

and

$$\Lambda = \lambda / \overline{NL_i}$$

$$\overline{NL_i} - \lambda \leqslant NL_i \leqslant \overline{NL_i} + \lambda$$

$$\overline{C_{MM}} - \psi \leqslant C_{MM} \leqslant \overline{C_{MM}} + \psi$$

$$\overline{ACT_i} - \alpha_i \leqslant ACT_i \leqslant \overline{ACT_i} + \alpha_i$$

Note that:

(1) If $I \geqslant 8$, say, then C_{SWM} will be Normal.
(2) If $I \leqslant 7$, then a guide to the risk would be as before.

11.6.1.3 *Operating costs*

The operating costs for N equipments of the same type are calculated by

$$C_{op} = HC_H + MS_M + N_M C_M$$

where H = operating hours;

C_H = cost per operating hour for power;

M = number of operators;

S_M = operator salary;

N_M = number of missions;

C_M = cost per mission.

For $N > 7$ say, C_{op} will be Normally distributed with mean

$$E\{C_{op}\} = \mu_{op} = H\bar{C}_H + M\bar{S}_M + N_M \bar{C}_M$$

and variance

$$\sigma_{op}^2 = \frac{H^2}{3}\sum_{i=1}^{N}\delta_i^2 + \frac{M^2}{3}\sum_{i=1}^{N}\gamma_i^2 + \frac{N_M^2}{3}\sum_{i=1}^{N}\psi^2$$

where

$$\bar{C}_H - \delta \leqslant C_H \leqslant \bar{C}_H + \delta$$
$$\bar{S}_M - \gamma \leqslant S_M \leqslant \bar{S}_M + \gamma$$
$$\bar{C}_M - \psi \leqslant C_M \leqslant \bar{C}_M + \psi$$

Thus, for probability (risk) α_0

$$C = \mu_{op} - \beta_0 \sigma_{op}$$

where $\beta_0 = \phi^{-1}\{\alpha_0\}$ and $\phi^{-1} =$ inverse cumulative Normal distribution function.

11.6.1.4 *Logistic costs*

Often the Poisson distribution is used to determine depot stock levels for spares. More generally, it can be shown that the Normal distribution function is more appropriate, and under less restrictive conditions too. For the purposes of this example we shall take the Normal approximation to the Poisson distribution. Thus

$$\mu = \sigma^2 = m\lambda T_R$$

where $m =$ number of identical equipments served by one intermediate depot;

$\lambda =$ failure rate of typical LRU (LRU = Line Replaceable Unit);

$T_R =$ repair turnaround time.

Let $\alpha^* =$ required availability of spares, and $\beta^* = \phi^{-1}\{\alpha^*\}$, then

$$E\{N_S\} = m\lambda T_R + \beta^*\sqrt{m\lambda T_R} + \tfrac{1}{2}$$

where $N_S =$ number of spares for one LRU type, and the 1/2 is the standard correction for integer solutions. Hence, $E\{N_S\}$ and $E\{N_S^2\}$ may be found, and used to give Var $\{N_S\}$.

Let the cost of spares be

$$C = \sum_{i=1}^{N_S} c_i$$

where

$$\bar{c} - \delta \leqslant c \leqslant \bar{c} + \delta$$

Then

$$E\{C\} = E\{N_S\}E\{c\}$$

and

$$\text{Var}\{C\} = \bar{c}^2 \text{ Var}\{N_S\} + \frac{\delta^2}{3} E\{N_S\}$$

Since this result applies to one LRU type, the cost of all spares for m identical equipments being served by one intermediate depot will be Normal, i.e.

$$E\{C_{SP}\} = L \cdot E\{C\}$$

and

$$\text{Var}\{C_{SP}\} = L \cdot \text{Var}\{C\}$$

where L = number of LRUs per equipment type (and is assumed to be known).

Similarly, for the cost of repairs,

$$\mu = \sigma^2 = n\lambda T_H$$

where T_H = total operating time, and the other nomenclature is as above, which gives $E\{N_R\}$ where N_R = number of repair actions and $\text{Var}\{N_R\}$.

If cost of repair

$$C_R = \sum_{i=1}^{N_R} c_{Ri} \quad \text{where } \bar{c}_R - \delta \leqslant c_R \leqslant \bar{c}_R + \delta$$

then we can find $E\{C_R\}$ and $\text{Var}\{C_R\}$. Again this result applies to one LRU, hence total cost of repair is Normally distributed and

$$E\{\text{Total cost of repair}\} = L \cdot E\{C_R\}$$

$$\text{Var}\{\text{Total cost of repair}\} = L \cdot \text{Var}\{C_R\}$$

11.6.1.5 *Training*
A similar calculation to that for operating costs gives that

$$E\{C_T\} = M \sum_{i=1}^{N} \bar{C}_{Mi} + O \sum_{i=1}^{N} \bar{C}_{Oi}$$

and

$$\text{Var}\{C_T\} = \frac{M^2}{3} \sum_{i=1}^{N} \delta_i^2 + \frac{O^2}{3} \sum_{i=1}^{N} \gamma_i^2$$

where C_T = total cost of training;

M = number of maintenance personnel requiring training;

O = number of operators requiring training;

C_{Mi} = cost of training one maintenance person;

C_{Ti} = cost of training one operator;

$$\overline{C_{Mi}} - \delta_i \leqslant C_{Mi} \leqslant \overline{C_{Mi}} + \delta_i$$
$$\overline{C_{Oi}} - \gamma_i \leqslant C_{Oi} \leqslant \overline{C_{Oi}} + \gamma_i$$

and C_T is again Normally distributed.

11.6.2 Combination of cost risk

A theorem frequently used in the preceding theory is that the sum of any number, including a random number, of independent Normally distributed random variables is itself Normally distributed. In the case of a fixed number of variates, the joint distribution has mean and variance equal to the sum of the individual means and variances, respectively. For a random number of variates, the Random Sum Theorem should be used. Thus, any combination of cost elements can be analysed using this result and the results presented above, e.g. by cost element, equipment type or complete option.

11.6.3 Other risks

The above analysis of cost risk essentially assumes that the considered system is viable technically, that it will be delivered according to the initial schedule, and that the economic climate will remain as originally perceived. Risks associated with departures from these initial projections are difficult to assess, let alone quantify, and the association of costs is even more tenuous. Nevertheless, we give a brief discussion on how these can be dealt with.

11.6.3.1 *Technical risk*

Technical risk is a somewhat more elusive concept than cost risk. The quantitative expression of technical risk is an essentially heuristic attempt to evaluate the relative difficulty of the successful development of a new item or project.

One way to quantify the technical risk of an item is to assign a risk factor that is a function of the current status of that item. An example of risk factors is given in Table 11.4.

Each element from a proposed system is assigned a risk factor, and the geometric mean of these factors is computed. A value of 1 would indicate minimum risk, whereas a value of 5 would indicate a great risk. This method at least allows relative risk comparison between possible options.

11.6.3.2 *Schedule risk*

Schedule risk lies midway between cost risk and technical risk in difficulty. Quantification and analysis of schedule risk can be handled in much the same

Table 11.4. Technical risk factor by life-cycle stage

Status of item	Risk factor
Concept	5
Engineering model	4
Prototype	3
In production	2
Fielded	1

way as for cost risk. However, it is much more difficult to combine the risks of each item of a programme than it is to give the risk to the programme as a whole. Therefore, schedule risk is usually determined only for each individual item and converted to an equivalent cost. The sum of these cost variations will give a simple measure of the schedule risk of the entire programme.

11.6.3.3   *Economic and acquisition concept risk*

Inflation and currency conversion risks can have effects upon the actual budgetary requirements for a project. A quantitative analysis is sometimes feasible by performing a sensitivity analysis on the life-cycle costs, but these considerations are not usually essential for the comparison of options for the realization of a system.

11.7   Summary

In this chapter we have discussed the issues of cost modelling and estimation both from the viewpoint of software project control and that of systems engineering. Appendix D gives detailed descriptions of various cost-estimation models; this chapter has concentrated on describing the practical problems that are faced by users of the models, and the extension of basic software cost modelling into the wider realm of systems estimation and risk analysis. In particular, we have tried to explain and justify the following points.

- Cost estimation is part of basic project control.
- Software cost models may give very poor predictions unless they are tuned to the environment in which they are to be used.
- Developing, tuning, and using software cost models depends on adequate data collection and analysis.
- Models that use estimates as input parameters will usually give less accurate predictions than models that use direct measurements.
- Estimates are probabilistic in nature. They have a basic uncertainty that can be modelled statistically and that should be used in software and system risk assessment.

12

Software Engineering Environments

Ian Sommerville

12.1	Introduction	377
12.2	Environment Facilities	378
12.3	Environment Architecture	381
12.4	Ada Support Environments	389
12.5	CASE Workbenches	391
12.6	Introducing an IPSE	394
12.7	Environments and Reliability Management	396
12.8	Summary	397
12.9	Further Reading	398

12.1 Introduction

Historically, the most significant productivity increases in manufacturing or building processes have come about when human skills are augmented by powerful tools. For example, one man and a bulldozer can probably shift more earth in a day than fifty men working with hand tools. The practice of software development has some similarities with manufacturing, and supporting software engineers with automated tools can lead to dramatic improvements in productivity.

Before the widespread introduction of timesharing computer systems, the majority of program development was carried out off-line. Programs were prepared and debugged without the aid of the computer system. Preparing a program involved punching it onto cardboard cards, submitting the cards to a batch processing system and then retrieving the cards along with a listing of the results of executing or compiling the program. Program modifications were made by repunching those cards in the deck that contained the program statements to be modified.

Even in this situation, some programming tools were available. Apart from compilers, assemblers and other language processors, most systems provided a link editor that allowed parts of the program to be independently compiled then linked together to form an executable program. Link editors are used to put together routines from different libraries. If a generally useful subroutine is prepared by one individual, that routine can be entered in a public library of subroutines and any other user may refer to that subroutine in his program. The link editor searches the appropriate subroutine libraries, abstracts the code of the called routine and links the referenced routine with the calling program.

As well as these tools, a variety of other software to assist the process of program development has now been developed. The use of timesharing systems allows interactive editors and debugging tools to be used and large amounts of backing store means that library programs to keep track of code and documentation can be developed. However, timesharing systems offer a restricted amount of computational power to each user and it is only now, with the introduction of powerful, networked single-user workstations to support software development, that the full productivity benefits from tool use can be realized.

12.2   Environment Facilities

The term *environment* is used as an abstract description of all of the automated facilities the software engineer has available to assist with the task of software development. As well as tools to assist with program preparation and development, an environment may also include design tools, management tools, documentation support tools, an electronic mail system, and so on. There are a number of different classes of environment, such as language-oriented environments intended to support programming in one particular programming language, educational environments that are intended to help beginners learn to program and software engineering environments to support the development of large software systems. Surveys by Howden (1982) and more recently, by Dart *et al.* (1987) describe these in broad terms.

The environments that are of most interest to us here are those for supporting large system development and these really fall into two classes, manely, programming environments such as Unix/PWB (Ivie, 1977; Dolotta *et al.*, 1978) and larger-scale software engineering environments such as ASPECT (Hall *et al.*, 1985), ISTAR (Dowson, 1987) and AWB-ADE (Childs & Vokolos, 1987).

There are implementation differences between these classes of environment, but the most important logical difference is that programming environments support the later stages of the software development process (implementation and testing) and do not provide special-purpose tools to support requirements specification, software design, management and other activities critical to the success of large software projects.

Software engineering environments, on the other hand, are intended to support all stages of the software process from initial feasibility studies through to operation and maintenance. Because of this wide-ranging support, such environments are sometimes called *integrated project support environments* (IPSEs).

The best known *programming* environment is probably the Unix Programmers Workbench (Unix/PWB) System. This system was designed to support the development of software for IBM, UNIVAC, XDS, and DIGITAL computers and now supports development of software for a vast range of machines. The system developers point out that, as well as providing an environment conducive to program development, the use of the Unix/PWB system means that the same system interface is presented to the programmer irrespective of which machine is actually being used for program execution. The programmer need not learn the details of several different systems and is also preserved from disruptions caused by changes in the target hardware.

The success of the Unix/PWB environment and the tools that have been developed for use in that environment is a major factor in the adoption of Unix as a host operating system for many IPSEs. Other, equally important, factors are the portability of the Unix system, which reduces the cost of rehosting an IPSE across a range of machines, and the fact that Unix has become a *de facto* standard for personal workstations such as those available from Sun, Apollo, Hewlett-Packard and other vendors. Such workstations are widely used as host systems for IPSEs because of their computing power and because of their bit-mapped, graphical interface capabilities.

Although Unix is probably the most widely used IPSE host operating system, this does not, of course, mean that the use of this system is critical for IPSE development. A number of IPSEs such as GENOS (Higgs & Stevens, 1986) and ISTAR (Dowson, 1987) are available that are offered with either Unix or some other operating system as a base. Unix-based systems are discussed here because these reflect the author's experience, but comparable examples could be drawn from other operating systems.

The key characteristic of an IPSE is the notion of *integration*. It is possible to identify three levels of integration that can be supported in an IPSE, namely:

(1) *Tool integration*. Rather than using *ad hoc* facilities for data storage, all data in an IPSE is under the control of an object-management system. In principle, this means that the outputs from any one tool may act as inputs for other tools and hence tools can be used in conjunction.

(2) *User interface integration*. User interface integration implies that the user interfaces of all of the IPSE facilities are consistent, so that an IPSE user is not presented with a set of tools that require learning various different interface styles.

(3) *Activity integration*. Activity integration implies that the IPSE includes facilities to model the process of software development and to intervene actively in support of that process by initiating or terminating process activities.

It can be argued that for an IPSE to be truly effective, all of these integration levels should be supported. However, the current state of IPSE development is such that there are still many problems associated with integration, particularly interface and activity integration. Present IPSE products may not be completely integrated, yet, as discussed below, their use may still be cost-effective.

The advantages of using an IPSE for large software project development may be listed as follows.

(1) All available software tools are interfaced to an object-management system (OMS) so that the output of any one tool can potentially be an input to any other tool. Whilst it is normally the case that tool interactions are predictable, there are many cases of serendipitious tool combinations and the IPSE database allows these combinations to occur when required.

(2) Project management has direct access to project information and management tools can use actual data collected during the course of a project.

(3) All of the documents produced in the course of a project from feasibility studies to fault reports can be put under configuration control and managed by the configuration-management tools that are an integral part of the IPSE. Furthermore, the data-management facilities are rich enough to allow relationships between documents to be recorded so that designs (say) can be linked to their associated code and changes to each automatically tracked. It is the author's opinion that this is probably the single most important reason for adopting an IPSE.

(4) If the IPSE is properly integrated, all of the support tools will present the user with a consistent interface, so that the task of learning to use new tools is reduced.

(5) The use of an object-management system allows fine-grain (small) objects to be recorded, named and subjected to configuration control. This means that the structure of the storage system can reflect the structure of the system rather than an artificial file organization being imposed on the program.

(6) It becomes possible to build more powerful software tools because these tools can make use of the relationships recorded in the OMS.

(7) The IPSE may offer process-modelling facilities and may be used to ensure that a known and documented process is used for system development.

An integrated project support environment is intended to support all of the activities in the software process through all phases from initial feasibility studies to software maintenance and evolution. At the time of writing, there are few IPSEs in use and many IPSEs under construction in North America, Europe and Japan. It is clear that, by 1990, a great many of these current development projects will probably be in operation.

To be realistic, however, whilst these IPSEs may not preclude the support of any software process activity, our current tool technology is such that many activities will not be supported except in a very rudimentary way. Understanding the underlying process fragments is still the subject of research and hence we cannot yet provide significant tool support for these activities.

12.3 Environment Architecture

The structure of an IPSE can be viewed (simplistically) as like that of an onion, where there are a number of layers of functionality provided by different levels in the system. Although it can be argued (Blair *et al.*, 1986) that IPSEs should be built in conjunction with a special-purpose operating system tailored to IPSE requirements, requirements such as the need for portability have meant that the innermost kernel in the 'IPSE-onion' is usually a standard operating system.

A typical structure for an integrated project support environment is shown in Fig. 12.1. It must be emphasized that this view of an IPSE, which evolved from work on Ada-specific environments, is a simplistic one and that, although some IPSE architectures fit this model, there are many alternative approaches. The 'onion' model presented in Fig. 12.1 is a convenient model for discussing IPSE facilities and separate sections below are included to cover each of the layers.

An alternative view of an IPSE architecture is suggested by Penedo & Riddle (1988) where they suggest that a further layer is appropriate namely an adaptation layer, which is concerned with adapting the IPSE to support a particular software process, application domain and user population.

It is quite clear that there is a need for adaptation capabilities in an IPSE, but it is not yet clear how these might best be provided. Adaptation capabilities required are:

(1) *Method-support capabilities.* IPSEs may be adapted to support a particular method of software development such as MASCOT. This

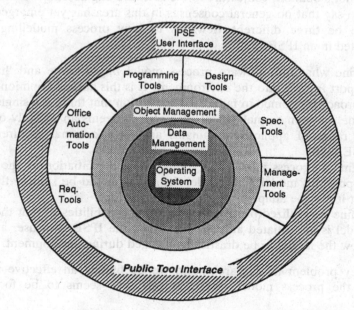

Fig. 12.1. A logical view of an IPSE.

involves incorporating knowledge of the MASCOT method into the IPSE and using this knowledge to drive the development process.

(2) *Tool-configuration capabilities.* Clearly not all IPSE instantiations will include all possible toolsets, and means of configuring an IPSE with a particular toolset are required.

(3) *Process-modelling capabilities.* These allow the software process to be modelled and captured in an IPSE and this model is then used to derive and control the development process. To some extent, method-support capabilities incorporate implicit process modelling but a more general modelling capability is clearly of value.

(4) *User interface adaptation capabilities.* These allow differ user interfaces to be generated, depending on the class of IPSE user. Of course, these should be variants of an integrated interface rather than completely different interface systems.

At the time of writing, there are vast discrepancies in the procedures and techniques adopted by different vendors to provide method support. Some vendors market IPSEs that are tailored explicitly for a particular method and for a particular process model using that method. Others provide support for a number of methods but little in the way of process-modelling capabilities, and yet others have concentrated on process modelling but offer a relatively limited range of tools.

Because of the assumption that a reliable process is more likely to lead to reliable products, the ability to adapt an IPSE to a particular process model is perhaps the most important adaptation capability from the point of view of this book. Process modelling is subject of a great deal of discussion, research and, in this author's opinion, conjecture in the software engineering community and it is fair to say that no general consensus in this area has yet emerged. There appear to be three different views as to how process modelling can be incorporated in an IPSE.

(1) Define what the software process model *ought* to be and 'hard-wire' support for this into the environment. It is this author's opinion that this approach is doomed to failure, as the notion that there is a single process model or even a small set of such models seems an unlikely one given the range of application domains and organizational requirements of IPSE users.

(2) Define a process model and configure an instantiation of the IPSE to support this model. The model definition should be sufficiently flexible that it may be adapted as the process develops.

(3) Define generalized process-programming capabilities so that the process model is instantiated at 'run-time' when the IPSE is in use, and which allow the model to be drastically changed during development.

The key problem in this area seems to be finding an effective means to describe the process model. Work in this area seems to be focusing on object-oriented description (Ould and Roberts, 1988), but much research remains to be carried out before process-modelling capabilities mature. We do not discuss process modelling further here because it is very difficult to make general observations about this topic. Although some IPSEs include process-modelling capabilities, these have not been widely documented. However, it is reasonable to predict that process modelling and other adaptation capabilities will be key constituents of many future IPSEs. Further reading in the area of process support is suggested at the end of the chapter.

The primary basis that distinguishes an IPSE from a software toolkit (collection of tools) is the object-management layer. This layer is responsible for controlling and managing all of the entities (conventionally termed 'objects' although these are different from the objects of object-oriented programming) produced during software development. Broadly, the object-management layer allows objects to be named and to exist in a number of different versions, and it provides facilities for typed relationships (such as *part-of*) to be recorded between objects.

The next layer out is the tool layer and the tools supported by an IPSE normally fall into three categories:

(1) *Integrated tools*. Tools that have been built or modified by the IPSE developers so that they can make intimate use of the facilities provided by the object-management system. In essence, these are tools that have been written to operate with a particular IPSE and OMS and are tailored to that system.
(2) *Imported tools*. These are tools that are less tightly integrated with the object-management system and that communicate with the IPSE via the PTI (public tools interface). Such tools may communicate using system objects but will generally not be able to make use of inbuilt information about objects in the same way as integrated tools.
(3) *Foreign tools*. These are tools that do not integrate with the object-management system but that interface directly to the underlying operating system. In order for IPSEs to be viable, they must support an upgrade path from existing toolkit machines, so that users can continue to use familiar file-based tools when an IPSE is introduced. Thus, most IPSEs support file-based tools and, in particular, support the tools provided with Unix.

The final layer in Fig. 12.1 is the user interface layer. If an IPSE is to be considered as an integrated system, is is not acceptable for that integration to be simply concerned with tool communication. It is equally important that the tools provided by the IPSE should be integrated at the user interface level so that users are not faced with the daunting cognitive taks of learning lots of different tool interfaces. In fact, this 'layer' is pervasive and should offer a direct interface to the object management system as well as interfaces to the tools provided in the IPSE.

12.3.1 The operating-system layer

The operating-system layer is the lowest IPSE layer and, as discussed above, Unix or one of its variants is the most common base for IPSE development. It is likely that this situation will persist well into the 1990s. The undoubted advantages of Unix are its availability on a wide range of machines and the vast amount of existing software available that runs under Unix.

Unix, in common with other operating systems such as VMS, suffers, however, from its ancestry as an operating system for single-processor systems. Although networked versions of current operating systems that operate on a cluster of processors are available, none of these are truly distributed operating systems and the lack of capability in this area is likely to retard the development of distributed IPSEs.

However, current research and standardization efforts concerned with the development of heterogeneous systems are addressing some of these distribution problems and it is increasingly likely that IPSEs operating on collections of different processors running different operating systems will be available in the relatively near future.

It is not appropriate to discuss particular operating system facilities here, as any of the current operating systems offered by major vendors can serve as an adequate although not an ideal basis for an IPSE.

12.3.2 The data-management layer

The data management built into an IPSE provides all of the data-storage facilities for project information and allows relationships between project entities to be specified and maintained. This layer is the foundation for the IPSE object-management system and should offer the following classes of facility:

(1) Facilities to create, modify, destroy and create attributed entities of a number of basic types such as TEXT, NUMBER, DATE, etc. Notice that these types are general types and the OMS typically offers a much richer type system.

(2) Facilities to create and destroy attributed relations between system entities.

(3) Facilities that allow managed entities to be uniquely identified.

(4) Facilities to control access to individual system entities at a fine level of granularity. Individual entity control is required because, unlike commercial systems, transactions in an IPSE are typically long transactions and it is unacceptable to lock large sections of the data store during a transaction.

(5) Facilities for rollback and recovery to allow the consistency of the data store to be maintained in the event of system failure and to allow for data to be recovered after user errors.

There are two approaches which have been adopted to providing the data-management facilities provided by an IPSE. One approach is suggested in Fig. 12.1 where the data-management facilities are implemented as a separate layer and the object-management system is built using these facilities. The advantage of this approach is that it allows a commercial database system to be used to provide data management and many current IPSEs use this strategy in their implementation. Relational databases are favoured by some IPSE vendors who have adopted this approach to data management.

An alternative approach to data management is to integrate data-management facilities with the object-management system (discussed below) so that, in essence, the OMS is built directly on top of the host operating system. This sometimes has performance advantages, as the data management can be optimized to the requirements of the OMS. However, it can lead to significantly higher implementation and maintenance costs. If the performance of commercial database systems continues to improve, it may well be the case that the performance advantages gained from this integrated approach become less important.

A futher development in this area that may impact IPSE evolution is the availability of object-oriented databases, which would allow direct implementation of an object-management system in the data-management layer.

12.3.3 The object-management system

The object-management system (OMS) is that part of the IPSE that provides control over the IPSE name space and provides a basis for the provision of configuration control on IPSE objects. Given the existence of an object-management system, the user may simply refer to environment objects using some local name and the OMS handles all of the problems of mapping that name to the unique identifier of the entity. The user should not need to have any knowledge of how the underlying data is structured and, in general, the name space model provided by the OMS is much simpler than the data schema.

In addition, the OMS must provide typing facilities that allow types to be defined, related to other system types and associated with objects managed by the system. These typing facilities are absolutely essential as the type information is used to control tool access to entities and also in the management and control of the activities involving these entities.

It is the object-management system's responsibility to maintain and name the different versions of system entities as they are created. It is generally good practice to support the notion of immortal entities, so that when an object is changed it is never overwritten but a new version of that object is created. Clearly, this normally leads to many thousands of entities being created and the underlying data-management system must be able to support entities that are held on some kind of archival medium, such as optical disk or magnetic tape.

To provide a basis for configuration control where objects exist in a number of different versions (the term 'version' here includes the notion of a variant), the OMS must provide for three basic classes of relationship to be supported:

(1) Object–object relationships where all versions of one object have the same relationship with all versions of another object. An example of such a relationship is the relationship between design descriptions and associated program components. Given that they are updated in step, it is sufficient simply to maintain the relationship between the objects and to compute which versions of each object correspond.

(2) Object–version relationships where all versions of an object have a relationship with a single version of another object. An example of such a relationship is where an object represents a component that is intended for use on a specific operating system. The relationship may be between that object and a version of a library component for that operating system. Another example of such a relationship is where a component makes use of another component but always wishes to use the most up-to-date version of that component. By utilizing sensible defaults, the user of the component need not be informed when new versions of the 'used' component are produced.

(3) Version–version relationships where a version of an object has a relationship with a version of another object. An example of such a relationship is where a component uses another specific component. Given that the combined component works in a predictable way, it is important to ensure that changes to either component do not affect the particular workings of an instantiation.

Some IPSEs include a purpose-built OMS that is tailored to the requirements of the particular system. However, an alternative approach is to factor-out the OMS and data-management facilities and to offer these as a standard basis for constructing a range of IPSEs. In essence, these systems offer a Public Tool Interface (PTI) to which a variety of different tools can be interfaced. There are two important developments in this area in Europe and the USA. These are the PCTE (Portable Common Tool Interface), whose definition was sponsored by the ESPRIT programme, and the CAIS (Common APSE Interface Set), which is tailored to Ada support environments and whose development was sponsored by the US Department of Defense.

PCTE (Gallo *et al.*, 1987) is emerging as a European standard for IPSE developments. In short, PCTE is an interface definition that can be implemented on a range of machines. As well as database facilities, based on an entity–relationship–attribute (ERA) model, it includes primitives for object-management, distribution and user-interface management. Environments based on PCTE can therefore, in principle at least, be ported to any machine supporting that standard. Objects in PCTE may be considered as entities with attributes that participate in relationships, which means that the ERA database may act as a basis for representation of the software process.

PCTE is an interface definition and not an implementation. There are a number of implementations of the PCTE on various computers, although, at the time of writing, these are relatvely immature and in need of improvement.

CAIS (Oberndorf, 1988) is comparable to PCTE in many ways, although the initial version of the system lacks effective support for user-defined typing, transactions, distribution and bit-mapped graphics facilities. All of these are provided in the PCTE. However, a revised version of the CAIS standard is currently available from the US Department of Defense.

12.3.4 IPSE tools

The term 'integrated project support environment' implies that a range of tools is available to support all of the activities that are involved in the software process. In practice, given our current understanding of that process, it is unlikely that such a range of tools will be available. Whilst programming tools such as compilers, debuggers and program analysers are well developed, specialized tools to support activities such as requirements analysis, design transformation and program maintenance are either undeveloped or in a very early stage of development and are unlikely to be included in an IPSE.

Current IPSEs, however, are much more than programming environments and most of them incorporate tools to assist with particular approaches to system design. Such tools might include graphical editors and design checkers where a graphics-based method such as Structured Design is supported (Willis, 1981; Sommerville *et al.*, 1987) or tools to support formal transformations and program proving where a design method based on formal specification is supported.

It is not possible to be definitive about the range of tools that should be provided in an IPSE because so much depends on the application domain, the development method and the approach to software development that is adopted. However, the following classes of tool might be expected to be available on most IPSEs.

(a) Tools to assist with any special-purpose notations used for requirements or functional specification.
(b) Software design support tools such as graphical editing systems. These are comparable with the design tools available in CASE workbenches.
(c) Project management tools—these software tools allow estimates of the time required for a project and the cost of that project to be made. They may also provide facilities for generating management reports on the status of a project at any time.
(d) If proper account is being taken of reliability, tools to gather and analyse system metrics, reliability modelling tools, etc. should be included. Reliability growth modelling and metrics are discussed elsewhere in this handbook in Chapters 6 and 10, respectively.

(e) Data dictionary support. Data dictionaries are particularly valuable in large, long-lifetime projects when used to record details of module interfaces. The availability of such information (given that organizational procedures ensure its use) means that interface integrity can be preserved over many years.

(f) Tools to assist with configuration management. These should include tools for version and release management, change control and system building.

(g) Documentation tools. These allow documentation to be developed on the same machine as the program. This simplifies the task of producing and updating documentation as the system is developed.

(h) An electronic mail system allowing straightforward information exchange between system developers.

(i) Editors and program-preparation systems.

(j) Compilers, link editors, interpreters and other tools associated with programming language translation.

(k) Testing and debugging tools—these might include test drivers, dynamic and static program analysers and test output analysis programs.

(l) Communications software linking the development computer (the host machine) to the computer on which the software is to execute (the target machine).

(m) Target machine simulators used in the development of microprocessor software.

The toolset provided with an IPSE is dependent on the application domain that the IPSE is intended to support and the development paradigm that is used in that domain. It is clear that whilst some facilities such as object management are required by all classes of system, other tools are specific to particular application domains and it is impossible or at least impractical for all tools to be supported in an IPSE.

12.3.5 The IPSE user interface

The IPSE user interface is the means by which users actually carry out productive work and it is now recognized that effective user interfaces have a very significant effect indeed on productivity. The designer of an IPSE interface is faced with some particular problems.

(1) The activities involved in software development are diverse. How can a user interface be produced that integrates the different facilities provided by these tools? For example, can a word-processor and a program debugger effectively share interface concepts?

(2) IPSE users vary tremendously in background, knowledge and experience. They range from project secretaries with no training in software engineering through to project managers who may have little recent technical experience to software engineers who use the system for

several hours every day. These users may have quite different requirements—secretaries may prefer non-technical terminology, managers may only use the IPSE occasionally and so prefer a helpful interface, and software engineers prefer an interface that maximizes their speed of interaction. It is not clear whether a single interface suitable for all of these classes of user can be built.

(3) The entities repesented in an IPSE may be very abstract and it may be difficult to represent these entities in such a way that they may be readily understood. For example, say one entity is composed of twenty others—how might this be displayed on a user's screen?

As well as these particular problems, IPSEs are like all large information-processing systems in that it is difficult to navigate around the system information space. It is the responsibility of the user interface to provide facilities, such as user views and virtual data structures, to support such navigation.

One approach to assisting with the problems of user-interface construction is to adopt a metaphor for interaction (the desktop metaphor is now well known) and to ensure that all tools in the IPSE conform to this metaphor. Such an approach has been adopted in the ECLIPSE IPSE (Reid & Welland, 1986), where the metaphor is a control panel, as is used in other complex hardware systems such as aircraft, power stations, etc. The presumption is that interacting with a complex entity such as an IPSE is analogous to interacting with other complex systems and that if the user is provided with buttons, switches, signs, etc., this provides a consistent means of interacting with the system in general and with specific tools.

It is now clear that effective interfaces can only be derived after much experimentation and we have not yet sufficient experience of IPSE usage to derive general interface guidelines and standards. It is to be expected that this particular area of IPSE development will be volatile, as new research results and user feedback influences the development of IPSE interfaces.

12.4 Ada Support Environments

The Ada programming language was specifically designed for the construction of embedded systems and its main design objectives were to increase the reliability of systems and reduce their overall life-cycle costs. Ada has been adopted as a mandatory standard for defence system implementation in both the US and the UK. It is certain that an increasing number of systems where high reliability is required will be developed using this language. For this reason, it is worth considering the special case of Ada support environments.

When the Ada programming language was under development, the need for an associated support environment was recognized and a number of requirements documents for such an environment were developed. This was probably the first organizational recognition of the importance of environments and the process culminated in the publication of the STONEMAN environment specification for Ada (Buxton, 1980). However, the requirements for an integrated generic support environment and an Ada support environment overlap to such an extent that it is now unlikely that future environments will be built specifically for Ada support. Rather, general-purpose environments will be configured in such a way that they are oriented towards the development of Ada systems.

The Stoneman proposals for an Ada programming environment (APSE) envisage that the APSE should be portable and available on a variety of different machines. To achieve this degree of portability, three levels of program support are required—a kernel environment (KAPSE), a minimal environment (MAPSE) and the full Ada support environment (APSE). The proposed organization of the APSE is shown in Fig. 12.2.

The innermost level of the APSE is the Kernel-APSE, which provides the interface between Ada programs and the underlying operating system. Thus, the KAPSE must include an Ada run-time support system, data management primitives and the interface to peripheral devices such as terminals. In principle, the KAPSE should insulate the remainder of the APSE from the underlying machine. Therefore, to transfer the APSE from machine to machine should simply require a reimplementation of the KAPSE system.

The next level in the APSE is the so-called Minimal-APSE. This is built on top of the KAPSE and should provide facilities for the development of Ada programs. Obviously, the MAPSE must include an Ada compiler, an editor and a loader, but other tools such as static and dynamic program analysers, command interpreters and configuration management systems are also to be provided at this level.

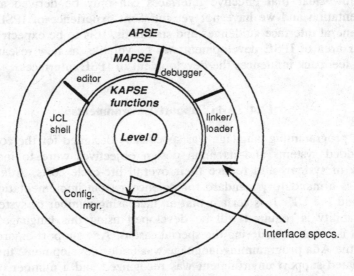

Fig. 12.2. The organization of an APSE.

The top-level APSE was defined in a very general way and, even now, it can be argued that no examples of a *complete* APSE, as anticipated in the Stoneman document, have been developed and put into use. As described in the requirements document, the APSE might provide tools to support all phases of the software life cycle and tools to support particular development methodologies. As well as providing a comprehensive toolkit to support the development of Ada programs, an APSE must also provide data-management facilities for tools to communicate and to allow relationships between objects to be recorded and maintained. The data in the system may be used to produce management reports detailing the current state of a project, project development cost, etc. A more detailed description of an APSE is provided in McDermid and Ripkin (1984).

It was never envisaged that there would be a single definitive APSE for all Ada support. Rather, it was intended that a number of different APSEs would evolve to support different classes of application domain. The Stoneman document was a very general document, which unfortunately included some quite specific requirements. It has not been updated to reflect changes in technology, such as the widespread use of personal workstations, and the general feeling now is that an APSE is simply an IPSE that is configured to support Ada. In fact, careful reading of the Stoneman report reveals that the majority of the Ada support tools are generic rather than specific, so viewing an APSE as a specific IPSE does not conflict with the majority of the requirements in that document.

12.5 CASE Workbenches

Recently, a class of software tool or environment that has gained a great deal of publicity and has been adopted in the DP community is that of CASE workbench systems. The acryonym CASE stands for Computer Aided Software Engineering and this buzzword suggests that these systems are designed to support software-engineering activities. There are many commercial products in this area and the majority of these are concerned with providing support for analysis and design. Other 'workbenches', such as project-management workbenches have also been developed. In a short chapter such as this, it is not possible to discuss these systems in detail and only a very general overview of design workbenches is provided here.

Design workbench systems are intended to support the analysis and design stages of the software process. These systems are oriented towards the support of graphical notations such as used in the various design methods. They are either intended for the support of a specific method, such as Structured Design (Constantine and Yourdon, 1979), or support a range of diagram types that encompasses those used in the most common methods.

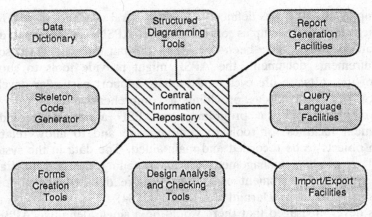

Fig. 12.3. CASE workbench facilities.

Typical components of a CASE workbench (Fig. 12.3) are:

(1) A design editing system that is used to create data-flow diagrams, structure charts, entity-relationship diagrams, etc. The editor is not just a simple drafting tool but is aware of the types of entities in the diagram. It captures information about these entities and saves this information in a central repository (sometimes called an encyclopaedia).

(2) Design analysis and checking facilities that process the design and report on errors and anomalies. As far as possible these are integrated with the editing system so that the user may be informed of errors during diagram creation.

(3) Query language facilities that allow the user to browse the stored information and examine completed designs.

(4) Data dictionary facilities that maintain information about named entities used in a system design.

(5) Report-generation facilities that take information from the central store and automatically generate system documentation.

(6) Forms-generation tools that allow screen and document formats to be specified.

(7) Import/export facilities that allow the interchange of information from the central repository with other development tools.

(8) Some systems support skeleton-code generators that generate code or code segments automatically from the design captured in the central store.

CASE workbench systems, like structured methods, have mostly been used in the development of data-processing systems, but there is no reason why they cannot be used in the development of other classes of system. Chikofsky & Rubenstein (1988) suggest that productivity improvements of up to 40% may be achieved with the use of such systems. They also suggest that, as well as these improvements, the quality of the developed systems is higher with fewer errors and inconsistencies and is more appropriate to the user's needs.

Martin (1988) has identified a number of deficiencies in the current generation of CASE workbenches.

(1) Some design workbenches are not integrated with other document-preparation tools such as word-processors and desktop-publishing systems. Import/export facilities are usually confined to ASCII text.
(2) There is a lack of standardization that makes information interchange across different workbenches difficult or impossible.
(3) They lack facilities that allow a method to be tailored to a particular application or class of application. For example, it is not usually possible for users to override a built-in rule and replace it with their own.
(4) The quality of the hard-copy documentation that is produced is often low. Martin observes that simply producing copies of screens is not good enough and that the requirements for paper documentation are distinct from those for screen documentation.
(5) The diagramming facilities can be slow to use, so that even a moderately complex diagram can take several hours to input and arrange. He suggests that there is a need for automated diagramming and diagram arrangement given a textual input.

This is a general list and, as systems are developed, it is undoubtedly the case that many of these deficiencies will be rectified.

A more serious omission, from the point of view of large-scale software engineering is the lack of support for configuration management provided by these systems. Large software systems are in use for many years and, in that time, are subject to many changes and exist in many versions. The argument put forward is that CASE workbenches may be integrated with existing configuration-management systems, although this clearly depends on compatible data organizations.

There is a lack of data standards, which makes it difficult or impossible to transfer information in the central repository to other workbench systems. This means that users may be faced with the prospect of maintaining obsolete CASE workbenches and their supporting computers for many years in order to maintain existing systems. This problem has not yet manifested itself because of the relative newness of these systems, but is likely to arise as new, second-generation CASE products come onto the market.

Although sometimes hyped as such, current CASE workbenches are not integrated project support environments in the sense discussed here. They do not support all project activities nor do they collect together all process documents in one repository. They are undoubtedly useful tools but they should be viewed as a component of a software-engineering environment rather than environments in their own right. However, as these systems are developed they will acquire more and more IPSE capabilities and the line between IPSEs and CASE workbenches is likely to become increasingly blurred.

A trend that appears to be emerging in some of the more advanced workbench systems is the notion of modelling a business using the workbench and then using this model to generate appropriate systems. Rather than follow the familiar software process of requirements, design, implementation, etc., this approach embodies business constraints and allows prototypes and upgrades to systems to be generated. When maintenance is required, a new system is generated from modifications made to high-level information. Lower-level code is not modified. This is an interesting approach that may well be effective for small-scale systems. It is not clear at the moment whether it can be applied outside the business-systems domain.

12.6 Introducing an IPSE

At the time of writing, IPSE system products have only been available for a short time and there is little reported experience on the organizational difficulties posed by such systems or of IPSE costs and cost savings. However, it is reasonable to postulate that moving software development to an IPSE will involve considerable disruption and costs and it is useful to try to anticipate what these might be. Some of these difficulties are clearly comparable with those experienced when changing operating systems and database systems, so we can learn from these experiences when introducing IPSEs.

The first obvious difficulty that is likely to arise is user resistance. With very few exceptions, humans are innately conservative and tend to resist new developments unles they have very obvious advantages. The present generation of IPSEs have clear advantages for software management as they provide more control over the software process, but the advantages for the individual software developer are less clear. Indeed, it can be argued that IPSEs are prescriptive and constrain the creativity of the individual engineer. It is suggested, pessimistically, that they do not obviously enhance his or her working environment but deskill the process of software engineering and hence reduce the overall satisfaction to be gained from software development.

This author does not accept this argument in general, although it may well be the case that some poorly designed IPSEs have this effect. A properly designed IPSE provides tools that take over or assist with some of the tedious chores that are inherent in software development, thus leaving individual engineers more time for the creative and fulfilling parts of their job.

A further reason for user resistance is that some engineers may feel that the new developments are somehow difficult to understand. This is likely to be a particular problem with staff who have learned by experience and have little or no formal training in computer science or software engineering. Furthermore, the pace of change in software development has been such that they may have just adapted to working with some new operating system and they may be reluctant to spend time learning another new system.

Some management, too, may be resistant to introducing an IPSE into a known development process. The reason for this is that much of the activity of software management is fundamentally concerned with cost control and that the cost advantages of introducing an IPSE are unquantifiable. Thus, they may argue that using an IPSE increases the risk associated with a project and, indeed, it is unlikely that there will be development cost advantages for IPSE pioneers.

Although we cannot be sure, it may well be the case that the use of an IPSE will increase the development costs for some projects. However, if cost distribution over the whole system life cycle is considered, the cost savings from an IPSE may be most apparent during system maintenance. Indeed, an IPSE may be the only way of ensuring that the system is maintainable! However, quantifying such long-term cost benefits is even more difficult than quantifying the effect of an IPSE on development costs, so the introduction of an IPSE on this basis must be largely an act of informed judgement rather than objective analysis.

Apart from user resistance, the other major problem of moving to an IPSE is the cost of converting existing development projects to work in the IPSE context. It may not be possible to justify the costs of the IPSE unless it is generally used, yet the costs and upheaval associated with converting to this development may be very great indeed. The reason for this is that the IPSE records and stores a great deal of project information that might be collected automatically but which, without an IPSE, may only exist on paper or in people's heads. For projects that are in progress, this must be collected, encoded and input to the IPSE—a very expensive process indeed.

These difficulties mean that management must adopt a sensitive approach when introducing an IPSE and must make realistic estimates of the start-up costs of moving to such an environment. Attempts to impose an IPSE without an understanding of the concerns of the software developer will simply lead to an exodus of the workforce, and attempting to introduce an IPSE on the cheap will simply lead to disgruntled users and financial problems. The cost advantages of an IPSE ensue in the long term rather than the short term and this must be understood by all levels of company management.

It is important that an adequate budget is available for training and that the move to IPSE-based development is incremental. Rather than move all projects to an IPSE at one time, the IPSE should be introduced in conjunction with existing support systems and, as new projects are started, they should make use of IPSE support. As the cost advantages of the IPSE become quantifiable, the costs of converting existing project work to an IPSE-based development may be assessed and a decision made on whether this conversion should be made or whether parallel development support should continue until project completion.

A related problem to that of initially moving to IPSE-based development is the problem of moving development from one IPSE to another. It is quite clear that this will be necessary in many organizations for the following reasons.

(1) The first available IPSEs have limited functionality and will be super-
    seded by improved versions relatively quickly.
(2) Mistakes will be made in choosing an IPSE product and incorporated
    tools and these may not become apparent until that product is put into
    use.
(3) External software purchasers may make it a condition of contract that a
    particular IPSE system is used for software development. This is most
    likely if an IPSE standard emerges and government agencies insist on the
    use of this standard as part of their terms of contract.

Clearly, the problems of moving from one IPSE to another are akin to those
of moving to IPSE-based development, but the conversion costs may be even
greater. Different object relationships may be supported and these may have
to be derived from existing relationships. Users may have learned a rich set of
facilities and may have to repeat this process for a new IPSE. From cost
studies of moving from one database management system to another, it is
reasonable to postulate that moving from one IPSE to another is a slow and
expensive process that may last three or four years.

The inevitability of multiple-IPSE support implies that the use of agreed or
de facto standards should be a major factor in choosing an IPSE as these may
allow later conversion without major disruption. On the other hand, we know
from experience that computing standards are rarely technically innovative and
superior functionality may be offered by non-standard IPSEs.

12.7 Environments and Reliability Management

From the point of view of reliability management, support environments must
be considered in the context of their relationship to the software process and
the importance of that process in achieving system reliability. In this book
there is an assumption that process reliability is critical if product reliability is
to be achieved and the importance of environments comes in helping to ensure
the reliability of the software process.

At the time of writing, the activity of ensuring process reliability is one of
quality assurance and it relies on a great deal of expensive, tedious,
time-consuming checking that standards have been followed, that appropriate
documentation has been produced, that proper records have been kept, and so
on. Fortunately, many of these QA activities are exactly those activities that
are readily supported in an IPSE, so the adoption of a support environment
will reduce the costs of process reliability and allow more effective, less
obtrusive checks and record keeping to be carried out.

Consider how the following QA activities that affect process reliability are
simplified by the existence of an IPSE with a powerful OMS and supporting
toolset.

(1) *Adherence to standards.* Many standards such as language-use standards can be embedded in the support tools used to produce the software. Thus, the standards-checking activity is greatly simplified as those standards that are simply syntactic (and often the most tedious to observe) are automatically enforced. Checking becomes unnecessary if it is impossible to produce a system that does not conform to the standard.

(2) *Status reporting.* The status of all system documents can be recorded in the environment database and inbuilt report-generation tools used to produce status reports as required. Thus, if a document has not been 'signed off', this can be made apparent by the reporting tools.

(3) *Change control.* Change control requests can be submitted on electronic forms, distributed electronically to the appropriate technical and managerial staff and maintained along with the software module with which they are associated. Reports on changes that are outstanding can easily be produced.

It is clear that the use of environments will simplify the problem on ensuring process reliability and there are undoubtedly many other examples apart from those above where automated tool support will be available. However, most existing environments do not appear to have considered the particular problems of supporting quality assurance and it may be some time before effective QA tools are integrated with these environment products.

Given the need for process reliability, perhaps the most important IPSE facilities are those facilities that are provided to define and integrate software process activities. An IPSE should require a process model to be set up and adherence to this model can then be monitored by the support environment. At the time of writing, some IPSEs, such as GENOS and, to a lesser extent, ISTAR, provide process-modelling and monitoring capabilities.

However, the notion of process modelling is not supported in either of the proposed Public Tool Interface standards (PCTE and CAIS) and this author is not aware of any proposals to add these capabilities to the standards. Thus, such capabilities will necessarily be IPSE-specific and this may cause particular problems in environments, such as systems houses, where multiple IPSEs are used depending on client requirements and when a decision is made to migrate from one IPSE to another.

Where process reliability is critical, it is recommended that the use of an IPSE is likely to have immediate benefit in supporting quality assurance and should be considered for adoption by reliability management.

12.8 Summary

This chapter has presented an overview of integrated project support environments. It has suggested that the use of such environments to support software development can lead to increased product reliability, partly because automation reduces the scope for programmer error and partly because they offer process support and thus help ensure the reliability of the process. The main points made in the chapter are:

- Software engineering environments should incorporate tools to support all aspects of software development. Examples of such tools are design editing systems, various program and text editors, document preparation tools, electronic mail and language-processing systems, configuration management and project management tools.
- Tool interworking is supported because all information is maintained in an object-management system that is accessible to all tools.
- PCTE is emerging as a European standard for a public tool interface. CAIS is a comparable US development.
- The object management system provides facilities to support configuration management. For large systems, these are probably the critically important IPSE facilities.
- Integration should not simply be at the tool level. The IPSE user interface should also be integrated so that tools present a consistent interface to users. Furthermore, activity integration may also be supported where knowledge of the software process is embedded in the IPSE.
- Ada support environments can be built by configuring a general-purpose IPSE.
- CASE workbenches are useful programming tools but, in themselves, they are not integrated project support environments.
- The costs of introducing an IPSE are high but long-term benefits ensue from moving to IPSE support.
- IPSEs are useful for reliability management because they help define, control and manage the quality of the software process. IPSEs that incorporate process-modelling facilities and support are of particular value in ensuring a reliable process.

12.9 Further Reading

The STARTS Guide (2nd edition), (National Computing Centre, 1987). This guide started out as a handbook of tools available to support real-time systems development but has now broadened and expanded to describe general support for software engineering. It contains useful chapters on IPSE facilities as well as details of IPSE products available at the time the handbook was prepared. These are now somewhat outdated but will be updated in a new edition.

Howden, W. E. (1982). Contemporary software development environments. *Commun. ACM*, **25**(5), 318–29. Although some of the details in this paper are somewhat out of data, this survey of the principles underlying environments remains a good starting point for reading in this area.

IEEE Software and IEEE Computer, November 1987. These two readable journals combined to make a joint presentation on software development environments. As is common in US journals, there is little emphasis given to work going on outside North America. In essence then, the articles summarize the state of US work in this area, which has a rather different orientation from European work.

Brereton, P. (ed.) (1988). *Software Engineering Environments*. Ellis Horwood, Chichester. The proceedings of a conference on environments provides a picture of work in this area that is going on in the UK and in Europe.

IEEE Transactions on Software Engineering, **SE-14**(6), June 1988. This special issue is concerned with environment architectures and presents some interesting articles discussing research in this area. It also contains one of the few published articles on the CAIS interface.

ACM Sigsoft, Software Engineering Notes, Volume **13**(5), November 1988. The proceedings of a US conference on practical software development environments that presents recent work in the area. Many of the papers are concerned with process modelling and reflect the growing research interest in this aspect of environments.

Appendix A
Software Reliability Growth Models

Bev Littlewood

A.1 Jelinski–Moranda (JM) Model 401
A.2 Bayesian Jelinski–Moranda (BJM) Model 403
A.3 Littlewood (L) Model 404
A.4 Littlewood–Verrall (LV) Model. 405
A.5 Duane (D) Model 406
A.6 Goel–Okumoto (GO) Model 407
A.7 Littlewood Nonhomogeneous Poisson Process (LNHPP)
Model 407
A.8 Musa–Okumoto (MO) Model 407
A.9 The u-Plot Method for Detecting Consistent Bias 408
A.10 The Prequential Likelihood Ratio for Detecting Noise and
Bias 409

A.1 Jelinski–Moranda (JM) Model

This model (Jelinski & Moranda, 1972) is justifiably credited with being the first reliability growth model specifically created for software. The Musa model (Musa, 1975) introduces extra refinements, and has been fairly widely used, but its foundations are essentially identical to JM.

The JM model assumes that T_1, $T_2, \ldots$, are independent random variables with exponential probability density functions

$$p(t_i \mid \lambda_i) = \lambda_i e^{-\lambda_i t_i} \qquad t_i > 0 \tag{A.1}$$

where

$$\lambda_i = (N - i + 1)\phi \tag{A.2}$$

The rationale for the model is as follows. When our observation of the reliability growth (debugging) begins, the program contains N faults. Removal of a fault occurs whenever a failure occurs, and at each such event the rate of occurrence of failures is reduced by an amount ϕ. Thus, ϕ can be taken to represent the size of a fault.

Another way to consider the model is via competing risks. All faults in a program can be considered to be waiting for discovery. Their discoveries will occur at times $X_1, X_2, \ldots, X_n, \ldots$ (for some arbitrary labelling of the faults) measured from the beginning of debugging. It is assumed that all faults are similar, so the X_i can be treated as identically distributed. It is further assumed (quite reasonably) that the X_i are independent and that the common distribution is

$$p(x_i) = \phi e^{-\phi x_i} \qquad x_i > 0 \tag{A.3}$$

The observed stochastic process is thus that process consisting of the first, second, third, . . . events (fault discoveries). The times of these events are the order statistics $X_{(1)}, X_{(2)}, X_{(3)}, \ldots$. The inter-event times are the spacings between the order statistics

$$T_i = X_{(i)} - X_{(i-1)} \tag{A.4}$$

for $i = 2, 3, \ldots$ with $T_1 = X_{(1)}$. It is easy to show that this formulation via order statistics agrees with eqns (A.1) and (A.2).

The unknown parameters of the model, N and ϕ, are estimated by maximum likelihood. This forms step (ii) of the prediction system (Chapter 6, Section 6.3). Predictions are made (step (iii)) by the 'plug-in' rule: substitution of these maximum-likelihood estimates into the appropriate model expressions. Thus, for example, when $t_1, t_2, \ldots, t_{i-1}$ are the observed data, the predicted (current) reliability is

$$\bar{R}_i(t) = e^{-(\hat{N}-i+1)\hat{\phi}t} \tag{A.5}$$

which is an estimate of $R_i(t) \equiv P(T_i < t)$.

The most serious criticism of this model is that it assumes the debugging process is purely deterministic and that all faults contribute equally to the unreliability of a program. This seems to be very implausible, and recent empirical studies (Adams, 1984; Nagel & Skrivan, 1981) suggest that in reality the sizes of ϕs corresponding to different faults will differ by orders of magnitude. If this is the case, we would expect that the earlier bugs to be encountered would be larger, on average, than the later ones. This would imply, when taken with the other assumptions of the model, that earlier fixes would tend to improve the reliability of the program more than later ones. This does seem to accord with practical experience in which bugs that are discovered late in the life of a system are ones associated with a mode of use that is infrequently encountered. If we were incorrectly to use this model in a context where the ϕs really are very variable, it can be shown that there will be a tendency to obtain reliability predictions that are too optimistic. Not only that, the estimate of N will generally be too low and will increase as the sample size increases: essentially the model will persistently suggest that only a few bugs remain. These effects have been observed in several real data sets, and they suggest that the assumption of equal bug rates is rarely satisfied.

A.2 Bayesian Jelinski–Moranda (BJM) Model

There has been considerable research into properties of the ML parameter estimates of JM (Joe & Reid, 1985). This was motivated by the apparently poor predictions of the model in many cases, and the suspicion that this poor predictive capability might be the fault of steps (ii) and (iii), rather than step (i), of the prediction system.

BJM (Littlewood & Sofer, 1987) is an attempt to remove the problems of using ML and a plug-in rule for (ii) and (iii) by using a proper Bayesian predictive set-up. For reasons of mathematical tractability, BJM is a slightly different model from JM, being parametrized as (λ, ϕ) with $\lambda \equiv N\phi$. Here λ can be regarded as the initial rate of occurrence of failures, and ϕ the improvement resulting from a fix. The modelling difference is that λ is not constrained to be an integer multiple of ϕ. It is unlikely that this slight difference in the underlying models will be sufficient to account for significant differences in reliability predictions.

The Bayesian analysis proceeds in the usual way. We start with a prior distribution for (λ, ϕ): this represents the initial beliefs of the experimenter about the magnitudes of the model parameters before they have seen any failures of the program under study. In Littlewood & Sofer (1987) this is taken to be of independent gamma type; here we shall take the 'ignorance prior' member of this gamma family, which is intended to represent the (likely) absence of an opinion about these magnitudes on the part of the experimenter. Given data $t_1, \ldots, t_{i-1}$, the posterior distribution

$$p(\lambda, \phi \mid t_1, \ldots, t_{i-1}) \tag{A.6}$$

can be computed in the usual way to form step (ii) of the prediction system. This represents the experimenter's new beliefs about the magnitudes of the parameters of the model after the failure data $t_1, \ldots, t_{i-1}$ has been seen. Bayesian predictive distributions are used for step (iii) (Aitchison & Dunsmore, 1975) so that, for example, the current reliability function is

$$\bar{R}_i(t) = \iint R_i(t \mid \lambda, \phi) p(\lambda, \phi \mid t_1, \ldots, t_{i-1}) \, d\lambda \, d\phi \tag{A.7}$$

where the conditional reliability is

$$R_i(t \mid \lambda, \phi) = e^{-(\lambda - [i-1]\phi)t} \tag{A.8}$$

Our experience with this prediction system is that it generally only offers marginally improved predictions compared with JM itself. As was stated in the previous section, JM itself usually underestimates the number of remaining bugs; occasionally it does this catastrophically by suggesting that there are *no* bugs left! In such extreme cases, when JM is telling us that there will be no more failures and the program is perfectly reliable, BJM will do better. In fact, a feature of this Bayesian approach is that we can estimate the chance that the last bug has been removed at any stage. Apart from these cases where JM is predicting that a failure-free program has been achieved, BJM rarely appears to offer significant improvement over JM: in fact the actual reliability predictions from the two are usually very close. This would suggest that the *model* itself, stage (i) of the prediction system, is at fault, rather than merely the method of statistical analysis.

A.3   Littlewood (L) Model

This model (Littlewood, 1981) is an attempt to answer the criticisms of JM/BJM whilst retaining the finite fault-count, order statistic approach. The major drawback of JM/BJM is that it treats debugging as a deterministic process: each fix is effective with certainty and all fixes have the same effect on the reliability. In L, it is assumed that faults contribute different amounts to the unreliability of the software. Thus, although it is still assumed that fixes are effective with certainty, the sequence of (improving) failure rates forms a stochastic process, since the magnitude of each improvement is unpredictable. There will be a *tendency* for the earlier changes in the rate of occurrence of failures to be larger than the later ones, but this is not a deterministic process.

In detail, the model assumes, as before

$$p(t_i \mid \Lambda_i = \lambda_i) = \lambda_i e^{-\lambda_i t_i} \tag{A.9}$$

where the random variables $\{\Lambda_i\}$ represent the successive ROCOFs arising from the gradual elimination of faults. Here

$$\Lambda_i = \Phi_1 + \Phi_2 + \cdots + \Phi_{N-i+1} \tag{A.10}$$

where N is the initial number of faults and Φ_j represents the (random variable) rate associated with fault j (in arbitrary labelling).

The initial rates $\Phi_1, \ldots, \Phi_N$ are assumed to be independent, identically distributed gamma (α, β) random variables. When the program has executed for a total time τ, use of Bayes theorem shows that the *remaining* rates are independent identically distributed gamma $(\alpha, \beta + \tau)$ random variables. This reflects our intuitive belief that the early fixes will tend to be associated with faults having larger rates: the initial average fault size (i.e. rate) is α/β, which becomes $\alpha/(\beta + \tau)$ for the faults remaining at time τ. We can say that as the program executes for longer it more quickly depletes the program of larger faults than smaller ones.

As was the case for JM, this model can be interpreted via order statistics. If we let X_i represent the time to detect fault i (in our arbitrary labelling), then

$$p(x_i \mid \Phi_i = \phi_i) = \phi_i e^{-\phi_i x_i} \qquad (x_i > 0) \tag{A.11}$$

and Φ_i is a gamma (α, β) variate. Thus unconditionally the pdf of X_i is Pareto:

$$p(x_i) = \frac{\alpha \beta^\alpha}{(\beta + x_i)^{\alpha+1}} \qquad (x_i > 0) \tag{A.12}$$

by mixing eqn (A.11) over the gamma distribution of Φ_i. This can be thought of as the distribution of the time needed to uncover a randomly selected bug (i.e. one whose rate is unknown). The observed stochastic process of inter-failure times $T_1, T_2, \ldots$ is then the process of *spacings*

$$T_i = X_{(i)} - X_{(i-1)} \quad (i = 2, 3, \ldots)$$

$$T_1 = X_{(1)}$$

(A.13)

of the order statistics of the independent, identically distributed Pareto Xs.

Estimation of the unknown parameter is by ML and prediction by substituting these into appropriate model expressions via the 'plug-in' rule. The estimated current reliability, based on data $t_1, t_2, \ldots, t_{i-1}$, is then

$$\tilde{R}_i(t) = \left(\frac{\hat{\beta} + t}{\hat{\beta} + \tau + t} \right)^{(\hat{N}-i+1)\hat{\alpha}}$$

(A.14)

where

$$\tau = \sum_{j=1}^{i-1} t_j$$

(A.15)

is total elapsed time.

A proper Bayesian analysis of this model seems difficult, largely because of the role played by β in the likelihood function. We have considered briefly elsewhere (Abdel-Ghaly, 1986) an *ad hoc* approach. This begins by assuming initially that β is known, whereupon it is possible to perform a conventional Bayesian analysis of the unknown (λ, ϕ), where $\lambda = N\alpha$. This uses independent gamma priors and the posterior analysis can be conducted analytically. For any given β it is then possible to form the usual predictive distributions. Finally, an estimator of β is used based on a maximum likelihood (ML) approach. Although it would be preferable to have a complete Bayesian analysis of any model, it is likely that, for fairly large sample sizes, the ML and Bayes predictors are close.

A.4 Littlewood–Verrall (LV) Model

This model (Littlewood & Verrall, 1973) again treats the successive rates of occurrence of failures, as fixes take place, as random variables. As in JM and BJM, it assumes

$$p(t_i \mid \Lambda_i = \lambda_i) = \lambda_i e^{-\lambda_i t_i} \quad (t_i > 0)$$

(A.16)

The sequence of rates Λ_i is treated as a sequence of independent *stochastically decreasing* random variables. This reflects the likelihood, but not certainty, that a fix will be effective. It is assumed that

$$p(\lambda_i) = \frac{[\psi(i)]^\alpha \lambda_i^{\alpha-1} e^{-\psi(i)\lambda_i}}{\Gamma(\alpha)}$$

(A.17)

a gamma distribution with parameters α, $\psi(i)$.

The function $\psi(i)$ determines the reliability growth. If, as is usually the case, $\psi(i)$ is an increasing function of i, it is easy to show that $\{\Lambda_i\}$ forms a stochastically decreasing sequence. Notice how this contrasts with the JM/BJM case where fixes are *certain* (and of equal magnitude). Even in the L model, it is assumed that a fix will improve the reliability, although the magnitude of the improvement is uncertain and depends on the rate of the bug that has been removed. In the LV model, the rate of occurrence of failures is itself modelled directly, rather than via the individual bug rates. Treating this as a random sequence means that a fix *may make the program less reliable,* and even if an improvement takes place it is of uncertain magnitude. Of course, the way in which the model represents this possibility of fallible fixes is quite crude. The difficulty here is that we know so little about the nature of fault-fixing and, in particular, how the bugs that are introduced in this way differ from 'ordinary' bugs that are present from the inception of the program.

The choice of parametric family for $\psi(i)$ is under the control of the user. Here we shall take

$$\psi(i) = \psi(i, \beta) = \beta_1 + \beta_2 i \tag{A.18}$$

Predictions are made by ML estimation of the unknown parameters α, β_1, β_2 and use of the 'plug-in' rule. Thus, the estimate of the current reliability function after seeing inter-failure times $t_1, t_2, \ldots, t_{i-1}$ is

$$\bar{R}_i(t) = \left(\frac{\psi(i, \hat{\beta})}{t + \psi(i, \hat{\beta})} \right)^{\hat{\alpha}} \tag{A.19}$$

where α, β are the ML estimates of the parameters.

A.5 Duane (D) Model

The Duane model originated in hardware reliability studies. Duane (1964) claimed to have observed in several disparate applications that the reliability growth in hardware systems showed the ROCOF having a power-law form in operating time. Crow (1977) took this observation and added the assumption that the failure process was a nonhomogeneous Poisson process (NHPP) with rate

$$kbt^{b-1} \qquad (k, b, t > 0) \tag{A.20}$$

There is a sense in which an NHPP is inappropriate for software reliability growth. We know that it is the fixes that change the reliability, and these occur at a finite number of known times. The true rate presumably changes discontinuously at these fixes, whereas the NHPP rate changes continuously. However, it is known (Miller, 1986) that for a single realization it is not possible to distinguish between an order statistic model and an NHPP with appropriate rate.

Prediction from this model involves ML estimation and the 'plug-in' rule.

A.6 Goel–Okumoto (GO) Model

It is easy to show (Miller, 1986) that if we treat the parameter N in the JM model as a Poisson random variable with mean m, the unconditional process is exactly an NHPP with rate function

$$m\phi e^{-\phi t} \tag{A.21}$$

Presumably such a mixture over a distribution for N only makes sense to a subjective Bayesian, for which this distribution could be taken to represent 'his' uncertainty about N.

Prediction for this model is, again, via ML estimation and the 'plug-in' rule. Details can be found elsewhere (Goel & Okumoto, 1979).

Miller (1986), in an interesting paper, shows that this NHPP and the JM model are indistinguishable on the basis of a single realization of the stochastic process, $t_1, t_2, \ldots$. He notes, however, that inferences for the two would differ, since they have different likelihood functions. This implies that *predictions* based on ML inference and the 'plug-in' rule would be different.

This is a very curious situation. We have two different prediction systems, giving different predictions, but based upon *models* that are indistinguishable on the basis of the data.

A.7 Littlewood Nonhomogeneous Poisson Process (LNHPP) Model

This model is an NHPP with rate function

$$\frac{m\alpha\beta^\alpha}{(\beta + t)^{\alpha+1}} \tag{A.22}$$

Again this can be interpreted as the Littlewood model mixed over a Poisson distributed N variable. Prediction is via ML estimation and the 'plug-in' rule. Similar indistinguishability conditions exist between L and LNHPP as were considered earlier, but again the detailed predictions would differ.

A.8 Musa–Okumoto (MO) Model

This is another nonhomogeneous Poisson process with rate $\zeta/(\beta + t)$. Its authors claim that this rate takes account of the tendency for the larger rate faults to be found earlier; specifically that the successive changes in the rate of the process decrease exponentially. Of course, such statements are really only meaningful in an average sense: like all NHPPs this process exhibits *continuous* change in its rate. The actual differences in the instantaneous rate at the successive times of failures will fluctuate randomly with a decreasing trend.

Prediction is, once again, by substitution of the maximum likelihood estimates of ζ, β into appropriate expressions obtained from the model.

A.9   The u-Plot Method for Detecting Consistent Bias

We shall concentrate, for convenience, upon the simplest prediction of all: that concerning current reliability. Most techniques for the analysis of predictive accuracy can be adapted easily to some problems of longer-term prediction, but there are also novel difficulties arising from these problems.

Having observed $t_1, t_2, \ldots, t_{i-1}$ we want to predict the random variable T_i. More precisely, we want a good estimate of

$$F_i(t) = P(T_i < t) \tag{A.23}$$

or, equivalently, of the reliability function

$$R_i(t) = 1 - F_i(t) \tag{A.24}$$

From one of the prediction systems described earlier we can calculate a predictor $\tilde{F}_i(t)$. A user is interested in the 'closeness' of $\tilde{F}_i(t)$ to the unknown true $F_i(t)$. In fact, the user may be only interested in summary statistics such as mean (or median) time to failure, ROCOF, etc. However, the quality of these summarized predictions will depend upon the quality of $\tilde{F}_i(t)$, so we shall concentrate on the latter.

Clearly, the difficulty of analysing the closeness of $\tilde{F}_i(t)$ to $F_i(t)$ arises from our never knowing, even at a later stage, the true $F_i(t)$. If this were available (for example, if we have simulated the reliability growth data from a sequence of known distributions), it would be possible to use measures of closeness based upon entropy and information, or distance measures such as those due to Kolmogorov or Cramer–von Mises.

In fact, the only information we shall obtain will be a single realization of the random variable T_i when the software next fails. That is, after making the prediction $\tilde{F}_i(t)$ based upon $t_1, t_2, \ldots, t_{i-1}$, we shall eventually observe t_i, which is a sample of size one from the true distribution $F_i(t)$. We must base all our analysis of the quality of the predictions upon these pairs $\{\tilde{F}_i(t), t_i\}$.

Our method will be an emulation of how a user would informally respond to a sequence of predictions and outcomes. The user would inspect the pairs $\{\tilde{F}_i(t), t_i\}$ to see whether there is any evidence to suggest that the t_i are not realizations of random variables from the $F_i(t)$. If such evidence were found, it would suggest that there are significant differences between $\tilde{F}_i(t)$ and $F_i(t)$, i.e. that the predictions are not in accord with actual behaviour.

Consider the following sequence of transformations:

$$u_i = \tilde{F}_i(t_i) \tag{A.25}$$

Each is a probability integral transform of the observed t_i, using the previously calculated predictor $\tilde{F}_i$ based upon $t_1, t_2, \ldots, t_{i-1}$. Now, if each $\tilde{F}_i$ were identical to the true F_i, it is easy to see that the u_i would be realizations of independent uniform $U(0, 1)$ random variables. Consequently, we can reduce the problem of examining the closeness of $\tilde{F}_i$ to F_i (for some range of values of i) to the question of whether the sequence $\{u_i\}$ 'looks like' a random sample from $U(0, 1)$.

We consider now one way in which the $\{u_i\}$ sequence can be examined. Since the u_i should look like a random sample from $U(0, 1)$ if the prediction system is working well, the first thing to examine is whether they appear uniformly distributed. We do this by plotting the sample cumulant distribution function (cdf) of the u_i and comparing it with the cdf of $U(0, 1)$, which is the line of unit slope through the origin. The 'distance' between them can be summarized in various ways. We shall use the Kolmogorov distance, which is the maximum absolute vertical difference.

In Fig. 6.7 are shown the u-plots for LV, JM and LNHPP predictions for the data of Table 6.1. The predictions here are $\tilde{F}_{36}(t)$ through $\tilde{F}_{135}(t)$. The Kolmogorov distances for the u-plots are 0·187 (JM) and 0·144 (LV). In tables of the Kolmogorov distribution the JM result is significant at the 1% level, LV only at the 5% level. That is, there is very strong evidence to suggest that the u_i from the JM predictions are *not* uniformly distributed. There is also evidence, less strong, that the LV predictions give non-uniform u_i. The Kolmogorov distance for the u-plot of LNHPP predictions is 0·081, which is not statistically significant. That is, there is no evidence on the basis of this analysis that the LNHPP predictions give non-uniform u_i.

From this analysis it appears that JM is significantly worse than LV, but that neither is performing well on this data. In fact, the detailed plots tell us more than this. The JM plot is everywhere above the line of unit slope (the $U(0, 1)$ cdf); the LV plot almost everywhere below it. This means that the u_i from JM tend to be too small and those from LV too large. But u_i represents the predicted probability that T_i will be less than t_i, so consistently too small u_i suggest that the predictions are underestimating the chance of small ts. That is, the JM plot tells us that these predictions are too optimistic. A similar argument suggests that the LV predictions are too pessimistic (although to a less pronounced degree).

There is evidence from this simple analysis, then, that the truth might lie somewhere between the predictions from JM and LV, but probably closer to LV. In particular, the true median plot probably lies between the JM and LV plots of Fig. 6.6 and the Kolmogorov distance of 0·081 for LNHPP indicates that it is closer to the truth than either of JM or LV for this data source.

A.10 The Prequential Likelihood Ratio for Detecting Noise and Bias

Before tackling the prediction problem directly, it is instructive to consider the estimation problem in classical statistics. There we have a random sample (independent, *identically distributed* random variables) from a population with an unknown parameter, θ. If we assume, for simplicity, that θ is scalar, it is usual to seek an estimator for θ, say $\tilde{\theta}$, that has small *mean square error*:

$$\text{mse}(\theta) = E\{(\tilde{\theta} - \theta)^2\}$$
$$= \text{Var}(\tilde{\theta}) + (\text{bias } \tilde{\theta})^2 \tag{A.26}$$

There is thus a trade-off between the variance of the estimator and its bias. It is not obvious, without adopting extra criteria, how one would choose among estimators with the same mean square error but different variances and biases.

In our prediction problem the situation is much more complicated: we wish at each stage to estimate a function, $F_i(t)$, not merely a scalar; and the context is non-stationary since the $F_i(t)$ are changing with i.

However, the analogy with the classical case has some value. We can think of the u-plot as similar to an investigation of bias. Indeed, it is easy to show that, if $E\{\tilde{F}_i(t)\} = F_i(t)$ for all i, the expected value of the u-plot is the line of unit slope. Thus a systematic deviation between $E\{\tilde{F}_i(t)\}$ and $F_i(t)$ will be detected by the u-plot.

The fact that we are making a sequence of predictions in a non-stationary context complicates matters. Thus, a prediction system could be biased in one direction for early predictions and in the other direction for later predictions (and, of course, more complicated deviations from reality are possible). Simple ways of detecting this kind of non-stationarity of bias are described elsewhere (Abdel-Ghaly et al., 1986).

The question now arises as to whether it is possible not only to detect bias in predictions, but also to detect 'noisiness'.

The median plot of Fig. 6.6, for example, shows JM to be more variable than LV. This suggests that the $\{\tilde{F}_i(t)\}$ sequence for JM is more variable than that for LV. The important question is whether this extra variability of JM is an accurate reflection of what happens to the true $\{F_i(t)\}$. Is $\{\tilde{F}_i(t)\}$ fluctuating rapidly in order to track the truly fluctuating $\{F_i(t)\}$, or is it exhibiting random sampling fluctuations about a slowly changing $\{F_i(t)\}$ sequence?

If we had the true $\{F_i(t)\}$ sequence available, it would be relatively easy to obtain measures akin to variance. We could, for example, average the Cramer–von Mises distances between $\tilde{F}_i(t)$ and $F_i(t)$ over some range of i. Unfortunately, the $\{F_i(t)\}$ sequence is not known, and we have been unsuccessful in our attempts to obtain good measures of the variability between $\{\tilde{F}_i(t)\}$ and $\{F_i(t)\}$. It is possible to obtain simple measures of the actual variability of predictions (Abdel-Ghaly et al., 1986), but these do not distinguish between warranted and unwarranted variation. This difficulty leads us to consider the prequential likelihood function and, in particular, the *prequential likelihood ratio* (PLR). We shall use PLR as an investigative tool to decide on the relative plausibility of the predictions emanating from two models.

The PL is defined as follows. The predictive distribution $\tilde{F}_i(t)$ for T_i based on $t_1, t_2, \ldots, t_{i-1}$ will be assumed to have a probability density function (pdf) $\tilde{f}_i(t) = \tilde{F}'_i(t)$. For predictions of $T_{j+1}, T_{j+2}, \ldots, T_{j+n}$, the *prequential likelihood* is

$$\mathrm{PL}_n = \prod_{i=j+1}^{j+n} \tilde{f}_i(t_i) \qquad (\text{A.27})$$

A comparison of two prediction systems, A and B, can be made via their

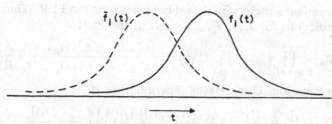

Fig. A.1. The predictor pdf, $\tilde{f}_i(t)$, is here in error since it does not coincide with the true pdf, $f_i(t)$.

prequential likelihood ratio

$$\text{PLR}_n = \frac{\displaystyle\prod_{i=j+1}^{j+n} \tilde{f}_i^A(t_i)}{\displaystyle\prod_{i=j+1}^{j+n} \tilde{f}_i^B(t_i)} \tag{A.28}$$

It can be shown that, if $\text{PLR}_n \to \infty$ as $n \to \infty$, prediction system B is discredited in favour of A.

To get an intuitive feel for the behaviour of the prequential likelihood, consider Fig. A.1. Here the predictor $\tilde{f}_i(t)$ differs markedly from $f_i(t)$: it is too pessimistic in our reliability context. Since the actual observation t_i will probably lie in the main body of $f_i(t)$, it will consequently probably lie in the right tail of $\tilde{f}_i(t)$ and so make a small contribution to the overall PL. In the case where the true f_i are not noisy (i.e. the sequence of $f_i(t)$ moves slowly to the right with few reversals of order), but the $\tilde{f}_i$ are noisy, it is easy to see that the observed t_i will fall in the tails (left or right) of the $\tilde{f}_i(t)$. The same argument applies when the f_i really are noisy and the $\tilde{f}_i$ are too smooth. Thus unwarranted noisiness, or unwarranted smoothness, of the predictor sequence will result in small PL. More details can be found in (Abdel-Ghaly *et al.*, 1986).

Clearly, PL will also detect bias. If, for example, the $\tilde{f}_i$ are consistently too pessimistic, the observed t_i will tend to lie in the right-hand tail of $\tilde{f}_i$, giving small PL.

The prequential likelihood, then, should allow us to detect both consistent deviations between prediction and reality ('bias'), and large variability in the distance between prediction and reality ('noise'). In this sense it is analogous to mean square error in parameter estimation.

One interpretation of the PLR, when A and B are *Bayesian prediction systems* (Aitchison & Dunsmore, 1975), is as an approximation to the posterior odds of model A against model B. Suppose that the user believes that either model A is true, with prior probability $p(A)$, or model B is true with prior probability $p(B)$ $(= 1 - p(A))$. He now observes the failure behaviour of the system; in particular, he makes predictions from the two prediction systems and compares them with actual behaviour via the PLR. Thus, when he has made predictions for $T_{j+1}, T_{j+2}, \ldots, T_{j+n}$, the PLR is

$$\text{PLR}_n = \prod_{i=j+1}^{j+n} \tilde{f}_{i(t_i)}^A \bigg/ \prod_{i=j+1}^{j+n} \tilde{f}_i^B(t_i) = \frac{p(t_{j+n}, \ldots, t_{j+1} \mid t_j \ldots t_1, A)}{p(t_{j+n}, \ldots, t_{j+1} \mid t_j \ldots t_1, B)} \quad (A.29)$$

in an obvious notation. Using Bayes' Theorem this is

$$\frac{[p(A \mid t_{j+n}, \ldots, t_1) p(t_{j+n}, \ldots, t_{j+1} \mid t_j \ldots t_1)] / [p(A \mid t_j, \ldots, t_1)]}{[p(B \mid t_{j+n}, \ldots, t_1) p(t_{j+n}, \ldots, t_{j+1} \mid t_j \ldots t_1,)] / [p(B \mid t_j, \ldots, t_1)]}$$

$$= \frac{p(A \mid t_{j+n}, \ldots, t_1) \, p(B \mid t_1, \ldots, t_j)}{p(B \mid t_{j+n}, \ldots, t_1) \, p(A \mid t_1, \ldots, t_j)} \quad (A.30)$$

If the initial predictions were based only on prior belief ($j = 0$), the second term in eqn (A.30) is merely the *prior odds ratio*. If the user is indifferent between A and B at this stage, this takes the value 1 since $p(A) = p(B) = 1/2$. thus eqn (A.30) becomes

$$\frac{w_A}{1 - w_A} \quad (A.31)$$

the posterior odds ratio, with w_A representing his posterior belief that A is true after seeing the data (i.e. after making predictions and comparing them with actual outcomes).

Of course, the prediction systems considered in Sections (A.1) to (A.8) are not all Bayesian ones. It is more usual to estimate the parameters via ML and use the 'plug-in' rule for prediction. It can be shown, however, that this procedure and the Bayesian predictive approach are asymptotically equivalent, so the above interpretation may be a reasonable approximation.

It is, in addition, not usual to allow $j = 0$ in practice. Although Bayesians can predict via prior belief without data, non-Bayesians usually insist that predictions are based on actual evidence. In practice, though, the value of j may be quite small.

With these reservations, we do think that eqn (A.31) can be used as an intuitive interpretation of PLR.

Appendix B

Software Development Process Models

Paul Rook

B.1 The Waterfall Model. 413
B.2 Classical Life-Cycle Phases 416
B.3 Interaction between Teams 418
B.4 Software Development Activities 420
B.5 Matrix of Phases and Activities 422
B.6 Software Development within System Development 426
B.7 Software Project Organizational Structure 428
B.8 The Contractual Model 429
B.9 Object-oriented Processes of Software Development 430
B.10 Prototyping 431
B.11 Incremental Development 433
B.12 The Spiral Model for defining Development Phases 435
B.13 The Ada Process Model 437
B.14 Conclusion 440

B.1 The Waterfall Model

This model was derived from the thinking of the late 1960s and one of the best papers describing the principles of the model is by Royce (Royce (1970), reprinted in the *IEEE Tutorial on Software Engineering Project Management* (Thayer, 1988)). Whilst the model has been overtaken by further development, the paper is still worth reading.

The starting principle was to decide that the first step from a totally unstructured process was to define a two-step structure consisting of deciding what to do and then doing it. This is shown for software development in Fig. B.1. Refining this further produces Fig. B.2, with the justification for the different steps being based upon the distinctly different ways they are planned and staffed for best utilization of resources on a large project.

Clearly, simply following the sequence of steps in Fig. B.2 is simplistic on any practical software development. It is most unlikely that the required product can be completely specified, and then completely designed without any realization of need to rework the specification. It will be necessary for

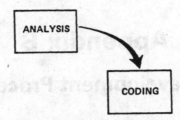

Fig. B.1 Implementation steps to deliver a small computer program for internal operations. (Reproduced from Royce (1970) with permission of the IEEE.)

clarification, even if there are no changes to the customers requirements in the meantime. Similarly, coding will usually involve sorting out unexpected problems in the design, and testing will find all sorts of surprises which require reworking of the previous steps. This leads then to the well-known and often-reproduced waterfail diagram shown in Fig. B.3.

The intention is that the process remains under control if all rework needs only to go back one step for the team to retrieve the situation and then have a basis for further progress. However, this is generally not so easily controllable, leading to the sort of situations shown in Fig. B.4, with consequent problems in the cost of correcting the software and loss of control of the project.

This model of the process of working makes perfectly good sense when the software is developed by an individual, or by a team acting cohesively like an individual with the management perception being limited primarily to 'started', 'working' and 'finished product'. When there is a larger organization and more attempt to gain management insight and control of progress, then there is a significant problem in the meaning of the backward arrows. Clearly, the fact of

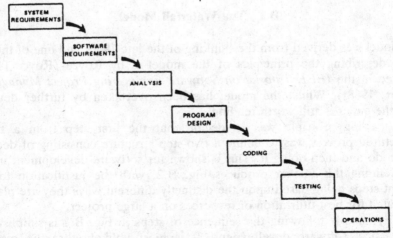

Fig. B.2. Implementation steps to develop a large computer program for delivery to a customer. (Reproduced from Royce (1970) with permission of the IEEE.)

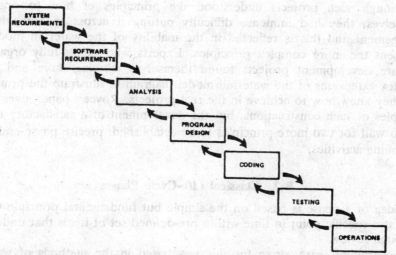

Fig. B.3. Hopefully, the iterative interactions between the various phases are confined to successive steps. (Reproduced from Royce (1970) with permission of the IEEE.)

rework is unarguable. But if the steps represent progress in time, then the backward arrows cannot represent reverse time, so the diagram must mean that any step can be revisited as required and at any point in time anyone in the team can be working on any of the steps on any part of the product. Thus there is no control of a software development team—management waits with bated breath until they have finished. By the late 1960s this was no longer acceptable and software development projects were becoming organized and controllable.

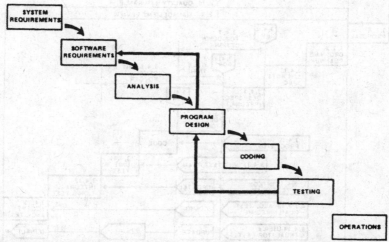

Fig. B.4. Unfortunately, for the process illustrated, the design iterations are never confined to the successive steps. (Reproduced from Royce (1970) with permission of the IEEE.)

Although such projects understood the principles of how to organize themselves, they had immense difficulty putting it across to non-software management and this is reflected in the inability of the waterfall model to represent the more complex principles. Experts who successfully organized software development projects found themselves creating more and more complex extensions of the waterfall model diagram to illustrate the principles that they knew how to achieve in the real projects. Royce's paper gives some examples of such constructions, but the development of a satisfactory model had to wait for two more principles to be established: precise phase-ends and continuing activities.

B.2 Classical Life-Cycle Phases

The idea of a phase is based on the simple but fundamental principle that it ends at a specific point in time with a pre-defined set of items that undergo a thorough review.

The strongest early drive for this was based in the methods of working developed between the Department of Defense and its suppliers, and defined in American Military Standards. The resulting philosophy of a method of working has been extensively documented, the example in Fig. B.5 being taken from a paper from TRW (Goldberg, 1977) also reprinted in the *IEEE Tutorial on Software Engineering Project Management*.

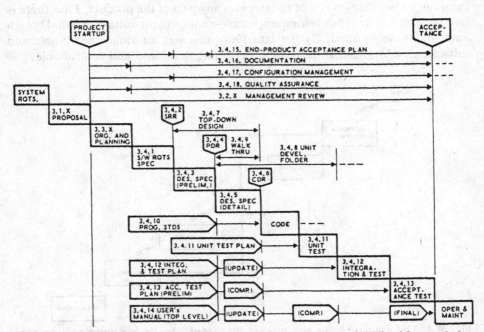

Fig. B.5. The software life cycle. (Reproduced from Goldberg (1977) with permission of the IEEE.)

Goldberg's paper lists sets of deliverable subproducts to be reviewed against checklists at each phase, and this naturally leads to thorough definitions of the form of the reviews, the standards and procedures and a whole method of working which can be understood and supported by management and the customer. Also, the staff on the software development team can clearly see a structure of what is expected of them, and when, and can expect training in an explicit way of working.

The set of phases shown in Fig. B.5, or something similar, is what has become known as the classical life cycle, and organizations which work on these principles refer to the Life-Cycle Model. They know what they mean, and concentrate on refining and interpreting the definitions and standards for the phase deliverables, ensuring thorough reviews and finding errors early so that the software development process is effective. But, when trying to explain to management, or to really look at the 'model', or investigate the process with the intention of improving what often continue to be inadequately controllable software development projects, there are still problems. These usually stem from relating the life-cycle phases to the waterfall model and getting into complications with the idea of reworking based on 'iteration of phases'.

In the original waterfall model the team did indeed move a step (or more) back, as represented by the backward arrows, and rework before moving forward again. In Fig. B.5 the phases end at project milestones and the waterfall model is reinterpreted, as shown in Fig. B.6 (Boehm, 1976), with the

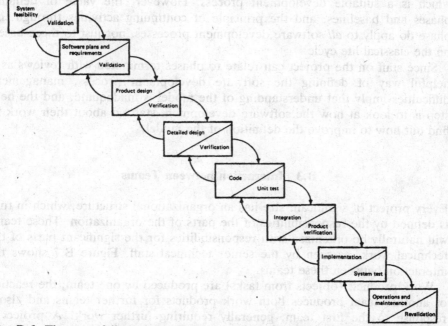

Fig. B.6. The waterfall model with V&V added to each phase. (Reproduced from Boehm (1976) with permission of the IEEE.)

backward arrows representing back-*references* for V&V against baselines. There is now no 'iteration of phases' implied in this new version of the waterfall model, since the end of a phase is a point in time and no-one is suggesting time travel

Rework may be controlled within a phase when it is realized at the intended end of a phase that the review shows that the phase products are inadequate and further work must be done on them and the review held again before the phase can be decided to be finished. In fact, some organizations deliberately hold a series of informal reviews through which the work of completing the phase is really controlled before reaching the formal phase end review. Iteration of phase-products in the following phase(s), i.e. rework to correct errors in the baselined phase-products is explained, in Section B.3, as a function of continuing activities.

Another basis for a wish to 'iterate phases' arises when the software project involves a significant element of research into what is wanted and how it should be designed and implemented. However, the conclusion that should be drawn is that it is inappropriate to try to use the classical life-cycle phases for such a project, rather than to pretend to use them as a gloss on the actuality of a different process. The proper basis for feasibility studies, prototyping and incremental development for projects involving uncertainty and risk is worked out in the later sections of this Appendix, the principles being combined in the Spiral Model (Section B.12). For the next three sections, the discussion is illustrated by reference to the classical life-cycle phases assuming projects for which is a suitable development process. However, the value of defining phases and baselines, and the principle of continuing activities through the phase do apply to *all* software development processes, not just to those based on the classical life cycle.

Since staff on the project can relate to phases terminated with reviews as a helpful way of defining the software development process, management difficulties imply that understanding of the model is inadequate, and the next step is to look at how the software development staff go about their work to find out how to improve the definition of the model.

B.3   Interaction between Teams

Every project of significant size has an organizational structure, which in turn is defined by the responsibilities of the parts of the organization. These teams will naturally be organized with responsibilities for the significant parts of the technical work, as seen by the senior technical staff. Figure B.7 shows the interaction between these teams.

Work products (objects from tasks) are produced by one team; the reaction of another team produces both work products for further teams and also a response to the first team, generally requiring further work. A project is brought under control by the project manager setting a structure to these

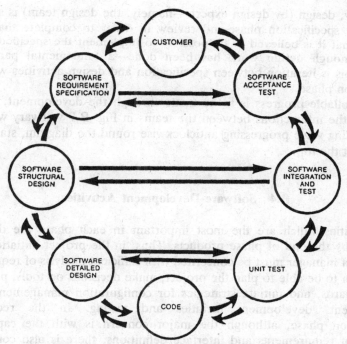

Fig. B.7. Team interaction in software development.

interactions which includes the need for decisions, responsibilities and control of changes.

This is the basis for defining the meaning of rework in the model. Each team performs an activity, and it is the iteration of work on specific objects between teams which is the essence of correcting problems in products that had been thought to be finished. If a phase product was thought to be correct at the phase-end review, but subsequently found to be faulty in the next, or even later, phase, then (subject to management decision and change control) the phase product is returned to the originating team to be corrected and updated. This goes on as an activity in parallel with the major activities of the phase. The iteration of work between teams implies that all activities associated with the teams carry on throughout all phases.

Confusion can arise from giving the phases the same names as the activities (and the teams).

There should not be any serious thought that specification is done only in the specification phase—it is simply the primary activity (or one of the primary activities) of that phase, and it does not stop at the end of that phase but is carried on to update the specification documents during subsequent phases. These updates may be due to changes from the customer, realization of errors or inconsistencies, or changes to the specification (with the customer's agreement) in the light of unexpected design difficulties.

Similarly, design (by design experts—namely, the design team) is necessary before the specification phase-end review in order to complete that review knowing that it is believed to be possible to implement the specified product because enough design work has been done—a fundamental part of the review. This is iteration between specification and design activities within the specification phase.

If controllable progress is to be made through the development, then the weight of the interactions between the teams in Fig. B.7 will vary with time, with a rolling wave progressing anticlockwise round the diagram, starting and finishing at the top.

B.4   Software-Development Activities

The activities which are the most important in each phase are defined in principle by the end of phase products. Thus, in the project initiation phase, the project manager must be concerned with sufficient analysis of requirements and design to be able to plan the project, make decisions on tools, procedures and standards, and initiate strategies for configuration management, quality management, development facilities and testing. In the requirement specification phase, although the major concern is with the capture and analysis of requirements and interface definitions, there is also considerable work required on updating the detail of the project plans. In the design phase the emphasis must not only be on completing the design but also on the quality of the design for reliability, efficiency and maintainability with a major concentration on technical control (reference Section 7.2.5 in Chapter 7).

Similar shifts in emphasis can be deduced for the subsequent phases, but, having stated this, it must be clear that all activities continue across all phases of the project. Even if most of the attention of the project is concentrated on the major concern of a phase, there must be staff working on other activities also during each phase.

An obvious example is structural design; not only must significant work be carried out on this during the requirement specification phase, and it is the primary activity in the structural design phase, but also there must be a continuing strong design control to maintain design integrity during the phases following completion of the review at the end of the structural design phase.

Although coding of a module does not properly commence before completion of the detailed design of that module, there are still programming activities to be performed during the early phases, such as planning the coding methods and facilities, acquisition and testing of tools and database development, and, in some cases, there may be exploratory investigations into algorithms and operations.

The primary activities of each of the phases should be thought of as continuing through the whole project; not as of fixed duration and stopping at the end of the phase. In a large software development, each activity should be

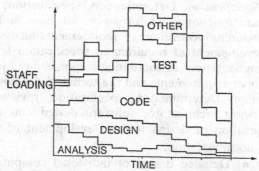

Fig. B.8. Allocation of effort to technical activities during development.

staffed by a distinct group of people whose numbers might grow and shrink but whose existence is identifiable from project start to project end.

Figure B.8 shows the allocation of effort to technical activities during development on a number of projects in the Yourdon survey (DeMarco, 1981). Whilst the shape of the curve and balance between the activities will vary for different projects, the principle shown in the figure is valid for all software development projects. Note that Fig. B.8 only covers the activities of technical development—it does not include project management, configuration management or quality assurance; 'other' in Fig. B.8 covers unanticipated and unclassified technical activities in the Yourdon survey data. It can be seen that the activities are continuous throughout the development, although with the expected humps at the appropriate phases in the development life cycle. This spread of the activities does assume the inclusion of the preparation for a task with the execution of the task, which is entirely rational since the work is done by the same team and therefore the work of the team corresponds to the definition of an activity.

For a better understanding of the software development process, we need a more precise definition of software development activities than the simple terms used in Fig. B.8. The following definition, derived from one given in *Software Engineering Economics* (Boehm, 1981), is an example of a suitable set of representative activities for software development.

- *Project Management.* Project level management functions. Includes project level planning and control, contract and subcontract management, customer interface, cost/schedule performance management, management reviews and audits, and includes acquisition of management tools.
- *Technical Control.* Responsibility for the technical correctness and quality of the complete product. Responsibility for maintaining the integrity of the whole design during the detailed design, programming and testing phases. Specification, review and update of integration test and acceptance test and acceptance test plans and procedures. Acquisition of requirements and design verification and validation tools. Acquisition and support of test drivers, test tools and test data.

- *Requirement Specification*. Determination, specification, review and update of software functional, performance, interface and verification requirements, including acquisition of requirements analysis and specification tools. Development of requirement specification level defining and describing documentation. A continuing responsibility for communication between customer requirements and the technical development.
- *Structural Design*. Determination, specification, review and update of hardware–software architecture, software design and database design, including acquisition of design tools. Development of structural design level defining documentation.
- *Detailed Design*. Detailed design of individual computer-program components. Development of detail design level defining documentation. When a significant number of staff are involved, this activity includes team-level management functions.
- *Code and Unit Test*. Code, unit test and integration of individual computer-program components including tool acquisition. When a significant number of staff are involved, this activity includes team-level management functions.
- *Verification, Validation and Testing*. Performance of independent requirements validation, design verification and validation, integration test and acceptance test, including test reports.
- *Manuals Production*. Development and update of product support documentation—User Manual, Operations Manual and Maintenance Manual.
- *Configuration Management*. Product identification, operation of change control, status accounting, operation of program support library.
- *Quality Assurance*. Consultancy on project standards and procedures, monitoring of project procedures in operation and quality audits of products.

The use of precise definitions of phases and activities such as those above (see Section 7.5.1 in Chapter 7 for a matching set of phase definitions) allows data to be collected and plans to be made with much more detail than the crude diagram shown in Fig. B.8. An example of planned staffing for a project, based on these detailed definitions, is shown in Fig. B.9. The size of the teams is shown through the project time-scale. It can be seen that the humps in the team-size curves represent peaks in their activities corresponding to the appropriate phase, with the emphasis shifting from activity to activity as the project proceeds through the phases.

B.5 Matrix of Phases and Activities

Having defined phases and activities, we can now return to the Life-Cycle Model and see how it corresponds to the process of software development. Using the activities defined above and the classical life-cycle phases, a matrix

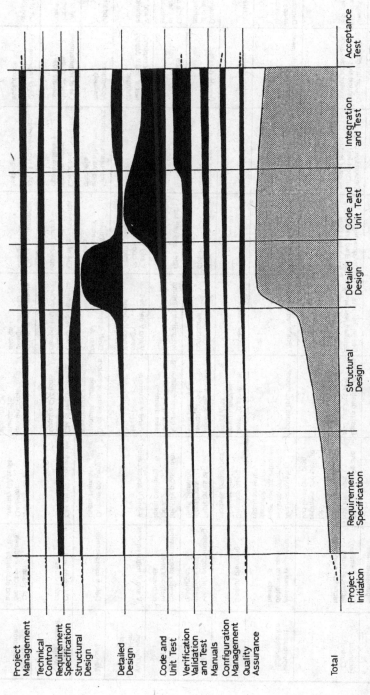

Fig. B.9. Software development teams. (Reproduced from Rook (1986) with permission of the Institution of Electrical Engineers.)

Activity \ Phase	Project Initiation	Reqmnt Specification	Structural Design	Detailed Design	Code and Unit Test	Integration & Test	Acceptance Test	Maintenance
Project Management	Project estimating, planning, scheduling, procedures, organisation etc.	Project management, project planning, contracts, liaison, etc.	Project management, status monitoring, contracts, liaison, etc.	Project management, status monitoring, contracts, liaison, etc.	Project management, status monitoring, contracts, liaison, etc.	Project management, status monitoring, contracts, liaison, etc.	Project management, status monitoring, contracts, liaison, etc.	Support management, status monitoring, contracts, liaison, etc.
Technical Control	Technical strategy, technical plans, technical standards	System models and risk analysis, acceptance test plan, acquire V and V tools for reqmnts and design, top-level test plan	Design quality, models and risk analysis, acquire test tools	Design integrity, detailed test plans, acquire test tools	Design integrity, detailed test plans, install test tools	Design integrity, support test tools, monitor testing	Design integrity, support test tools, monitor acceptance	Design integrity, risk analysis test plans
Requirement Specification	Analyse requirements determine user needs	Analyse existing system, determine user needs, integrate document and iterate requirements	Update requirements	Update requirements	Update requirements	Update requirements	Update requirements	Determine user needs and problems, update requirements
Structural Design	Design planning	Develop basic architecture, models, prototypes	Develop structural design, models, prototypes	Update design	Update design	Update design	Update design	Update design
Detailed Design	Identify programming methods and resources	Prototypes of algorithms, team planning	Models, algorithms investigation, team planning	Detailed design, component documentation	Update detailed design	Update detailed design	Update detailed design	Detailed design of changes and enhancements
Code and Unit Test	Identify programming methods and resources	Identify programming tools, team planning	Acquire programming tools and utilities, team planning	Integration planning	Code and unit test	Integrate software, update code	Update code	Code and unit test of changes and enhancements
Verification, Validation and Test	V and V requirements	V and V specification	V and V structural design	V and V detailed design, V and V design changes	V and V top portions of code, V and V design changes	Perform product test V and V design changes	Perform acceptance test, V and V design changes	V and V changes and enhancements
Manuals	Define users manual	Outline portions of users manual	Draft users, operators manuals, outline maintenance manual	Draft maintenance manual	Full draft users and operators manuals	Final users, operators and maintenance manuals	Acceptance of manuals	Update manual
Configuration Management	CM plans and procedures	CM plans, procedures, identify CM tools	CM of requirements, design, acquire CM tools	CM of requirements, design, detailed design, install CM tools, set up library	CM of requirements, design, code, operate library	CM of requirements, design, code, operate library	CM of requirements, design, code, operate library	CM of all documentation, operate library
Quality Assurance	QA plans, project procedures and standards	Standards, procedures, QA plans, identify QA tools	QA of requirements, design, project standards, acquire QA tools	QA of requirements, design, detailed design	QA of requirements, design, code	QA of requirements, design, testing	QA of requirements, design, code, acceptance	QA of maintenance updates

Fig. B.10. Software-development tasks by activity and phase. (Reproduced from Rook (1986) with permission of the Institution of Electrical Engineers.)

can be drawn out, as shown in Fig. B.10, defining tasks for the teams corresponding to the specific work of an activity in a phase. The tasks can be subdivided, where relevant, to subsystems and modules of the product.

Note that this is only a simple basis for seeing the definition of the tasks, the standards and procedures that should be in use and the appropriate tools, etc. for every box in the matrix. The matrix is not the Life-Cycle model—it is only the outworking of the model for a particular set of phases and activities. The more precisely defined the phases and activities, the more precisely the process can be defined in the terms of a matrix.

However, even with considerable precision, good management and skilful, responsible technical staff to ensure that the intended process is actually followed, the matrix needs interpretation to correspond to reality. The vertical lines for the ends of the first three phases do indeed correspond to phase ends for the whole of the project. Once past the end of the structural design phase, by definition the design is now sufficiently baselined that it no longer has to be the property of a single team and parts of the design can be worked on by separate teams, relying on defined interfaces. This is the distinction between the two design phases; not some arbitrary level of design decomposition. The central design team will still have the activity of maintaining design integrity over the work of the teams working on the detailed designs; for example, participating in the detailed design walkthroughs. However, the work of the teams will proceed in parallel through detailed design, coding and unit test, producing their finished modules at different times. This would be deliberately planned, with the assignment of teams to the parts of the implementation organized so that they arrive in the required sequence for the integration and test team to proceed according to a planned (probably top-down) integration. Thus, the ends of the two phases of detailed design and code and unit test in the matrix do not correspond to single points in time for the whole project, though they are very real points in time for the teams working on each group of modules, with thorough reviews (probably based on walkthroughs, code readings and unit test data).

Also, the phases of the software development process have a relationship that is not brought out in the linear progressions used in the diagrams shown so far in this appendix. As can be seen in the V-diagram in Chapter 7 (Fig. 7.6), there are tasks of producing test specifications, test plans, and test data derived from the specifications and designs in the earlier phases, which progress in parallel with and independently of the middle phases, but necessarily have to be completed for the work of the later testing phases. The appropriate matrix for the chosen phases and activities of any well-defined process is an excellent reference point, but must not be interpreted simplistically as being the model of the process.

The interactions between the activities and phases determine the tasks and phase products to be baselined. This provides the technical basis to underpin the principles of project control described in Chapter 7. The more precise the definitions (backed by procedures) of the activities and the definitions (backed by standards) for the products to be reviewed at the end of each phase, the more precisely is the process defined and the more closely can it be planned with technically meaningful milestones, monitored and controlled, and the easier is it to collect data for project analysis. The matrix and the V-diagram are useful to illustrate the principles, but, for each specific project, it is necessary to work through the detail to a level such that a diagram like Fig. 7.7 can be drawn before there is a sufficient basis for project control.

It should be emphasized that the principles of phases and activities discussed above are entirely general. Although the example uses the classical life-cycle phases and the graphs show the type of curves usually associated with large real-time software projects using traditional coding languages, the principles apply just as well to different development methods and applications.

Use of a 4GL or a code generator leads naturally to less emphasis on coding and unit testing phases and more emphasis on analysis and design, with correspondingly different shapes in the curves. Small (even one-person) teams working on parts of the software in the sort of development process usually applied in commercial data-processing require different definitions of activities and phases from those used for large real-time projects. The resulting process will be defined by different versions of the diagrams exemplified in Fig. 7.7, different definitions against which the project data is to be collected, and different staff-time profiles. However the principles are universal: what is necessary is that, for the different processes used on different projects in different styles of development, they are fully worked out and defined in order to provide the basis for successful estimating, planning and project control.

B.6 Software Development within System Development

Software is frequently only one element in a total system. To an increasing extent, computers and microprocessors are being used to provide system functions that were previously provided by non-computing hardware. Even in a dedicated computer environment there are many examples of programs that have to be designed in parallel with the development of the computing hardware. In these cases, it is essential that the approach to reliability takes a total system view, both for the product and for the development process.

Figures B.11 and B.12 illustrate integration of software and hardware development phases into an effective system development process. The essential differences between hardware and software must be recognized, but the principles of the Life-Cycle Model are just as applicable in the combined development that relies on the technical skills and professionalism of the staff to carry through well-defined and robust processes to produce the software and hardware that successfully integrate to form the system product.

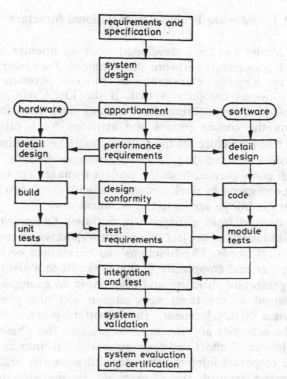

Fig. B.11. Software and hardware development within system development. (Reproduced from Wingrove (1986) with permission of the Institution of Electrical Engineers.)

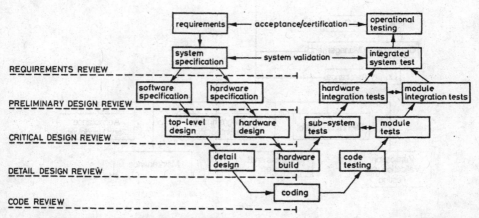

Fig. B.12. The system development life cycle. (Reproduced from Wingrove (1986) with permission of the Institution of Electrical Engineers.)

B.7 Software Project Organizational Structure

The Life-Cycle Model has been developed from an attempt at best understanding of good (successful) software development. Particular emphasis has
been placed on the way the relationships of the tasks between the teams are
organized. The obvious corollary is that, if the Life-Cycle model and the
principles of Software Engineering are credible, then once the appropriate
process based on the chosen phases and activities for a project has been
determined, the team structure for the project should be organized ('designed',
reference Section 7.3.2 and Fig. 7.3) to correspond. This will have the
immensely useful consequence, from the project manager's point of view, that
responsibilities correspond to work assignments and strengthen management's
understanding of the bridge across to the technical work.

Figure B.13, derived from a diagram in *Software Engineering Economics,*
shows a generalized software project organization chart which can be tailored to
fit particular project needs. The functions can be merged or further divided
according to the size and complexity of the work. Boehm gives guidelines for
tailoring the organization structure and also shows an example of how it can
suitably be changed as the team sizes change with the project's progress
through the phases of development. The important point is that the precise
definitions of the activities and the tasks to produce the phase-products lead
naturally to estimates of effort and team sizes which fit into an organizational
structure where responsibilities match delegated authority and the principles
that enable project control are represented in the structure of project
management.

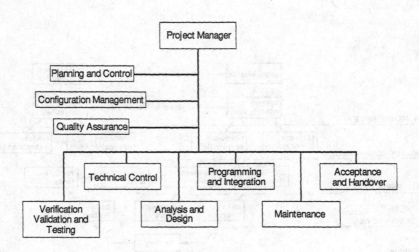

Fig. B.13. Generalized software project organization chart.

B.8 The Contractual Model

So far the discussion of the Life-Cycle Model has emphasized structuring and visibility for the purposes of management of the process. This is necessary for successful projects, but not sufficient. A successful software product depends fundamentally on the technical quality of the work, as does the productivity of the team. Originally, the technical quality was seen as the essence, with management almost a spectator. Software engineering has restored the balance, but the principles of the Life-Cycle Model do depend on there being a bridge between two strong forces working in harness. This bridge is based, from the project-management point of view, on phases and baselines. The Life-Cycle Model is used to understand and define the project manager's relationship to the software development activities and hence the tasks to be assigned to the teams. However, although the project manager is responsible for the technical correctness of the product under development, project management will fail if it tries to structure the work down to mere elementary tasks and must depend on a strong technical control function as discussed in Chapter 7 (Section 7.2.4).

Technical control deals with the process of transformations in the technical development that can be modelled using the Contractual Model (Cohen, 1982). This is used in Chapter 3 as the basis for the use of formal specification (Section 3.3 and Fig. 3.1). The principle is that of transformations as contracts between teams, with alternations of specification and design, the result from one stage of design being then explicitly written as contractual specification(s) for the next stage. The contractual model is an excellent basis for the technical controller to structure the significant technical complexity of the transformations from requirements specification through design and down through detailed design to modules for implementation. Properly used, it provides the structured documentation basis for the interactions between the teams shown in Fig. B.7. It can be used to deal with transformations as contracts between teams.

The contractual model of technical transformation and decomposition is orthogonal to the principle of progress through time-based phases and cannot be relied upon as the basis for project control. Any attempt to do so for large projects founders on questions of predefined levels of decomposition, 'goodness' of design and design 'finished'.

The life-cycle phases can be referred to as 'horizontal' time progression through suitable review milestones. The contractual model is concerned with 'vertical' levels of abstraction and there is no requirement that there be a one-to-one mapping between them. Reference the usual six levels in Mascot; one normally only enters detailed design with multiple teams when the design is reduced from parallel processes to purely procedural code. The levels of abstraction may be preplanned, or their determination may be part of the design process itself—they do not have to correspond to multiple design phases, though it is clearly wise to define phases and phase product reviews at planned key achievements in the design process. It is the responsibility of the technical control team that the 'best' design techniques are used. The recursive nature of the contractual model works with data-based and process-based design techniques just as well, provided the design team bring good design thinking to the task instead of allowing the levels of abstraction to be led merely by decomposing the functions.

Having said this, it should be clear that the contractual model is not in conflict with the Life-Cycle Model and is in fact an excellent way of representing the structuring of good design as the technical side of the bridge between technical control and project management. This point is brought out strongly as underlying the techniques of technical development discussed in Chapters 2 to 5 (Sections 2.1, 3.3, 4.2 and 5.2.1). The documents of the decomposed design structure are, of course, the task products for baselining that enables the phase-product based approach to give a measure of progress which includes technical quality.

B.9 Object-oriented Processes of Software Development

The transformations of the design process lead naturally to an object-oriented Work Breakdown Structure (WBS). The activities of the teams are broken down by the WBS into tasks which produce the objects required for phase-end reviews, which are the major milestones of progress—with the principle of designing the organizational structure in an object-oriented way (reference Fig. 7.7). The whole drive of the organization, and its motivation to respond to the perceived demands made by the project manager, should be on the basis of producing objects which within the process structure, progress to combine into the whole product required. Not 'I program (verb intransitive, i.e. for the fun of it or because it seems to be what I should be doing)', but 'I program items (verb transitive, i.e. with the aim of producing a defined object that will be the only way of satisfying the demand made of me by my manager)'. The logic applies not only to programming but also to *all* the other activities such as writing documents, reviewing, testing, etc.

Here we are using 'object-oriented' not in the sense of applying it to the technical design, but to bring exactly the same principles to the 'design' of the process, the organization and the WBS. To put the message explicitly, the goal is: object-oriented managers, object-oriented processes, object-oriented organizational structures, object-oriented tasks for object-oriented development staff working with object-oriented design techniques and supported by object-oriented environments which possess all the objects with an object management system (OMS). This provides the means of structuring the relationship of technical development to project management to enable the definition of the basis for project control. It completes the first stage of the purpose of this appendix in underpinning Chapter 7 with the principles of the technical internal structure of the Life-Cycle Model to fit the external relationships to phases and baselines used by Chapter 7 to describe the control and management of software development projects.

B.10   Prototyping

The process models discussed so far in this Appendix have assumed a sufficiently well-defined and well-known product that the phases for the project can be predetermined in a form such as the classical life cycle. This is unrealistic for many large and complex software developments, which are usually tackling unprecedented problems at considerable risk from unknown technical and environmental factors. Increasingly, for large software development projects, the trend is to move away from the single shot approach to evolutionary development. Where the project is dealing with unknown technology, an uncertain statement of requirements or an unprecedented situation in any significant way, then it may be more suitable to use a process where the phases are iterated around a cycle based on prototyping.

There are many forms of prototype, ranging from a one-off version that will be thrown away when it has served its purpose, through a mock-up/simulation that will have its internal operations reprogrammed and 4GL working models which, once proved, will be rewritten in a procedural language, to a basic system which will be enhanced and refined over time until it is user-acceptable. The purpose of prototyping may be for research into the feasibility of a system or issues of performance, and as such may be treated as a feasibility study prior to the planning of a traditional development once the technical risks have been reduced to an acceptable level.

More often, prototyping (usually referred to as rapid prototyping in this context) is used to improve poorly understood purposes of the planned product or to determine the user interfaces in a much more effective way than can be achieved by working on tightening a written specification—to deal with the genuine situation of 'I can't tell you exactly what I want, but I'll know it when I see it'. The principle involved in a software development process based on prototyping stages with user involvement is the reduction of risk so that a product can be successfully produced without, on final delivery to the customer, running into the response 'You gave me what I asked for, not what I now realize I wanted'.

Of the many ways of defining a prototyping development process, Fig. B.14 is just an example. All such prototyping processes show a form of iteration, or cycling through an evolution of creation, evaluation, approval, refinement and derivation/tuning for further versions, see Zelkowitz & Squires (1982) for examples and papers on prototyping processes for software development.

The emphasis on iteration is the strength of prototyping methods (which underlies the oft-expressed wish to 'iterate phases' in the waterfall model, mentioned in Section B.2) and is the basis of the approach to minimizing the

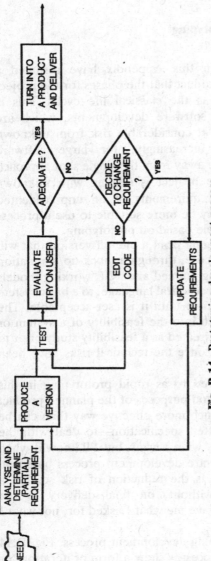

Fig. B.14. Prototyping development process.

Project Environment	Personnel	Technical
Undefined Responsibilities and Authorities	Wrong People Available – not the right grade – not the right training – not the right expertise	Requirement Changes – genuine change of mind by customer – hidden implication emerges
Undefined Procedures		
Unknown Quality of Development Products		Failure to Meet Requirement – cannot produce a feasible design – acceptance test fails
Inadequate Control of Development Products	Wrong Availability – too many people for the current tasks – too few people for the current tasks	
Problems and Errors Detected Late		Problem or Error Detected – design inconsistent – missing component – inadequate computer time for testing
Inadequate Technical Approaches		
Inadequate Support Facilities and Services		
Lack of "Visibility"		

Fig. B.15. Major components of risk.

technical risk in producing a successful product. However, there are difficulties in scaling the methods up to very large systems (problems of spaghetti code, ensuring that the code is maintainable and flexible enough to accommodate unplanned evolution), avoiding the undisciplined hacker syndrome that the life-cycle model has been trying to cure and ensuring process visibility for project control. Designing the process to be able to manage risk must take into account not only technical risk but also the project environment and personnel risks (reference Fig. B.15) to ensure reliable (control of) development of a successful product.

The remainder of this appendix deals with the more sophisticated models of the software development process which provide for phases designed to deal with all aspects of risk.

B.11 Incremental Development

Incremental development, as a further refinement of the software development process, is based on developing the software in increments of functional capability with a series of overlapping developments and a series of staggered deliveries to the customer. The advantages of incremental development are often emphasized in software engineering and it has been used successfully on many projects, especially those for very large software products. The principle is shown in Fig. B.16.

The team sizes shown in Figs B.8 and B.9 are based on the production of the software as a single delivery, and show the classic rise and fall in numbers of staff employed on the project. There is also a transfer of numbers of staff from design to programming to test as the project progresses through the phases (or alternatively a turnover of staff if different expertise is deemed to be required for work in the different teams). This can present problems simply in staffing the project, in addition to the technical problems inherent in the single-shot approach to developing a software product.

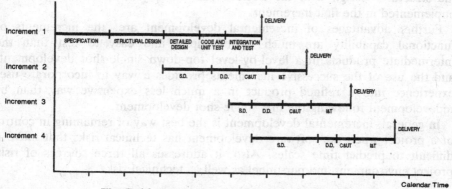

Fig. B.16. Incremental development sequence.

If the software is developed incrementally, then provided proper top-down techniques are used, not only is the project under better technical control (especially when there is considerable technical uncertainty and research is required) but also staffing problems are eased. The design, programming and test teams can remain at relatively constant strength, dealing with the work of each increment in turn. The main result is to level out the labour distribution curve on a software project. Instead of the classical humped curve distribution of labour over time, the labour-distribution graph is much more flattened.

If the increments of a large product development are very distinct, both in time and function, then the project organization approximates to a functional organization dealing with a series of projects going through. This implies that the full organizational structure would need to be permanently in operation and the manager needs then to be concerned with the span of control that this implies. Moreover, the manager has to give attention to all the functions in parallel, whereas with a single development going through each phase in turn the project manager can give most attention to the primary activity corresponding to the current phase. Thus, while incremental development decouples the project from the single driving pressure inherent in the single-shot development, when carried sufficiently far it may result in many pressures in parallel with all the dangers of a functional organization. When this threatens, the solution is either to strengthen the project office to deal with the increments separately, or to appoint subproject managers for each increment to preserve the project-oriented drive. These problems only arise for a large project with very separate increments.

Although the diagram shows increments based on the classical life-cycle phases, it is just as relevant to use prototyping methods in the development of the increments. Technical risk may also be dealt with by partitioning and moving, as far as possible, the less well-understood parts of the functionality to later increments. Of course, this cannot be applied to anything that is crucial to the central design, which must be completed in the first increment. The splitting of the product into increments must not be done solely on consideration of priorities of user-perceived functions, but must also be based on a cut at the structural design with the nucleus and primary structure designed and implemented in the first increment.

Further advantages of incremental development are: the increments of functional capability are much more helpful and easy to test than the intermediate products in a level-by-level top-down single-shot development; and the use of the successive increments provides a way to incorporate user experience into a refined product in a much less expensive way than by redevelopment following the first single-shot development.

In general, incremental development is the best way of remaining in control of a project when the software development has technical risks that make it difficult to predict time scales. Also, it addresses all three sources of risk; project environment and personnel as well as technical risks.

B.12 The Spiral Model for defining Development Phases

Figure B.17 shows a 'spiral model' as a general meta-model for processes, which includes most of the previously discussed models as special cases. It can be used to discuss the principles of processes to fit a wide variety of circumstances and provides guidance as to which sequence of phases best fits a given software situation. The spiral model has been developed at TRW over a number of years, based on experience on large government software projects. The diagram and following explanation of the principles of the spiral model are taken from a paper by Boehm (1988*a*) updated and reprinted in the *IEEE Tutorial on Software Engineering Project Management,* which gives further details and describes the experience of applying the model to the TRW Software Productivity Project.

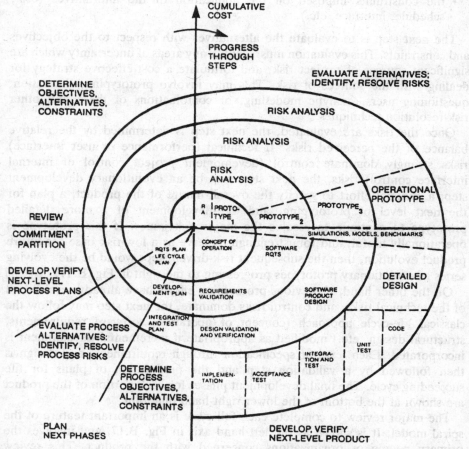

Fig. B.17. Spiral model of the software process. (Reproduced from Boehm (1988*a*) with permission of the IEEE.)

The radial dimension in Fig. B.17 represents the cumulative cost (with some artistic licence) incurred in accomplishing the steps to date; the angular dimension represents the progress made in completing each cycle of the spiral. The model holds that each cycle involves a progression through the same sequence of steps, for each portion of the product and for each of its levels of elaboration, from an overall concept of operation document down to the coding of each individual program.

Following the commitment to go ahead, each cycle of the spiral begins, in the top left-hand quadrant, with the determination of:

- the objectives of the portion of the product being elaborated (performance, functionality, ability to accommodate change, etc.);
- the alternative means of implementing this portion of the product (alternative designs, re-use, purchase, etc.);
- the constraints imposed on the application of the alternatives (cost, schedule, interface, etc.).

The next step is to evaluate the alternatives with respect to the objectives and constraints. This evaluation must identify any areas of uncertainty which are significant sources of project risk, and formulate a cost-effective strategy for dealing with the sources of risk. This may involve prototyping, simulation, questioning users, analytic modelling, or combinations of these and other risk-resolution techniques.

Once the risks are evaluated, the next step is determined by the relative balance of the perceived risks. If technical (performance or user interface) risks strongly dominate control (development project control or internal interface control) risks, the next step may be an evolutionary development step: a minimal effort to specify the overall nature of the product, a plan for the next level of prototyping, and the development of a more detailed prototype to continue to resolve the major risk issues. If this prototype is operationally useful, and robust enough to serve as a low-risk base for future product evolution, then the subsequent risk-driven steps would be the evolving series of evolutionary prototypes progressing to the right in Fig. B.17.

On the other hand, if previous prototyping efforts have already resolved all of the technical risks, and control risks dominate, the next step may follow the classical life-cycle approach (concept of operation, software requirements, structural design, etc.) modified as appropriate if incremental development is incorporated. Each level of specification through requirements and design is then followed by a validation step and the preparation of plans for the succeeding cycle. The final development phases for each portion of the product are shown at the bottom of the lower right-hand quadrant.

The major review to complete each full cycle is an important feature of the spiral model. It is shown as the left-hand axis in Fig. B.17, and involves the primary people or organizations concerned with the product. This review covers all of the products developed during the previous cycle, including the plans for the next cycle and the resources required to carry them out. The major objective is to ensure that all concerned parties are mutually committed to the approach to be taken for the next cycle. The plans for the succeeding phases may include a partition of the product into increments for successive development, or components to be developed by separate organizations, teams, or individuals. Thus, the review and commitment step may range from an individual walkthrough of the design of a single programmer's component, to a major requirements review involving developer, customer, user, and maintenance organizations.

The most significant emphasis of the diagram of the spiral model is on decision making to ensure management of *all* aspects of risk. The plans developed in the lower left-hand quadrant to achieve the commitment review decision undergo further analysis in the upper parts of the diagram before the plans are finalized to a level of detail for the actual development. Planning, decision making, and determining, evaluating and resolving alternatives for detailed plans is not a simple linear progression but must be iterated for risk management planning in each cycle as necessary. The principle of the spiral model is valid without confusing the diagram with an attempt to show more detail of the decision-making process (that is part of the project management activity). The diagram of the spiral model is concerned with the development process. The emphasis of a large area of Fig. B.17 on decision making and risk analysis is consistent with the application of the model to determining processes for risky projects—once risk is controlled for the development of all, or (more usually) a portion, of the product then that portion goes through into the lower right-hand part of the model to progress through a straightforward process to implementation. The lack of uncontrollable risk at this stage should mean that there is no need for a major review to commit to progress through each of these final phases.

The spiral model can be used to accommodate the choice of any appropriate mixture of specification-oriented, automatic transformation-oriented, simulation-oriented, prototype-oriented, incremental, or other approach to software development, where the appropriate mixed strategy is chosen by considering the relative magnitude of the program risks, and the relative effectiveness of the various techniques in resolving the risks. Risk management and the choice of a suitable process for a particular project from the risk-management perspective are dealt with in Section 7.6.

B.13 The Ada Process Model

Figure B.18 is taken from a paper by Boehm (1988*b*), and compares an 'all too frequent process model' with an 'Ada process model'. The former, condemned, process suffers from unrealistically early schedules for completing software requirements and design, with the consequential inefficiencies of process thrashing and interpersonal communication overhead brought on when large numbers of project personnel are working in parallel on tasks which are

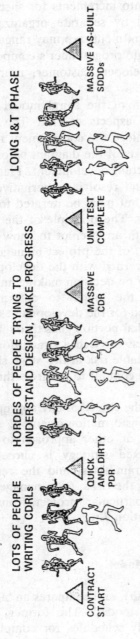

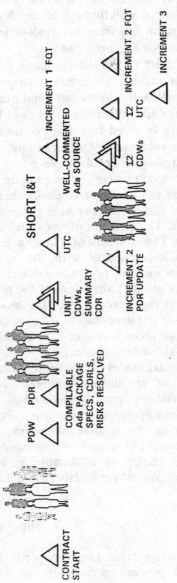

Fig. B.18. Ada process model: key distinctions. (Reproduced from Boehm (1988b) with permission of the IEEE.)

closely intertwined, incompletely defined, continually changing, and not well prepared for downstream integration.

The 'Ada Process Model' is so-called by Boehm because the Ada language constructs (primarily, compiler-checkable package specifications) fit neatly into the process. However, it should be emphasized that the virtues of this process model (an orderly structure of work for small teams and incremental development to deal with unprecedented and unknown aspects of the work, thus reducing project communications overhead and rework) in not only appropriate for Ada development. It is an example of good development practices, fits with good design techniques, is highly appropriate for object-oriented methods and is valid for any language environment.

The primary features of the 'Ada process model', as defined by Boehm, are:

- compilable package specifications produced before program design review (PDR);
- major risk items resolved by PDR;
- planned incremental development with stabilized requirements for each increment;
- small up-front system engineering and design teams;
- intermediate technical walkthroughs (SSW, PDW) in the early requirements and design phases;
- individual detailed design walkthroughs (CDWs) instead of a massive Critical Design Review (CDR);
- efficient CDR covering CDW highlights;
- continuous integration via Ada package specifications;
- well-commented Ada code and high-level design information instead of massive as-built Software Detailed Design Documents.

The first three features listed above ensure that large numbers of people can work on a software project in parallel (a necessary feature for achieving timely schedules), without the thrashing and inefficiencies usually experienced. Because of the reduction in project communications overhead and diseconomies of scale, the use of this process leads to an overall reduction in project effort. The overall schedule is lengthened somewhat compared with a single-shot development, but the use of incremental development means that users receive their initial operating capability earlier. The phase distribution of effort and schedule also changes. Use of this process involves more effort and schedule for requirements analysis and design, and considerably less for code, integration and test. The result is a controlled and manageable process of software development.

This model for a software development process is an outworking of the principles of incremental development, the spiral model, and good software development practices (both technical and managerial). It links precisely back into Chapter 7 for the discussion of project control founded on baselines, well-defined processes and risk management.

B.14 Conclusion

The software development process can be modelled by a Life-Cycle Model depending on phases, with baselined phase products, provided these are related to the software development activities under effective technical control. An object-oriented approach should be used for work-breakdown structure, task assignment and technical development, using principles such as those in the contractual model. The organization, reviews and phase control should be geared to explicit risk management. For a sufficiently large and uncertain project, the risks should be reduced by the techniques discussed for incremental development and the spiral model of the process. All the necessary principles are illustrated in these generalized models and, taken together with adequate decision making and risk management, can be used to define the appropriate process for any project. The specific process model chosen for the project needs to be defined at least to the level of detail shown in Fig. 7.7 to enable successful project control with the techniques described in Chapter 7.

Appendix C

Software Development Metrics and Models

Barbara Kitchenham

C.1 Introduction 441
C.2 Selection Criteria 442
C.3 Software Science 447
C.4 Software Metrics 449
C.5 Quantitative Software Models 476

C.1 Introduction

This appendix describes a number of software metrics and a number of quantitative models. The selection of metrics and models is not intended to be complete, it is meant to illustrate the various types of models and metrics that are currently available.

For convenient reference from Chapter 10, the metrics and models are listed below, in alphabetical order, with references to the page number on which they appear in this appendix.

	Page number
Change request classification schema (event attribute)	475
Design-to-code expansion rate (product attribute of relationships between products)	466
DeYoung/Kampen's readability measure (product attribute of software understandability)	464
Fan-in/fan-out (product attribute of software modularity)	460
Fault and change rates (product attribute of stability)	468
Fault-classification schemas (event attributes)	473
Fault-detection rates (process attribute of checking efficiency)	472
Gunning's fog Index (product attribute of document understandability)	465
Halstead's Software Science (model of software metrics)	447
Huff, Sroka & Struble's test and fix model 1 (process model of bug clearance)	482
Huff, Sroka & Struble's test and fix model 2 (process model of testcase passage)	485
Lines of code (product attribute of software size)	451

McCall, Walters & Richards' quality model (quality model)   480
McCabe's Cyclomatic number (product attribute of software structure)   455
Module strength (product attribute of software modularity)   459
Number·of words (product attribute of document size)   452
Oviedo's complexity measure (product attribute of software structure)   458
Remus & Zilles' defect-removal model (fault introduction and detection
   model)   478
Small & Faulkener's system design and integration model (fault introduction
   and detection model)   476
Yin & Winchester's measure of software design complexity (product attribute
   of software structure)   453
Woodward/Hedley/Hennell's test effectiveness measures (process attributes of
   checking completeness)   470

C.2   Selection Criteria

C.2.1   Selection criteria for software metrics

Metric types have been selected by reference to a model of software development. The model chosen is a simplified version of the model developed by the Alvey Software Data Library (Ross, 1986), to support the development of a data model for their software metrics database. The full Software Data Library (SWDL) model considers organizational characteristics of software production, as well as the products, processes and events that are observed for a particular project. This is because SWDL requires classificatory information to provide the comparability data that is needed for valid industry-wide data collection and analysis. For the identification of metric types, a model that considers only the products, process, and events that make up software production is sufficient.

Ross provides a full Entity-Relationship model for SWDL, together with a Data Dictionary. For those who prefer a more informal approach, a description of the product, process and event part of the model follows.

Products include not only the final delivered product but also the intermediate documents that are created as part of the software development process. Products are therefore of two basic types: executable software and text. Executable software includes not only source code listings and object code, but also executable specifications and design-language statements. Executable software may be described in terms of its structure or components, which can be subsystems and/or modules. Textual components may be classified with respect to the stage in the development process or the particular task that generated them. Thus, textual documents include requirements specifications, design documents including pictorial design representations, project and test plans, test reports and final product manuals. Products are inputs to and outputs from processes.

Processes are of two types: tasks and operations. Tasks are work items such as the design of a specified subsystem, or unit testing of a specified module, which are identified explicitly as a part of the production process and would be cross-referenced in project plans. Tasks themselves are of two main types: production tasks and checking tasks. Production tasks are all those tasks that are concerned with the production of products. Checking tasks include all validation, verification and testing activities that are used to assess products. Operations are procedures that are performed in response to unscheduled events (for example responding to a module failure during testing), and are examples of contingency planning, as distinct from project planning, since the times at which a particular operation may be activated cannot be determined in a project plan.

Events are signals that cause processes to be activated. Events that trigger tasks are planned, in the sense that the criteria for starting a task can be determined in advance and once the criteria are satisfied the task may be initiated. This view of planned events may be slightly novel to some people, but arises from process-modelling ideas that support much of the work on integrated project support environments (IPSEs), see for example Hurst (1986). Events that trigger operations are unpredictable incidents that occur during the development and support of a product. The view of events as unpredictable incidents is usually seen as a maintenance view, since the maintenance activity is driven by fault reports from customers. However, it is equally applicable throughout the development process. It is not only relevant to recording and handling the faults that are revealed by all the various checking tasks; it is also important to recognize that the failue to initiate a planned event is itself an unplanned incident, which should be subject to contingency planning.

Quantifiable attributes of products, processes and events, excluding cost metrics, which are covered in Chapter 11, are as follows.

PRODUCTS
Both text and executable software products possess two main quantifiable attributes: *size* and *structure*. Size is measured in terms of simple counts of some component part of the item being measured (e.g. lines of code in a code listing of a module, machine-code instructions in the object code of a module, English words in a document). Structure is usually measured in terms of attributes of the relationships between components where the relationships are often modelled in terms of mathematical graphs (e.g. control-flow diagrams to show the relationship between executable statements in a module, or data-flow diagrams to show the movement of data among modules).

Executable software can be quantified with respect to component interface characteristics. These are often measured in terms of simple counts, for example the number of different input and output parameters, or the number of different functions performed by the module. Such metrics are meant to provide a measure of system decomposition or *modularity*.

Textual products and human-readable software products may also be quantified with respect to *understandability*. Measures of the understandability of text are available in terms of readability indexes. The understandability of software components is more difficult to measure; in practice this may be done by subjective assessment as part of a quality assurance programme, but objective metrics are difficult to construct. It should be noted that program structure is often regarded as an important feature of the understandability of programs, i.e. a program with a convoluted control flow diagram is believed to be more difficult to understand than a program with a straightforward control flow. However, this is a conceptual model of understandability rather than a metric, and most metrics derived from control flow graphs are not equated directly with measures of understandability.

Products do not exist in isolation; for example, a design document will be related to a particular module or set of modules, or a requirements specification will be related to a number of specification and design documents and via those documents to specific code modules. Some metrics attempt to measure some attribute of the *relationship between products*. One example of a measurable attribute of the relationship between products is the *expansion rate* between products, which measures, for example, the relationship between the size of a design document and the size of the related code modules. This type of metric indicates the rather fuzzy nature of the product/process split. Some people might prefer to regard expansion rates as attributes of the processes that, for example, take detailed design documents as inputs and output coded modules. This viewpoint regards expansion ratios almost as a measure of the size of the transformation process. In my view, overall expansion rates, based on total design statements to total code statements, which can only be interpreted in terms of the metric values obtained from other similar products, are best regarded as measures of process attributes. In contrast, expansion rates for individual modules, which can be interpreted in terms of comparisons among modules in order to identify abnormal modules, are best regarded as measures of product attributes.

Finally, all products are subject to amendment during development and maintenance, both as a result of the discovery of faults and as a result of requirements changes. Metrics that record the rate and amount of change are used to measure the *stability* (or perhaps more accurately the instability) of a product.

PROCESSES

The most common measurable attributes of processes are cost- and schedule-related metrics. Other than those, most process metrics are obtained from checking tasks. Metrics related to checking include those that are related to assessing the *completeness of the checking activity* (e.g. test coverage metrics that indicate the amount of a product that has been checked), and those which indicate the *efficiency of the checking activity* (e.g. the number and nature of faults discovered by each type of checking task).

EVENTS

Most event-based metrics are derived from fault counts and change request counts obtained within the context of some classification scheme. Additional information collected about individual faults and change requests allows fault and change request counts to be used for product and process assessment, by cross-referencing faults and change requests to product components to indicate error-prone and change-prone components, and by using data about the time at which events occur, to indicate the rate at which faults are discovered by particular checking methods and the rate of changes the product as a whole is subjected to.

Although the concept of events is essential to the organization of data-collection activities, the metrics obtained from events are usually incorporated into synthetics (e.g. rates such as faults per 100 lines of code or faults found per calendar week), and are incorporated into product and process measures. In this document, fault and change-request classification schemes will be identified, but the use of fault and change-request counts will be incorporated into stability metrics for products and efficiency metrics for processes.

There are usually a number of different metrics that measure the same attribute of software development, particularly in the case of product metrics. In this document, the actual metrics described have been selected on the basis that they exhibit at least one of the following characteristics.

- The metric has proved particularly useful in practice.
- The metric has been extensively validated.
- The metric is well-known but may be misleading.
- The metric fulfils a vital need.

C.2.2 Criteria for metric description

Each metric will be described in the terms recommended by the software data library (Ross, 1986), with some adaptations. The SWDL recommendations are to define metrics in the following terms.

- *Name.*
- *Explanation,* which gives a short summary of the basis of the metric.
- *Elaboration,* which defines the entities which may be measured using this metric.
- *Measure,* which indicates what attribute of the entity is being measured, what units are used, or what classification scheme is being used.
- *Comparability data,* which indicates what information is needed to ensure that measurements can be determined unambiguously and compared validly with measurements from other projects.
- *Examples,* which provides some concrete examples of the metric, and its comparability data.
- *Uses,* which lists the possible uses of the metrics.

In this appendix, the elaboration section of the definition will identify whether the metric is a control metric, a predictor metric or both. The uses section will include control and/or predictor uses as appropriate. The examples section will be omitted, but when the metric is used as a predictor, two additional sections will be included.

- *Evaluation*, which will describe the type of evaluation that the metric has been subjected to, and the results. This section will indicate whether the evaluation was direct or indirect, and whether it was supported by single or double cross-validation. In this context, an investigation of the metric in more than one study will be regarded as double cross-validation.
- *Problems*, which will indicate any additional difficulties with the use of the metric in practice.

For all metrics, there will be a final section, *recommendations*, that will indicate whether use of the metric is recommended or not, and whether any such recommendation is dependent on particular circumstances. In addition, other possible uses of the metric will be considered, and other related metrics will be identified (although not fully defined).

C.2.3 Selection criteria for quantitative models

The quantitative models selected for inclusion in this section of the handbook were chosen to provide examples of the three main classes of analytical models of software development:

- fault/error introduction and detection models;
- quality models;
- process models.

The one exception is Maurice Halstead's Software Science (Halstead, 1977). A description of Software Science concepts is included because many other metrics and models are based on Software Science metrics and cannot be evaluated unless Software Science is evaluated first.

C.2.4 Criteria for model description

Each model will be described in the following terms:

- *Name.*
- *Exaplanation*, which identifies the type of model and its main aims.
- *Model inputs*, which identifies the inputs to the model.
- *Model outputs*, which identifies the outputs from the model.
- *Formula*, which identifies the formula or procedure used to transform the model inputs to the required outputs.
- *Evaluation*, which describes the type of evaluation the model has been subjected to, and the results.

- *Problems,* which indicate any known difficulties with the model.
- *Recommendations,* which indicates whether the model is recommended or not, and whether the recommendation is dependent upon any particular circumstances. Other related, or similar, models may be discussed in this section, but will not be fully defined.

C.3 Software Science

Since Software Science is closer to a field of study than a particular metric or model, and because many metrics and models are based on Software Science concepts, the theory of Software Science is treated before other metrics and models.

EXPLANATION

In Software Science, Halstead (1977) attempts to identify a number of program attributes from a small number of simple metrics derived from the implementation, in a programming language, of an algorithm or program. The attributes of a program include size, mental effort to create the program, time to create the program, and the number of delivered bugs in the program.

MODEL INPUTS

Software Science is based on four fundamental measurements:

- n_1, which is defined as the number of unique operators in a program;
- n_2, which is defined as the number of unique operands in a program;
- N_1, which is defined as the total number of operators in a program;
- N_2, which is defined as the total number of operands in a program.

From the four basic measures, three other simple metrics are derived:

- $n = n_1 + n_2$, which is called the program *vocabulary*;
- $N = N_1 + N_2$, which is called the program *length*;
- $V = N \log_2 n$, which is called the program *volume*.

N is a measure of size that is similar to the more conventional count of executable statements. However, Halstead preferred V as a size metric, where V is supposed to measure the number of bits needed to encode the program in a notation with a separate identifier for each operator and operand.

MODEL OUTPUTS

Software Science attempts to characterize a number of program attributes.

- L, which is called the *Level of abstraction* and is believed to be the inverse of the difficulty experienced during the coding process.
- I, which is called the *Intelligence content* of a program, and which is meant to be an implementation-independent measure of the functionality of a program.

- λ, which is called the *Language level,* and is meant to be a program-independent measure of the implementation language used.
- *E,* which is called the *Mental effort,* and is believed to measure the number of 'elementary mental discriminations' needed to code a program.
- *T,* the time in seconds to code a program.
- *B,* the number of 'delivered bugs' in a program, where delivered bugs are those remaining in a program, at the completion of some phase in the development process, which according to Halstead, does not have to coincide with delivery to the ultimate customer.

FORMULA

L is not directly measurable and so is estimated using the following formula:

$$L_{est} = (2/n_1)(n_2/N_2)$$

L_{est} is used to replace *L* in all the remaining formulae.

$$I = LV \qquad \lambda = L^2 V \qquad E = V/L$$

B and *T* are estimated using

$$T_{est} = E/18 \qquad B_{est} = E^{2/3}/3000 = V/3000$$

EVALUATION

There have been a large number of evaluation studies of Software Science reported by Halstead (1977) and Fitzsimmons & Love (1978). Unfortunately, the majority of these studies confused correlation studies, which indicate the existence of a relationship, with regression studies, which indicate the nature of a relationship. In addition, in many cases there was no attempt to test formally any of the hypotheses under consideration, using appropriate statistical methods.

A complete re-evaluation of the initial Software Science evaluation studies has been performed by Hamer & Frewin (1981, and 1982). They conclude that 'the claimed experimental support is largely illusionary'.

Other researchers have both criticized the psychological arguments used to derive the equation for *T* (Coulter, 1983) and suggested that the Software Science metrics offer no more information about the characteristics of a program than do simple size metrics such as instruction counts—see Kitchenham (1981) or Gremillion (1984).

PROBLEMS

A basic problem with Software Science is that to obtain any of the metrics it is necessary to determine what constitutes an operator and what constitutes an operand in a particular programming language. For example, Halstead defines 'goto label' as a single operator, such that each goto statement with a different label counts as a separate operator, i.e. 'goto here' and 'goto there' are regarded as separate operators. Many people might prefer to define 'goto' as a single operator, and each distinct label as a distinct operand of the goto operator. Hamer and Frewin comment that 'The counting rules for the basic metrics are ill-defined, arbitrary and not applicable to languages with structured and abstract data types'.

A separate problem with theory of Software Science is the distinction between L and L_{est}. Hamer and Frewin conclude:

'There is a major division between Software Science theory and practice in the alternative families of metrics based on L and L_{est}. The theory does not explain the existence of two such similar concepts, nor does it define them adequately.

The family of metrics based on L is almost certainly spurious since it depends on another ill-defined (and probably provably undefinable) metric.'

RECOMMENDATIONS

There does not appear to be any sound evidence that the complex Software Science formulae are valid, or provide good measures of the product attributes they are meant to characterize. The use of any Software Science metrics, except perhaps the simple counts and size metrics, cannot be advised.

Equally, any other metrics that are based on L, I, λ, E, B or T cannot be justified in terms of the theory of Software Science. In addition, studies, that attempt to validate new metrics in terms of their relationship with Software Science metrics cannot be regarded as valid.

For the above reasons, no metrics that are derived from Software Science metrics will be described in this appendix.

C.4 Software Metrics

The metrics described in this section are as follows.

PRODUCT ATTRIBUTES
* SIZE
  —software
  Lines of code (*LOC*)
  —text
  Number of words
* STRUCTURE
  —software
  Characteristics of module connections
    Yin and Winchester's measure of software design complexity
  Internal module characteristics
    McCabe's cyclomatic number
    Oviedo's complexity measure
  —text
  no metrics included

- MODULARITY
  —software
    Module strength
    Fan-in/fan-out
  —text
    not applicable
- UNDERSTABILITY
  —software
    De Young/Kampen's readability measure
  —text
    Gunning's fog index
- RELATIONSHIPS BETWEEN PRODUCTS
  —software
    Design to code expansion rate
  —text
    no metrics included
- STABILITY
  —software and text
    Fault and change rates

PROCESS ATTRIBUTES
  - CHECKING COMPLETENESS
    Woodward/Hedley/Hennell's test effectiveness measures
  - CHECKING EFFICIENCY
    Fault detection rates

EVENT ATTRIBUTES
N.B. the items noted below are not metrics in themselves; they provide the framework within which fault counts and change request counts may be accumulated.
  - FAULTS
    Fault classification schemas
  - CHANGE REQUESTS
    Change request classification schema

The metrics identified above only present a small sample of the software metrics that have been generated over the last 10 to 15 years. The interested reader will find many other metrics described in the literature. In particular, the survey documents by Hocker *et al.* (1984), and Sherif *et al.* (1985) describe a great many quality indicator metrics, and Troy & Zweben (1981), suggest a large number of possible design metrics. In addition, the *IEEE Transactions on Software Engineering* and the *Journal of Systems and Software* publish a substantial number of papers dealing with software metrics.

C.4.1 Metric descriptions—product attributes

C.4.1.1 *Lines of code (LOC)*

EXPLANATION

LOC is a static measure of the physical size of source code of a software component.

ELABORATION

LOC is used to measure modules, subsystems and complete systems. It is used both as a control metric and as a predictor metric.

MEASURE

LOC counts the number of lines in a software component, and where possible classifies them as;

- new lines
- amended lines
- reused lines
- comment lines
- blank lines

COMPARABILITY DATA

The method by which the counts are obtained must indicate whether blank lines, comment lines, data declarations, reused lines, and lines of code that are not intended for delivery (i.e. test harness code) are included or not.

It is also necessary to indicate whether multiple statements on one line are counted as one or many lines, and whether statements that span several lines are treated as one or many lines.

The language that is being measured should also be identified.

USES

LOC is used as a control metric to measure task completion. It it used to predict control metrics such as the effort and time scales required to produce a product, and to identify fault-prone components. It should be noted that in order to act as effort predictors, size metrics will often be based on estimates rather than actual measurements.

EVALUATION

Evaluation of LOC as a predictor of costs and schedule is included in Chapter 11.

A number of studies have reported examples of a positive association between component size and the number of errors found in a component (see for example Kafura & Canning (1985) or Kitchenham (1986)). There is no indication that there is a consistent relationship in different environments, or even for products produced in the same environment.

PROBLEMS

Jones, T. C. (1977) has pointed out that attempts to compare the productivity and quality of programs in terms of production rates and fault rates based on lines of code can be extremely misleading if comparisons are made for programs written in different languages.

LOC is also extremely sensitive to programming style.

RECOMMENDATIONS

LOC can be recommended for use both as a control metric and as a predictor metric, as long as it is used with care. The metric must be properly defined, and should only be used for comparison purposes when it is being used to compare modules written in the same language, and when it is certain that style differences between programmers will not invalidate any conclusions.

LOC is a useful measure of size for four basic reasons:

- It is applicable both to new code and code amendments.
- It is relatively simple to collect.
- It is used in most cost models.
- It is as good an indicator of anomalous components as more sophisticated metrics.

LOC is usually applied to source code, but there is no reason why the basic concept should not be extended to software specifications and designs if they are represented in formal notations.

Other metrics related to product size are Halstead's program length, N, or number of executable statements, or number of machine-code instructions (for high-level languages), or number of bytes of object code.

C.4.1.2 *Number of words*

EXPLANATION

Number of words is a static measure of the physical size of a document written in a natural language.

ELABORATION

The measure applies to any text document, produced at any stage in the development process. It is used as a control metric.

MEASURE

The measure is self-explanatory.

COMPARABILITY DATA

The procedures for data collection must specify whether or not words used to annotate diagrams are to be included. In addition, the procedure for dealing with hyphenated words and acronyms must be specified.

Uses

The metric can be used as a control metric to monitor the progress of document production with respect to percentage completeness.

Recommendations

We are not aware of any published work recording the use of this metric in software development. The analogy to LOC implies that such a metric might be useful, particularly if it were applied to natural language specification and design documents. There are no overpowering reasons not to collect this metric, it must depend upon whether it is believed that the information it provides can or will be used.

Equivalent metrics are number of sentences and number of pages.

C.4.1.3 *Software design complexity*

Yin & Winchester's measure of Software design complexity (Yin & Winchester, 1978).

Explanation

This measures the complexity of a software system in terms of the number of modules in the design and the connections between them.

Elaboration

The measure compares the actual design structure of a system with the 'ideal' structure, which is assumed to be a tree structure.

The metric may be applied to systems or subsystems. It is a quality indicator metric that is believed to influence the clarity, understandability and maintainability of the product.

Measurement

The basic measurements which are needed to construct the metric are:

- A_i, which is the number of module arcs from level 0 to level i in the actual module structure;
- N_i, which is the total number of modules from level 0 to level i.

The number of module arcs in the ideal tree structure (i.e. a structure in which each module is called by only one module) is one less than the number of modules:

- $T_i = N_i - 1$

From these metrics, the three measures of design quality are calculated:

- $C_i = A_i - T_i$ is assumed to measure the absolute complexity of the ith level of the module network.
- $R_i = C_i/A_i$ is assumed to measure the relative complexity of the ith level of the module network (relative tree impurity).
- $D_i = (C_i - C_{i-1})/(A_i - A_{i-1})$ is assumed to measure the relative complexity of a hierarchy level (differential tree impurity).

The measured quantities may be obtained from design structure charts.

COMPARABILITY DATA

The way in which recursive modules are represented in the structure diagram must be specified.

USES

The metrics are meant to indicate areas of a design that are suboptimum and therefore, potentially of poor quality.

EVALUATION

Correlation studies from two systems indicated that there was an association between both C_i and R_i and error rate. No other evaluation studies have been performed.

PROBLEMS

There has been no validation that the measures are directly related to clarity, understandability, or maintainability.

The measures are based on the underlying assertion that a tree-based design is 'optimum'. This assumption is not shared by the proponents of the data-flow design method that led to the use of structure diagrams. Constantine & Yourdon (1979) and Myers (1978) recommend identifying general-purpose modules at the bottom level of the system structure, which can be used to perform frequently-needed, general-purpose functions, and which will, therefore be called by a number of other modules.

The presence of functions that are called by more than one module prevents a structure diagram from conforming to the constraints of a tree, but it could be reasonably argued that this does not harm the clarity or understandability of the design, since there is a reduction in unnecessary duplication. Such a non-tree structure is also of positive benefit when identifying modules suitable for re-use and when specifying unit tests, and is likely to reduce coding effort. However, it can be argued that integration testing becomes more difficult, since modules can be invoked by a number of different calling sequences. In addition, it is likely that a structure will be more complex if levels other than the lowest level in the hierarchy depart from a strict tree structure.

RECOMMENDATIONS

Few design metrics have been subjected to widespread validation, so there is little to choose between these metrics and other metrics based on structure diagrams. These measures are fairly simple to obtain and will appeal to software engineers who agree with the importance of tree structures.

Troy & Zweben (1981) have identified 21 metrics that can be obtained from a structure diagram and identified that those related to coupling (i.e. the type of data linkage between modules) were most strongly associated with subsequent error rates. The coupling metrics identified by Troy & Zweben were as follows:

- the maximum number of interconnections per node in the structure diagram;
- the average number of interconnections per node;
- the total number of interconnections per node;
- the number of nodes accessing a common interconnection;
- the number of unique common interconnections in a structure chart;
- the number of nodes accessing control interconnections;
- the number of nodes accessing control interconnections other than OK/FAIL, where OK/FAIL indicates successful or unsuccessful completion of processing of a module;
- the number of interconnections to the top node;
- the number of data structure interconnections to the top node;
- the number of simple connections to the top node.

The potential importance of design metrics as early indicators of software quality, even if the term 'quality' in this sense only implies potentially error-prone components, is very great. The use of any of the above metrics or Yin and Winchester's metrics can therefore be recommended to those who use structure diagrams. However, it will be the responsibility of the potential user of the metrics to validate that they are useful in his or her environment.

C.4.1.4 *Cyclomatic complexity*
McCabe's Cyclomatic Number (McCabe, 1976).

EXPLANATION
This measure is derived from the equivalent control flow graph of a program and measures the number of linearly independent paths through a program.

ELABORATION
This metric is a quality predictor metric that is meant to be a measure of the testability of a program. It may also be used as a control metric to assess the completeness of the testing process.

MEASUREMENT
The cyclomatic number, $V(G)$, is determined from the following formula:

$$V(G) = e - n + 2p$$

where e is the number of edges in the control graph, where an edge is equivalent to a branching point in the program;

n is the number of vertices in the control graph, where a vertex is equivalent to a sequential block of code in the program;

p is the number of connected components usually 1.

In structured programs (i.e. programs that do not permit jumps into and out of the body of loops), $V(G)$ is equivalent to the number of predicates plus 1, where compound predicates such as IF a AND b THEN are treated as two. This is equivalent to the number of decision points in a program.

COMPARABILITY DATA

The method by which a program is converted into its equivalent control-flow diagram must be specified. Such a transformation may be quite straightforward for languages such as BASIC and FORTRAN, but may be very complicated for more complex languages such as Ada or Algol 68. For example the control flow implications of the following Algol 68 structures are extremely difficult to specify:

- Compound Boolean control structures in the context of a language compiler that permits lazy evaluation of compound Booleans.
- The evaluation of compound Booleans outside loop structures; for example consider the following sequence of statements

$$a := c \text{ or } d$$

```
{a sequence of statements}
if
    a
then
    . . .
```

- Conditional structures embedded in assignment statements.
- Sequential blocks of code embedded in control structure, for example

```
if
    a or
        begin
            {sequence of statements}
            b
        end
then
    . . .
```

USES

The metric may be used to identify testing requirements for a program in terms of test completion criteria aimed at exercising each independent path at least once.

McCabe has suggested that a program with a high level of the metric is likely to be difficult to produce and maintain. For his FORTRAN environment, he recommended an upper limit of 10.

EVALUATION

The metric has been evaluated both as a test metric (Paige, 1980), and in terms of its relation to understandability and modifiability of programs (Curtis & Sheppard, 1979).

It has been shown to be associated with module error rates, but has not been demonstrated to provide much better identification of error-prone modules than LOC (see Kafura & Canning, 1985; Kitchenham, 1981).

A full and critical evaluation of the metric has been provided by Shepperd (1988) from the viewpoint of its lack of an explicit model and poor empirical performance. He concludes that 'there must exist considerable doubts about the utility of McCabe's cyclomatic complexity metric'.

PROBLEMS

The practical difficulties that are sometimes encountered when attempting to determine the equivalent flow graph of a program mean that very often the flow graph of an *equivalent program* is obtained rather than that of the program as originally written. This must cast some doubt as to what is actually being measured.

The metric must be regarded as a very superficial complexity measure, since it regards all program structures as equivalent. Thus, a sequence of three loops will provide the same cyclomatic number as three nested loops.

Another fundamental problem with the use of the metric as a measure of testability is that it is entirely based on control flow and ignores data flow. Many programs can be written to avoid the use of control structures, by the use of look-up tables and arrays and other data-oriented programming practices instead (see Humpphrey, 1986). Thus, the value of the metric may be strongly influenced by programming style, and may give very misleading estimates of the amount of testing required.

RECOMMENDATIONS

The cyclomatic number cannot in general be recommended for use as a complexity metric, and must be used with caution when it is regarded as a testability measure.

In an environment where the metric can be obtained from detailed design representations before code production, it might prove more useful, since it could be used as an early indicator of large and potentially fault-prone programs. It might also be useful in conjunction with Jackson's approach to structured programming. The value of the cyclomatic number obtained from the data-structure diagrams should match exactly the cyclomatic number obtained from the schematic logic (Jackson, 1975). Thus, the cyclomatic number could provide a consistency check between stages in the JSP process.

This metric is important historically, since McCabe's idea of analysing the structure of programs using equivalent mathematical graphs stimulated a large amount of software metrics research; see for example Fenton *et al.* (1985).

A related metric is the program Knot count (Woodward *et al.*, 1979), which counts the number of times the control flow paths in a program intersect one another.

C.4.1.5 *Oviedo's complexity measure*

EXPLANATION
Oviedo's complexity measure is a weighted sum of a control-flow metric and a data-flow metric (Ovideo, 1980).

ELABORATION
Oviedo's measure attempts to capture overall program complexity by including control-flow and data-flow measures. The control-flow metric is based on the number of edges in the equivalent control-flow graph. The data-flow metric is based on the number of variables referenced but not defined in a program block (i.e. sequence of statements between branches). A variable definition is defined to be the assignment of a value to a variable; variable reference is defined to be the use of a variable in an expression or as an output.

The metric is intended to be a quality indicator that measures the complexity of a program.

MEASURE
Oviedo's metric C is calculated from the formula:

$$C = aCF + bDF$$

where CF is the control flow complexity measured in terms of the total number of edges in the control flow graph;

DF is the data flow complexity, which is measured in terms of the sum of data flow complexity of each block in the program. The data flow complexity of each block is the number of variables referenced but not defined in each block;

a, b are weighting factors that may be assumed to be 1.

COMPARABILITY DATA
The comparability data for the control flow metric is the same as that required for McCabe's metric.

For data flow complexity, it is necessary to determine how references to individual elements in complex data structures are to be assessed, i.e. is each element of a data structure counted as a separate variable?

USES
The metric can be used to identify complex modules that may require redesign or extra testing.

EVALUATION
This metric has not been evaluated at all. A similar metric has been shown to be related to subjective views of program complexity (Whitworth & Szulewski, 1980).

PROBLEMS

The metric faces the same problems as other metrics that depend on extracting an equivalent control-flow diagram; see the comments directed at McCabe's metric above.

In addition, the identification of the data flow metric is likely to be extremely time-consuming unless an automatic tool is provided.

There is also the problem of adding together two different items. Theoretically it means that the units of measurement for the metric are not clear; practically, it means that the interpretation of unusual metric values is more difficult. It is usually necessary to know what the contributions of each count are to the overall synthetic, in order to determine whether there are any problems with a program, so it is perhaps unnecessary to construct the synthetic.

RECOMMENDATIONS

It seems essential to develop measures of program structure that consider both control-flow and data-flow. Oviedo's metric or Whitworth and Szulewski's metric appear to be the only options available, although it may be simpler to keep control-flow metrics and data-flow metrics as separate counts rather than create a combined metric.

A simple data-flow metric, based for example on Oviedo's DF metric, can therefore, be recommended for use, with the caution that evaluation of the usefulness of the metric is the responsibility of the metric user.

C.4.1.6 *Module strength*

EXPLANATION

Module strength (i.e. cohesion) is a measure of the extent to which a module has a single function.

ELABORATION

It is assumed that a well-modularized system attempts to ensure that each module performs a single function. It is also assumed that modules that perform a number of functions are over-complex and indicate that the system has not been properly decomposed. Module strength is, therefore, an indicator of both the quality of decomposition and the complexity of individual modules.

MEASURE

Card *et al.* (1985) measured module strength by requiring programmers to indicate how many of the following functions a module performed:

- input/output;
- login/control;
- algorithmic processing.

Their measure could therefore only take the values 1, 2, or 3, where a value of 1 is regarded as high strength, 2 as medium strength, and 3 as low strength.

COMPARABILITY DATA

It is hard to imagine a module that did not perform some aspects of each of the itemized processes. It is necessary, therefore, to have some guidelines about how much of a program (e.g. percentage executable statements) needs to be devoted to a particular type of processing before it contributes to the module strength metric.

USES

The metric is used to identify badly modularized components.

EVALUATION

In a study of 453 new FORTRAN programs, Card *et al.* found that high-strength modules were less error-prone and cost less to code than low-strength modules, allowing for the effect of module size.

PROBLEMS

Although there is no *a priori* objection to subjective metrics, organizing the collection of subjective metrics is difficult, and it is difficult to ensure that values are comparable.

RECOMMENDATIONS

Although the concept of the metric is interesting, the difficulty associated with subjective metrics implies that use of the metric cannot be recommended.

C.4.1.7 *Fan-in and fan-out*

EXPLANATION

These metrics are counts of the interconnections that a module has with other modules in a system.

ELABORATION

The terms fan-in and fan-out are used ambiguously in the software metrics lietrature to refer to different concepts:

(i) to describe the calling relationship between modules in a structure chart derived as steps in Constantine & Yourdon's structured design method (1979) (fan-in and fan-out measures based on this concept will be referred to as structural fan-in and fan-out);

(ii) to describe the information-flow relationship between procedures, and the relationship between procedures and data items, as suggested by Henry & Kafura (1981) (fan-in and fan-out measures based on this concept will be referred to as informational fan-in and fan-out).

Structural fan-in and fan-out metrics derived from structure diagrams indicate the interconnections between modules, where a module is a single compilable unit (i.e. a procedure). Structural fan-in metrics count the number of modules that call a given module. Structural fan-out metrics count the number of modules that a given module calls.

Structural fan-in and fan-out metrics are quality indicator metrics in the sense that it is assumed that modules with large metric values may be both complex and system-critical.

Informational fan-in and fan-out metrics are based on the information flow between procedures, which includes not only flow based on the fact that one procedure calls another (which Henry & Kafura call *direct local flow* of information), but also information based by means of return values (which they call *indirect local flow* of information) and information that is passed between procedures via a global data structure (which they call *global flow* of information).

Henry and Kafura derive a complexity metric for procedures, based on informational fan-in and fan-out counts. They also consider the complexity of *modules,* where they define a module, in terms of data structures not procedures, to consist of those procedures that either directly update a specified data structure or directly retrieve information from it.

MEASURE

1. *Structural fan-in and fan-out*

   Structural fan-in is measured in terms of the number of lines emanating upwards from a node in a structure chart. Structural fan-out is measured in terms of the number of lines emanating downwards from a node in a structure chart.

2. *Informational fan-in and fan-out*

   Informational fan-in of a procedure is a count of the number of local data flows into the procedure plus the count of the number of data structures from which the procedure retrieves information (Henry & Kafura, 1981). Informational fan-out of a procedure is a count of the number of local data flows from a procedure plus the number of data structures that the procedure updates (Henry & Kafura, 1981).

Local data flows occur if any one of the following three conditions hold:

- a procedure calls another procedure;
- a procedure calls another, and then makes use of a value returned to it (this is considered to be a fan-in to the calling procedure, and fan-out from the called procedure);
- a procedure calls two procedures (A and B) and the output from A is passed as input B (this is considered to be a fan-out from A and a fan-in to B).

The structural fan-in and fan-out counts, therefore, are one element of the informational fan-in and fan-out counts.

Henry & Kafura use the following formula to indicate the complexity of a procedure:

$$\text{length} \times [(\text{fan-in} \times \text{fan-out})^2]$$

where length is any metric of size (e.g. lines of code, or Halstead counts, or McCabe's cyclomatic number).

COMPARABILITY DATA

1. *Structural fan-in and fan-out*
   It is necessary to know whether recursive procedures are included in the structure diagram.
2. *Informational fan-in and fan-out*
   (i) Any tool used to collect data flow information should be specified.
   (ii) The level to which indirect data flow is monitored should be specified, e.g. will a local indirect data flow be recognized if the input from one procedure is included in an equation before being passed to another procedure?

USES

The metrics may be used to identify potentially complex and critical parts of a system.

Henry & Kafura suggest that their complexity metric can be used to identify stress points in a system, and that high informational fan-out and fan-in counts may indicate procedures that either perform more than one function or are inadequately refined in the sense of missing an appropriate level of abstraction.

EVALUATION

1. *Structural fan-in and fan-out*

   The fan-out metric appears to be useful for detecting potentially large and error-prone modules before coding, while the fan-in metric indicates widely used, and/or critical, modules that should be subject to particularly stringent V&V activities. Although the metrics have not often been the subject of formal, statistically based validation exercises, they have been widely used as criteria for evaluating and refining structure charts by software developers who use the data-flow analysis methods recommended by Constantine & Yourdon (1979) and Myers (1978).

   Troy & Zweben (1981) included fan-in and fan-out metrics in their study of design metrics and observed that fan-out was correlated with subsequent error-proneness of modules, whereas fan-in was not.

2. *Informational fan-in and fan-out*
   Henry & Kafura have validated their metrics using the UNIX operating system. They found that (fan-in × fan-out) was associated with the number of changes (Henry & Kafura, 1981), and that consideration of the complexities of *modules* could indicate both the need for, and a method of evaluating, a redesign of certain procedures (Henry & Kafura, 1984).

PROBLEMS

1. *Structural fan-in and fan-out*
   There are no particular difficulties with structural fan-in and fan-out.
2. *Informational fan-in and fan-out*
   Henry and Kafura introduce a degree of difficulty with the use of their
   metrics because they use different definitions in their 1981 and 1984
   papers. In the former paper, informational fan-in and fan-out are defined
   to include counts of read and write accesses to external data items; in the
   later paper accesses to data structures are not included in the relevant
   definitions.

Far more importantly, their suggested procedure complexity metric has two
major problems and one minor problem. The major problems are:

- The metric is difficult to interpret except in terms of the values of its
  component metrics.
- The metric gives a value of zero for non-trivial procedures if they have no
  fan-in or fan-out. This occurs in the case of interface procedures that may
  have a zero fan-in because they are called by system users not by other
  system procedures, and in the case of the lowest-level system procedures
  that may have a zero fan-out because they do not call any other
  procedures.

The minor problem is that the formula for the procedure complexity will
generate *very* large numbers for some procedures, which may cause some
computational difficulties unless the values are transformed prior to any data
analysis.

The three problems that may be encountered with the procedure-complexity
metric all suggest that it may be more practical to investigate informational
fan-in and fan-out metrics separately for each procedure and to avoid using the
single procedure-complexity metric.

However, the straightforward information-flow metrics suffer from the usual
difficulties of synthetic metrics, which are that the measurement is not clear
and that, in practice, the component counts are important to determine
whether an abnormal value is likely to imply that a procedure is potentially
dangerous. For example, a procedure that is called by a large number of other
procedures is likely to have stringent performance and reliability requirements,
whereas this is not likely to be the case for a procedure that reads from a large
number of data items, although both types of procedure would have a large
informational fan-in value.

RECOMMENDATIONS

The structurally based metrics seem well-suited to software design methods
that use structure diagrams and can be recommended for use in the evaluation
of such diagrams.

The informationally based metrics seem to provide a much greater insight into potential design problems compared with the structurally based metrics, and can, therefore, be recommended, provided a tool to extract the relevant counts is available. However, it may be preferable to collect all the component counts separately and not to construct the synthetics.

The concept of fan-in and fan-out can be extended to data structures as well as to modules by constructing diagrams indicating which components read from and write to a data item (see Henry & Kafura, 1981).

C.4.1.8 *Readibility formula*
De Young/Kampen's readability measure (De Young & Kampen, 1979).

EXPLANATION
This metric uses features of the code and its structure to predict the readability of programs.

ELABORATION
The metric is a quality predictor. It is intended for use with medium-sized programs written in block-structured languages (e.g. PL/1, ALGOL, PASCAL).

MEASURE
The readibility, *R,* of a set of programs was calculated using regression analysis to be:

$$R = 0.295VAR - 0.499NSL + 0.13CYCLO$$

where *VAR* is the average normalized length of variables;
    NSL is the number of lines containing statements;
    CYCLO is the total number of program branches + 1.

COMPARABILITY DATA
The usual comparability data is needed to determine NSL (see LOC) and CYCLO (see McCabe's cyclomatic number).

USES
A readability measure for programs may be used to assess the maintainability and extendability of programs.

EVALUATION
The formulation of the readability equation was based on a subjective evaluation of the readability of programs, and thus confirms the existence of the association between the program characteristics and readability.

The regression formula was not subjected to a single-cross validation study, so the coefficients in the equation should be treated with caution. For example, it is a little surprising to see a relationship that implies that a program becomes more readable as the number of branches in the program increases.

PROBLEMS

This form of synthetic metric, i.e. one derived by regression studies, is very likely to be environment-specific. Thus, even if the association between the program variables and the quality of readability is confirmed in other studies, it is extremely unlikely that the coefficients in the equation will be the same. This implies that the use of this metric depends on a preliminary calibration study to determine the nature of the relationship in a particular environment.

RECOMMENDATIONS

A measure of the readability of programs is potentially very useful, particularly for programs that are expected to be maintained and enhanced over a long period of time. It is also reasonable to assume that the use of meaningful variable names, module size, and module control flow influence the readability of modules. However, there are likely to be many other factors, such as the use of indentation, the inclusion of meaningful comments, module cross-references, data dictionaries etc. Thus, De Young & Kampen's formula must be treated with considerable caution, and could only be used after a preliminary study to confirm the existence of the relationship and calibrate the regression equation.

Another equivalent metric, based on the same principles but including more program characteristics, is Joergenson's (1980) readability measure.

C.4.1.9 *Fog index*
Gunning's fog index (Gunning, 1962).

EXPLANATION

This metric assesses the readability of text written in English in terms of the length of sentences and the number of 'hard' words.

ELABORATION

The fog index is applicable to any textual components, and is a quality indicator metric.

MEASURE

The measure is calculated on the basis of sampling text at the rate of about 100 lines per four pages. The characteristics of the text sample measured are as follows:

sen, the number of sentences;
wrd, the number of words;
syl, the number of syllables.

The fog index, FI, is calculated as follows:

$$FI = 0 \cdot 4(wrd/sen + (hrd/wrd)100)$$

where *hrd* is the number of words of three or more syllables.

COMPARABILITY DATA
None.

USES
This metric can be used to assess the quality of user documentation. It may also be particularly useful for large software projects where many specialists are involved at separate stages in the development process. In this type of project, different staff will be responsible for different stages in the process and will be dependent on written documentation of the previous stages to delineate their required contribution to the project, and will need to prepare written documentation to record their actual contribution. In this sort of project, a means of assessing the readability and understandability of documents is very important.

EVALUATION
The fog index has not been evaluated for software documentation. It has only been evaluated for US magazines.

PROBLEMS
Software documentation is full of long words (even 'computer' is a three-syllable word). It may be that the definition of 'hard words' used in the fog index is over-simplistic within the context of a particular technical discipline that has its own specialist jargon.

RECOMMENDATIONS
The potential usefulness of a measure of document's readability means that the metric must be recommended for use. However, its use must be preceded by some validation studies within any particular software development environment.

There are a fairly large number of readability indexes applicable to natural languages. The fog index has the virtue of simplicity, but there is no reason to assume it is inherently preferable to other measures; see for example the Dale–Chall readability formula (Dale & Chall, 1948), or the Flesch–Kincaid index (Kincaid *et al.*, 1981).

C.4.1.10 *Design-to-code expansion rate*

EXPLANATION
This is the average number of lines of code that correspond to a single design statement.

ELABORATION
This metric can only be used if the design of a software component is recorded in some formal or semi-formal notation. This could be in terms of pseudo-code statements on a flow diagram, statements in a design language, simplified natural language statements, or a formal specification language.

MEASURE

The expansion rate, E, for a software component is calculated as

$$E = LOC/DS$$

where LOC is the total number of lines of code in a software component;
DS is the corresponding total number of design statements.

COMPARABILITY DATA

The comparability data for lines of code has been discussed previously, similar rules need to be determined to ensure that design-statement counts are also comparable. For example, in designs that are expressed in simplified natural English, a design statement might be defined to be a sentence. For design statements based on pseudo-code, it must be determined whether or not pseudo-code comments will be included in the counts.

USES

This metric may be regarded as a measure of the relationship between component representations. It may be used to assess the consistency of the transformation between representations, by comparing the value obtained for groups of similar components, e.g. modules in the same product, in order to identify any modules that have abnormal expansion rates.

The overall expansion rate for all components in a product can be compared with the values obtained for other similar products. In this case a particularly unusual value would indicate that the transformation process had changed in some respect.

In both these cases, abnormal values should not be interpreted as being indicative of a *problem* with a particular module or a particular process. The underlying cause of an abnormal value can usually only be identified after further investigation and may equally well be a favourable as an unfavourable circumstance.

EVALUATION

There have been no evaluation studies for this metric.

PROBLEMS

None.

RECOMMENDATIONS

This metric is one of the few metrics that considers the relationship between products, and as such can be recommended for use in projects that record design statements. However, it is up to the user of the metric to assess whether the metric proves useful in practice.

The concept of expansion rates can be extended to link any related textual or software products. For example, test plans and code may be linked in terms of the expansion rate between number of test cases and lines of code, and requirements documents and design documents in natural English may be linked in terms of the expansion rate in sentences between the two documents.

C.4.1.11 *Fault and change rates*

EXPLANATION
This name is given to a family of metrics which measure the amount of unplanned changes a component is subjected to during product development.

ELABORATION
Fault and change rate metrics may be calculated for any product, textual and software. The metrics are used to record the number of times a component is changed with respect to some baseline version of the component (e.g. the version of the component that is first put under configuration control), and/or the amount of change incorporated into a component in terms of amended lines or statements.

Fault and change rates are used primarily as control metrics, but are intended to indicate the stability or otherwise of components during development and are also considered indicators of final product reliability.

MEASUREMENT
A number of different fault and change metrics can be derived from basic fault and change counts as follows:

- total faults found for a component;
- total faults of a particular type found for a component;
- fault rate = (total faults)/(component size);
- fault rate for a particular type of fault;
- size of component amendments due to faults;
- size of component amendments due to faults of a particular type.

The types of faults that may be considered include:

- faults that were introduced into the component by a particular process (e.g. design faults);
- faults that were revealed by a particular process (e.g. inspections);
- faults of a particular nature (e.g. due to something missing, or due to something present that is incorrect);
- faults related to a particular type of software function (e.g. I/O faults or logic faults).

A number of fault types are described in the fault classification schemas in Section C.4.3.1.

In addition to changes due to faults, there are also changes to a product that are not related to faults, the most important of which are changes due to requirements changes. It is, therefore, possible to construct a series of metrics equivalent to the above fault metrics for non-fault-induced changes. A classification schema, identifying the different reasons for non-fault-induced changes to products is given in Section C.4.3.2.

It should be noted that a single change request or fault can cause a number of different documents and products to be amended. This means that fault counts or change counts accumulated against system components may not add up to the total number of faults or change requests accumulated against the system as a whole.

COMPARABILITY DATA

The classification schemas used to identify types of fault and change requests must be identified.

In addition, it is important to identify the point at which change and fault data begins to be collected. For example, is is from the point at which a version of a component exists, or the point at which some official or recognized version of the component exists, or the point at which the component is used as an input to a planned checking activity, or the point at which the component is released to its user(s)?

USES

Fault and change counts and rates may be used to identify particularly error-prone or change-prone components, since it is assumed that identification of such components may encourage software engineers to consider either re-design or additional testing of such components before they are released to users.

Additional classification of counts and rates may indicate possible reasons for change- or error-proneness. In particular, a large number of changes attributed to requirements changes may indicate a potentially unstable and, therefore, unreliable system or system component.

The size of changes due to faults and change requests can be used to assess the cost of defects and unplanned work, in terms of additional unplanned code production.

Basili & Weiss (1982b) have used information about changes to analyse software development in the software engineering laboratory.

EVALUATION

Walston & Felix (1977) identified requirements changes as a factor that influenced production costs in an IBM study. Boehm, however, did not observe a significant effect of this in his COCOMO studies (Boehm, 1981).

Belady & Lehman (1976) confirmed the problem associated with system changes for systems that undergo long-term modification and enhancement, with thier report of the breakdown in the development of IBM's OS360 system. Lehman (1978) has confirmed the generality of the result with analyses of other systems.

In a system released periodically to its customers with enhanced facilities, modules that were change-prone during the production of one release were found to be more likely to be changed in subsequent releases than normal modules (Kitchenham, 1986).

In a study of 30 programs, Takahashi & Kamayachi (1985) found a correlation between changes, resulting from requirements changes, and fault rate (i.e. faults per thousand lines of code).

Grady & Caswell (1987) reported the results of tracking pre- and post-release faults on a module basis, and found that the modules that exhibited most faults before release were the same modules that exhibited most faults after release.

PROBLEMS

The collection of data about faults requires software engineers to record objectively data about their mistakes. This requires a very professional approach to software production, not only by software engineers, but also by software managers, and it is not surprising that such an approach is not accepted whole-heartedly by all members of the profession. It must, therefore, be recognized that information about faults and unplanned changes prior to system release may be incomplete and subject to recording errors.

RECOMMENDATIONS

When trustworthy information about change and fault rates is available, the use of these metrics can be recommended on the basis of normal quality assurance practice in any industry.

A prudent project manager would be well advised to concentrate some extra effort on components with a bad historical record, and we would recommend such an approach.

C.4.2 Metrics descriptions—process attributes

C.4.2.1 *Test effectiveness measures*
Woodward/Hedley/Hennell's test effectiveness measures (Woodward *et al.*, 1979).

EXPLANATION

This family of metrics characterize the completeness of testing on the basis of the 'amount' of a software product tested with respect to some criteria that indicates the 'amount' of a product available for testing.

ELABORATION

These metrics are used to measure the test coverage of executable software components. The metrics are control metrics that monitor test progress, but are also sometimes regarded as indicators of product reliability.

MEASURE

The test coverage metrics are based on identifying the following features of a program:

- *NI*, the number of instructions in the program;
- *NB*, the number of branches in the program;
- *NLCSAJ*, the number of LCSAJs (linear code sequence and jump);
- NPP_i, the number of partial paths consisting of i LCSAJs;
- NCP_i, the number of complete paths consisting of a maximum of i LCSAJs.

Then, for any test case or set of test cases, the test coverage metrics are obtained by identifying which parts of the program are executed by the test case(s), in terms of the identified program features.

The test coverage metrics are as follows:

- TER_1 = number of instructions executed/*NI*;
- TER_2 = number of branches executed/*NB*;
- TER_3 = number of LSCAJs executed/*NLCSAJ*;
- TER_{i+2} = (number of different partial paths with i LCSAJs executed at least once + number of different complete paths with a maximum of i LCSAJs executed at least once)/$(NPP_i + NCP_i)$.

Woodward *et al.* note that it is increasingly difficult to obtain a value of 1 of the TER_i metrics as the value of i increases beyond 3 or 4.

COMPARABILITY DATA

Instruction counts and branch counts need to be defined as indicated in the LOC and McCabe's cyclomatic number descriptions, respectively. Similarly, what is meant by an LCSAJ (particularly with respect to the evaluation of compound Boolean statements with lazy evaluation), needs to be unambiguously defined.

USES

The metrics are used to establish minimum testing criteria for programs, in order to monitor the testing process.

It is also often assumed that achieving values of the coverage metrics close to or equal to 1 implies that the product is in some sense 'well-tested'. Thus, the metric values are assumed to be indicators of final reliability.

PROBLEMS

These metrics suffer from many of the same problems as McCabe's cyclomatic number, a particular problem for measures of testedness is that they only measure control-flow coverage and do not consider data flow.

These metrics cannot practically be evaluated by hand. They must be supported by a test harness that identifies the program structures and analyses the execution history of the program when the program is tested.

EVALUATION

There have been no evaluation studies aimed at assessing the relationship between levels of reliability and the various test coverage metrics.

RECOMMENDATIONS

If a test bed is available to support the extraction of coverage metrics, these metrics can be recommended as a means by which criteria for testing activities can be established and the testing activity can be monitored. However, it must be recognized that achieving a particular test coverage value does not guarantee achieving product reliability. Thus, there is no objective criterion for choosing to aim for one coverage target or another. Validated, cost-effective test strategies for achieving required levels of reliability are desperately required, but are not currently available.

Other useful metrics are those that relate test coverage metrics both to the number of test cases planned and to the number of test cases actually run. These metrics allow the effectiveness of test planning to be assessed.

C.4.2.2 *Fault detection rates*

EXPLANATION

This name is given to a family of metrics that measure the fault-detection effectiveness of test cases and checking techniques.

ELABORATION

Fault detection rates can be calculated for any checking activity. They are used as control metrics, to track the progress of checking activities and evaluate the effectiveness of checking methods and test planning.

MEASUREMENTS

A number of different fault rate metrics can be derived from basic fault counts:

- Total faults found during a particular checking activity, normalized with respect to the size of the component(s) being checked (e.g. three faults per 100 LOC for unit testing all modules).
- Normalized number of faults of a particular type found during a particular checking activity.
- Percentage of total faults and/or faults of a particular type, found by a particular checking activity (e.g. 20% of design faults found during development were found by unit testing).
- The rate (which may be normalized with respect to the size of the product being checked) at which all faults and/or faults of a particular type are found during a particular checking activity (e.g. during integration testing faults were detected at a rate of three per week per 1000 LOC).
- The effort per fault detected for a particular checking activity (one person-hour per fault detected during design inspections).
- The average number of faults detected per test case.

The type of faults that may be considered include:

- faults that were introduced by a particular production process;
- faults of a particular nature;
- faults related to type of software function.

A classification schema for fault types is given in Section C.4.3.1.

COMPARABILITY DATA
The comparability data is the same as that given in Section C.4.1.11 for fault and change rates.

USES
Fault-detection rates are used to monitor the progress and assess the efficiency of checking activities. It is usual to establish expected rates from past records of other similar projects and plan the checking activities in terms of those rates. The actual progress of checking is then monitored with respect to those plans.

Fault-detection rates have been used to diagnose problems with software development methods and to assess the effects of changes (see Kitchenham & Kitchenham, 1984; Kitchenham *et al.*, 1986).

RECOMMENDATIONS
It is recommended that fault-detection rates are used to plan and monitor checking activities. Use of such metrics can in the long run provide information about the cost-effectiveness of various checking activities to assist in the development of effective checking strategies.

A related metric is fault latency that measures the delay between fault introduction and fault detection (Boehm *et al.*, 1978).

C.4.3 Classification schemas—event attributes

C.4.3.1 *Fault classification schemas*

EXPLANATION
These schemas identify a number of different ways in which a fault may be described.

ELABORATION
The classification schemas identify a number of major attributes of a fault. For each attribute, a number of mutually exclusive categories are suggested that can be used to describe the characteristics of any fault.

CLASSIFICATION SCHEMAS
Source of fault

- requirements analysis
- technical specification of product
- high-level design
- detailed design
- coding
- fault correction activities introduced a new fault
- amendments to a component caused unchanged code to exhibit a fault

Process that revealed fault

- requirements definition review/inspection
- technical specification review/inspection
- high-level design/inspection
- detailed design review/inspection
- code review/inspection
- unit testing
- integration test
- system test
- field trial/acceptance test
- live-use of the system
- other

Nature of fault

- component missing
- component incorrect
- clerical error
- complex combinatorial fault

Software function

- timing
- initialization
- logic/control
- interface (external)
- interface (internal)
- data (value or structure)
- computation
- other

COMPARABILITY DATA

The above classification schemas assume a particular underlying view of the life cycle. Any classification process must reflect the reality of the life cycle within which it is to be used. The above schemas should therefore be calibrated to the specific features of any particular environment before use.

The specific meaning of each category in each schema must be properly defined: for example, in the above schema computation means calculation of mathematical formulae, whereas logic/control refers to the direction of the program through the correct paths; for a discussion of the other terms see Basili *et al.* (1977) and Basili & Weiss (1982*a*).

OTHER FAULT DATA
In order to construct fault rates and fault-detection rates it is necessary to keep additional information about individual faults. Such information includes the date and time of fault occurrence, and the system components and documents that must be amended as a result of the fault.

C.4.3.2 *Change-request classification schema*

EXPLANATION
This classification schema provides a series of categories to describe the type of change requests that can occur.

CLASSIFICATION SCHEMA
Nature of change request

- fault correction
- planned enhancement or new facility
- correction of design deficiency
- implementation of requirements change
- improvement of clarity, maintainability, or documentation
- improvement of user service
- insertion or deletion of debug code
- optimization
- adaptation to environment change

COMPARABILITY DATA
The above schema must be calibrated to the particular features of any environment in which it is to be used. The meaning of each category must be fully described.

OTHER CHANGE-REQUEST DATA
In addition to classifying change requests, it is necessary to collect additional data about change requests in order to calculate the change-rate metrics indicated in Section C.4.1.11. In particular, information about the software components and documents that need to be amended and the size of the amendments should be collected.

C.5   Quantitative Software Models

The models described in this section are related to the control of the development process in terms of the defects found during testing and the organization of the testing process, and the evaluation of intermediate products from the viewpoint of progress towards final product characteristics (not just reliability, but other qualities such as maintainability, usability, performance, etc.). The issue of measuring the reliability of an executing product is covered fully in Chapter 6.

The quantitative models described in this section are as follows:

- *Fault introduction and detection models*
  Small and Faulkener's system design and integration model
  Remus and Zilles defect removal model
- *Quality models*
  McCall, Walters & Richards quality model
- *Process models*
  Huff, Sroka & Struble's test and fix model 1 (bug clearance)
  Huff, Sroka & Struble's test and fix model 2 (testcase passage)

C.5.1   Fault introduction and detection models

C.5.1.1   *System design and integration*
Small & Faulkener's system design and integration model (Small & Faulkener, 1983).

EXPLANATION
This model regards system development as a two-stage process of system design and system construction.

System design is regarded as a hierarchy. At each level of the hierarchy a number of components are identified that describe the system in more detailed terms, until at the lowest level of the hierarchy the basic building blocks of the system are reached (these may be gates, cells, MSI ICs, order code instructions, etc.). This model regards system design at each level of the hierarchy to be the process of partitioning the design into a set of components and specifying both the components and the interfaces between components. It is assumed that during the design process, faults are introduced that if allowed to remain in a high-level component will propagate through all the related lower-level components.

System integration is the process of progressive assembly of components and interfaces, starting from the lowest level until the full system is assembled. It is assumed that during the process of integration, test and repair takes place. At each level, each component is tested with respect to its internal characteristics and the level as a whole is tested to attempt to reveal faults that exist in the interfaces between components.

The model investigates the implication for final product quality of alternative testing strategies. It also indicates either the final quality of the system, given information about the test strategy being used and the fault detection characteristics of the tests used, or indicates the fault detection rates that are necessary to achieve a desired final system quality.

MODEL INPUTS
The model requires an estimate of the expected number of fault classes, n, and the expected number of faults per class, per basic system component, f_{ij}, $i = 1, \ldots, N$ components, $j = 1, \ldots, n$ classes.

In addition, the number of levels in the design, $r + 1$, and the number of basic components, N, in the whole system must be counted. It is assumed that for $r + 1$ levels there are r possible independent test stages during system integration. For each test stage used, the fault-detection rate for each class at each stage, d_{jk}, must be estimated, where $k = 1, \ldots, r$ stages.

MODEL OUTPUTS
The model outputs either an estimate of the total number of faults in the system after the specified number of tests, or the required fault-detection rates needed to achieve a specified residual fault count.

FORMULA
The model relates fault rates and fault-detection rates per test stage with the following formulae:

$$F'_j = F_j(1 - D_j)$$

where F'_j is the total number of faults in fault class j remaining after integration and

$$D_j = 1 - \prod (1 - d_{jk}) \qquad F_j = \left(\sum f_{ij} \right)(1 - d_{jk})$$

EVALUATION
The model has not undergone any formal evaluation studies.

PROBLEMS
The model was originally developed to model hardware design quality, where the concept of system integration as an assembly task based on basic components of equal quality is much more reasonable than it is for software.

Like all fault-counting models, it does not address the issue of reliability, which depends not on the number of faults but on the likelihood of the faults being invoked while the system is in use. In addition, although Small & Faulkener discuss the generation of faults in terms of a Poisson process, no statistical analysis of the accuracy of the model outputs is provided.

The model also relies on a number of inputs that are difficult if not impossible to estimate accurately.

Small & Faulkener note that there is a practical problem in obtaining independent tests for each test stage as is assumed by the model, and that the model does not represent the way in which inter-component errors become more likely as the system size increases.

RECOMMENDATIONS
As it currently exists, the model can not be recommended as a predictor of residual faults. However, it is an interesting model for two reasons:

- It is one of the few models that acknowledges the existence of hardware design faults, and offers a broad enough view of *system* development to be applicable to hardware and software faults.
- Under simplifying assumptions, it has demonstrated the superiority of testing during design decomposition by illustrating that the testing efficiency for each test stage can be substantially less to achieve the same final quality if testing occurs during design decomposition rather than only during system integration.

C.5.1.2 *Remus and Zilles defect-removal model*

EXPLANATION
Remus & Zilles model assumes that each piece of software starts with an original set of defects (*OD*), that are introduced when the first version is written (Remus & Zilles, 1979). They assume that the number of defects depends primarily on the size of the code.

They then assume that there is a sequence of defect-removal steps in which defects are detected and corrected. Methods of defect detection include design reviews/inspections, code inspections, testing, and the processing of defects found in the field. During each defect-detection stage, some fraction of the defects present on entry to the stage are detected. They assume that all defects detected in a stage are removed, but allow some fraction of the repairs to introduce new defects. Thus, on exit from each stage, the total number of defects remaining is the sum of the defects that were not detected and the defects that were introduced as a result of incorrect repairs.

Assuming that the fraction of defects detected at each stage and the proportion of bad fixes at each stage are constant and given the number of defects found at the first two defect-detection stages, the model provides an estimate of the total lifetime defects in the product and the defects remaining on exit from the second stage.

MODEL INPUTS
The model requires the following inputs:

- *MP*, which is the number of major problems recorded during reviews and inspections;
- *PTM*, which is the number of defects discovered during testing.

The model then requires either estimates of the proportion of bad fixes at each stage ε_i and the fraction of defects detected at each stage P_i or assumes that ε_i and P_i are constant for all stages.

MODEL OUTPUT

The model provides a measure of the total lifetime defects in the product, TD, and the defects remaining after the second defect detection stage, Q_2. The model provides a measure of the cumulative removal efficiency (CRE) of the defect-removal steps, assuming that there are only two steps in the process i.e. reviews/inspections and testing.

FORMULA

Assuming constant bad-fix and defect-detection rates,

$$TD = MP\mu/(\mu - 1)$$
$$Q_2 = TD/\mu^2$$
$$CRE = (\mu^2 - 1)/\mu^2$$

where $\mu = MP/PTM$.

EVALUATION

Remus & Zilles presented no form of evaluation for their model.

It has been found that the model provides unstable estimates of TD and Q_2 when the assumption that ε_i and P_i are constant is invalid (Kitchenham, 1986).

PROBLEMS

The usual criticism of fault-counting models, that they do not offer genuine reliability predictions, applies to this model. In addition, this is a strictly deterministic model, so it provides no estimate of the accuracy of its predictions.

A conceptual problem with the model is its confused view of defect introduction and detection during the design stage of software production. Design inspections are directed at different representations of software from those of code inspections and conventional testing. The view that a 'piece of software' contains an original set of defects that are removed by a series of defect-detection stages, which includes design inspections, seems, therefore, to be inconsistent with the reality of software-production and defect-introduction processes.

RECOMMENDATIONS

The model is reasonably simple to use, and it is likely that it would be more stable if estimates for ε_i and P_i were available from similar projects, so that the simplifying assumptions can be dispensed with.

The model can be recommended, with caution, as an initial rough assessment of product quality. This type of 'qualitative number' might have a use as an explanatory variable or a Bayesian prior in genuine reliability models.

C.5.2 Quality models

C.5.2.1 *McCall, Walters & Richards quality model*

EXPLANATION

This model predicts the value of a number of final product qualities, using measurements taken during software development (McCall *et al.*, 1977).

The model assumes a hierarchical model of quality, in which a quality of the final product, called a *quality factor* (e.g. reliability), is assumed to depend on a number of *quality criteria* that are under the control of software developers (e.g. the criteria underlying reliability are asserted to be consistency, accuracy, error tolerance and simplicity). For each quality criterion, a set of quality metrics are provided that may be obtained during software development. The metrics have the following characteristics:

- There are system-based metrics and module-based metrics.
- Many of the metrics are checklist-based (e.g. are answers to questions of the type 'Does the module have only one entry and exit point?'). Checklist items are converted into measurements by using the ratio of the number of items with a 'yes' answer, to the total number of items. The checklists were devised so that a value close to 1 would correspond to a high level of quality, and a value close to 0 would correspond to low quality.
- Metrics were developed for requirements, design and implementation, to allow the development of a product to be monitored with respect to quality achievement from an early stage in the lifecycle.

The qualities identified by McCall *et al.* were:

- correctness
- reliability
- efficiency
- integrity
- usability
- maintainability
- testability
- flexibility
- portability
- re-usability
- interoperability

These were supported by 23 different quality criteria, where each criterion could support a number of different quality factors. McCall *et al.* developed 41 metrics to measure the quality criteria and hence the quality factors.

MODEL INPUTS

Rather than list all 41 different checklists, we will illustrate the nature of the model with one example, the completeness metric. Completeness is one of the criteria underlying correctness and is measured with the following checklist.

1. Unambiguous references (input, function, output) [R, D, I].
2. All data references defined, computed, or obtained from an external source [R, D, I].
3. All defined functions used [R, D, I].
4. All referenced functions defined [R, D, I].
5. All conditions and processing defined for each decision point [R, D, I].
6. All defined and referenced calling sequence parameters agree [D, I].
7. All problem reports resolved [R, D, I].
8. Design agrees with requirements [D].
9. Code agrees with design [I].

The letters R, D, or I in square brackets indicates whether the checklist element is applicable to requirements, design and/or implementation. The checklist is converted into a metric by assigning a 1 to each 'yes' answer and 0 to each 'no' answer, counting the number of 1s and dividing that by the number of checklist items used. For example, the requirements metric is based on 6 checklist items.

To provide a measure of a quality factor, the metric values of all the related quality criteria are required.

MODEL OUTPUTS
The model outputs a number in the range 0 to 1 for each quality factor.

FORMULA
The formula for each quality factor is based on the same principle; as an example, the formula for Correctness is given:

Correctness = (Traceability + Completeness + Consistency)/3

where Traceability, Completeness, and Consistency are constructed from checklists, as described for Completeness above.

The value of Correctness will depend on the stage of the development process at which it is calculated.

EVALUATION
McCall *et al.* performed an indirect evaluation of some of the quality factors using single cross-validation. They evaluated metrics for module maintainability and module reliability, and then used linear regression analysis to relate the quality metrics to module debugging effort and fault rate, respectively. They had data from two systems and used part of the data to establish the nature of the relationship and the remaining data to evaluate the accuracy of the relationship.

PROBLEMS
Many of the checklist items require subjective assessment, which implies that procedures must be established to make such assessments as repeatable as possible.

In addition, the construction of the checklists assumes a conventional development cycle and conventional programming languages; it may, therefore, be necessary to reformulate the checklists for non-standard environments.

The McCall *et al.* model is one of a series of quality models based on the quality factor, quality criteria, quality metric model; see Boehm *et al.* (1978), and Bowen *et al.* (1984). A general problem with the models is that each research group identifies a different set of quality factors, and when they do agree on a factor (for example, all the studies include reliability), they then disagree on the number and nature of the criteria that are meant to support the factor, and disagree further on the metrics which are meant to measure the criteria. (For a general discussion of the problems of this type of model, see Kitchenham and Walker (1986a).)

A particular problem with the model is the form of the model output. It is hardly plausible to assert that all qualities are measures in the range 0 to 1; for example, maintainability is likely to be specified and measured in terms of effort or time to diagnose and/or debug a system failure. Since McCall *et al.*'s model does not predict the quality factors measures directly, it is impossible to validate the model directly and impossible to understand what the model means in terms of the way in which genuine quality requirements are likely to be specified. Also, it is rather unlikely that each element in each of the checklists that define the quality metrics contributes an exactly equal amount to software quality.

RECOMMENDATIONS
The problems with the nature of the model output means that the model cannot be recommended as a predictor of quality. However, there is no doubt that the production of the checklists is in itself an extremely useful contribution to software quality assurance, and they are likely to be of great assistance to validation activities, for example as the basis of inspection checklists (Fagan, 1976).

C.5.3   Process models

C.5.3.1   *Test and fix model 1*
Huff, Sroka & Struble's test and fix model 1 (bug clearance) (Huff *et al.*, 1986).

EXPLANATION
This model is used to describe the test and fix activity for a product that is being developed incrementally, with each intermediate release having its own test and fix period.

Test and fix is a period during which test cases are run and analysed, bugs that are reported are assigned, analysed, fixed and eventually cleared. It is assumed that a separate team runs and analyses the test cases and reports officially on the status of bugs. The work of fixing the bugs is assumed to be the responsibility of the programmers who wrote the code.

It is assumed that the exit criteria from the test and fix stage is that a given percentage of previously specified test cases are eventually run without failure.

The model permits bugs to vary with respect to ease of fixing. It also notes that some so-called 'bugs' will not be faults at all. The model allows for the effect of 'parallel processing', whereby programmers will work on several bugs at once when the queue of outstanding bugs is full.

The model identifies the total number of bugs that will be cleared during the test and fix period, the elapsed calendar days required for the test and fix activity, and the percentage of programmer time that will not be required for bug handling during the test and fix period.

MODEL INPUTS

The model inputs are as follows:

- S, the number of programmers who wrote the code being tested and are taking part in the test and fix activity;
- T, the number of test cases in the test suite;
- B, the average number of new bugs detected in the product per test case;
- PC, the percentage of cases required to run successfully to complete the test and fix period;
- $L1$, $L2$, $L3$, $L4$, the respective likelihood of bugs that are easy, average, hard, or spurious (the sum of the Ls should be 1);
- $D1$, $D2$, $D3$, $D4$, the respective effort to handle each class of bug, in person-days;
- $ED1$, $ED2$, $ED3$, $ED4$, the respective elapsed times to handle each class of bug in calendar days;
- $M1$, $M2$, the rates at which bugs can be multiprocessed during the early stage and later stage, respectively, of the test and fix period. $M1$ corresponds to the period when the queue is assumed to be full, $M2$ corresponds to the period when the queue is assumed to be empty;
- C, the number of bugs remaining to be cleared at the switchover from $M1$ to $M2$.

MODEL OUTPUTS

The outputs from the model are:

- NBC, the number of bugs to be cleared by the end of the test and fix period;
- ECD, the elapsed calendar days for the test and fix period;
- PDT, the percentage of programmer time not required for bug handling during the test and fix period.

FORMULA

The model outputs are calculated using the following formulae:

$$NBC = PC \times T \times B,$$
$$ECD = ((NBC - C) \times W)/(S \times M1) + (C \times W)/(S \times M2),$$
$$PDT = 1 - V/(ECD \times S)$$

where

$$W = (L1 \times ED1 + L2 \times ED2 + L3 \times ED3 + L4 \times ED4);$$
$$V = NBC \times (L1 \times D1 + L2 \times D2 + L3 \times D3 + L4 \times D4).$$

EVALUATION

Huff *et al.* report having used the model in their own environment but do not present any formal evaluation studies.

PROBLEMS

Huff *et al.* point out that the model depends on a large number of input metrics that are difficult to estimate accurately. They also note that the model makes the unstated assumption that the rate at which bugs are discovered per test case and the rates at which test cases are run and bugs discovered are all constant.

RECOMMENDATIONS

Huff *et al.* regard process modelling as a method by which activities are planned, and would not expect any particular model to be used in another environment without modifications appropriate to the particular environment. This model should be regarded as one possible model of the test and fix process that might be useful in particular circumstances.

Huff *et al.* themselves recommend an alternative model to calculate the number of bugs available to be cleared (*NBA*). The model they suggest uses the following inputs:

- *NL*, the number of new lines of code to be tested in the test and fix period;
- *OL*, the number of old lines (i.e. the number of lines tested in previous test and fix periods);
- *EB*, the expected number of bugs per line of code (total over all test and fix periods);
- *H1*, the percentage of bugs in new code that will be found in this test and fix period;
- *H2*, the percentage of bugs in old code that will be found in this test and fix period;
- *F*, the actual number of bugs cleared during previous test and fix periods;
- *U*, the number of known, uncleared bugs at the beginning of this test and fix period.

The estimate of the number of bugs available to be cleared during the test and fix period is obtained from the following formula:

$$NBA = U + H1 \times NB + H2 \times RB$$

where

$$NB = NL \times EB;$$
$$RB = (OL \times EB) - F - U.$$

C.5.3.2 *Test and fix model 2*

Huff, Sroka & Struble's test and fix model 2 (testcase passage) (Huff *et al.*, 1986).

EXPLANATION

This model views the test and fix period in terms of the requirement to run successfully a certain percentage of test cases, rather than in terms of clearing an expected number of bugs, which is the viewpoint taken in Huff *et al.*'s first model.

This model assumes that progress is made at one rate initially and that the rate slows down at the end of the test and fix period. The rationale for the assumption in this case is that the bugs encountered first will be the ones that are detected by many test cases, and removal of these bugs pays off in terms of the advancement of multiple test cases towards running successfully. Bugs detected at the end of the test and fix period are likely to be those that only affect one test case, so clearing bugs of this sort will result in slower overall progress.

This model includes the concept of the time of initial exposure to the test cases, *EX*. This is meant to capture any delay in achieving the normal early test case passage rate due to problems with the test suite itself.

The model again provides an estimate of the elapsed calendar days needed for the test and fix period.

MODEL INPUTS

The inputs to the model are as follows:

- *T*, the total number of test cases in the test suite;
- *PC*, the percentage of test cases that must be run successfully in order to complete the test and fix period;
- *R*1, the rate, in days per case, at which tests are made to run successfully during the first stage of the test and fix period;
- *R*2, the rate, in days per case, at which tests are made to run successfully during the later stage of the test and fix period;
- *C*, the number of test cases remaining to be passed when the switchover from *R*1 to *R*2 occurs;
- *EX*, the time period, in days, during which the test suite is first exposed to the product;
- *G*, the number of test cases that run successfully first time.

MODEL OUTPUTS

The model provides an estimate of elapsed calendar days for the test and fix period, *ECD*.

FORMULA

The model estimates *ECD* using the following equation:

$$ECD = EX + (NTC - C) \times R1 + C \times R2$$

where $NTC = PC \times T - G$.

EVALUATION

Huff *et al.* report that the model is used in their organization, but they do not present any formal evaluation.

PROBLEMS

Huff *et al.* feel that a weakness of the model is that it does not provide equations relating progress to effort expended, which means that a manager cannot judge whether a lower progress rate than expected is due to understaffing or to underestimating the volume of work.

Again, it must be noted that the model depends on a large number of difficult-to-calculate metrics.

RECOMMENDATIONS

This model provides a different view of the test and fix process from the first model, which may be useful to project managers when there is experience of closely related projects available.

Huff *et al.* note that it can be reconciled with their first model (ignoring *EX* and *G*), by letting

$$R1 = (W/(S \times M1)) \times B$$
$$R2 = (W/(S \times M2)) \times B$$

Appendix D

Software Development Cost Models

Barbara Kitchenham

D.1 Introduction 487
    D.1.1 Model Validation and Verification Criteria 487
D.2 Examples of Empirical Factor Models 489
    D.2.1 COCOMO—the COnstructive COst MOdel 489
    D.2.2 TRW Wolverton Model 498
    D.2.3 The SDC Model 498
    D.2.4 Walston–Felix 499
    D.2.5 SOFTCOST 501
    D.2.6 PRICE SP 503
    D.2.7 ESTIMACS 504
    D.2.8 Bailey–Basili Meta Model 505
D.3 Examples of Constraint Models 507
    D.3.1 Putnam's Model 507
    D.3.2 Parr 515
    D.3.3 Jensen 515
    D.3.4 COCOMO Schedule Equation 516
    D.3.5 COPMO 516

D.1 Introduction

This appendix covers some of the well-known cost models in terms of their underlying assumptions, their advantages, and their difficulties. In addition, a few newer cost models are described that may be of theoretical interest to readers with wider experience of cost modelling.

The COCOMO and Putnam models are described in the greatest detail because they are in a sense archetypical models of the empirical factor and constraint model classes; other models are described in less detail. COCOMO and Putnam's model are also evaluated in terms of the model validation and verification criteria described below.

D.1.1 Model validation and verification criteria

Model validation is the process of determining how useful a models is. Model verification is the process of determining how accurate estimates made by the

487

model are. If usefulness is equated to accuracy of prediction, then validation and verification are the same thing, but it is usually more realistic to accept that there are factors other than accuracy that are important to consider. For example, it is preferable to have a less accurate but timely estimate than a more accurate estimate too late.

There have been a number of suggestions of the subjective criteria that should be used to validate a model (e.g. Boehm, 1981; Conte *et al.*, 1986). These include:

- *Input parameter objectivity*, which considers whether the model inputs are measurable and objective, or are based on subjective assessment that would vary substantially from individual to individual.
- *Ease of use*, which considers the difficulty and cost of obtaining the input data, and whether or not the input data is well enough defined to allow the model to be used at all.
- *Model generality*, which considers whether a model is general enough for use in different environment, or is 'overfitted' to a particular dataset.
- *Input parameter availability*, which considers the point in the life cycle at which the input data for the model is available or may be estimated accurately.
- *Robustness* (stability), which indicates whether small changes in input parameters have disproportionate effects on model outputs.
- *Comprehensiveness*, which indicates how much of the life cycle and how many of the project-related activities are included in the estimates. It also considers the level of detail and the relevance of the outputs of the model.
- *Decision-making facilities*, which indicates how well the model can support 'what if' analysis and decision making.
- *Validity* of model assumptions (in contrast to the *accuracy* of the model predictions, which is discussed below).

Conte *et al.* also indicate a number of objective measures to assess the predictive accuracy of models. They recommend three measures in particular that can be used to assess the performance of a model over a set of n projects.

(1) *Mean magnitude of relative error (MMRE)*

$$MMRE = \left[\sum_{i=1}^{n} MRE_i \right] \Big/ n \qquad \text{(D.1)}$$

where $MRE = |E_i - \hat{E}_i|/E_i$ is the magnitude of the relative error for project i;

E_i is the actual value of a cost parameter for the ith project;

$\hat{E}_i$ is the estimate of the cost parameter for the ith project.

Conte *et al.* suggest that $MMRE \leq 0.25$ is acceptable for effort-prediction models.

(2) *Prediction at level l (PRED(l))*

$$PRED(l) = k/n \qquad \text{(D.2)}$$

where k is the number of projects in a set n for which $MRE \leq l$.

Conte *et al.* suggest $PRED(\cdot 25) \geqslant 0 \cdot 75$ is acceptable for effort-prediction models.

(3) *Relative root means square error (RRMS)*

$$RRMS = RMS \Big/ \left[\left(\sum_{i=1}^{n} (E_i) \right) \Big/ n \right\} \tag{D.3}$$

where $RMS = (\overline{MSE})^{1/2}$ is the root mean square error;

$\overline{MSE} = \left[\sum_{i=1}^{n} (E_i - \hat{E}_i)^2 \right] \Big/ n$ is the mean squared error.

Conte *et al.* suggest that $RRMS \leqslant 0 \cdot 25$ is acceptable for effort-prediction models.

Conte *et al.* note that a particular model may perform well on one of their criteria and badly on another. Therefore, they suggest a composite criteria of the form:

$$MMRE \leqslant 0 \cdot 25 \text{ and } PRED(\cdot 25) \geqslant 0 \cdot 75 \tag{D.4}$$

These objective criteria offer a good means of verifying a model but three points need to be remembered.

(1) Models should perform well on the dataset that generated them. Verification studies using the above metrics are only really meaningful when performed on independent data sets. Cross-validation studies are needed to validate a model on its own data set (see the comments on cross-validation in Chapter 10).

(2) Verification studies will overestimate the predictive accuracy of models even when independent datasets are used, if the inputs to the models are actual values for verification purposes, but model use depends on estimating the input values, i.e. if a model requires an estimate of lines of code, but is verified using the actual lines of code from past projects, it will seem to be better than it actually is.

(3) Using single metrics to assess predictive accuracy will fail to detect any systematic bias such as consistent under- or over-estimation or a tendency to predict larger projects less accurately than smaller projects. A detailed verification study should consider plotting both actual values against estimates, and residuals (actuals − estimates) against actual values, in order to detect systematic estimating bias.

The description of cost models that follows will indicate the results of reported model evaluation studies concentrating on verification studies.

D.2 Examples of Empirical Factor Models

D.2.1 COCOMO—the COnstructive COst MOdel

COCOMO is one of the best-known, and almost certainly one of the best-documented, of all the software cost models. It was developed by Barry

Boehm, and described in his book *Software Engineering Economics* (Boehm, 1981). In this section, we will discuss only the COCOMO effort equations; the COCOMO schedule equations will be discussed in the section describing constraint models.

COCOMO is a set of three modelling systems, Basic COCOMO, Intermediate COCOMO and Detailed COCOMO, each of which includes a number of algorithms relating product size in thousand lines of delivered source instructions ($KDSI$) to development effort in months (MM_{nom}).

Intermediate and Detailed COCOMO estimates are refined by a number of multiplicative corrections (which indicate the project-specific effect on effort of the factors that influence cost). They may therefore be classified as corrected single-factor models. Basic COCOMO does not use any corrections, so is simply a single-factor model.

D.2.1.1 *The COCOMO effort algorithms*

All the COCOMO effort algorithms have the same basic form:

$$MM_{nom} = \alpha(KDSI)^{\beta} \tag{D.5}$$

where the effort estimates excludes feasibility and requirements analysis, installation and maintenance effort. It refers to all project-based effort.

The values of coefficients α and β depend both on the COCOMO modelling system being used (i.e. Basic, Intermediate, or Detailed), and on the *mode* of the project. The values adopted by Boehm are shown in Table D.1. The coefficients can be understood by noting that the value of α is approximately the time in months to deliver 1000 lines of source instructions (ignoring comments and blank lines). The value of β being greater than 1 indicates that larger projects achieve a somewhat lower productivity than the basic productivity indicated by the coefficient α. The more stringent the constraints on the development, as indicated by the mode, the lower the basic level of productivity and the more large projects are penalized.

The coefficient values (and the cost driver adjustments described in the next section) were determined by expert opinion. The COCOMO database of 63 historical projects was used to refine the values provided by the experts.

Table D.1. COCOMO coefficient values

Mode	Basic		Intermediate and Detailed	
	α	β	α	β
Organic	2·4	1·05	3·2	1·05
Semi-detached	3·0	1·12	3·0	1·12
Embedded	3·6	1·20	2·8	1·20

- The mode of the project is one of three possibilities, 'organic', 'embedded' or 'semi-detached', which describe three different types of software development.
- 'Organic' is used to describe the situation of relatively small software teams, developing software in a highly familiar in-house environment.
- 'Embedded' is used to describe a project that needs to operate within tight constraints. The software may have limited main store, and timing constraints, and there may be stringent requirements to meet specifications. There may also be regulations concerning the methods of product development and testing.
- 'Semi-detached' is meant to imply a mid-point between the extremes of the organic and embedded modes.

COCOMO provide tables of the distribution of effort across the main phases of software development, and the distribution of effort for each activity in each phase. Using these tables, the effort estimate can be converted into detailed activity estimates for project planning.

D.2.1.2 *Intermediate and Detailed COCOMO*

Intermediate and Detailed COCOMO permit the basic effort estimate to be adjusted by means of multiplicative correction factors. These corrections are intended to account for the features of the particular project that make it different from the 'average' project.

The adjustments are based on the 'rating' given to each of 15 cost drivers and a multiplicative adjustment corresponding to each rating. For example, 'Use of software tools' is one of the 15 cost drivers, and has associated with it five possible ratings: 'Very low', 'Low', 'Nominal', 'High', or 'Very High'. Each rating has associated with it a numerical value; very low equates to 1·24, low equates to 1·10, nominal equates to 1·0, high equates to 0·91, very high equates to 0·83. To adjust the basic effort estimate MM_{nom}, the appropriate rating must be selected and MM_{nom} multiplied by the associated numerical value. Thus, a less than average use of software tools will increase the effort estimate, and a greater than average use will decrease the estimate.

The 15 cost drivers used by Intermediate and Detailed COCOMO are divided into four groups, product attributes, computer attributes, personnel attributes and project attributes as follows.

1. PRODUCT ATTRIBUTES
   RELY: Required Software Reliability
   DATA: Data Base Size
   CPLX: Product Complexity
2. COMPUTER ATTRIBUTES
   TIME: Execution Time Constraint (target machine)
   STOR: Main Storage Constraint (target machine)
   VIRT: Virtual Machine Volatility (target machine)
   TURN: Computer Turnaround Time (development machine)

3. PERSONNEL ATTRIBUTES
    ACAP: Analyst Capability
    AEXP: Applications Experience
    PCAP: Programming Capability
    VEXP: Virtual Machine Experience
    LEXP: Programming Language Experience
4. PROJECT ATTRIBUTES
    MODP: Use of modern programming practices
    TOOL: Use of software tools
    SCED: Required development schedule

The ratings and the numerical multipliers for Intermediate COCOMO are shown in Table D.2.

The important points about Intermediate and Detailed COCOMO are not just the introduction of cost drivers. Intermediate COCOMO is intended to be used at the point at which the major components of the software product have been identified. This permits effort estimates to be made on a component basis using the size estimates and cost drivers ratings appropriate to each component. The adjusted effort estimates for each component are summed to give an overall estimate. Thus, effort estimates are refined not only by the introduction of cost drivers, but also by the use of more detailed knowledge of the internal characteristics of the product.

Detailed COCOMO takes the process of refined estimation a step further. It uses cost driver multipliers that differ for each major development phase, and it recommends that some drivers be applied at a module level and some at

Table D.2. Intermediate COCOMO effort multipliers

Cost drivers	Ratings					
	Very low	Low	Nominal	High	Very high	Extra high
RELY	0·75	0·88	1·00	1·15	1·40	
DATA		0·94	1·00	1·08	1·16	
CPLX	0·70	0·85	1·00	1·15	1·30	1·65
TIME			1·00	1·11	1·30	1·66
STOR			1·00	1·06	1·21	1·56
VIRT		0·87	1·00	1·15	1·30	
TURN	0·79	0·87	1·00	1·07	1·15	
ACAP	1·46	1·19	1·00	0·86	0·71	
AEXP	1·29	1·13	1·00	0·91	0·82	
PCAP	1·42	1·17	1·00	0·86	0·71	
VEXP	1·21	1·10	1·00	0·90		
LEXP	1·14	1·07	1·00	0·95		
MODP	1·24	1·10	1·00	0·91	0·82	
TOOL	1·24	1·10	1·00	0·91	0·83	0·77
SCED	1·23	1·08	1·00	1·04	1·10	

subsystem level. Drivers that are applied at a module level are module complexity, programmer capability, language experience and virtual machine experience. In addition, adjustments for code reuse are applied at a module level.

The final important features of the original version of COCOMO are the algorithms for handling adapted code and assessing maintenance effort. They are discussed in the next two sections.

Boehm has recently developed an improved version of COCOMO, which is based on a more modern process model (refer to Section B.11 of Appendix B), includes risk management, and can be used to predict the costs of Ada projects (Boehm, 1987*b*, 1988*c*).

D.2.1.3 *Code adaptation*
COCOMO handles the effect of re-using code from previously developed software by calculating an *equivalent number of delivered source instructions* (*EDSI*), and using *EDSI* in place of *DSI* in the effort algorithms.

EDSI is based on an adjustment to the *adapted DSI*, which is the number of delivered source instructions adapted from existing software. *EDSI* is calculated using an intermediate quantity the *adaptation adjustment factor* (*AAF*) as follows:

$$AAF = 0{\cdot}40(DM) + 0{\cdot}30(CM) + 0{\cdot}30(IM) \tag{D.6}$$

where *DM* is the percentage of the adapted software's design that is modified
   in order to adapt it to the new system;
   CM is the percentage of the adapted software's code that is modified in
   order to adapt it to the new system;
   IM is the percentage of effort required to integrate the adapted
   software into the new system and to test the resulting product, as
   compared to the normal amount of integration and test effort for
   software of comparable size.

$$EDSI = ADSI \times AAF/100 \tag{D.7}$$

The coefficients in the *AAF* equation are based on the assumption that development effort is split on a 40%, 30%, 30% basis among design, implementation and integration, respectively, and may be altered if a different split is found in practice.

D.2.1.4 *Maintenance effort estimation*
COCOMO restricts software maintenance effort estimates to effort expended on the following activities:

- redesign and development of small portions of a product (less than 50% new code);
- design and development of small interface packages that require some redesign of the product (less than 20%);
- modification of the software product's code, documentation, or database structure.

The Basic COCOMO estimate for annual software maintenance is calculated in terms of the *annual change traffic (ACT)*, which is the fraction of the software product's source instructions that undergo change during a (typical) year, either through addition or modification:

$$(MM)_{AM} = ACT \times (MM_{nom}) \tag{D.8}$$

where $(MM)_{AM}$ is the estimated annual maintenance effort;

MM_{nom} is the estimated development effort.

Boehm suggests that the annual maintenance effort estimate may be refined by use of the Intermediate COCOMO cost drivers with the following adaptions.

- *SCED* is not used as a driver.
- Personnel ratings and computer turnaround are related to the maintenance staff and the maintenance computer, respectively.
- New effort multipliers are used for *RELY* and *MODP*.

D.2.1.5 *An assessment of COCOMO*

SUBJECTIVE CRITERIA

COCOMO may be assessed in terms of the subjective evaluation criteria identified in Section D.1.1 as follows:

- *Input parameter objectivity*. The model depends on estimates of *DSI* but encourages re-estimation as knowledge of the product increases during project development. The *ACT* and *AAF* are highly subjective. In addition, unlike *DSI* and *ACT*, the *AAF* estimate can never be objectively verified.

  The model also depends on being able to rate the 15 cost drivers, and determine the mode of development. These are subjective estimates. The model does provide extended explanations to reduce the variability of the subjective assessments. However, it is still not easy to be certain that ratings provided by different project managers will be consistent, since many projects have mixed characteristics compared with Boehm's explanations. Another area of difficulty with Intermediate COCOMO, is that there are no clear instructions on how individual experience and capability ratings are applied at a team rather than an individual level.

  Thus, in summary, COCOMO rates poorly on input parameter objectivity, but well on providing procedures to help cope with subjectivity.
- *Ease of use*. An outstanding feature of COCOMO is the care with which the input and output parameters are defined.

  To use Basic COCOMO the amount of data required is very small (i.e. mode and *KDSI*). For Intermediate COCOMO, substantially more data is needed, since *KDSI*, and 15 cost driver ratings are required for each identified component. The problems with obtaining the cost driver ratings have already been described but, assuming that these can be overcome,

Table D.3. Number of projects in COCOMO database with given *TIME* and mode characteristics

TIME rating	Mode		
	Embedded	*Semi-detached*	*Organic*
Extra High	4	0	0
Very High	9	1	0
High	13	4	3
Nominal	3	7	19

the amount of data required for Intermediate COCOMO is unlikely to be prohibitive.

For Detailed COCOMO, data is required about each module in the system, and for a large system this may begin to reach an unacceptable overhead.

In summary, COCOMO performs well with respect to ease of use.

• *Model generality*. Basic COCOMO is applicable to most conventional projects assuming that the same counting rules for *DSI* and effort are used.

Intermediate and Detailed COCOMO both show signs of over-fitting. There are more potential combinations of driver values for Intermediate COCOMO than there are points in the COCOMO database, and there are even more possible combinations for Detailed COCOMO.

Another problem is that there are signs that various input parameters are correlated; for example embedded-mode software is more likely to have timing, storage constraints, and stringent reliability requirements than organic-model software. Thus, the effect of some drivers may already have been partially accounted for by the mode selection, and certain drivers may be highly correlated. Tables D.3 and D.4 show the overlap between the *TIME* cost driver and mode, and the *TIME* and *STOR* drivers respectively. These tables confirm the relationships between the factors (if there were no relationships, the number of projects in each cell of a particular column would be approximately equal). The issue is important

Table D.4. Number of projects in COCOMO database with given *TIME* and *STOR* characteristics

TIME rating	*STOR* rating			
	Nominal	*High*	*Very High*	*Extra High*
Nominal	18	9	2	0
High	1	9	9	2
Very High	0	2	4	3
Extra High	0	0	1	3

because relationships among input parameters will make any model unstable.

To summarize, Basic COCOMO appears to be a very general model, but Intermediate and Detailed COCOMO show signs of over-fitting to the particular COCOMO dataset.

- *Input parameter availability.* The mode parameter and many of the cost drivers should be readily identifiable from the start of the requirements phase of the project.

The most important input parameter to COCOMO is *KDSI*, and that will not be measurable until after implementation, although estimates of the parameter may be expected to become more accurate as the project moves from requirements analysis to high level and then detailed design. In addition, drivers such as product complexity and database size will be difficult to determine early in the project life cycle.

To summarize, although a number of the effort-correction factors should be capable of evaluation early in the life cycle, the most important model input cannot be measured until the completion of coding.

- *Robustness.* A sensitivity analysis of the COCOMO equations (Kitchenham & Taylor, 1984) indicated that COCOMO effort equations were fairly robust with respect to mis-estimates in size, but fairly sensitive to mode mis-estimates, and potentially very vulnerable to mis-estimates of cost drivers. Conte *et al.* (1986) confirm this point by noting that the effect of the cost drivers is to give a range between the minimum and maximum estimated effort of 800 times the minimum.

- *Comprehensiveness.* COCOMO is an extremely comprehensive model. It provides direct estimates of all project-related development activities, an algorithm to cater for maintenance, and an adjustment for code re-use.

It also provides a method of detailed activity planning by indicating the percentage of effort for each activity in each phase.

- *Decision-making facilities.* The original version of COCOMO does not include any specific risk-management features, but it does permit the effect of changes to cost drivers to be assessed.

- *Validity of model assumptions.* The basic assumption behind the effort algorithm is an exponential relationship between size and effort. This type of relationship has been observed in a number of empirical studies summarized by Basili & Freburger (1981).

The values used for the exponential coefficient β are characteristic of such studies; however, the multiplicative coefficient α varies significantly among different studies. This implies that different datasets exhibit different basic productivity levels. This could be a genuine difference resulting from the product application, language and development differences between organizations, or a result of different counting rules used for lines of code and effort. In either case, it is not surprising.

The choice of cost drivers is also consistent with the results of empirical studies.

Assumptions built into COCOMO with respect to the breakdown of effort for each activity and each phase have not been subject to any empirical validation. The higher-level breakdown of effort across phases seems to confirm to many software engineers' 'best guesses' and was confirmed by Kitchenham & Taylor (1984).

We are not aware of any studies which have tested the assumptions used in the code adaption formula or the maintenance effort formula.

VERIFICATION OF PREDICTIVE ACCURACY
Boehm analysed the performance of the COCOMO models on the COCOMO database (i.e. the database that was used to assist with the construction of the model) and found:

- for Basic COCOMO, $PRED(\cdot2) = 0\cdot25$ which is quite poor;
- for Intermediate COCOMO, $PRED(\cdot2) = 0\cdot68$ which is very good;
- for Detailed COCOMO, $PRED(\cdot2) = 0\cdot70$ which is very good.

He also provided plots of actuals against estimates, and histograms of the relative error that make it clear that the model exhibits no systematic bias on the COCOMO dataset.

However, validations performed on other datasets have not always obtained such good results:

- Conte *et al.* (1986) used the Basic COCOMO on five other datasets and found that it worked extremely badly on one data set and reasonably well on two. They point out that there are many possible reasons for poor results, for example different counting rules for source instructions and effort.
- Kemerer (1987) evaluated Basic, Intermediate and Detailed COCOMO on a dataset of 15 projects. He found the performance of the models was very poor for all versions of the model. The *MMRE* values were $6\cdot1$ for Basic, $5\cdot8$ for Intermediate, and $6\cdot1$ for Detailed COCOMO. He found the model biased, with a systematic tendency to over-estimate effort. He also found that the Intermediate and Detailed versions of COCOMO did not improve the accuracy of the estimates. A failure of Intermediate COCOMO to improve estimates compared with Basic COCOMO was also observed by Kitchenham & Taylor (1984).
- Miyazaki & Mori (1985) report an *MMRE* of $1\cdot66$ for a dataset of 43 projects and observed a systematic bias to underestimate effort.

AVAILABILITY OF SUPPORT TOOLS
Several automated versions of COCOMO exist. A simple version was produced by the Wang Institute (WICOMO), a more sophisticated version was developed by GEC Software (GECOMO).

D.2.2   TRW Wolverton model

The TRW model (Wolverton, 1974) is one of the few models that actually estimates the cost of a project in dollars. It uses a software cost matrix (shown in Table D.5) to provide a cost per instruction for a module based on the type of module (Control, Input/output, Pre/post processor, Algorithm, Data management, Time critical), the difficulty (Easy, Medium, Hard), and the novelty of the application (New or Old). The cost per instruction is multiplied by an estimate of the module size to obtain the cost of producing the module.

The model provides a breakdown of project effort by phase and activity.

The model is mainly of historical interest because it is clearly of very limited generality (since its output is monetary costs), and is only applicable for use after a product has been broken down to module level. However, the software cost matrix may be of use, not as a cost matrix, but as a complexity weighting for module-size estimates.

In addition, Boehm (1981) reports that the model is well calibrated to a class of US government control and command projects, but is less accurate for other classes of project.

D.2.3   The SDC model

The Software Development Corporation model (Nelson, 1966) is another model that is of mainly historical interest. It is a multiple-parameter linear model that curiously enough does not include lines of code as a parameter. It was obtained by multiple regression analysis of 104 attributes of 169 software projects.

The model took the following form:

$$
\begin{aligned}
MM = -33{\cdot}63 \\
+9{\cdot}15 \text{ (lack of requirements) } (0-2) \\
+10{\cdot}73 \text{ (stability of design) } (0-3) \\
+0{\cdot}51 \text{ (percent math instructions)} \\
+0{\cdot}46 \text{ (percent storage/retrieval instructions)} \\
+0{\cdot}40 \text{ (number of subprograms)} \\
+7{\cdot}28 \text{ (programming language) } (0-1) \\
-21{\cdot}45 \text{ (business application) } (0-1) \\
+13{\cdot}53 \text{ (stand-alone program) } (0-1) \\
+12{\cdot}35 \text{ (first program on computer) } (0-1) \\
+58{\cdot}82 \text{ (concurrent hardware development) } (0-1) \\
+30{\cdot}61 \text{ (random access device used) } (0-1) \\
+29{\cdot}55 \text{ (different host, target hardware)} \\
+0{\cdot}54 \text{ (number of personnel trips)} \\
-25{\cdot}20 \text{ (developed by military organization) } (0-1)
\end{aligned}
\tag{D.9}
$$

where the numbers in parentheses indicate the ratings that must be made by the estimator.

Table D.5. An example of the software cost matrix

Type	Difficulty					
	O–E	O–M	O–H	N–E	N–M	N–H
Control	21	27	30	33	40	49
I/O	17	24	27	28	35	43
Pre/post processor	16	23	26	28	34	42
Algorithm	15	20	22	25	30	35
Data management	24	31	35	37	46	57
Time critical	75	75	75	75	75	75

The model is clearly incorrect, since zero values of all the input parameters would indicate that it takes -33.63 months to produce nothing. In fact this type of effect implies that there are relationships among the input parameters that cause the effort to be over-estimated when all the parameters are treated as if they were independent. The model can, however, be viewed as identifying a number of potential cost drivers, and from that viewpoint did contribute to the production of later models.

D.2.4 Walston–Felix

Walston & Felix (1977) collected data on 60 IBM projects in order to investigate effort prediction and factors that affect productivity. Initially they attempted to produce an estimation model based on size alone. They anticipated a model of the form:

$$E = \alpha S^\beta \tag{D.10}$$

where E refers to effort and S refers to size.

In order to obtain the values of the coefficients, they performed a simple linear regression on the logarithms of E and S. This is done as follows:

$$\log_{10} E = \log_{10} \alpha + \beta \log_{10} S \tag{D.11}$$

Letting $Y = \log E$, $A = \log \alpha$, and $X = \log S$, the following linear relationship is obtained:

$$Y = A + \beta X$$

which can be solved for a dataset of Y and X values by least-squares analysis. The α that is required in the original equation is obtained by taking anti-logs.

The final equation they obtained was:

$$\hat{E} = 5.2 S^{0.91} \tag{D.12}$$

This is one of the few equations of this type with an exponential value less than 1. The implication of the exponential value is that larger projects achieve greater productivity than smaller projects.

However, Walston & Felix found that their basic effort equation performed relatively badly on their dataset, so they investigated the effect of a number of factors that might have been responsible for the large deviations between actual and estimated effort. They considered 68 factors and used multiple linear regression to reduce the number to 29.

Project leaders were then asked to indicate to what extent the factors had affected their project. For each factor the responses were rated as normal, below normal, or above normal. For all projects with the same rating for a particular factor, the average productivity was calculated. From these figures, Walston & Felix were able to calculate the change in productivity that could be attributed to those factors (defined as the difference between the higher and lower productivity values) and the productivity range (defined to be the ratio of the higher and lower productivity values). The results for the six factors exhibiting the largest productivity change are shown in Table D.6.

Walston & Felix used their complete set of 29 factors to define a productivity index I for each project:

$$I = \sum_{i=1}^{29} W_i X_i \tag{D.13}$$

where W_i is a weighting defined as

$$W_i = \tfrac{1}{2} \log_{10}(\Delta L_i) \tag{D.14}$$

$X_i = 1$ if the rating for variable i increased productivity;
$\quad\ = 0$ if the rating for variable i was nominal;
$\quad\ = -1$ if the rating for variable i lowered productivity.

They then used linear regression to find the best fit to the equation:

$$\log L = \alpha + \beta I \tag{D.15}$$

where L is project productivity.

Table D.6. The six factors exhibiting the largest productivity ranges in the Walston–Felix study

Factor	Response group mean productivity			Productivity change (ΔL)	Productivity range (L_{high}/L_{low})
	< Normal	Normal	> Normal		
Customer interface complexity	500	295	124	376	4·03
Programming language experience	122	225	385	263	3·16
Personnel experience	132	257	410	278	3·11
Customer originated changes	297		196	101	2·94
Customer experience of area	318	340	206	112	2·84
Experience of application	146	221	410	264	2·81

Then, the effort needed to produce a product can be calculated from the formula:

$$E = S/L \qquad (D.16)$$

where S is lines of code.

Formula (D.16) for effort uses a size estimate as a scaling factor to convert an effort-per-line productivity estimate into an overall effort estimate. This is analogous to Wolverton's model, which uses size as a scaling factor to convert a dollars-per-instruction estimate into an overall cost estimate.

The Walston & Felix approach exhibits the usual problem of over-fitting, since many correlated variables are incorporated into the model and the number of projects in the data set is smaller than the range of possible variable levels. In adition, the values of α and β for the productivity model were not published, so the model has not been validated on an independent data set.

The important feature of the model is that it suggests a number of potential cost drivers, and a methodology for assessing the impact of those drivers. It is also the case that IBM have continued to refine their approach to cost estimation by continuing the collection of project data, and now claim extremely high precision for their cost estimates. (An account of discussions with IBM FSD researchers can be found in Dale & Kitchenham, 1985.)

D.2.5 SOFTCOST

Researchers at the Jet Propulsion Laboratory produced the SOFTCOST model (Tausworthe, 1981), in an attempt to develop a model that incorporated the good points of a number of different models. They incorporate the 29 factors from the Walston–Felix model plus seven factors from the GRC model (Carriere & Thibodeau, 1979), and make use of a modified Rayleigh-curve model to check the feasibility of resource estimates and resource allocation.

The model is implemented as an interactive computer program that can deduce its 68 parameter values from 47 questions it poses to the user of the system. The 68 parameters relate to productivity, duration, staffing level, documentation and computer resources.

The program outputs the following information:

- development effort and schedule broken down into a standard Work Breakdown Structure, with variances for each estimate;
- staffing level;
- pages of documentation (as a function of size);
- CPU requirements (as a function of size).

The model assumes a linear relationship between size and effort:

$$E = S/P_1 \qquad (D.17)$$

where S is the total equivalent lines of code in thousands;

P_1 is the average productivity in KLOC/(person-month).

SOFTCOST concentrates on estimating the average productivity factor P_1, using various technology and environmental factors. It therefore uses the same approach as the second Walston–Felix model (D.16).

The productivity rate has the form:

$$P_1 = P_0 A_1 A_2 \qquad\qquad (D.18)$$

where P_0 is a constant;

A_1 is a multiplicative factor incorporating six factors used in the GRC model;

A_2 is a multiplicative factor incorporating the 29 factors used in the Walston–Felix model.

$$A_1 = [(1 + A_l + A_{tc} + A_{cc})A_d A_s A_e]^w \qquad\qquad (D.19)$$

where w is chosen to produce a 50:1 spread in P_1;

A_l is a language adjustment factor;

A_{tc} is a timing criticality adjustment factor;

A_{cc} is a capacity criticality adjustment factor;

A_d is a difficulty adjustment factor;

A_s is the requirements and design stability adjustment factor;

A_e is an experience adjustment factor.

$$A_2 = \exp[\omega \sum x_i \log (PH_i/PL_i)] \qquad\qquad (D.20)$$

where ω is chosen to produce a 50:1 spread in P_1;

PH_i/PL_i is the ratio of productivities for factor i found by Walston & Felix;

x_i takes on the values 1, 0, or -1.

We are not aware of any studies that have indicated the accuracy of the model, but it clearly has a number of potential problems.

- It includes an even larger selection of correlated factors than its 'parent models', and some of the factors may be as difficult to estimate at an early stage in the development as size (e.g. difficulty and stability from the GRC model, and factors such as ratio of staff/size to duration, percentage of code for delivery, number of classes of items in database per 1000 lines of code, and number of pages of documentation per 1000 LOC, from the Walston–Felix model).
- It appears over-complex, because it treats the two factor groups in different ways.
- It does not make direct use of the effect of size on effort; it uses size as a scaling factor only.

However, the model provides a very comprehensive set of outputs and a commercial version of the model (SOFTCOST R) is available. There is also a version of SOFTCOST adapted for use on Ada projects that has been developed from a reasonably large amount of empirical data (Reifer, 1988).

D.2.6 PRICE SP

PRICE SP is a proprietary model developed and supported by RCA PRICE Systems, which is part of General Electric. The internal workings of the model are not public domain, although a fairly detailed description of the basic assumptions of the model was presented recently by one of its developers (Park, 1988).

The model can, therefore, only be described in terms of its inputs and outputs. There are 10 inputs to the model that can be divided into two groups. The first group, comprising six variables describes the product to be developed. The second group describes the development process. The inputs are as follows.

PRODUCT VARIABLES

- Instructions (i.e. the size of the program in lines of code or object code instructions).
- New code (i.e. the proportion of the code that must be produced from scratch on a scale 0 to 1).
- New design (i.e. the proportion of the design which must be produced from scratch on a scale 0 to 1).
- Application (i.e. one of the seven application types identified: operating system, interactive operations, real-time command and control, on-line communications, data storage and retrieval, string manipulation, mathematical applications).
- Utilization (i.e. hardware restrictions such as limited memory space).
- Platform (i.e. the environment in which the software will be used, which is one of the following eight types: production centre internally developed software, production centre contracted software, MIL-spec ground, military mobile (van or shipboard), commercial avionics, MIL-spec avionics, unmanned space, manned space).

DEVELOPMENT PROCESS VARIABLES

- Productivity index, which is determined by analysis of a number of completed products.
- Manload (i.e. the average number of staff on the project).
- Fractional time (i.e. the proportion of their time staff will devote to the project).
- Complexity, which is meant to describe the project characteristics that affect lead time. It includes consideration of personnel experience, product familiarity, and other 'complicating factors'.

The model outputs are effort in man-months and project lead time.

In order to determine the value of the productivity index, data from 5–10 projects is used, in effect, to run the model backwards with effort and lead time as inputs and the productivity index as the output. If the different values of the productivity index are similar, the average value can be used in future estimates. If the index varies significantly from project to project, the model cannot be used. PRICE SP is, therefore, appropriate for use in an environment where similar products are developed using similar techniques.

An advantage of PRICE SP is that it can only be used if it is tuned (calibrated) to a particular homogeneous environment, which should ensure that it provides reasonable predictions. However, we are not aware of any published data describing the accuracy of the model.

The disadvantages of the model are primarily related to the subjectivity and availability of the input parameters. Cuelenaere *et al.* (1987) provide a vivid description of the difficulty of ensuring that the input parameters are understood and used in a consistent manner. In fact, they have developed an expert system as a front end to PRICE SP to help users provide correct, consistent inputs to the model. In addition, the model requires an estimate of size that may be inaccurate. It also uses manload as an input parameter, whereas many project managers might have hoped to obtain the value of the parameter as an output!

D.2.7 ESTIMACS

ESTIMACS is a proprietary model developed by Howard Rubin (Rubin, 1985), and, like PRICE SP, internal details of the model are not available. The most important feature of the model is that it uses a 'function point-like' measure to provide an estimate of the 'size' of the system rather than lines of code. Function-point counts are based on features of the product that are determined at an early stage in the development process, such as the number of inputs, outputs, internal files and inquiries. They were first suggested by Albrecht (1979) and are discussed in Chapter 11, Sections 11.4.1.6 and 11.4.2.2.

The model uses 25 questions to generate its model inputs. Kemerer divides the ESTIMACS inputs into six groups as follows.

SIZE VARIABLES

- number of major subsystems (functions)
- number of major logical groupings of external inputs to the system
- number of major logical groupings of outputs from the system
- number of internal logical databases
- number of categories of inquiry

PRODUCT VARIABLES

- system type
- error detection and correction requirements
- complexity
- back-up and recovery requirements
- stringency of performance requirements
- stringency of reliability requirements

ENVIRONMENT VARIABLES

- development mode
- telecommunication requirements
- distributed processing

PERSONNEL VARIABLES

- familiarity with application type
- relocation

PROJECT VARIABLES

- travel
- requirements volatility

USER FACTORS

- number of user organizations involved
- number of users
- percentage of user participation
- user DP knowledge

The output from the model includes:

- effort in hours, schedule in months, and peak staffing level
- work breakdown for staff level, effort, and cost
- function point counts
- maintenance effort
- risk assessment
- financial information
- upper and lower bounds for the estimate

The main advantage of the ESTIMACS model is that it uses product characteristics as its main 'size' measure, providing a main input parameter that should be determined much earlier in the development process than lines of code. However, this advantage is also its main limitation, because it restricts the model to use on conventional DP applications. This tuning of the model to DP applications is also noticeable from its use of several user variables as inputs.

Kemerer investigated the predictive accuracy of the model on nine projects and found an *MMRE* of 0·85 and *PRED*(·25) = 0·22.

D.2.8 Bailey–Basili meta model

Bailey & Basili (1981) were not interested in developing a model, but wanted to derive a methodology for effort estimation that could be used at a specific location. They assumed that the coefficients in any effort equation would be highly dependent on the environment and personnel at a particular installation, and that coefficients derived from a local database would lead to a much more accurate model.

In order to demonstrate their methodology, they used a database of 18 projects developed at the NASA Goddard Space Flight Center. Bailey & Basili used a basic model of the form:

$$E = \alpha + \beta S^\gamma \qquad \text{(D.21)}$$

where α is interpreted as initial preparation time required to understand the design before programming begins.

In order to determine the values of the coefficients for a particular data set, the method of taking logarithms is not effective. Therefore, Bailey & Basili used the method of minimizing the 'standard error of the estimate' (*SEE*) using non-linear least-squares regression. The function minimized was

$$SEE = \sum_{i=1}^{N} [1 - (\alpha + \beta S_i^\gamma)/E_i]^{1/2} \qquad \text{(D.22)}$$

The equation they obtained was

$$\hat{E} = 3 \cdot 5 + 0 \cdot 73 S^{1 \cdot 16} \qquad \text{(D.23)}$$

which gave an *SEE* of $1 \cdot 25$. The *SEE* is a multiplicative factor, so the 68% bounds on any estimate made using the function can be obtained by multiplying the estimate by $1 \cdot 25$ and dividing the estimate by $1 \cdot 25$. The equation is very accurate when applied to its own database, giving an *MMRE* of $0 \cdot 18$ and a *PRED*$(0 \cdot 25)$ of $0 \cdot 78$.

They also indicated a procedure for improving the basic estimate by taking into account other project factors (i.e. cost drivers) such as methodology, complexity, and experience.

They determine the multiplicative adjustment factor (ER_{adj}) that relates the estimate $\hat{E}_i$ to the actual value E_i for each project using the formula:

$$E_{adj} = \begin{cases} R - 1 & \text{if } R > 0 \\ 1 - 1/R & \text{if } R < 0 \end{cases}$$

where $R = E/\hat{E}$. ER_{adj} is related to actual effort by the following relationship (the effort adjustment equation):

$$E = \begin{cases} (1 + ER_{adj})\hat{E} & \text{if } ER_{adj} > 0 \\ \hat{E}/(1 + |ER_{adj}|) & \text{if } ER_{adj} < 0 \end{cases} \qquad \text{(D.24)}$$

They use multiple linear regression to estimate the coefficients in the equation (the adjustment factor equation):

$$ER_{adj} = \alpha + \beta METH + \gamma CPLX + \delta EXP \qquad \text{(D.25)}$$

where *METH* is an assessment of the methodology being used obtained by rating nine characteristics on a scale from 0 to 5 (the characteristics include the use of tree charts, top-down design, formal documentation, chief programmer teams, formal test plans, formal training, design formalisms, code reading and unit development folders). *CPLX* is an assessment of complexity obtained by rating seven characteristics on a scale from 0 to 5 (the characteristics include customer interface complexity, application complexity, program flow complexity, internal communication complexity, database complexity, external communication complexity, and customer-initiated design changes). *EXP* is an assessment of personnel experience based on rating five characteristics on a scale from 0 to 5 (the characteristics include programmer qualifications, programmer machine experience, programmer application experience, and team experience).

Having determined both the basic effort equation (D.23) and the adjustment factor equation (D.25), a new project can be costed by obtaining the basic effort estimate and then refining it using the estimated adjustment factor (obtained from the adjustment factor equation D.25) in the effort adjustment equation (D.24).

This model is important not because the specific effort equation or the particular cost drivers are important, but because it provides a methodology by which individual organizations may construct their own models that are tuned to their particular environment and working practices. Their results demonstrate that even straightforward unadjusted effort models will provide good results (at least on their generating dataset), if the dataset is homogeneous. This result confirms the basic approach used in PRICE SP.

It should be noted that the basic methodology has a few potential problems.

- Adding ranks of various subfactors to obtain an overall measure of the factor assumes that each subfactor has an equivalent and independent effect on the factor. This is sometimes difficult to ensure. Is the use of chief programmer teams equivalent to the use of tree charts? Is the use of formal documentation independent of the use of formal test plans, or design formalisms, or unit development folders?
- As it is formulated, the effort equation appears to relate to implementation and test, so the model's good fit may be due to the fact that lines of code is a particularly good predictor for the later phases of the life cycle. Locally derived models that include the earlier phases might not be so accurate.

D.3 Examples of Constraint Models

D.3.1 Putnam's model

D.3.1.1 *The origin of the Rayleigh-curve model*
In the early 1960s, Norden performed a study of the staff build-up for engineering and development projects in IBM (Norden, 1963). Plots of manpower curves of the staff working on a project each month showed a

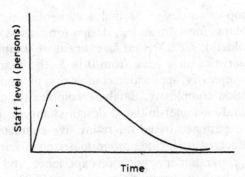

Fig. D.1. The basic Rayleigh curve.

pattern similar to that shown in Fig. D.1. The characteristic curve resembled a probability curve, and comparisons with known probability curves indicated that the Rayleigh curve was the best fit.

Putnam (1978) suggested that the Rayleigh curve could be used to model staffing levels on large software projects. The basic Rayleigh curve is modelled by the differential equation

$$\mathrm{d}y/\mathrm{d}t = 2\,Kat\,\exp\,(-at^2) \qquad (\text{D.26})$$

where $\mathrm{d}y/\mathrm{d}t$ is the staff build-up rate;
  t is the elapsed time from the start of design to product replacement;
  K is the area under the curve in the interval $[0, \infty)$
  a is constant that determines the shape of the curve.
Integrating (D.26) over the interval $[0, t]$, we obtain

$$y(t) = K(1 - \exp\,\{-at^2\}) \qquad (\text{D.27})$$

where $y(t)$ is the cumulative number of staff used to time t.

From (D.27) it can be seen that as $t \to \infty$, $y \to K$. Thus, K represents the total life-cycle effort including maintenance. It should be noted that Putnam explicitly excludes feasibility studies and requirements analysis from the life cycle.

Putnam assumed that the point in time when the staff level is at its peak (the maximum of the curve) should correspond reasonably closely to the project development time (i.e. the time from the start of design to product release). Project development time (t_d) is therefore obtained by differentiating (D.26) and letting $\mathrm{d}^2y/\mathrm{d}t^2 = 0$. This corresponds to

$$t_d = (1/2a)^{1/2} \qquad (\text{D.28})$$

Thus, project development effort can be estimated by calculating the value of eqn (D.27) when $t = t_d$. Substituting for a and t in (D.27) we obtain

$$y(t_d) = K[1 - \exp(-\tfrac{1}{2})]$$

Thus, project development effort (E) is approximately $0 \cdot 3945K$.

D.3.1.2 *Extensions to the basic model*

Putnam investigated a number of US Army projects and found that projects that exhibited a high productivity had a relatively slow initial staff build-up and projects that exhibited a low productivity had a relatively fast initial staff build-up. The initial rate of staff build-up corresponds to the gradient of the Rayleigh curve at time $t = 0$, which Putnam denoted the difficulty (D) of the project. The initial gradient can be obtained by differentiating eqn (D.26) and putting $t = 0$. This gives

$$D = K/(t_d)^2 \tag{D.29}$$

Putnam assumed that there must be a relationship between D and productivity (L) of the form:

$$L = \alpha D^\beta \tag{D.30}$$

L is defined as

$$L = S_s/E \tag{D.31}$$

where S_s is the number of lines of code produced in thousands;
$E = y(t_d) = 0.3945K$ is the development effort.

Using non-linear regression, Putnam found that the exponential constant β in equation (D.30) was $-2/3$. Substituting for L in eqn (D.30) gives:

$$S_s = \alpha D^{-2/3}(0.3945K) \tag{D.32}$$

Substituting D from (D.29) into (D.32) gives

$$S_s = \begin{cases} C[K/(t_d)^2]^{-2/3}K \\ CK^{1/3}(t_d)^{4/3} \end{cases} \tag{D.33}$$

where C is called the *technology factor*.

Putnam regards eqn (D.33) as the basic underlying relationship between effort and time. Differences among projects are reflected by factors such as hardware constraints, personnel experience and programming environment and are represented by a variety of different values of C. Putnam suggests using 20 different values of C ranging from 610 to 57 314 (assuming K is measured in programmer years and t_d is measured in years).

In addition, Putnam also uses the following equation:

$$D_0 = K/\{t_d\}^3 \tag{D.34}$$

where D_0 is constant called the 'manpower acceleration', which can take a number of discrete values depending on the type of project. A value of 7.3 is meant to be appropriate for new software with many interfaces and interaction with other system; 15 for new standalone systems; 27 for rebuilt software. In all, six different values of D_0 are used.

Equation (D.34) is derived by differentiating the difficulty equation (D.29) with respect to t_d, the values attributed to the ratio were those Putnam observed in his data set. A relationship between the cube root of effort and the development time has been observed in a number of different empirical studies (e.g. Basili & Freburger, 1981; Kitchenham & Taylor, 1984). Thus, the relationship is reasonable on empirical if not theoretical grounds.

Equation (D.34) is essential for the Putnam model to be used as an estimating model since eqns (D.34) and (D.33) can be combined to form an equation including only one cost parameter (K or t_d):

$$t_d = [(S_s)^3/(D_0 C^3)]^{1/7} \qquad (D.35)$$

$$K = (S_s/C)^{9/7}(D_0)^{4/7} \qquad (D.36)$$

Equation (D.36) implies that effort is proportional to a size taken to the power 1·29, which is quite similar to the COCOMO model assumptions.

D.3.1.3 *Components of the life cycle*

Putnam suggested that each phase in the life cycle could be modelled as a mini-Rayleigh curve with the overall life-cycle curve viewed as a composite curve as shown in Fig. D.2. The design and code curve is, therefore, represented by the following equation:

$$dy_1/dt = 2K_1 bt \exp(-bt^2) \qquad (D.37)$$

where K_1 is the total effort for design and code;
  $b = 1/[2(t_{1d})^2]$ by analogy with (D.28).
  The design and development curve starts at time $t = 0$ with the same initial gradient as the overall curve, thus,

$$K/(t_d)^2 = K_1/(t_{1d})^2 \qquad (D.38)$$

Putnam assumes that the project development time, t_d, will correspond to the time at which the design and code is 95% complete. Integrating eqn (D.35) from 0 to t_d will therefore equal $0·95K_1$. This implies that:

$$1 - \exp[-b(t_d)^2] = 0·95$$

Substituting for b:

$$0·05 = \exp[-(t_d)^2/\{2(t_{1d})^2\}]$$

$$2\ln(0·05) = (t_d/t_{1d})^2$$

$$t_d/t_{1d} \simeq 6^{1/2} \qquad (D.39)$$

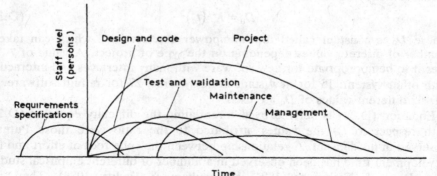

Fig. D.2. The life-cycle phases as Rayleigh curves.

Using (D.39) to simplify eqn (D.38) gives

$$K_1 = K/6 \qquad (D.40)$$

D.3.1.4 *Time–effort trade-off*
The most important (and frequently quoted) effect of Putnam's basic equation (D.33) is that for a particular product in a particular environment, K varies inversely as the fourth power of the development time. This can be seen by rewriting (D.33) as

$$K = (S_s/C)^3/(t_d)^4 \qquad (D.41)$$

This relationship has been strongly disputed by researchers. Putnam himself reported investigating 750 software systems and found that eqn (D.39) held for only 251 of them. This investigation involved using the values of K, t_d, and S_s in eqn (D.38) in order to determine the value of C before using eqn (D.38) to estimate K, which is *not* an independent validation of the equation.

D.3.1.5 *Estimation procedures*
To use the Putnam model in practice it is necessary to determine C, S_s, and D_0. The value of C may be determined in two different ways:

- by using the values of S_s, K, and t_d obtained from other similar project(s) and calculating C using eqn (D.33);
- by using a facility of the SLIM package (which Putnam markets to support his modelling approach) to estimate C from a set of parameters that describe the development environment, product and staff characteristics.

The value of D_0 is determined from the type of product as described above, and S_s must be estimated in terms of non-comment source statements (NCSS).

D.3.1.6 *Project size and code re-use adjustments*
The Rayleigh curve applies to 'large' projects and some adjustments need to be made to apply the estimating procedures to small projects. For small projects (comprising up to 18 000 NCSS), it is assumed that the project life cycle is almost equivalent to the design-and-code life cycle, so that the estimates of development schedule and development effort are determined from eqns (D.39) and (D.40), respectively. (This implies that for small projects the test-and-validation life cycle is subsumed into the design-and-code life cycle.)

For 'medium' size projects, (between 18 000 and 70 000 NCSS), an additional sub life cycle called the 'project life cycle' is required. This project life cycle includes the design-and-code life cycle as shown in Fig. D.3. The adjustment to the basic estimation procedures needed for medium-sized projects are described by Londeix (1987)

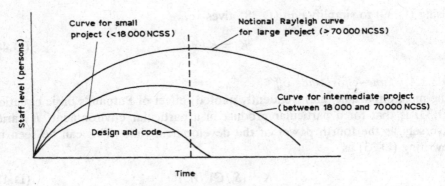

Fig. D.3. The project curve.

Code re-use is described by Londeix and is based on the following formula:

$$S_{equ} = 43\% \ S_i$$
$$+ 6\% \ S_p$$
$$+ 100\% \ S_a \qquad\qquad (D.42)$$
$$+ 51\% \ S_c$$
$$- 49\% \ S_d$$

where S_i is the size of the unchanged system modules;
S_p is the size of the changed modules;
S_a is the number of source statement added;
S_c is the number of source statements changed;
S_d is the number of source statements deleted.

Equation (D.42) is based on assumptions about the distribution of effort required for various activities and may therefore need to be tailored to different environments.

D.3.1.7 *An assessment of Putnam's model*
In this section, we evaluate Putnam's model in terms of the criteria discussed in Section D.1.1.

SUBJECTIVE ASSESSMENT

- *Input parameter objectivity.* To use Putnam's model, it is necessary to estimate system size in terms of non-comment source statements, S_s, and to determine which values of the technology factor, C, and D_0 are appropriate.

    S_s is obtained by subjective assessment, but C and D_0 can be obtained objectively. When information about other 'similar' projects is available, C may be calculated from the values found in the other projects. The value of D_0 should be objectively determined on the basis of the type of project.

• *Ease of use.* The major difficulty associated with the input data concerns the calculation of *C*. It is necessary to obtain cost data from a number of similar projects in order to estimate *C* from eqn (D.33). However, past data is unlikely to be collected in the format used in (D.33). For example, development costs will be available rather than total life-cycle costs. The elapsed time to delivery may be collected rather than the elapsed time to peak manning, so t_d may need to be estimated as elapsed time corresponding to 95% use of design and code effort.

Further complications arise if the project is small or intermediate in size, because the development costs will not correspond to $0.39K$, and the estimation of *K* becomes more complex.

There are methods of calculating *C* from a description of the project that are built into the SLIM estimating tool, but Kemerer (1987) reported very large discrepancies between *C* values calculated from eqn (D.33) and *C* values estimated from project descriptions. He found that the estimates of *C* based on project descriptions resulted in very inaccurate cost predictions.

• *Model generality.* Putnam's model is a general model for large (70 000 NCSS) projects. The model as stated in eqn D.33 represents a large number of specific models, depending on which of the 20 possible values of *C* and the six possible values of D_0 are used.

Variants of the basic model are necessary for small and intermediate-sized projects.

• *Input parameter availability.* The size input is only available for measurement after coding, but *C* and D_0 are never directly measurable, although they can be calculated at the end of design and code when estimates of t_d and *K* are available.

• *Robustness.* The effort estimates obtained from the model are very sensitive to mis-estimates of the technology factor. A mis-estimate of one level on the scale of 20 possible values can cause a change in the effort estimate of 100%. The model is also quite sensitive to mis-estimates of size: a 14% mis-estimate of size can cause a 50% mis-estimate of effort.

Kitchenham & Taylor (1984) point out that the sensitivity of the model to mis-estimates depends on the value of the technology factor; with a small technology factor, the effects are very large. The model is much more robust if the technology factor is average or above average.

• *Comprehensiveness.* The basic Rayleigh curve model provides the effort, schedule, and staffing information for the total life cycle and the development part of the life cycle. It does not consider detailed phase and activity work breakdown.

The SLIM tool provides information in terms of the effort per major activity per month throughout development. The activities identified are detailed design, code, integration, V&V, documentation and management. The SLIM tool provides many additional outputs including error estimates and feasibility analyses.

The outputs of the model need to be interpreted carefully to avoid confusion between the time to peak staffing and the time at which the system is ready for delivery.

- *Decision-making facilities.* The basic model is aimed at allowing the relationships among staffing levels, schedule and effort to be investigated and the effects of changes to be assessed.

  The SLIM tool provides extensive facilities for investigating trade-off among the cost parameters and the effects of the uncertainty inherent in the size estimate.

- *Validity of the model assumptions.* The Putnam model is based on four critical assumptions:

  (1) that project manpower curves are well approximated by the Rayleigh curve;
  (2) that there is a relationship between the difficulty D and productivity of the form given in eqn (D.30), with the exponent $\beta = -2/3$;
  (3) that eqn (D.34) holds;
  (4) that the discrete values of D_0 (in eqn D.34) are correct.

The assumptions of the model lead to the fourth-power relationship between effort and schedule shown in eqn (D.40), and the relationships between t_d and size, and effort and size shown in eqns (D.35) and (D.36), respectively.

A number of studies have disputed the basic Rayleigh-curve assumption (Basili & Beane, 1981; Basili & Zelkowitz, 1978; Kitchenham & Taylor, 1985). However, the projects used in these studies were relatively small.

Conte *et al.* (1986) investigated the productivity/difficulty relationship on six data sets and found little evidence for a value of β close to $-2/3$. The average value of β for their data sets was -0.256.

There does appear to be empirical support for eqn (D.34). Most researchers have reported relationships between effort and schedule of the form:

$$\text{effort} = \alpha \, \text{schedule}^{\beta}$$

where β is in the range 0·3–0·4. However, Kitchenham & Taylor (1984) investigated the values of $K/(t_d)^3$, and found a large variation, with little support for the suggested D_0 values.

In terms of the model implications, the fourth-power law has not been independently substantiated, but eqns (D.35) and (D.36) have empirical support for the values of exponents (Kitchenham & Taylor, 1984; Basili & Freburger, 1981; Boehm, 1981).

VERIFICATION OF PREDICTIVE ACCURACY

Conte *et al.* (1986) investigated the predictive accuracy of Putnam's model on their six data sets and found uniformly poor performance. This result was confirmed by Kemerer (1987) who found that the model consistently over-estimated effort by an average of 772%. He noted that the over-estimation could have been due to under-estimating C, and that the estimates *correlated* well with the actuals even though they did not *predict* the actuals well.

AVAILABILITY OF SUPPORT TOOLS

The Rayleigh-curve model is part of the SLIM cost-estimation and project management tool.

D.3.2 Parr

The Rayleigh-curve model has been criticized by some managers because its assumption of a staff build-up starting from zero and fading away to zero during maintenance is unrealistic. It is argued that most projects start with a finite non-zero staffing level, and stabilize at some non-zero level during maintenance. The Parr model (Parr, 1980) is an attempt to adjust the Rayleigh curve model to cater for these criticisms using the sech^2 curve as follows:

$$m(t) = \tfrac{1}{4} \mathrm{sech}^2[(at + c)/2] \tag{D.43}$$

where $m(t)$ is the staffing level at time t (which is equivalent to dy/dt in the Rayleigh curve model);

a and c are parameters that determine the shape of the curve.

DeMarco (1982) reports that empirical results from the Yourdon 1978–1980 project survey supported the Parr model. He recommends using the basic Rayleigh curve with a graphical Parr 'adjustment' at the start to allow an initial non-zero staffing level. However, we are not aware of any commercial cost-estimation system that makes use of the model, and it does not appear to be used in practice.

D.3.3 Jensen

The Jensen model (Jensen, 1984) uses a basic equation adapted from Putnam's basic model (D.33) with a 'technology' factor similar to Boehm's multiplicative cost drivers. The basic equation is

$$S_s = C_{te} t_d K^2 \tag{D.44}$$

where S_s, t_d, and K are the size, development time, and total effort, respectively;

C_{te} is called the effective technology constant.

$$C_{te} = C_{tb} \prod_{i=1}^{1s} f_i \tag{D.45}$$

where f_i is a measure of the ith cost driver used in the COCOMO model.

In order to provide an estimating model as well as a constraint model, Jenson uses the manpower acceleration eqn (D.34):

$$D_0 = K/(t_d)^3$$

Jensen's basic equation (D.44) is an attempt to reduce severity of the effort/schedule relationship used in Putnam's model.

Conte *et al.* (1986) assessed the Jensen model on six data sets. They found the predictive accuracy of the model better than Putnam's model, but still very poor.

D.3.4 COCOMO schedule equation

COCOMO uses a relationship between schedule (development time) and development effort of the following kind:

$$TDEV = \alpha(MM)^\beta \qquad (D.46)$$

where *TDEV* is the development time in months;

  MM is the estimated effort to produce the product in man-months;

  α and β are constants that depend on the mode of the development as shown in Table D.7. The same values are used for Basic, Intermediate and Detailed COCOMO.

The values used for the exponent value β are similar to those observed in empirical studies.

A problem with the COCOMO model is that the Intermediate and Detailed effort equations include schedule compression as a cost driver, so there is a potential for confusion when the separate schedule equation is used. In fact, it is best to view the COCOMO effort equations as cost equations with 14 drivers and one constraint. The schedule compression driver provides discrete adjustments, which are equivalent to point estimates on the curve representing the schedule/effort function.

D.3.5 COPMO

The COPMO model is described in detail in Conte *et al.* (1986). It was developed by Thebaut (1983) and models the relationships between staffing level, schedule, effort and size.

Although staffing level changes with time, COPMO (COoperative Programming MOdel) considers only the average personnel level (P_a):

$$P_a = E/T \qquad (D.47)$$

where *E* is the effort in person months;

  T is the project duration in months.

COPMO uses a basic effort equation of the following form:

$$E = E_P(S) + E_c(P_a) \qquad (D.48)$$

Table D.7. Constants in the COCOMO schedule equation

Mode	Multiplier (α)	Exponent (β)
Organic	2·5	0·38
Semi-detached	2·5	0·35
Embedded	2·5	0·32

where $E_P(S)$ is the effort required by one or more persons working independently on modules which require no interaction with other modules;

S is the total size of the software product in terms of thousands of lines of code;

$E_c(P_a)$ is the effort required to coordinate the development process with other programmers in the team;

P_a is the average team size computed from eqn (D.47).

The model further assumes that

$$E_P(S) = a + bS \tag{D.49}$$

$$E_c(P_a) = c(P_a)^d \tag{D.50}$$

This means that (D.48) can be rewritten as

$$E = a + bS + c(P_a)^d \tag{D.51}$$

In order to estimate the coefficients a, b, and c, Thebaut suggests a two-stage least-squares process.

(1) Determine the parameters a and b from historical projects for which $P_a \simeq 1$.

(2) With a and b fixed, use the remaining historical projects to determine c and d by fitting

$$E - \hat{E}_P(S) = c(P_a)^d \tag{D.52}$$

Conte *et al.* report that an evaluation of COPMO on their six data sets indicated that the model performed reasonably well but was not acceptable in terms of their basic evaluation criteria.

They pointed out that COPMO does not cater for differences in complexity among projects. They showed that a version of COPMO adjusted to handle projects sorted into a number of complexity classes gave very good predictions on the COCOMO dataset ($MMRE = 0{\cdot}25$, $PRED({\cdot}25) = 0{\cdot}78$).

We are not aware of any other direct evaluations of COPMO, but Jeffery (1987) proposed an alternative model relating size (S), productivity ($L = E/T$), and maximum staffing level (M) of the form:

$$L = aS^b M^{-c} \tag{D.53}$$

This model was fitted to three separate data sets and accounted for between 60 and 80% of the variation in productivity. Jeffery's model shows that productivity decreases as the maximum staffing level increases. This agrees with the COPMO finding that effort increases as the average staffing level increases.

References

Abdel-Ghaly, A. A. (1986). Analysis of predictive quality of software reliability models. PhD Thesis, City University, London.

Abdel-Ghaly, A. A., Chan, P. Y. & Littlewood, B. (1986). Evaluation of competing software reliability predictions. *IEEE Trans. Software Eng.*, **SE-12**(9), 950–67.

Adams, E. N. (1984). Optimizing preventive service of software products. *IBM J. Res. Develop.*, **28**, 1.

Aitchison, J. & Dunsmore, I. R. (1975). *Statistical Prediction Analysis*. Cambridge University Press, Cambridge.

Albrecht, A. J. (1979). Measuring application development productivity. In *Proceedings of the IBM Applications Development Symposium, GUIDE/SHARE*, October 1979.

Albrecht, A. J. & Gaffney Jnr. J. (1983). Software function, source lines of code, and development effort prediction: A software science validation. *IEEE Trans. Software Eng.*, **SE-9**(6), 639–47.

Anderson, T. (1985). Can design faults be tolerated? *Software and Microsystems*, **4**(3), 59–62.

Anderson, T. & Lee, P. A. (1981). *Fault Tolerance: Principles and Practice*, Prentice-Hall, Englewood Cliffs, NJ.

Anderson, T. Barrett, P. A., Halliwell, D. N. & Moulding, M. R. (1985). Software fault tolerance: an evaluation. *IEEE Trans. Software Eng.*, **SE-11** (12) 1502–10.

Avizienis, A. (1985). The *N*-version approach to fault tolerant software. *IEEE Trans. Software Eng.*, **SE-11**(12), 1491–501.

Avizienis, A. & Kelly, J. P. J. (1984). Fault tolerance by design diversity: concepts and experiments. *IEEE Computer*, **17**, 67–80.

Avizienis, A. Lyn, M. R. T., Schutz, W., Tso, K. S. & Voges, U. (1988). DEDIX 87—a supervisory system for design diversity experiments at UCLA. In *Software Diversity in Computerized Control Systems,* ed. U. Voges, Springer-Verlag, Berlin, pp. 129–68.

Babich, W. A. (1986). *Software Configuration Management.* Addison-Wesley, Reading, MA.

Bailey, J. W. (1983) *Human Error in Computer Systems,* Prentice-Hall, Englewood Cliffs, NJ.

Bailey, J. W. & Basili, V. R. (1981). A meta-model for software development resource expenditures. In *Proceedings of Fifth International Conference on Software Engineering.* IEEE Computer Society Press, New York, pp. 107–16.

Barringer, H. (1985). *A Survey of Verification Techniques for Parallel Programs.* Lecture Notes in Computer Science, 191. Springer-Verlag, Berlin.

Barringer, H. (1986). Using temporal logic in compositional specification of concurrent systems. Report UMCS-86-10-1, Department of Computer Science, University of Manchester.

Basili, V. R. & Beane, J. (1981). Can the Parr curve help with manpower distribution and resource estimation problems? *J. Systems and Software*, **2**.

Basili, V. R. & Freburger, K. (1981). Programming measurement and estimation in the software engineering laboratory. *J. Systems Software*, **2**, 47–57.

Basili, V. R. & Weiss, D. M. (1982a). A methodology for collecting valid software engineering data. Report TR-1235, University of Maryland, MD.

Basili, V. R. & Weiss, D. M. (1982*b*). Evaluating software development by analysis of changes: the data from the software engineering laboratory. Report TR-1236, University of Maryland, MD.

Basili, V. R. & Zelkowitz, M. V. (1978). Analysing medium-scale software development. In *Proceedings 3rd International Conference on Software Engineering*. IEEE Computer Society Press, New York, pp. 116–23.

Basili, V. R., Zelkowitz, M. & McGarry, F. (1977). The software engineering laboratory. Report TR-535, University of Maryland, MD.

Belady, L. A. & Lehman, M. M. (1976). A model of large program development. *IBM Systems J.*, **15**, 3.

Bergstra, J. A., Heering, J. & Klint, P. (eds) (1989). *Algebraic Specification*, Frontier Series, Addison-Wesley, Reading, MA.

Bersoff, E. H., Henderson, V. D. & Siegel, S. G. (1980). *Software Configuration Management and Investment in Product Integrity*. Prentice-Hall, Englewood Cliffs, NJ.

Bishop, P., Esp, D. G., Barnes, M., Humphreys, P., Dahll, G. & Lahti, J. (1986). PODS—a project on diverse software. *IEEE Trans. Software Eng.*, **SE-12**(9), 929–40.

Bjorner, D. & Jones, C. B. (eds) (1982). *Formal Specification and Software Development*, Series in Computer Science. Prentice-Hall, Englewood Cliffs, NJ.

Bjorner, D. & Jones, C. B. (eds) (1987). *VDM '87: VDM–A Formal Method at Work, VDM Europe Symposium, Brussels, Belgium*. Lecture Notes in Computer Science, 252. Springer-Verlag, Berlin.

Blair, G. S., Lea, R., Mariani, J. A., Nicol, J. & Wylie, C. (1986). Total system design in IPSEs. In *Software Engineering Environments*, ed. I. Sommerville. Peter Perigrinus Ltd., Stevenage, UK.

Bloomfield, R. E. & Froome, P. K. D. (1986). The application of formal methods to the assessment of high integrity software. *IEEE Trans. Software Eng.*, **SE-12**(9), 988–93.

Bochmann, G. *et al.* (1982). Experience with formal specifications using an extended state transition model. *IEEE Trans. Commun.* **COM-30** (Dec.), 2506–13.

Boehm, B. W. (1976). Software Engineering, *IEEE Transactions on Computers* (Dec.), 1226–41.

Boehm, B. W. (1981). *Software Engineering Economics*. Prentice-Hall, Englewood Cliffs, NJ.

Boehm, B. W. (1987*a*). Improving software productivity. *IEEE Computer* (Sept.), 43–57; reprinted in Thayer (1988), pp. 93–107, and extended in Boehm & Papaccio (1988).

Boehm, B. W. (1987*b*). Ada COCOMO: TRW IOC version. Third COCOMO User's Group Meeting, November 1987.

Boehm, B. W. (1988*a*). A spiral model of software development and enhancement. *IEEE Computer* (May), 61–72; updated and reprinted in Thayer (1988, pp. 128–42).

Boehm, B. W. (1988*b*). Rapid prototyping, risk management, 2167 and the Ada process model. AWIS Ada Workshop, Sept. 1988.

Boehm, B. W. (1988*c*). Ada COCOMO refinements. Fourth COCOMO Users' Group Meeting. November, 1988.

Boehm, B. W. (1989). *Software risk management*. IEEE Tutorial.

Boehm, B. W. & Papaccio, P. N. (1988). Understanding and controlling software costs. *IEEE Trans. Software Eng.*, **SE-14**(10) (Oct.), 1462–77.

Boehm, B. W., Brown, J. R., Kaspar, H., Lipow, M., Macleod, G. J. & Merritt, M. J. (1978). *Characteristics of Software Quality*. TRW Series of Software Technology, North Holland, Amsterdam.

Booch, G. (1987). *Software Engineering with Ada* (2nd edition). Benjamin Cummings, Menlo Park, CA.

Boudel, G., Roucairol, G. & de-Simons, R. (1985). Petri nets and algebraic calculi of processes. In Rozenberg (1985).

Bowen, T. P., Wigle, G. B. & Tsai, J. (1984). *Specification of Quality Attributes,* Vols. I, II, and III. Boeing Aerospace Company, Seattle.

Boyer, R. S. & Moore, J. S. (eds) (1981). *The Correctness Problem in Computer Science.* Academic Press, New York.

Bozoki, G. (1987). Software Sizing Models. Third COCOMO User's Group Meeting, November 1987.

Brereton, P. (ed.) (1988). *Software Engineering Environments,* Ellis Horwood, Chichester.

Britcher, R. N. (1988). Using inspections to investigate program correctness, *IEEE Computer* (Nov.), 38–44.

Britcher, R. N. & Gaffney Jr., J. E. (1985). Reliable size estimates for software systems decomposed as state machines. *Proceedings of COMPSAC '85.* IEEE Computer Society Press, New York.

British Standards Institution (1987). *Quality Systems,* BS-5750, Parts 0 (0.1 & 0.2), 1, 2 and 3.

Bromell, J. Y. & Sadler, S. J. (1987). A strategy for the development of safety critical software. In *Achieving Safety and Reliability with Computer Systems. Proc. SARSS,* vol. 87. Elsevier Applied Science, London.

Brooks, F. P. (1975). *The Mythical Man-month.* Addison-Wesley, Reading, MA.

Brooks, F. P. (Jr) (1987). No silver bullet. *IEEE Computer* (April).

Broy, M., Geser, A. & Hussman, H. (1986). Towards advanced programming environments based on algebraic concepts. In Conradi *et al.* (1986).

Buckle, J. K. (1982). *Software Configuration Management.* Macmillan, New York.

Burstall, R. M. & Goguen, J. A. (1981). An informal introduction to specification using CLEAR. In Boyer & Moore (1981).

Buxton, J. (1980). Requirements for Ada programming support environments: STONEMAN. U.S. Department of Defence (Ada Joint Program Office).

Campbell, R. H., Horton, K. H. & Belford, G. C. (1979). Simulations of a fault tolerant deadline mechanism. *Digest FTCS-9,* pp. 95–101, Madison, WI.

Card, D. N., Page, G. T. & McGarry, F. L. (1985). Criteria for modularization. In *Proceedings of the 8th International Conference on Software Engineering.* IEEE Computer Society Press, New York, pp. 372–7.

Carre, B. A. & Debney, C. W. (1985). Spade-Pascal. Program Validation Ltd.

Carre, B. A. & Jennings, T. J. (1988). Spark—the Spade Ada Kernel. University of Southampton.

Carriere, W. M. & Thibodeau, R. (1979). Development of a logistics software cost estimating technique for foreign military sales. Report CR-3-839, General Research Corporation.

Checkland, P. (1981). *Systems Thinking, Systems Practice.* Wiley, Chichester.

Chedgey, Chr., Kearney, S. & Kugler, H.-J. (1987). Using VDM in an object oriented development method for Ada software. In Bjorner & Jones (1987).

Chen, L. & Avizienis, A. (1978). *N*-version programming: a fault-tolerance approach to reliability of software operation. *Digest FTCS-8,* pp. 3–9, Toulouse.

Cheung, R. C. (1980). A user-oriented software reliability model. *IEEE Trans. Software Eng.,* SE-6(3), 118–25.

Chikofsky, E. J. & Rubenstein, B. L. (1988). CASE: reliability engineering for information systems. *IEEE Software,* 5(2), 11–17.

Childs, C. & Vokolos, F. I. (1987). AWB-ADE: an application development environment for interactive, integrated systems. *ACM Sigplan Notices,* 22(1), 111–21.

Clemmensen, G. B. & Oest, O. N. (1983). Formal specification and development of an Ada compiler—a VDM case study. Dansk Datamatik Center.

Cohen, B. (1982). Justification of formal methods for system specification. *IEE Software and Microsystems* 5.

Cohen, B., Harwood, W. T. & Jackson, M. I. (1986). *The Specification of Complex Systems*. Addison Wesley, Reading, MA.

Comparin, G., Lanzarone, G. A., Lautenbach, K., Pagnoni, A., Panzeri, W. & Torgano, A. (1985). Guidelines on using net analysis techniques with large specifications. In Rozenberg (1985).

Conradi, R., Didiriksen, T. M. & Wanvik, D. H. (eds) (1986). *Advanced Programming Environments*: *Proc. Int. Workshop. Trondheim, Norway*, Lecture Notes in Computer Science, 244. Springer-Verlag, Berlin.

Constantine, L. L. & Yourdon, E. (1979). *Structured Design*. Prentice-Hall, Englewood Cliffs, NJ.

Conte, S. D., Dunsmore, H. E. & Shen, V. Y. (1986). *Software Engineering Metrics and Models*. Benjamin Cummings, Menlo Park, California.

Coulter, N. S. (1983). Software science and cognitive psychology. *IEEE Trans. Software Eng.*, **SE-9**(2).

Cowderoy, A. J. C. & Jenkins, J. O. (1988). Cost-estimation by analogy as good management practice. *Proceedings of Software Engineering '88*. IEEE, London, pp. 80–4.

Cowderoy, A. J. C. & Jenkins, J. O. (1989) New trends in cost-estimation. In *Measurement for Software Control and Assurance*, ed. B. A. Kitchenham & B. Littlewood. Elsevier, London, pp. 63–88.

Crispin, R. J. (1987). Experience using VDM in STC. In Bjorner & Jones (1987).

Crosby, P. B. (1979). *Quality is Free*. McGraw Hill, New York.

Crow, L. H. (1977). Confidence interval procedures for reliability growth analysis. US Army Material Systems Analysis Activity, Aberdeen, MD, Report 197.

Cuelenaere, A. M. E., van Genuchten, M. J. I. M. & Heemstra, F. J. (1987). Calibrating a software estimation model: why and how. *Information and Software Technology*, **29**(10).

Cullyer, W. J. & Pygott, C. H. (1987). Application of formal methods to the Viper microprocessor. *IEE Proceedings*, **134**, part E, no. 3, pp. 133–42.

Cunningham, J., Finkelstein, A., Goldsack, S., Maibaum, T. & Potts, C. (1985). Formal requirements specification—the FOREST project. In *Proc. 3rd IWSSD*, IEEE CS Press, pp. 186–91.

Curritt, P. A., Dyer, M. & Mills, H. D. (1986). Certifying the reliability of software, *IEEE Trans. Software Eng.*, **SE-12**(1), 3–11.

Curtis, B. & Sheppard, S. B. (1979). Identification and validation of quantitative measure of the psychological complexity of software. TR-79-388100-7. General Electric Company, Arlington, VA.

Cutts, G. (1987). *SSADM, Structured Systems Analysis and Design Methodology*. Paradigm Publishing.

DACS (1987). A descriptive evaluation of software sizing models. Data and Analysis Centre for Software, RADC/COED, Griffiss AFB, New York.

Dale, C. J. & Kitchenham, B. A. (1985). Report on visit to USA. Software Data Library Report to the Alvey Directorate.

Dale, E. & Chall, J. S. (1948). A formula for predicting readability. *Educational Res. Bull.*, **27**, 221–33.

Dart, S. A., Ellison, R. J., Feiler, P. H. & Habermann, A. N. (1987). Software development environments. *IEEE Computer*, **20**(11), 18–28.

DeMarco, T. (1978). *Structured Analysis and System Specification*. Yourdon Press, New York.

DeMarco, T. (1981). *Yourdon 1978–80 Project Survey Final Report*. Yourdon Press, New York.

DeMarco, T. (1982). *Controlling Software Projects*: *Management, Measurement and Estimation*. Prentice-Hall, Englewood Cliffs, NJ.

DeMarco, T. & Lister, T. (1987). *Peopleware: Productive Projects and Teams*. Dorset House, New York.

Denvir, T. (1986). *Introduction to Discrete Mathematics for Software Engineering*. Macmillan, London.

Department of Trade and Industry (1985). *Benefits of Software Engineering Methods and Tools*. (June 1985). HMSO, London.

De Young, G. E. & Kampen, G. R. (1979). Program factors as predictors of program readability. In *Proceedings of the Computer Software and Applications Conference*. IEEE Computer Society Press, New York, pp. 668–73.

Dick, A. J. J. (1985). ERIL—equational reasoning: an interactive laboratory. Report RAL-86-010, Rutherford Appleton Laboratory, Oxon.

Doerflinger, C. W. & Basili, V. R. (1983). Monitoring Software Development through dynamic variables. In *Proceedings of the IEEE Conference on Computer Software and Applications (COMPSAC) 1983*. IEEE Computer Society Press, New York.

Dolotta, T. A., Haight, R. C. & Mashey, J. R. (1978). The programmer's workbench. *Bell Sys. Tech. J.*, **57**(6), 2177–200.

Downs, E., Clare, P. & Coe, I. (1988). *SSADM: Application and Context*. Prentice-Hall, Englewood Cliffs, NJ.

Dowson, M. (1987). Integrated project support with ISTAR. *IEEE Software*, **4**(6), 6–15.

Duane, J. T. (1964). Learning curve approach to reliability monitoring. *IEEE Trans. Aerospace*, (April), 563–6.

Dunn, R. & Ullman, R. (1982). *Quality Assurance for Computer Software*. McGraw Hill, New York.

Duran, J. W. & Ntafos, S. (1980). A report on random testing. UTD Tech. Rept. 83, University of Texas at Dallas.

Dyer, M. (1987). The IBM Clean Room experiment. In *Centre for Software Reliability Symposium, Bristol*. Blackwell, Oxford.

Earl, A. N., Whittington, R. P., Hitchcock, P. & Hall, A. (1986). Specifying a semantic model for use in an integrated project support environment. In *Software Engineering Environments*, ed. I. Sommerville. Peter Perigrinus, London.

Elphick, M. J. (ed.) (1983). Formal specification. *Proceedings of the Joint IBM/University of Newcastle-upon-Tyne seminar*. University Computing Laboratory, Newcastle upon Tyne.

Evans, M. W. (1984). *Productive Software Test Management*. Wiley, Chichester.

Fagan, M. E. (1976). Design and code inspections to reduce errors in program development. *IBM Systems J.*, **15**(3), 182–211.

Fairley, R. E. (1987). A guide for preparing software project management plans. In Thayer (1988) pp. 257–264.

Fenton, N. E., Whitty, R. W. & Kaposi, A. A. (1985). A generalised mathematical theory of structured programming. *Theor. Comput. Sci.*, **36**.

Finkelstein, A. & Potts, C. (1986) Structured common sense: The elicitation and formalisation of systems requirements. In *Proc SE T86*, ed. by D. Barnes & P. Brown, Peter Perigrinus, pp. 236–50.

Fitzsimmons, A. & Love, T. (1978). A review and evaluation of software science. *Comput. Surv.*, **10**(1), 3–18.

Fourman, M., Palmer, W. & Zimmer, R. (1988*a*). Interactive behavioural synthesis. In *Proc. Electronic Design Automation Conference, Wembley*, Electronic Design Automation, London.

Fourman, M., Harris & Musgrave, J. (Abstract Hardware Ltd.) (1988*b*). Core tools for the next generation of electronic CAD. In *Proc. Electronic Design Automation Conference, Wembley*, Electronic Design Automation, London.

Freeman, P. & Wasserman, A. I. (1982). *Software Development Methodologies and*

Ada; *Concepts and Requirements*. Ada Joint Program Office, U.S. Department of Defense.

Gaffney Jr., J. E. (1984). Estimation of software code size based on quantitative aspects of function (with application of expert systems technology). *J. Parametrics*, **4**(3).

Gallo, F., Minot, R. & Thomas, I. (1987). The object management system of PCTE as a software engineering database management system. *ACM Sigplan Notices*, **22**(1), 12–16.

Gehani, N. & McGettrick, A. D. (eds) (1986). *Software Specification Techniques*, International Computer Science Series. Addison Wesley, Reading, MA.

Geser, A. & Hussman, H. (1986). Experience with the RAP system—a specification interpreter combining term rewriting and resolution techniques. In *Proc. ESOP 86 Conf*, Lecture Notes in Computer Science, 213. Springer-Verlag, Berlin.

Gilb, T. (1985). *Design by Objectives*. North-Holland, Amsterdam.

Gilb, T. (1986). Tools for 'Design by objectives'. In *Software: Requirements, Specification and Testing*. Blackwell Scientific, Oxford.

Gilb, T. (1988). *Software Engineering Management*. Addison-Wesley, Reading, MA.

Glass, R. L. & Noiseux, R. A. (1981). *Software Maintenance Guidebook*. Prentice-Hall, Englewood Cliffs, NJ.

Goel, A. L. & Okumoto, K. (1979). A time-dependent error detection rate model for software reliability and other measures. *IEEE Trans. Reliability*, **R-28**(3), 206–11.

Goguen, J. & Burstall, R. (1984). Introducing institutions. In *Logics of Programs*, ed. E. Clarke & D. Kozen. Springer-Verlag, Berlin, pp. 221–56.

Goguen, J. & Meseguer, J. (1982). Rapid prototyping in the OBJ executable specification language. *ACM SIGSOFT—Software Engineering Notes*, **7**(5), 75.

Goguen, J. A., Thatcher, J. W. & Wagner, E. G. (1978). An initial algebra approach to the specification, correctness and implementation of abstract data types. In *Current Trends in Programming Methodology*, ed. R. I. Yeh, Vol. IV, Data Structuring. Prentice-Hall, Englewood Cliffs, NJ.

Goldberg, E. A. (1977). Applying Corporate Software Development Policies. TRW Defense and Space Systems Group, Dec. 1977; reprinted in Thayer (1988) pp. 186–203.

Goldberg, A. & Robson, D. (1983). *Smalltalk-80. The Language and its Implementation*. Addison Wesley, Reading, MA.

Good, D. I. (1983*a*). Reusable problem domain theories. In Elphick (1983).

Good, D. I. (1983*b*). The proof of a distributed system in Gypsy. In Elphick (1983).

Grady, R. B. & Caswell, D. L. (1987). *Software metrics: Establishing a company-wide program*. Prentice-Hall, Englewood Cliffs, NJ.

Gremillion, L. L. (1984). Determinants of program repair maintenance requirements. *Commun. ACM*, **27**(8), 826–32.

Gunning, R. (1962). *Technique of Clear Writing* (revised edition), McGraw-Hill, New York.

Guttag, J. V. (1975). The specification and application to programming of abstract data types. Ph.D. Dissertation Report No. CSRG-59, Computational Sciences Group, University of Toronto.

Guttag, J. V. & Horning, J. J. (1980). Formal specification as a design tool. *7th Annual ACM Symposium on Principles of Programming Languages*, pp. 251–61. (Also reproduced in Gehani & McGettrick (1986).)

Guttag, J. V., Horning, J. J. & Wing, J. M. (1985). LARCH in five easy pieces. Report 5, Digital Systems Research Center, December, Palo Alto, California.

Haglin, G. (1988). ERICSSON safety system for railway control. In *Software Diversity in Computerized Control Systems*, ed. U. Voges. Springer-Verlag, Berlin, pp. 11–22.

Hall, J. A., Hitchcock, P. & Took, R. (1985). An overview of the ASPECT architecture. In *Integrated Project Support Environments,* ed. J. McDermid. Peter Perigrinus Ltd., Stevenage, UK.

Halliwell, D. N. (1984). An investigation into the use of software fault tolerance in a MASCOT-based Naval command and control system, Reference A049/DD.17/1, MARI, Newcastle upon Tyne.

Halstead, M. H. (1977). *Elements of Software Science.* Elsevier North-Holland, Amsterdam.

Hamer, P. G. & Frewin, G. D. (1981). M. H. Halstead's software science—a critical examination. ITT Technical Report No. STL 1341. Standard Telecommunication Laboratories.

Hamer, P. G. & Frewin, G. D. (1982). M. H. Halstead's software science—a critical examination. In *Proceedings of the 6th International Conference on Software Engineering.* IEEE Computer Society Press, New York, pp. 197–206.

Hamer, P. G., Frewin, G. D., Andersen, O. & Davies, S. P. (1986). The constructive quality modelling system. REQUEST Report R1.8.0 CEC ESPRIT Programme, Brussels.

Harper, R., MacQueen, D. & Milner, R. (1986). Standard ML. Report ECS-LFCS-86-2, Computer Science Department, Edinburgh University.

Hayes, I. (1985). Applying formal specification to software development in industry. *IEEE Trans. Software Eng.,* **SE-11**(2), 169–178. (Reprinted in Hayes (1987).)

Hayes, I. (ed.) (1987). *Specification Case Studies,* Series in Computer Science. Prentice-Hall, Englewood Cliffs, NJ.

Health and Safety Executive (1987). *Programmable Electronic Systems in Safety Related Applications.* HMSO, London.

Henderson, P. (1986). Functional programming; formal specifications and rapid prototyping. *IEEE Trans. Software Eng.,* **SE-12**(2), 241–50.

Henderson, P. & Minkowitz, C. (1984). The 'Me Too' method of software design. Tech. Report TR 14, Department of Computer Science, University of Stirling.

Heninger, K. L. (1980). Specifying software requirements for complex systems: new techniques and their application. *IEEE Trans. Software Eng.,* **SE-6**(1), 2–13.

Henry, S. & Kafura, D. (1981). Software structure metrics based on information flow. *IEEE Trans. Software Eng.,* **SE-7**(5) pp. 510–18.

Henry, S. & Kafura, D. (1984). The evaluation of software systems' structure using quantitative software metrics. *Software—Practice and Experience,* **14**(6), 561–73.

Hetzel, W. (1984). *The Complete Guide to Software Testing.* Collins, London.

Higgs, M. & Stevens, P. (1986). Developing an environment manager for an IPSE. In *Software Engineering Environments,* ed. I. Sommerville. Peter Perigrinus Ltd., Stevenage.

Hoaglin, D. C., Mosteller, F. & Tukey, J. W. (1983). *Understanding Exploratory Data Analysis.* Wiley, New York.

Hoare, C. A. R. (1985). *Communicating Sequential Processes,* Series in Computer Science. Prentice-Hall, Englewood Cliffs, NJ.

Hocker, H., Itzfeldt, W. D., Schmidt, M. & Timm, M. (1984). *Comparative Descriptions of Software Quality Measures.* GMD-Studien Nr 81.

Horning, J. J. (1983). Some notes on putting formal specifications to productive use. In Elphick (1983).

Howden, W. E. (1982). Contemporary software development environments. *Commun. ACM,* **25**(5), 318–29.

Huff, K. E., Sroka, J. V. & Struble, D. D. (1986). Quantitative models for managing software development processes. *IEE/BCS Software Eng. J.,* **1**(1), 17–23.

Humphrey, R. A. (1986). Control flow as a measure of programming complexity. *Alvey Club on Software Reliability and Metrics Newsletter,* Issue 4.

Hurst, R. S. (1986). SPMMS—information structures in software management. *IEE/BCS Software Eng. J.,* **1**(1), 50–7.

Hyland, I. (1985). A backward recoverable MC 68000 microcomputer. Final Year Undergraduate Project, The Hatfield Polytechnic.

IEEE (1983). *Software Test Documentation*, ANSI/IEEE Std 829-1983.

IEEE (1984). *Guide to Software Requirements Specifications*. ANSI/IEEE, Std 830-1984.

International Organization for Standardization (1986). *Quality Management and Quality System Elements—Guidelines* (First edition): ISO 9004.

International Organization for Standardization (1987). *Quality Systems—Model for Quality Assurance* (First edition): ISO 9001.

International Organization for Standardization (1988). Information processing systems, open system interconnections, LOTOS—a formal description technique based on the temporal ordering of observational behaviour. DIS 8807 TEC JTC 1/SC 21 N2987.

Ivie, E. L. (1977). The programmer's workbench—a machine for software development. *Commun. ACM*, **20**(10), 746–53.

Jackson, M. A. (1975). *Principles of Program Design*. Academic Press, New York.

Jeffery, D. R. (1987). The relationship between team size, experience, and attitudes and software development productivity. In *Proceedings COMPSAC '87*, IEEE Computer Society Press, New York.

Jelinski, Z. & Moranda, P. B. (1972). Software reliability research. In *Statistical Computer Performance Evaluation*, ed. W. Freiberger. Academic Press, New York, pp. 465–84.

Jensen, R. W. (1984). A comparison of the Jensen and COCOMO schedule and cost estimation models. *Proceedings of the International Society of Parametric Analysis*, pp. 96–106.

Joe, H. & Reid, N. (1985). Estimating the number of faults in a system. *J. Amer. Statist. Soc.*, **80**, 222–6.

Joergenson, A. H. (1980). A methodology for measuring the readability and modifiability of computer programs. *BIT*, **20**, 394–405.

Johnson, P. (1988). Experience of formal development in CICS. IBM Report, Hursley Park.

Jones, C. B. (1980). *Software Development a Rigorous Approach*, Series in Computer Science. Prentice-Hall, Englewood Cliffs, NJ.

Jones, C. B. (1983). Specification and design of (parallel) programs. In *IFIP*, North Holland, Amsterdam.

Jones, C. B. (1986). *Systematic Software Development Using VDM*, Series in Computer Science. Prentice-Hall, Englewood Cliffs, NJ.

Jones, C. B. & Shaw, R. C. (1988). *Case Studies in Systematic Software Development*. Prentice-Hall, Englewood Cliffs, NJ.

Jones, C. B., Lindsay, P. A. & Wadsworth, C. (1986). IPSE 2.5 theorem proving concepts paper. Manchester University and RAL. Report to the Alvey Directorate.

Jones, T. C. (1977). Program quality and programmer productivity. IBM report, TR02.764.

Jones, T. C. (1986). *Programming Productivity*. McGraw Hill, New York.

Kafura, D. & Canning, J. (1985). A validation of software metrics using many metrics and two resources. *Proceedings of the 8th International Conference on Software Engineering*. IEEE Computer Society Press. New York, pp. 378–85.

Kemerer, C. F. (1987). An empirical validation of software cost estimation models. *Commun. ACM*, **30**(5), 416–29.

Keravnou, E. & Johnson, L. (1986). *Competent Expert Systems*. Kogan Page, London.

Kincaid, J. P., Aagard, J. A., O'Hara, J. W. & Cottrell, L. K. (1981). Computer readability editing system. *IEEE Trans. Professional Commun.*, **PC-24**, pp. 38–41.

Kitchenham, B. A. (1981). Measures of programming complexity. *ICL Tech. J.*, **2**, 298–316.

Kitchenham, B. A. (1984). Program history records; a system of software data collection and analysis. *ICL Tech. J.*, May 1984, pp. 103–14.

Kitchenham, B. A. (1986). *Metrics in Practice*. In *Software Reliability*, ed. A. Bendell & P. Mellor. Infotech State of the Art Report, 14:2, Pergamon Infotech Ltd, Berkshire, UK.

Kitchenham, B. A. & Kitchenham, A. P. (1984). The use of measurements to evaluate software production methods. In *Proceedings of the Seminar Approches Quantitative en Génie Logiciel*. AFCET, Sophia-Antipolis, France, pp. 203–216.

Kitchenham, B. A. & Taylor, N. R. (1984). Software cost models. *ICL Tech. J.*, (May), 73–102.

Kitchenham, B. A. & Taylor, N. R. (1985). Software project development cost estimation. *J. Systems Software*, **5**, 267–78.

Kitchenham, B. A. & Walker, J. G. (1986a). The meaning of quality. In *Proceedings of BCS/IEE Conference on Software Engineering*, ed. D. Barnes, O. P. Brown. IEE Computing Series, Peter Perigrinus Ltd, pp. 393–406.

Kitchenham, B. A. & Walker, J. G. (1986b). An information model for software quality management. Test Specification and Quality Management Project Report A24 to the Alvey Directorate.

Kitchenham, B. A. & Wood, L. M. (1986). Statistical techniques for modelling software quality. REQUEST report R1.6.8, CEC ESPRIT Programme, Brussels.

Kitchenham, B. A., Kitchenham, A. P. & Fellows, J. P. (1986). The effects of inspections on software quality and productivity. *ICL Tech. J.*, (May) pp. 112–22.

Knight, J. C. & Leveson, N. G. (1986a). An experimental evaluation of the assumption of independence in multiversion programming. *IEEE Trans. Software Eng.*, **SE-12**(1), 96–109.

Knight, J. C. & Leveson, N. G. (1986b). An empirical study of failure probabilities in multi-version software. *Proc. 16th International Conference on Fault Tolerant Computing*. IEEE Computer Society, New York, pp. 165–70.

Lambert, J. M. (1986). A software sizing model. *J. Parametrics*, **6**, 4.

Larsen, K. G. & Milner, R. (1986). A complete protocol verification using relativised bisimulation. Report ECS-LFS-86-13. Laboratory for Foundations of Computer Science, Edinburgh University.

Lee, P. A., Ghani, N. & Heron, K. (1980). A recovery cache for the PDP-11. *IEEE Trans. Computers*, **C-29**(6), 546–9.

Lehman, M. M. (1978). Laws of program evolution—rules and tools for programming management. In Infotech State of the Art Report *Why Software Projects Fail*.

Lescanne, P. (1983). Computer experiments with the REVE term rewriting system generator. *Proceedings 10th ACM Symposium on Principles of Programming Languages*, Austin, Texas, pp. 99–108.

Lindsay, P. A., Moore, R. C. & Ritchie, B. (1986). IPSE 2.5 review of existing theorem provers. Manchester University and RAL. Report to the Alvey Directorate.

Littlewood, B. (1978). How to measure software reliability and how not to . . . . In *Proceedings of the Third International Conference on Software Engineering*, IEEE Computer Society Press, New York, pp. 37–45.

Littlewood, B. (1979a). Software reliability model for modular program structure. *IEEE Trans. Reliability*, **R-28**(3), 241–6.

Littlewood, B. (1979b). How to measure software reliability and how not to. *IEEE Trans. Reliability*, **R-28**(2), 103–10.

Littlewood, B. (1981). Stochastic reliability growth: a model for fault-removal in computer programs and hardware designs. *IEEE Trans. Reliability*, **R-30**, 313–20.

Littlewood, B. (1989). Forecasting Software Reliability, Lecture Notes in Computer Science, No. 341, Springer-Verlag, Berlin.

Littlewood, B. & Keiller, P. A. (1984). Adaptive software reliability modelling. In

Proceedings 14th International Conference on Fault-Tolerant Computing. IEEE Computer Society, New York, pp. 108–13.

Littlewood, B. & Sofer, A. (1987). A Bayesian modification to the Jelinski–Moranda software reliability model. *IEE/BCS Software Eng. J.*, **2** (March), 30–41.

Littlewood, B. & Verrall, J. L. (1973). A Bayesian reliability growth model for computer software. *J. Royal Statist. Soc., Appl. Statist.*, **22**(3), 332–46.

Londeix, B. (1987). Cost estimation for software development. Addison-Wesley, Reading, MA.

Maibaum, T. (1988). *A Logic for the Formal Requirements Specification of Real-Time/Embedded Systems,* FOREST Report R3 to the Alvey Directorate.

Markusz, S. & Kaposi, A. A. (1985). Complexity control of logic based programming. *Computer J.*, **28,** 5.

Martin, C. F. (1988). Second-generation CASE tools: a challenge to vendors. *IEEE Software,* **5**(2)**,** 46–9.

Martin, D. J. (1982). Dissimilar software in high integrity applications in flight controls. In *Proc. AGARD Symposium on Software for Avionics.* The Hague, Netherlands, pp. 36:1–36:13.

MASCOT Suppliers Association (1980). *The Official Handbook of MASCOT.* RSRE, Malvern.

McCabe, T. J. (1976). A complexity measure. *IEEE Trans. Software Eng.,* **SE-2**(4).

McCall, J. A., Richards, P. K. & Walters, G. F. (1977). *Factors in Software Quality.* Rome Air Development Center, Griffiss AFB, NY. RADC Reports, pp. 308–20.

McDermid, J. & Ripkin, K. (1984). *Life Cycle Support in the Ada Environment.* Cambridge University Press, Cambridge.

Melliar-Smith, P. M. (1983). Development of software fault tolerance techniques. NASA Contractor Report 172122.

Melliar-Smith, P. M. & Schwarz, R. L. (1982). Formal specification and mechanical verification of SIFT: a fault tolerant flight control system. *IEEE Trans. Computers,* **C-31**(7), 616–29.

Meyer, B. (1985). On formalism in specification. *IEEE Software* **2**(1)**,** 6–26.

Meyer, B. (1988). *Object-Oriented Software Construction,* Series in Computer Science. Prentice-Hall, Englewood Cliffs, NJ.

Miller, D. R. (1986). Exponential order statistic models of software reliability growth. *IEEE Trans. Software Eng.,* **SE-12**(1)**,** 12–24.

Mills, H. D., Dyer, M. & Linger, R. (1987). Cleanroom Software Engineering. *IEEE Software,* **4**(5)**,** 19–25.

Milner, R. (1980). *A Calculus of Communicating Systems.* Lecture Notes in Computer Science, 92. Springer-Verlag, Berlin.

Milner, R. (1988). Operational and algebraic semantics of concurrent processes. Report ECS-LFCS-88-46. Laboratory for Foundations of Computer Science, Edinburgh University.

Ministry of Defence, (1984). *Guide to the Achievement of Quality in Software.* Defence Standard 00-16, (Issue 1). HMSO, London.

Ministry of Defence (1988). *Safety Critical Computing Systems: The Procurement of Safe Computer Systems.* UK Interim Defence Standard 00-55, HMSO, London.

Miyazaki, Y. & Mori, K. (1985). COCOMO evaluation and tailoring. In *Proceedings 8th International Conference on Software Engineering.* IEEE Computer Society Press, New York, pp. 292–9.

Mohanty, S. N. (1981). Software cost estimation: present and future. *Software Practice & Experience,* **11,** 103–21.

Mohr, W. L. & Mohr, H. (1983). *Quality Circles.* Addison Wesley, Reading, MA.

Moulding, M. R. (1986). An architecture to support software fault tolerance and an evaluation of its performance in a command and control application. *Digest IEE Colloquium on Performance Measurement and Prediction,* Feb. 1986.

Moulding, M. R. & Barrett, P. (1987). An investigation into the application of software fault tolerance to air traffic control systems: project final report. Ref. 1049/TD.6 Version 2, RMCS, Shrivenham, Wilts, UK.

Musa, J. D. (1975). A theory of software reliability and its application. *IEEE Trans. Software Eng.*, **SE-1**, 312–27.

Musa, J. D. (1980). Software reliability data. Report available from DACS, Rome Air Development Center, Griffiss AFB, NY.

Musa, J. D. & Okumoto, K. (1984). A logarithmic Poisson execution time model for software reliability measurement. *Proceedings 7th International Conference on Software Engineering*. IEEE Computer Society Press, New York, pp. 230–8.

Musser, D. R. (1979). Abstract data type specification in the AFFIRM system. In *IEEE Proceedings of Specification of Reliable Software* (*Cambridge, Mass., Apr. 3–5*), pp. 47–57. IEEE, New York.

Myers, G. J. (1978). *Composite Structured Design*. Van Nostrand Reinhold, New York.

Myers, G. (1979). *The Art of Software Testing*. Wiley, New York.

Nagel, P. N. & Skrivan, J. A. (1981). Software reliability: repetitive run experimentation and modelling. BCS-40399, Boeing Computer Services Company, Seattle.

National Computing Centre (1987). *The STARTS Guide*, (2nd edition). National Computing Centre, Manchester.

Nelson, E. A. (1966). Management handbook for the estimation of computer programming costs. AD-A648750. Systems Development Corporation.

Neumann, B. de (1983). Computerised life cycle cost models. In *Electronic Systems Effectiveness and Life Cycle Costing*, ed. J. K. Skwirzynski. Springer-Verlag, Berlin.

Nielson, D. S. (1988). Hierarchical refinement of a Z specification. In *Refinement Workshop, University of York* (digest of papers), Jan. 1988.

Norden, P. V. (1963). Useful tools for project management. In *Operations Research in Research and Development*, John Wiley & Sons, New York.

Oberndorf, P. A. (1988). The common APSE interface set. *IEEE Trans. Software Eng.*, **SE-14**(6), 742–9.

Ould, M. A. & Roberts, C. (1988). Defining formal models of the software development process. In *Software Engineering Environments*, ed. P. Brereton. Ellis Horwood, Chichester.

Ould, M. & Unwin, C. (eds) (1986). *Testing in Software Development*, British Computer Society Monographs in Informatics. Cambridge University Press, Cambridge.

Oviedo, E. I. (1980). Control flow, data flow and program complexity. In *Proceedings of the 4th Computer Software and Application Conference* (*COMPSAC* 80). IEEE Computer Society Press, New York, pp. 146–52.

Paige, M. (1980). A metric for software test planning. In *Proceedings Computer Software and Applications*. IEEE Computer Society Press, New York, pp. 499–504.

Parikh, G. & Zvegintzov, Z. (1983). *Tutorial on Software Maintenance*, IEEE Computer Society Press, New York.

Park, R. (1988). The central equations of the PRICE Software cost model. Fourth COCOMO Users' Group Meeting, November, 1988.

Parnas, D. (1972). On the criteria to be used in decomposing systems into modules. *Commun. ACM.*, **15**(2), 1053–8.

Parr, F. N. (1980). An alternative to the Rayleigh curve model for software development effort. *IEEE Trans. Software Eng.*, **SE-6**(3), 291–6.

Parrow, J. (1986). Verifying a CSMA/CD protocol with CCS. Report ECS-LFCS-87-18. Laboratory for Foundations of Computer Science, Edinburgh University.

Partsch, H. & Steinbruggen, R. (1983). Program transformation systems. *ACM Computing Surveys*, **15**(3), 199–236.

Penedo, M. H. & Riddle, W. E. (1988). Software engineering environment architectures. *IEEE Trans. Software Eng.*, **SE-14**(6), 689–97.

Pepper, P. (ed.) (1984). *Program Transformation and Programming Environments.* NATO ASI Series (F), 8. Springer-Verlag, Berlin.

Petersen, P. G. & Kitchenham, B. A. (1988). The development of a software quality model. *First European Seminar on Software Quality*, Brussels, 1988, pp. 74–89.

Petersen, P. G., Andersen, O., Heillesen, J. H., Klim, S. & Schmidt, J. (1989). Software quality drivers and indicators. In *Proceedings 22nd Hawaii International Conference on System Sciences, 1989.*

Prehn, S. (1987). From VDM to RAISE. In Bjorner & Jones (1987).

Putnam, L. H. (1978). A general empirical solution to the macro software sizing and estimation problem. *IEEE Trans. Software Eng.*, **SE-4**(4), 345–61.

Putnam, L. (1987). Size Planner, an Automated Sizing Model. Third COCOMO User's Group Meeting, November 1987.

Putnam, L. H. & Putnam, D. T. (1984). A data verification of the software power trade-off law. In *Proceedings of the International Society of Parametric Analysis*, **3**(1), 443–71.

Randell, B. (1975). System structuring for software fault tolerance. *IEEE Trans. Software Eng.*, **SE-1**(2), 220–32.

Rapp, W. (1985). RCA PRICE parametric software sizing—a state-of-the-art approach. In *Proceedings of the International Society of Parametric Analysts Seventh Annual Conference*, **4**(1).

Reade, C. M. P. (1989). *Elements of Functional Programming.* Addison-Wesley, Reading, MA.

Redmill, F. J. (1987). Difficulties of specifying users' requirements for computer systems and methods of mitigating them. *Br. Telecommun. Eng.*, **6** (April), 60–7.

Refinement Workshop, University of York (digest of papers), Jan. 1988.

Reid, P. & Welland, R. C. (1986). Software development in view. In *Software Engineering Environments*, ed. I. Sommerville. Peter Perigrinus Ltd., Stevenage.

Reifer, D. J. (1986). Predicting the size of real-time systems. In *Proceedings of the NIS Software Cost and Quality Management Conference*, October 1986.

Reifer, D. (1988). Softcost-Ada: An update. Fourth COCOMO User' Group Meeting, November, 1988.

Reisig, W. (1985). *Petri Nets: An Introduction*, EATCS Monographs in Theoretical Computer Science. Springer-Verlag, Berlin.

Reliability and Statistical Consultants Ltd. (1985). *Software Reliability Modelling Programs*. Details from Reliability and Statistical Consultants Ltd., 5 Jocelyn Road, Richmond, Surrey TW9 2TJ.

Remus, H. & Zilles, S. (1979). Prediction and management of program quality. In *Proceedings of the 4th International Conference on Software Engineering.* IEEE Computer Society Press, New York, pp. 341–50.

Rook, P. E. (1986). Controlling software projects. *IEE/BCS Software Eng. J.*, **1**(1), 7–16.

Ross, N. (1986). Data Definitions. Software Data Library Report 2.2.2 to the Alvey Directorate.

Royce, W. W. (1970). Managing the development of large software systems. In *Proceedings of IEEE WESCON 1970*, pp. 1–9; reprinted in Thayer (1988, pp. 118–27).

Rozenberg, G. (ed.) (1985). *Advances in Petri Nets 1985*, Lecture Notes in Computer Science, 222. Springer-Verlag, Berlin.

RTCA (1985). Software Considerations in Airborne Systems and Equipment Certification: Report DO 178A. Radio Technical Commission for Aeronautics.

Rubin, H. A. (1983). Macroestimation of software development parameters: the Estimacs system. In *SOFTFAIR Conference on Software Development Tools, Techniques and Alternatives, Arlington, July 1983*, IEEE Press, New York, pp. 109–18.

Rubin, H. A. (1985). A comparison of cost estimation tools. (A panel session). In

Proceedings of the 8th International Conference on Software Engineering, IEEE Computer Society Press, New York, pp. 174–80.

Saaty, T. L. (1980). *The Analytical Hierarchy Process.* McGraw-Hill, New York.

Samson, W. B., Dugard, P. I., Nevill, D. G., Oldfield, P. E., Smith, A. W. & Titterington, G. (1989). The relationship between specification and implementation metrics. In *Measurement for Software Control and Assurance,* ed. B. A. Kitchenham & B. Littlewood. Elsevier Science Publishers Ltd, London, pp. 335–84.

Sarikaya, B. & Bochmann, G. V. (eds) (1987). *Protocol Specification, Testing, & Verification.* North-Holland, Amsterdam.

Sen, D. (1987). Objectives of the British standardisation of a language to support VDM. In Bjorner & Jones (1987).

Shephard, D. (1988). Using formal methods in VLSI design. In *Refinement Workshop, University of York* (digest of papers), Jan. 1988.

Shepperd, M. (1988). A critique of cyclomatic complexity as a software metric. *Software Eng. J.,* **3**(2), 30–6.

Sherif, Y. S., Ng, E. & Steinbacher, J. (1985). Computer software quality measures and metrics. *Microelectron. Reliab.,* **25**(6), 1105–50.

Shin, K. G. & Lee, Y. H. (1984). Evaluation of error recovery blocks used for co-operating processes. *IEEE Trans. Software Eng.,* **SE-10**(6), 692–700.

Shooman, M. L. (1976). Structural models for software reliability prediction. In *Proceedings of the 2nd International Conference on Software Engineering,* IEEE, New York, pp. 268–80.

Simpson, H. (1986). The MASCOT method. *BCS/IEE Software Eng. J.,* **1**(3), 103–20.

Small, M. & Faulkener, T. L. (1983). A quality model of system design and integration. In *FTCS 13th Annual International Symposium on Fault Tolerant Computing.* IEEE Computer Society Press, New York, pp. 412–19.

Sommerville, I., Beer, S. & Welland, R. C. (1987). The ECLIPSE design editing system. In *Proceedings 1st European Software Engineering Conference, Strasbourg.* Springer-Verlag, Berlin.

Spivey, J. M. (1988a). *The Z Notation—A Reference Manual.* Prentice-Hall, Englewood Cliffs, NJ.

Spivey, J. M. (1988b). *Understanding Z.* Cambridge University Press, Cambridge.

Staunstrup, J. (1982). *Program Specification: Proceedings of a Workshop, Aarhus, Denmark,* Lecture Notes in Computer Science, 134. Springer-Verlag, Berlin.

Symons, C. R. (1988). Function point analysis: difficulties and improvements. *IEEE Trans. Software Eng.,* **14**(1), 2–11.

Systems-Designers, plc. (1986). *Aspect: Specification of the Public Tool Interface.*

Takahashi, M. & Kamayachi, Y. (1985). An empirical study of a model for program error prediction. In *Proceedings of the 8th International Conference on Software Engineering.* IEEE Computer Society Press, New York, pp. 330–6.

Tapscott, D. (1982). *Office Automation: a User-driven Method.* Plenum Press, New York.

Tausworthe, R. C. (1981). Deep space network software cost estimation model. Publication 81-7, Jet Propulsion Laboratory, Pasadena.

Taylor, D. J., Morgan, D. E. & Black, J. P. (1980). Redundancy in data structures: improving software fault tolerance. *IEEE Trans. Software Eng.,* **SE-6**(6), 585–94.

Taylor, J. R. (1981). Letter from the editor. *ACM Software Eng. Notes,* **6**(1), 1–2.

Thatcher, J. W., Wagner, E. G. & Wright, J. B. (1978). Data type specification: parameterisation and the power of specification techniques. In *ACM Proc. SIGACT 10th Symposium on Theory of Computing.*

Thayer, R. H. (1988). *Software Engineering Project Management.* IEEE Tutorial EH0263-4.

Thebaut, S. M. (1983). The saturation effect in large-scale software development: its impact and control. PhD Thesis, Department of Computer Science, Purdue University.

Titterington, G. C. (1986). Application of formal methods in an industrial environment. Report to Alvey Directorate (Software Engineering), Software Sciences Ltd.

Traverse, P. (1988). AIRBUS and ATR system architecture and specification. In *Software Diversity in Computerized Control Systems* (ed. U. Voges), Springer-Verlag, Berlin.

Troy, D. A. & Zweben, S. H. (1981). Measuring the quality of structured designs. *J. Systems Software*, **2**, 113–20.

Turner, D. A. (1985). *Miranda: A non strict functional language with polymorphic types*. Lecture Notes in Computer Science, No. 20, Springer-Verlag, Berlin.

Turski, W. M. & Maibaum, T. S. E. (1987). *The Specification of Complex Programs*, International Computer Science Series. Addison Wesley, Reading, MA.

VIP Project Team (1988*a*). Kernel Interface: Final Specification Report VIP T.E.8.2. VIP, CEC ESPRIT Programme, Brussels.

VIP Project Team (1988*b*). Man–Machine Interface: Final Specification Report VIP T.E.8.3. VIP, CEC ESPRIT Programme, Brussels.

Voges, U. (ed.) (1988). *Software Diversity in Computerized Control Systems*. Springer-Verlag, Berlin.

Walker, M. G. (1981). *Managing Software Reliability: the Paradigmatic Approach*. Elsevier North-Holland, Amsterdam.

Walston, C. E. & Felix, C. P. (1977). A method of programming measurement and estimation. *IBM Systems J.*, **16**(1), 54–73.

Warnier, J. D. (1976). *Logical Construction of Programs* (3rd edition), trans B. M. Flanagan, Van Nostrand Reinhold, New York.

Weinberg, G. M. & Freedman, D. P. (1984). Reviews, walkthroughs and inspections. *IEEE Trans. Software Eng.* **SE-10**(1) (Jan.), 68–72; reprinted in Thayer (1988), pp. 399–403.

Whitworth, M. H. & Szulewski, P. A. (1980). The measurement of control flow and data flow complexity in software designs. In *Proceedings of the 4th Computer Software and Applications Conference (COMPSAC 80)*. IEEE Computer Society Press, New York, pp. 735–43.

Wightman, D. W. & Bendell, A. (1985). The practical application of proportional hazards modelling. In *Proceedings of Reliability '85*.

Willis, R. R. (1981). AIDES: computer-aided design of software systems. In *Software Engineering Environments*, ed. H. Hunke, North-Holland, Amsterdam.

Wingrove, A. A. (1986). The problems of managing software projects, *IEE/BCS Software Eng. J.*, **1**(1), 3–6.

Wolverton, R. W. (1974). The cost of developing large-scale software. *IEEE Trans. Computers*, **C-23**(6), 615–36.

Woodstock, J. C. P. & Dickson, B. (1988). Using VDM with Rely- and Guarantee-Conditions: Experience from a real project (preliminary draft). *Refinement Workshop, University of York*.

Woodward, M. R., Hennell, M. A. & Hedley, D. (1979). A measure of control flow complexity in program text. *IEEE Trans. Software Eng.*, **SE-5**(1), 45–50.

Woodward, M. R., Hennell, M. A. & Hedley, D. (1980). Experience with path analysis and testing programs. *IEEE Trans. Software Eng.*, **SE-6**(3), 278–86.

Yeh, R. T. (1980). Specifying software requirements. *Proc. IEEE*, **68**(9), 1077–84.

Yin, B. H. & Winchester, J. W. (1978). The establishment and use of measures to evaluate the quality of software designs. *ACM Software Eng. Notes*, **3**(5), 45–52.

Zelkowitz, M. & Squires, S. (1982). *Proceedings of ACM Rapid Prototyping Symposium*, ACM, October 1982.

Index

Acceptance
  procedures, 229–30
  test, 122, 197
Achievability of reliability requirements,
  6–8
Acquisition
  concept risk, 376
  costs, 334
ACT ONE, 74
Activity integration, 379
Ada, 30–2, 44–6, 49, 61, 71, 78, 92–6,
  132, 386, 389–91, 456
Ada process model, 437–9
Adaptation adjustment factor (*AAF*), 493
AFFIRM, 63
Algol-68, 456
Analytical models, 315
Animation, 56–7
Annual change traffic (*ACT*), 494
APSE, 390–1
ARCH, 352
ASCII, 393
ASPECT, 70, 378
Assembler, 351
ASSET-R, 351–3, 354, 356
Asynchronous components, 84, 86
Audits, 266–7, 287–8, 295–6
Automatic rebuild tools, 119
Availability, 3, 5
Avionics industry, 108
AWB-ADE, 378

Backward recovery, 91, 100, 104
Bailey–Basili meta-model, 505–7

Bang metrics, 357–8, 366
Baselines
  concept of, 178–80
  documentation, 237
  maintenance, 237–9, 241
  monitoring project progress with
    respect to, 309
BASIC, 456
Bayes theorem, 404, 412
Bayesian analysis, 405
Bayesian Jelinski–Moranda (BJM)
  model, 403–4
Bayesian prediction systems, 411
Bench marking, 231
Bias
  noisiness, and, 151
  detection, 408, 409–12
Bisimulation proof technique, 74
BJM Model, 144
Box-plots, 311–12
BYL (before you leap), 351

C language, 48, 351
CAIS (Common APSE Interface Set),
  386, 387, 397, 398
CASE (Computer Aided Software
  Engineering), 391–4
Cash-dispenser system, 35
CCS, 73, 74
Certification, 9–11
Change control, 397
Change instruction, 118
Change-request classification schema, 475
Chebyshev inequality, 370
Checking activity, 444

Checklists, 7
CHILL, 71
CICS, 69
CIRCAL, 74
Classification schemas, 473–5
CLEAR, 63, 75, 76, 82
COBOL, 351, 356
COCOMO, 342–3, 356, 361, 364–5, 368, 369, 469, 487, 489–97, 516
　assessment, 494–7
　improved version, 493
　intermediate and detailed, 491–3
　maintenance, 372–3
　original version, 493
　subjective criteria, 494
　verification of predictive accuracy, 497
Code, 422
　adaptation, 493
　metrics, 325–6, 366
　re-use, 512
　re-use adjustments, 511
Code of practice, 190, 208
Coding checks, 100
Coding phase products, 196
Common-mode effects, 8
Communications, 267–9, 288–9, 296
Comparison of application functions, 349
Comparison of project attributes, 350
Complexity measure, 458–9
Compliance table or matrix, 115
Component faults, 89
Computer Economic Inc. Sizer (CEIS), 350
Conceptual models, 315
Concurrent systems, 73–5
Configuration management, 164–5, 239, 265, 286, 294–5, 380, 382, 388, 422
Constraint models, 341, 507–17
Contingency plans, 364
Contract
　management, 224
　software procurement, 216
Contractual model, 429–30
Conversations, 104–5
COPMO, 516–17
COQUAMO, 368
CORAL, 109
CORE, 120
Corrected single-factor cost models, 341
Corrective actions, 318, 329–31
Correctness, 9, 11, 481

Cost
　analysis, 334–5
　elements, 370
Cost–benefit analysis, 226
Cost–benefit considerations, 8
Cost-effective defect control, 307
Cost-effectiveness of formal specifications, 29
Cost estimation, 333–76
　risk analysis, and, 368–76
　improving, 361–2
　political and technical issues, 338–40
　problems of, 336–8
　project control, 364
Cost implications of lowering reliability requirements, 8
Cost measurement, problems of, 336–8
Cost models, 206, 333–76, 487–517
　calibration, 363–5
　classification, 340–1
　COCOMO, 342–3
　construction of local cost models, 365–7
　familiarization and consolidation, 363–4
　installation, 363
　practical problems, 343–4
　procedures for improving model accuracy, 364
　Putnam's, 342
　tuning, 363–5
Cost–quality interactions, 206
Cost-reduction strategies, 206–7
Cross-validation, 316
CSP, 73, 74
Current reliability, 138
Customer acceptance review, 198
Cyclomatic complexity, 455–8
Cyclomatic number, 455–8

Dale–Chall readability formula, 466
Damage assessment, 88, 97
Data collection, 14–17, 139, 266, 286–7, 295, 309–10
　analysis and use, 243
　mechanisms of, 153
Data dictionary support, 388
Data management, 380, 384, 385
Data structures, 25
Deadline mechanism, 106
Decision making, 159
Defect analysis, 307
Defect avoidance, 307

Defect detection and correction, 111–36, 307
  cost-effective, 307
  development and testability, 115–16
  general principles of, 114–20
  requirements and testability, 115
  see also Life-cycle
Defect-removal model, 478–9
Defensive programming, 92
Definition/specification phase, 123–5
Delphi technique, 345–6
Design, 21–49
  characteristics, 24
  complexity, 453–5
  coupling, 24
  diagram, 25
  documentation, 25
  formal methods of, 28
  phase, 128–9
  process, contractual description of, 54
  specification, 194
  stages in process, 22
  structured, 24, 27
  visibility, 24, 25
  see also Detailed design; Object-oriented design; Structural design
Design-to-code expansion rate, 466–8
Design weight metrics, 358–9, 366
Destructive testing, 232
Detailed design, 131–2, 195, 422
  products, 195–6
  use of metrics in, 322–5
Disposal costs, 335
Documentation, 119, 123, 422
  control, 265–6, 286, 294–5
  tools, 388
Domino effect, 103, 104
Driver module, 96
Dual-version programming, 108
Duane (D) model, 406

ECLIPSE, 389
Economic risk, 376
Electronic mail system, 25, 27, 388
Embedded software systems, 27
EML-I, 367
Empirical factor models, 341
Entity-relationship model, 442
Entity-relationship-attribute (ERA) model, 386

Environment
  architecture, 381–9
  facilities, 378–80
  reliability management, and, 396–7
Equivalent number of delivered source instructions (*EDSI*), 493
ERIL, 77
Erroneous transition, 87
Error detection, 88, 90, 100, 105–6
Error-free state, 91
Error recovery, 88, 92, 97
ESTIMACS, 344, 356, 504–5
Estimating for software development, 161
Estimating Quality Factor (*EQF*), 361
Estimation procedures, 511
Evaluation, 446
Events and event attributes, 443, 445, 450, 473–5
Exception-handling facilities, 92–6
Expansion rate, 444
Expected, definition, 3
External state, 87

Factor models, 489–507
Failure
  behaviour prediction, 138
  data, 12, 13, 16
  definition, 2
  exceptions, 91
  process, 138–43
Fan-in and fan-out, 460–4
Fault analysis, 307
Fault and change rates, 468–70
Fault classification, 307, 473–5
Fault counting, 307
Fault detection rates, 472–3
Fault identification, 118
Fault introduction and detection models, 476–9
Fault location, 118, 119
Fault tolerance, 8, 83–110
  controller, 88, 91, 97
  implementation framework for, 90–2
  object of, 87
  overview of, 84–90
  systems, 108
Fault treatment, 88
Feasibility studies, 191, 260–1, 282, 291, 299
Feedback loops, 157
Flesch–Kincaid index, 466

Floating-point unit, 71
FOCUS, 351
Fog index, 465-6
FOREST Project, 72, 81
Formal development tools and systems, 28, 76-7
Formal methods, 28, 51-82
  algebraic approach, 62-3
  approaches to, 58-69
  current use of, 69-72
  example, 63-9
  important issues for effective use of, 72-9
  mandatory use of, 51
  model-based approach, 59-62
  nature of, 52-3
  present application, 51
  prospects and conclusions, 80-2
  reliability, and, 53, 56-8
  role in software development, 58
Formal specifications, 53, 57, 58
Formal system specification, 28-9
Formal verification, 28, 52
Fortran, 351, 456, 460
Forward recovery, 91, 100
Function box, 348
Function point analysis, 355-6
Function points, 351, 360, 366
Functional Primitives (FP), 357
Functional specification, 125
Functionally degraded alternates, 102-3

Gantt charts, 183
Generic phase, 114-15
Generic risks, 201, 202
GENOS, 379, 386, 397
Goel-Okumoto (GO) Model, 407
Goods-inwards test, 119
Graphical interfaces, 79
Guidelines, 7, 14
GYPSY, 70

Halstead Volume formula, 357
Halstead's Software Science metrics, 347, 351, 353
Health and Safety Executive, 13, 14
Heating control system, 33, 34
High-level languages, 78-9
Higher Order Logic, 71
Human ingenuity, 23

IBM Cleanroom concept, 58, 70-1
IEEE Guide to Software Requirements Specifications, 217
IEEE standard on testing, 116
IEEE Tutorial on Software Engineering Project Management, 159, 162, 413, 416, 435
IEEE Tutorial on Software Risk Management, 200
Incoming tests, 119, 121, 123, 125, 127, 129, 131, 132, 134-5
Incremental development, 433-4
Information hiding, 29, 32-5
Informational fan-in and fan-out, 460-4
Installation, 229-30
Integrated Project Support Environments (IPSEs), 173-4, 270, 276, 378-89, 394-6, 398, 443
Integration, 196-7
Integration testing, 197
  use of metrics in, 327-8
Interaction between teams, 418-20
Interface exceptions, 90
Internal states, 87
IPSE 2.5, 80
ISO, 74
ISTAR, 379

Jelinski-Moranda (JM) model, 144, 147-9, 151, 152, 401-2
Jensen model, 515-16
JSD, 72
JSP, 27
Justification, 288-9, 296

KAPSE, 390
Knuth-Bendix algorithm, 77

Language-use standards, 397
LARCH, 63, 76
Large-scale specifications, 75-6
Law of diminishing returns, 8
LCF/LSM, 71
LCSAJ, 471
Legal problems, 11-14
Life-cycle, 112-14, 176-9, 190-9, 203, 416-18, 511
  components, 510
  costs, 334
  curve, 510

Life-cycle—*contd.*
  defect detection and correction
    throughout, 120–35
  models, 112, 177, 182–3, 417, 422–6,
    428–30
  use of metrics throughout, 317
  vee-model, 113–14
Linear regression, 366
Lines of code (LOC), 205–6, 312, 319,
  320, 325, 451–2
  estimation methods, 345–54
  predictive model, 349–53
Link editors, 377–8
Littlewood (L) model, 144, 404–5
Littlewood nonhomogeneous Poisson
  process (LNHPP) model, 145,
  147–9, 151, 152, 407
Littlewood–Verrall (LV) model, 144,
  147–9, 151, 152, 405–6
Local specification, 55, 57
Logarithmic transformation, 313
Logistic costs, 373
LOTOS, 74

Maintenance of software, 211, 234–44
  baseline establishment, 237–9
  baseline maintenance, 241
  build management, 241–2
  change control, 240–1
  continuous assessment of product
    status, 243
  effort estimation, 493–4
  managing changes against baseline,
    239–43
  manual, 195
  problems of, 236
  role in achieving reliable software,
    244–5
  specific actions in, 237
  support for future procurement, 243
Management
  control, 170
  decisions, 117–18, 121, 123, 125, 126,
    129, 131–4
  reporting, 162–3
  structure, 169
Manpower acceleration, 509
MAPSE, 390
Mark II Function Points, 360
MASCOT, 27, 109, 381–2
Maximum-likelihood estimates, 144, 153,
  405, 407

Mean magnitude of relative error
  (MMRE), 356, 488
Mean square error, 409
Median, definition, 3
Menu object, 46–7
Meta-model, 366
Method-support capabilities, 381–2
Metrics, 112, 205, 207, 276, 441–75
  analysis of, 310–14
  classes of, 304
  code, use in, 325–6
  control, 305, 315
  criteria for description, 445–6
  datasets, 311
  definitions, 310
  detailed design, use in, 322–5
  dual-purpose, 306–7
  evaluation, 315–7
  guidelines for integrating values,
    328–31
  Halstead's Software Science, 347, 351,
    353
  integration testing, use in, 327–8
  interpretation of values, 308–9
  module-based analysis, use in, 322, 324,
    326–8
  nature and use of, 304
  predictor, 305–6, 315
  requirements specification, use in, 319
  scope of, 314
  selection criteria, 442–5
  size, 306
  structural design, use in, 320–2
  term, use of, 303–4
  throughout life-cycle, 317
  unit testing, use in, 326–7
  see also under specific metrics
Mini-Rayleigh curve, 510
Miranda, 78, 79
ML, 70
MMRE (mean magnitude of relative
  error), 356, 488
Model formulation, 316
Modula-2, 46, 93
Modularity, 443
Modularization, 115–16
Module-based analysis, 322, 324, 326, 327
Module code and test, 132–5
Module strength, 459–60
MTBF (mean time between failures), 2–3
MTTF (mean time to failure), 2, 4
Multivariate regression, 312
Musa–Okumoto (MO) model, 407

MVOL, 353
Mythical Man-Month, 167, 170

Network of processes, 85
Noise and noise detection, 151, 409–12
Non-comment source statements (NCSS), 511
Non-Gaussian data, 311
Nonhomogeneous Poisson process (NHPP), 145, 406
Non-parametric techniques, 312
Number of words, 452–3
N-version programming, 92, 96–9
  comparison with recovery blocks, 105–7
  experimental evaluations, 108
  practical application of, 107–9

OBJ, 63, 70, 314
Object implementation, 44–8
Object management system (OMS), 173, 380, 385–7, 430
Object–object relationships, 386
Object-oriented design, 21, 23, 27, 29–44, 72, 75, 184, 190
  advantages of, 29
  example, 36–44
  inappropriate, 35–6
Object-oriented processes, 430
Object-oriented programming, 23
Object–version relationships, 386
Observational equality, 74
Operating-system layer, 384
Operation (in-service and maintenance), 199
Operational reliability, 17
Operational test, 198
Operations, 442–3
Operations manual, 195
Organizational details, 310
Organizational specifications, 55
Organizational structure diagram, 183

Pascal, 47, 78, 93, 351
Past predicting accuracy, 147–52
PCTE (Portable Common Tool Interface), 70, 386–7, 397, 398
Performance testing, 230
Petri Nets, 75
PL/1, 61, 71
Planning for software development, 161–3

Plug-in rule, 402, 407, 412
Poisson distribution, 373
Poisson process models, 145
Prediction
  level 1, at, 488–9
  past accuracy, 147–52
  procedures, 143
  systems, 143–4
Prequential likelihood ratio (PLR), 151, 409–12
PRICE SP model, 344, 364, 502–4, 507
PRICE SZ model, 345, 353–4
Prime Mission Equipment Costs, 369, 371
Prior odds ratio, 412
Probability distribution, 140
Process algebras, 73, 74
Process attributes, 470–3
Process control, 275
Process Definition Diagram, 169, 183–90
Process design, 272–5
Process engineering, 269–79, 283, 292, 300–1
  introducing new processes, 277–9
  selecting and improving available processes, 269–71
Process improvement, 120, 121, 123, 125, 127, 129, 131, 132, 135
Process instrumentation, 275–7
Process introduction, 283, 292, 300–1
Process modelling, 382, 482–6
Process requirement specification, 271
Process selection, 282, 291, 299–300
Processes, 442–4
Procurement of software, 211–34
  analysis, 234
  contract for, 216
  contract management, 224
  inputs from potential users, 228–9
  interfaces between supplier, users, and procurer, 227–8
  product development and testing, 226–7
  product handover, 234
  progress reporting and control, 232–3
  role in achieving reliable software, 244–5
  roles and responsibilities in, 212–13
  supplier evaluation and selection, 218–20
  supplier roles in forming requirements, 220–2
Product, 443
  attributes, 449–70

Product—*contd.*
  operation review, 198
  phaseout, 199
  reliability measurement, 12
Productivity, 207
  quality, and, 367–8
Program development, 378
Programming environments, 378, 379
Programming tools, 377
Progress monitoring, 162
Project completion phase, 198–9
Project completion review, 199
Project control and management 155–209,
      275, 380, 421, 428, 434
  contractural basis, 174–6
  cost measurement and estimation in,
      336–8, 364
  interacting tasks, 159–63
  primary structure, 157–9
Project initiation, 169–72, 190, 193
  phase products, 193
Project specific risks, 201–2
PROLOG, 79, 314
Prototyping, 431–4
Public Tool Interface (PTI), 70, 386
Putnam's model, 487, 507–15

QSM Size Planner, 349, 351
Quality Circles, 266–7, 291
Quality management, 14, 163–4, 233,
      247–302, 292, 368, 397, 422, 444,
      480
  basic functions, 260, 279–80
  company or entire organization,
      296–301
  company-based, 280
  cost estimation in, 340
  definition, 249–52, 279
  definition and support, 281, 290–1,
      297–8
  design and implementation of, 260
  general elements of, 259–69
  group-based, 280, 289–96
  main objectives and strategies used, 259
  manual, 209
  models, 480–2
  plans, 174, 225–7, 233
  productivity, and, 367–8
  project-based, 280–9
  reasons for not using or not using well,
      254–8
  recommendation for, 258–9

Quality management—*contd.*
  report, 198
  reporting, 264–5, 285, 294
  role in process selection, engineering,
      and introduction, 261–2
  role in software development, 253–4
  standards, 206
  value of, 252–3
Quantitative models, 476–86
  criteria for description of, 446–7
  selection criteria, 446

RAISE, 61
RAP, 77
Rayleigh-curve model, 507–8, 510, 515
R & D costs, 334
Readability, 24, 444, 464–5
Reasonable checks, 101
Recommendations, 446
Record keeping, 119
Recover-last operation, 98
Recovery blocks, 92, 99–105
  acceptance tests, 100–1
  alternates, 101–3
  basic features, 99
  comparison with N-version
      programming, 105–7
  concurrent systems, 103–5
  design diversity within, 101–3
  long-term research programme, 109
  practical application, 107–9
Recovery lines, 104–5
Recovery points, 103
Redundancy, 116
Regression testing, 117, 231
Relative root mean square error (RRMS),
      489
Release note, 118
Release testing, 229–30
Reliability, 4
  assessment
    based on development process, 11–14
    based on observation of development
      process, 13
  concepts of, 1–19
  definition, 2
  design process, and, 23
  estimates, 17
  growth models, 3, 137–53, 401–12
    assumptions in, 139
    definition, 143
    example of use, 146–7

Reliability—*contd.*
  management, and environment, 396–7
  models, 16
    basic simple conceptual model
        underlying, 140
  operational, 17
  prediction, 143–4
  report, 198
Repair, 119
REQUEST, 319, 368
Requirements, 213
  statement of, 5–6, 213, 216–18
  testability, and, 120, 122–5, 128–32
Requirements/feasibility phase, 120–3
Requirements specification, 193–4, 422
  phase products, 194
  use of metrics in, 319
Research directions, 17–19
Reversal checks, 100
Reviews, 266–7, 287–8, 295–6
  baseline stages, at, 181–2
Re-work, 367
Rigorous verification, 52
Risk
  assessment, 201, 203
  checklist, 220–1
  components, 433
  exposure, 201
  management, 109–205
  monitoring, 203
  prioritization, 200–1
  technical, 375, 433, 434
Risk analysis, 118
  cost estimation, and, 368–76
Risk Reduction Leverage, 201–3
Rocof (rate of occurrence of failures), 2,
        4, 140, 145
Royal Military College of Science, 109
Run-time overheads, 106–7

Safety-related applications, 14
SCCS, 73
Schedule risk, 375–6
Scoping, 229–32
SDC model, 498–9
Selection criteria, 442–7
Sequential processes, 58
Sequential program, hierarchical structure
        chart for, 84–5
Service, 135
SIFT, 71
Size, 443
  adjustments, 511
Size-in–size-out techniques, 345–7

Size metrics, non-LOC, 355–60
Sizing
  analogy, by, 348–9
  models, 344–60
SLIM, 342, 349, 356, 364, 513–15
Smalltalk, 44, 49
Smalltalk-80, 23
SOFTCOST, 501–2
SOFTCOST-Ada, 356
SOFTCOST R, 353, 356
Software component construction nested
        phase(s), 129–31
Software Data Library (SWDL), 442, 445
Software design. *See* Design
Software development, 155
  activities, 183, 420–2
  assessment of, 13
  choice of process, 109–205
  contract-oriented, 205
  contracting for, 215
  definition of process, 168–9
  effectiveness of, 209
  establishing organization for, 169
  establishing process of, 167–76
  life-cycle of. *See* Life-cycle
  measuring, 303–31
  methodology, 207–8
  nested phase, 122–3
  phases of, 112
  potential incidence of trouble, 169
  process, 155
  process management, 176–7
  process models, 203, 413–40
  productivity of, 205
  reliability assessment based on, 11–14
  sample of, 190–9
  special studies, 222–3
  testability, and, 120, 122, 124, 125, 128,
        130–2
  third-generation approach, 317
  within system development, 426
Software diversity, 106
Software Engineering Economics, 161
Software engineering environments,
        377–99
Software engineering techniques, 10
Software implementation nested phase,
        125–8
Software maintenance. *See* Maintenance
        of software
Software metrics. *See* Metrics
Software problem reports (SPRs), 199
Software procurement. *See* Procurement
        of software

Software reliability. *See* Reliability
Software Science, 446, 447–9
Software system, abstract model of, 84, 87
Source code review, 196
Specification, checklist, 14
Specifications
  construction, 54, 57
  contractual nature of, 54
  faults, 89
  formal, 53, 56–8
  formal versus informal, 53–4
  languages, 57, 78
  local, 55, 57
  model-based, 59
  nature of, 53–5
  organizational, 55
  process requirement, 271
  property-based, 59, 62
  requirements, 193–4, 319, 422
  stages, 86
  structural, 55
  system, 54–5, 213, 229–32
  test, 116, 195
Spiral model, 418, 435–7
Stability, 444
Standard ML, 71, 78, 79
STARTS Guide, 111, 113, 180
State machine model, 348, 351
Statement of requirements, 213
  initial draft, 216–18
  reliability, 5–6
Statistical inference procedure, 143
Statistical techniques, 310–12, 316
Status reporting, 397
Stochastically decreasing random
        variables, 405
STONEMAN, 390
STP, 72
Stress testing, 230–1
Structural checks, 101
Structural decomposition, 347–8
Structural design, 194, 422
  phase products, 194–5
  review, 195
  use of metrics in, 320–2
Structural fan-in and fan-out, 460–4
Structural specifications, 55
Structure, 443
Structured design, 24, 27
Subsystems, 27
Supplier
  evaluation and selection, 218–20
  roles in forming requirements, 220–2

Supplier—*contd.*
  selection checklist, 220
Synchronous components, 84, 86
System design
  faults, 89
  integration model, and, 476
System development, 426
System failure, 86
System requirements, 86
System specifications, 54–5, 213, 229–32

Target setting, 318–20, 322, 325–7
Tasks, 442–3
  definitions, 183
Technical complexity factor (TCF), 355
Technical control, 165–7, 421, 429
Technical development, 165–7
Technical risk, 375, 433, 434
Technology factor, 342, 509
Temporal logics, 74
Test, 112, 181, 229–32, 422
  achievement, as, 140
  measurement, as, 140
  effectiveness measures, 470–2
  execution, 117, 121, 123, 124, 126, 129,
        131–3
  planning and preparation, 116, 121,
        122, 124–6, 129, 130, 132, 133,
        317
  procedures, 116
  requirements, 116
  specifications, 116, 195
Test and fix model 1, 482–4
Test and fix model 2, 485–6
Tested software items, 197
Tested software review, 197
Time-effort trade-off, 511
Time to target, 3, 5
Tool integration, 379
Tool selection, 208
Tool support, 172–4
Traceability, 115, 124
Transformation, 312–14, 429
  systems, 77
  tools, 57
Transformational programming, 52–3
TRW Wolverton model, 498
TRW Software Productivity Project, 435

u-plot method, 408
UK Interim Defence Standard 00–55, 81
Unadjusted function count (UFC), 355